THE LIFE OF
Samuel Johnson

THE LIFE OF
Samuel Johnson

BY JAMES BOSWELL

Illustrations by Gordon Ross

1946

Doubleday and Company, Inc.

GARDEN CITY, NEW YORK

ILLUSTRATIONS

DEDICATION TO
SIR JOSHUA REYNOLDS

My dear Sir,—

Every liberal motive that can actuate an Author in the dedication of his labours, concurs in directing me to you, as the person to whom the following Work should be inscribed.

If there be a pleasure in celebrating the distinguished merit of a contemporary, mixed with a certain degree of vanity not altogether inexcusable, in appearing fully sensible of it, where can I find one, in complimenting whom I can with more general approbation gratify those feelings? Your excellence not only in the Art over which you have long presided with unrivalled fame, but also in Philosophy and elegant Literature, is well known to the present, and will continue to be the admiration of future ages. Your equal and placid temper, your variety of conversation, your true politeness, by which you are so amiable in private society, and that enlarged hospitality which has long made your house a common centre of union for the great, the accomplished, the learned, and the ingenious; all these qualities I can, in perfect confidence of not being accused of flattery, ascribe to you.

If a man may indulge an honest pride, in having it known to the world that he has been thought worthy of particular attention by a person of the first eminence in the age in which he lived, whose company has been universally courted, I am justified in availing myself of the usual privilege of a Dedication, when I mention that there has been a long and uninterrupted friendship between us.

If gratitude should be acknowledged for favours received, I have this opportunity, my dear Sir, most sincerely to thank you for the many happy hours which I owe to your kindness,—for the cordiality with which you have at all times been pleased to welcome me,—for the number of valuable acquaintance to whom you have introduced me,—for the *noctes cænæque Deûm,* which I have enjoyed under your roof.

If a work should be inscribed to one who is master of the subject of it, and whose approbation, therefore, must insure it credit and success, the "Life of Dr. Johnson" is, with the greatest propriety, dedicated to Sir Joshua Reynolds, who was the intimate and beloved friend of that great man; the friend whom he declared to be "the most invulnerable man he knew; whom, if he should quarrel with him, he should find the most difficulty how to abuse." You, my dear Sir, studied him, and knew him well; you venerated and admired him. Yet, luminous as he was upon the whole, you perceived all the shades which mingled in the grand composition; all the little peculiarities and slight blemishes which marked the literary Colossus. Your very warm commendation of the specimen which I gave in my "Journal of a Tour to the Hebrides," of my being able to preserve his conversation in an authentic and lively manner, which opinion the Public has confirmed, was the best encouragement for me to persevere in my purpose of producing the whole of my stores.

In one respect, this Work will, in some passages, be different from the former. In my "Tour," I was almost unboundedly open in my communications, and from my eagerness to display the wonderful fertility and readiness of Johnson's wit, freely showed to the world its dexterity, even when I was myself the object of it. I trusted that I should be liberally understood, as knowing very well what I was about, and by no means as simply unconscious of the pointed effects of the satire. I own, indeed, that I was arrogant enough to suppose that the tenour of the rest of the book would sufficiently guard me against such a strange imputation. But it seems I judged too well of the world; for, though I could scarcely believe it, I have been undoubtedly informed that many persons, especially in distant quarters, not penetrating enough into Johnson's character, so as to understand his mode of treating his friends, have arraigned my judgment, instead of seeing that I was sensible of all that they could observe.

It is related of the great Dr. Clarke that when in one of his leisure hours he was unbending himself with a few friends in the most playful and frolicsome manner, he observed Beau Nash approaching; upon which he suddenly stopped;—"My boys (said he), let us be grave; here comes a fool." The world, my friend, I have found to be a great fool, as to that particular on which it has become necessary to speak very plainly. I have, therefore, in this Work been more reserved; and though I tell nothing but the truth, I have still kept in my mind that the whole truth is not always to be exposed. This, however, I have managed so as to occasion no diminution of the pleasure which my book should afford; though malignity may sometimes be disappointed of its gratifications.

I am, my dear Sir,
Your much obliged friend,
And faithful humble servant,
JAMES BOSWELL.

London, April 20, 1791.

Contents

Contents

Editor's Preface

FOR THE PURPOSES of this illustrated edition of Boswell's perennial classic, it has been necessary greatly to shorten the text. It was with definite trepidation and in a humble spirit that I accepted the assignment. To devotees of Boswell, any tampering with his text must seem sacrilegious; but viewed more dispassionately, a sympathetic abridgment can produce a volume more suited in length to these less leisured times, and one which yet retains the full flavor of that truly great biography.

It has been my careful effort to suppress no details which will contribute to an understanding of the highly complex and contradictory character of Dr. Johnson, and to omit nothing essential to the chronological presentation of the narrative. Fortunately the rich texture of Boswell's biographical skill includes a piling up, a repetition of detail, so that by exercising selection in the multiplicity of evidence, it was possible to effect the curtailment without risk of distorting the original.

There have been many great editors of Boswell's *Life of Johnson,* each of whom has added much to our knowledge of the titan; I hope that my simpler efforts at abridgment may bring enjoyment to new readers who might miss the pleasures of this book because of its rather overwhelming size. For as its subject was a great bear of a man, the original is a grizzly among biographies.

C. P. CHADSEY

CHAPTER I—1709–1728

Parentage and Early Days

SAMUEL JOHNSON was born at Lichfield, in Staffordshire, on the 18th of September, N.S. 1709; and his initiation into the Christian church was not delayed; for his baptism is recorded, in the register of St. Mary's parish in that city, to have been performed on the day of his birth: his father is there styled *Gentleman,* a circumstance of which an ignorant panegyrist has praised him for not being proud; when the truth is, that the appellation of Gentleman, though now lost in the indiscriminate assumption of *Esquire,* was commonly taken by those who could not boast of gentility. His father was Michael Johnson, a native of Derbyshire, of obscure extraction, who settled in Lichfield as a bookseller and stationer. His mother was Sarah Ford, descended from an ancient race of substantial yeomanry in Warwickshire. They were well advanced in years when they married, and never had more than two children, both sons; Samuel, their first-born, who lived to be the illustrious character whose various excellence I am to endeavour to record, and Nathaniel, who died in his twenty-fifth year.

Mr. Michael Johnson was a man of a large and robust body, and of a strong and active mind; yet, as in the most solid rocks veins of unsound substance are often discovered, there was in him a mixture of that disease, the nature of which eludes the most minute inquiry, though the effects are well known to be a weariness of life, an unconcern about those things which agitate the greater part of mankind, and a general sensation of gloomy wretchedness. From him, then, his son inherited, with some other qualities, "a vile melancholy," which in his too strong expression of any disturbance of the mind "made him mad all his life, at least not sober." Michael was, however, forced by the narrowness of his circumstances to be very diligent in business, not only in his shop, but by occasionally resorting to several towns in the neighbourhood, some of which were at a considerable distance from Lichfield. At that time booksellers' shops, in the provincial towns of England, were very rare; so that there was not one even in Birmingham, in which town old Mr. Johnson used to open a shop every market-day. He was a pretty good Latin scholar, and a citizen so creditable as to be made one of the magistrates of Lichfield; and being a man of good sense, and skill in his trade, he acquired a reasonable share of wealth, of which, however, he afterwards lost the greatest part, by engaging unsuccessfully in a manufacture of parchment. He was a zealous high-churchman and royalist, and retained his attachment to the unfortunate house of Stuart, though he reconciled himself, by casuistical arguments of expediency and necessity, to take the oaths imposed by the prevailing power.

There is a circumstance in his life somewhat romantic, but so well authenticated, that I shall not omit it. A young woman of Leek, in Staffordshire, while he served his apprenticeship there, conceived a violent passion for him; and though it met with no favourable return, followed him to Lichfield, where she took lodgings opposite to the house in which he lived, and indulged her hopeless flame. When he was informed that it so preyed upon her mind that her life was in danger, he with a generous humanity went to her and offered to marry her, but it was then too late: her vital power was exhausted; and she actually exhibited one of the very rare instances of dying for love. She was buried in the cathedral of Lichfield; and he, with a tender regard, placed a stone over her grave, with this inscription:

Here lies the body of
Mrs. Elizabeth Blaney, a stranger:
She departed this life
20th of September, 1694.

In following so very eminent a man [Samuel Johnson] from his cradle to his grave, every minute particular, which can throw light on the progress of his mind, is interesting. That he was remarkable, even in his earliest years, may easily be supposed; for, to use his own words in his Life of Sydenham, "That the strength of his understanding, the accuracy of his discernment, and the ardour of his curiosity, might have been remarked from his infancy, by a diligent observer, there is no reason to doubt. For there is no instance of any man, whose history has been minutely related, that did not in every part of life discover the same proportion of intellectual vigour."

Of the power of his memory, for which he was all his life eminent to a degree almost incredible, the following early instance was told me in his presence at Lichfield, in 1776, by his step-daughter, Mrs. Lucy Porter, as related to her by his mother. When he was a child in petticoats, and had learnt to read, Mrs. Johnson one morning put the Common Prayer Book into his hands, pointed to the collect for the day, and said, "Sam, you must get this by heart." She went up stairs leaving him to study it: but by the time she had reached the second floor, she heard him following her. "What's the matter?" said she. "I can say it," he replied; and repeated it distinctly, though he could not have read it more than twice.

Young Johnson had the misfortune to be much afflicted with the scrofula, or king's evil, which disfigured a countenance naturally well formed, and hurt his visual nerves so much, that he did not see at all with one of his eyes, though its appearance was little different from that of the other. There is amongst his prayers one inscribed *"When my* EYE *was restored to its use,"* which ascertains a defect that many of his friends knew he had, though I never perceived it. I supposed him to be only near-sighted: and indeed I must observe, that in no other respect could I discern any defect in his vision; on the contrary, the force of his attention and perceptive quickness made him see and distinguish all manner of objects, whether of nature or of art, with a nicety that is rarely to be found. When he and I were travelling in the Highlands of Scotland, and I pointed out to him a mountain which I observed resembled a cone, he corrected my inaccuracy, by showing me, that it was indeed pointed at the top, but that one side of it was larger than the other. And the ladies with whom he was acquainted, agree, that no man was more nicely and minutely critical in the elegance of female dress. When I found that he saw the romantic beauties of Ilam, in Derbyshire, much better than I did, I told him that he resembled an able performer upon a bad instrument. How false and contemptible then are all the remarks which have been made to the prejudice either of his candour or his philosophy, founded upon a supposition that he was almost blind! It has been said, that he contracted this grievous malady from his nurse. His mother yielding to the superstitious notion, which, it is wonderful to think, prevailed so long in this country, as to the virtue of the regal touch; a notion which our kings encouraged, and to which a man of such inquiry and such judgment as Carte could give credit; carried him to London, where he was actually touched by Queen Anne. Mrs. Johnson, indeed, as Mr. Hector informed me, acted by the advice of the celebrated Sir John Floyer, then a physician in Lichfield. Johnson used to talk of this very frankly; and Mrs. Piozzi has preserved his very picturesque description of the scene, as it remained in his fancy. Being asked if he could remember Queen Anne,—"He had (he said) a confused, but somehow a sort of solemn, recollection of a lady in diamonds, and a long black hood." This touch, however, was without any effect. I ventured to say to him, in allusion to the political principles in which he was educated, and of which he ever retained some odour, that "his mother had not carried him far enough, she should have taken him to Rome."

He was first taught to read English by Dame Oliver, a widow, who kept a school for young children in Lichfield. He told me she could read the black letter, and asked him to borrow for her, from his father, a Bible in that character. When he was going to Oxford, she came to take leave of him, brought him, in the simplicity of her kindness, a present of gingerbread, and said he was the best scholar she ever had. He delighted in mentioning this early compliment: adding, with a smile, that "this was as high a proof of his merit as he could conceive."

He began to learn Latin with Mr. Hawkins, usher, or under-master, of Lichfield school, "a man (said he), very skilful in his little way."

"This I do—to save you from the gallows!"

With him he continued two years, and then rose to be under the care of Mr. Hunter, the headmaster, who according to his account, "was very severe, and wrong-headedly severe. He used (said he) to beat us unmercifully; and he did not distinguish between ignorance and negligence; for he would beat a boy equally for not knowing a thing, as for neglecting to know it. He would ask a boy a question, and if he did not answer it, he would beat him, without considering whether he had an opportunity of knowing how to answer it. For instance, he would call up a boy and ask him Latin for a candlestick, which the boy could not expect to be asked. Now, Sir, if a boy could answer every question, there would be no need of a master to teach him."

It is, however, but just to the memory of Mr. Hunter to mention, that though he might err in being too severe, the school of Lichfield was very respectable in his time. The late Dr. Taylor, Prebendary of Westminster, who was educated under him, told me, that "he was an excellent master, and that his ushers were most of them men of eminence; that Holbrook, one of the most ingenious men, best scholars, and best preachers of his age, was usher during the greatest part of the time that Johnson was at school."

Indeed, Johnson was very sensible how much he owed to Mr. Hunter. Mr. Langton one day asked him how he had acquired so accurate a knowledge of Latin, in which, I believe, he was exceeded by no man of his time; he said, "My master whipped me very well. Without that, Sir, I should have done nothing." He told Mr. Langton, that while Hunter was flogging his boys unmercifully, he used to say, "And this I do to save you from the gallows." Johnson, upon all occasions, expressed his approbation of enforcing instruction by means of the rod. "I would rather (said he) have the rod to be the general terror to all, to make them learn, than tell a child, if you do thus, or thus, you will be more esteemed than your brothers or sisters. The rod produces an effect which terminates in itself. A child is afraid of being whipped, and gets his task, and there's an end on't; whereas, by exciting emulation and comparisons of superiority, you lay the foundation of lasting mischief; you make brothers and sisters hate each other."

That superiority over his fellows, which he maintained with so much dignity in his march through life, was not assumed from vanity and ostentation, but was the natural and constant effect of those extraordinary powers of mind, of which he could not but be conscious by comparison; the intellectual difference, which, in other cases of comparison by characters, is often a matter of undecided contest, being as clear in his case as the superiority of stature in some men above others. Johnson did not strut or stand on tiptoe; he only did not stoop. From his earliest years, his superiority was perceived and acknowledged. He was, from the beginning, ἄναξ ἀνδρῶν, a king of men. His schoolfellow, Mr. Hector, has obligingly furnished me with many particulars of his boyish days; and assured me that he never knew him corrected at school, but for talking and diverting other boys from their business. He seemed to learn by intuition; for though indolence and procrastination were inherent in his constitution, whenever he made an exertion, he did more than any one else. In short, he is a memorable instance of what has been often observed, that the boy is the man in miniature; and that the distinguishing characteristics of each individual are the same, through the whole course of life. His favourites used to receive very liberal assistance from him; and such was the submission and deference with which he was treated, such the desire to obtain his regard, that three of the boys, of whom Mr. Hector was sometimes one, used to come in the morning as his humble attendants and carry him to school. One in the middle stooped, while he sat upon his back, and one on each side supported him; and thus he was borne triumphant. Such a proof of the early predominance of intellectual vigour is very remarkable, and does honour to human nature.—Talking to me once himself of his being much distinguished at school, he told me, "they never thought to raise me by comparing me to any one: they never said, Johnson is as good a scholar as such a one; but such a one is as good a scholar as Johnson; and this was said but of one, but of Lowe; and I do not think he was as good a scholar."

He discovered a great ambition to excel, which roused him to counteract his indolence. He was uncommonly inquisitive; and his memory was so tenacious, that he never forgot anything that he either heard or read. Mr. Hector remembers having recited to him eighteen verses, which, after a little pause, he repeated verbatim, varying only one epithet, by which he improved the line.

He never joined with the other boys in their ordinary diversions; his only amusement was in winter, when he took a pleasure in being drawn upon the ice by a boy barefooted, who pulled him along by a garter fixed round him; no very easy operation, as his size was remarkably large. His defective sight, indeed, prevented him from enjoying the common sports; and he once pleasantly remarked to me, "how wonderfully well he had contrived to be idle without them." Lord Chesterfield, however, has justly observed in one of his letters, when earnestly cautioning a friend against the pernicious effects of idleness, that active sports are not to be reckoned idleness in young people; and that the listless torpor of doing nothing, alone deserves that name. Of this dismal inertness of disposition, Johnson had all his life too great a share. Mr. Hector relates, that "he could not oblige him more than by sauntering away the hours of vacation in the fields, during which he was more engaged in talking to himself than to his companion."

Lichfield Grammar School where Johnson attended school

After having resided for some time at the house of his uncle, Cornelius Ford, Johnson was, at the age of fifteen, removed to the school of Stourbridge in Worcestershire, of which Mr. Wentworth was then master. This step was taken by the advice of his cousin, the Rev. Mr. Ford, a man in whom both talents and good dispositions were disgraced by licentiousness, but who was a very able judge of what was right. At this school, he did not receive so much benefit as was expected. It has been said, that he acted in the capacity of an assistant to Mr. Wentworth, in teaching the younger boys. "Mr. Wentworth (he told me) was a very able man, but an idle man, and to me very severe; but I cannot blame him much. I was then a big boy; he saw I did not reverence him; and that he should get no honour by me. I had brought enough with me to carry me through; and all I should get at his school would be ascribed to my own labour, or to my former master. Yet he taught me a great deal."

He thus discriminated to Dr. Percy, Bishop of Dromore, his progress at his two grammar-schools. "At one, I learned much in the school, but little from the master; in the other, I learned much from the master, but little in the school."

The Bishop also informs me, that "Dr. Johnson's father, before he was received at Stourbridge, applied to have him admitted as a scholar and assistant to the Rev. Samuel Lea, M.A., headmaster of Newport school, in Shropshire (a very diligent good teacher, at that time in high reputation, under whom, Mr. Hollis is said, in the Memoirs of his life, to have been also educated). This application to Mr. Lea was not successful; but Johnson had afterwards the gratification to hear that the old gentleman, who lived to a very advanced age, mentioned it as one of the most memorable events of his life, that "he was *very near* having that great man for his scholar."

He remained at Stourbridge little more than a year, and then he returned home, where he may be said to have loitered, for two years, in a state very unworthy his uncommon abilities. He had already given several proofs of his poetical genius, both in his school exercises and in other occasional compositions.

The two years which he spent at home, after his return from Stourbridge, he passed in what he thought idleness, and was scolded by his father for his want of steady application. He had no settled plan of life, nor looked forward at all, but merely lived from day to day. Yet he read a great deal in a desultory manner, without any scheme of study; as chance threw books in his way, and inclination directed him through them. He used to mention one curious instance of his casual reading, when but a boy. Having imagined that his brother had hid some apples behind a large folio upon an upper shelf in his father's shop, he climbed up to search for them. There were no apples; but the large folio proved to be Petrarch, whom he had seen mentioned, in some preface, as one of the restorers of learning. His curiosity having been thus excited, he sat down with avidity, and read a great part of the book. What he read during these two years, he told me, was not works of mere amusement, "not voyages and travels, but all literature,

Sir, all ancient writers, all manly; though but little Greek, only some of Anacreon and Hesiod: but in this irregular manner (added he) I had looked into a great many books, which were not commonly known at the Universities, where they seldom read any books but what were put into their hands by their tutors; so that when I came to Oxford, Dr. Adams, now master of Pembroke College, told me I was the best qualified for the University that he had ever known come there."

In estimating the progress of his mind during these two years, as well as in future periods of his life, we must not regard his own hasty confession of idleness; for we see, when he explains himself, that he was acquiring various stores; and indeed he himself concluded the account with saying, "I would not have you think I was doing nothing then." He might, perhaps, have studied more assiduously; but it may be doubted, whether such a mind as his was not more enriched by roaming at large in the fields of literature, than if it had been confined to any single spot. The analogy between body and mind is very general, and the parallel will hold as to their food, as well as any other particular. The flesh of animals who feed excursively is allowed to have a higher flavour than that of those who are cooped up. May there not be the same difference between men who read as their taste prompts, and men who are confined in cells and colleges to stated tasks?

CHAPTER II—1728–1731

Oxford

THAT A MAN in Mr. Michael Johnson's circumstances should think of sending his son to the expensive University of Oxford, at his own charge, seems very improbable. The subject was too delicate to question Johnson upon; but I have been assured by Dr. Taylor, that the scheme never would have taken place, had not a gentleman of Shropshire, one of his schoolfellows, spontaneously undertaken to support him at Oxford, in the character of his companion, though, in fact, he never received any assistance whatever from that gentleman.

He, however, went to Oxford, and was entered a commoner of Pembroke College, on the 31st of October, 1728, being then in his nineteenth year.

The Reverend Dr. Adams, who afterward presided over Pembroke College with universal esteem, told me he was present, and gave me some account of what passed on the night of Johnson's arrival at Oxford. On that evening, his father, who had anxiously accompanied him, found means to have him introduced to Mr. Jorden, who was to be his tutor. His being put under any tutor, reminds us of what Wood says of Robert Burton, author of the "Anatomy of Melancholy," when

Entrance of Pembroke College, Oxford
(Johnson's College)

elected student of Christ Church; "for form's sake, *though he wanted not a tutor,* he was put under the tuition of Dr. John Bancroft, afterwards Bishop of Oxon."

His father seemed very full of the merits of his son, and told the company he was a good scholar, and a poet, and wrote Latin verses. His figure and manner appeared strange to them; but he behaved modestly, and sat silent, till, upon something which occurred in the course of conversation, he suddenly struck in and quoted Macrobius; and thus he gave the first impression of that more extensive reading in which he had indulged himself.

His tutor, Mr. Jorden, fellow of Pembroke, was not, it seems, a man of such abilities as we should conceive requisite for the instructor of Samuel Johnson, who gave me the following account of him. "He was a very worthy man, but a heavy man, and I did not profit much by his instructions. Indeed, I did not attend him much. The first day after I came to college, I waited upon him, and then stayed away four. On the sixth, Mr. Jorden asked me why I had not attended. I answered I had been sliding in Christ Church meadow, and this I said with as much *nonchalance* as I am now talking to you. I had no notion that I was wrong or irreverent to my tutor. BOSWELL: That, Sir, was great fortitude of mind. JOHNSON: No, Sir, stark insensibility.

The fifth of November was at that time kept with great solemnity at Pembroke College, and exercises upon the subject of the day were required. Johnson neglected to perform his, which is much to be regretted; for his vivacity of imagination, and force of language, would probably have produced something sublime upon the gunpowder-plot. To apologise for his neglect, he gave in a short copy of verses, entitled "Somnium," containing a common thought; "that the Muse had come to him in his sleep, and whispered, that it did not become him to write on such subjects as politics; he should confine himself to humbler themes"; but the versification was truly Virgilian.

He had a love and respect for Jorden, not for his literature, but for his worth. "Whenever (said he) a young man becomes Jorden's pupil, he becomes his son."

Having given such a specimen of his poetical powers, he was asked by Mr. Jorden to translate Pope's "Messiah" into Latin verse, as a Christmas exercise. He performed it with uncommon rapidity, and in so masterly a manner, that he obtained great applause from it, which ever after kept him high in the estimation of his College, and, indeed, of all the University.

It is said, that Mr. Pope expressed himself concerning it in terms of strong approbation. Dr. Taylor told me that it was first printed for old Mr. Johnson, without the knowledge of his son, who was very angry when he heard of it. "A Miscellany of Poems," collected by a person of the name of Husbands, was published at Oxford in 1731. In that "Miscellany" Johnson's translation of the "Messiah" appeared, with this modest motto from Scaliger's Poetics: *"Ex alieno ingenio poeta, ex suo tantum versificator."*

I am not ignorant that critical objections have been made to this and other specimens of Johnson's Latin poetry. I acknowledge myself not competent to decide on a question of such extreme nicety.

The "morbid melancholy," which was lurking in his constitution, and to which we may ascribe those particularities, and that aversion to regular life, which at a very early period marked his character, gathered such strength in his twentieth year, as to afflict him in a dreadful manner. While he was at Lichfield, in the College vacation of the year 1729, he felt himself overwhelmed with a horrible hypochondria, with perpetual irritation, fretfulness, and impatience; and with a dejection, gloom, and despair, which made existence misery. From this dismal malady he never afterward was perfectly relieved; and all his labours, and all his enjoyments, were but temporary interruptions of its baleful influence. How wonderful, how unsearchable, are the ways of God! Johnson, who was blest with all the powers of genius and understanding, in a degree far above the ordinary state of human nature, was at the same time visited with a disorder so afflictive, that they who know it by dire experience will not envy his exalted endowments. That it was, in some degree, occasioned by a defect in his nervous system, that inexplicable part of our frame, appears highly probable. He told Mr. Paradise that he was sometimes so languid and inefficient, that he could not distinguish the hour upon the town-clock.

Johnson, upon the first violent attack of this disorder, strove to overcome it by forcible exertions. He frequently walked to Birmingham and back again, and tried many other expedients; but all in vain. His expression concerning it to me was, "I did not then know how to manage it." His distress became so intolerable, that he applied to Dr. Swinfen, physician in Lichfield, his godfather, and put into his hands a state of his case, written in Latin. Dr. Swinfen was so much struck with the extraordinary acuteness, research, and eloquence of this paper, that, in his zeal for his godson, he showed it to several people. His daughter, Mrs. Desmoulins, who was many years humanely supported in Dr.

Johnson's house in London, told me, that upon his discovering that Dr. Swinfen had communicated his case, he was so much offended, that he was never afterward fully reconciled to him. He indeed had good reason to be offended; for, though Dr. Swinfen's motive was good, he inconsiderately betrayed a matter deeply interesting and of great delicacy, which had been intrusted to him in confidence; and exposed a complaint of his young friend and patient, which, in the superficial opinion of the generality of mankind, is attended with contempt and disgrace.

But let not little men triumph upon knowing that Johnson was an Hypochondriac, was subject to what the learned, philosophical, and pious Dr. Cheyne has so well treated under the title of "The English Malady." Though he suffered severely from it, he was not therefore degraded. The powers of his great mind might be troubled, and their full exercise suspended at times; but the mind itself was ever entire. As a proof of this, it is only necessary to consider, that, when he was at the very worst, he composed that state of his own case, which showed an uncommon vigour, not only of fancy and taste, but of judgment. I am aware that he himself was too ready to call such a complaint by the name of *madness;* in conformity with which notion, he has traced its gradations, with exquisite nicety, in one of the chapters of his RAS-SELAS. But there is surely a clear distinction between a disorder which affects only the imagination and spirits, while the judgment is sound, and a disorder by which the judgment itself is impaired.

It is a common effect of low spirits or melancholy, to make those who are afflicted with it imagine that they are actually suffering those evils which happen to be most strongly presented to their minds. Some have fancied themselves to be deprived of the use of their limbs, some to labour under acute diseases, others to be in extreme poverty; when, in truth, there was not the least reality in any of the suppositions; so that, when the vapours were dispelled, they were convinced of the delusion. To Johnson, whose supreme enjoyment was the exercise of his reason, the disturbance or obscuration of that faculty was the evil most to be dreaded. Insanity, therefore, was the object of his most dismal apprehension; and he fancied himself seized by it, or approaching to it, at the very time when he was giving proofs of a more than ordinary soundness and vigour of judgment. That his own diseased imagination should have so far deceived him is strange; but it is stranger still that some of his friends should have given credit to his groundless opinion, when they had such undoubted proofs that it was totally fallacious; though it is by no means surprising that those who wish to depreciate him, should, since his death, have laid hold of this circumstance, and insisted upon it with very unfair aggravation.

The history of his mind as to religion is an important article. I have mentioned the early impressions made upon his tender imagination by his mother, who continued her pious cares with assiduity, but, in his opinion, not with judgment. "Sunday (said he) was a heavy day with me when I was a boy. My mother confined me on that day, and made me read 'The Whole Duty of Man,' from a great part of which I could derive no instruction. When, for instance, I had read the chapter on theft, which, from my infancy, I had been taught was wrong, I was no more convinced that theft was wrong than before; so there was no accession of knowledge. A boy should be introduced to such books, by having his attention directed to the arrangement, to the style, and other excellences of composition; that the mind, being thus engaged by an amusing variety of objects, may not grow weary."

He communicated to me the following particulars upon the subject of his religious progress. "I fell into an inattention to religion, or an indifference about it, in my ninth year. The church at Lichfield, in which we had a seat, wanted reparation, so I was to go and find a seat in other churches; and having bad eyes, and being awkward about this, I used to go and read in the fields on Sunday. This habit continued till my fourteenth year; and still I find a great reluctance to go to church. I then became a sort of lax *talker* against religion, for I did not much *think* against it; and this lasted till I went to Oxford, where it would not be *suffered*. When at Oxford, I took up Law's 'Serious Call to a Holy Life,' expecting to find it a dull book (as such books generally are), and perhaps to laugh at it. But I found Law quite an overmatch for me; and this was the first occasion of my thinking in earnest of religion, after I became capable of rational inquiry."

From this time forward, religion was the predominant object of his thoughts; though, with the just sentiments of a conscientious Christian, he lamented that his practice of its duties fell far short of what it ought to be.

How seriously Johnson was impressed with a sense of religion, even in the vigour of his youth, appears from the following passage in his minutes, kept by way of a diary: "Sept. 7, 1736. I have this day entered upon my 28th year. Mayest thou, O God, enable me for Jesus Christ's sake, to spend this in such a manner, that I may receive comfort from it at the hour of death, and in the day of judgment! Amen."

The particular course of his reading while at Oxford, and during the
time of vacation which he passed at home, cannot be traced. Enough
has been said of his irregular mode of study. He told me, that from his
earliest years he loved to read poetry, but hardly ever read any poem
to an end; that he read Shakespeare at a period so early, that the speech
of the Ghost in Hamlet terrified him when he was alone; that Horace's
Odes were the compositions in which he took most delight, and it was
long before he liked his Epistles and Satires. He told me what he read
solidly at Oxford was Greek; not the Grecian historians, but Homer
and Euripides, and now and then a little Epigram; that the study of
which he was the most fond, was Metaphysics, but he had not read
much, even in that way. I always thought that he did himself injustice
in his account of what he had read, and that he must have been speaking with reference to the vast portion of study which is possible, and to
which few scholars in the whole history of literature have attained; for
when I once asked him whether a person, whose name I have now
forgotten, studied hard, he answered, "No, Sir. I do not believe he
studied hard. I never knew a man who studied hard. I conclude, indeed, from the effects, that some men have studied hard, as Bentley and
Clarke." Trying him by that criterion upon which he formed his judgment of others, we may be absolutely certain, both from his writings
and his conversation, that his reading was very extensive. Dr. Adam
Smith, than whom few were better judges on this subject, once
observed to me, that "Johnson knew more books than any man alive."
He had a peculiar facility in seizing at once what was valuable in any
book, without submitting to the labour of perusing it from beginning
to end. He had, from the irritability of his constitution, at all times,
an impatience and hurry when he either read or wrote. A certain apprehension arising from novelty, made him write his first exercise at
College twice over; but he never took that trouble with any other composition; and we shall see that his most excellent works were struck off
at a heat, with rapid exertion."

Yet he appears, from his early notes or memorandums in my possession, to have at various times attempted, or at least planned, a methodical course of study, according to computation, of which he was all his
life fond, as it fixed his attention steadily upon something without, and
prevented his mind from preying upon itself. Thus I find in his hand-
writing the number of lines in each of two of Euripides' Tragedies, of
the Georgics of Virgil, of the first six books of the Æneid, of Horace's
Art of Poetry, of three of the books of Ovid's Metamorphoses, of some

parts of Theocritus, and of the tenth Satire of Juvenal; and a table, showing at the rate of various numbers a day (I suppose verses to be read) what would be, in each case, the total amount in a week, month, and year.

No man had a more ardent love of literature, or a higher respect for it, than Johnson. His apartment in Pembroke College was that upon the second floor over the gateway. The enthusiast of learning will ever contemplate it with veneration. One day, while he was sitting in it quite alone, Dr. Panting, then master of the College, whom he called "a fine Jacobite fellow," overheard him uttering this soliloquy in his strong emphatic voice: "Well, I have a mind to see what is done in other places of learning. I'll go and visit the Universities abroad. I'll go to France and Italy. I'll go to Padua.—And I'll mind my business. For an *Athenian* blockhead is the worst of all blockheads."

Dr. Adams told me that Johnson, while he was at Pembroke College, "was caressed and loved by all about him, was a gay and frolicsome fellow, and passed there the happiest part of his life." But this is a striking proof of the fallacy of appearances, and how little any of us know of the real internal state even of those whom we see most frequently; for the truth is, that he was then depressed by poverty, and irritated by disease. When I mentioned to him this account as given me by Dr. Adams, he said, "Ah, Sir, I was mad and violent. It was bitterness which they mistook for frolic. I was miserably poor, and I thought to fight my way by my literature and my wit; so I disregarded all power and all authority."

The Bishop of Dromore observes, in a letter to me, "The pleasure he took in vexing the tutors and fellows has been often mentioned. But I have heard him say, what ought to be recorded to the honour of the present venerable master of that College, the Reverend William Adams, D.D., who was then very young, and one of the junior fellows, that the mild but judicious expostulations of this worthy man, whose virtue awed him, and whose learning he revered, made him really ashamed of himself, 'though I fear (said he) I was too proud to own it.'

"I have heard from some of his contemporaries that he was generally seen lounging at the College-gate, with a circle of young students round him, whom he was entertaining with wit, and keeping from their studies, if not spiriting them up to rebellion against the College discipline, which in his maturer years he so much extolled."

I do not find that he formed any close intimacies with his fellow-collegians. But Dr. Adams told me that he contracted a love and regard for Pembroke College, which he retained to the last. A short time before his death he sent to that College a present of all his works, to be deposited in their library; and he had thoughts of leaving to it his house at Lichfield; but his friends who were about him, very properly dissuaded him from it, and he bequeathed it to some poor relations. He took a pleasure in boasting of the many eminent men who had been educated at Pembroke.

He was not, however, blind to what he thought the defects of his own College: and I have, from the information of Dr. Taylor, a very strong instance of that rigid honesty which he ever inflexibly preserved. Taylor had obtained his father's consent to be entered of Pembroke, that he might be with his schoolfellow, Johnson, with whom, though some years older than himself, he was very intimate. This would have been a great comfort to Johnson. But he fairly told Taylor that he could not, in conscience, suffer him to enter where he knew he could not have an able tutor. He then made inquiry all round the University, and having found that Mr. Bateman, of Christ Church, was the tutor of highest reputation, Taylor was entered of that College. Mr. Bateman's lectures were so excellent, that Johnson used to come and get them at second-hand from Taylor, till his poverty being so extreme, that his shoes were worn out, and his feet appeared through them, he saw that this humiliating circumstance was perceived by the Christ-Church men, and he came no more. He was too proud to accept of money, and somebody having set a pair of new shoes at his door, he threw them away with indignation. How must we feel, when we read such an anecdote of Samuel Johnson!

The *res augusta domi* prevented him from having the advantage of a complete academical education. The friend to whom he had trusted for support had deceived him. His debts in College, though not great, were increasing; and his scanty remittances from Lichfield, which had all along been made with great difficulty, could be supplied no longer, his father having fallen into a state of insolvency. Compelled, therefore, by irresistible necessity, he left the College in autumn, 1731, without a degree, having been a member of it little more than three years.

Dr. Adams, the worthy and respectable master of Pembroke College, has generally had the reputation of being Johnson's tutor. The fact, however, is, that in 1731, Mr. Jorden quitted the College, and his pupils were transferred to Dr. Adams; so that had Johnson returned, Dr. Adams *would have been his tutor*. It is to be wished, that this connexion had taken place. His equal temper, mild disposition, and politeness of manners, might have insensibly softened the harshness of Johnson, and infused into him those more delicate charities, those *petites morales,* in which, it must be confessed, our great moralist was more deficient than his best friends could fully justify. Dr. Adams paid Johnson this high compliment. He said to me at Oxford, in 1776, "I was his nominal tutor; but he was above my mark." When I repeated it to Johnson, his eyes flashed with grateful satisfaction, and he exclaimed, "That was liberal and noble."

CHAPTER III—1731–1736

Matrimony and Authorship

AND NOW (I had almost said *poor*) Samuel Johnson returned to his native city, destitute, and not knowing how he should gain even a decent livelihood. His father's misfortunes in trade rendered him unable to support his son; and for some time there appeared no means by which he could maintain himself. In the December of this year, his father died.

The state of poverty in which he died, appears from a note in one of Johnson's little diaries of the following year, which strongly displays his spirit and virtuous dignity of mind. "1732, *Julii* 15. *Undecim aureos desposui, quo die quicquid ante matris funus (quod serum sit precor) de paternis bonis sperari licet, viginti scilicet libras, accepi. Usque adeo mihi fortuna fingenda est. Interea, ne paupertate vires animi languescant, nec in flagitia egestas abigat, cavendum.*—I laid by eleven guineas on this day, when I received twenty pounds, being all that I have reason to hope for out of my father's effects, previous to the death of my mother; an event which I pray God may be very remote. I now therefore see that I must make my own fortune. Meanwhile let me take care that the powers of my mind be not debilitated by poverty, and that indigence do not force me into any criminal act."

Johnson was so far fortunate, that the respectable character of his parents, and his own merit, had, from his earliest years, secured him a kind reception in the best families at Lichfield. Among these I can mention Mr. Howard, Dr. Swinfen, Mr. Simpson, Mr. Levett, Captain Garrick, father of the great ornament of the British stage; but, above all, Mr. Gilbert Walmsley, Registrar of the Ecclesiastical Court of Lichfield, whose character, long after his decease, Dr. Johnson has, in his life of Edmund Smith ("Lives of the Poets"), thus drawn in the glowing colours of gratitude:

"Of Gilbert Walmsley, thus presented to my mind, let me indulge myself in the remembrance. I knew him very early; he was one of the first friends that literature procured me, and I hope, that at least my gratitude made me worthy of his notice.

"He was of an advanced age, and I was only not a boy, yet he never received my notions with contempt. He was a Whig, with all the virulence and malevolence of his party; yet difference of opinion did not keep us apart. I honoured him, and he endured me.

"He had mingled with the gay world, without exemption from its vices or its follies; but had never neglected the cultivation of his mind. His belief of revelation was unshaken; his learning preserved his principles; he grew first regular, and then pious.

"His studies had been so various, that I am not able to name a man of equal knowledge. His acquaintance with books was great, and what he did not immediately know, he could, at least, tell where to find. Such was his amplitude of learning, and such his copiousness of communication, that it may be doubted whether a day now passes, in which I have not some advantage from his friendship.

"At this man's table I enjoyed many cheerful and instructive hours, with companions such as are not often found—with one who has lengthened, and one who has gladdened, life; with Dr. James, whose skill in physic will be long remembered; and with David Garrick, whom I hoped to have gratified with this character of our common friend. But what are the hopes of man? I am disappointed by that stroke of death, which has eclipsed the gaiety of nations, and impoverished the public stock of harmless pleasure."

In these families he passed much time in his early years. In most of them, he was in the company of ladies, particularly at Mr. Walmsley's, whose wife and sisters-in-law, of the name of Aston, and daughters of a baronet, were remarkable for good breeding; so that the notion which has been industriously circulated and believed, that he never was in good company till late in life, and consequently had been confirmed in coarse and ferocious manners by long habits, is wholly without foundation. Some of the ladies have assured me, they recollected him well when a young man, as distinguished for his complaisance.

In the forlorn state of his circumstances, he accepted of an offer to be employed as usher in the school of Market Bosworth, in Leicestershire, to which it appears, from one of his little fragments of a diary, that he went on foot, on the 16th of July.—*"Julii 16, Bosvortiam pedes petii."*

This employment was very irksome to him in every respect, and he complained grievously of it in his letters to his friend, Mr. Hector, who was now settled as a surgeon at Birmingham. The letters are lost; but Mr. Hector recollects his writing "that the poet had described the dull sameness of his existence in these words, *'Vitam continet una dies'* (one day contains the whole of my life); that it was unvaried as the note of the cuckoo; and that he did not know whether it was more disagreeable for him to teach, or the boys to learn, the grammar rules." His general aversion to this painful drudgery was greatly enhanced by a disagreement between him and Sir Wolstan Dixie, the patron of the school, in whose house, I have been told, he officiated as a kind of domestic chaplain, so far, at least, as to say grace at table, but was treated with what he represented as intolerable harshness; and, after suffering for a few months such complicated misery, he relinquished a situation which all his life afterward he recollected with the strongest aversion, and even a degree of horror. But it is probable that at this period, whatever uneasiness he may have endured, he laid the foundation of much future eminence by application to his studies.

Being now again totally unoccupied, he was invited by Mr. Hector to pass some time with him at Birmingham, as his guest, at the house of Mr. Warren, with whom Mr. Hector lodged and boarded. Mr. Warren was the first established bookseller in Birmingham, and was very attentive to Johnson, whom he soon found could be of much service to him in his trade, by his knowledge of literature; and he even obtained the assistance of his pen in furnishing some numbers of a periodical Essay printed in the newspaper, of which Warren was proprietor. After very diligent inquiry, I have not been able to recover those early specimens of that particular mode of writing by which Johnson afterward so greatly distinguished himself.

He continued to live as Mr. Hector's guest for about six months, and then hired lodgings in another part of the town, finding himself as well situated at Birmingham as he supposed he could be anywhere, while he had no settled plan of life, and very scanty means of subsistence. He made some valuable acquaintances there, amongst whom were Mr. Porter, a mercer, whose widow he afterward married, and Mr. Taylor, who, by his ingenuity in mechanical inventions, and his success in trade, acquired an immense fortune. But the comfort of being near Mr.

Hector, his old schoolfellow and intimate friend, was Johnson's chief inducement to continue here.

In what manner he employed his pen at this period, or whether he derived from it any pecuniary advantage, I have not been able to ascertain. He probably got a little money from Mr. Warren; and we are certain, that he executed here one piece of literary labour, of which Mr. Hector has favoured me with a minute account. Having mentioned that he had read at Pembroke College "A Voyage to Abyssinia," by Lobo, a Portuguese Jesuit, and that he thought an abridgment and translation of it from the French into English might be a useful and profitable publication, Mr. Warren and Mr. Hector joined in urging him to undertake it. He accordingly agreed; and the book not being to be found in Birmingham, he borrowed it of Pembroke College. A part of the work being very soon done, one Osborn, who was Mr. Warren's printer, was set to work with what was ready, and Johnson engaged to supply the press with copy as it should be wanted; but his constitutional indolence soon prevailed, and the work was at a stand. Mr. Hector, who knew that a motive of humanity would be the most prevailing argument with his friend, went to Johnson, and represented to him, that the printer could have no other employment till this undertaking was finished, and that the poor man and his family were suffering. Johnson upon this exerted the powers of his mind, though his body was relaxed. He lay in bed with the book, which was a quarto, before him, and dictated while Hector wrote. Mr. Hector carried the sheets to the press, and corrected almost all the proof sheets, very few of which were even seen by Johnson. In this manner, with the aid of Mr. Hector's active friendship, the book was completed, and was published in 1735, with London upon the title-page, though it was in reality printed at Birmingham, a device too common with provincial publishers. For this work, he had from Mr. Warren only the sum of five guineas.

This being the first prose work of Johnson, it is a curious object of inquiry how much may be traced in it of that style which marks his subsequent writings with so happy a union of force, vivacity, and perspicuity. I have perused the book with this view, and have found that here, as I believe in every other translation, there is in the work itself no vestige of the translator's own style; for the language of translation, being adapted to the thoughts of another person, insensibly follows their cast and as it were runs into a mould that is ready prepared.

But in the Preface, the Johnsonian style begins to appear; and though use had not yet taught his wing a permanent and equable flight, there are parts of it which exhibit his best manner in full vigour. I had once the pleasure of examining it with Mr. Edmund Burke, who confirmed me in this opinion by his superior critical sagacity, and was, I remember, much delighted with the following specimen:

"The Portuguese traveller, contrary to the general vein of his countrymen, has amused his reader with no romantic absurdities, or incredible fictions; whatever he relates, whether true or not, is at least probable; and he who tells nothing exceeding the bounds of probability, has a right to demand that they should believe him who cannot contradict him.

"He appears, by his modest and unaffected narration, to have described things as he saw them, to have copied nature from the life, and to have consulted his senses, not his imagination. He meets with no basilisks that destroy with their eyes; his crocodiles devour their prey without tears, and his cataracts fall from the rocks without deafening the neighbouring inhabitants.

"The reader will here find no regions cursed with irremediable barrenness, or blest with spontaneous fecundity; no perpetual gloom, or unceasing sunshine; nor are the nations here described either devoid of all sense of humanity, or consummate in all private or social virtues. Here are no Hottentots without religious policy or articulate language; no Chinese perfectly polite, and completely skilled in all sciences; he will discover, what will always be discovered by a diligent and impartial inquirer, that wherever human nature is to be found, there is a mixture of vice and virtue, a contest of passion and reason; and that the Creator doth not appear partial in his distributions, but has balanced, in most countries, their particular inconveniences by particular favours."

Here we have an early example of that brilliant and energetic expression, which, upon innumerable occasions in his subsequent life, justly impressed the world with the highest admiration.

Nor can anyone, conversant with the writings of Johnson, fail to discern his hand in this passage of the Dedication to John Warren, Esq., of Pembrokeshire, though it is ascribed to Warren, the bookseller. "A generous and elevated mind is distinguished by nothing more certainly than an eminent degree of curiosity; nor is that curiosity ever more agreeably or usefully employed, than in examining the laws and customs of foreign nations. I hope, therefore, the present I now presume to make, will not be thought improper; which, however, it is not my business as a dedicator to commend, nor as a bookseller to depreciate."

It is reasonable to suppose, that his having been thus accidentally led

Gordon Ross del.

New York, 1945

Samuel Johnson.

to a particular study of the history and manners of Abyssinia, was the remote occasion of his writing, many years afterward, his admirable philosophical tale, the principal scene of which is laid in that country.

Johnson returned to Lichfield early in 1734, and in August that year he made an attempt to procure some little subsistence by his pen; for he published proposals for printing by subscription the Latin poems of Politian. "*Angeli Politiani Poemata Latina, quibus Notas, cum historia Latinæ poeseos, a Petrarchæ ævo ad Politiani tempora deducta, et vita Politiani fusius quam antehac enarrata, addidit* SAM. JOHNSON."[1]

It appears that his brother Nathaniel had taken up his father's trade; for it is mentioned that "subscriptions are taken in by the Editor, or N. Johnson, bookseller, of Lichfield." Notwithstanding the merit of Johnson, and the cheap price at which his book was offered, there were not subscribers enough to ensure a sufficient sale; so the work never appeared, and probably never was executed.

We find him again this year at Birmingham, and there is preserved the following letter from him to Mr. Edward Cave, the original compiler and editor of the *Gentleman's Magazine:*

"TO MR. CAVE.

"*Nov. 25, 1734.*

"SIR,—

"As you appear no less sensible than your readers of the defects of your poetical article, you will not be displeased, if, in order to the improvement of it, I communicate to you the sentiments of a person, who will undertake, on reasonable terms, sometimes to fill a column.

"His opinion is, that the public would not give you a bad reception, if, beside the current wit of the month, which a critical examination would generally reduce to a narrow compass, you admitted not only poems, inscriptions, etc., never printed before, which he will sometimes supply you with; but likewise short literary dissertations in Latin or English, critical remarks on authors ancient or modern, forgotten poems that deserve revival, or loose pieces, like Floyer's, worth preserving. By this method, your literary article, for so it might be called, will, he thinks, be better recommended to the public than by low jests, awkward buffoonery, or the dull scurrilities of either party.

"If such a correspondence will be agreeable to you, be pleased to

[1]The book was to contain more than thirty sheets; the price to be two shillings and sixpence at the time of subscribing, and two shillings and sixpence at the delivery of a perfect book in quires.

inform me, in two posts, what the conditions are on which you shall expect it. Your late offer gives me no reason to distrust your generosity. If you engage in any literary projects besides this paper, I have other designs to impart, if I could be secure from having others reap the advantage of what I should hint.

"Your letter, by being directed to *S. Smith,* to be left at the Castle in Birmingham, Warwickshire, will reach

"Your humble servant."

Mr. Cave has put a note on this letter. "Answered Dec. 2." But whether anything was done in consequence of it, we are not informed.

Johnson had, from his early youth, been sensible to the influence of female charms. When at Stourbridge School, he was much enamoured of Olivia Lloyd, a young Quaker, to whom he wrote a copy of verses, which I have not been able to recover; but with what facility and elegance he could warble the amorous lay, will appear from the following lines which he wrote for his friend Mr. Edmund Hector.

VERSES *to a* LADY, *on receiving from her a* SPRIG *of* MYRTLE.

"What hopes, what terrors does thy gift create,
Ambiguous emblem of uncertain fate!
The Myrtle, ensign of supreme command,
Consign'd by Venus to Melissa's hand;
Not less capricious than a reigning fair,
Now grants, and now rejects, a lover's prayer.
In myrtle shades oft sings the happy swain;
In myrtle shades despairing ghosts complain;
The myrtle crowns the happy lovers' heads,
The unhappy lover's grave the myrtle spreads.
O then the meaning of thy gift impart,
And ease the throbbing of an anxious heart!
Soon must this bough, as you shall fix his doom,
Adorn Philander's head, or grace his tomb."

His juvenile attachments to the fair sex were, however, very transient; and it is certain that he formed no criminal connexion whatsoever. Mr. Hector, who lived with him in his younger days in the utmost intimacy and social freedom, has assured me, that even at that ardent season his conduct was strictly virtuous in that respect; and that though he loved to exhilarate himself with wine, he never knew him intoxicated but once.

In a man whom religious education has secured from licentious indulgences, the passion of love, when once it has seized him, is exceedingly strong; being unimpaired by dissipation, and totally concentrated in one object. This was experienced by Johnson, when he became the fervent admirer of Mrs. Porter, after her first husband's death. Miss Porter told me, that when he was first introduced to her mother, his appearance was very forbidding; he was then lean and lank, so that his immense structure of bones was hideously striking to the eye, and the scars of the scrofula were deeply visible. He also wore his hair, which was straight and stiff, and separated behind; and he often had, seemingly, convulsive starts and odd gesticulations, which tended to excite at once surprise and ridicule. Mrs. Porter was so much engaged by his conversation that she overlooked all these external disadvantages, and said to her daughter, "this is the most sensible man that I ever saw in my life."

Though Mrs. Porter was double the age of Johnson, and her person and manner, as described to me by the late Mr. Garrick, were by no means pleasing to others, she must have had a superiority of understanding and talents, as she certainly inspired him with a more than ordinary passion; and she having signified her willingness to accept of his hand, he went to Lichfield to ask his mother's consent to the marriage, which he could not but be conscious was a very imprudent scheme, both on account of their disparity of years, and her want of fortune. But Mrs. Johnson knew too well the ardour of her son's temper, and was too tender a parent to oppose his inclinations.

I know not for what reason the marriage ceremony was not performed at Birmingham; but a resolution was taken that it should be at Derby, for which place the bride and bridegroom set out on horseback, I suppose in very good humour. But though Mr. Topham Beauclerk used archly to mention Johnson's having told him, with much gravity, "Sir, it was a love marriage on both sides," I have had from my illustrious friend the following curious account of their journey to church upon the nuptial morn (9th July):—"Sir, she had read the old romances, and had got into her head the fantastical notion that a woman of spirit should use her lover like a dog. So, Sir, at first she told me that I rode too fast, and she could not keep up with me; and, when I rode a little slower, she passed me, and complained that I lagged behind. I was not to be made the slave of caprice; and I resolved to begin as I meant to end. I therefore pushed on briskly, till I was fairly out of her sight. The road lay between two hedges, so I was sure she could not miss it; and I contrived that she should soon come up with me. When she did, I observed her to be in tears."

This, it must be allowed, was a singular beginning of connubial felicity; but there is no doubt that Johnson, though he thus showed a manly firmness, proved a most affectionate and indulgent husband to the last moment of Mrs. Johnson's life: and in his "Prayers and Meditations" we find very remarkable evidence that his regard and fondness for her never ceased, even after her death.

He now set up a private academy, for which purpose he hired a large house, well situated, near his native city. In the *Gentleman's Magazine* for 1736, there is the following advertisement: "At Edial, near Lichfield, in Staffordshire, young gentlemen are boarded and taught the Latin and Greek languages, by SAMUEL JOHNSON." But the only pupils who were put under his care were the celebrated David Garrick and his brother George, and a Mr. Offely, a young gentleman of good fortune, who died early. As yet, his name had nothing of that celebrity which afterwards commanded the highest attention and respect of mankind. Had such an advertisement appeared after the publication of his "London," or his *Rambler,* or his "Dictionary," how would it have burst upon the world! with what eagerness would the great and the wealthy have embraced an opportunity of putting their sons under the learned tuition of SAMUEL JOHNSON! The truth, however, is, that he was not so well qualified for being a teacher of elements, and a conductor in learning by regular gradations, as men of inferior powers of mind. His own acquisitions had been made by fits and starts, by violent irruptions in the regions of knowledge; and it could not be expected that his impatience would be subdued, and his impetuosity restrained so as to fit him for a quiet guide to novices. The art of communicating instruction, of whatever kind, is much to be valued; and I have ever thought that those who devote themselves to this employment, and do their duty with diligence and success, are entitled to very high respect from the community, as Johnson himself often maintained. Yet I am of opinion that the greatest abilities are not only not required for this office, but render a man less fit for it.

Johnson was not more satisfied with his situation as the master of an academy, than with that of the usher of a school; we need not wonder, therefore, that he did not keep his academy above a year and a half. From Mr. Garrick's account he did not appear to have been profoundly reverenced by his pupils. His oddities of manner, and uncouth gesticulations, could not but be the subject of merriment to them; and in particular, the young rogues used to listen at the door of his bed-chamber, and peep through the key-hole, that they might turn into ridicule his tumultuous and awkward fondness for Mrs. Johnson, whom he used to name by the familiar appellation of *Tetty* or *Tetsey;* which, like *Betty* or *Betsey,* is provincially used as a contraction for *Elizabeth,* her Christian name, but which to us seems ludicrous, when applied to a woman of her age and appearance. Mr. Garrick described her to me as very fat, with a bosom of more than ordinary protuberance, with swelled cheeks, of a florid red, produced by thick painting, and increased by the liberal use of cordials; flaring and fantastic in her dress, and affected both in her speech and general behaviour. I have seen Garrick exhibit her, by his exquisite talent of mimicry, so as to excite the heartiest bursts of laughter; but he, probably, as is the case in all such representations, considerably aggravated the picture.

While Johnson kept his academy, there can be no doubt that he was insensibly furnishing his mind with various knowledge; but I have not discovered that he wrote anything, except a great part of his tragedy of "Irene." Mr. Peter Garrick, the elder brother of David, told me that he remembered Johnson's borrowing the Turkish history of him, in order to form his play from it. When he had finished some part of it, he read what he had done to Mr. Walmsley, who objected to his having already brought his heroine into great distress, and asked him, "How can you possibly contrive to plunge her into deeper calamity?" Johnson, in sly allusion to the supposed oppressive proceedings of the court of which Mr. Walmsley was registrar, replied, "Sir, I can put her into the Spiritual Court!"

Mr. Walmsley, however, was well pleased with this proof of Johnson's abilities as a dramatic writer, and advised him to finish the tragedy, and produce it on the stage.

CHAPTER IV—1737-1738

First Years in London

JOHNSON now thought of trying his fortune in London, the great field of genius and exertion, where talents of every kind have the fullest scope and the highest encouragement. It is a memorable circumstance that his pupil David Garrick went thither at the same time, with intent to complete his education, and follow the profession of the law, from which he was soon diverted by his decided preference for the stage.

How he employed himself upon his first coming to London is not particularly known.[1] I never heard that he found any protection or encouragement by the means of Mr. Colson, to whose academy David Garrick went. Mrs. Lucy Porter told me, that Mr. Walmsley gave him a letter of introduction to Lintot, his bookseller, and that Johnson wrote some things for him; but I imagine this to be a mistake, for I have discovered no trace of it, and I am pretty sure he told me, that Mr. Cave was the first publisher by whom his pen was engaged in London.

He had a little money when he came to town, and he knew how he could live in the cheapest manner. His first lodgings were at the house of Mr. Morris, a stay-maker, in Exeter-street, adjoining Catherine-street, in the Strand. "I dined," said he, "very well for eightpence, with very good company, at the Pine Apple, in New-street, just by. Several of them had travelled. They expected to meet every day; but did not know one another's names. It used to cost the rest a shilling, for they drank wine; but I had a cut of meat for sixpence, and bread for a penny, and gave the waiter a penny; so that I was quite well served, nay, better than the rest, for they gave the waiter nothing."

He at this time, I believe, abstained entirely from fermented liquors; a practice to which he rigidly conformed, for many years together, at different periods of his life.

His Ofellus in the "Art of Living in London," I have heard him relate, was an Irish painter, whom he knew at Birmingham, and who had practised his own precepts of economy for several years in the British capital. He assured Johnson, who, I suppose, was then meditating to try his fortune in London, but was apprehensive of the expense, "that thirty pounds a year was enough to enable a man to live there without being contemptible." He allowed ten pounds for clothes and linen. He said a man might live in a garret at eighteen pence a week; few people would inquire where he lodged; and if they did, it was easy to say, "Sir, I am to be found at such a place." By spending threepence in a coffee-house, he might be for some hours every day in very good company; he might dine for sixpence, breakfast on bread and milk for

---

[1]One curious anecdote was communicated by himself to Mr. John Nichols. Mr. Wilcox, the bookseller, on being informed by him that his intention was to get his livelihood as an author, eyed his robust frame attentively, and with a significant look, said, "You had better buy a porter's knot." He, however, added, "Wilcox was one of my best friends."

a penny, and do without supper. On *clean-shirt-day* he went abroad, and paid visits. I have heard him more than once talk of his frugal friend, whom he recollected with esteem and kindness, and did not like to have one smile at the recital. "This man (said he, gravely,) was a very sensible man, who perfectly understood common affairs; a man of a great deal of knowledge of the world, fresh from life, not strained through books. He borrowed a horse and ten pounds at Birmingham. Finding himself master of so much money, he set off for West Chester, in order to get to Ireland. He returned the horse, and probably the ten pounds too, after he got home."

Considering Johnson's narrow circumstances in the early part of his life, and particularly at the interesting era of his launching into the ocean of London, it is not to be wondered at, that an actual instance, proved by experience, of the possibility of enjoying the intellectual luxury of social life upon a very small income, should deeply engage his attention, and be ever recollected by him as a circumstance of much importance. He amused himself, I remember, by computing how much more expense was absolutely necessary to live upon the same scale with that which his friend described, when the value of money was diminished by the progress of commerce. It may be estimated that double the money might now with difficulty be sufficient.

Amidst this cold obscurity, there was one brilliant circumstance to cheer him; he was well acquainted with Mr. Henry Hervey, one of the branches of the noble family of that name, who had been quartered at Lichfield as an officer of the army, and had at this time a house in London, where Johnson was frequently entertained, and had an opportunity of meeting genteel company. Not very long before his death he mentioned this, among other particulars of his life, which he was kindly communicating to me; and he described this early friend, "Harry Hervey," thus: "He was a vicious man, but very kind to me. If you call a dog Hervey, I shall love him."

He told me he had now written only three acts of his "Irene," and that he retired for some time to lodgings at Greenwich, where he proceeded in it somewhat farther, and used to compose, walking in the Park; but did not stay long enough at that place to finish it.

At this period we find the following letter from him to Mr. Edward Cave, which, as a link in the chain of his literary history, it is proper to insert:

"TO MR. CAVE.

"Greenwich, next door to the Golden Heart,
"Church Street, July 12, 1737.

"SIR,—

"Having observed in your papers very uncommon offers of encouragement to men of letters, I have chosen, being a stranger in London, to communicate to you the following design, which, I hope, if you join in it, will be of advantage to both of us.

"The History of the Council of Trent having been lately translated into French and published with large Notes by Dr. Le Courayer, the reputation of that book is so much revived in England, that, it is presumed, a new translation of it from the Italian, together with Le Courayer's Notes from the French, could not fail of a favourable reception.

"If it be answered, that the History is already in English, it must be remembered, that there was the same objection against Le Courayer's undertaking, with this disadvantage, that the French had a version by one of their best translators, whereas you cannot read three pages of the English History without discovering that the style is capable of great improvements; but whether those improvements are to be expected from the attempt, you must judge from the specimen, which, if you approve the proposal, I shall submit to your examination.

"Suppose the merit of the versions equal, we may hope that the addition of the Notes will turn the balance in our favour, considering the reputation of the Annotator.

"Be pleased to favour me with a speedy answer, if you are not willing to engage in this scheme; and appoint me a day to wait upon you, if you are.

"I am, Sir, your humble servant,

"SAM. JOHNSON."

It should seem from this letter, though subscribed with his own name, that he had not yet been introduced to Mr. Cave. We shall presently see what was done in consequence of the proposal which it contains.

In the course of the summer he returned to Lichfield, where he has left Mrs. Johnson, and there he at last finished his tragedy, which was not executed with his rapidity of composition upon other occasions, but was slowly and painfully elaborated. A few days before his death, while burning a great mass of papers, he picked out from among them the original unformed sketch of this tragedy, in his own hand-writing, and gave it to Mr. Langton, by whose favour a copy of it is now in my possession. It contains fragments of the intended plot, and speeches for the different persons of the drama, partly in the raw materials of prose, partly worked up into verse; as also a variety of hints for illustration, borrowed from the Greek, Roman, and modern writers. The hand-writing is very difficult to be read, even by those who are best acquainted with Johnson's mode of penmanship, which at all times was very particular. The King having graciously accepted of this manuscript as a literary curiosity, Mr. Langton made a fair and distinct copy of it, which he ordered to be bound up with the original and the printed tragedy; and the volume is deposited in the King's library. His Majesty was pleased to permit Mr. Langton to take a copy of it for himself.

Johnson's residence at Lichfield, on his return to it at this time, was only for three months; and as he had as yet seen but a small part of the wonders of the metropolis, he had little to tell his townsmen. He related to me the following minute anecdote of this period: "In the last age, when my mother lived in London, there were two sets of people, those who gave the wall, and those who took it; the peaceable and the quarrelsome. When I returned to Lichfield, after having been in London, my mother asked me, whether I was one of those who gave the wall, or those who took it. *Now* it is fixed that every man keeps to the right; or, if one is taking the wall, another yields it; and it is never a dispute."

He now removed to London with Mrs. Johnson; but her daughter, who had lived with them at Edial, was left with her relations in the country. His lodgings were for some time in Woodstock-street, near Hanover-square, and afterwards in Castle-street, near Cavendish-square. As there is something pleasingly interesting, to many, in tracing so great a man through all his different habitations, I shall, before this work is concluded, present my readers with an exact list of his lodgings and houses, in order of time, which, in placid condescension to my respectful curiosity, he one evening dictated to me, but without specifying how long he lived at each. In the progress of his life, I shall have occasion to mention some of them as connected with particular incidents, or with the writing of particular parts of his works. To some, this minute attention may appear trifling; but when we consider the punctilious exactness with which the different houses in which Milton resided have been traced by the writers of his life, a similar enthusiasm may be pardoned in the biographer of Johnson.

His tragedy being by this time, as he thought, completely finished and fit for the stage, he was very desirous that it should be brought forward. Mr. Peter Garrick told me, that Johnson and he went together to the Fountain tavern, and read it over, and that he afterward solicited Mr. Fleetwood, the patentee of Drury-lane theatre, to have it acted at his house; but Mr. Fleetwood would not accept it, probably because it

St. John's Gate, Clerkenwell

was not patronised by some man of high rank; and it was not acted till 1749, when his friend David Garrick was manager of that theatre.

The *Gentleman's Magazine,* begun and carried on by Mr. Edward Cave, under the name of Sylvanus Urban, had attracted the notice and esteem of Johnson, in an eminent degree, before he came to London, as an adventurer in literature. He told me, that when he first saw St. John's Gate, the place where that deservedly popular miscellany was originally printed, he "beheld it with reverence." I suppose, indeed, that every young author has had the same kind of feeling for the magazine or periodical publication which has first entertained him, and in which he has first had an opportunity to see himself in print, without the risk of exposing his name. I myself recollect such impressions from the *Scots Magazine,* which was begun at Edinburgh in the year 1739, and has been ever conducted with judgment, accuracy, and propriety. I yet cannot help thinking of it with an affectionate regard. Johnson has dignified the *Gentleman's Magazine,* by the importance with which he invests the life of Cave; but he has given it still greater lustre by the various admirable Essays which he wrote for it.

Though Johnson was often solicited by his friends to make a complete list of his writings, and talked of doing it, I believe with a serious intention that they should all be collected on his own account, he put it off from year to year, and at last died without having done it perfectly. I have one in his own handwriting, which contains a certain number; I indeed doubt if he could have remembered every one of them, as they were so numerous, so various, and scattered in such a multiplicity of unconnected publications; nay, several of them published under the names of other persons, to whom he liberally contributed from the abundance of his mind. We must, therefore, be content to discover them, partly from occasional information given by him to his friends, and partly from internal evidence.[2]

His first performance in the *Gentleman's Magazine,* which for many years was his principal source for employment and support, was a copy of Latin verses, in March, 1738, addressed to the editor in so happy a style of compliment, that Cave must have been destitute both of taste and sensibility, had he not felt himself highly gratified.

[2]While in the course of my narrative I enumerate his writings, I shall take care that my readers shall not be left to waver in doubt, between certainty and conjecture, with regard to their authenticity; and, for that purpose, shall mark with an *asterisk* (*) those which he acknowledged to his friends, and with a *dagger* (†) those which are ascertained to be his by internal evidence. When any other pieces are ascribed to him, I shall give my reasons.

It appears that he was now enlisted by Mr. Cave, as a regular coadjutor in his magazine, by which he probably obtained a tolerable livelihood. At what time, or by what means, he had acquired a competent knowledge both of French and Italian, I do not know; but he was so well skilled in them, as to be sufficiently qualified for a translator. That part of his labour which consisted in emendation and improvement of the productions of other contributors, like that employed in levelling ground, can be perceived only by those who had an opportunity of comparing the original with the altered copy. What we certainly know to have been done by him in this way, was the Debates in both Houses of Parliament, under the name of "The Senate of Lilliput," sometimes with feigned denominations of the several speakers, sometimes with denominations formed of the letters of their real names, in the manner of what is called anagram, so that they might easily be deciphered. Parliament then kept the Press in a kind of mysterious awe, which made it necessary to have recourse to such devices. In our time it has acquired an unrestrained freedom, so that the people in all parts of the kingdom have a fair, open, and exact report of the actual proceedings of their representatives and legislators, which in our constitution is highly to be valued; though, unquestionably, there has of late been too much reason to complain of the petulance with which obscure scribblers have presumed to treat men of the most respectable character and situation.

This important article of the *Gentleman's Magazine* was, for several years, executed by Mr. William Guthrie, a man who deserves to be respectably recorded in the literary annals of this country. He was descended of an ancient family in Scotland; but having a small patrimony, and being an adherent of the unfortunate house of Stuart, he could not accept of any office in the state; he therefore came to London, and employed his talents and learning as an "Author by profession." His writings in history, criticism, and politics, had considerable merit.[3] He was the first English historian who had recourse to that authentic source of information, the Parliamentary Journals; and such was the power of his political pen, that, at an early period, government thought it worth their while to keep it quiet by a pension, which he enjoyed till his death. Johnson esteemed him enough to wish that his life should

---

[3]How much poetry he wrote, I know not: but he informed me that he was the author of the beautiful little piece, "The Eagle and Robin Redbreast," in the collection of poems entitled, "The Union," though it is there said to be written by Archibald Scott, before the year 1600.

be written. The details in Parliament, which were brought home and digested by Guthrie, whose memory, though surpassed by others who have since followed him in the same department, was yet very quick and tenacious, were sent by Cave to Johnson for his revision; and after some time, when Guthrie had attained to greater variety of employment, and the speeches were more and more enriched by the accession of Johnson's genius, it was resolved that he should do the whole himself, from the scanty notes furnished by persons employed to attend in both Houses of Parliament. Sometimes, however, as he himself told me, he had nothing more communicated to him than the names of the several speakers, and the part which they had taken in the debate.

Thus was Johnson employed during some of the best years of his life, as a mere literary labourer "for gain not glory," solely to obtain an honest support. He, however, indulged himself in occasional little sallies, which the French so happily express by the term *jeux d'esprit,* and which will be noticed in their order, in the progress of this work.

But what first displayed his transcendent powers, and "gave the world assurance of the Man," was his "London, a poem in Imitation of the Third Satire of Juvenal," which came out in May, this year, and burst forth with splendour, the rays of which will for ever encircle his name. Boileau had imitated the same satire with great success, applying it to Paris: but an attentive comparison will satisfy every reader that he is much excelled by the English Juvenal. Oldham had also imitated it, and applied it to London: all which performances concur to prove, that great cities in every age, and in every country, will furnish similar topics of satire. Whether Johnson had previously read Oldham's imitation, I do not know; but it is not a little remarkable, that there is scarcely any coincidence found between the two performances, though upon the very same subject.

Where, or in what manner, this poem was composed, I am sorry that I neglected to ascertain with precision, from Johnson's own authority. He has marked upon his corrected copy of the first edition of it, "Written in 1738"; and, as it was published in the month of May in that year, it is evident that much time was not employed in preparing it for the press. The history of its publication I am enabled to give in a very satisfactory manner; and, judging from myself, and many of my friends, I trust that it will not be uninteresting to my readers.

We may be certain, though it is not expressly named in the following letters to Mr. Cave, in 1738, that they all relate to it:

"to mr. cave.

"*Castle-street, Wednesday morning.*
[*No date.   1738.*]

"Sir,—

"When I took the liberty of writing to you a few days ago, I did not expect a repetition of the same pleasure so soon; for a pleasure I shall always think it, to converse in any manner with an ingenious and candid man; but having the inclosed poem in my hands to dispose of for the benefit of the author (of whose abilities I shall say nothing, since I send you his performance), I believed I could not procure more advantageous terms from any person than from you, who have so much distinguished yourself by your generous encouragement of poetry; and whose judgment of that art nothing but your commendation of my trifle[4] can give me any occasion to call in question. I do not doubt but you will look over this poem with another eye, and reward it in a different manner, from a mercenary bookseller, who counts the lines he is to purchase, and considers nothing but the bulk. I cannot help taking notice, that, besides what the author may hope for on account of his abilities, he has likewise another claim to your regard, as he lies at present under very disadvantageous circumstances of fortune. I beg, therefore, that you will favour me with a letter to-morrow, that I may know what you can afford to allow him, that he may either part with it to you, or find out (which I do not expect) some other way more to his satisfaction.

"I have only to add, that as I am sensible I have transcribed it very coarsely, which, after having altered it, I was obliged to do, I will, if you please to transmit the sheets from the press, correct it for you; and take the trouble of altering any stroke of satire which you may dislike.

"By exerting on this occasion your usual generosity, you will not only encourage learning, and relieve distress, but (though it be in comparison of the other motives of very small account) oblige in a very sensible manner, Sir, your very humble servant,

"Sam. Johnson."

"to mr. cave.

"*Monday, No. 6, Castle-street.*

"Sir,

"I am to return you thanks for the present you were so kind as to send by me, and to intreat that you will be pleased to inform me, by the

[4]His Ode "Ad Urbanum," probably. N.

[38]

penny-post, whether you resolve to print the poem. If you please to send it me by the post, with a note to Dodsley, I will go and read the lines to him, that we may have his consent to put his name in the title-page. As to the printing, if it can be set immediately about, I will be so much the author's friend, as not to content myself with mere solicitations in his favour. I propose, if my calculation be near the truth, to engage for the reimbursement of all that you shall lose by an impression of five hundred; provided, as you very generously propose, that the profit, if any, be set aside for the author's use, excepting the present you made, which, if he be a gainer, it is fit he should repay. I beg that you will let one of your servants write an exact account of the expense of such an impression, and send it with the poem, that I may know what I engage for. I am very sensible, from your generosity on this occasion, of your regard to learning, even in its unhappiest state; and cannot but think such a temper deserving of the gratitude of those who suffer so often from a contrary disposition.

> "I am, Sir, your most humble servant,
>
> "SAM. JOHNSON."

"TO MR. CAVE.

[*No date.*]

"SIR,

"I waited on you to take the copy to Dodsley's: as I remember the number of lines which it contains, it will be no longer than 'Eugenio,' with the quotations, which must be subjoined at the bottom of the page; part of the beauty of the performance (if any beauty be allowed it) consisting in adapting Juvenal's sentiments to modern facts and persons. It will, with those additions, very conveniently make five sheets. And since the expense will be no more, I shall contentedly insure it, as I mentioned in my last. If it be not therefore gone to Dodsley's, I beg it may be sent me by the penny-post, that I may have it in the evening. I have composed a Greek Epigram to Eliza, and think she ought to be celebrated in as many different languages as Lewis le Grand. Pray send me word when you will begin upon the poem, for it is a long way to walk. I would leave my Epigram, but have not day-light to transcribe it. I am, Sir,

> "Yours, etc.
>
> "SAM. JOHNSON."

"SIR,

"I am extremely obliged by your kind letter, and will not fail to attend you to-morrow with Irene, who looks upon you as one of her best friends.

"I was to-day with Mr. Dodsley, who declares very warmly in favour of the paper you sent him, which he desires to have a share in, it being, as he says, *a creditable thing to be concerned in.* I knew not what answer to make till I had consulted you, nor what to demand on the author's part, but am very willing that, if you please, he should have a part in it, as he will undoubtedly be more diligent to disperse and promote it. If you can send me word to-morrow what I shall say to him, I will settle matters, and bring the poem with me for the press, which, as the town empties, we cannot be too quick with. I am, Sir,

"Yours, etc.

"SAM. JOHNSON."

To us, who have long known the manly force, bold spirit, and masterly versification of this poem, it is a matter of curiosity to observe the diffidence with which its author brought it forward into public notice, while he is so cautious as not to avow it to be his own production; and with what humility he offers to allow the printer to "alter any stroke of satire which he might dislike." That any such alteration was made, we do not know. If we did, we could not but feel an indignant regret; but how painful is it to see that a writer of such vigorous powers of mind was actually in such distress, that the small profit which so short a poem, however excellent, could yield, was courted as a "relief."

It has been generally said, I know not with what truth, that Johnson offered his "London" to several booksellers, none of whom would purchase it. To this circumstance Mr. Derrick alludes in the following lines of his "Fortune, a Rhapsody":

> "Will no kind patron Johnson own?
> Shall Johnson friendless range the town?
> And every publisher refuse
> The offspring of his happy Muse?"

But we have seen that the worthy, modest, and ingenious Mr. Robert Dodsley had taste enough to perceive its uncommon merit, and thought it creditable to have a share in it. The fact is, that, at a future conference, he bargained for the whole property of it, for which he gave Johnson ten guineas; who told me, "I might perhaps have accepted of less; but that Paul Whitehead had a little before got ten guineas for a poem; and I would not take less than Paul Whitehead."

I may here observe, that Johnson appeared to me to undervalue Paul Whitehead upon every occasion when he was mentioned, and, in my opinion, did not do him justice; but when it is considered that Paul Whitehead was a member of a riotous and profane club, we may account for Johnson's having a prejudice against him. Paul Whitehead was, indeed, unfortunate in being not only slighted by Johnson, but violently attacked by Churchill, who utters the following imprecation:

> "May I (can worse disgrace on manhood fall?)
> Be born a Whitehead, and baptized a Paul!"

yet I shall never be persuaded to think meanly of the author of so brilliant and pointed a satire as "Manners."

Johnson's "London," was published in May, 1738; and it is remarkable that it came out on the same morning with Pope's satire, entitled "1738"; so that England had at once its Juvenal and Horace as poetical monitors. The Reverend Dr. Douglas, now Bishop of Salisbury, to whom I am indebted for some obliging communications, was then a student at Oxford, and remembers well the effect which "London" produced. Everybody was delighted with it; and there being no name to it, the first buzz of the literary circles was, "Here is an unknown poet, greater even than Pope." And it is recorded in the *Gentleman's Magazine* of that year, that it "got to the second edition in the course of a week."

One of the warmest patrons of this poem on its first appearance was General OGLETHORPE, whose "strong benevolence of soul" was unabated during the course of a very long life; though it is painful to think, that he had but too much reason to become cold, and callous, and discontented with the world, from the neglect which he experienced of his public and private worth, by those in whose power it was to gratify so gallant a veteran with marks of distinction. This extraordinary person was as remarkable for his learning and taste, as for his other eminent qualities; and no man was more prompt, active, and generous, in encouraging merit. I have heard Johnson gratefully acknowledge, in his presence, the kind and effectual support which he gave to his "London," though unacquainted with its author.

Pope, who then filled the poetical throne without a rival, it may reasonably be presumed, must have been particularly struck by the sudden appearance of such a poet; and, to his credit, let it be remembered, that his feelings and conduct on the occasion were candid and liberal. He requested Mr. Richardson, son of the painter, to endeavour to find out who this new author was. Mr. Richardson, after some inquiry, having informed him that he had discovered only that his name was Johnson, and that he was some obscure man, Pope said, "He will soon be *déterré.*" We shall presently see, from a note written by Pope, that he was himself, afterward, more successful in his inquiries than his friend.

We may easily conceive with what feeling a great mind like his, cramped and galled by narrow circumstances, uttered this last line, which he marked by capitals. The whole of the poem is eminently excellent, and there are in it such proofs of a knowledge of the world, and of a mature acquaintance with life, as cannot be contemplated without wonder, when we consider that he was then only in his twenty-sixth year, and had yet been so little in the "busy haunts of men."

Though thus elevated into fame, and conscious of uncommon powers, he had not that bustling confidence, or, I may rather say, that animated ambition, which one might have supposed would have urged him to endeavour at rising in life. But such was his inflexible dignity of character, that he could not stoop to court the great; without which, hardly any man has made his way to a high station. He could not expect to produce many such works as his "London," and he felt the hardships of writing for bread; he was, therefore, willing to resume the office of a schoolmaster, so as to have a sure, though moderate, income for his life; and an offer being made to him of the mastership of a school, provided he could obtain the degree of Master of Arts, Dr. Adams was applied to, by a common friend, to know whether that could be granted him as a favour from the University of Oxford.—But though he had made such a figure in the literary world, it was then thought too great a favour to be asked.

Pope, without any knowledge of him but from his "London," recommended him to Earl Gower, who endeavoured to procure for him a degree from Dublin, by the following letter to a friend of Dean Swift:

"SIR,

"Mr. Samuel Johnson (author of "London," a satire, and some other poetical pieces) is a native of this country, and much respected by some worthy gentlemen in his neighbourhood, who are trustees of a charity-school now vacant; the certain salary is sixty pounds a year, of which they are desirous to make him master; but unfortunately, he is not capable of receiving their bounty, which *would make him happy for life,* by not being *a Master of Arts;* which, by the statutes of this school, the master of it must be.

"Now these gentlemen do me the honour to think that I have interest enough in you, to prevail upon you to write to Dean Swift, to persuade the University of Dublin to send a diploma to me, constituting this poor man Master of Arts in their University. They highly extol the man's learning and probity; and will not be persuaded, that the University will make any difficulty of conferring such a favour upon a stranger, if he is recommended by the Dean. They say, he is not afraid of the strictest examination, though he is of so long a journey; and will venture it, if the Dean thinks it necessary: choosing rather to die upon the road *than be starved to death in translating for booksellers;* which has been his only subsistence for some time past.

"I fear there is more difficulty in this affair, than those good-natured gentlemen apprehend; especially as their election cannot be delayed longer than the 11th of next month. If you see this matter in the same light that it appears to me, I hope you will burn this, and pardon me for giving you so much trouble about an impracticable thing: but, if you think there is a probability of obtaining the favour asked, I am sure your humanity, and propensity to relieve merit in distress, will incline you to serve the poor man, without my adding any more to the trouble I have already given you, than assuring you that I am, with great truth, Sir,

"Your faithful servant,

"GOWER.

"Trentham, Aug. 1, 1739."

It was, perhaps, no small disappointment to Johnson that this respectable application had not the desired effect; yet how much reason has there been, both for himself and his country, to rejoice that it did not succeed, as he might probably have wasted in obscurity those hours in which he afterwards produced his incomparable works.

CHAPTER V—1738-1743

The Gentleman's Magazine

ABOUT THIS TIME he made one other effort to emancipate himself from the drudgery of authorship. He applied to Dr. Adams, to consult Dr. Smallbrooke of the Commons, whether a person might be permitted to practise as an advocate there, without a doctor's degree in Civil Law. "I am," said he, "a total stranger to these studies; but whatever is a profession, and maintains numbers, must be within the reach of common abilities, and some degree of industry." Dr. Adams was much pleased with Johnson's design to employ his talents in that manner, being confident he would have attained to great eminence. And, indeed, I cannot conceive a man better qualified to make a distinguished figure as a lawyer; for, he would have brought to his profession a rich store of various knowledge, an uncommon acuteness, and a command of language, in which few could have equalled, and none have surpassed him. He, who could display eloquence and wit in defence of the decision of the House of Commons upon Mr. Wilkes's election for Middlesex, and of the unconstitutional taxation of our fellow-subjects in America, must have been a powerful advocate in any cause. But here, also, the want of a degree was an insurmountable bar.

He was therefore under the necessity of persevering in that course into which he had been forced; and we find, that his proposal from Greenwich to Mr. Cave, for a translation of Father Paul Sarpi's History, was accepted.

Some sheets of this translation were printed off, but the design was dropped; for it happened, oddly enough, that another person of the name of Samuel Johnson, Librarian of St. Martin's in the Fields, and Curate of that Parish, engaged in the same undertaking, and was patronised by the Clergy, particularly by Dr. Pearce, afterwards Bishop of Rochester. Several light skirmishes passed between the rival translators, in the newspapers of the day; and the consequence was that they destroyed each other, for neither of them went on with the work. It is much to be regretted that the able performance of that celebrated genius Fra Paolo lost the advantage of being incorporated into British literature by the masterly hand of Johnson.

I have in my possession, by the favour of Mr. John Nichols, a paper in Johnson's handwriting, entitled "Account between Mr. Edward Cave and Sam. Johnson, in relation to a version of Father Paul, etc., begun August the 2nd, 1738"; by which it appears, that from that day to the 21st of April, 1739, Johnson received for this work £49 7s. in sums of one, two, three, and sometimes four guineas at a time, most frequently two. And it is curious to observe the minute and scrupulous accuracy with which Johnson had pasted upon it a slip of paper, which he has entitled "Small account," and which contains one article, "Sept. 9th, Mr. Cave laid down 2s. 6d." There is subjoined to this account, a list of some subscribers to the work, partly in Johnson's handwriting, partly in that of another person; and there follows a leaf or two on which are written a number of characters which have the appearance of a shorthand, which, perhaps, Johnson was then trying to learn.

"TO MR. CAVE.

"*Wednesday.*

"SIR,

"I did not care to detain your servant while I wrote an answer to your letter, in which you seem to insinuate that I had promised more than I am ready to perform. If I have raised your expectations by anything that may have escaped my memory, I am sorry; and if you remind me of it, shall thank you for the favour. If I made fewer alterations than usual in the Debates, it was only because there appeared, and still appears to be, less need of alteration. The verses to Lady Firebrace may be had when you please, for you know that such a subject neither deserves much thought, nor requires it.

"The Chinese Stories may be had folded down when you please to send, in which I do not recollect that you desired any alterations to be made.

"An answer to another query I am very willing to write, and had consulted with you about it last night, if there had been time; for I think it the most proper way of inviting such a correspondence as may be an advantage to the paper, not a load upon it.

"As to the Prize Verses, a backwardness to determine their degrees of merit is not peculiar to me. You may, if you please, still have what I can say; but I shall engage with little spirit in an affair, which I shall *hardly* end to my own satisfaction, and *certainly* not to the satisfaction of the parties concerned.

"As to Father Paul, I have not yet been just to my proposal, but have met with impediments, which, I hope, are now at an end; and if you find the progress hereafter not such as you have a right to expect, you can easily stimulate a negligent translator.

"If any or all of these have contributed to your discontent, I will endeavour to remove it; and desire you to propose the question to which you wish for an answer.

"I am, Sir, your humble servant,

"SAM. JOHNSON."

In 1739, beside the assistance which Johnson gave to the Parliamentary Debates, his writings in the *Gentleman's Magazine* were, "The Life of Boerhaave," [*] in which it is to be observed that he discovers that love of chemistry which never forsook him; "An Appeal to the Public in behalf of the Editor"; [†] "An Address to the *Reader*"; [†] "An Epigram both in Greek and Latin to Eliza," [*] and also English verses to her; [*] and, "A Greek Epigram to Dr. Birch." [*] His separate publications were, "A Complete Vindication of the Licensers of the Stage, from the malicious and scandalous Aspersions of Mr. Brooke, Author of Gustavus Vasa," [*] being an ironical Attack upon them for their Suppression of that Tragedy; and, "Marmor Norfolciense; or an Essay on an ancient prophetical Inscription, in monkish Rhyme, lately discovered near Lynne, in Norfolk, by Probus Britannicus." [*] In this performance, he, in a feigned inscription, supposed to have been found in Norfolk, the county of Sir Robert Walpole, then the obnoxious prime minister of this country, inveighs against the Brunswick succession, and the measures of government consequent upon it. To this supposed prophecy he added a Commentary, making each expression apply to the times, with warm Anti-Hanoverian zeal.

This anonymous pamphlet, I believe, did not make so much noise as was expected, and, therefore, had not a very extensive circulation. Sir John Hawkins relates that "Warrants were issued, and messengers employed to apprehend the author; who, though he had forborne to subscribe his name to the pamphlet, the vigilance of those in pursuit of him had discovered"; and we are informed that he lay concealed in Lambeth-marsh till the scent after him grew cold. This, however, is altogether without foundation; for Mr. Steele, one of the Secretaries of the Treasury, who, amidst a variety of important business, politely obliged me with his attention to my inquiry, informed me that "He directed every possible search to be made in the records of the Treasury and Secretary of State's Office, but could find no trace whatever of any warrant having been issued to apprehend the author of this pamphlet."

"Marmor Norfolciense" became exceedingly scarce, so that I, for many years, endeavoured in vain to procure a copy of it. At last I was indebted to the malice of one of Johnson's numerous petty adversaries, who, in 1775, published a new edition of it, "with Notes, and a Dedication to Samuel Johnson, LL.D., by Tribunus"; in which some puny scribbler invidiously attempted to found upon it a charge of inconsistency against its author, because he had accepted of a pension from his present Majesty, and had written in support of the measures of government. As a mortification to such impotent malice, of which there are so many instances towards men of eminence, I am happy to relate that this *telum imbelle* did not reach its exalted object, till about a year after it thus appeared, when I mentioned it to him, supposing that he knew of the re-publication. To my surprise, he had not yet heard of it. He requested me to go directly and get it for him, which I did. He looked at it, and laughed, and seemed to be much diverted with the feeble efforts of his unknown adversary, who, I hope, is alive to read this account. "Now (said he) here is somebody who thinks he has vexed me sadly; yet, if it had not been for you, you rogue, I should probably never have seen it."

As Mr. Pope's note concerning Johnson, alluded to in a former page, refers both to his "London," and his "Marmor Norfolciense," I have deferred inserting it till now. I am indebted for it to Dr. Percy, the Bishop of Dromore, who permitted me to copy it from the original in his possession. It was presented to his Lordship by Sir Joshua Reynolds, to whom it was given by the son of Mr. Richardson the painter, the person to whom it was addressed. I have transcribed it with minute exactness, that the peculiar mode of writing, and imperfect spelling of that celebrated poet, may be exhibited to the curious in literature. It justifies Swift's epithet of "paper-sparing Pope," for it is written on a slip no larger than a common message-card, and was sent to Mr. Richardson, along with the imitation of Juvenal.

"This is imitated by one Johnson who put in for a Publick-school in Shropshire, but was disappointed. He has an infirmity of the convulsive kind, that attacks him sometimes, so as to make Him a sad Spectacle. Mr. P. from the Merit of This Work which was all the knowledge he had of Him endeavour'd to serve Him without his own application; & wrote to my L^d gore, but he did not succeed. Mr. Johnson published afterw^dᵃ another Poem in Latin with Notes the whole very Humerous call'd the Norfolk Prophecy.

"P."

Johnson had been told of this note; and Sir Joshua Reynolds informed him of the compliment which it contained, but, from delicacy, avoided showing him the paper itself. When Sir Joshua observed to Johnson that he seemed very desirous to see Pope's note, he answered, "Who would not be proud to have such a man as Pope so solicitous in inquiring about him?"

The infirmity to which Mr. Pope alludes appeared to me also, as I have elsewhere observed, to be of the convulsive kind, and of the nature of that distemper called St. Vitus's dance; and in this opinion I am confirmed by the description which Sydenham gives of that disease. "This disorder is a kind of convulsion. It manifests itself by halting or unsteadiness of one of the legs, which the patient draws after him like an idiot. If the hand of the same side be applied to the breast, or any other part of the body, he cannot keep it a moment in the same posture, but it will be drawn into a different one by a convulsion, notwithstanding all his efforts to the contrary." Sir Joshua Reynolds, however, was of a different opinion, and favoured me with the following paper.

"These motions or tricks of Dr. Johnson are improperly called convulsions. He could sit motionless, when he was told to do so, as well as any other man. My opinion is, that it proceeded from a habit which he had indulged himself in, of accompanying his thoughts with certain untoward actions, and those actions always appeared to me as if they were meant to reprobate some part of his past conduct. Whenever he was not engaged in conversation, such thoughts were sure to rush into his mind; and, for this reason, any company, any employment whatever, he preferred to being alone. The great business of his life, he said, was to escape from himself; this disposition he considered as the disease of his mind, which nothing cured but company.

"One instance of his absence and particularity, as it is characteristic of the man, may be worth relating. When he and I took a journey together into the West, we visited the late Mr. Banks, of Dorsetshire; the conversation turning upon pictures, which Johnson could not well see, he retired to a corner of the room, stretching out his right leg as far as he could reach before him, then bringing up his left leg, and stretching his right still further on. The old gentleman observing him, went up to him, and in a very courteous manner assured him, though it was not a new house, the flooring was perfectly safe. The Doctor started from his reverie, like a person waked out of his sleep, but spoke not a word."

While we are on this subject, my readers may not be displeased with another anecdote, communicated to me by the same friend, from the relation of Mr. Hogarth.

Johnson used to be a pretty frequent visitor at the house of Mr. Richardson, author of "Clarissa," and other novels of extensive reputation. Mr. Hogarth came one day to see Richardson, soon after the execution of Dr. Cameron, for having taken arms for the House of Stuart in 1745–6; and being a warm partizan of George the Second, he observed to Richardson that certainly there must have been some very unfavourable circumstances lately discovered in this particular case, which had induced the King to approve of an execution for rebellion so long after the time when it was committed, as this had the appearance of putting a man to death in cold blood, and was very unlike his Majesty's usual clemency. While he was talking, he perceived a person standing at the window in the room, shaking his head, and rolling himself about in a strange, ridiculous manner. He concluded that he was an idiot, whom his relations had put under the care of Mr. Richardson, as a very good man. To his great surprise, however, this figure stalked forwards to where he and Mr. Richardson were sitting, and all at once took up the argument, and burst out into an invective against George the Second, as one, who, upon all occasions, was unrelenting and barbarous; mentioning many instances, particularly, that when an officer of high rank had been acquitted by a Court Martial, George the Second had with his own hand struck his name off the list. In short, he displayed such a power of eloquence, that Hogarth looked at him with astonishment, and actually imagined that this idiot had been at the moment inspired. Neither Hogarth nor Johnson were made known to each other at this interview.

In 1741 he wrote for the *Gentleman's Magazine* the "Preface," [†] "Conclusion of his lives of Drake and Barretier," [*] "A free translation of the Jests of Hierocles, with an Introduction"; [†] and, I think, the following pieces: "Debate on the Proposal of Parliament to Cromwell, to assume the title of King, abridged, modified, and digested"; [†] "Translation of Abbé Guyon's Dissertation on the Amazons"; [†] "Translation of Fontenelle's Panegyric on Dr. Morin." [†] Two notes upon this appear to me undoubtedly his. He this year, and the two following, wrote the Parliamentary Debates. He told me himself that he was the sole composer of them for those three years only. He was not, however, precisely exact in his statement, which he mentioned from hasty recollection; for it is sufficiently evident that his composition of them began November 19, 1740, and ended February 23, 1742-3.

It appears from some of Cave's letters to Dr. Birch, that Cave had better assistance for that branch of his Magazine than had been generally supposed; and that he was indefatigable in getting it made as perfect as he could.

There is no reason, I believe, to doubt the veracity of Cave. It is, however, remarkable that none of these letters are in the years during which Johnson alone furnished the Debates, and one of them is in the very year after he ceased from that labour. Johnson told me, that as soon as he found that the speeches were thought genuine, he determined that he would write no more of them; "For he would not be accessory to the propagation of falsehood." And such was the tenderness of his conscience, that a short time before his death he expressed his regret for his having been the author of fictions, which had passed for realities.

He nevertheless agreed with me in thinking that the Debates which he had framed were to be valued as orations upon questions of public importance. They have accordingly been collected in volumes, properly arranged, and recommended to the notice of parliamentary speakers by a preface, written by no inferior hand. I must, however, observe, that although there is in those Debates a wonderful store of political information, and very powerful eloquence, I cannot agree that they exhibit the manner of each particular speaker, as Sir John Hawkins seems to think. But, indeed, what opinion can we have of his judgment, and taste in public speaking, who presumes to give, as the characteristics of two celebrated orators, "the deep-mouthed rancour of Pulteney, and the yelping pertinacity of Pitt."

This year I find that his tragedy of "Irene" had been for some time ready for the stage, and that his necessities made him desirous of getting as much as he could for it, without delay; for there is the following letter from Mr. Cave to Dr. Birch, in the same volume of manuscripts in the British Museum, from which I copied those above quoted. They were most obligingly pointed out to me by Sir William Musgrave, one of the Curators of that noble repository.

"Sept. 9, 1741.

"I have put Mr. Johnson's play into Mr. Gray's hands, in order to sell it to him, if he is inclined to buy it; but I doubt whether he will or not. He would dispose of the copy, and whatever advantage may be made by acting it. Would your society, or any gentleman, or body of men that you know, take such a bargain? He and I are very unfit to deal with theatrical persons. Fleetwood was to have acted it last season, but Johnson's diffidence or ¹ prevented it."

I have already mentioned that "Irene" was not brought into public notice till Garrick was manager of Drury-lane theatre.

In 1742 he wrote for the *Gentleman's Magazine* the "Preface," [†] the "Parliamentary Debates," [*] "Essay on the Account of the Conduct of the Duchess of Marlborough," [*] then the popular topic of conversation. This Essay is a short but masterly performance. We find him, in No. 13 of his *Rambler,* censuring a profligate sentiment in that "Account"; and again insisting upon it strenuously in conversation. "An Account of the Life of Peter Burman," [*] I believe chiefly taken from a foreign publication; as, indeed, he could not himself know much about Burman; "Additions to his Life of Barretier"; [*] "The Life of Sydenham," [*] afterwards prefixed to Dr. Swan's edition of his works; "Proposals for printing Bibliotheca Harleiana, or a Catalogue of the Library of the Earl of Oxford." [*] His account of that celebrated collection of books, in which he displays the importance to literature, of what the French call a *catalogue raisonné,* when the subjects of it are extensive and various, and it is executed with ability, cannot fail to impress all his readers with admiration of his philological attainments. It was afterwards prefixed to the first volume of the Catalogue, in which the Latin accounts of books were written by him. He was employed in this business by Mr. Thomas Osborne, the bookseller, who purchased the library for £13,000, a sum which Mr. Oldys says, in one of his manuscripts, was not more than the binding of the books had cost; yet, as Dr. Johnson assured me, the slowness of the sale was such, that there was not much gained by it. It has been confidently related, with many embellishments, that Johnson one day knocked Osborne down in his shop, with a folio, and put his foot upon his neck. The simple truth I had from Johnson himself. "Sir, he was impertinent to me, and I beat him. But it was not in his shop; it was in my own chamber."

A very diligent observer may trace him where we should not easily suppose him to be found. I have no doubt that he wrote the little abridgment entitled "Foreign History," in the Magazine for December.

I am obliged to Mr. Astle for his ready permission to copy the two following letters, of which the originals are in his possession. Their con-

¹There is no erasure here, but a mere blank; to fill up which may be an exercise for ingenious conjecture.

tents show that they were written about this time, and that Johnson was now engaged in preparing an historical account of the British Parliament.

"TO MR. CAVE.

[*No date.*]

"SIR,—

"I believe I am going to write a long letter, and have therefore taken a whole sheet of paper. The first thing to be written about is our historical design.

"You mentioned the proposal of printing in numbers, as an alteration in the scheme, but I believe you mistook, some way or other, my meaning; I had no other view than that you might rather print too many of five sheets than of five-and-thirty.

"With regard to what I shall say on the manner of proceeding, I would have it understood as wholly indifferent to me, and my opinion only, not my resolution. *Emptoris sit eligere.*

"I think the insertions of the exact dates of the most important events in the margin, or of so many events as may enable the reader to regulate the order of facts with sufficient exactness, the proper medium between a journal, which has regard only to time, and a history which ranges facts according to their dependence on each other, and postpones or anticipates according to the convenience of narration. I think the work ought to partake of the spirit of history, which is contrary to minute exactness, and of the regularity of a journal, which is inconsistent with spirit. For this reason, I neither admit numbers or dates, nor reject them.

"I am of your opinion with regard to placing most of the resolutions, etc., in the margin, and think we shall give the most complete account of parliamentary proceedings that can be contrived. The naked papers, without an historical treatise interwoven, require some other book to make them understood. I will date the succeeding facts with some exactness, but I think in the margin. You told me on Saturday that I had received money on this work, and found set down £13 2s. 6d. reckoning the half-guinea of last Saturday. As you hinted to me that you had many calls for money, I would not press you too hard, and therefore shall desire only, as I send it in, two guineas for a sheet of copy; the rest you may pay me when it may be more convenient; and even by this sheet-payment I shall, for some time, be very expensive.

"The 'Life of Savage' I am ready to go upon; and in Great Primer, and Pica notes, I reckon on sending in half a sheet a day; but the money for that shall likewise lie by in your hands till it is done. With the debates, shall not I have business enough? if I had but good pens.

"Towards Mr. Savage's Life what more have you got? I would willingly have his trial, etc., and know whether his defence be at Bristol, and would have his collection of poems, on account of the Preface;— "The Plain Dealer,"—all the magazines that have anything of his or relating to him.

"I thought my letter would be long, but it is now ended; and

"I am, Sir, yours, etc.,

"SAM. JOHNSON."

"The boy found me writing this almost in the dark, when I could not quite easily read yours.

"I have read the Italian:—nothing in it is well.

"I had no notion of having any thing for the inscription. I hope you don't think I kept it to extort a price. I could think of nothing, till to-day. If you could spare me another guinea for the history, I should take it very kindly, to-night; but if you do not I shall not think it an injury. . . . I am almost well again."

"TO MR. CAVE.

"SIR,—

"You did not tell me your determination about the "Soldier's Letter," which I am confident was never printed. I think it will not do by itself, or in any other place, so well as the Mag. Extraordinary. If you will have it all, I believe you do not think I set it high, and I will be glad if what you give you will give quickly.

"You need not be in care about something to print, for I have got the State Trials, and shall extract Layer, Atterbury, and Macclesfield from them, and shall bring them to you in a fortnight; after which I will try to get the South Sea Report."

[*No date, nor signature.*]

I would also ascribe to him an "Essay on the Description of China," from the French of Du Halde.[†]

His writings in the *Gentleman's Magazine* in 1743 are the Preface, [†] the Parliamentary Debates, [†] "Considerations on the Dispute between Crousaz and Warburton, on Pope's 'Essay on Man' "; [†] in which, while he defends Crousaz, he shows an admirable metaphysical acuteness and temperance in controversy; "Ad Lauram parituram

Epigramma"; [*] and, "A Latin Translation of Pope's Verses on his Grotto"; [*] and, as he could employ his pen with equal success upon a small matter as a great, I suppose him to be the author of an advertisement for Osborne, concerning the great Harleian Catalogue.

Johnson had now an opportunity of obliging his schoolfellow, Dr. James, of whom he once observed, "no man brings more mind to his profession." James published this year his "Medicinal Dictionary," in three volumes folio. Johnson, as I understood from him, had written, or assisted in writing, the proposals for this work; and being very fond of the study of physic, in which James was his master, he furnished some of the articles. He, however, certainly wrote for it the Dedication to Dr. Mead, [†] which is conceived with great address, to conciliate the patronage of that very eminent man.

His circumstances were at this time embarrassed; yet his affection for his mother was so warm, and so liberal, that he took upon himself a debt of hers, which, though small in itself, was then considerable to him. This appears from the following letter which he wrote to Mr. Levett, of Lichfield, the original of which lies now before me.

"TO MR. LEVETT; IN LICHFIELD.

"*December 1, 1743.*

"Sir,—

"I am extremely sorry that we have encroached so much upon your forbearance with respect to the interest, which a great perplexity of affairs hindered me from thinking of with that attention that I ought, and which I am not immediately able to remit to you, but will pay it (I think twelve pounds) in two months. I look upon this, and on the future interest of that mortgage, as my own debt; and beg that you will be pleased to give me directions how to pay it, and not mention it to my dear mother. If it be necessary to pay this in less time, I believe I can do it; but I take two months for certainty, and beg an answer whether you can allow me so much time. I think myself very much obliged to your forbearance, and shall esteem it a great happiness to be able to serve you. I have great opportunities of dispersing any thing that you may think it proper to make public. I will give a note for the money, payable at the time mentioned, to any one here that you shall appoint.

"I am, Sir, your most obedient
"And most humble servant,
"SAM. JOHNSON.

"*At Mr. Osborne's, bookseller, in Gray's Inn.*"

CHAPTER VI—1744–1748

Richard Savage

IT DOES NOT APPEAR that he wrote anything in 1744 for the *Gentleman's Magazine* but the Preface. [*] His "Life of Barretier" was now re-published in a pamphlet by itself. But he produced one work this year, fully sufficient to maintain the high reputation which he had acquired. This was "The Life of Richard Savage"; [*] a man, of whom it is difficult to speak impartially, without wondering that he was for some time the intimate companion of Johnson; for his character[1] was marked by profligacy, insolence, and ingratitude: yet, as he undoubtedly had a warm and vigorous, though unregulated mind, had seen life in all its varieties, and been much in the company of the statesmen and wits of his time, he could communicate to Johnson an abundant supply of such materials as his philosophical curiosity most eagerly desired; and, as Savage's misfortunes and misconduct had reduced him to the lowest state of wretchedness as a writer for his bread, his visit to St. John's Gate naturally brought Johnson and him together.[2]

[1]As a specimen of his temper, I insert the following letter from him to a noble lord, to whom he was under great obligations, but who, on account of his bad conduct, was obliged to discard him. The original was in the hands of the late Francis Cockayne Cust, Esq., one of his Majesty's Counsel learned in the law:
"*Right Honourable* BRUTE *and* BOOBY,—

"I find you want (as Mr. ———— is pleased to hint) to swear away my life, that is, the life of your creditor, because he asks you for a debt.—The public shall soon be acquainted with this, to judge whether you are not fitter to be an Irish Evidence, than to be an Irish Peer.—I defy and despise you. I am,
"Your determined adversary,
"R. S."

[2]Sir John Hawkins gives the world to understand that Johnson, "being an admirer of genteel manners, was captivated by the address and demeanour of Savage, who, as to his exterior, was to a remarkable degree accomplished."—Hawkins's "Life," p. 52. But Sir John's notions of gentility must appear somewhat ludicrous, from his stating the following circumstance as presumptive evidence that Savage was a good swordsman: "That he understood the exercise of a gentleman's weapon, may be inferred from the use made of it in that rash encounter which is related in his life." The dexterity here alluded to was, that Savage, in a nocturnal fit of drunkenness, stabbed a man at a coffee-house, and killed him: for which he was tried at the Old Bailey and found guilty of murder.
Johnson, indeed, describes him as having "A grave and manly deportment, a solemn dignity of mien; but which, upon a nearer acquaintance, softened into an engaging easiness of manners."

It is melancholy to reflect, that Johnson and Savage were sometimes in such extreme indigence, that they could not pay for a lodging; so that they have wandered together whole nights in the streets. Yet, in these almost incredible scenes of distress, we may suppose that Savage mentioned many of the anecdotes with which Johnson afterwards enriched the life of this unhappy companion, and those of other Poets.

He told Sir Joshua Reynolds, that one night in particular, when Savage and he walked round St. James's-square for want of a lodging, they were not at all depressed by their situation; but, in high spirits and brimful of patriotism, traversed the square for several hours, inveighed against the minister, and "resolved they would *stand by their country*."

I am afraid, however, that by associating with Savage, who was habituated to the dissipation and licentiousness of the town, Johnson, though his good principles remained steady, did not entirely preserve that conduct for which, in days of greater simplicity, he was remarked by his friend Mr. Hector; but was imperceptibly led into some indulgences which occasioned much distress to his virtuous mind.

That Johnson was anxious that an authentic and favourable account of his extraordinary friend should first get possession of the public attention, is evident from a letter which he wrote in the *Gentleman's Magazine* for August of the year preceding its publication.

"Mr. Urban,—

"As your collections show how often you have owed the ornaments of your poetical pages to the correspondence of the unfortunate and ingenious Mr. Savage, I doubt not but you have so much regard to his memory as to encourage any design that may have a tendency to the preservation of it from insults or calumnies; and therefore, with some degree of assurance, entreat you to inform the public, that his life will speedily be published by a person who was favoured with his confidence, and received from himself an account of most of the transactions which he proposes to mention, to the time of his retirement to Swansea in Wales.

"From that period, to his death in the prison of Bristol, the account will be continued from materials still less liable to objection; his own letters, and those of his friends, some of which will be inserted in the work, and abstracts of others subjoined in the margin.

"It may reasonably be imagined that others may have the same design; but as it is not credible that they can obtain the same materials, it must be expected they will supply from invention the want of in-

Gordon Ross del.

New York, 1945

The house in Lichfield where Johnson was born.

telligence; and that under the title of 'The Life of Savage,' they will publish only a novel, filled with romantic adventures and imaginary amours. You may therefore, perhaps, gratify the lovers of truth and wit, by giving me leave to inform them in your Magazine, that my account will be published in 8vo by Mr. Roberts, in Warwick Lane."

[*No signature.*]

In February, 1744, it accordingly came forth from the shop of Roberts, between whom and Johnson I have not traced any connexion, except the casual one of this publication. In Johnson's "Life of Savage," although it must be allowed that its moral is the reverse of—"*Respicere exemplar vitæ morumque jubelo,*" a very useful lesson is inculcated to guard men of warm passions from a too free indulgence of them; and the various incidents are related in so clear and animated a manner, and illuminated throughout with so much philosophy, that it is one of the most interesting narratives in the English language. Sir Joshua Reynolds told me that upon his return from Italy he met with it in Devonshire, knowing nothing of its author, and began to read it while he was standing with his arm leaning against a chimney-piece. It seized his attention so strongly, that, not being able to lay down the book till he had finished it, when he attempted to move, he found his arm totally benumbed. The rapidity with which this work was composed is a wonderful circumstance. Johnson has been heard to say, "I wrote forty-eight of the printed octavo pages of the 'Life of Savage' at a sitting; but then I sat up all night."

It is remarkable, that in this biographical disquisition there appears a very strong symptom of Johnson's prejudice against players; a prejudice which may be attributed to the following causes: first, the imperfection of his organs, which were so defective that he was not susceptible of the fine impressions which theatrical excellence produces upon the generality of mankind; secondly, the cold rejection of his tragedy; and, lastly, the brilliant success of Garrick, who had been his pupil, who had come to London at the same time with him, not in a much more prosperous state than himself, and whose talents he undoubtedly rated low, compared with his own. His being outstripped by his pupil in the race of immediate fame, as well as of fortune, probably made him feel some indignation, as thinking that whatever might be Garrick's merits in his art, the reward was too great when compared with what the most successful efforts of literary labour could attain. At all periods of his life, Johnson used to talk contemptuously of players, but in this work he speaks of them with peculiar acrimony; for which, perhaps, there was formerly too much reason, from the licentious and dissolute manners of those engaged in that profession. It is but justice to add, that in our own time such a change has taken place, that there is no longer room for such an unfavourable distinction.

His schoolfellow and friend, Dr. Taylor, told me a pleasant anecdote of Johnson's triumphing over his pupil, David Garrick. When that great actor had played some little time at Goodman's fields, Johnson and Taylor went to see him perform, and afterwards passed the evening at a tavern with him and old Giffard. Johnson, who was ever depreciating stage-players, after censuring some mistakes in emphasis, which Garrick had committed in the course of that night's acting, said, "The players, Sir, have got a kind of rant, with which they run on, without any regard either to accent or emphasis." Both Garrick and Giffard were offended at this sarcasm, and endeavoured to refute it; upon which Johnson replied, "Well, now, I'll give you something to speak, with which you are little acquainted, and then we shall see how just my observation is. That shall be the criterion. Let me hear you repeat the ninth Commandment, 'Thou shalt not bear false witness against thy neighbour.'" Both tried at it, said Dr. Taylor, and both mistook the emphasis which should be upon *not* and *false witness*. Johnson put them right, and enjoyed his victory with great glee.

He this year wrote the "Preface to the Harleian Miscellany." [*] The selection of the pamphlets of which it was composed was made by Mr. Oldys, a man of eager curiosity and indefatigable diligence, who first exerted that spirit of inquiry into the literature of the old English writers, by which the works of our great dramatic poet have of late been so signally illustrated.

In 1745 he published a pamphlet entitled, "Miscellaneous Observations on the Tragedy of Macbeth, with Remarks on Sir T. H.'s (Sir Thomas Hanmer's) Edition of Shakspeare." [*] To which he affixed proposals for a new edition of that poet.

As we do not trace any thing else published by him during the course of this year, we may conjecture that he was occupied entirely with that work. But the little encouragement which was given by the public to his anonymous proposals for the execution of a task which Warburton was known to have undertaken, probably damped his ardour. His pamphlet, however, was highly esteemed, and was fortunate enough to obtain the approbation even of the supercilious Warburton himself, who, in the Preface to his Shakspeare published two years afterwards, thus mentioned it: "As to all those things which have been published under the titles of *Essays, Remarks, Observations,* etc., on Shakspeare, if you except some Critical Notes on Macbeth, given as a specimen of a projected edition, and written, as appears, by a man of parts and genius, the rest are absolutely below a serious notice."

Of this flattering distinction shown to him by Warburton, a very grateful remembrance was ever entertained by Johnson, who said, "He praised me at a time when praise was of value to me."

In 1746 it is probable that he was still employed upon his Shakspeare, which perhaps he laid aside for a time, upon account of the high expectations which were formed of Warburton's edition of that great poet. It is somewhat curious that his literary career appears to have been almost totally suspended in the years 1745 and 1746, those years which were marked by a civil war in Great Britain, when a rash attempt was made to restore the House of Stuart to the throne. That he had a tenderness for that unfortunate House, is well known; and some may fancifully imagine that a sympathetic anxiety impeded the exertion of his intellectual powers: but I am inclined to think that he was, during this time, sketching the outlines of his great philological work.

None of his letters during those years are extant, so far as I can discover. This is much to be regretted. It might afford some entertainment to see how he then expressed himself to his private friends concerning State affairs. Dr. Adams informs me, that "At this time a favourite object which he had in contemplation was 'The Life of Alfred'; in which, from the warmth with which he spoke about it, he would, I believe, had he been master of his own will, have engaged himself, rather than on any other subject."

In 1747 it is supposed that the *Gentleman's Magazine* for May was enriched by him with five short poetical pieces, distinguished by three asterisks. The first is a translation, or rather a paraphrase, of a Latin Epitaph on Sir Thomas Hanmer. Whether the Latin was his, or not, I have never heard, though I should think it probably was, if it be certain that he wrote the English; as to which, my only cause of doubt is, that his slighting character of Hanmer as an editor, in his "Observations on Macbeth," is very different from that in the Epitaph. It may be said that there is the same contrariety between the character in the Observations, and that in his own Preface to Shakspeare; but a considerable time elapsed between the one publication and the other, whereas the Observations and the Epitaph came close together. The others are, "To Miss ——, on her giving the Author a gold and silk network Purse of her own weaving"; "Stella in Mourning"; "The Winter's Walk"; "An Ode"; and, "To Lyce, an elderly Lady." I am not positive that all these were his productions; but as "The Winter's Walk" has never been controverted to be his, and all of them have the same mark, it is reasonable to conclude that they are all written by the same hand. Yet to the Ode, in which we find a passage very characteristic of him, being a learned description of the gout,

> "Unhappy, whom to beds of pain
> *Arthritick* tyranny consigns";

there is the following note, "The author being ill of the gout"; but Johnson was not attacked with that distemper till a very late period of his life. May not this, however, be a poetical fiction? Why may not a poet suppose himself to have the gout as well as suppose himself to be in love, of which we have innumerable instances, and which has been admirably ridiculed by Johnson in his "Life of Cowley"? I have also some difficulty to believe that he could produce such a group of *conceits* as appear in the verses to Lyce, in which he claims for this ancient personage as good a right to be assimilated to *heaven,* as nymphs whom other poets have flattered: he therefore ironically ascribes to her the attributes of the *sky,* in such stanzas as this:

> "Her teeth the *night* with *darkness* dies,
> She's *starr'd* with pimples o'er;
> Her tongue like nimble *lightning* plies,
> And can with *thunder* roar."

But as at a very advanced age he could condescend to trifle in *namby-pamby* rhymes, to please Mrs. Thrale, and her daughter, he may have, in his earlier years, composed such a piece as this.

It is remarkable, that in this first edition of "The Winter's Walk," the concluding line is much more Johnsonian than it was afterwards printed; for in subsequent editions, after praying Stella to "snatch him to her arms," he says,

> "And *shield* me from the *ills* of life."

Whereas in the first edition it is

> "And *hide* me from the *sight* of life."

A horror at life in general is more consonant with Johnson's habitual gloomy cast of thought.

This year his old pupil and friend, David Garrick, having become joint patentee and manager of Drury-lane theatre, Johnson honoured his opening of it with a Prologue, [*] which for just and manly dramatic criticism on the whole range of the English stage, as well as for poetical excellence, is unrivalled. Like the celebrated Epilogue to the "Distressed Mother," it was, during the season, often called for by the audience. The most striking and brilliant passages of it have been so often repeated and are so well recollected by all the lovers of the drama, and of poetry, that it would be superfluous to point them out. In the *Gentleman's Magazine* for December this year, he inserted an "Ode on Winter," which is, I think, an admirable specimen of his genius for lyric poetry.

But the year 1747 is distinguished as the epoch, when Johnson's arduous and important work, his "Dictionary of the English Language," was announced to the world, by the publication of its Plan or "Prospectus."

How long this immense undertaking had been the object of his contemplation, I do not know. I once asked him by what means he had attained to that astonishing knowledge of our language, by which he was enabled to realise a design of such extent and accumulated difficulty. He told me that "it was not the effect of particular study; but that it had grown up in his mind insensibly." I have been informed by Mr. James Dodsley that several years before this period, when Johnson was one day sitting in his brother Robert's shop, he heard his brother suggest to him that a Dictionary of the English Language would be a work that would be well received by the public; that Johnson seemed at first to catch at the proposition, but, after a pause, said, in his abrupt decisive manner, "I believe I shall not undertake it." That he, however, had bestowed much thought upon the subject, before he published his "Plan," is evident from the enlarged, clear, and accurate views which it exhibits; and we find him mentioning in that tract that many of the writers whose testimonies were to be produced as authorities, were selected by Pope; which proves that he had been furnished, probably by Mr. Robert Dodsley, with whatever hints that eminent poet had contributed towards a great literary project, that had been the subject of important consideration in a former reign.

The booksellers who contracted with Johnson, single and unaided, for the execution of a work, which in other countries has not been effected but by the co-operating exertions of many, were Mr. Robert Dodsley, Mr. Charles Hitch, Mr. Andrew Millar, the two Messieurs

Longman, and the two Messieurs Knapton. The price stipulated was £1,575.

The "Plan" was addressed to Philip Dormer, Earl of Chesterfield, then one of his Majesty's Principal Secretaries of State; a nobleman who was very ambitious of literary distinction, and who, upon being informed of the design, had expressed himself in terms very favourable to its success. There is, perhaps in everything of any consequence, a secret history which it would be amusing to know, could we have it authentically communicated. Johnson told me, "Sir, the way in which the plan of my Dictionary came to be inscribed to Lord Chesterfield, was this: I had neglected to write it by the time appointed. Dodsley suggested a desire to have it addressed to Lord Chesterfield. I laid hold of this as a pretext for delay, that it might be better done, and let Dods-

Lord Chesterfield

ley have his desire. I said to my friend, Dr. Bathurst, "Now, if any good comes of my addressing to Lord Chesterfield, it will be ascribed to deep policy, when, in fact, it was only a casual excuse for laziness."

It is worthy of observation, that the "Plan" has not only the substantial merit of comprehension, perspicuity, and precision, but that the language of it is unexceptionally excellent; it being altogether free from that inflation of style, and those uncommon but apt and energetic words, which in some of his writings have been censured, with more petulance than justice; and never was there a more dignified strain of compliment than that in which he courts the attention of one who, he had been persuaded to believe, would be a respectable patron.

"With regard to question of purity or propriety [says he], I was once in doubt whether I should not attribute to myself too much in attempting to decide them, and whether my province was to extend beyond the proposition of the question, and the display of the suffrages on each side; but I have been since determined by your Lordship's opinion, to interpose my own judgment, and shall therefore endeavour to support what appears to me most consonant to grammar and reason. Ausonius thought that modesty forbade him to plead inability for a task to which Cæsar had judged him equal:

Cur me posse negem, posse quod ille putat?

And I may hope, my Lord, that since you, whose authority in our language is so generally acknowledged, have commissioned me to declare my own opinion, I shall be considered as exercising a kind of vicarious jurisdiction; and that the power which might have been denied to my own claim, will be readily allowed me as the delegate of your Lordship."

This passage proves that Johnson's addressing his "Plan" to Lord Chesterfield was not merely in consequence of the result of a report by means of Dodsley, that the Earl favoured the design; but that there had been a particular communication with his Lordship concerning it. Dr. Taylor told me that Johnson sent his "Plan" to him in manuscript, for his perusal; and that when it was lying upon his table, Mr. William Whitehead happened to pay him a visit, and being shown it, was highly pleased with such parts of it as he had time to read, and begged to take it home with him, which he was allowed to do; that from him it got into the hands of a noble Lord, who carried it to Lord Chesterfield. When Taylor observed this might be an advantage, Johnson replied, "No, Sir, it would have come out with more bloom, if it had not been seen before by anybody."

The opinion conceived of it by another noble author, appears from the following extract of a letter from the Earl of Orrery to Dr. Birch:

"Caledon, Dec. 30, 1747.

"I have just now seen the specimen of Mr. Johnson's Dictionary, addressed to Lord Chesterfield. I am much pleased with the plan, and I think the specimen is one of the best that I have ever read. Most specimens disgust, rather than prejudice us in favour of the work to follow; but the language of Mr. Johnson's is good, and the arguments are properly and modestly expressed. However, some expressions may be cavilled at, but they are trifles. I'll mention one: the *barren* Laurel. The laurel is not barren, in any sense whatever; it bears fruit and flowers. *Sed hæ sunt nugæ,* and I have great expectations from the performance."

That he was fully aware of the arduous nature of the undertaking, he acknowledges; and shows himself perfectly sensible of it in the conclusion of his "Plan"; but he had a noble consciousness of his own abilities, which enabled him to go on with undaunted spirit.

Dr. Adams found him one day busy at his Dictionary, when the following dialogue ensued. ADAMS: This is a great work, Sir. How are you to get all the etymologies? JOHNSON: Why, Sir, here is a shelf with Junius, and Skinner, and others; and there is a Welsh gentleman who has published a collection of Welsh proverbs, who will help me with the Welsh. ADAMS: But, Sir, how can you do this in three years? JOHNSON: Sir, I have no doubt that I can do it in three years. ADAMS: But the French Academy, which consists of forty members, took forty years to compile their Dictionary. JOHNSON: Sir, thus it is. This is the proportion. Let me see; forty times forty is sixteen hundred. As three to sixteen hundred, so is the proportion of an Englishman to a Frenchman. With so much ease and pleasantry could he talk of that prodigious labour which he had undertaken to execute.

The public has had from another pen[3] a long detail of what had been done in this country by prior Lexicographers; and no doubt Johnson was wise to avail himself of them, so far as they went; but the learned, yet judicious research of etymology, the various, yet accurate display of definition, and the rich collection of authorities, were reserved for the superior mind of our great philologist. For the mechanical part he employed, as he told me, six amanuenses; and let it be remembered by the natives of North Britain, to whom he is supposed to have been

[3]See Sir John Hawkins's "Life of Johnson."

so hostile, that five of them were of that country. There were two Messieurs Macbean; Mr. Shiels, who we shall hereafter see partly wrote the "Lives of the Poets," to which the name of Cibber is affixed; Mr. Stewart, son of Mr. George Stewart, bookseller at Edinburgh; and a Mr. Maitland. The sixth of these humble assistants was Mr. Peyton, who, I believe, taught French, and published some elementary tracts.

To all these painful labourers Johnson showed a never-ceasing kindness, so far as they stood in need of it. The elder Mr. Macbean had afterwards the honour of being Librarian to Archibald Duke of Argyle, for many years, but was left without a shilling. Johnson wrote for him a Preface to "A System of Ancient Geography"; and, by the favour of Lord Thurlow, got him admitted a poor brother of the Charterhouse. For Shiels, who died of a consumption, he had much tenderness; and it has been thought that some choice sentences in the "Lives of the Poets" were supplied by him. Peyton, when reduced to penury, had frequent aid from the bounty of Johnson, who at last was at the expense of burying him and his wife.

While the Dictionary was going forward, Johnson lived part of the time in Holborn, part in Gough-square, Fleet-street; and he had an upper room fitted up like a counting-house for the purpose, in which he gave to the copyists their several tasks. The words, partly taken from other dictionaries, and partly supplied by himself, having been first written down with spaces left between them, he delivered in writing their etymologies, definitions, and various significations. The authorities were copied from the books themselves, in which he had marked the passages with a black-lead pencil, the traces of which could easily be effaced. I have seen several of them, in which that trouble had not been taken; so that they were just as when used by the copyists. It is remarkable that he was so attentive in the choice of the passages in which words are authorized, that one may read page after page of his Dictionary with improvement and pleasure; and it should not pass unobserved, that he has quoted no author whose writings had a tendency to hurt sound religion and morality.

The necessary expense of preparing a work of such magnitude for the press, must have been a considerable deduction from the price stipulated to be paid for the copyright. I understand that nothing was allowed by the booksellers on that account; and I remember his telling me, that a large portion of it having, by mistake, been written upon both sides of the paper, so as to be inconvenient for the compositor, it cost him twenty pounds to have it transcribed upon one side only.

He is now to be considered as "tugging at his oar," as engaged in a steady continued course of occupation, sufficient to employ all his time for some years; and which was the best preventive of that constitutional melancholy which was ever lurking about him, ready to trouble his quiet. But his enlarged and lively mind could not be satisfied without more diversity of employment, and the pleasure of animated relaxation. He therefore not only exerted his talents in occasional compositions very different from Lexicography, but formed a club in Ivy-lane, Paternoster-row, with a view to enjoy literary discussion, and amuse his evening hours. The members associated with him in this little society were his beloved friend, Dr. Richard Bathurst, Mr. Hawkesworth, afterwards well known by his writing, Mr. John Hawkins, an attorney, and a few others of different professions.

CHAPTER VII—1749–1750

The "Rambler"

IN JANUARY, 1749, he published "The Vanity of Human Wishes, being the Tenth Satire of Juvenal imitated." [*] He, I believe, composed it the preceding year. Mrs. Johnson, for the sake of country air, had lodgings at Hampstead, to which he resorted occasionally, and there the greatest part, if not the whole, of this Imitation was written. The fervid rapidity with which it was produced, is scarcely credible. I have heard him say that he composed seventy lines of it in one day, without putting one of them upon paper till they were finished. I remember, when I once regretted to him that he had not given us more of Juvenal Satires, he said he probably should give more, for he had them all in his head; by which I understood, that he had the originals and correspondent allusions floating in his mind, which he could, when he pleased, embody and render permanent without much labour. Some of them, however, he observed, were too gross for imitation.

The profits of a single poem, however excellent, appear to have been very small in the last reign, compared with what a publication of the same size has since been known to yield. I have mentioned, upon Johnson's own authority, that for his "London" he had only ten guineas; and now, after his fame was established, he got for his "Vanity of

Human Wishes," but five guineas more, as is proved by an authentic document in my possession.

It will be observed that he reserves to himself the right of printing one edition of this satire, which was his practice upon occasion of the sale of all his writings; it being his fixed intention to publish at some period, for his own profit, a complete collection of his works.

Garrick being now vested with theatrical power, by being manager of Drury-lane Theatre, he kindly and generously made use of it to bring out Johnson's tragedy, which had been long kept back for want of encouragement. But in this benevolent purpose he met with no small difficulty from the temper of Johnson, which could not brook that a drama which he had formed with much study, and had been obliged to keep more than the nine years of Horace, should be revised and altered at the pleasure of an actor. Yet Garrick knew well, that without some alterations it would not be fit for the stage. A violent dispute having ensued between them, Garrick applied to the Reverend Dr. Taylor to interpose. Johnson was at first very obstinate. "Sir (said he), the fellow wants me to make Mahomet run mad, that he may have an opportunity of tossing his hands and kicking his heels." He was, however, at last, with difficulty, prevailed on to comply with Garrick's wishes, so as to allow of some changes; but still there were not enough.

Dr. Adams was present the first night of the representation of "Irene," and gave me the following account: "Before the curtain drew up, there were catcalls and whistling, which alarmed Johnson's friends. The Prologue, which was written by himself, in a manly strain, soothed the audience, and the play went off tolerably, till it came to the conclusion, when Mrs. Pritchard, the Heroine of the piece, was to be strangled upon the stage, and was to speak two lines with the bow-string round her neck. The audience cried out *'Murder! Murder!'* She several times attempted to speak; but in vain. At last she was obliged to go off the stage alive." This passage was afterwards struck out, and she was carried off to be put to death behind the scenes, as the play now has it. The Epilogue, as Johnson informed me, was written by Sir William Yonge. I know not how his play came to be thus graced by the pen of a person then so eminent in the political world.

Notwithstanding all the support of such performers as Garrick, Barry, Mrs. Cibber, Mrs. Pritchard, and every advantage of dress and decoration, the tragedy of "Irene" did not please the public. Mr. Garrick's zeal carried it through for nine nights, so that the author had his three nights' profits; and from a receipt signed by him, now in the hands of Mr. James Dodsley, it appears that his friend, Mr. Robert Dodsley, gave him £100 for the copy, with his usual reservation of the right of one edition.

"Irene," considered as a poem, is entitled to the praise of superior excellence. Analysed into parts, it will furnish a rich store of noble sentiments, fine imagery, and beautiful language; but it is deficient in pathos, in that delicate power of touching the human feelings, which is the principal end of the drama. Indeed, Garrick has complained to me that Johnson not only had not the faculty of producing the impressions of tragedy, but that he had not the sensibility to perceive them. His great friend Mr. Walmsley's prediction, that he would "turn out a fine tragedy writer," was, therefore, ill-founded. Johnson was wise enough to be convinced that he had not the talents necessary to write successfully for the stage, and never made another attempt in that species of composition.

When asked how he felt upon the ill-success of his tragedy, he replied, "Like the Monument"; meaning, that he continued firm and unmoved as that column. And let it be remembered, as an admonition to the *genus irritabile* of dramatic writers, that this great man, instead of peevishly complaining of the bad taste of the town, submitted to its decision without a murmur. He had, indeed, upon all occasions a great deference for the general opinion: "A man," said he, "who writes a book thinks himself wiser or wittier than the rest of mankind; he supposes that he can instruct or amuse them, and the public, to whom he appeals, must, after all, be the judges of his pretensions."

On occasion of this play being brought upon the stage, Johnson had a fancy that as a dramatic author his dress should be more gay than what he ordinarily wore; he therefore appeared behind the scenes, and even in one of the side boxes, in a scarlet waistcoat, with rich gold lace, and a gold-laced hat. He humorously observed to Mr. Langton "that when in that dress he could not treat people with the same ease as when in his usual plain clothes." Dress, indeed, we must allow, has more effect even upon strong minds than one should suppose, without having had the experience of it. His necessary attendance while his play was in rehearsal, and during its performance, brought him acquainted with many of the performers, of both sexes, which produced a more favourable opinion of their profession than he had harshly expressed in his "Life of Savage." With some of them he kept up an acquaintance as long as he and they lived, and was ever ready to show them acts of kindness. He for a considerable time used to frequent the

Green-Room, and seemed to take delight in dissipating his gloom, by mixing in the sprightly chit-chat of the motley circle then to be found there. Mr. David Hume related to me from Mr. Garrick that Johnson at last denied himself that amusement, from considerations of rigid virtue; saying: "I'll come no more behind your scenes, David; for the silk stockings and white bosoms of your actresses excite my amorous propensities."

In 1750, he came forth in the character for which he was eminently qualified, a majestic teacher of moral and religious wisdom. The vehicle which he chose was that of a periodical paper, which he knew had been, upon former occasions, employed with great success. The *Tatler, Spectator,* and *Guardian* were the last of the kind published in England, which had stood the test of a long trial; and such an interval had now elapsed since their publication as made him justly think that, to many of his readers, this form of instruction would, in some degree, have the advantage of novelty. A few days before the first of his Essays came out, there started another competitor for fame in the same form, under the title of *The Tatler Revived,* which I believe was "born but to die." Johnson was, I think, not very happy in the choice of his title—the *Rambler;* which certainly is not suited to a series of grave and moral discourses; which the Italians have literally, but ludicrously, translated by *Il Vagabondo;* and which has been lately assumed as the denomination of a vehicle of licentious tales, the *Rambler's Magazine.* He gave Sir Joshua Reynolds the following account of its getting this name: "What *must* be done, Sir, *will* be done. When I was to begin publishing that paper, I was at a loss how to name it. I sat down at night upon my bedside, and resolved that I would not go to sleep till I had fixed its title. The *Rambler* seemed the best that occurred, and I took it."

The first paper of the *Rambler* was published on Tuesday, the 20th of March, 1749–50; and its author was enabled to continue it, without interruption, every Tuesday and Saturday, till Saturday, the 17th of March, 1752, on which day it closed. This is a strong confirmation of the truth of a remark of his, which I have had occasion to quote elsewhere, that "a man may write at any time, if he will set himself doggedly to it"; for, notwithstanding his constitutional indolence, his depression of spirits, and his labour in carrying on his Dictionary, he answered the stated calls of the press twice a week from the stores of his mind during all that time; having received no assistance, except four billets in No. 10, by Miss Mulso, now Mrs. Chapone; No. 30, by Mrs.

Catharine Talbot; No. 97, by Mr. Samuel Richardson, whom he describes in an introductory note' as "An author who has enlarged the knowledge of human nature and taught the passions to move at the command of virtue"; and Nos. 44 and 100, by Mrs. Elizabeth Carter.

Posterity will be astonished when they are told, upon the authority of Johnson himself, that many of these discourses, which we should suppose had been laboured with all the slow attentions of literary leisure, were written in haste as the moment pressed, without even being read over by him before they were printed. It can be accounted for only in this way: that by reading and meditation, and a very close inspection of life, he had accumulated a great fund of miscellaneous knowledge, which, by a peculiar promptitude of mind, was ever ready at his call, and which he had constantly accustomed himself to clothe in the most apt and energetic expression. Sir Joshua Reynolds once asked him by what means he had attained his extraordinary accuracy and flow of language. He told him, that he had early laid it down as a fixed rule to do his best on every occasion, and in every company; to impart whatever he knew in the most forcible language he could put it in; and that by constant practice, and never suffering any careless expressions to escape him, or attempting to deliver his thoughts without arranging them in the clearest manner, it became habitual to him.

As the *Rambler* was entirely the work of one man, there was, of course, such a uniformity in its texture, as very much to exclude the charm of variety; and the grave and often solemn cast of thinking, which distinguished it from other periodical papers, made it, for some time, not generally liked. So slowly did this excellent work, of which twelve editions have now issued from the press, gain upon the world at large, that even in the closing number the author says, "I have never been much of a favourite of the public."

Yet, very soon after its commencement, there were those who felt and acknowledged its uncommon excellence. Verses in its praise appeared in the newspapers; and the editor of the *Gentleman's Magazine* mentions, in October, his having received several letters to the same purpose from the learned. *The Student, or Oxford and Cambridge Miscellany,* in which Mr. Bonnel Thornton and Mr. Colman were the principal writers, describes it as "a work that exceeds any thing of the kind ever published in this kingdom, some of the *Spectators* excepted —if indeed they may be excepted." And afterwards, "May the public favours crown his merits, and may not the English, under the auspicious reign of George the Second, neglect a man, who, had he lived in the first century, would have been one of the greatest favourites of Augustus." This flattery of the monarch had no effect. It is too well known, that the second George never was an Augustus to learning or genius.

Johnson told me, with an amiable fondness, a little pleasing circumstance relative to this work. Mrs. Johnson, in whose judgment and taste he had great confidence, said to him, after a few numbers of the *Rambler* had come out, "I thought very well of you before; but I did not imagine you could have written any thing equal to this." Distant praise, from whatever quarter, is not so delightful as that of a wife whom a man loves and esteems. Her approbation may be said to "come home to his *bosom*"; and being so near, its effect is most sensible and permanent.

Mr. James Elphinston, who has since published various works, and who was ever esteemed by Johnson as a worthy man, happened to be in Scotland while the *Rambler* was coming out in single papers at London. With a laudable zeal at once for the improvement of his countrymen, and the reputation of his friend, he suggested and took the charge of an edition of those Essays at Edinburgh, which followed progressively the London publication.[1]

The *Rambler* has increased in fame as in age. Soon after its first folio edition was concluded, it was published in six duodecimo volumes, and its author lived to see ten numerous editions of it in London, beside those of Ireland and Scotland.

I profess myself to have ever entertained a profound veneration for the astonishing force and vivacity of mind which the *Rambler* exhibits. That Johnson has penetration enough to see, and seeing would not disguise, the general misery of man in this state of being, may have given rise to the superficial notion of his being too stern a philosopher. But men of reflection will be sensible that he has given a true representation of human existence, and that he has, at the same time, with a generous benevolence displayed every consolation which our state affords us; not only those arising from the hopes of futurity, but such as may be attained in the immediate progress through life. He has not depressed the soul to despondency and indifference. He has everywhere

---

[1] It was executed in the printing-office of Sands, Murray, and Cochran, with uncommon elegance, upon writing paper, of a duodecimo size, and with the greatest correctness; and Mr. Elphinston enriched it with translations of the mottoes. When completed, it made eight handsome volumes. It is, unquestionably, the most accurate and beautiful edition of this work; and there being but a small impression, it is now become scarce, and sells at a very high price.

inculcated study, labour, and exertion. Nay, he has shown, in a very odious light, a man whose practice is to go about darkening the views of others, by perpetual complaints of evil, and awakening those considerations of danger and distress, which are, for the most part, lulled into a quiet oblivion. This he has done very strongly in his character of Suspirius, from which Goldsmith took that of Croker, in his comedy of "The Good-natured Man," as Johnson told me he acknowledged to him, and which is, indeed, very obvious.

To point out the numerous subjects which the *Rambler* treats, with a dignity and perspicuity which are there united in a manner which we shall in vain look for anywhere else, would take up too large a portion of my book, and would, I trust, be superfluous, considering how universally those volumes are now disseminated. Even the most condensed and brilliant sentences which they contain, and which have very properly been selected under the name of "Beauties," are of considerable bulk. But I may shortly observe, that the *Rambler* furnishes such an assemblage of discourses on practical religion and moral duty, of critical investigations, and allegorical and oriental tales, that no mind can be thought very deficient that has, by constant study and meditation, assimilated to itself all that may be found there. No. 7, written in Passion-week, on abstraction and self-examination, and No. 119, on penitence and the placability of the Divine Nature, cannot be too often read. No. 54, on the effect which the death of a friend should have upon us, though rather too dispiriting, may be occasionally very medicinal to the mind. Every one must suppose the writer to have been deeply impressed by a real scene; but he told me that was not the case; which shows how well his fancy could conduct him to the "house of mourning." Some of these more solemn papers, I doubt not, particularly attracted the notice of Dr. Young, the author of "The Night Thoughts," of whom my estimation is such, as to reckon his applause an honour even to Johnson. I have seen volumes of Dr. Young's copy of the *Rambler,* in which he has marked the passages which he thought particularly excellent, by folding down a corner of the page; and such as he rated in a super-eminent degree, are marked by double folds. I am sorry that some of the volumes are lost. Johnson was pleased when told of the minute attention with which Young had signified his approbation of his Essays.

Though instruction be the predominant purpose of the *Rambler,* yet it is enlivened with a considerable portion of amusement. Nothing can be more erroneous than the notion which some persons have entertained, that Johnson was then a retired author, ignorant of the world; and, of consequence, that he wrote only from his imagination, when he described characters and manners. He said to me, that before he wrote that work, he had been "running about the world," as he expressed it, more than almost anybody; and I have heard him relate, with much satisfaction, that several of the characters in the *Rambler* were drawn so naturally, that when it first circulated in numbers, a club, in one of the towns of Essex, imagined themselves to be severally exhibited in it, and were much incensed against a person who, they suspected, had thus made them objects of public notice; nor were they quieted till authentic assurance was given them, that the *Rambler* was written by a person who had never heard of any one of them. Some of the characters are believed to have been actually drawn from the life, particularly that of Prospero from Garrick, who never entirely forgave its pointed satire. For instances of fertility of fancy, and accurate description of real life, I appeal to No. 19, a man who wanders from one profession to another, with most plausible reasons for every change: No. 34, female fastidiousness and timorous refinement: No. 82, a Virtuoso who has collected curiosities: No. 98, petty modes of entertaining a company, and conciliating kindness: No. 182, fortune-hunting: No. 194–195, a tutor's account of the follies of his pupil: No. 197–198, legacy-hunting: He has given a specimen of his nice observation, of the mere external appearances of life, in the following passage in No. 179, against affectation, that frequent and most disgusting quality: "He that stands to contemplate the crowds that fill the streets of a populous city, will see many passengers, whose air and motions it will be difficult to behold without contempt and laughter; but if he examine what are the appearances that thus powerfully excite his risibility, he will find among them neither poverty nor disease, nor any involuntary or painful defect. The disposition to derision and insult is awakened by the softness of foppery, the swell of insolence, the liveliness of levity, or the solemnity of grandeur; by the sprightly trip, the stately stalk, the formal strut, and the lofty mien; by gestures intended to catch the eye, and by looks elaborately formed as evidences of importance."

Every page of the *Rambler* shows a mind teeming with classical allusion and poetical imagery: illustrations from other writers are, upon all occasions, so ready, and mingle so easily in his periods, that the whole appears of one uniform vivid texture.

The style of this work has been censured by some shallow critics as involved and turgid, and abounding with antiquated and hard words. So ill-founded is the first part of this objection, that I will challenge all who may honour this book with a perusal, to point out any English writer whose language conveys his meaning with equal force and perspicuity. It must, indeed, be allowed, that the structure of his sentences is expanded, and often has somewhat of the inversion of Latin; and that he delighted to express familiar thoughts in philosophical language; being in this the reverse of Socrates, who, it is said, reduced philosophy to the simplicity of common life. But let us attend to what he himself says in his concluding paper: "When common words were less pleasing to the ear, or less distinct in their signification, I have familiarized the terms of philosophy, by applying them to popular ideas." And, as to the second part of this objection, upon a late careful revision of the work, I can with confidence say, that it is amazing how few of these words, for which it has been unjustly characterised, are actually to be found in it; I am sure, not the proportion of one to each paper. This idle charge has been echoed from one babbler to another, who have confounded Johnson's Essays with Johnson's Dictionary; and because he thought it right in a Lexicon of our language to collect many words which had fallen into disuse, but were supported by great authorities, it has been imagined that all of these have been interwoven into his own compositions. That some of them have been adopted by him unnecessarily, may, perhaps, be allowed; but, in general, they are evidently an advantage, for without them his stately ideas would be confined and cramped. "He that thinks with more extent than another, will want words of larger meaning." He once told me that he had formed his style upon that of Sir William Temple, and upon Chambers's Proposal for his Dictionary. He certainly was mistaken; or, if he imagined at first that he was imitating Temple, he was very unsuccessful; for nothing can be more unlike than the simplicity of Temple, and the richness of Johnson. Their styles differ as plain cloth and brocade.

The style of Johnson was, undoubtedly, much formed upon that of the great writers in the last century, Hooker, Bacon, Sanderson, Hakewell, and others; those "Giants," as they were well characterised by *a great Personage,* whose authority were I to name him, would stamp a reverence on the opinion.

Yet Johnson assured me that he had not taken upon him to add more than four or five words to the English language, of his own information; and he was very much offended at the general licence by no means "modestly taken" in his time, not only to coin new words, but to use many words in senses quite different from their established meaning, and those frequently very fantastical.

Sir Thomas Browne, whose life Johnson wrote, was remarkably fond of Anglo-Latin diction; and to his example we are to ascribe Johnson's sometimes indulging himself in this kind of phraseology. Johnson's comprehension of mind was the mould for his language. Had his conceptions been narrower, his expression would have been easier. His sentences have a dignified march; and it is certain that his example has given a general elevation to the language of his country, for many of our best writers have approached very near to him; and, from the influence which he has had upon our composition, scarcely any thing is written now that is not better expressed than was usual before he appeared to lead the national taste.

Johnson's language, however, must be allowed to be too masculine for the delicate gentleness of female writing. His ladies, therefore, seem strangely formal, even to ridicule; and are well denominated by the names which he has given them, as Misella, Zozima, Properantia, Rhodoclia.

It has of late been the fashion to compare the style of Addison and Johnson, and to depreciate, I think, very unjustly, the style of Addison as nerveless and feeble, because it has not the strength and energy of that of Johnson. Their prose may be balanced like the poetry of Dryden and Pope. Both are excellent, though in different ways. Addison writes with the ease of a gentleman. His readers fancy that a wise and accomplished companion is talking to them; so that he insinuates his sentiments and taste into their minds by an imperceptible influence. Johnson writes like a teacher. He dictates to his readers as if from an academical chair. They attend with awe and admiration; and his precepts are impressed upon them by his commanding eloquence. Addison's style, like a light wine, pleases everybody from the first. Johnson's, like a liquor of more body, seems too strong at first, but, by degrees, is highly relished; and such is the melody of his periods, so much do they captivate the ear, and seize upon the attention, that there is scarcely any writer, however inconsiderable, who does not aim, in some degree, at the same species of excellence. But let us not ungratefully undervalue that beautiful style, which has pleasingly conveyed to us much instruction and entertainment. Though comparatively weak, opposed to Johnson's Herculean vigour, let us not call it positively feeble. Let us remember the character of his style, as given by Johnson himself: "What he attempted, he performed: he is *never feeble,* and he did not wish to be energetic; he is never rapid, and he never stagnates. His sentences have neither studied amplitude, nor affected brevity: his periods, though not diligently rounded, are voluble and easy. Whoever wishes to attain an English style, familiar but not coarse, and elegant but not ostentatious, must give his days and nights to the volumes of Addison."

Though the *Rambler* was not concluded till the year 1752, I shall, under this year, say all that I have to observe upon it. Some of the translations of the mottoes by himself, are admirably done. He acknowledges to have received "elegant translations" of many of them from Mr. James Elphinston; and some are very happily translated by a Mr. *F. Lewis,* of whom I never heard more, except that Johnson thus described him to Mr. Malone:—"Sir, he lived in London, and hung loose upon society." The concluding paper of his *Rambler* is at once dignified and pathetic. I cannot, however, but wish that he had not ended it with an unnecessary Greek verse, translated also into an English couplet. It is too much like the conceit of those dramatic poets, who used to conclude each act with a rhyme; and the expression in the first line of his couplet, "Celestial Powers," though proper in Pagan poetry, is ill suited to Christianity, with "a conformity" to which he consoles himself. How much better would it have been to have ended with the prose sentence, "I shall never envy the honours which wit and learning obtain in any other cause, if I can be numbered among the writers who have given ardour to virtue and confidence to truth."

His friend, Dr. Birch, being now engaged in preparing an edition of Ralegh's smaller pieces, Dr. Johnson wrote the following letter to that gentleman:

"TO DR. BIRCH.

"*Gough-square, May 12, 1750.*

"SIR,—

"Knowing that you are now preparing to favour the public with a new edition of Ralegh's miscellaneous pieces, I have taken the liberty to send you a Manuscript, which fell by chance within my notice. I perceive no proofs of forgery in my examination of it; and the owner tells me that, as he has heard, the hand-writing is Sir Walter's. If you should find reason to conclude it genuine, it will be a kindness to the owner, a blind person, to recommend it to the booksellers.

"I am, Sir, your most humble servant,

"SAM. JOHNSON."

His just abhorrence of Milton's political notions was ever strong. But this did not prevent his warm admiration of Milton's great poetical merit, to which he has done illustrious justice, beyond all who have written upon the subject. And this year he not only wrote a Prologue, which was spoken by Mr. Garrick before the acting of "Comus" at Drury-lane Theatre, for the benefit of Milton's grand-daughter, but took a very zealous interest in the success of the charity. On the day preceding the performance, he published the following letter in the *General Advertiser,* addressed to the printer of that paper.

"Sir,—
"That a certain degree of reputation is acquired merely by approving the works of genius, and testifying a regard to the memory of authors, is a truth too evident to be denied; and therefore to ensure a participation of fame with a celebrated poet, many, who would, perhaps, have contributed to starve him when alive, have heaped expensive pageants on his grave.

"It must, indeed, be confessed, that this method of becoming known to posterity with honour, is peculiar to the great, or at least to the wealthy; but an opportunity now offers for almost every individual to secure the praise of paying a just regard to the illustrious dead, united with the pleasure of doing good to the living. To assist industrious indigence, struggling with distress and debilitated by age, is a display of virtue, and an acquisition of happiness and honour.

"Whoever, then, would be thought capable of pleasure in reading the works of our incomparable Milton, and not so destitute of gratitude as to refuse to lay out a trifle in rational and elegant entertainment, for the benefit of his living remains, for the exercise of their own virtue, the increase of their reputation, and the pleasing consciousness of doing good, should appear at Drury-lane Theatre to-morrow, April 5, when 'Comus' will be performed for the benefit of Mrs. Elizabeth Foster, grand-daughter to the author, and the only surviving branch of the family.

"N.B.—There will be a new prologue on the occasion, written by the author of 'Irene,' and spoken by Mr. Garrick; and, by particular desire, there will be added to the Masque, a dramatic satire, called 'Lethe,' in which Mr. Garrick will perform."

CHAPTER VIII—1751-1754

Johnson's Circle of Friends

IN 1751 we are to consider him as carrying on both his Dictionary and *Rambler*. But he also wrote "The Life of Cheynel" [*] in the miscellany called *The Student;* and the Reverend Dr. Douglas having with uncommon acuteness clearly detected a gross forgery and imposition upon the public by William Lauder, a Scotch schoolmaster, who had, with equal impudence and ingenuity, represented Milton as a plagiary from certain modern Latin poets, Johnson, who had been so far imposed upon as to furnish a Preface and Postcript to his work, now dictated a letter for Lauder, addressed to Dr. Douglas, acknowledging his fraud in terms of suitable contrition.[1]

This extraordinary attempt of Lauder was no sudden effort. He had brooded over it for many years; and to this hour it is uncertain what his principal motive was, unless it were a vain notion of his superiority, in being able, by whatever means, to deceive mankind. To effect this, he produced certain passages from Grotius, Masenius, and others, which had a faint resemblance to some parts of the "Paradise Lost." In these he interpolated some fragments of Hog's Latin translation of that poem, alleging that the mass thus fabricated was the archetype from which Milton copied. These fabrications he published from time to time in the *Gentleman's Magazine;* and, exulting in his fancied success, he in 1750 ventured to collect them into a pamphlet entitled, "An Essay on Milton's Use and Imitation of the Moderns in his 'Para-

---

[1]Lest there should be any person, at any future period, absurd enough to suspect that Johnson was a partaker in Lauder's fraud, or had any knowledge of it, when he assisted him with his masterly pen, it is proper here to quote the words of Dr. Douglas, now Bishop of Salisbury, at the time when he detected the imposition. "It is to be hoped, nay it is *expected,* that the elegant and nervous writer, whose judicious sentiments and inimitable style point out the author of Lauder's Preface and Postscript, will no longer allow one to *plume himself with his feathers,* who appeareth so little to deserve assistance: an assistance which I am persuaded would never have been communicated, had there been the least suspicion of those facts which I have been the instrument of conveying to the world in these sheets." "Milton no Plagiary," 2d edit., p. 78. And his Lordship has been pleased now to authorise me to say, in the strongest manner, that there is no ground whatever for any unfavourable reflection against Dr. Johnson, who expressed the strongest indignation against Lauder.

dise Lost.' " To this pamphlet Johnson wrote a Preface, in full persuasion of Lauder's honesty, and a Postscript recommending, in the most
persuasive terms, a subscription for the relief of a grand-daughter of
Milton, of whom he thus speaks: "It is yet in the power of a great
people to reward the poet whose name they boast, and from their alliance to whose genius they claim some kind of superiority to every other
nation of the earth; that poet, whose works may possibly be read when
every other monument of British greatness shall be obliterated; to reward him, not with pictures or with medals, which, if he sees, he sees
with contempt, but with tokens of gratitude, which he, perhaps, may
even now consider as not unworthy the regard of an immortal spirit."
Surely this is inconsistent with "enmity towards Milton," which Sir
John Hawkins imputes to Johnson upon this occasion, adding, "I could
all along observe that Johnson seemed to approve not only of the design, but of the argument; and seemed to exult in a persuasion, that
the reputation of Milton was likely to suffer by this discovery. That he
was not privy to the imposture, I am well persuaded; that he wished
well to the argument, may be inferred from the Preface, which in-
dubitably was written by Johnson." Is it possible for any man of clear
judgment to suppose that Johnson, who so nobly praised the poetical
excellence of Milton in a postscript to this very "discovery," as he then
supposed it, could, at the same time, exult in a persuasion that the great
poet's reputation was likely to suffer by it? This is an inconsistency of
which Johnson was incapable; nor can any thing more be fairly inferred from the Preface, than that Johnson, who was alike distinguished for ardent curiosity and love of truth, was pleased with an
investigation by which both were gratified. That he was actuated by
these motives, and certainly by no unworthy desire to depreciate our
great epic poet, is evident from his own words; for, after mentioning
the general zeal of men of genius and literature, "to advance the honour, and distinguish the beauties, of 'Paradise Lost,' " he says, "Among
the inquiries to which this ardour of criticism has naturally given occasion, none is more obscure in itself, or more worthy of rational
curiosity, than a retrospect of the progress of this mighty genius in the
construction of his work; a view of the fabric gradually rising, perhaps,
from small beginnings, till its foundation rests in the centre, and its
turrets sparkle in the skies; to trace back the structure through all its
varieties, to the simplicity of its first plan; to find what was first projected, whence the scheme was taken, how it was improved, by what
assistance it was executed, and from what stores the materials were col-

lected; whether its founder dug them from the quarries of Nature, or demolished other buildings to embellish his own."—Is this the language of one who wished to blast the laurels of Milton?

Though Johnson's circumstances were at this time far from being easy, his humane and charitable disposition was constantly exerting itself. Mrs. Anna Williams, daughter of a very ingenious Welsh physician, and a woman of more than ordinary talents and literature, having come to London in hopes of being cured of a cataract in both her eyes, which afterwards ended in total blindness, was kindly received as a constant visitor at his house while Mrs. Johnson lived; and after her death, having come under his roof in order to have an operation upon her eyes performed with more comfort to her than in lodgings, she had an apartment from him during the rest of her life, at all times when he had a house.

In 1752, he was almost entirely occupied with his Dictionary. But, in the same year, Dr. Hawkesworth, who was his warm admirer, and a studious imitator of his style, and then lived in great intimacy with him, began a periodical paper, entitled, *The Adventurer,* in connexion with other gentlemen, one of whom was Johnson's much-loved friend, Dr. Bathurst; and, without doubt, they received many valuable hints from his conversation, most of his friends having been so assisted in the course of their works.

That there should be a suspension of his literary labours during a part of the year 1752 will not seem strange when it is considered that, soon after closing his *Rambler,* he suffered a loss which, there can be no doubt, affected him with the deepest distress for, on the 17th of March, O. S. his wife died. Why Sir John Hawkins should unwarrantably take upon him even to *suppose* that Johnson's fondness for her was *dissembled* (meaning simulated or assumed), and to assert, that if it was not the case, "it was a lesson he had learned by rote," I cannot conceive; unless it proceeded from a want of similar feelings in his own breast. To argue, from her being much older than Johnson, or any other circumstances, that he could not really love her, is absurd; for love is not a subject of reasoning, but of feeling, and therefore there are no common principles upon which one can persuade another concerning it. Every man feels for himself, and knows how he is affected by particular qualities in the person he admires, the impressions of which are too minute and delicate to be substantiated in language.

That his love for his wife was of the most ardent kind, and, during the long period of fifty years, was unimpaired by the lapse of time, is evident from various passages in the series of his "Prayers and Meditations," published by the Reverend Mr. Strahan, as well as from other memorials, two of which I select, as strongly marking the tenderness and sensibility of his mind.

"March 28, 1753. I kept this day as the anniversary of my Tetty's death, with prayer and tears in the morning. In the evening I prayed for her conditionally, if it were lawful."

"April 23, 1753. I know not whether I do not too much indulge the vain longings of affection; but I hope they intenerate my heart, and that when I die like my Tetty, this affection will be acknowledged in a happy interview, and that in the meantime I am incited by it to piety. I will, however, not deviate too much from common and received methods of devotion."

Her wedding-ring, when she became his wife, was, after her death, preserved by him, as long as he lived, with an affectionate care, in a little round wooden box, in the inside of which he pasted a slip of paper, thus inscribed by him in fair characters, as follows:

"Eheu !
Eliz. Johnson,
Nupta Jul. 9° 1736.
Mortua, eheu !
Mart. 17° 1752."

After his death, Mr. Francis Barber, his faithful servant, and residuary legatee, offered this memorial of tenderness to Mrs. Lucy Porter, Mrs. Johnson's daughter; but she having declined to accept of it, he had it enamelled as a mourning-ring, for his old master, and presented it to his wife, Mrs. Barber, who now has it.

I have, indeed, been told by Desmoulins, who, before her marriage, lived for some time with Mrs. Johnson at Hampstead, that she indulged herself in country air and nice living, at an unsuitable expense, while her husband was drudging in the smoke of London, and that she by no means treated him with that complacency which is the most engaging quality in a wife. But all this is perfectly compatible with his fondness of her, especially when it is remembered that he had a high opinion of her understanding, and that the impressions which her beauty, real or imaginary, had originally made upon his fancy, being continued by habit, had not been effaced, though she herself was doubtless much altered for the worse. The dreadful shock of separation took place in the night; and he immediately despatched a letter to his friend, the Reverend Dr. Taylor, which, as Taylor told me, expressed grief in the strongest manner he had ever read; so that it is much to be regretted it has not been preserved. The letter was brought to Dr. Taylor, at his house in the Cloisters, Westminster, about three in the morning; and as it signified an earnest desire to see him, he got up, and went to Johnson as soon as he was dressed, and found him in tears and in extreme agitation. After being a little while together, Johnson requested him to join with him in prayer. He then prayed extempore, as did Dr. Taylor; and thus, by means of that piety which was ever his primary object, his troubled mind was, in some degree, soothed and composed.

That his sufferings upon the death of his wife were severe, beyond what are commonly endured, I have no doubt, from the information of many who were then about him, to none of whom I give more credit than to Mr. Francis Barber, his faithful negro servant,[2] who came into his family about a fortnight after the dismal event. These sufferings were aggravated by the melancholy inherent in his constitution: and although he probably was not oftener in the wrong than she was, in the little disagreements which sometimes troubled his married state, during which, he owned to me, that the gloomy irritability of his existence was more painful to him than ever, he might very naturally, after her death, be tenderly disposed to charge himself with slight omissions and offences, the sense of which would give him much uneasiness. The kindness of his heart, notwithstanding the impetuosity of his temper, is well known to his friends; and I cannot trace the smallest foundation for the following dark and uncharitable assertion by Sir John Hawkins: "The apparition of his departed wife was altogether of the terrific kind, and hardly afforded him a hope that she was in a state of happiness."

He deposited the remains of Mrs. Johnson in the church of Bromley in Kent, to which he was probably led by the residence of his friend Hawkesworth at that place. The funeral sermon which he composed

---

[2]Francis Barber was born in Jamaica, and was brought to England in 1750 by Colonel Bathurst, father of Johnson's very intimate friend, Dr. Bathurst. He was sent, for some time, to the Reverend Mr. Jackson's school, at Barton, in Yorkshire. The Colonel by his will left him his freedom, and Dr. Bathurst was willing that he should enter into Johnson's service, in which he continued from 1752 till Johnson's death, with the exception of two intervals; in one of which, upon some difference with his master, he went and served an apothecary in Cheapside, but still visited Dr. Johnson occasionally; in another, he took a fancy to go to sea. Part of the time, indeed, he was, by the kindness of his master, at a school in Northamptonshire, that he might have the advantage of some learning. So early and so lasting a connexion was there between Dr. Johnson and this humble friend.

for her, which was never preached, but having been given to Dr. Taylor, has been published since his death, is a performance of uncommon excellence, and full of rational and pious comfort to such as are depressed by that severe affliction which Johnson felt when he wrote it. When it is considered that it was written in such an agitation of mind, and in the short interval between her death and burial, it cannot be read without wonder.

From Mr. Francis Barber I have had the following authentic and artless account of the situation in which he found him recently after his wife's death: "He was in great affliction. Mrs. Williams was then living in his house, which was in Gough-square. He was busy with the Dictionary. Mr. Shiels, and some others of the gentlemen who had formerly written for him, used to come about him. He had then little for himself, but frequently sent money to Mr. Shiels when in distress. The friends who visited him at that time were chiefly Dr. Bathurst, and Mr. Diamond, an apothecary in Cork-street, Burlington-gardens, with whom he and Mrs. Williams generally dined every Sunday. There was a talk of his going to Iceland with him, which would probably have happened, had he lived. There were also Mr. Cave, Dr. Hawkesworth, Mr. Ryland, merchant on Tower-hill, Mrs. Masters, the poetess, who lived with Mr. Cave, Mrs. Carter, and sometimes Mrs. Macaulay; also, Mrs. Gardiner, wife of a tallow-chandler on Snow-hill, not in the learned way, but a worthy good woman; Mr. (now Sir Joshua) Reynolds; Mr. Miller, Mr. Dodsley, Mr. Bouquet, Mr. Payne, of Paternoster-row, booksellers; Mr. Strahan, the printer; the Earl of Orrery, Lord Southwell, Mr. Garrick."

Many are, no doubt, omitted in this catalogue of friends, and, in particular, his humble friend Mr. Robert Levet, an obscure practiser in physic amongst the lower people, his fees being sometimes very small sums, sometimes whatever provisions his patients could afford him; but of such extensive practice in that way, that Mrs. Williams has told me his walk was from Houndsditch to Marybone. It appears from Johnson's diary, that their acquaintance commenced about the year 1746; and such was Johnson's predilection for him, and fanciful estimation of his moderate abilities, that I have heard him say he should not be satisfied, though attended by all the College of Physicians, unless he had Mr. Levet with him. Ever since I was acquainted with Dr. Johnson, and many years before, as I have been assured by those who knew him earlier, Mr. Levet had an apartment in his house, or his chambers, and waited upon him every morning, through the whole course of his late and tedious breakfast. He was of a strange grotesque appearance, stiff and formal in his manner, and seldom said a word while any company was present.

The circle of his friends, indeed, at this time, was extensive and various, far beyond what has been generally imagined. To trace his acquaintance with each particular person, if it could be done, would be a task, of which the labour would not be repaid by the advantage. But exceptions are to be made; one of which must be a friend so eminent as Sir Joshua Reynolds, who was truly his *dulce decus,* and with whom he maintained an uninterrupted intimacy to the last hour of his life. When Johnson lived in Castle-street, Cavendish-square, he used frequently to visit two ladies who lived opposite to him, Miss Cotterells, daughters of Admiral Cotterell. Reynolds used also to visit there, and thus they met. Mr. Reynolds, as I have observed above, had, from the first reading of his "Life of Savage," conceived a very high admiration of Johnson's powers of writing. His conversation no less delighted him; and he cultivated his acquaintance with the laudable zeal of one who was ambitious of general improvement. Sir Joshua, indeed, was lucky enough at their very first meeting to make a remark, which was so much above the common-place style of conversation, that Johnson at once perceived that Reynolds had the habit of thinking for himself. The ladies were regretting the death of a friend, to whom they owed great obligations; upon which Reynolds observed, "You have, however, the comfort of being relieved from a burden of gratitude." They were shocked a little at this alleviating suggestion, as too selfish; but Johnson defended it in his clear and forcible manner, and was much pleased with the *mind,* the fair view of human nature, which it exhibited, like some of the reflections of Rochefoucault. The consequence was, that he went home with Reynolds, and supped with him.

Sir Joshua told me a pleasant characteristical anecdote of Johnson, about the time of their first acquaintance. When they were one evening together at the Miss Cotterells', the then Duchess of Argyle, and another lady of high rank, came in. Johnson, thinking that the Miss Cotterells were too much engrossed by them, and that he and his friend were neglected, as low company of whom they were somewhat ashamed, grew angry; and resolving to shock their supposed pride, by making their great visitors imagine that his friend and he were low indeed, he addressed himself in a loud tone to Mr. Reynolds, saying, "How much do you think you and I could get in a week, if we were to *work as hard* as we could?"—as if they had been common mechanics.

His acquaintance with Bennet Langton, Esq., of Langton, in Lincolnshire, another much valued friend, commenced soon after the conclusion of his *Rambler;* which that gentleman, then a youth, had read with so much admiration, that he came to London chiefly with a view of endeavouring to be introduced to its author. By a fortunate chance he happened to take lodgings in a house where Mr. Levet frequently visited; and having mentioned his wish to his landlady, she introduced him to Mr. Levet, who readily obtained Johnson's permission to bring Mr. Langton to him; as, indeed, Johnson, during the whole course of his life, had no shyness, real or affected, but was easy of access to all who were properly recommended, and even wished to see numbers at his *levée,* as his morning circle of company might, with strict propriety, be called. Mr. Langton was exceedingly surprised when the sage first appeared. He had not received the smallest intimation of his figure, dress, or manner. From perusing his writings, he fancied he should see a decent, well-drest, in short a remarkably decorous, philosopher. Instead of which, down from his bed-chamber, about noon, came, as newly risen, a huge uncouth figure, with a little dark wig which scarcely covered his head, and his clothes hanging loose about him. But his conversation was so rich, so animated, and so forcible, and his religious and political notions so congenial with those in which Langton had been educated, that he conceived for him that veneration and attachment which he ever preserved. Johnson was not the less ready to love Mr. Langton, for his being of a very ancient family; for I have heard him say, with pleasure, "Langton, Sir, has a grant of free warren from Henry the Second; and Cardinal Stephen Langton, in King John's reign, was of his family."

Mr. Langton, afterwards, went to pursue his studies at Trinity College, Oxford, where he formed an acquaintance with his fellow-student, Mr. Topham Beauclerk; who, though their opinions and modes of life were so different, that it seemed utterly improbable that they should at all agree, had so ardent a love of literature, so acute an understanding, such elegance of manners, and so well discerned the excellent qualities of Mr. Langton, a gentleman eminent not only for worth and learning, but for an inexhaustible fund of entertaining conversation, that they became intimate friends.

Johnson, soon after this acquaintance began, passed a considerable time at Oxford. He at first thought it strange that Langton should associate so much with one who had the character of being loose, both in his principles and practice: but, by degrees, he himself was fascinated. Mr. Beauclerk's being of the St. Alban's family, and having, in some particulars, a resemblance to Charles the Second,[3] contributed, in Johnson's imagination, to throw a lustre upon his other qualities; and, in a short time, the moral, pious Johnson, and the gay, dissipated Beauclerk, were companions. "What a coalition!" said Garrick, when he heard of this: "I shall have my old friend to bail out of the Round-house." But I can bear testimony that it was a very agreeable association. Beauclerk was too polite, and valued learning and wit too much, to offend Johnson by sallies of infidelity or licentiousness; and Johnson delighted in the good qualities of Beauclerk, and hoped to correct the evil. Innumerable were the scenes in which Johnson was amused by these young men. Beauclerk could take more liberty with him than anybody with whom I ever saw him; but, on the other hand, Beauclerk was not spared by his respectable companion, when reproof was proper. Beauclerk had such a propensity to satire, that at one time Johnson said to him, "You never open your mouth but with intention to give pain; and you have often given me pain, not from the power of what you said, but from seeing your intention." At another time applying to him, with a slight alteration, a line of Pope, he said,

"Thy love of folly and thy scorn of fools——

Everything thou dost shows the one, and everything thou say'st the other." At another time he said to him, "Thy body is all vice, and thy mind all virtue." Beauclerk not seeming to relish the compliment, Johnson said, "Nay, Sir, Alexander the Great, marching in triumph into Babylon, could not have desired to have had more said to him."

Johnson was some time with Beauclerk at his house at Windsor, where he was entertained with experiments in natural philosophy. One Sunday, when the weather was very fine, Beauclerk enticed him, insensibly, to saunter about all the morning. They went into a churchyard, in the time of divine service, and Johnson laid himself down at his ease upon one of the tombstones. "Now, Sir (said Beauclerk), you are like Hogarth's 'Idle Apprentice.' " When Johnson got his pension, Beauclerk said to him, in the humorous phrase of Falstaff, "I hope you'll now purge and live cleanly, like a gentleman."

One night, when Beauclerk and Langton had supped at a tavern in London, and sat till about three in the morning, it came into their heads to go and knock up Johnson, and see if they could prevail on

[3]He was the only son of Lord Sidney Beauclerk, third son of the first Duke of St. Albans, and consequently the great grandson of Charles II and Nell Gwynn.

him to join them in a ramble. They rapped violently at the doors of his chambers in the Temple, till at last he appeared in his shirt, with his little black wig on the top of his head instead of a nightcap, and a poker in his hand, imagining, probably, that some ruffians were coming to attack him. When he discovered who they were, and was told their errand, he smiled, and with great good humour agreed to their proposal: "What, is it you, you dogs! I'll have a frisk with you." He was soon drest, and they sallied forth together into Covent-Garden, where the green-grocers and fruiterers were beginning to arrange their hampers, just come in from the country. Johnson made some attempts to help them; but the honest gardeners stared so at his figure and manner, and odd interference, that he soon saw his services were not relished. They then repaired to one of the neighbouring taverns, and made a bowl of that liquor called *Bishop,* which Johnson had always liked: while in joyous contempt of sleep, from which he had been roused, he repeated the festive lines,

> "Short, O short, then be thy reign,
> And give us to the world again!"

They did not stay long, but walked down to the Thames, took a boat, and rowed to Billingsgate. Beauclerk and Johnson were so well pleased with their amusement, that they resolved to persevere in dissipation for the rest of the day: but Langton deserted them, being engaged to breakfast with some young ladies. Johnson scolded him for "leaving his social friends, to go and sit with a set of wretched *un-idea'd* girls." Garrick being told of this ramble, said to him smartly, "I heard of your frolic t'other night. You'll be in the *Chronicle*." Upon which Johnson afterwards observed, *"He* durst not do such a thing. His *wife* would not *let* him!"

He entered upon this year, 1753, with his usual piety, as appears from the following prayer, which I transcribed from that part of his diary which he burnt a few days before his death:

"Jan. 1, 1753, N.S. which I shall use for the future.

"Almighty God, who hast continued my life to this day, grant that, by the assistance of thy Holy Spirit, I may improve the time which thou shalt grant me, to my eternal salvation. Make me to remember, to thy glory, thy judgments and thy mercies. Make me to consider the loss of my wife, whom thou hast taken from me, that it may dispose me, by thy grace, to lead the residue of my life in thy fear. Grant this, O Lord, for Jesus Christ's sake. Amen."

[87]

He now relieved the drudgery of his Dictionary, and the melancholy of his grief, by taking an active part in the composition of the *Adventurer,* in which he began to write April 10, marking his essays with the signature T, by which most of his papers in that collection are distinguished: those, however, which have that signature, and also that of "Mysargyrus," were not written by him, but, as I suppose, by Dr. Bathurst. Indeed, Johnson's energy of thought and richness of language are still more decisive marks than any signature. Let me add that Hawkesworth's imitations of Johnson are sometimes so happy, that it is extremely difficult to distinguish them with certainty, from the compositions of his great archetype. Hawkesworth was his closest imitator, a circumstance of which that writer would once have been proud to be told; though, when he had become elated by having risen into some degree of consequence, he, in a conversation with me, had the provoking effrontery to say he was not sensible of it.

Johnson was truly zealous for the success of the *Adventurer;* and very soon after his engaging in it, he wrote the following letter:

"TO THE REVEREND DR. JOSEPH WARTON.

"DEAR SIR,—

"I ought to have written to you before now, but I ought to do many things which I do not; nor can I, indeed, claim any merit from this letter; for, being desired by the authors and proprietors of the *Adventurer* to look out for another hand, my thoughts necessarily fixed upon you, whose fund of literature will enable you to assist them, with very little interruption of your studies.

"They desire you to engage to furnish one paper a month, at two guineas a paper, which you may very readily perform. We have considered that a paper should consist of pieces of imagination, pictures of life, and disquisitions of literature. The part which depends on the imagination is very well supplied, as you will find when you read the paper; for descriptions of life, there is now a treaty almost made with an author and an authoress; and the province of criticism and literature they are very desirous to assign to the commentator on Virgil.

"I hope this proposal will not be rejected, and that the next post will bring us your compliance. I speak as one of the fraternity, though I have no part in the paper, beyond now and then a motto; but two of the writers are my particular friends, and I hope the pleasure of seeing

Gordon Ross del.

New York, 1945

Lichfield, Dr. Johnson's Birthplace.

a third united to them, will not be denied to, dear Sir, your most obędient

"And most humble servant,
"SAM. JOHNSON.

"March 8, 1753."

The consequence of this letter was, Dr. Warton's enriching the collection with several admirable essays.

Johnson's saying, "I have no part in the paper beyond now and then a motto," may seem inconsistent with his being the author of the papers marked T. But he had, at this time, written only one number; and besides, even at any after period, he might have used the same expression, considering it as a point of honour not to own them; for Mrs. Williams told me that, "as he had *given* those essays to Dr. Bathurst, who sold them at two guineas each, he never would own them: nay, he used to say he did not *write* them: but the fact was, that he *dictated* them, while Bathurst wrote." I read to him Mrs. Williams's account; he smiled and said nothing.

I am not quite satisfied with the casuistry by which the productions of one person are thus passed upon the world for the productions of another. I allow that not only knowledge, but powers and qualities of mind, may be communicated; but the actual effect of individual exertion never can be transferred, with truth, to any other than its own original cause. One person's child may be made the child of another person by adoption, as among the Romans, or by the ancient Jewish mode of a wife having children borne to her upon her knees, by her handmaid. But these were children in a different sense from that of nature. It was clearly understood that they were not of the blood of their nominal parents. So, in literary children, an author may give the profits and fame of his composition to another man, but cannot make that the real author.

In one of the books of his diary, I find the following entry:
"Apr. 3, 1753. I began the second vol. of my Dictionary, room being left in the first for Preface, Grammar, and History, none of them yet begun.

"O God, who hast hitherto supported me, enable me to proceed in this labour, and in the whole task of my present state; that when I shall render up, at the last day, an account of the talent committed to me, I may receive pardon for the sake of Jesus Christ. Amen."

CHAPTER IX—1754-1755

The Dictionary

In 1754, I can trace nothing published by him, except his numbers of the *Adventurer* and "The Life of Edward Cave," [*] in the *Gentleman's Magazine* for February. In biography, there can be no question that he excelled, beyond all who have attempted that species of composition; upon which, indeed, he set the highest value. To the minute selection of characteristical circumstances, for which the ancients were remarkable, he added a philosophical research, and the most perspicuous and energetic language.

The Dictionary, we may believe, afforded Johnson full occupation this year. As it approached to its conclusion, he probably worked with redoubled vigour, as seamen increase their exertion and alacrity when they have a near prospect of their haven.

Lord Chesterfield, to whom Johnson had paid the high compliment of addressing to his Lordship the Plan of his Dictionary, had behaved to him in such a manner as to excite his contempt and indignation. The world has been for many years amused with a story confidently told, and as confidently repeated with additional circumstances, that a sudden disgust was taken by Johnson upon occasion of his having been one day kept long in waiting in his Lordship's antechamber, for which the reason assigned was, that he had company with him; and that at last, when the door opened, out walked Colley Cibber; and that Johnson was so violently provoked when he found for whom he had been so long excluded, that he went away in a passion, and never would return. I remember having mentioned this story to George Lord Lyttelton, who told me he was very intimate with Lord Chesterfield; and holding it as a well-known truth, defended Lord Chesterfield by saying that "Cibber, who had been introduced familiarly by the back-stairs, had probably not been there above ten minutes." It may seem strange even to entertain a doubt concerning a story so long and so widely current, and thus implicitly adopted, if not sanctioned, by the authority which I have mentioned; but Johnson himself assured me that there was not the least foundation for it. He told me that there was never any particular incident which produced a quarrel between Lord Chesterfield and him;

but that his Lordship's continued neglect was the reason why he resolved to have no connexion with him. When the Dictionary was upon the eve of publication, Lord Chesterfield, who, it is said, had flattered himself with expectations that Johnson would dedicate the work to him, attempted, in a courtly manner, to soothe and insinuate himself

Dr. Johnson fumes in the antechamber of Lord Chesterfield

with the Sage, conscious, as it should seem, of the cold indifference with which he had treated its learned author; and farther attempted to conciliate him, by writing two papers in the *World*, in recommendation of the work; and it must be confessed that they contain some studied compliments, so finely turned, that if there had been no previous offence, it is probable that Johnson would have been highly delighted. Praise, in general, was pleasing to him; but by praise from a man of rank and elegant accomplishments, he was peculiarly gratified.

His Lordship says, "I think the public in general, and the republic of letters in particular, are greatly obliged to Mr. Johnson, for having undertaken and executed so great and desirable a work. Perfection is not to be expected from man; but if we are to judge by the various works of Mr. Johnson already published, we have good reason to believe that he will bring this as near to perfection as any man could do. The Plan of it, which he published some years ago, seems to me to be a proof of it. Nothing can be more rationally imagined, or more accurately and elegantly expressed. I therefore recommend the previous perusal of it to all those who intend to buy the Dictionary, and who, I suppose, are all those who can afford it."

* * *

"It must be owned, that our language is, at present, in a state of anarchy, and hitherto, perhaps, it may not have been the worse for it. During our free and open trade, many words and expressions have been imported, adopted, and naturalized from other languages, which have greatly enriched our own. Let it still preserve what real strength and beauty it may have borrowed from others; but let it not, like the Tarpeian maid, be overwhelmed and crushed by unnecessary foreign ornaments. The time for discrimination seems to be now come. Toleration, adoption, and naturalization, have run their lengths. Good order and authority are now necessary. But where shall we find them, and, at the same time, the obedience due to them? We must have recourse to the old Roman expedient in times of confusion, and choose a dictator. Upon this principle, I give my vote for Mr. Johnson to fill that great and arduous post. And I hereby declare, that I make a total surrender of all my rights and privileges in the English language, as a freeborn British subject, to the said Mr. Johnson, during the term of his dictatorship. Nay, more, I will not only obey him like an old Roman, as my dictator, but, like a modern Roman, I will implicitly believe in him as my Pope, and hold him to be infallible while in the chair, but no longer. More than this he cannot well require; for I presume that obedience can never be expected, when there is neither terror to enforce, nor interest to invite it."

* * *

"But a Grammar, a Dictionary, and a History of our Language through its several stages, were still wanting at home, and importunately called for from abroad. Mr. Johnson's labours will now, I dare say, very fully supply that want, and greatly contribute to the farther spreading of our language in other countries. Learners were discouraged by finding no standard to resort to; and, consequently, thought it incapable of any. They will now be undeceived and encouraged."

This courtly device failed of its effect. Johnson, who thought that "all was false and hollow," despised the honey words, and was even indignant that Lord Chesterfield should, for a moment, imagine that he could be the dupe of such an artifice. His expression to me concerning Lord Chesterfield, upon this occasion, was, "Sir, after making great professions, he had, for many years, taken no notice of me; but when my Dictionary was coming out, he fell a scribbling in the *World* about it. Upon which, I wrote him a letter, expressed in civil terms, but such as might show him that I did not mind what he said or wrote, and that I had done with him."

This is that celebrated letter of which so much has been said, and about which curiosity has been so long excited, without being gratified. I for many years solicited Johnson to favour me with a copy of it, that so excellent a composition might not be lost to posterity. He delayed from time to time to give it me;[1] till at last, in 1781, when we were on a visit at Mr. Dilly's, at Southill in Bedfordshire, he was pleased to dictate it to me from memory. He afterwards found among his papers a copy of it, which he had dictated to Mr. Baretti, with its title and corrections, in his own hand-writing. This he gave to Mr. Langton; adding, that if it were to come into print, he wished it to be from that copy. By Mr. Langton's kindness, I am enabled to enrich my work with a perfect transcript of what the world has so eagerly desired to see.

"TO THE RIGHT HONOURABLE THE EARL OF CHESTERFIELD.

"*February 7, 1755.*

"My Lord,—

"I have been lately informed, by the proprietor of the *World*, that two papers, in which my Dictionary is recommended to the public, were written by your Lordship. To be so distinguished, is an honour, which, being very little accustomed to favours from the great, I know not well how to receive, or in what terms to acknowledge.

"When, upon some slight encouragement, I first visited your Lordship, I was overpowered, like the rest of mankind, by the enchantment of your address, and could not forbear to wish that I might boast myself *Le vainqueur du vainqueur de la terre;*—that I might obtain that regard for which I saw the world contending; but I found my attendance so little encouraged, that neither pride nor modesty would suffer me to

---

[1]Dr. Johnson appeared to have had a remarkable delicacy with respect to the circulation of this letter; for Dr. Douglas, Bishop of Salisbury, informed me that having many years ago pressed him to be allowed to read it to the second Lord Hardwicke, who was very desirous to hear it (promising, at the same time, that no copy of it should be taken), Johnson seemed much pleased that it had attracted the attention of a nobleman of such a respectable character; but, after pausing some time, declined to comply with the request, saying, with a smile, "No, Sir; I have hurt the dog too much already"; or words to that purpose.

continue it. When I had once addressed your Lordship in public, I had exhausted all the art of pleasing which a retired and uncourtly scholar can possess. I had done all that I could; and no man is well pleased to have his all neglected, be it ever so little.

"Seven years, my Lord, have now past, since I waited in your outward rooms, or was repulsed from your door; during which time I have been pushing on my work through difficulties, of which it is useless to complain, and have brought it, at last, to the verge of publication, without one act of assistance,[2] one word of encouragement, or one smile of favour. Such treatment I did not expect, for I never had a Patron before.

"The shepherd in Virgil grew at last acquainted with Love, and found him a native of the rocks.

"Is not a Patron, my Lord, one who looks with unconcern on a man struggling for life in the water, and, when he has reached ground, encumbers him with help? The notice which you have been pleased to take of my labours, had it been early, had been kind; but it has been delayed till I am indifferent, and cannot enjoy it; till I am solitary, and cannot impart it; till I am known, and do not want it. I hope it is no very cynical asperity not to confess obligations where no benefit has been received, or to be unwilling that the public should consider me as owing that to a Patron, which Providence has enabled me to do for myself.

"Having carried on my work thus far with so little obligation to any favourer of learning, I shall not be disappointed though I should conclude it, if less be possible, with less; for I have been long wakened from that dream of hope, in which I once boasted myself with so much exultation, my Lord,

"Your Lordship's most humble,
"Most obedient servant,
"SAM. JOHNSON."[3]

[2] The following note is subjoined by Mr. Langton. "Dr. Johnson, when he gave me this copy of his letter, desired that I would annex it to his information to me, that whereas it is said in the letter that 'no assistance has been received,' he did once receive from Lord Chesterfield the sum of £10, but as that was so inconsiderable a sum, he thought the mention of it could not properly find a place in a letter of the kind that this was."

[3] Upon comparing this copy with that which Dr. Johnson dictated to me from recollection, the variations are found to be so slight, that this must be added to the many other proofs which he gave of the wonderful extent and accuracy of his memory. To gratify the curious in composition, I have deposited both the copies in the British Museum.

"While this was the talk of the town," says Dr. Adams, in a letter to me, "I happened to visit Dr. Warburton, who, finding that I was acquainted with Johnson, desired me earnestly to carry his compliments to him, and to tell him that he honoured him for his manly behaviour in rejecting these condescensions of Lord Chesterfield, and for resenting the treatment he had received from him with a proper spirit. Johnson was visibly pleased with this compliment, for he had always a high opinion of Warburton." Indeed, the force of mind which appeared in this letter, was congenial with that which Warburton himself amply possessed.

There is a curious minute circumstance which struck me, in comparing the various editions of Johnson's "Imitations of Juvenal." In the tenth Satire, one of the couplets upon the vanity of wishes, even for literary distinction, stood thus:

> "Yet think what ills the scholar's life assail,
> Toil, envy, want, the *garret*, and the jail."

But after experiencing the uneasiness which Lord Chesterfield's fallacious patronage made him feel, he dismissed the word *garret* from the sad group, and in all the subsequent editions the line stands,

> "Toil, envy, want, the *Patron*, and the jail."

That Lord Chesterfield must have been mortified by the lofty contempt, and polite, yet keen, satire with which Johnson exhibited him to himself in this letter, it is impossible to doubt. He, however, with that glossy duplicity which was his constant study, affected to be quite unconcerned. Dr. Adams mentioned to Mr. Robert Dodsley that he was sorry Johnson had written his letter to Lord Chesterfield. Dodsley, with the true feelings of trade, said, "he was very sorry too; for that he had a property in the Dictionary, to which his Lordship's patronage might have been of consequence." He then told Dr. Adams that Lord Chesterfield had shown him the letter. "I should have imagined (replied Dr. Adams) that Lord Chesterfield would have concealed it." "Poh! (said Dodsley) do you think a letter from Johnson could hurt Lord Chesterfield? Not at all, Sir. It lay upon his table, where anybody might see it. He read it to me; said, 'this man has great powers,' pointed out the severest passages, and observed how well they were expressed." This air of indifference, which imposed upon the worthy Dodsley, was certainly nothing but a specimen of that dissimulation which Lord Chesterfield inculcated as one of the most essential lessons for the conduct of life. His Lordship endeavoured to justify himself to Dodsley from the charges brought against him by Johnson; but we may judge of the flimsiness of his defence, from his having excused his neglect of Johnson, by saying that "he had heard he had changed his lodgings, and did not know where he lived"; as if there could have been the smallest difficulty to inform himself of that circumstance, by inquiring in the literary circle with which his Lordship was well acquainted, and was, indeed, himself, one of its ornaments.

Dr. Adams expostulated with Johnson, and suggested that his not being admitted when he called on him was probably not to be imputed to Lord Chesterfield; for his Lordship had declared to Dodsley that "he would have turned off the best servant he ever had, if he had known that he denied him to a man who would have been always more than welcome"; and in confirmation of this, he insisted on Lord Chesterfield's general affability and easiness of access, especially to literary men. "Sir (said Johnson), that is not Lord Chesterfield; he is the proudest man this day existing." "No (said Dr. Adams), there is one person, at least, as proud; I think, by your own account, you are the prouder man of the two." "But mine (replied Johnson instantly) was *defensive* pride." This, as Dr. Adams well observed, was one of those happy turns for which he was so remarkably ready.

Johnson, having now explicitly avowed his opinion of Lord Chesterfield, did not refrain from expressing himself concerning that nobleman with pointed freedom: "This man (said he) I thought had been a Lord among wits; but, I find, he is only a wit among Lords." And when his Letters to his natural son were published, he observed that "they teach the morals of a whore, and the manners of a dancing master."[4]

[4]That collection of letters cannot be vindicated from the serious charge of encouraging, in some passages, one of the vices most destructive to the good order and comfort of society, which his Lordship represents as mere fashionable gallantry; and, in others, of inculcating the base practice of dissimulation, and recommending, with disproportionate anxiety, a perpetual attention to external elegance of manners. But it must, at the same time, be allowed that they contain many good precepts of conduct, and much genuine information upon life and manners, very happily expressed; and that there was considerable merit in paying so much attention to the improvement of one who was dependent upon his Lordship's protection: it has, probably, been exceeded in no instance by the most exemplary parent; and though I can by no means approve of confounding the distinction between lawful and illicit offspring, which is, in effect, insulting the civil establishment of our country, to look no higher; I cannot help thinking it laudable to be kindly attentive to those, of whose existence we have, in any way, been the cause. Mr. Stanhope's character has been unjustly represented as diametrically opposite to what Lord Chesterfield wished him to be. He has been called dull, gross, and awkward: but I knew him at Dresden, when he was Envoy to that court; and though he could not boast of the *graces,* he was, in truth, a sensible, civil, well-behaved man.

Johnson this year found an interval of leisure to make an excursion to Oxford, for the purpose of consulting the libraries there. Of this, and of many interesting circumstances concerning him, during a part of his life when he conversed but little with the world, I am enabled to give a particular account, by the liberal communications of the Reverend Mr. Thomas Warton, who obligingly furnished me with several of our common friends' letters, which he illustrated with notes. These I shall insert in their proper places.

"TO THE REV. MR. THOMAS WARTON.

"SIR,—

"It is but an ill-return for the book with which you were pleased to favour me, to have delayed my thanks for it till now. I am too apt to be negligent; but I can never deliberately show my disrespect to a man of your character; and I now pay you a very honest acknowledgment, for the advancement of the literature of our native country. You have shown to all, who shall hereafter attempt the study of our ancient authors, the way to success; by directing them to the perusal of the books which those authors had read. Of this method, Hughes, and men much greater than Hughes, seem never to have thought. The reason why the authors, which are read, of the sixteenth century, are so little understood, is, that they are read alone; and no help is borrowed from those who lived with them, or before them. Some part of this ignorance I hope to remove by my book, which now draws towards its end; but which I cannot finish to my mind, without visiting the libraries of Oxford, which I therefore hope to see in a fortnight. I know not how long I shall stay, or where I shall lodge: but shall be sure to look for you at my arrival, and we shall easily settle the rest. I am, dear Sir,

"Your most obedient, etc.,

"SAM. JOHNSON.

"[*London*], *July 16, 1754.*"

The degree of Master of Arts, which, it has been observed, could not be obtained for him at an early period of his life, was now considered as an honour of considerable importance, in order to grace the title-page of his Dictionary; and his character in the literary world being by this time deservedly high, his friends thought that, if proper exertions were made, the University of Oxford would pay him the compliment.

[97]

"TO THE REV. MR. THOMAS WARTON.

"DEAR SIR,—

"I am extremely obliged to you and to Mr. Wise, for the uncommon care which you have taken of my interest: if you can accomplish your kind design, I shall certainly take me a little habitation among you.

"The books which I promised to Mr. Wise, I have not been able to procure; but I shall send him a Finnick Dictionary, the only copy, perhaps, in England, which was presented me by a learned Swede: but I keep it back, that it may make a set of my own books of the new edition, with which I shall accompany it, more welcome. You will assure him of my gratitude.

"Poor dear Collins!—Would a letter give him any pleasure? I have a mind to write.

"I am glad of your hindrance in your Spenserian design, yet I would not have it delayed. Three hours a day stolen from sleep and amusement will produce it. Let a Servitour transcribe the quotations, and interleave them with references, to save time. This will shorten the work, and lessen the fatigue.

"Can I do anything to promoting the diploma? I would not be wanting to co-operate with your kindness: of which, whatever be the effect, I shall be, dear Sir,

"Your most obliged, etc.,

"SAM. JOHNSON.

"[*London*], *Nov. 28, 1754.*"

In 1755 we behold him to great advantage; his degree of Master of Arts conferred upon him, his Dictionary published, his correspondence animated, his benevolence exercised.

"TO THE REVEREND MR. THOMAS WARTON.

"DEAR SIR,—

"I wrote to you some weeks ago, but believe did not direct accurately, and therefore know not whether you had my letter. I would, likewise, write to your brother, but know not where to find him. I now begin to see land, after having wandered, according to Mr. Warburton's phrase, in this vast sea of words. What reception I shall meet with on the shore, I know not; whether the sound of bells, and acclamations of the people, which Ariosto talks of in his last Canto, or a general murmur of dislike, I know not: whether I shall find upon the coast a Calypso that will court, or a Polypheme that will resist. But if Polypheme comes, have at his eye. I hope, however, the critics will let me be at peace; for though I do not much fear their skill and strength, I am a little afraid of myself, and would not willingly feel so much ill-will in my bosom as literary quarrels are apt to excite.

"Mr. Baretti is about a work for which he is in great want of Crescimbeni, which you may have again when you please.

"There is nothing considerable done or doing among us here. We are not, perhaps, as innocent as villagers, but most of us seem to be as idle. I hope, however, you are busy; and should be glad to know what you are doing. I am, dearest Sir,

"Your humble servant,
"SAM. JOHNSON.

"[*London*], *Feb. 4, 1755.*"

"TO THE SAME.

"DEAR SIR,—

"I received your letter this day, with great sense of the favour that has been done me; for which I return my most sincere thanks; and entreat you to pay to Mr. Wise such returns as I ought to make for so much kindness so little deserved.

"I sent Mr. Wise the Lexicon, and afterwards wrote to him; but know not whether he had either the book or letter. Be so good as to contrive to inquire.

"But why does my dear Mr. Warton tell me nothing of himself? Where hangs the new volume? Can I help? Let not the past labour be lost, for want of a little more: but snatch what time you can from the Hall, and the pupils, and the coffee-house, and the parks, and complete your design.

"I am, dear Sir, etc.,
"SAM. JOHNSON.

"[*London*], *Feb. 4, 1755.*"

"TO THE SAME.

"DEAR SIR,—

"After I received my diploma, I wrote you a letter of thanks, with a letter to the Vice-Chancellor, and sent another to Mr. Wise: but have heard from nobody since, and begin to think myself forgotten. It is true, I sent you a double letter, and you may fear an expensive correspondent; but I would have taken it kindly, if you had returned it treble: and what is a double letter to a *petty king*, that, having *fellowship and fines*, can sleep without a *Modus in his head?*

"Dear Mr. Warton, let me hear from you, and tell me something, I care not what, so I hear it but from you. Something, I will tell you: I hope to see my Dictionary bound and lettered, next week; *vastâ mole superbus.* And I have a great mind to come to Oxford at Easter; but you will not invite me. Shall I come uninvited, or stay here where nobody perhaps would miss me if I went? A hard choice. But such is the world to, dear Sir, yours, etc.,

"SAM. JOHNSON.

"[*London*], *March 20, 1755.*"

"TO DR. BIRCH.

"*March 29, 1755.*

"SIR,—

"I have sent some parts of my Dictionary, such as were at hand, for your inspection. The favour which I beg is, that if you do not like them, you will say nothing. I am, Sir,

"Your most affectionate humble servant,

"SAM. JOHNSON."

"TO MR. SAMUEL JOHNSON.

"*Norfolk Street, April 23, 1755.*

"SIR,—

"The part of your Dictionary which you have favoured me with the sight of has given me such an idea of the whole, that I most sincerely congratulate the public upon the acquisition of a work long wanted, and now executed with an industry, accuracy, and judgment, equal to the importance of the subject. You might, perhaps, have chosen one in which your genius would have appeared to more advantage, but you could not have fixed upon any other in which your labours would have done such substantial service to the present age and to posterity. I am glad that your health has supported the application necessary to the performance of so vast a task; and can undertake to promise you as one (though perhaps the only) reward of it, the approbation and

thanks of every well-wisher to the honour of the English language. I am, with the greatest regard, Sir, your most faithful, and
"Most affectionate humble servant,
"Tho. Birch."

Mr. Charles Burney, who has since distinguished himself so much in the science of Music, and obtained a Doctor's degree from the University of Oxford, had been driven from the capital by bad health, and was now residing at Lynne Regis in Norfolk. He had been so much delighted with Johnson's *Rambler,* and the plan of his Dictionary, that when the great work was announced in the newspapers as nearly finished, he wrote to Dr. Johnson, begging to be informed when and in what manner his Dictionary would be published; entreating, if it should be by subscription, or he should have any books at his own disposal, to be favoured with six copies for himself and friends.

In answer to this application, Dr. Johnson wrote the following letter, of which (to use Dr. Burney's own words), "If it be remembered that it was written to an obscure young man, who at this time had not much distinguished himself even in his own profession, but whose name could never have reached the author of the *Rambler,* the politeness and urbanity may be opposed to some of the stories which have been lately circulated of Dr. Johnson's natural rudeness and ferocity.

"TO MR. BURNEY, IN LYNNE REGIS, NORFOLK.

"Sir,—

"If you imagine that by delaying my answer I intended to show any neglect of the notice with which you have favoured me, you will neither think justly of yourself nor of me. Your civilities were offered with too much elegance not to engage attention; and I have too much pleasure in pleasing men like you, not to feel very sensibly the distinction which you have bestowed upon me.

"Few consequences of my endeavours to please or to benefit mankind have delighted me more than your friendship thus voluntarily offered, which now I have it I hope to keep, because I hope to continue to deserve it.

"I have no Dictionaries to dispose of for myself, but shall be glad to have you direct your friends to Mr. Dodsley, because it was by his recommendation that I was employed in the work.

"When you have leisure to think again upon me, let me be favoured with another letter; and another yet, when you have looked into my Dictionary. If you find faults, I shall endeavour to mend them; if you find none, I shall think you blinded by kind partiality; but to have made you partial in his favour, will very much gratify the ambition of, Sir, your most obliged

"And most humble servant,
"SAM. JOHNSON.

"Gough Square, Fleet Street, April 8, 1755."

Mr. Andrew Millar, bookseller, in the Strand, took the principal charge of conducting the publication of Johnson's Dictionary; and as the patience of the proprietors was repeatedly tried and almost exhausted by their expecting that the work would be completed within the time which Johnson had sanguinely supposed, the learned author was often goaded to despatch, more especially as he had received all the copy-money, by different drafts, a considerable time before he had finished his task. When the messenger who carried the last sheet to Millar returned, Johnson asked him, "Well, what did he say?"—"Sir (answered the messenger), he said, Thank God, I have done with him."—"I am glad (replied Johnson with a smile) that he thanks God for any thing." It is remarkable that those with whom Johnson chiefly contracted for his literary labours were Scotchmen, Mr. Millar and Mr. Strahan. Millar, though himself no great judge of literature, had good sense enough to have for his friends very able men, to give him their opinion and advice in the purchase of copyright; the consequence of which was his acquiring a very large fortune with great liberality. Johnson said of him, "I respect Millar, Sir; he has raised the price of literature." The same praise may be justly given to Panckoucke, the eminent bookseller of Paris. Mr. Strahan's liberality, judgment, and success, are well known.

"TO BENNET LANGTON, ESQ., AT LANGTON NEAR SPILSBY,
LINCOLNSHIRE.

"SIR,—
"It has been long observed, that men do not suspect faults which they do not commit; your own elegance of manners, and punctuality of complaisance, did not suffer you to impute to me that negligence of which I was guilty, and which I have not since atoned. I received both your letters, and received them with pleasure proportionate to the

esteem which so short an acquaintance strongly impressed, and which I hope to confirm by nearer knowledge, though I am afraid that gratification will be for a time withheld.

Bennet Langton

"I have, indeed, published my Book, of which I beg to know your father's judgment, and yours; and I have now stayed long enough to watch its progress in the world. It has, you see, no patrons, and, I think, has yet had no opponents, except the critics of the coffee-house, whose outcries are soon dispersed into the air, and are thought on no more: from this, therefore, I am at liberty, and think of taking the opportunity of this interval to make an excursion, and why not then into Lincolnshire? or, to mention a stronger attraction, why not to dear Mr. Langton? I will give the true reason, which I know you will approve:—I have a mother more than eighty years old, who has counted the days to the publication of my book in hopes of seeing me; and to her, if I can disengage myself here, I resolve to go.

"As I know, dear Sir, that to delay my visit for a reason like this, will not deprive me of your esteem, I beg it may not lessen your kindness. I have very seldom received an offer of friendship which I so earnestly desire to cultivate and mature. I shall rejoice to hear from you, till I can see you, and will see you as soon as I can; for when the duty that calls me to Lichfield is discharged, my inclination will carry me to Langton. I shall delight to hear the ocean roar, or see the stars twinkle, in the company of men to whom Nature does not spread her volumes or utter her voice in vain.

"Do not, dear Sir, make the slowness of this letter a precedent for delay, or imagine that I approved the incivility that I have committed; for I have known you enough to love you, and sincerely to wish a farther knowledge; and I assure you, once more, that to live in a house that contains such a father, and such a son, will be accounted a very uncommon degree of pleasure, by, dear Sir,

"Your most obliged, and

"Most humble servant,

"SAM. JOHNSON.

"*May 6, 1755.*"

The Dictionary, with a Grammar and History of the English Language, being now at length published, in two volumes folio, the world contemplated with wonder so stupendous a work achieved by one man, while other countries had thought such undertakings fit only for whole academies. Vast as his powers were, I cannot but think that his imagination deceived him, when he supposed that by constant application he might have performed the task in three years. Let the Preface be attentively perused, in which is given, in a clear, strong, and glowing style, a comprehensive yet particular view of what he had done; and it will be evident, that the time he employed upon it was comparatively short. I am unwilling to swell my book with long quotations from what is in everybody's hands, and I believe there are few prose compositions in the English language that are read with more delight, or are more impressed upon the memory, than that preliminary discourse. One of its excellences has always struck me with peculiar admiration; I mean the perspicuity with which he has expressed abstract scientific notions. As an instance of this, I shall quote the following sentence: "When the radical idea branches out into parallel ramifications, how can a consecutive series be formed of senses in their nature collateral?" We have here an example of what has been often said, and I believe with justice, that there is for every thought a certain nice adaptation of words which none other could equal, and which when a man has been so fortunate as to hit, he has attained, in that particular case, the perfection of language.

The extensive reading which was absolutely necessary for the accumulation of authorities, and which alone may account for Johnson's retentive mind being enriched with a very large and various store of knowledge and imagery, must have occupied several years. The Preface furnishes an eminent instance of a double talent, of which Johnson was fully conscious. Sir Joshua Reynolds heard him say, "There are two things which I am confident I can do very well: one is an introduction to any literary work, stating what it is to contain, and how it should be executed in the most perfect manner; the other is a conclusion, showing from various causes why the execution has not been equal to what the author promised to himself and to the public."

How should puny scribblers be abashed and disappointed, when they find him displaying a perfect theory of lexicographical excellence, yet at the same time candidly and modestly allowing that he "had not satisfied his own expectations." Here was a fair occasion for the exercise of Johnson's modesty, when he was called upon to compare his own arduous performance, not with those of other individuals (in which case his inflexible regard to truth would have been violated had he affected diffidence), but with speculative perfection; as he, who can outstrip all his competitors in the race, may yet be sensible of his deficiency when he runs against time. Well might he say, that "the English Dictionary was written with little assistance of the learned"; for he told me that the only aid which he received was a paper containing twenty etymologies, sent to him by a person then unknown, who he was afterwards informed was Dr. Pearce, Bishop of Rochester. The etymologies, though they exhibit learning and judgment, are not, I think, entitled to the first praise amongst the various parts of this immense work. The definitions have always appeared to me such astonishing proofs of acuteness of intellect and precision of language, as indicate a genius of the highest rank. This it is which marks the superior excellence of Johnson's Dictionary over others equally or even more voluminous, and must have made it a work of much greater mental labour than mere Lexicons, or *Word-Books,* as the Dutch call them. They, who will make the experiment of trying how they can define a few words of whatever nature, will soon be satisfied of the unquestionable justice of this observation, which I can assure my readers is founded upon much study, and upon communication with more minds than my own.

A few of his definitions must be admitted to be erroneous. Thus, *Windward,* and *Leeward,* though directly of opposite meaning, are defined identically the same way; as to which inconsiderable specks it is enough to observe, that his Preface announces that he was aware there might be many such in so immense a work; nor was he at all disconcerted when an instance was pointed out to him. A lady once asked him how he came to define *Pastern* the *knee* of a horse: instead of making an elaborate defence, as she expected, he at once answered, "Ignorance, Madam, pure ignorance." His definition of *Network* has often been quoted with sportive malignity, as obscuring a thing in itself very plain. But to these frivolous censures no other answer is necessary than that with which we are furnished by his own Preface. "To explain, requires the use of terms less abstruse than that which is to be explained, and such terms cannot always be found. For as nothing can be proved but by supposing something intuitively known, and evident without proof, so nothing can be defined but by the use of words too plain to admit of a definition. Sometimes easier words are changed into harder; as, *burial,* into *sepulture* or *interment; dry,* into *desiccative; dryness,* into *siccity* or *aridity; fit,* into *paroxysm;* for, the *easiest* word, whatever it be, can never be translated into one more easy."

His introducing his own opinions, and even prejudices, under general definitions of words, while at the same time the original meaning of the words is not explained, as his *Tory, Whig, Pension, Oats, Excise,* and a few more, cannot be fully defended, and must be placed to the account of capricious and humorous indulgence. Talking to me upon this subject when we were at Ashbourne in 1777, he mentioned a still stronger instance of the predominance of his private feelings in the composition of this work, than any now to be found in it. "You know, Sir, Lord Gower forsook the old Jacobite interest. When I came to the word *Renegado,* after telling that it meant 'one who deserts to the enemy, a revolter,' I added, *Sometimes we say a* Gower. Thus it went to the press: but the printer had more wit than I, and struck it out."

Let it, however, be remembered, that this indulgence does not display itself only in sarcasm towards others, but sometimes in playful allusion to the nations commonly entertained of his own laborious task. Thus: "*Grub Street,* the name of a street in London, much inhabited by writers of small histories, *dictionaries,* and temporary poems, whence any mean production is called *Grub Street.*"—"*Lexicographer,* a writer of dictionaries, a *harmless drudge.*"

At the time when he was concluding his very eloquent Preface, Johnson's mind appears to have been in such a state of depression, that we cannot contemplate without wonder the vigorous and splendid thoughts, which so highly distinguish that performance. "I (says he) may surely be contented without the praise of perfection, which if I could obtain in this gloom of solitude, what would it avail me? I have protracted my work till most of those whom I wished to please have sunk into the grave; and success and miscarriage are empty sounds. I therefore dismiss it with frigid tranquillity, having little to fear or hope from censure or from praise." That this indifference was rather a temporary than an habitual feeling, appears, I think, from his letters to Mr. Warton; and however he may have been affected for the moment, certain it is that the honours which his great work procured him, both at home and abroad, were very grateful to him. His friend, the Earl of Cork and Orrery, being at Florence, presented it to the *Academia della Crusca.* That Academy sent Johnson their *Vocabulario,* and the French Academy sent him their *Dictionnaire,* which Mr. Langton had the pleasure to convey to him.

It must undoubtedly seem strange, that the conclusion of his Preface should be expressed in terms so desponding, when it is considered that the author was then only in his forty-sixth year. But we must ascribe its gloom to that miserable dejection of spirits to which he was constitutionally subject, and which was aggravated by the death of his wife two years before. I have heard it ingeniously observed by a lady of rank and elegance, that "his melancholy was then at its meridian." It pleased God to grant him almost thirty years of life after this time; and once, when he was in a placid frame of mind, he was obliged to own to me that he had enjoyed happier days, and had many more friends, since that gloomy hour, than before.

The celebrated Mr. Wilkes, whose notions and habits of life were very opposite to his, but who was ever eminent for literature and vivacity, sallied forth with a little *Jeu d'Esprit* upon the following passage in his Grammar of the English Tongue, prefixed to the Dictionary: "*H* seldom, perhaps never, begins any but the first syllable." In an essay printed in *The Public Advertiser,* this lively writer enumerated many instances in opposition to this remark; for example, "The author of this observation must be a man of quick *appre-hension,* and of a most *compre-hensive* genius." The position is undoubtedly expressed with too much latitude.

CHAPTER X—1756–1758

Dr. Burney

IN 1756 Johnson found that the great fame of his Dictionary had not set him above the necessity of "making provisions for the day that was passing over him." No royal or noble patron extended a munificent hand to give independence to the man who had conferred stability on the language of his country. We may feel indignant that there should have been such unworthy neglect; but we must, at the same time, congratulate ourselves, when we consider, that to this very neglect, operating to rouse the natural indolence of his constitution, we owe many valuable productions, which otherwise, perhaps, might never have appeared.

He had spent, during the progress of the work, the money for which he had contracted to write his Dictionary. We have seen that the reward of his labour was only fifteen hundred and seventy-five pounds; and when the expense of amanuenses and paper, and other articles, are deducted, his clear profit was very inconsiderable. I once said to him, "I am sorry, Sir, you did not get more for your Dictionary." His answer was, "I am sorry, too. But it was very well. The booksellers are generous, liberal-minded men." He, upon all occasions, did ample justice to their character in this respect. He considered them as the patrons of literature; and, indeed, although they have eventually been considerable gainers by his Dictionary, it is to them that we owe its having been undertaken and carried through at the risk of great expense, for they were not absolutely sure of being indemnified.

On the first day of this year we find, from his private devotions, that he had then recovered from sickness, and in February that his eye was restored to its use.

His works this year were, an abstract or epitome, in octavo, of his folio Dictionary, and a few essays in a monthly publication, entitled, *The Universal Visiter*. Christopher Smart, with whose unhappy vacillation of mind he sincerely sympathised, was one of the stated undertakers of this miscellany; and it was to assist him that Johnson sometimes employed his pen.

He engaged also to superintend and contribute largely to another monthly publication, entitled *The Literary Magazine, or Universal Review;* [*] the first number of which came out in May this year. What were his emoluments from this undertaking, and what other writers were employed in it, I have not discovered. He continued to write in it, with intermissions, till the fifteenth number; and I think that he never gave better proofs of the force, acuteness, and vivacity of his mind, than in this miscellany, whether we consider his original essays, or his reviews of the works of others. The "Preliminary Address" [†] to the public, is a proof how this great man could embellish, with the graces of superior composition, even so trite a thing as the plan of a magazine.

His original essays are, "An Introduction to the Political State of Great Britain"; [†] "Remarks on the Militia Bill"; [†] "Observations on his Britannic Majesty's Treaties with the Empress of Russia and the Landgrave of Hesse Cassel"; [†] "Observations on the Present State of Affairs"; [†] and, "Memoirs of Frederick III, King of Prussia." [†] In all these he displays extensive political knowledge and sagacity, expressed with uncommon energy and perspicuity, without any of those words which he sometimes took a pleasure in adopting, in imitation of Sir Thomas Browne; of whose "Christian Morals" he this year gave an edition, with his "Life" [*] prefixed to it, which is one of Johnson's best biographical performances. In one instance only in these essays has he indulged his *Brownism*. Dr. Robertson, the historian, mentioned it to me, as having at once convinced him that Johnson was the author of the "Memoirs of the King of Prussia." Speaking of the pride which the old King, the father of his hero, took in being master of the tallest regiment in Europe, he says, "To review this *towering* regiment was his daily pleasure; and to perpetuate it was so much his care, that when he met a tall woman he immediately commanded one of his *Titanian* retinue to marry her, that they might *propagate procerity.*" For this Anglo-Latin word *procerity,* Johnson had, however, the authority of Addison.

It is worthy of remark, in justice to Johnson's political character, which has been misrepresented as abjectly submissive to power, that his "Observations on the Present State of Affairs" glow with as animated a spirit of constitutional liberty as can be found anywhere.

Here we have it assumed as an incontrovertible principle, that in this country the people are the superintendents of the conduct and measures of those by whom government is administered; of the beneficial effect of which the present reign afforded an illustrious example, when addresses from all parts of the kingdom controlled an audacious attempt to introduce a new power subversive of the crown.

A still stronger proof of his patriotic spirit appears in his review of an "Essay on Waters," by Dr. Lucas, of whom, after describing him as a man well known to the world for his daring defiance of power, when he thought it exerted on the side of wrong, he thus speaks: "The Irish ministers drove him from his native country by a proclamation, in which they charge him with crimes of which they never intended to be called to the proof, and oppressed him by methods equally irresistible by guilt and innocence.

"Let the man thus driven into exile, for having been the friend of his country, be received in every other place as a confessor of liberty; and let the tools of power be taught in time, that they may rob, but cannot impoverish."

His defence of tea against Mr. Jonas Hanway's violent attack upon that elegant and popular beverage, shows how very well a man of genius can write upon the slightest subject, when he writes, as the Italians say, *con amore:* I suppose no person ever enjoyed with more relish the infusion of that fragrant leaf than Johnson. The quantities which he drank of it at all hours were so great, that his nerves must have been uncommonly strong, not to have been extremely relaxed by such an intemperate use of it. He assured me that he never felt the least inconvenience from it; which is a proof that the fault of his constitution was rather a too great tension of fibres, than the contrary. Mr. Hanway wrote an angry answer to Johnson's review of his "Essay on Tea," and Johnson, after a full and deliberate pause, made a reply to it; the only instance, I believe, in the whole course of his life, when he condescended to oppose any thing that was written against him.

Johnson's most exquisite critical essay in the *Literary Magazine,* and indeed anywhere, is his review of Soame Jenyns's "Inquiry into the Origin of Evil." Jenyns was possessed of lively talents, and a style eminently pure and easy, and could very happily play with a light subject, either in prose or verse; but when he speculated on that most difficult and excruciating question, the Origin of Evil, he "ventured far beyond his depth," and, accordingly, was exposed by Johnson, both with acute argument and brilliant wit. I remember when the late Mr. Bicknell's humorous performance, entitled "The Musical Travels of Joel Collyer," in which a slight attempt is made to ridicule Johnson, was ascribed to Soame Jenyns. "Ha! (said Johnson) I thought I had given *him* enough of it."

His triumph over Jenyns is thus described by my friend Mr. Courtenay in his "Poetical Review of the Literary and Moral Character of Dr. Johnson"; a performance of such merit, that, had I not been honoured with a very kind and partial notice in it, I should echo the sentiments of men of the first taste loudly in its praise:

"When specious sophists with pre-
 sumption scan
The source of evil hidden still
 from man;
Revive Arabian tales, and vainly
 hope
To rival St. John, and his scholar
 Pope:
Though metaphysics spread the
 gloom of night,

By reason's star he guides our ach-
 ing sight;
The bounds of knowledge marks,
 and points the way
To pathless wastes, where wilder'd
 sages stray;
Where, like a farthing link-boy,
 Jenyns stands,
And the dim torch drops from his
 feeble hands."[1]

This year Mr. William Payne, brother of the respectable book-seller of that name, published "An Introduction to the Game of Draughts," to which Johnson contributed a Dedication to the Earl of Rochford, [*] and a Preface, [*] both of which are admirably adapted to the treatise to which they are prefixed. Johnson, I believe, did not play at draughts after leaving College, by which he suffered; for it would have afforded him an innocent soothing relief from the melan-

[1]Some time after Dr. Johnson's death there appeared in the newspapers and magazines an illiberal and petulant attack upon him, in the form of an Epitaph, under the name of Mr. Soame Jenyns, very unworthy of that gentleman, who had quietly submitted to the critical lash while Johnson lived. It assumed, as character-istics of him, all the vulgar circumstances of abuse which had circulated amongst the ignorant. It was an unbecoming indulgence of puny resentment, at a time when he himself was at a very advanced age, and had a near prospect of descending to the grave. I was truly sorry for it; for he was then become an avowed, and (as my Lord Bishop of London, who had a serious conversation with him on the subject, assures me) a sincere Christian. He could not expect that Johnson's numerous friends would patiently bear to have the memory of their master stigmatised by no mean pen, but that, at least, one would be found to retort. Accordingly, this unjust and sarcastic Epitaph was met in the same public field by an answer, in terms by no means soft, and such as wanton provocation only could justify:

"EPITAPH,

"Prepared for a creature not quite dead *yet.*

"Here lies a little ugly nauseous elf,
 Who judging only from its wretched
 self,
Feebly attempted, petulant and vain,
The 'Origin of Evil' to explain.
A mighty Genius, at this elf displas'd,
With a strong critic grasp the urchin
 squeez'd.

For thirty years its coward spleen it
 kept,
Till in the dust the mighty Genius
 slept;
Then stunk and fretted in expiring
 snuff,
And blink'd at Johnson with its last
 poor puff."

choly which distressed him so often. I have heard him regret that he had not learnt to play at cards; and the game of draughts we know is peculiarly calculated to fix the attention without straining it. There is a composure and gravity in draughts which insensibly tranquillizes the mind; and, accordingly, the Dutch are fond of it, as they are of smoking, of the sedative influence of which, though he himself never smoked, he had a high opinion. Besides, there is in draughts some exercise of the faculties; and, accordingly, Johnson wishing to dignify the subject in his Dedication with what is most estimable in it, observes, "Triflers may find or make anything a trifle: but since it is the great characteristic of a wise man to see events in their causes, to obviate consequences, and ascertain contingencies, your Lordship will think nothing a trifle by which the mind is inured to caution, foresight, and circumspection."

As one of the little occasional advantages which he did not disdain to take by his pen, as a man whose profession was literature, he this year accepted of a guinea from Mr. Robert Dodsley, for writing the introduction to *The London Chronicle,* an evening newspaper; and even in so slight a performance exhibited peculiar talents. This *Chronicle* still subsists, and from what I observed, when I was abroad, has a more extensive circulation upon the Continent than any of the English newspapers. It was constantly read by Johnson himself; and it is but just to observe that it has all along been distinguished for good sense, accuracy, moderation, and delicacy.

Another instance of the same nature has been communicated to me by the Reverend Dr. Thomas Campbell, who has done himself considerable credit by his own writings. "Sitting with Dr. Johnson one morning alone, he asked me if I had known Dr. Madden, who was the author of the premium-scheme in Ireland. On my answering in the affirmative, and also that I had for some years lived in his neighbourhood, etc., he begged of me, that when I returned to Ireland, I would endeavour to procure for him a poem of Dr. Madden's, called 'Boulter's Monument.' The reason (said he) why I wish for it is this: when Dr. Madden came to London, he submitted that work to my castigation; and I remember I blotted a great many lines, and might have blotted many more without making the poem worse. However, the Doctor was very thankful, and very generous, for he gave me ten guineas, *which to me at that time was a great sum.*"

He this year resumed his scheme of giving an edition of Shakspeare with notes. He issued proposals of considerable length, in which he showed that he perfectly well knew what a variety of research such an undertaking required; but his indolence prevented him from pursuing it with that diligence which alone can collect those scattered facts, that genius, however acute, penetrating, and luminous, cannot discover by its own force. It is remarkable that at this time his fancied activity was for the moment so vigorous, that he promised his work should be published before Christmas, 1757. Yet nine years elapsed before it saw the light. His throes in bringing it forth had been severe and remittent; and at last we may almost conclude that the Cæsarean operation was performed by the knife of Churchill, whose upbraiding satire, I dare say, made Johnson's friends urge him to despatch.

> "He for subscribers baits his hook,
> And takes your cash; but where's the book?
> No matter where; wise fear, you know,
> Forbids the robbing of a foe;
> But what, to serve our private ends,
> Forbids the cheating of our friends?"
> *The Ghost,* iii. 801.

About this period he was offered a living of considerable value in Lincolnshire if he were inclined to enter into holy orders. It was a rectory in the gift of Mr. Langton, the father of his much-valued friend. But he did not accept of it; partly I believe from a conscientious motive, being persuaded that his temper and habits rendered him unfit for that assiduous and familiar instruction of the vulgar and ignorant, which he held to be an essential duty in a clergyman; and partly because his love of a London life was so strong, that he would have thought himself an exile in any other place, particularly if residing in the country. Whoever would wish to see his thoughts upon that subject displayed in their full force, may peruse the *Adventurer,* Number 126.

Mr. Burney having enclosed to him an extract from the review of his Dictionary in the *Bibliothèque des Savans,* and a list of subscribers to his Shakspeare, which Mr. Burney had procured in Norfolk, he wrote the following answer:

"TO MR. BURNEY, IN LYNNE, NORFOLK.

"SIR,—
"That I may show myself sensible of your favours, and not commit the same fault a second time, I make haste to answer the letter which I received this morning. The truth is, the other likewise was received,

and I wrote an answer; but being desirous to transmit you some proposals and receipts, I waited till I could find a convenient conveyance, and day was passed after day, till other things drove it from my thoughts; yet not so, but that I remember with great pleasure your commendation of my Dictionary. Your praise was welcome, not only because I believe it was sincere, but because praise has been very scarce. A man of your candour will be surprised when I tell you, that among all my acquaintance there were only two who upon the publication of my book did not endeavour to depress me with threats of censure from the public, or with objections learned from those who had learned them from my own preface. Yours is the only letter of goodwill that I have received; though, indeed, I am promised something of that sort from Sweden.

"How my new edition will be received I know not; the subscription has not been very successful. I shall publish about March.

"If you can direct me how to send proposals, I should wish that they were in such hands.

"I remember, Sir, in some of the first letters with which you favoured me, you mentioned your lady. May I inquire after her? In return for the favours which you have shown me, it is not much to tell you, that I wish you and her all that can conduce to your happiness. I am, Sir, your most obliged

"And most humble servant,

"Sam. Johnson.

"Gough Square, Dec. 24, 1757."

In 1758 we find him, it should seem, in as easy and pleasant a state of existence as constitutional unhappiness ever permitted him to enjoy.

"TO THE SAME.

"Sir,—

"Your kindness is so great, and my claim to any particular regard from you so little, that I am at a loss how to express my sense of your favours; but I am, indeed, much pleased to be thus distinguished by you.

"I am ashamed to tell you that my Shakspeare will not be out so soon as I promised my subscribers: but I did not promise them more than I promised myself. It will, however, be published before summer.

"I have sent you a bundle of proposals, which, I think, do not pro-

fess more than I have hitherto performed. I have printed many of the
plays, and have hitherto left very few passages unexplained; where I
am quite at a loss, I confess my ignorance, which is seldom done by
commentators.

"I have, likewise, enclosed twelve receipts; not that I impose upon
you the trouble of pushing them, with more importunity than may
seem proper, but that you may rather have more than fewer than you
shall want. The proposals you will disseminate as there shall be an opportunity. I once printed them at length in the *Chronicle,* and some of
my friends (I believe Mr. Murphy, who formerly wrote the *Gray's Inn
Journal*) introduced them with a splendid encomium.

"Since the 'Life of Browne' I have been a little engaged, from time
to time, in the *Literary Magazine,* but not very lately. I have not the
collection by me, and therefore cannot draw out a catalogue of my
own parts, but will do it, and send it. Do not buy them, for I will gather
all those that have any thing of mine in them, and send them to Mrs.
Burney, as a small token of gratitude for the regard which she is pleased
to bestow upon me. I am, Sir, your most obliged

"And most humble servant,

"SAM. JOHNSON.

"London, March 8, 1758."

CHAPTER XI—1758–1759

The "Idler"

ON THE FIFTEENTH OF APRIL he began a new periodical paper, entitled
the *Idler* [*] which came out every Saturday in a weekly newspaper,
called *The Universal Chronicle, or Weekly Gazette,* published by New-
bery. These essays were continued till April 5, 1760. Of one hundred
and three, their total number, twelve were contributed by his friends;
of which, Numbers 33, 93, and 96, were written by Mr. Thomas Warton; No. 67, by Mr. Langton; and No. 76, 79, and 82, by Sir Joshua
Reynolds: the concluding words of No. 82, "and pollute his canvas
with deformity," being added by Johnson; as Sir Joshua informed me.

The *Idler* is evidently the work of the same mind which produced
the *Rambler,* but has less body and more spirit. It has more variety of

[115]

real life, and greater facility of language. He describes the miseries of idleness, with the lively sensations of one who has felt them: and in his private memoranda while engaged in it, we find, "This year I hope to learn diligence." Many of these excellent essays were written as hastily as an ordinary letter. Mr. Langton remembers Johnson, when on a visit at Oxford, asking him one evening how long it was till the post went out; and on being told about half an hour, he exclaimed, "Then we shall do very well." He upon this instantly sat down and finished an *Idler,* which it was necessary should be in London the next day. Mr. Langton having signified a wish to·read it, "Sir (said he), you shall not do more than I have done myself." He then folded it up, and sent it off.

A casual coincidence with other writers, or an adoption of a sentiment or image which has been found in the writings of another; and afterwards appears in the mind as one's own, is not unfrequent. The richness of Johnson's· fancy, which could supply his page abundantly on all occasions, and the strength of his memory, which at once detected the real owner of any thought, made him less liable to the imputation of plagiarism than, perhaps, any of our writers. In the *Idler,* however, there is a paper, in which conversation is assimilated to a bowl of punch, where there is the same train of comparison as in a poem by Blacklock, in his collection published in 1756; in which a parallel is ingeniously drawn between human life and that liquor. It ends.

> "Say, then, physicians of each kind,
> Who cure the body or the mind,
> What harm in drinking can there be,
> Since punch and life so well agree?"

To the *Idler,* when collected in volumes, he added, beside the Essay on Epitaphs, and the Dissertation on those of Pope, an Essay on the Bravery of the English common Soldiers. He, however, omitted one of the original papers, which, in the folio copy, is No. 22.

"TO BENNET LANGTON, ESQ., AT LANGTON, NEAR SPILSBY, LINCOLNSHIRE.

"DEAR SIR,—

"I should be sorry to think that what engrosses the attention of my friend, should have no part of mine. Your mind is now full of the fate of Dury;[1] but his fate is past, and nothing remains but to try what reflection will suggest to mitigate the terrors of a violent death, which is more formidable at the first glance, than on a nearer and more steady view. A violent death is never very painful; the only danger is, lest it should be unprovided. But if a man can be supposed to make no provision for death in war, what can be the state that would have awakened him to the care of futurity? When would that man have prepared himself to die, who went to seek death without preparation? What then can be the reason why we lament more, him that dies of a wound, than him that dies of a fever? A man that languishes with disease, ends his life with more pain, but with less virtue: he leaves no example to his friends, nor bequeaths any honour to his descendants. The only reason why we lament a Soldier's death, is, that we think he might have lived longer; yet this cause of grief is common to many other kinds of death, which are not so passionately bewailed. The truth is, that every death is violent which is the effect of accident; every death, which is not gradually brought on by the miseries of age, or when life is extinguished for any other reason than that it is burnt out. He that dies before sixty, of a cold or consumption, dies, in reality, by a violent death; yet his death is borne with patience, only because the cause of his untimely end is silent and invisible. Let us endeavour to see things as they are, and then inquire whether we ought to complain. Whether to see life as it is, will give us much consolation, I know not; but the consolation which is drawn from truth, if any there be, is solid and durable; that which may be derived from error, must be, like its original, fallacious and fugitive.

"I am, dear, dear Sir,

"Your most humble servant,

"SAM. JOHNSON.

"*Sept. 21, 1758.*"

In 1759, in the month of January, his mother died at the great age of ninety, an event which deeply affected him; not that "his mind had acquired no firmness by the contemplation of mortality"; but that his reverential affection for her was not abated by years, as indeed he retained all his tender feelings even to the latest period of his life. I have

---

[1] Major-General Alexander Dury, of the first regiment of Foot-Guards, who fell in the gallant discharge of his duty, near St. Cas, in the well-known unfortunate expedition against France, in 1758. His lady and Mr. Langton's mother were sisters. He left an only son, Lieutenant-Colonel Dury, who has a company in the same regiment.

been told that he regretted much his not having gone to visit his mother for several years previous to her death. But he was constantly engaged in literary labours which confined him to London; and though he had not the comfort of seeing his aged parent, he contributed liberally to her support.

"TO MRS. JOHNSON, IN LICHFIELD.

"HONOURED MADAM,—

"The account which Miss [Porter] gives me of your health, pierces my heart. God comfort, and preserve you, and save you, for the sake of Jesus Christ.

"I would have Miss read to you from time to time the Passion of our Saviour, and sometimes the sentences in the Communion Service, beginning—*Come unto me, all ye that travail and are heavy laden, and I will give you rest.*

"I have just now read a physical book, which inclines me to think that a strong infusion of the bark would do you good. Do, dear Mother, try it.

"Pray send me your blessing, and forgive all that I have done amiss to you. And whatever you would have done, and what debts you would have paid first, or anything else that you would direct, let Miss put it down; I shall endeavour to obey you.

"I have got twelve guineas to send you, but unhappily am at a loss how to send it to-night. If I cannot send it to-night, it will come by the next post.

"Pray, do not omit anything mentioned in this letter. God bless you for ever and ever. I am, your dutiful Son,

"SAM. JOHNSON.

"Jan. 13, 175[9]."

"TO MISS PORTER, AT MRS. JOHNSON'S, IN LICHFIELD.

"MY DEAR MISS,—

"I think myself obliged to you beyond all expression of gratitude for your care of my dear mother. God grant it may not be without success. Tell Kitty, that I shall never forget her tenderness for her mistress. Whatever you can do, continue to do. My heart is very full.

"I hope you received twelve guineas on Monday. I found a way of sending them by means of the Postmaster, after I had written my let-

[118]

ter, and hope they came safe. I will send you more in a few days. God bless you all.

"I am, my dear,

"Your most obliged and most humble servant,

"SAM. JOHNSON.

"Jan. 16, 1759.

"Over the leaf is a letter to my Mother.

"DEAR HONOURED MOTHER,—

"Your weakness afflicts me beyond what I am willing to communicate to you. I do not think you unfit to face death, but I know not how to bear the thought of losing you. Endeavour to do all you [can] for yourself. Eat as much as you can.

"I pray often for you; do you pray for me.—I have nothing to add to my last letter.

"I am, dear, dear Mother,

"Your dutiful Son,

"SAM. JOHNSON.

"Jan. 16, 1759."

"TO MRS. JOHNSON, IN LICHFIELD.

"DEAR HONOURED MOTHER,—

"I fear you are too ill for long letters; therefore I will only tell you, you have from me all the regard that can possibly subsist in the heart. I pray God to bless you for evermore, for Jesus Christ's sake. Amen.

"Let Miss write to me every post, however short.

"I am, dear Mother,

"Your dutiful Son,

"SAM. JOHNSON.

"Jan. 18, 1759."

"TO MISS PORTER, AT MRS. JOHNSON'S, IN LICHFIELD.

"DEAR MISS,—

"I will, if it be possible, come down to you. God grant I may yet [find] my dear mother breathing and sensible. Do not tell her, lest I disappoint her. If I miss to write next post, I am on the road.

"I am, my dearest Miss,

"Your most humble servant,

"SAM. JOHNSON.

"Jan. 20, 1759."

"On the other side."

"DEAR HONOURED MOTHER,—

"Neither your condition nor your character make it fit for me to say much. You have been the best mother, and I believe, the best woman in the world. I thank you for your indulgence to me, and beg forgiveness of all that I have done ill, and all that I have omitted to do well. God grant you His Holy Spirit, and receive you to everlasting happiness, for Jesus Christ's sake. Amen. Lord Jesus receive your spirit. Amen.

"I am, dear, dear Mother,
"Your dutiful Son,
"SAM. JOHNSON.

"Jan. 20, 1759."

"TO MISS PORTER, IN LICHFIELD.

"You will conceive my sorrow for the loss of my mother, of the best mother. If she were to live again, surely I should behave better to her. But she is happy, and what is past is nothing to her; and for me, since I cannot repair my faults to her, I hope repentance will efface them. I return you and all those that have been good to her my sincerest thanks, and pray God to repay you all with infinite advantage. Write to me, and comfort me, dear child. I shall be glad likewise, if Kitty will write to me. I shall send a bill of £20 in a few days, which I thought to have brought to my mother; but God suffered it not. I have not power or composure to say much more. God bless you, and bless us all.

"I am, dear Miss,
"Your affectionate humble servant,
"SAM. JOHNSON.

"Jan. 23, 1759."

Soon after this event, he wrote his "Rasselas, Prince of Abyssinia"; [*] concerning the publication of which, Sir John Hawkins guesses vaguely and idly, instead of having taken the trouble to inform himself with authentic precision. Not to trouble my readers with a repetition of the Knight's reveries, I have to mention that the late Mr. Strahan, the printer, told me that Johnson wrote it, that with the profits he might defray the expense of his mother's funeral, and pay some little debts which she had left. He told Sir Joshua Reynolds that he composed it in the evenings of one week, sent it to the press in portions as it

Gordon Ross del.

New York, 1945

Oxford in Johnson's day.

was written, and had never since read it over. Mr. Strahan, Mr. Johnson, and Mr. Dodsley, purchased it for a hundred pounds, but afterwards paid him twenty-five pounds more, when it came to a second edition.

Considering the large sums which have been received for compilations, and works requiring not much more genius than compilations, we cannot but wonder at the very low price which he was content to receive for this admirable performance; which, though he had written nothing else, would have rendered his name immortal in the world of literature. None of his writings have been so extensively diffused over Europe; for it has been translated into most, if not all, of the modern languages.

The fund of thinking which this work contains is such, that almost every sentence of it may furnish a subject of long meditation. I am not satisfied if a year passes without my having read it through; and at every perusal, my admiration of the mind which produced it is so highly raised, that I can scarcely believe that I had the honour of enjoying the intimacy of such a man.

Notwithstanding my high admiration of "Rasselas," I will not maintain that the "morbid melancholy" in Johnson's constitution may not, perhaps, have made life appear to him more insipid and unhappy than it generally is; for I am sure that he had less enjoyment from it than I have. Yet, whatever additional shade his own particular sensations may have thrown on his representation of life, attentive observation and close inquiry have convinced me that there is too much reality in the gloomy picture. The truth, however, is that we judge of the happiness and misery of life differently at different times, according to the state of our changeable frame. I always remember a remark made to me by a Turkish lady, educated in France: *"Ma foi, Monsieur, notre bonheur dépend de la façon que notre sang circule."* This have I learnt from a pretty hard course of experience, and would, from sincere benevolence, impress upon all who honour this book with a perusal, that until a steady conviction is obtained, that the present life is an imperfect state, and only a passage to a better, if we comply with the divine scheme of progressive improvement; and also that it is a part of the mysterious plan of Providence, that intellectual beings must "be made perfect through suffering"; there will be a continual recurrence of disappointment and uneasiness. But if we walk with hope in "the mid-day sun" of revelation, our temper and disposition will be such, that the comforts and enjoyments in our way will be relished, while we patiently support the inconveniences and pains. After much speculation and various reasoning, I acknowledge myself convinced of the truth of Voltaire's conclusion, *"Après tout, c'est un monde passable."*

I would ascribe to this year the following letter to a son of one of his early friends at Lichfield, Mr. Joseph Simpson, Barrister, and author of a tract entitled "Reflections on the Study of the Law."

"TO JOSEPH SIMPSON, ESQ.

"DEAR SIR,—

"Your father's inexorability not only grieves but amazes me: he is your father: he was always accounted a wise man; nor do I remember anything to the disadvantage of his good nature; but in his refusal to assist you there is neither good nature, fatherhood, nor wisdom. It is the practice of good nature to overlook faults which have already, by the consequences, punished the delinquent. It is natural for a father to think more favourably than others of his children; and it is always wise to give assistance, while a little help will prevent the necessity of greater.

"If you married imprudently, you miscarried at your own hazard, at an age when you had a right of choice. It would be hard if the man might not choose his own wife, who has a right to plead before the Judges of his country.

"If your imprudence has ended in difficulties and inconveniences, you are yourself to support them; and, with the help of a little better health, you would support them and conquer them. Surely, that want which accident and sickness produces is to be supported in every region of humanity, though there were neither friends nor fathers in the world. You have certainly from your father the highest claim of charity, though none of right: and therefore I would counsel you to omit no decent nor manly degree of importunity. Your debts in the whole are not large, and of the whole but a small part is troublesome. Small debts are like small shot; they are rattling on every side, and can scarcely be escaped without a wound; great debts are like cannon; of loud noise, but little danger. You must, therefore, be enabled to discharge petty debts, that you may have leisure, with security, to struggle with the rest. Neither the great nor the little debts disgrace you. I am sure you have my esteem for the courage with which you contracted them, and the spirit with which you endure them. I wish my esteem could be of more use. I have been invited, or have invited myself, to several parts of the kingdom; and will not incommode my dear Lucy by coming to Lichfield, while her present lodging is of any use to her. I hope, in a few days, to be at leisure, and to make visits. Whither I shall fly is matter of no importance. A man unconnected is at home everywhere; unless he may be said to be at home nowhere. I am sorry, dear Sir, that where you have parents, a man of your merits should not have a home. I wish I could give it you.

"I am, my dear Sir,

"Affectionately yours,

"SAM. JOHNSON."

His negro servant, Francis Barber, having left him, and been some time at sea, not pressed as has been supposed, but with his own consent, it appears from a letter to John Wilkes, Esq., from Dr. Smollett, that his master kindly interested himself in procuring his release from a state of life of which Johnson always expressed the utmost abhorrence. He said, "No man will be a sailor who has contrivance enough to get himself into a jail; for being in a ship is being in a jail, with the chance of being drowned." And at another time, "A man in jail has more room, better food, and commonly better company." The letter was as follows:

"Chelsea, March 16, 1759.

"DEAR SIR,—

"I am again your petitioner, in behalf of that great Cham of literature, Samuel Johnson. His black servant, whose name is Francis Barber, has been pressed on board the *Stag* Frigate, Captain Angel, and our lexicographer is in great distress. He says, the boy is a sickly lad, of a delicate frame, and particularly subject to a malady in his throat, which renders him very unfit for his Majesty's service. You know what matter of animosity the said Johnson has against you: and I dare say you desire no other opportunity of resenting it than that of laying him under an obligation. He was humble enough to desire my assistance on this occasion, though he and I were never cater-cousins; and I gave him to understand that I would make application to my friend Mr. Wilkes, who, perhaps, by his interest with Dr. Hay and Mr. Elliot, might be able to procure the discharge of his lacquey. It would be superfluous to say more on the subject, which I leave to your own consideration; but I cannot let slip this opportunity of declaring that I am, with the most inviolable esteem and attachment, dear Sir,

"Your affectionate obliged humble servant,

"T. SMOLLETT."

Mr. Wilkes, who upon all occasions has acted as a private gentleman, with most polite liberality, applied to his friend Sir George Hay, then one of the Lords Commissioners of the Admiralty; and Francis Barber was discharged, as he told me, without any wish of his own. He found his old master in Chambers in the Inner Temple, and returned to his service.

At this time there being a competition among the architects of London to be employed in the building of Blackfriars-bridge, a question was very warmly agitated whether semicircular or elliptical arches were preferable. In the design offered by Mr. Mylne the elliptical form was adopted, and therefore it was the great object of his rivals to attack it. Johnson's regard for his friend Mr. Gwyn induced him to engage in this controversy against Mr. Mylne; and after being at considerable pains to study the subject, he wrote three several letters in the *Gazetteer,* in opposition to his plan.

If it should be remarked that this was a controversy which lay quite out of Johnson's way, let it be remembered, that after all, his employing his powers of reasoning and eloquence upon a subject which he had studied on the moment, is not more strange than what we often observe in lawyers, who as *Quicquid agunt homines* in the matter of law-suits, are sometimes obliged to pick up a temporary knowledge of an art or science, of which they understood nothing till their brief was delivered, and appear to be much masters of it. In like manner, members of the Legislature frequently introduce and expatiate upon subjects of which they have informed themselves for the occasion.

CHAPTER XII—1760–1763

Johnson's Pension

IN 1760 he wrote "an Address of the Painters to George III on his accession to the Throne of these Kingdoms," [†] which no monarch ever ascended with more sincere congratulations from his people. Two generations of foreign princes had prepared their minds to rejoice in having again a King, who gloried in being "born a Briton." He also wrote for Mr. Baretti the Dedication [†] of his Italian and English

Dictionary, to the Marquis of Abreu, then Envoy-Extraordinary from Spain at the Court of Great Britain.

In this year I have not discovered a single private letter written by him to any of his friends. It should seem, however, that he had at this period a floating intention of writing a history of the recent and wonderful successes of the British arms in all quarters of the globe; for among his resolutions or memorandums, September 18, there is, "Send for books for Hist. of War." How much is it to be regretted that this intention was not fulfilled! His majestic expression would have carried down to the latest posterity the glorious achievements of his country, with the same fervent glow which they produced on the mind at the time. He would have been under no temptation to deviate in any degree from truth, which he held very sacred, or to take a licence, which a learned divine told me he once seemed in a conversation jocularly to allow to historians. "There are (said he) inexcusable lies, and consecrated lies. For instance, we are told that on the arrival of the news of the unfortunate battle of Fontenoy, every heart beat, and every eye was in tears. Now we know that no man eat his dinner the worse, but there *should* have been all this concern; and to say there was (smiling), may be reckoned a consecrated lie."

"TO BENNET LANGTON, ESQ., AT LANGTON, NEAR SPILSBY, LINCOLNSHIRE.

"DEAR SIR,—

"You, that travel about the world, have more materials for letters, than I who stay at home: and should, therefore, write with frequency equal to your opportunities. I should be glad to have all England surveyed by you, if you would impart your observations in narratives as agreeable as your last. Knowledge is always to be wished to those who can communicate it well. While you have been riding and running, and seeing the tombs of the learned, and the camps of the valiant, I have only stayed at home, and intended to do great things, which I have not done. Beau went away to Cheshire, and has not yet found his way back. Chambers passed the vacation at Oxford.

"I am very sincerely solicitous for the preservation or curing of Mr. Langton's sight, and am glad that the chirurgeon at Coventry gives him so much hope. Mr. Sharpe is of opinion that the tedious maturation of the cataract is a vulgar error, and that it may be removed as soon as it is formed. This notion deserves to be considered; I doubt whether it be universally true; but if it be true in some cases, and those cases can be distinguished, it may save a long and uncomfortable delay.

"Of dear Mrs. Langton you gave me no account; which is the less friendly, as you know how highly I think of her, and how much I interest myself in her health. I suppose you told her of my opinion, and likewise suppose it was not followed; however, I still believe it to be right.

"Let me hear from you again, wherever you are, or whatever you are doing; whether you wander or sit still, plant trees or make 'Rustics,' play with your sisters or muse alone; and in return I will tell you the success of Sheridan, who at this instant is playing *Cato,* and has already played *Richard* twice. He had more company the second than the first night, and will make, I believe, a good figure in the whole, though his faults seem to be very many; some of natural deficience, and some of laborious affectation. He has, I think, no power of assuming either that dignity or elegance which some men, who have little of either in common life, can exhibit on the stage. His voice, when strained, is unpleasing, and when low is not always heard. He seems to think too much on the audience, and turns his face too often to the galleries.

"However, I wish him well; and among other reasons, because I like his wife.

"Make haste to write to, dear Sir,

"Your most affectionate servant,

"SAM. JOHNSON.

"*Oct. 18, 1760.*"

In 1761, Johnson appears to have done little. He was still, no doubt, proceeding in his edition of "Shakspeare"; but what advances he made in it cannot be ascertained. He certainly was at this time not active; for in his scrupulous examination of himself on Easter eve, he laments, in his too-rigorous mode of censuring his own conduct, that his life, since the communion of the preceding Easter, had been "dissipated and useless." He, however, contributed this year the Preface [*] to "Rolt's Dictionary of Trade and Commerce," in which he displays such a clear and comprehensive knowledge of the subject, as might lead the reader to think that its author had devoted all his life to it. I asked him whether he knew much of Rolt, and of his work. "Sir (said he), I never saw the man, and never read the book. The booksellers wanted a Preface to a Dictionary of Trade and Commerce. I knew very well what such a Dictionary should be, and I wrote a Preface accordingly."

Johnson had now for some years admitted Mr. Baretti to his intimacy; nor did their friendship cease upon their being separated by Baretti's revisiting his native country, as appears from Johnson's letters to him.

"TO MR. JOSEPH BARETTI, AT MILAN.

"You reproach me very often with parsimony of writing; but you may discover, by the extent of my paper, that I design to recompense rarity by length. A short letter to a distant friend is, in my opinion, an insult like that of a slight bow or cursory salutation; a proof of unwillingness to do much, even where there is a necessity of doing something. Yet it must be remembered, that he who continues the same course of life in the same place, will have little to tell. One week and one year are very like one another. The silent changes made by him are not always perceived, and, if they are not perceived, cannot be recounted. I have risen and lain down, talked and mused, while you have roved over a considerable part of Europe; yet I have not envied my Baretti any of his pleasures, though, perhaps, I have envied others his company: and I am glad to have other nations made acquainted with the character of the English, by a traveller who has so nicely inspected our manners, and so successfully studied our literature. I received your kind letter from Falmouth, in which you gave me notice of your departure for Lisbon; and another from Lisbon, in which you told me that you were to leave Portugal in a few days. To either of these how could any answer be returned? I have had a third from Turin, complaining that I have not answered the former. Your English style still continues in its purity and vigour. With vigour your genius will supply it; but its purity must be continued by close attention. To use two languages familiarly, and without contaminating one by the other, is very difficult: and to use more than two, is hardly to be hoped. The praises which some have received for their multiplicity of languages may be sufficient to excite industry, but can hardly generate confidence.

"I know not whether I can heartily rejoice at the kind reception which you have found, or at the popularity to which you are exalted. I am willing that your merit should be distinguished; but cannot wish that your affections may be gained. I would have you happy wherever you are: yet I would have you wish to return to England. If you ever visit us again, you will find the kindness of your friends undiminished. To tell you how many inquiries are made after you, would be tedious, or, if not tedious, would be vain; because you may be told in a very few words, that all who knew you wish you well; and that all that you embraced at your departure will caress you at your return: therefore do not let Italian academicians nor Italian ladies drive us from your thoughts. You may find among us what you will leave behind, soft smiles and easy sonnets. Yet I shall not wonder if all our invitations should be rejected; for there is a pleasure in being considerable at home, which is not easily resisted.

"By conducting Mr. Southwell to Venice, you fulfilled, I know, the original contract: yet I would wish you not wholly to lose him from your notice, but to recommend him to such acquaintance as may best secure him from suffering by his own follies, and to take such general care, both of his safety and his interest, as may come within your power. His relations will thank you for any such gratuitous attention: at least they will not blame you for any evil that may happen, whether they thank you or not for any good.

"You know that we have a new King and a new Parliament. Of the new Parliament, Fitzherbert is a member. We were so weary of our old King, that we are much pleased with his successor; of whom we are so much inclined to hope great things, that most of us begin already to believe them. The young man is hitherto blameless; but it would be unreasonable to expect much from the immaturity of juvenile years, and the ignorance of princely education. He has been long in the hands of the Scots, and has already favoured them more than the English will contentedly endure. But, perhaps, he scarcely knows whom he has distinguished, or whom he has disgusted.

"The Artists have instituted a yearly Exhibition of pictures and statues, in imitation, as I am told, of foreign academies. This year was the second Exhibition. They please themselves much with the multitude of spectators, and imagine that the English School will rise in reputation. Reynolds is without a rival, and continues to add thousands to thousands, which he deserves, among other excellences, by retaining his kindness for Baretti. This Exhibition has filled the heads of the Artists and lovers of art. Surely life, if it be not long, is tedious, since we are forced to call in the assistance of so many trifles to rid us of our time, of that time which never can return.

"I know my Baretti will not be satisfied with a letter in which I give him no account of myself: yet what account shall I give him? I have not since the day of our separation, suffered or done anything considerable. The only change in my way of life is, that I have frequented the theatre more than in former seasons. But I have gone thither only to escape from myself. We have had many new farces, and the comedy called 'The Jealous Wife,' which, though not written with much genius, was yet so well adapted to the stage, and so well exhibited by the actors, that it was crowded for near twenty nights. I am digressing from myself to the playhouse; but a barren plan must be filled with episodes. Of myself I have nothing to say, but that I have hitherto lived without the concurrence of my own judgment; yet I continue to flatter myself, that, when you return, you will find me mended. I do not wonder that, where the monastic life is permitted, every order finds votaries, and every monastery inhabitants. Men will submit to any rule, by which they may be exempted from the tyranny of caprice and of chance. They are glad to supply by external authority their own want of constancy and resolution, and court the government of others, when long experience has convinced them of their own inability to govern themselves. If I were to visit Italy, my curiosity would be more attracted by convents than by palaces; though I am afraid that I should find expectation in both places equally disappointed, and life in both places supported with impatience and quitted with reluctance. That it must be soon quitted, is a powerful remedy against impatience; but what shall free us from reluctance? Those who have endeavoured to teach us to die well, have taught few to die willingly: yet I cannot but hope that a good life might end at last in a contented death.

"You see to what a train of thought I am drawn by the mention of myself. Let me now turn my attention upon you. I hope you take care to keep an exact journal, and to register all occurrences and observations; for your friends here expect such a book of travels as has not been often seen. You have given us good specimens in your letters from Lisbon. I wish you had stayed longer in Spain, for no country is less known to the rest of Europe; but the quickness of your discernment must make amends for the celerity of your motions. He, that knows which way to direct his view, sees much in a little time.

"Write to me very often, and I will not neglect to write to you; and I may, perhaps, in time, get something to write: at least, you will know by my letters, whatever else they may have or want, that I continue to be your most affectionate friend,

"SAM. JOHNSON.

"*London, June 10, 1761.*"

The following letter, which, on account of its intrinsic merit, it would have been unjust both to Johnson and the public to have withheld was obtained for me by the solicitation of my friend Mr. Seward:

"TO DR. STAUNTON (NOW SIR GEORGE STAUNTON, BARONET).

"DEAR SIR,—

"I make haste to answer your kind letter, in hope of hearing again from you before you leave us. I cannot but regret that a man of your qualifications should find it necessary to seek an establishment in Guadaloupe, which if a peace should restore to the French, I shall think it some alleviation of the loss, that it must restore likewise Dr. Staunton to the English.

"It is a melancholy consideration, that so much of our time is necessarily to be spent upon the care of living, and that we can seldom obtain ease in one respect but by resigning it in another; yet I suppose we are by this dispensation not less happy in the whole, than if the spontaneous bounty of Nature poured all that we want into our hands. A few, if they were left thus to themselves, would, perhaps, spend their time in laudable pursuits; but the greater part would prey upon the quiet of each other, or, in the want of other subjects, would prey upon themselves.

"This, however, is our condition, which we must improve and solace as we can; and though we cannot choose always our place of residence, we may in every place find rational amusements, and possess in every place the comforts of piety and a pure conscience.

"In America there is little to be observed except natural curiosities. The new world must have many vegetables and animals with which philosophers are but little acquainted. I hope you will furnish yourself with some books of natural history, and some glasses and other instruments of observation. Trust as little as you can to report; examine all you can by your own senses. I do not doubt but you will be able to add much to knowledge, and, perhaps, to medicine. Wild nations trust to simples; and, perhaps, the Peruvian bark is not the only specific which those extensive regions may afford us.

"Wherever you are, and whatever be your fortune, be certain, dear Sir, that you carry with you my kind wishes; and that whether you return hither, or stay in the other hemisphere, to hear that you are happy will give pleasure to, Sir,

"Your most affectionate humble servant,
"SAM. JOHNSON.

"*June 1, 1762.*"

A lady having at this time solicited him to obtain the Archbishop of Canterbury's patronage to have her son sent to the University, one of those solicitations which are too frequent, where people, anxious for a particular object, do not consider propriety, or the opportunity which the persons whom they solicit have to assist them, he wrote to her the following answer; with a copy of which I am favoured by the Reverend Dr. Farmer, Master of Emmanuel College, Cambridge.

"MADAM,—

"I hope you will believe that my delay in answering your letter could proceed only from my unwillingness to destroy any hope that you had formed. Hope is itself a species of happiness, and, perhaps, the chief happiness which this world affords: but, like all other pleasures immoderately enjoyed, the excesses of hope must be expiated by pain: and expectations, improperly indulged, must end in disappointment. If it be asked, what is the improper expectation which it is dangerous to indulge, experience will quickly answer, that it is such expectation as is dictated not by reason, but by desire; expectation raised, not by the common occurrences of life, but by the wants of the expectant; an expectation that requires the common course of things to be changed, and the general rules of action to be broken.

"When you made your request to me, you should have considered, Madam, what you were asking. You ask me to solicit a great man, to whom I never spoke, for a young person whom I had never seen, upon a supposition which I had no means of knowing to be true. There is no reason why, amongst all the great, I should choose to supplicate the Archbishop, nor why, among all the possible objects of his bounty, the Archbishop should choose your son. I know, Madam, how unwillingly conviction is admitted, when interest opposes it; but surely, Madam, you must allow, that there is no reason why that should be done by me, which every other man may do with equal reason, and which, indeed, no man can do properly, without some very particular relation both to the Archbishop and to you. If I could help you in this exigence by any proper means, it would give me pleasure; but this proposal is so very remote from usual methods, that I cannot comply with it, but at the risk of such answer and suspicions as I believe you do not wish me to undergo.

"I have seen your son this morning; he seems a pretty youth, and will, perhaps, find some better friend than I can procure him; but

[131]

though he should at last miss the University, he may still be wise, useful, and happy.

> "I am, Madam,
> > "Your most humble servant,
> > > "SAM. JOHNSON.

"*June 8, 1762.*"

"*London, July 20, 1762.*

"SIR,—

"However justly you may accuse me for want of punctuality in correspondence, I am not so far lost in negligence as to omit the opportunity of writing to you, which Mr. Beauclerk's passage through Milan affords me.

"I suppose you received the *Idlers,* and I intend that you shall soon receive 'Shakspeare,' that you may explain his works to the ladies of Italy and tell them the story of the editor, among the other strange narratives with which your long residence in this unknown region has supplied you.

"As you have now been long away, I suppose your curiosity may pant for some news of your old friends. Miss Williams and I live much as we did. Miss Cotterell still continues to cling to Mrs. Porter, and Charlotte is now big of the fourth child. Mr. Reynolds gets six thousands a year. Levet is lately married, not without much suspicion that he has been wretchedly cheated in his match. Mr. Chambers is gone this day, for the first time, the circuit with the Judges. Mr. Richardson is dead of an apoplexy, and his second daughter has married a merchant.

"My vanity or my kindness makes me flatter myself that you would rather hear of me than of those whom I have mentioned; but of myself I have very little which I care to tell. Last winter I went down to my native town, where I found the streets much narrower and shorter than I thought I had left them, inhabited by a new race of people, to whom I was very little known. My playfellows were grown old, and forced me to suspect that I was no longer young. My only remaining friend has changed his principles, and was become the tool of the predominant faction. My daughter-in-law, from whom I expected most, and whom I met with sincere benevolence, has lost the beauty and gaiety of youth, without having gained much of the wisdom of age. I wandered about for five days, and took the first convenient opportunity of returning to a place, where, if there is not much happiness, there is, at least, such a diversity of good and evil, that slight vexations do not fix upon the heart.

"I think in a few weeks to try another excursion; though to what end? Let me know, my Baretti, what has been the result of your return to your own country: whether time has made any alteration for the better, and whether, when the first raptures of salutation were over, you did not find your thoughts confessed their disappointment.

"Moral sentences appear ostentatious and tumid, when they have no greater occasions than the journey of a wit to his own town; yet such pleasures and such pains make up the general mass of life; and as nothing is little to him that feels it with great sensibility, a mind able to see common incidents in their real state is disposed by very common incidents to very serious contemplations. Let us trust that a time will come, when the present moment shall be no longer irksome; when we shall not borrow all our happiness from hope, which at last is to end in disappointment.

"I beg that you will show Mr. Beauclerk all the civilities which you have in your power; for he has always been kind to me.

"I have lately seen Mr. Stratico, Professor of Padua, who has told me of your quarrel with an Abbot of the Celestine order; but had not the particulars very ready in his memory. When you write to Mr. Marsili, let him know that I remember him with kindness.

"May you, my Baretti, be very happy at Milan, or some other place nearer to, Sir,

"Your most affectionate humble servant,

"SAM. JOHNSON."

The accession of George the Third to the throne of these kingdoms opened a new and brighter prospect to men of literary merit, who had been honoured with no mark of royal favour in the preceding reign. His present Majesty's education in this country, as well as his taste and beneficence, prompted him to be the patron of science and the arts; and early this year Johnson having been represented to him as a very learned and good man, without any certain provision, his Majesty was pleased to grant him a pension of three hundred pounds a year. The Earl of Bute, who was then Prime Minister, had the honour to announce this instance of his Sovereign's bounty, concerning which, many and various stories, all equally erroneous, have been propagated; maliciously representing it as a political bribe to Johnson, to desert his avowed principles, and become the tool of a government which he held to be founded in usurpation. I have taken care to have it in my power to refute them from the most authentic information. Lord Bute told me that Mr. Wedderburn, now Lord Loughborough, was the person who first mentioned this subject to him. Lord Loughborough told me that the pension was granted to Johnson solely as the reward of his literary merit, without any stipulation whatever, or even tacit understanding that he should write for the Administration. His Lordship added that he was confident the political tracts which Johnson afterwards did write, as they were entirely consonant with his own opinions, would have been written by him, though no pension had been granted to him.

Mr. Thomas Sheridan and Mr. Murphy, who then lived a good deal both with him and Mr. Wedderburn, told me that they previously talked with Johnson upon this matter, and that it was perfectly understood by all parties that the pension was merely honorary. Sir Joshua Reynolds told me that Johnson called on him after his Majesty's intention had been notified to him, and said he wished to consult his friends as to the propriety of his accepting this mark of the royal favour, after the definitions which he had given in his Dictionary of *pension* and *pensioners*. He said he should not have Sir Joshua's answer till the next day, when he would call again, and desired he might think of it. Sir Joshua answered that he was clear to give his opinion then, that there could be no objection to his receiving from the King a reward for literary merit; and that certainly the definitions in his Dictionary were not applicable to him. Johnson, it should seem, was satisfied, for he did not call again till he had accepted the pension, and waited on Lord Bute to thank him. He then told Sir Joshua that Lord Bute said to him expressly, "It is not given you for anything you are to do, but for what you have done." His Lordship, he said, behaved in the handsomest manner. He repeated the words twice that he might be sure Johnson heard them, and thus set his mind perfectly at ease. This nobleman, who has been so virulently abused, acted with great honour in this instance, and displayed a mind truly liberal. A minister of a more narrow and selfish disposition would have availed himself of such an opportunity to fix an implied obligation on a man of Johnson's powerful talents to give him his support.

Mr. Murphy and the late Mr. Sheridan severally contended for the distinction of having been the first who mentioned to Mr. Wedderburn that Johnson ought to have a pension. When I spoke of this to Lord Loughborough, wishing to know if he recollected the prime mover in the business, he said, "All his friends assisted": and when I told him that Mr. Sheridan strenuously asserted his claim to it, his Lordship said, "He rang the bell." And it is but just to add that Mr. Sheridan told me that when he communicated to Dr. Johnson that a pension was to be granted him, he replied in a fervour of gratitude, "The English language does not afford me terms adequate to my feelings on this occasion. I must have recourse to the French. I am *pénétré* with his Majesty's goodness." When I repeated this to Dr. Johnson, he did not contradict it.

His definitions of *pension* and *pensioner*, partly founded on the satirical verses of Pope, which he quotes, may be generally true; and yet everybody must allow that there may be, and have been, instances of pensions given and received upon liberal and honourable terms. Thus, then, it is clear, that there was nothing inconsistent or humiliating in Johnson's accepting of a pension so unconditionally and so honourably offered to him.

But I shall not detain my readers longer by any words of my own, on a subject on which I am happily enabled, by the favour of the Earl of Bute, to present them with what Johnson himself wrote; his Lordship having been pleased to communicate to me a copy of the following letter to his late father, which does great honour both to the writer, and to the noble person to whom it is addressed:

"TO THE RIGHT HONOURABLE THE EARL OF BUTE.

"MY LORD,—

"When the bills were yesterday delivered to me by Mr. Wedderburn, I was informed by him of the future favours which his Majesty has, by your Lordship's recommendation, been induced to intend for me.

"Bounty always receives part of its value from the manner in which it is bestowed; your Lordship's kindness includes every circumstance that can gratify delicacy, or enforce obligation. You have conferred your favours on a man who has neither alliance nor interest, who has not merited them by services, nor courted them by officiousness; you have spared him the shame of solicitation, and the anxiety of suspense.

"What has been thus elegantly given, will, I hope, not be reproachfully enjoyed; I shall endeavour to give your Lordship the only recompense which generosity desires—the gratification of finding that your benefits are not improperly bestowed.

"I am, my Lord,
"Your Lordship's most obliged,
"Most obedient, and most humble servant,
"Sam. Johnson.

"*July 20, 1762.*"

"TO MR. JOSEPH BARETTI, AT MILAN.

"*London, Dec. 21, 1762.*

"Sir,—

"You are not to suppose, with all your conviction of my idleness, that I have passed all this time without writing to my Baretti. I gave a letter to Mr. Beauclerk, who in my opinion, and in his own, was hastening to Naples for the recovery of his health; but he has stopped at Paris, and I know not when he will proceed. Langton is with him.

"I will not trouble you with speculations about peace and war. The good or ill success of battles and embassies extends itself to a very small part of domestic life: we all have good and evil, which we feel more sensibly than our petty part of public miscarriage or prosperity. I am sorry for your disappointment, with which you seem more touched than I should expect a man of your resolution and experience to have been, did I not know that general truths are seldom applied to particular occasions; and that the fallacy of our self-love extends itself as wide as our interest or affections. Every man believes that mistresses are unfaithful, and patrons capricious; but he excepts his own mistress, and his own patron. We have all learned that greatness is negligent and contemptuous, and that in Courts life is often languished away in ungratified expectation; but he that approaches greatness, or glitters in a Court, imagines that destiny has at last exempted him from the common lot.

"Do not let such evils overwhelm you as thousands have suffered, and thousands have surmounted; but turn your thoughts with vigour to some other plan of life, and keep always in your mind that, with due submission to Providence, a man of genius has been seldom ruined but by himself. Your patron's weakness or insensibility will finally do you little hurt, if he is not assisted by your own passions. Of your love I know not the propriety, nor can estimate the power; but in love, as in every other passion of which hope is the essence, we ought always to remember the uncertainty of events. There is, indeed, nothing that so much seduces reason from vigilance, as the thought of passing life with an amiable woman; and if all would happen that a lover fancies, I know not what other terrestrial happiness would deserve pursuit. But love and marriage are different states. Those who are to suffer the evils together, and to suffer often for the sake of one another, soon lose that tenderness of look, and that benevolence of mind, which arose from the participation of unmingled pleasure and successive amusement. A woman, we are sure, will not be always fair; we are not sure she will always be virtuous: and man cannot retain through life that respect and assiduity by which he pleases for a day or for a month. I do not, however, pretend to have discovered that life has anything more to be desired than a prudent and virtuous marriage; therefore know not what counsel to give you.

"If you can quit your imagination of love and greatness, and leave your hopes of preferment and bridal raptures to try once more the fortune of literature and industry, the way through France is now open. We flatter ourselves that we shall cultivate, with great diligence, the arts of peace; and every man will be welcome among us who can teach us anything we do not know. For your part, you will find all your old friends willing to receive you.

"Reynolds still continues to increase in reputation and in riches. Miss Williams, who very much loves you, goes on in the old way. Miss Cotterell is still with Mrs. Porter. Miss Charlotte is married to Dean Lewis, and has three children. Mr. Levet has married a street-walker. But the gazette of my narration must now arrive to tell you, that Bathurst went physician to the army, and died at the Havannah.

"I know not whether I have not sent you word that Huggins and Richardson are both dead. When we see our enemies and friends gliding away before us, let us not forget that we are subject to the general law of mortality, and shall soon be where our doom will be fixed for ever. I pray God to bless you, and am, Sir,

"Your most affectionate humble servant,

"SAM. JOHNSON.

"Write soon."

CHAPTER XIII—1763

Enter Boswell

[1763.] THIS IS TO ME a memorable year; for in it I had the happiness to obtain the acquaintance of that extraordinary man whose memoirs I am now writing; an acquaintance which I shall ever esteem as one of the most fortunate circumstances in my life. Though then but two-and-twenty, I had for several years read his works with delight and instruction, and had the highest reverence for their author, which had grown up in my fancy into a kind of mysterious veneration, by figuring to myself a state of solemn elevated abstraction, in which I supposed him to live in the immense metropolis of London. Mr. Gentleman, a native of Ireland, who passed some years in Scotland as a player, and as an instructor in the English language, a man whose talents and worth were depressed by misfortunes, had given me a representation of the figure and manner of Dictionary Johnson! as he was then generally called; and during my first visit to London, which was for three months in 1760, Mr. Derrick the Poet, who was Gentleman's friend and countryman, flattered me with hopes that he would introduce me to Johnson, an honour of which I was very ambitious. But he never found an opportunity; which made me doubt that he had promised to do what was not in his power; till Johnson some years afterwards told me, "Derrick, Sir, might very well have introduced you. I had a kindness for Derrick, and am sorry he is dead."

In the summer of 1761, Mr. Thomas Sheridan was at Edinburgh, and delivered lectures upon the English Language and Public Speaking to large and respectable audiences. I was often in his company, and heard him frequently expatiate on Johnson's extraordinary knowledge, talents and virtues, repeat his pointed sayings, describe his particularities, and boast of his being his guest sometimes till two or three in the morning. At his house I hoped to have many opportunities of seeing the Sage, as Mr. Sheridan obligingly assured me I should not be disappointed.

When I returned to London in the end of 1762, to my surprise and regret I found an irreconcilable difference had taken place between Johnson and Sheridan. A pension of two hundred pounds a year had been given to Sheridan. Johnson, who, as has already been mentioned, thought slightingly of Sheridan's art, upon hearing that he was also pensioned, exclaimed, "What! have they given *him* a. pension? Then it is time for me to give up mine." Whether this proceeded from a momentary indignation, as if it were an affront to his exalted merit, that a player should be rewarded in the same manner with him, or was the sudden effect of a fit of peevishness, it was unluckily said, and, indeed, cannot be justified. Mr. Sheridan's pension was granted to him not as a player, but as a sufferer in the cause of Government, when he was manager of the Theatre Royal in Ireland, when parties ran high in 1753. And it must also be allowed that he was a man of literature, and had considerably improved the arts of reading and speaking with distinctness and propriety.

Johnson complained that a man who disliked him repeated his sarcasm to Mr. Sheridan, without telling him what followed, which was, that, after a pause, he added, "However, I am glad that Mr. Sheridan has a pension, for he is a very good man." Sheridan could never forgive his hasty contemptuous expression. It rankled in his mind; and though I informed him of all that Johnson said, and that he would be very glad to meet him amicably, he positively declined repeated offers which I made, and once went off abruptly from a house where he and I were engaged to dine, because he was told that Dr. Johnson was to be there. I have no sympathetic feeling with such persevering resentment. It is painful when there is a breach between those who have lived together socially and cordially; and I wonder there is not, in all such cases, a mutual wish that it should be healed. I could perceive that Mr. Sheridan was by no means satisfied with Johnson's acknowledging him to be a good man. That could not soothe his injured vanity. I could not but smile, at the same time that I was offended, to observe Sheridan, in the "Life of Swift," which he afterwards published, attempting, in the writhings of his resentment, to depreciate Johnson, by characterising him as "A writer of gigantic fame, in these days of little men"; that very Johnson, whom he once so highly admired and venerated.

This rupture with Sheridan deprived Johnson of one of his most agreeable resources for amusement in his lonely evenings; for Sheridan's well-informed, animated, and bustling mind never suffered conversation to stagnate; and Mrs. Sheridan was a most agreeable companion to an intellectual man. She was sensible, ingenious, unassuming, yet communicative. I recollect, with satisfaction, many pleasing hours which I passed with her under the hospitable roof of her husband, who was to me a very kind friend. Her novel, entitled "Memoirs of Miss Sydney Biddulph," contains an excellent moral, while it inculcates a future state of retribution; and what it teaches is impressed upon the mind by a series of as deep distress as can affect humanity, in the amiable and pious heroine who goes to her grave unrelieved, but resigned, and full of hope of "Heaven's mercy." Johnson paid her this high compliment upon it: "I know not, Madam, that you have a right, upon moral principles, to make your readers suffer so much."

Mr. Thomas Davies, the actor, who then kept a bookseller's shop in Russell-street, Covent Garden, told me that Johnson was very much his friend, and came frequently to his house, where he more than once invited me to meet him; but by some unlucky accident or other he was prevented from coming to us.

Mr. Thomas Davies was a man of good understanding and talents, with the advantage of a liberal education. Though somewhat pompous, he was an entertaining companion; and his literary performances have no inconsiderable share of merit. He was a friendly and very hospitable man. Both he and his wife (who has been celebrated for her beauty), though upon the stage for many years, maintained a uniform decency of character: and Johnson esteemed them, and lived in as easy an intimacy with them as with any family he used to visit. Mr. Davies recollected several of Johnson's remarkable sayings, and was one of the best of the many imitators of his voice and manner, while relating them. He increased my impatience more and more to see the extraordinary man whose works I highly valued, and whose conversation was reported to be so peculiarly excellent.

At last, on Monday the 16th of May, when I was sitting in Mr. Davies's back-parlour, after having drunk tea with him and Mrs. Davies, Johnson unexpectedly came into the shop; and Mr. Davies having perceived him through the glass-door in the room in which we were sitting, advancing towards us—he announced his awful approach to me, somewhat in the manner of an actor in the part of Horatio, when he addresses Hamlet on the appearance of his father's ghost, "Look, my lord, it comes." I found that I had a very perfect idea of Johnson's figure, from the portrait of him painted by Sir Joshua Reynolds soon after he had published his Dictionary, in the attitude of sitting in his easy chair in deep meditation; which was the first picture his friend did for him, which Sir Joshua very kindly presented to me, and from which an engraving has been made for this work. Mr. Davies mentioned my name, and respectfully introduced me to him. I was much agitated; and recollecting his prejudice against the Scotch, of which I had heard much, I said to Davies, "Don't tell where I come from."—"From Scotland," cried Davies, roguishly. "Mr. Johnson (said I), I do, indeed, come from Scotland, but I cannot help it." I am willing to flatter myself that I meant this as light pleasantry to soothe and conciliate him, and not as a humiliating abasement at the expense of my country. But however that might be, this speech was somewhat unlucky; for with that quickness of wit for which he was so remarkable, he seized the expression "come from Scotland," which I used in the sense of being of that country; and, as if I had said that I had come away from it, or left it, retorted, "That, Sir, I find, is what a very great many of your countrymen cannot help." This stroke stunned me a good deal; and when we had sat down, I felt myself not a little embarrassed, and apprehensive of what might come next. He then addressed himself to Davies: "What do you think of Garrick? he has refused me an order for the play for Miss Williams, because he knows the house will be full, and that an order would be worth three shillings." Eager to take any opening to get into conversation with him, I ventured to say, "O, Sir, I cannot think Mr. Garrick would grudge such a trifle to you."—"Sir (said he, with a stern look), I have known David Garrick longer than you have done: and I know no right you have to talk to me on the subject." Perhaps I deserved this check; for it was rather presumptuous in me, an entire stranger, to express any doubt of the justice of his animadversion upon his old acquaintance and pupil.[1] I now felt myself much mortified, and began to think that the hope which I had long indulged of obtaining his acquaintance was blasted. And, in truth, had not my ardour been uncommonly strong and my resolution uncommonly persevering, so rough a reception might have deterred me for ever from making any farther attempts. Fortunately, however, I remained upon the field not wholly discomfited; and was soon rewarded by hearing some of his conversation, of which I preserved the following short minute, without marking the questions and observations by which it was produced.

[1] That this was a momentary sally against Garrick there can be no doubt; for at Johnson's desire he had, some years before, given a benefit night at his theatre to this very person, by which she had got two hundred pounds. Johnson, indeed, upon all other occasions, when I was in his company, praised the very liberal charity of Garrick. I once mentioned to him, "It is observed, Sir, that you attack Garrick yourself, but will suffer nobody else to do it." JOHNSON (smiling): "Why, Sir, that is true."

"People (he remarked) may be taken in once, who imagine that an author is greater in private life than other men. Uncommon parts require uncommon opportunities for their exertion.

"In barbarous society, superiority of parts is of real consequence. Great strength or great wisdom is of much value to an individual. But in more polished times there are people to do everything for money; and then there are a number of other superiorities, such as those of birth and fortune, and rank, that dissipate men's attention, and leave no extraordinary share of respect for personal and intellectual superiority. This is wisely ordered by Providence to preserve some equality among mankind."

"Sir, this book ('The Elements of Criticism,' which he had taken up) is a pretty essay, and deserves to be held in some estimation, though much of it is chimerical."

Speaking of one who with more than ordinary boldness attacked public measures and the royal family, he said, "I think he is safe from the law; but he is an abusive scoundrel; and instead of applying to my Lord Chief Justice to punish him, I would send half a dozen footmen, and have him well ducked."

"The notion of liberty amuses the people of England, and helps to keep off the *tædium vitæ*. When a butcher tells you that *his heart bleeds for his country,* he has, in fact, no uneasy feeling."

I was highly pleased with the extraordinary vigour of his conversation, and regretted that I was drawn away from it by engagement at another place. I had, for a part of the evening, been left alone with him, and had ventured to make an observation now and then, which he received very civilly; so that I was satisfied that, though there was a roughness in his manner, there was no ill-nature in his disposition. Davies followed me to the door, and when I complained to him a little of the hard blows which the great man had given me, he kindly took upon him to console me, by saying, "Don't be uneasy. I can see he likes you very well."

A few days afterwards I called on Davies, and asked him if he thought I might take the liberty of waiting on Mr. Johnson at his chambers in the Temple. He said I certainly might, and that Mr. Johnson would take it as a compliment. So upon Tuesday the 24th of May, after having been enlivened by the witty sallies of Messieurs Thornton, Wilkes, Churchill, and Lloyd, with whom I had passed the morning, I boldly repaired to Johnson. His chambers were on the first floor of No. 1 Inner Temple Lane, and I entered them with an impression, given me by the Rev. Dr. Blair, of Edinburgh, who had been introduced to him not long before, and described his having "found the Giant in his den"; an expression which, when I came to be pretty well acquainted with Johnson, I repeated to him, and he was diverted at this picturesque account of himself.

He received me very courteously; but it must be confessed that his apartment, and furniture, and morning dress, were sufficiently uncouth. His brown suit of clothes looked very rusty; he had on a little old shrivelled unpowdered wig, which was too small for his head; his shirt-neck and knees of his breeches were loose; his black worsted stockings ill drawn up; and he had a pair of unbuckled shoes by way of slippers. But all these slovenly particularities were forgotten the moment that he began to talk. Some gentlemen, whom I do not recollect, were sitting with him; and when they went away, I also rose; but he said to me,

No. 1 Inner Temple Lane

"Nay, don't go."—"Sir (said I), I am afraid that I intrude upon you. It is benevolent to allow me to sit and hear you." He seemed pleased with this compliment, which I sincerely paid him, and answered, "Sir, I am obliged to any man who visits me."—I have preserved the following short minute of what passed this day:

"Madness frequently discovers itself merely by unnecessary deviation from the usual modes of the world. My poor friend Smart showed the disturbance of his mind by falling upon his knees, and saying his prayers in the street, or in any other unusual place. Now although, rationally speaking, it is greater madness not to pray at all than to pray as Smart did, I am afraid there are so many who do not pray, that their understanding is not called in question."

Concerning this unfortunate poet, Christopher Smart, who was confined in a madhouse, he had, at another time, the following conversation with Dr. Burney.—BURNEY: "How does poor Smart do, Sir; is he likely to recover?" JOHNSON: "It seems as if his mind had ceased to struggle with the disease; for he grows fat upon it." BURNEY: "Perhaps, Sir, that may be from want of exercise." JOHNSON: "No, Sir; he has partly as much exercise as he used to have, for he digs in the garden. Indeed, before his confinement, he used for exercise to walk to the ale-house; but he was *carried* back again. I did not think he ought to be shut up. His infirmities were not noxious to society. He insisted on people praying with him; and I'd as lief pray with Kit Smart as anyone else. Another charge was, that he did not love clean linen; and I have no passion for it."—

Talking of Garrick, he said, "He is the first man in the world for sprightly conversation."

When I rose a second time he again pressed me to stay, which I did.

He told me that he generally went abroad at four in the afternoon, and seldom came home till two in the morning. I took the liberty to ask if he did not think it wrong to live thus, and not make more use of his great talents. He owned it was a bad habit. On reviewing, at the distance of many years, my journal of this period, I wonder how, at my first visit, I ventured to talk to him so freely, and that he bore it with so much indulgence.

Before we parted, he was so good as to promise to favour me with his company one evening at my lodgings; and as I took my leave, shook me cordially by the hand. It is almost needless to add that I felt no little elation at having now so happily established an acquaintance of which I had been so long ambitious.

My readers will, I trust, excuse me for being thus minutely circumstantial, when it is considered that the acquaintance of Dr. Johnson was to me a most valuable acquisition, and laid the foundation of whatever instruction and entertainment they may receive from my collections concerning the great subject of the work which they are now perusing.

I did not visit him again till Monday, June 13, at which time I recollect no part of his conversation, except that when I told him I had been to see Johnson ride upon three horses, he said, "Such a man, Sir, should be encouraged; for his performances show the extent of the human powers in one instance, and thus tend to raise our opinion of the faculties of man. He shows what may be attained by persevering application; so that every man may hope that by giving as much application, although perhaps he may never ride three horses at a time, or dance upon a wire, yet he may be equally expert in whatever profession he has chosen to pursue."

He again shook me by the hand at parting, and asked me why I did not come oftener to him. Trusting that I was now in his good graces, I answered that he had not given me much encouragement, and reminded him of the check I had received from him at our first interview. "Poh, Poh! (said he with a complacent smile), never mind these things. Come to me as often as you can. I shall be glad to see you."

I had learnt that his place of frequent resort was the Mitre Tavern in Fleet Street, where he loved to sit up late, and I begged I might be allowed to pass an evening with him there soon, which he promised I should. A few days afterwards I met him near Temple Bar about one o'clock in the morning, and asked if he would then go to the *Mitre*. "Sir (said he), it is too late; they won't let us in. But I'll go with you another night with all my heart."

A revolution of some importance in my plan of life had just taken place; for instead of procuring a commission in the Foot-Guards, which was my own inclination, I had, in compliance with my father's wishes, agreed to study the law, and was soon to set out for Utrecht, to hear the lectures of an excellent Civilian in that university, and then to proceed on my travels. Though very desirous of obtaining Johnson's advice and instruction on the mode of pursuing my studies, I was at this time so occupied, shall I call it? or so dissipated, by the amusements of London, that our next meeting was not till Saturday, June 25, when happening to dine at Clifton's eating-house in Butcher-row I was surprised to perceive Johnson come in and take his seat at another table.

The mode of dining, or rather being fed, at such houses in London, is well known to many to be particularly unsocial, as there is no Ordinary, or united company, but each person has his own mess, and is under no obligation to hold any intercourse with any one. A liberal and full-minded man, however, who loves to talk, will break through this

The Mitre Tavern
A favorite lunch place for Johnson and Boswell

churlish and unsocial restraint. Johnson and an Irish gentleman got into a dispute concerning the cause of some part of mankind being black. "Why, Sir (said Johnson), it has been accounted for in three ways: either by supposing that they are the posterity of Ham, who was cursed; or that God at first created two kinds of men, one black and another white; or that by the heat of the sun the skin is scorched, and so acquires a sooty hue. This matter has been much canvassed among naturalists, but has never been brought to any certain issue." What the Irishman said is totally obliterated from my mind; but I remember that he became very warm and intemperate in his expressions: upon which Johnson rose, and quietly walked away. When he had retired, his antagonist took his revenge, as he thought, by saying, "He has a most ungainly figure, and an affectation of pomposity, unworthy of a man of genius."

Johnson had not observed that I was in the room. I followed him, however, and he agreed to meet me in the evening at the *Mitre*. I called on him, and we went thither at nine. We had a good supper, and port wine, of which he then sometimes drank a bottle. The orthodox high-church sound of the *Mitre*—the figure and manner of the celebrated Samuel Johnson—the extraordinary power and precision of his conversation, and the pride arising from finding myself admitted as his companion, produced a variety of sensations, and a pleasing elevation of mind beyond what I had ever before experienced. I find in my journal the following minute of our conversation, which, though it will but give a very faint notion of what passed, is, in some degree, a valuable record; and it will be curious in this view, as showing how habitual to his mind were some opinions which appear in his works.

"Colley Cibber, Sir, was by no means a blockhead; but by arrogating to himself too much, he was in danger of losing that degree of estimation to which he was entitled. His friends gave out that he *intended* his birthday Odes should be bad: but that was not the case, Sir; for he kept them many months by him, and a few years before he died, he showed me one of them, with great solicitude to render it as perfect as might be, and I made some corrections, to which he was not very willing to submit. I remember the following couplet in allusion to the King and himself:

> 'Perch'd on the eagle's soaring wing,
> The lowly linnet loves to sing.'

Sir, he had heard something of the fabulous tale of the wren sitting upon the eagle's wing, and he had applied it to a linnet. Cibber's familiar style, however, was better than that which Whitehead has assumed. *Grand* nonsense is insupportable. Whitehead is but a little man to inscribe verses to players."

I did not presume to controvert this censure, which was tinctured with his prejudice against players, but I could not help thinking that a dramatic poet might with propriety pay a compliment to an eminent performer, as Whitehead has very happily done in his verses to Mr. Garrick.

"Sir, I do not think Gray a first-rate poet. He has not a bold imagination, nor much command of words. The obscurity in which he has involved himself will not persuade us that he is sublime. His 'Elegy in a Churchyard' has a happy selection of images, but I don't like what are called his great things. His 'Ode' which begins:

> 'Ruin seize thee, ruthless King,
> Confusion on thy banners wait!'

has been celebrated for its abruptness, and plunging into the subject all at once. But such arts as these have no merit, unless when they are original. We admire them only once; and this abruptness has nothing new in it. We have had it often before. Nay, we have it in the old song of Johnny Armstrong:

> 'Is there ever a man in all Scotland
> From the highest estate to the lowest degree,' etc.

And then, Sir,

> 'Yes, there is a man in Westmoreland,
> And Johnny Armstrong they do him call.'

There, now, you plunge at once into the subject. You have no previous narration to lead you to it.—The two next lines in that 'Ode' are, I think, very good:

> 'Though fann'd by conquest's crimson wing,
> They mock the air with idle state.' "[2]

Here let it be observed, that although his opinion of Gray's poetry was widely different from mine, and I believe from that of most men of taste, by whom it is with justice highly admired, there is certainly much absurdity in the clamour which has been raised, as if he had been culpably injurious to the merit of that bard, and had been actuated by envy. Alas! ye little short-sighted critics, could Johnson be envious of the talents of any of his contemporaries? That his opinion on this subject was what in private and in public he uniformly expressed, regardless of what others might think, we may wonder, and perhaps regret; but it is shallow and unjust to charge him with expressing what he did not think.

Finding him in a placid humour, and wishing to avail myself of the opportunity which I fortunately had of consulting a sage, to hear whose wisdom, I conceived in the ardour of youthful imagination, that men filled with a noble enthusiasm for intellectual improvement would

[2]My friend Mr. Malone, in his valuable comments on Shakspeare, has traced in that great poet the *disjecta membra* of these lines.

gladly have resorted from distant lands;—I opened my mind to him ingenuously, and gave him a little sketch of my life, to which he was pleased to listen with great attention.

I acknowledged, that though educated very strictly in the principles of religion, I had for some time been misled into a certain degree of infidelity; but that I was come now to a better way of thinking, and was fully satisfied of the truth of the Christian revelation, though I was not clear as to every point considered to be orthodox. Being at all times a curious examiner of the human mind, and pleased with an undisguised display of what had passed in it, he called to me with warmth. "Give me your hand; I have taken a liking to you." He then began to descant upon the force of testimony, and the little we could know of final causes; so that the objections of, Why was it so? or, Why was it not so? ought not to disturb us: adding, that he himself had at one period been guilty of a temporary neglect of religion, but that it was not the result of argument, but mere absence of thought.

After having given credit to reports of his bigotry, I was agreeably surprised when he expressed the following very liberal sentiment, which has the additional value of obviating an objection to our holy religion, founded upon the discordant tenets of Christians themselves: "For my part, Sir, I think all Christians, whether Papists or Protestants, agree in the essential articles, and that their differences are trivial, and rather political than religious."

Our conversation proceeded. "Sir (said he), I am a friend to subordination, as most conducive to the happiness of society. There is a reciprocal pleasure in governing and being governed."

"Dr. Goldsmith is one of the first men we now have as an author, and he is a very worthy man too. He has been loose in his principles, but he is coming right."

I mentioned Mallet's tragedy of "Elvira," which had been acted the preceding winter at Drury Lane, and that the Honourable Andrew Erskine, Mr. Dempster, and myself, had joined in writing a pamphlet, entitled "Critical Strictures" against it. That the mildness of Dempster's disposition had, however, relented; and he candidly said, "We have hardly a right to abuse this tragedy; for, bad as it is, how vain should either of us be to write one not near so good." JOHNSON: "Why, no, Sir; that is not just reasoning. You *may* abuse a tragedy, though you cannot write one. You may scold a carpenter who has made you a bad table, though you cannot make a table. It is not your trade to make tables."

He proceeded: "Your going abroad, Sir, and breaking off idle habits may be of great importance to you. I would go where there are Courts and learned men. There is a good deal of Spain that has not been perambulated. I would have you go thither. A man of inferior talents to yours may furnish us with useful observations upon that country." His supposing me, at that period of life, capable of writing an account of my travels that would deserve to be read, elated me not a little.

I appeal to every impartial reader whether this faithful detail of his frankness, complacency, and kindness to a young man, a stranger and a Scotchman, does not refute the unjust opinion of the harshness of his general demeanour. His occasional reproofs of folly, impudence, or impiety, and even the sudden sallies of his constitutional irritability of

The famous "Ghost House" in Cock Lane

temper, which have been preserved for the poignancy of their wit, have produced that opinion among those who have not considered that such instances, though collected by Mrs. Piozzi, into a small volume, and read over in a few hours, were, in fact, scattered through a long series of years: years in which his time was chiefly spent in instructing and delighting mankind by his writings and conversation, in acts of piety to God, and good-will to men.

I complained to him that I had not yet acquired much knowledge, and asked his advice as to my studies. He said, "Don't talk of study now. I will give you a plan; but it will require some time to consider of it." "It is very good in you (I replied), to allow me to be with you thus. Had it been foretold to me some years ago that I should pass an evening with the author of the *Rambler,* how should I have exulted!" What I then expressed was sincerely from the heart. He was satisfied that it was, and cordially answered, "Sir, I am glad we have met. I hope we shall pass many evenings and mornings too, together." We finished a couple of bottles of port, and sat till between one and two in the morning.

CHAPTER XIV—1763

Oliver Goldsmith

As DR. OLIVER GOLDSMITH will frequently appear in this narrative, I shall endeavour to make my readers in some degree acquainted with his singular character. He was a native of Ireland, and a contemporary with Mr. Burke, at Trinity College, Dublin, but did not then give much promise of future celebrity. He, however, observed to Mr. Malone that "though he made no great figure in mathematics, which was a study in much repute there, he could turn an 'Ode' of Horace into English better than any of them." He afterwards studied physic at Edinburgh, and upon the Continent, and I have been informed, was enabled to pursue his travels on foot, partly by demanding at Universities to enter the lists as a disputant, by which, according to the custom of many of them, he was entitled to the premium of a crown, when luckily for him his challenge was not accepted; so that, as I once observed to Dr. Johnson, he *disputed* his passage, through Europe. He then came to

England, and was employed successively in the capacities of an usher to an academy, a corrector of the press, a reviewer, and a writer for a newspaper. He had sagacity enough to cultivate assiduously the acquaintance of Johnson, and his faculties were gradually enlarged by the contemplation of such a model. To me and many others it appeared that he studiously copied the manner of Johnson, though, indeed, upon a smaller scale.

He, I am afraid, had no settled system of any sort, so that his conduct must not be strictly scrutinized; but his affections were social and generous, and when he had money he gave it away very liberally. His desire of imaginary consequence predominated over his attention to truth. When he began to rise into notice, he said he had a brother who was Dean of Durham, a fiction so easily detected, that it was wonderful how he should have been so inconsiderate as to hazard it. He boasted to me at this time of the power of his pen in commanding money, which I believe was true in a certain degree, though in the instance he gave he was by no means correct. He told me that he had sold a novel for four hundred pounds. This was his "Vicar of Wakefield." But Johnson informed me that he had made the bargain for Goldsmith, and the price was sixty pounds. "And, Sir (said he), a sufficient price too, when it was sold; for then the fame of Goldsmith had not been elevated, as it afterward was, by his 'Traveller'; and the bookseller had such faint hopes of profit by his bargain, that he kept the manuscript by him a long time, and did not publish it till after the 'Traveller' had appeared. Then, to be sure, it was accidentally worth more money."

Mrs. Piozzi and Sir John Hawkins had strangely mis-stated the history of Goldsmith's situation and Johnson's friendly interference, when this novel was sold. I shall give it authentically from Johnson's own exact narration:

"I received one morning a message from poor Goldsmith that he was in great distress, and as it was not in his power to come to me, begging that I would come to him as soon as possible. I sent him a guinea, and promised to come to him directly. I accordingly went as soon as I was drest, and found that his landlady had arrested him for his rent, at which he was in a violent passion. I perceived that he had already changed my guinea, and had got a bottle of Madeira and a glass before him. I put the cork into the bottle, desired he would be calm, and began to talk to him of the means by which he might be extricated. He then told me that he had a novel ready for the press,

New York, 1945.

Johnson sets out on his honeymoon.

which he produced to me. I looked into it, and saw its merit; told the landlady I should soon return, and having gone to a bookseller, sold it for sixty pounds. I brought Goldsmith the money, and he discharged his rent, not without rating his landlady in a high tone for having used him so ill."

Goldsmith, while reading the mss. of "The Vicar of Wakefield" to Johnson, was interrupted by his landlady and the bailiff. Johnson came to the rescue and the reading was resumed

My next meeting with Johnson was on Friday, the 1st of July, when he and I and Dr. Goldsmith supped at the *Mitre*. I was before this time pretty well acquainted with Goldsmith, who was one of the brightest ornaments of the Johnsonian school. Goldsmith's respectful attachment to Johnson was then at its height; for his own literary reputation had not yet distinguished him so much as to excite a vain desire of competition with his great Master. He had increased my admiration of the goodness of Johnson's heart, by incidental remarks in the course of conversation; such as, when I mentioned Mr. Levet, whom he entertained under his roof, "He is poor and honest, which is recommendation enough to Johnson"; and when I wondered that he was very kind to a man of whom I had heard a very bad character, "He is now become miserable, and that insures the protection of Johnson."

Goldsmith attempting this evening to maintain, I suppose from an affectation of paradox, "that knowledge was not desirable on its own account, for it often was a source of unhappiness";—JOHNSON: "Why, Sir, that knowledge may in some cases produce unhappiness, I allow. But, upon the whole, knowledge, *per se*, is certainly an object which every man would wish to attain, although, perhaps, he may not take the trouble necessary for attaining it."

He talked very contemptuously of Churchill's poetry, observing that "it had a temporary currency, only from its audacity of abuse, and being filled with living names, and that it would sink into oblivion." I ventured to hint that he was not quite a fair judge, as Churchill had attacked him violently. JOHNSON: "Nay, Sir, I am a very fair judge. He did not attack me violently till he found I did not like his poetry; and his attack on me shall not prevent me from continuing to say what I think of him, from an apprehension that it may be ascribed to resentment. No, Sir, I called the fellow a blockhead at first, and I will call him a blockhead still. However, I will acknowledge that I have a better opinion of him now than I once had; for he has shown more fertility than I expected. To be sure, he is a tree that cannot produce good fruit; he only bears crabs. But, Sir, a tree that produces a great many crabs is better than a tree which produces only a few."

Bonnell Thornton had just published a burlesque "Ode on St. Cecilia's Day," adapted to the ancient British music, viz., the salt-box, the jew's-harp, the marrow-bones and cleaver, the hum-strum or hurdy-gurdy, etc. Johnson praised its humour, and seemed much diverted with it. He repeated the following passage:

"In strains more exhalted the salt-box shall join,
    And clattering and battering and clapping combine;
    With a rap and a tap while the hollow side sounds,
    Up and down leaps the flap, and with rattling rebounds."

Let me here apologize for the imperfect manner in which I am obliged to exhibit Johnson's conversation at this period. In the early part of my acquaintance with him I was so rapt in admiration of his extraordinary colloquial talents, and so little accustomed to his peculiar mode of expression, that I found it extremely difficult to recollect and record his conversation with its genuine vigour and vivacity. In progress of time, when my mind was, as it were, *strongly impregnated with the Johnsonian æther,* I could, with much facility and exactness, carry in my memory and commit to paper the exuberant variety of his wisdom and wit.

At this time *Miss* Williams, as she was then called, though she did not reside with him in the Temple under his roof, but had lodgings in Bolt Court, Fleet Street, had so much of his attention, that he every night drank tea with her before he went home, however late it might be, and she always sat up for him. This, it may be fairly conjectured, was not alone a proof of his regard for *her,* but of his own unwilling-ness to go into solitude, before that unseasonable hour at which he had habituated himself to expect the oblivion of repose. Dr. Goldsmith, being a privileged man, went with him this night, strutting away, and calling to me with an air of superiority, like that of an esoterick over an exoterick disciple of a sage of antiquity, "I go to Miss Williams." I confess, I then envied him this mighty privilege, of which he seemed so proud; but it was not long before I obtained the same mark of dis-tinction.

On Tuesday, the 5th of July, I again visited Johnson. He told me he had looked into the poems of a pretty voluminous writer, Mr. (now Dr.) John Ogilvie, one of the Presbyterian ministers of Scotland, which had lately come out, but could find no thinking in them. BOSWELL: "Is there not imagination in them, Sir?" JOHNSON: "Why, Sir, there is in them what *was* imagination, but it is no more imagination in *him* than sound is sound in the echo. And his diction, too, is not his own. We have long ago seen *white-robed innocence,* and *flower-bespangled meads."*

Talking of London, he observed, "Sir, if you wish to have a just notion of the magnitude of this city, you must not be satisfied with seeing its great streets and squares, but must survey the innumerable little lanes and courts. It is not in the showy evolutions of buildings, but in the multiplicity of human habitations, which are crowded together, that the wonderful immensity of London consists."—I have often amused myself with thinking how different a place London is to dif-ferent people. They, whose narrow minds are contracted to the con-sideration of some one particular pursuit, view it only through that medium. But the intellectual man is struck with it as comprehending the whole of human life in all its variety, the contemplation of which is inexhaustible.

On Wednesday, July 6th, he was engaged to sup with me at my lodgings in Downing Street, Westminster. But on the preceding night, my landlord having behaved very rudely to me and some company who were with me, I resolved not to remain another night in his house. I was exceedingly uneasy at the awkward appearance I supposed I should make to Johnson and the other gentlemen whom I had invited, not being able to receive them at home, and being obliged to order supper at the *Mitre.* I went to Johnson in the morning, and talked of it as of a serious distress. He laughed, and said, "Consider, Sir, how insignificant this will appear a twelvemonth hence."—Were this consideration to be applied to most of the little vexatious incidents of life, by which our quiet is too often disturbed, it would prevent many painful sensations. I have tried it frequently with good effect. "There is nothing (continued he) in this mighty misfortune; nay, we shall be better at the *Mitre.*" I told him that I had been at Sir John Fielding's office, complaining of my landlord, and had been informed that though I had taken my lodgings for a year, I might, upon proof of his bad behaviour, quit them when I pleased, without being under an obligation to pay rent for any longer time than while I possessed them. The fertility of Johnson's mind could show itself even upon so small a matter as this. "Why, Sir (said he), I suppose this must be the law, since you have been told so in Bow-street. But, if your landlord could hold you to your bargain, and the lodgings should be yours for a year, you may certainly use them as you think fit. So, Sir, you may quarter two life-guardsmen upon him; or you may send the greatest scoundrel you can find into your apartments; or you may say that you want to make some experiments in natural philosophy, and may burn a large quantity of assafœtida in his house."

I had, as my guests this evening at the Mitre Tavern, Dr. Johnson, Dr. Goldsmith, Mr. Thomas Davies, Mr. Eccles, an Irish gentleman, for whose agreeable company I was obliged to Mr. Davies, and the Reverend Mr. John Ogilvie, who was desirous of being in company with my illustrious friend, while I, in my turn, was proud to have the honour of showing one of my countrymen upon what easy terms Johnson permitted me to live with him.

Goldsmith, as usual, endeavoured, with too much eagerness, to *shine,* and disputed very warmly with Johnson against the well-known maxim of the British constitution, "the King can do no wrong"; affirming that "what was morally false could not be politically true; and as the King might, in the exercise of his regal power, command and cause the doing of what was wrong, it certainly might be said, in sense and in reason, that he could do no wrong." JOHNSON: "Sir, you are to consider that in our constitution, according to its true principles, the King is the head, he is supreme; he is above everything, and there is no power by which he can be tried. Therefore, it is, Sir, that we hold the King can do no wrong; that whatever may happen to be wrong in government may not be above our reach, by being ascribed to Majesty. Redress is always to be had against oppression by punishing the immediate agents. The King, though he should command, cannot force a Judge to condemn a man unjustly; therefore it is the Judge whom we prosecute and punish. Political institutions are formed upon the consideration of what will most frequently tend to the good of the whole, although now and then exceptions may occur. Thus it is better in general that a nation should have a supreme legislative power, although it may at times be abused. And then, Sir, there is this consideration, that *if the abuse be enormous, Nature will rise up, and, claiming her original rights, overturn a corrupt political system.*" I mark this animated sentence with peculiar pleasure, as a noble instance of that truly dignified spirit of freedom which ever glowed in his heart, though he was charged with slavish tenets by superficial observers; because he was at all times indignant against that false patriotism, that pretended love of freedom, that unruly restlessness, which is inconsistent with the stable authority of any good government.

Mr. Ogilvie was unlucky enough to choose for the topic of his conversation the praises of his native country. He began with saying that there was very rich land around Edinburgh. Goldsmith, who had studied physic there, contradicted this, very untruly, with a sneering laugh. Disconcerted a little by this, Mr. Ogilvie then took new ground, where, I suppose, he thought himself perfectly safe; for he observed that Scotland had a great many noble wild prospects. JOHNSON: "I believe, Sir, you have a great many. Norway, too, has noble wild prospects; and Lapland is remarkable for prodigious noble wild prospects. But, Sir, let me tell you, the noblest prospect which a Scotchman ever sees is the high road that leads him to England!" This unexpected and pointed sally produced a roar of applause. After all, however, those who admire the rude grandeur of Nature cannot deny it to Caledonia.

On Saturday, July 9, I found Johnson surrounded with a numerous *levée*, but have not preserved any part of his conversation. On the 14th we had another evening by ourselves at the *Mitre*. It happening to be a very rainy night, I made some common-place observations on the relaxation of nerves and depression of spirits which such weather occasioned; adding, however, that it was good for the vegetable creation. Johnson, who, as we have already seen, denied that the temperature of the air had any influence on the human frame, answered, with a smile of ridicule, "Why, yes, Sir, it is good for vegetables, and for the animals who eat those vegetables, and for the animals who eat those animals." This observation of his aptly enough introduced a good supper; and I soon forgot, in Johnson's company, the influence of a moist atmosphere.

Feeling myself now quite at ease as his companion, though I had all possible reverence for him, I expressed a regret that I could not be so easy with my father, though he was not much older than Johnson, and certainly, however respectable, had not more learning and greater abilities to depress me. I asked him the reason of this. JOHNSON: "Why, Sir, I am a man of the world. I live in the world, and I take, in some degree, the colour of the world as it moves along. Your father is a Judge in a remote part of the island, and all his notions are taken from the old world. Besides, Sir, there must always be a struggle between a father and son, while one aims at power and the other at independence." I said I was afraid my father would force me to be a lawyer. JOHNSON: "Sir, you need not be afraid of his forcing you to be a laborious practising lawyer; that is not in his power. For as the proverb says, 'One man may lead a horse to the water, but twenty cannot make him drink.' He may be displeased that you are not what he wishes you to be; but that displeasure will not go far. If he insists only on your having as much law as is necessary for a man of property, and then endeavours to get you into Parliament, he is quite in the right."

"Idleness is a disease which must be combated; but I would not advise a rigid adherence to a particular plan of study. I myself have never persisted in any plan for two days together. A man ought to read just as inclination leads him; for what he reads as a task will do him little good. A young man should read five hours in a day, and so may acquire a great deal of knowledge."

To such a degree of unrestrained frankness had he now accustomed me, that in the course of this evening I talked of the numerous reflections which had been thrown out against him on account of his having accepted a pension from his present Majesty. "Why, Sir (said he, with a hearty laugh), it is a mighty foolish noise that they make.[1] I have accepted of a pension as a reward which has been thought due to my literary merit; and now that I have this pension, I am the same man in every respect that I have ever been; I retain the same principles. It is true, that I cannot now curse (smiling) the House of Hanover; nor would it be decent for me to drink King James's health in the wine that King George gives me money to pay for. But, Sir, I think that the

[1] When I mentioned the same idle clamour to him several years afterwards, he said, with a smile, "I wish my pension were twice as large, that they might make twice as much noise."

pleasure of cursing the House of Hanover, and drinking King James's health, are amply overbalanced by £300 a year."

Sir David Dalrymple, now one of the Judges of Scotland by the title of Lord Hailes, had contributed much to increase my high opinion of Johnson, on account of his writings, long before I attained to a personal acquaintance with him; I, in return, had informed Johnson of Sir David's eminent character for learning and religion; and Johnson was so much pleased, that at one of our evening meetings he gave him for his toast. I at this time kept up a very frequent correspondence with Sir David; and I read to Dr. Johnson to-night the following passage from the letter which I had last received from him:

"It gives me pleasure to think that you have obtained the friendship of Mr. Samuel Johnson. He is one of the best moral writers which England has produced. At the same time, I envy you the free and un-disguised converse with such a man. May I beg you to present my best respects to him, and to assure him of the veneration which I entertain for the author of the *Rambler* and of 'Rasselas'? Let me recommend this last work to you; with the *Rambler* you certainly are acquainted. In 'Rasselas' you will see a tender-hearted operator, who probes the wound only to heal it. Swift, on the contrary, mangles human nature. He cuts and slashes, as if he took pleasure in the operation, like the tyrant who said, *Ita feri, ut se sentiat emori*." Johnson seemed to be much gratified by this just and well-turned compliment.

He recommended me to keep a journal of my life, full and unre-served. He said it would be a very good exercise, and would yield me great satisfaction when the particulars were faded from my remem-brance. I was uncommonly fortunate in having had a previous coin-cidence of opinion with him upon this subject, for I had kept such a journal for some time; and it was no small pleasure to me to have this to tell him, and to receive his approbation. He counselled me to keep it private, and said I might surely have a friend who would burn it in case of my death. From this habit I have been enabled to give the world so many anecdotes, which would otherwise have been lost to posterity. I mentioned that I was afraid I put into my journal too many little incidents. JOHNSON: "There is nothing, Sir, too little for so little a creature as man. It is by studying little things that we attain the great art of having as little misery and as much happiness as possible."

Next morning Mr. Dempster happened to call on me, and was so much struck even with the imperfect account which I gave him of Dr. Johnson's conversation, that to his honour be it recorded, when I complained that drinking port and sitting up late with him affected my nerves for some time after, he said, "One had better be palsied at eighteen than not keep company with such a man."

On Tuesday, July 18, I found tall Sir Thomas Robinson sitting with Johnson. Sir Thomas said that the King of Prussia valued himself upon three things:—upon being a hero, a musician, and an author. JOHNSON: "Pretty well, Sir, for one man. As to his being an author, I have not looked at his poetry; but his prose is poor stuff. He writes just as you would suppose Voltaire's foot-boy to do, who has been his amanuensis. He has such parts as the valet might have, and about as much of the colouring of the style as might be got by transcribing his works." When I was at Ferney, I repeated this to Voltaire, in order to reconcile him somewhat to Johnson, whom he, in affecting the English mode of expression, had previously characterized as "a superstitious dog"; but after hearing such a criticism on Frederick the Great, with whom he was then on bad terms, he exclaimed, "An honest fellow!"

Mr. Levet this day showed me Dr. Johnson's library, which was contained in two garrets over his Chambers, where Lintot, son of the celebrated bookseller of that name, had formerly his warehouse. I found a number of good books, but very dusty and in great confusion. The floor was strewed with manuscript leaves, in Johnson's own handwriting, which I beheld with a degree of veneration, supposing they perhaps might contain portions of the *Rambler,* or of "Rasselas." I observed an apparatus for chymical experiments, of which Johnson was all his life very fond.

The place seemed to be very favourable for retirement and meditation. Johnson told me that he went up thither without mentioning it to his servant when he wanted to study, secure from interruption; for he would not allow his servant to say he was not at home when he really was. "A servant's strict regard to truth (said he) must be weakened by such a practice. A philosopher may know that it is merely a form of denial; but few servants are such nice distinguishers. If I accustom a servant to tell a lie for *me,* have I not reason to apprehend that he will tell many lies for *himself?*"

Mr. Alexander Donaldson, bookseller of Edinburgh, had for some time opened a shop in London, and sold his cheap editions of the most popular English books, in defiance of the supposed common-law right of *Literary Property.* Johnson, though he concurred in the opinion which was afterwards sanctioned by a judgment of the House of Lords, that there was no such right, was at this time very angry that the booksellers of London, for whom he uniformly professed much regard, should suffer from an invasion of what they had ever considered to be secure; and he was loud and violent against Mr. Donaldson. "He is a fellow who takes advantage of the law to injure his brethren; for notwithstanding that the statute secures only fourteen years of exclusive right, it has always been understood by *the trade* that he who buys the copyright of a book from the author obtains a perpetual property; and upon that belief, numberless bargains are made to transfer that property after the expiration of the statutory term. Now Donaldson, I say, takes advantage here of people who have really an equitable title from usage; and if we consider how few of the books, of which they buy the property, succeed so well as to bring profit, we should be of opinion that the term of fourteen years is too short; it should be sixty years." DEMPSTER: "Donaldson, Sir, is anxious for the encouragement of literature. He reduces the price of books, so that poor students may buy them." JOHNSON (laughing): "Well, Sir, allowing that to be his motive, he is no better than Robin Hood, who robbed the rich in order to give to the poor."

It is remarkable that when the great question concerning Literary Property came to be ultimately tried before the supreme tribunal of this country, in consequence of the very spirited exertions of Mr. Donaldson, Dr. Johnson was zealous against a perpetuity; but he thought that the term of exclusive right of authors should be considerably enlarged. He was then for granting a hundred years.

Mr. Dempster having endeavoured to maintain that intrinsic merit *ought* to make the only distinction amongst mankind:—JOHNSON: "Why, Sir, mankind have found that this cannot be. How shall we determine the proportion of intrinsic merit? Were that to be the only distinction amongst mankind, we should soon quarrel about the degrees of it. Were all distinctions abolished, the strongest would not long acquiesce, but would endeavour to obtain a superiority by their bodily strength. But, Sir, as subordination is very necessary for society, and contentions for superiority very dangerous, mankind, that is to say, all civilized nations, have settled it upon a plain invariable principle. A man is born to hereditary rank; or his being appointed to certain offices, gives him a certain rank. Subordination tends greatly to human happiness. Were we all upon an equality, we should have no other enjoyment than mere animal pleasure."

I said, I considered distinction or rank to be of so much importance in civilized society, that if I were asked on the same day to dine with the first duke in England, and with the first man in Britain for genius, I should hesitate which to prefer. JOHNSON: "To be sure, Sir, if you were to dine only once, and it were never to be known where you dined, you would choose rather to dine with the first man of genius; but to gain most respect, you should dine with the first duke in England. For nine people in ten that you meet would have a higher opinion of you for having dined with a duke; and the great genius himself would receive you better because you had been with the great duke."

He took care to guard himself against any possible suspicion that his settled principles of reverence for rank and respect for wealth were at all owing to mean or interested motives; for he asserted his own independence as a literary man. "No man (said he) who ever lived by literature, has lived more independently than I have done." He said he had taken longer time than he needed to have done in composing his Dictionary. He received our compliments upon that great work with complacency, and told us that the Academy *della Crusca* could scarcely believe that it was done by one man.

At night, Mr. Johnson and I supped in a private room at the Turk's Head Coffee House, in the Strand. "I encourage this house (said he), for the mistress of it is a good, civil woman, and has not much business."

"Sir, I love the acquaintance of young people; because, in the first place, I don't like to think myself growing old. In the next place, young acquaintances must last longest, if they do last; and then, Sir, young men have more virtue than old men; they have more generous sentiments in every respect. I love the young dogs of this age, they have more wit and humour and knowledge of life than we had; but then the dogs are not so good scholars. Sir, in my early years I read very hard. It is a sad reflection, but a true one, that I knew almost as much at eighteen as I do now. My judgment, to be sure, was not so good; but, I had all the facts. I remember very well, when I was at Oxford, an old gentleman said to me, 'Young man, ply your book diligently now, and acquire a stock of knowledge; for when years come unto you, you will find that poring upon books will be but an irksome task.' "

This account of his reading, given by himself in plain words, sufficiently confirms what I have already advanced upon the disputed question as to his application. It reconciles any seeming inconsistency in his way of talking upon it at different times; and shows that idleness and reading hard were with him relative terms, the import of which, as used by him, must be gathered from a comparison with what scholars of different degrees of ardour and assiduity have been known to do. And let it be remembered that he was now talking spontaneously, and expressing his genuine sentiments; whereas at other times he might be induced, from his spirit of contradiction, or more properly from his love of argumentative contest, to speak lightly of his own application to study.

He mentioned to me now, for the first time, that he had been distressed by melancholy, and for that reason had been obliged to fly from study and meditation to the dissipating variety of life. Against melancholy he recommended constant occupation of mind, a great deal of exercise, moderation in eating and drinking, and especially to shun drinking at night. He said melancholy people were apt to fly to intemperance for relief, but that it sunk them much deeper in misery. He observed that labouring men who work hard, and live sparingly, are seldom or never troubled with low spirits.

He again insisted on the duty of maintaining subordination of rank. "Sir, I would no more deprive a nobleman of his respect, than of his money. I consider myself as acting a part in the great system of society, and I do to others as I would have them to do to me. I would behave to a nobleman, as I should expect he would behave to me, were I a nobleman, and he Sam. Johnson. Sir, there is one Mrs. Macaulay in this town, a great republican. One day when I was at her house I put on a very grave countenance, and said to her, 'Madam, I am now become a convert to your way of thinking. I am convinced that all mankind are upon an equal footing; and to give you an unquestionable proof, Madam, that I am in earnest here is a very sensible, civil, well-behaved fellow-citizen, your footman; I desire that he may be allowed to sit down and dine with us.' I thus, Sir, showed her the absurdity of the levelling doctrine. She has never liked me since. Sir, your levellers wish to level *down* as far as themselves; but they cannot bear levelling *up* to themselves. They would all have some people under them; why not then have some people above them?" I mentioned a certain author who disgusted me by his forwardness, and by showing no deference to noblemen into whose company he was admitted. JOHNSON: "Suppose a shoemaker should claim an equality with him, as he does with a lord, how he would stare. 'Why, Sir, do you stare? (says the shoemaker); I do great service to society. 'Tis true, I am paid for doing it; but so are you, Sir; and I am sorry to say it, better paid than I am, for doing something not so necessary. For mankind could do better without your books than without my shoes.' Thus, Sir, there would be a perpetual struggle for precedence, were there no fixed invariable rules for the distinction of rank, which creates no jealousy, as it is allowed to be accidental."

I spoke of a Sir James Macdonald as a young man of most distinguished merit, who united the highest reputation at Eton and Oxford, with the patriarchal spirit of a great Highland Chieftain. I mentioned that Sir James had said to me that he had never seen Mr. Johnson, but he had a great respect for him though at the same time it was mixed with some degree of terror. JOHNSON: "Sir, if he were to be acquainted with me it might lessen both."

The mention of this gentleman led us to talk of the Western Islands of Scotland, to visit which he expressed a wish that then appeared to me a very romantic fancy, which I little thought would be afterwards realized. He told me that his father had put Martin's account of those islands into his hands when he was very young, and that he was highly pleased with it; that he was particularly struck with the St. Kilda man's notion, that the high church of Glasgow had been hollowed out of a rock; a circumstance to which old Mr. Johnson had directed his attention. He said he would go to the Hebrides with me, when I returned from my travels, unless some very good companion should offer when I was absent, which he did not think probable: adding, "There are few people whom I take so much to as to you." And when I talked of my leaving England, he said with a very affectionate air, "My dear Boswell, I should be very unhappy at parting, did I think we were not to meet again." I cannot too often remind my readers that although such instances of his kindness are doubtless very flattering to me, yet I hoped my recording them will be ascribed to a better motive than to vanity; for they afford unquestionable evidence of his tenderness and complacency, which some, while they were forced to acknowledge his great powers, have been so strenuous to deny.

He maintained that a boy at school was the happiest of human beings. I supported a different opinion, from which I have never yet varied, that a man is happier; and I enlarged upon the anxiety and sufferings which are endured at school. JOHNSON: "Ah! Sir, a boy's being flogged is not so severe as a man's having the hiss of the world against him. Men have a solicitude about fame; and the greater share they have of it the more afraid they are of losing it." I silently asked myself, "Is it possible that the great Samuel Johnson really entertains any such apprehension, and is not confident that his exalted fame is established upon a foundation never to be shaken?"

He this evening drank a bumper to Sir David Dalrymple, "as a man of worth, a scholar, and a wit."—"I have (said he) never heard of him, except from you; but let him know my opinion of him; for as he does not show himself much in the world, he should have the praise of the few who hear of him."

CHAPTER XV—1763–1765

The Literary Club

ON TUESDAY, JULY 26, I found Mr. Johnson alone. We talked of the education of children; and I asked him what he thought was best to teach them first. JOHNSON: "Sir, it is no matter what you teach them first, any more than what leg you shall put into your breeches first. Sir, you may stand disputing which is best to put in first, but in the meantime your breech is bare. Sir, while you are considering which of two things you should teach your child first, another boy has learnt them both."

On Thursday, July 28, we again supped in private at the Turk's Head Coffee House. JOHNSON: "Swift has a higher reputation than he deserves. His excellence is strong sense; for his humour, though very well, is not remarkably good. I doubt whether the 'Tale of a Tub' be his; for he never owned it, and it is much above his usual manner."

He laughed heartily when I mentioned to him a saying of his concerning Mr. Thomas Sheridan, which Foote took a wicked pleasure to circulate. "Why, Sir, Sherry is dull, naturally dull; but it must have taken him a great deal of pains to become what we now see him. Such an excess of stupidity, Sir, is not in Nature."—"So (said he), I allowed him all his own merit."

The conversation then took a philosophical turn. JOHNSON: "Human experience, which is constantly contradicting theory, is the greatest test of truth. A system, built upon the discoveries of a great many minds, is always of more strength than what is produced by the mere workings of any one mind, which, of itself, can do little. There is not so poor a book in the world that would not be a prodigious effort were it wrought out entirely by a single mind, without the aid of prior investigators. The French writers are superficial, because they are not scholars, and so proceed upon the mere power of their own minds; and we see how very little power they have."

"As to the Christian religion, Sir, besides the strong evidence which we have for it, there is a balance in its favour from the number of great men who have been convinced of its truth, after a serious consideration of the question. Grotius was an acute man, a lawyer, a man accustomed to examine evidence, and he was convinced. Grotius was not a recluse, but a man of the world, who certainly had no bias to the side of religion. Sir Isaac Newton set out an infidel, and came to be a very firm believer."

I expressed my opinion of my friend Derrick as but a poor writer. JOHNSON: "To be sure, Sir, he is: but you are to consider that his being a literary man has got for him all that he has. It has made him King of Bath. Sir, he has nothing to say for himself but that he is a writer. Had he not been a writer he must have been sweeping the crossings in the streets, and asking halfpence from everybody that passed."

In justice, however, to the memory of Mr. Derrick, who was my first tutor in the ways of London, and showed me the town in all its variety of departments, both literary and sportive, the particulars of which Dr. Johnson advised me to put in writing, it is proper to mention what Johnson, at a subsequent period, said of him both as a writer and an editor: "Sir, I have often said that if Derrick's letters had been written by one of a more established name, they would have been thought very pretty letters." And, "I sent Derrick to Dryden's relations to gather materials for his life; and I believe he got all that I myself should have got."

Johnson said once to me, "Sir, I honour Derrick for his presence of mind. One night, when Floyd, another poor author, was wandering about the streets in the night, he found Derrick fast asleep upon a bulk; upon being suddenly waked, Derrick started up, 'My dear Floyd, I am sorry to see you in this destitute state; will you go home with me to *my lodgings?*'"

I again begged his advice as to my method of study at Utrecht. "Come (said he), let us make a day of it. Let us go down to Greenwich and dine, and talk of it there." The following Saturday was fixed for this excursion.

As we walked along the Strand to-night, arm-in-arm, a woman of the town accosted us, in the usual enticing manner. "No, no, my girl (said Johnson), it won't do." He, however, did not treat her with harshness; and we talked of the wretched life of such women, and agreed that much more misery than happiness, upon the whole, is produced by illicit commerce between the sexes.

On Saturday, July 30, Dr. Johnson and I took a sculler at the Temple Stairs, and set out for Greenwich. I asked him if he really thought a knowledge of the Greek and Latin languages an essential requisite to a good education. JOHNSON: "Most certainly, Sir; for those who know them have a very great advantage over those who do not. Nay, Sir, it is wonderful what a difference learning makes upon people even in the

A Voyage to Greenwich

common intercourse of life, which does not appear to be much connected with it." "And yet (said I), people go through the world very well, and carry on the business of life to good advantage without learning."—JOHNSON: "Why, Sir, that may be true in cases where learning cannot possibly be of any use; for instance, this boy rows us as well without learning as if he could sing the song of Orpheus to the Argonauts, who were the first sailors." He then called to the boy, "What would you give, my lad, to know about the Argonauts?" "Sir (said the boy), I would give what I have." Johnson was much pleased with his answer, and we gave him a double fare. Dr. Johnson then turning to me, "Sir (said he), a desire of knowledge is the natural feeling of mankind; and every human being, whose mind is not debauched, will be willing to give all that he has, to get knowledge."

We landed at the *Old Swan*, and walked to Billingsgate, where we took oars and moved smoothly along the silver Thames. It was a very fine day. We were entertained with the immense number and variety of ships that were lying at anchor, and with the beautiful country on each side of the river.

I talked of preaching, and of the great success which those called Methodists have. JOHNSON: "Sir, it is owing to their expressing themselves in a plain and familiar manner which is the only way to do good to the common people, and which clergymen of genius and learning ought to do from a principle of duty, when it is suited to their congregation; a practice for which they will be praised by men of sense. To insist against drunkenness as a crime because it debases reason, the noblest faculty of man, would be of no service to the common people; but to tell them that they may die in a fit of drunkenness, and show them how dreadful that would be, cannot fail to make a deep impression. Sir, when your Scotch clergy give up their homely manner, religion will soon decay in that country." Let this observation, as Johnson meant it, be ever remembered.

Afterwards he entered upon the business of the day, which was to give me his advice as to a course of study. And here I am to mention with much regret that my record of what he said is miserably scanty. I recollect with admiration an animating blaze of eloquence, which roused every intellectual power in me to the highest pitch, but must have dazzled me so much that my memory could not preserve the substance of his discourse; for the note which I find of it is no more than this:—"He ran over the grand scale of human knowledge; advised me to select some particular branch to excel in, but to acquire a little of every kind." The defects of my minutes will be fully supplied by a long letter upon the subject, which he favoured me with, after I had been some time at Utrecht, and which my readers will have the pleasure to peruse in its proper place.

We walked in the evening in Greenwich Park. He asked me, I suppose, by way of trying my disposition, "Is not this very fine?" Having no exquisite relish of the beauties of Nature, and being more delighted with "the busy hum of men," I answered, "Yes, Sir, but not equal to Fleet Street." JOHNSON: "You are right, Sir."

We stayed so long at Greenwich, that our sail up the river, in our return to London, was by no means so pleasant as in the morning; for the night air was so cold that it made me shiver. I was the more sensible of it from having sat up all the night before, recollecting and writing in my Journal what I thought worthy of preservation; an exertion, which, during the first part of my acquaintance with Johnson, I frequently made. I remember having sat up four nights in one week without being much incommoded in the day time.

Johnson, whose robust frame was not in the least affected by the cold, scolded me, as if my shivering had been a paltry effeminacy, saying, "Why do you shiver?" Sir William Scott, of the Commons, told me that when he complained of a headache in the post-chaise, as they were travelling together to Scotland, Johnson treated him in the same manner: "At your age, Sir, I had no headache."

We concluded the day at the Turk's Head Coffee House very socially. He was pleased to listen to a particular account which I gave him of my family, and of its hereditary estate, as to the extent and population of which he asked questions, and made calculations; recommending, at the same time, a liberal kindness to the tenantry, as people over whom the proprietor was placed by Providence. He took delight in hearing my description of the romantic seat of my ancestors. "I must be there, Sir (said he), and we will live in the old castle; and if there is not a room in it remaining, we will build one." I was highly flattered, but could scarcely indulge a hope that Auchinleck would indeed be honoured by his presence, and celebrated by a description, as it afterwards was, in his "Journey to the Western Islands."

After he had again talked of my setting out for Holland, he said, "I must see thee out of England; I will accompany you to Harwich." I could not find words to express what I felt upon this unexpected and very great mark of his affectionate regard.

Next day, Sunday, July 31, I told him I had been that morning at a meeting of the people called Quakers, where I had heard a woman preach. JOHNSON: "Sir, a woman's preaching is like a dog's walking on his hind legs. It is not done well; but you are surprised to find it done at all."

On Tuesday, August 2 (the day of my departure from London having been fixed for the 5th), Dr. Johnson did me the honour to pass a part of the morning with me at my chambers. He said that "he always felt an inclination to do nothing." I observed that it was strange to think that the most indolent man in Britain had written the most laborious work, "The English Dictionary."

I mentioned an imprudent publication, by a certain friend of his, at an early period of life, and asked him if he thought it would hurt him. JOHNSON: "No, Sir, not much. It may, perhaps, be mentioned at an election."

I had now made good my title to be a privileged man, and was carried by him in the evening to drink tea with Miss Williams, whom, though under the misfortune of having lost her sight, I found to be agreeable in conversation, for she had a variety of literature, and expressed herself well; but her peculiar value was the intimacy in which she had long lived with Johnson, by which she was acquainted with his habits, and knew how to lead him on to talk.

After tea he carried me to what he called his walk, which was a long narrow paved court in the neighbourhood, overshadowed by some trees. There we sauntered a considerable time, and I complained to him that my love of London and of his company was such, that I shrunk almost from the thought of going away even to travel, which is generally so much desired by young men. He roused me by manly and spirited conversation. He advised me, when settled in any place abroad, to study with an eagerness after knowledge, and to apply to Greek an hour every day; and when I was moving about to read diligently the great book of mankind.

On Wednesday, August 3, we had our last social evening at the Turk's Head Coffee House, before my setting out for foreign parts. I had the misfortune, before we parted, to irritate him unintentionally. I mentioned to him how common it was in the world to tell absurd stories of him, and to ascribe to him very strange sayings. JOHNSON: "What do they make me say, Sir?" BOSWELL: "Why, Sir, as an instance very strange indeed (laughing heartily as I spoke), David Hume told me you said that you would stand before a battery of cannon to restore the Convocation to its full powers."—Little did I apprehend that he had actually said this: but I was soon convinced of my error; for, with a determined look, he thundered out—"And would I not, Sir? Shall the Presbyterian *Kirk* of Scotland have its General Assembly, and the Church of England be denied its Convocation?" He was walking up and down the room, while I told him the anecdote; but when he uttered this explosion of High-Church zeal, he had come close to my chair, and his eyes flashed with indignation. I bowed to the storm, and diverted the force of it by leading him to expatiate on the influence which religion derived from maintaining the Church with great external respectability.

On Friday, August 5, we set out early in the morning in the Harwich stage coach. A fat elderly gentlewoman, and a young Dutchman, seemed the most inclined among us to conversation. At the inn where we dined, the gentlewoman said that she had done her best to educate her children; and, particularly, that she had never suffered them to be a moment idle. JOHNSON: "I wish, Madam, you would educate me too: for I have been an idle fellow all my life." "I am sure, Sir (said she), you have not been idle." JOHNSON: "Nay, Madam, it is very true; and that gentleman there (pointing to me) has been idle. He was idle at Edinburgh. His father sent him to Glasgow, where he continued to be idle. He then came to London, where he has been very idle; and now he is going to Utrecht, where he will be as idle as ever." I asked him privately how he could expose me so. JOHNSON: "Poh, poh! (said he); they knew nothing about you, and will think of it no more." Though by no means niggardly, his attention to what was generally right was so minute, that having observed at one of the stages that I ostentatiously gave a shilling to the coachman, when the custom was for each passenger to give only sixpence, he took me aside and scolded me, saying that what I had done would make the coachman dissatisfied with all the rest of the passengers, who gave him no more than his due. This was a just reprimand; for in whatever way a man may indulge his generosity or his vanity in spending his money, for the sake of others he ought not to raise the price of any article for which there is a constant demand.

At supper this night he talked of good eating with uncommon satisfaction. "Some people (said he) have a foolish way of not minding, or pretending not to mind, what they eat. For my part, I mind my belly very studiously, and very carefully; for I look upon it that he who does not mind his belly will hardly mind anything else." He now appeared to me *Jean Bull philosophe,* and he was, for the moment, not only serious but vehement. Yet I have heard him, upon other occasions, talk with great contempt of people who were anxious to gratify their palates; and the 206th number of his *Rambler* is a masterly essay against gulosity. His practice, indeed, I must acknowledge, may be considered as casting the balance of his different opinions upon this subject; for I never knew any man who relished good eating more than he did. When at table, he was totally absorbed in the business of the moment; his looks seemed riveted to his plate; nor would he, unless when in very high company, say one word, or even pay the least attention to what was said by others, till he had satisfied his appetite; which was so fierce, and indulged with such intenseness, that while in the act of eating, the veins of his forehead swelled, and generally a strong perspiration was visible. To those whose sensations were delicate, this could not but be disgusting; and it was doubtless not very suitable to the character of a philosopher, who should be distinguished by self-command. But it must be owned that Johnson, though he could be rigidly *abstemious,* was not a *temperate* man either in eating or drinking. He could refrain, but he could not use moderately. He told me that he had fasted two days without inconvenience, and that he had never been hungry but once. They who beheld with wonder how much he ate upon all occasions when his dinner was to his taste, could not easily conceive what he must have meant by hunger; and not only was he remarkable for the extraordinary quantity which he ate, but he was, or affected to be, a man of very nice discernment in the science of cookery. He used to descant critically on the dishes which had been at table where he had dined or supped, and to recollect very minutely what he had liked. I remember, when he was in Scotland, his praising *"Gordon's palates"* (a dish of palates at the Honourable Alexander Gordon's), with a warmth of expression which might have done honour to more important subjects. "As for Maclaurin's imitation of a *made dish,* it was a wretched attempt." He about the same time was so much displeased with the performance of a nobleman's French cook that he exclaimed with vehemence, "I'd throw such a rascal into the river"; and he then proceeded to alarm a lady at whose house he was to sup by the following manifesto of his skill: "I, Madam, who live at a variety of good tables, am a much better judge of cookery than any person who has a very tolerable cook, but lives much at home; for his palate is gradually adapted to the taste of his cook; whereas, Madam, in trying by a wider range, I can more exquisitely judge."—When invited to dine, even with an intimate friend, he was not pleased if something better than a plain dinner was not prepared for him. I have heard him say on such an occasion, "This was a good dinner enough, to be sure; but it was not a dinner to *ask* a man to." On the other hand he was wont to express, with great glee, his satisfaction when he had been entertained quite to his mind. One day, when he had dined with his neighbour and landlord in Bolt-court, Mr. Allen, the printer, whose old housekeeper had studied his taste in every thing, he pronounced this eulogy: "Sir, we could not have had a better dinner had there been a *Synod of Cooks.*"

While we were left by ourselves, after the Dutchman had gone to bed, Dr. Johnson talked of that studied behaviour which many have recommended and practised. He disapproved of it: and said, "I never considered whether I should be a grave man, or a merry man, but just let inclination, for the time, have its course."

He flattered me with some hopes that he would, in the course of the following summer, come over to Holland, and accompany me in a tour through the Netherlands.

I teased him with fanciful apprehensions of unhappiness. A moth having fluttered round the candle, and burnt itself, he laid hold of this little incident to admonish me; saying, with a sly look, and in a solemn but a quiet tone, "That creature was its own tormentor, and I believe its name was Boswell."

Next day we got to Harwich to dinner; and my passage in the packet-boat to Helvoetsluys being secured, and my baggage put on board, we dined at our inn by ourselves. I happened to say it would be terrible if he should not find a speedy opportunity of returning to London, and be confined in so dull a place. JOHNSON: "Don't, Sir, accustom yourself to use big words for little matters. It would *not* be *terrible,* though I *were* to be detained some time here. The practice of using words of disproportionate magnitude is, no doubt, too frequent everywhere; but I think most remarkable among the French, of which, all who have travelled in France must have been struck with innumerable instances."

We went and looked at the church, and having gone into it, and walked up to the altar, Johnson, whose piety was constant and fervent, sent me to my knees, saying, "Now that you are going to leave your native country, recommend yourself to the protection of your Creator and Redeemer."

My revered friend walked down with me to the beach, where we embraced and parted with tenderness, and engaged to correspond by letters. I said, "I hope, Sir, you will not forget me in my absence." JOHNSON: "Nay, Sir, it is more likely you should forget me, than that I should forget you." As the vessel put out to sea, I kept my eyes upon him for a considerable time, while he remained rolling his majestic frame in the usual manner; and at last I perceived him walk back into the town, and he disappeared.

Utrecht seeming at first very dull to me, after the animated scenes of London, my spirits were grievously affected; and I wrote to Johnson a plaintive and desponding letter, to which he paid no regard. Afterwards, when I had acquired a firmer tone of mind, I wrote him a second letter, expressing much anxiety to hear from him. At length I received the following epistle, which was of important service to me, and, I trust, will be so to many others.

"*A* MR. BOSWELL, *à la Cour de l'Empereur, Utrecht.*

"DEAR SIR,—

"You are not to think yourself forgotten, or criminally neglected, that you have had yet no letter from me. I love to see my friends, to hear from them, to talk to them, and to talk of them; but it is not without a considerable effort of resolution that I prevail upon myself to write. I would not, however, gratify my own indolence by the omission of any important duty, or any office of real kindness.

"To tell you that I am or am not well, that I have or have not been in the country, that I drank your health in the room in which we last sat together, and that your acquaintance continue to speak of you with their former kindness, topics with which those letters are commonly filled which are written only for the sake of writing I seldom shall think worth communicating; but if I can have it in my power to calm any harassing disquiet, to excite any virtuous desire, to rectify any important opinion, or fortify any generous resolution, you need not doubt but I shall at least wish to prefer the pleasure of gratifying a friend much less esteemed than yourself, before the gloomy calm of idle vacancy. Whether I shall easily arrive at an exact punctuality of correspondence, I cannot tell. I shall, at present, expect that you will receive this in return for two which I have had from you. The first, indeed, gave me an account so hopeless of the state of your mind, that it hardly admitted or deserved an answer; by the second I was much better pleased; and the pleasure will still be increased by such a narrative of the progress of your studies, as may evidence the continuance of an equal and rational application of your mind to some useful inquiry.

"You will, perhaps, wish to ask, what study I would recommend. I shall not speak of theology, because it ought not to be considered as a question whether you shall endeavour to know the will of God.

"I shall, therefore, consider only such studies as we are at liberty to pursue or to neglect; and of these I know not how you will make a better choice, than by studying the civil law as your father advises, and the ancient languages, as you had determined for yourself; at least resolve, while you remain in any settled residence, to spend a certain number of hours every day amongst your books. The dissipation of thought of which you complain is nothing more than the vacillation of a mind suspended between different motives, and changing its direction as any motive gains or loses strength. If you can but kindle in your mind any strong desire, if you can but keep predominant any wish for some particular excellence or attainment, the gusts of imagination will break away, without any effect upon your conduct, and commonly without any traces left upon the memory.

"There lurks, perhaps, in every human heart a desire of distinction, which inclines every man first to hope, and then to believe, that nature has given him something peculiar to himself. This vanity makes one mind nurse aversion, and another actuate desires, till they rise by art much above their original state of power; and as affectation in time improves to habit, they at last tyrannize over him who at first encouraged them only for show. Every desire is a viper in the bosom, who, while he was chill, was harmless; but when warmth gave him strength, exerted it in poison. You know a gentleman, who, when first he set his foot in the gay world, as he prepared himself to whirl in the vortex of pleasure, imagined a total indifference and universal negligence to be the most agreeable concomitants of youth, and the strongest indication of an airy temper and a quick apprehension. Vacant to every object, and sensible of every impulse, he thought that all appearance of diligence would deduct something from the reputation of genius; and hoped that he should appear to attain, amidst all the ease of carelessness, and all the tumult of diversion, that knowledge and those accomplishments which mortals of the common fabric obtain only by mute abstraction and solitary drudgery. He tried this scheme of life awhile, was made weary of it by his sense and his virtue; he then wished to return to his studies; and finding long habits of idleness and pleasure harder to be cured than he expected, still willing to retain his claim to some extraordinary prerogatives, resolved the common consequences of irregularity into an unalterable decree of destiny, and concluded that Nature had originally formed him incapable of rational employment.

"Let all such fancies, illusive and destructive, be banished henceforward from your thoughts for ever. Resolve, and keep your resolution; choose, and pursue your choice. If you spend this day in study, you will find yourself still more able to study to-morrow; not that you are to expect that you shall at once obtain a complete victory. Depravity is not very easily overcome. Resolution will sometimes relax, and diligence will sometimes be interrupted; but let no accidental surprise or deviation, whether short or long, dispose you to despondency. Consider these failings as incident to all mankind. Begin again where you left off, and endeavour to avoid the seducements that prevailed over you before.

"This, my dear Boswell, is advice which, perhaps, has been often given you, and given you without effect. But this advice, if you will not take from others, you must take from your own reflections, if you purpose to do the duties of the station to which the bounty of Providence has called you.

"Let me have a long letter from you as soon as you can. I hope you continue your journal, and enrich it with many observations upon the country in which you reside. It will be a favour if you can get me any books in the Frisick language, and can inquire how the poor are maintained in the Seven Provinces.

"I am,

"Dear Sir, your most affectionate servant,

"SAM. JOHNSON.

"London, Dec. 8, 1763."

Early in 1764, Johnson paid a visit to the Langton family, at their seat of Langton, in Lincolnshire, where he passed some time, much to his satisfaction. His friend, Bennet Langton, it will not be doubted, did everything in his power to make the place agreeable to so illustrious a guest: and the elder Mr. Langton and his lady, being fully capable of understanding his value, were not wanting in attention. He, however, told me that old Mr. Langton, though a man of considerable learning, had so little allowance to make for his occasional "laxity of talk," that, because in the course of discussion he sometimes mentioned what might be said in favour of the peculiar tenets of the Romish Church, he went to his grave believing him to be of that communion.

Johnson, during his stay at Langton, had the advantage of a good library, and saw several gentlemen of the neighbourhood. I have obtained from Mr. Langton the following particulars of this period.

He was now fully convinced that he could not have been satisfied with a country living; for, talking of a respectable clergyman in Lincolnshire, he observed, "This man, Sir, fills up the duties of his life well. I approve of him, but could not imitate him."

So socially accommodating was he that once when Mr. Langton and he were driving together in a coach, and Mr. Langton complained of being sick, he insisted that they should go out, and sit on the back of it in the open air, which they did. And being sensible how strange the appearance must be, observed, that a countryman whom they saw in a field would probably be thinking, "If these two madmen should come down, what would become of me?"

Soon after his return to London, which was in February, was founded that Club which existed long without a name, but at Mr.

Garrick's funeral became distinguished by the title of the Literary Club. Sir Joshua Reynolds had the merit of being the first proposer of it, to which Johnson acceded, and the original members were Sir Joshua Reynolds, Dr. Johnson, Mr. Edmund Burke, Dr. Nugent, Mr. Beauclerk, Mr. Langton, Dr. Goldsmith, Mr. Chamier, and Sir John Hawkins. They met at the Turk's Head, in Gerrard Street, Soho, one evening in every week, at seven, and generally continued their conversation till a pretty late hour. This club has been gradually increased to its present number, thirty-five. After about ten years, instead of supping weekly, it was resolved to dine together once a fortnight during the meeting of Parliament. Their original tavern having been converted into a private house, they moved first to Prince's in Sackville Street, then to Le Telier's in Dover Street, and now meet at Parsloe's, St. James's Street. Between the time of its formation, and the time at which this work is passing through the press (June 1792), the following persons, now dead, were members of it: Mr. Dunning (afterwards Lord Ashburton), Mr. Samuel Dyer, Mr. Garrick, Dr. Shipley, Bishop of St. Asaph, Mr. Vesey, Mr. Thomas Warton, and Dr. Adam Smith. The present members are, Mr. Burke, Mr. Langton, Lord Charlemont, Sir Robert Chambers, Dr. Percy, Bishop of Dromore, Dr. Barnard, Bishop of Killaloe, Dr. Marlay, Bishop of Clonfert, Mr. Fox, Dr. George Fordyce, Sir William Scott, Sir Joseph Banks, Sir Charles Bunbury, Mr. Windham of Norfolk, Mr. Sheridan, Mr. Gibbon, Sir William Jones, Mr. Colman, Mr. Steevens, Dr. Burney, Dr. Joseph Warton, Mr. Malone, Lord Ossory, Lord Spencer, Lord Lucan, Lord Palmerston, Lord Eliot, Lord Macartney, Mr. Richard Burke, junior, Sir William Hamilton, Dr. Warren, Mr. Courtenay, Dr. Hinchliffe, Bishop of Peterborough, the Duke of Leeds, Dr. Douglas, Bishop of Salisbury, and the writer of this account.

About this time he was afflicted with a very severe return of the hypochondriac disorder, which was ever lurking about him. He was so ill, as, notwithstanding his remarkable love of company, to be entirely averse to society, the most fatal symptom of that malady. Dr. Adams told me that as an old friend he was admitted to visit him, and that he found him in a deplorable state, sighing, groaning, talking to himself, and restlessly walking from room to room. He then used this emphatical expression of the misery which he felt: "I would consent to have a limb amputated to recover my spirits."

Talking to himself was, indeed, one of his singularities ever since I knew him. I was certain that he was frequently uttering pious ejaculations: for fragments of the Lord's Prayer have been distinctly overheard. His friend, Mr. Thomas Davies, of whom Churchill says—

"That Davies hath a very pretty wife":

when Dr. Johnson muttered "lead us not into temptation"; used with waggish and gallant humour to whisper to Mrs. Davies, "You, my dear, are the cause of this."

He had another particularity, of which none of his friends even ventured to ask an explanation. It appeared to me some superstitious habit, which he had contracted early, and from which he had never called upon his reason to disentangle him. This was his anxious care to go out or in at a door or passage, by a certain number of steps from a certain point, or at least so as that either his right or his left foot (I am not certain which) should constantly make the first actual movement when he came close to the door or passage. Thus I conjecture: for I have, upon innumerable occasions, observed him suddenly stop, and then seem to count his steps with a deep earnestness; and when he had neglected or gone wrong in this sort of magical movement, I have seen him go back again, put himself in a proper posture to begin the ceremony, and, having gone through it, break from his abstraction, walk briskly on, and join his companion. A strange instance of something of this nature, even when on horseback, happened when he was in the Isle of Sky. Sir Joshua Reynolds has observed him to go a good way about rather than cross a particular alley in Leicester-fields; but this Sir Joshua imputed to his having had some disagreeable recollection associated with it.

That the most minute singularities which belonged to him and made very observable parts of his appearance and manner may not be omitted, it is requisite to mention that while talking or even musing as he sat in his chair, he commonly held his head to one side towards his right shoulder, and shook it in a tremulous manner, moving his body backwards and forwards, and rubbing his left knee in the same direction, with the palm of his hand. In the intervals of articulating he made various sounds with his mouth, sometimes as if ruminating, or what is called chewing the cud, sometimes giving half a whistle, sometimes making his tongue play backwards from the roof of his mouth, as if clucking like a hen, and sometimes protruding it against his upper gums in front, as if pronouncing quickly under his breath, *too, too, too;* all this accompanied sometimes with a thoughtful look, but more frequently with a smile. Generally when he had concluded a period, in the course of a dispute, by which time he was a good deal exhausted by violence and vociferation, he used to blow out his breath like a whale. This I suppose was a relief to his lungs; and seemed in him to be a contemptuous mode of expression, as if he had made the arguments of his opponent fly like chaff before the wind.

I am fully aware how very obvious an occasion I here give for the sneering jocularity of such as have no relish of an exact likeness; which to render complete he who draws it must not disdain the slightest strokes. But if witlings should be inclined to attack this account, let them have the candour to quote what I have offered in my defence.

Early in the year 1765 he paid a short visit to the University of Cambridge, with his friend Mr. Beauclerk. There is a lively picturesque account of his behaviour on this visit, in the *Gentleman's Magazine* for March, 1785, being an extract of a letter from the late Dr. John Sharp. The two following sentences are very characteristical: "He drank his large potations of tea with me, interrupted by many an indignant contradiction, and many a noble sentiment."—"Several persons got into his company the last evening at Trinity, where, about twelve, he began to be very great; stripped poor Mrs. Macaulay to the very skin, then gave her for his toast, and drank her in two bumpers."

No man was more gratefully sensible of any kindness done to him than Johnson. There is a little circumstance in his diary this year which shows him in a very amiable light.

"July 2. I paid Mr. Simpson ten guineas, which he had formerly lent me in my necessity, and for which Tetty expressed her gratitude."

"July 8. I lent Mr. Simpson ten guineas more."

Here he had a pleasing opportunity of doing the same kindness to an old friend which he had formerly received from him. Indeed his liberality as to money was very remarkable. The next article in his diary is, "July 16th, I received £75. Lent Mr. Davies £25."

Trinity College, Dublin, at this time surprised Johnson with a spontaneous compliment of the highest academical honours, by creating him Doctor of Laws.

This unsolicited mark of distinction, conferred on so great a literary character, did much honour to the judgment and liberal spirit of that learned body. Johnson acknowledged the favour in a letter to Dr. Leland, one of their number; but I have not been able to obtain a copy of it.

This year was distinguished by his being introduced into the family of Mr. Thrale, one of the most eminent brewers in England, and

Member of Parliament for the borough of Southwark. Foreigners are not a little amazed when they hear of brewers, distillers, and men in similar departments of trade, held forth as persons of considerable consequence. In this great commercial country it is natural that a situation which produces much wealth should be considered as very respectable; and, no doubt, honest industry is entitled to esteem. But, perhaps, the too rapid advances of men of low extraction tends to lessen the value of that distinction by birth and gentility, which has ever been found beneficial to the grand scheme of subordination. Johnson used to give this account of the rise of Mr. Thrale's father: "He worked at six shillings a week for twenty years in the great brewery, which afterwards was his own. The proprietor of it had an only daughter, who was married to a nobleman. It was not fit that a peer should continue the business. On the old man's death, therefore, the brewery was to be sold. To find a purchaser for so large a property was a difficult matter; and, after some time, it was suggested that it would be advisable to treat with Thrale, a sensible, active, honest man, who had been employed in the house, and to transfer the whole to him for £30,000, security being taken upon the property. This was accordingly settled. In eleven years Thrale paid the purchase-money. He acquired a large fortune, and lived to be a Member of Parliament for Southwark. But what was most remarkable was the liberality with which he used his riches. He gave his son and daughters the best education. The esteem which his good conduct procured him from the nobleman who had married his master's daughter, made him be treated with much attention; and his son, both at school and at the University of Oxford, associated with young men of the first rank. His allowance from his father, after he left College, was splendid; not less than a thousand a year. This, in a man who had risen as old Thrale did, was a very extraordinary instance of generosity. He used to say, 'If this young dog does not find so much after I am gone as he expects, let him remember that he has had a great deal in my own time.'"

The son, though in affluent circumstances, had good sense enough to carry on his father's trade, which was of such extent that I remember he once told me he would not quit it for an annuity of ten thousand a year; "Not (said he) that I get ten thousand a year by it, but it is an estate to a family." Having left daughters only, the property was sold for the immense sum of £135,000; a magnificent proof of what may be done by fair trade in a long period of time.

Mr. Thrale had married Miss Hesther Lynch Salusbury, of good

Welsh extraction, a lady of lively talents, improved by education. That Johnson's introduction into Mr. Thrale's family, which contributed so much to the happiness of his life, was owing to her desire for his conversation, is a very probable and the general supposition; but it is not the truth. Mr. Murphy, who was intimate with Mr. Thrale, having spoken very highly of Dr. Johnson, he was requested to make them acquainted. This being mentioned to Johnson, he accepted an invitation to dinner at Thrale's, and was so much pleased with his reception, both by Mr. and Mrs. Thrale, and they so much pleased with him, that his invitations to their house were more and more frequent, till at last he became one of the family, and an apartment was appropriated to him, both in their house at Southwark and in their villa at Streatham.

Johnson had a very sincere esteem for Mr. Thrale, as a man of excellent principles, a good scholar, well skilled in trade, of a sound understanding, and of manners such as presented the character of a plain independent English Squire. As this family will frequently be mentioned in the course of the following pages, and as a false notion has prevailed that Mr. Thrale was inferior, and in some degree insignificant, compared with Mrs. Thrale, it may be proper to give a true state of the case from the authority of Johnson himself, in his own words.

"I know no man (said he) who is more master of his wife and family than Thrale. If he but holds up a finger, he is obeyed. It is a great mistake to suppose that she is above him in literary attainments. She is more flippant; but he has ten times her learning: he is a regular scholar; but her learning is that of a schoolboy in one of the lower forms." My readers may naturally wish for some representation of the figures of this couple. Mr. Thrale was tall, well proportioned, and stately. As for *Madam,* or *my Mistress,* by which epithets Johnson used to mention Mrs. Thrale, she was short, plump, and brisk. She has herself given us a lively view of the idea which Johnson had of her person, on her appearing before him in a dark-coloured gown: "You little creatures should never wear those sort of clothes, however; they are unsuitable in every way. What! have not all insects gay colours?" Mr. Thrale gave his wife a liberal indulgence, both in the choice of their company, and in the mode of entertaining them. He understood and valued Johnson without remission, from their first acquaintance to the day of his death. Mrs. Thrale was enchanted with Johnson's conversation for its own sake, and had also a very allowable vanity in appearing to be honoured with the attention of so celebrated a man.

Nothing could be more fortunate for Johnson than this connexion. He had at Mr. Thrale's all the comforts and even luxuries of life; his melancholy was diverted, and his irregular habits lessened by association with an agreeable and well-ordered family. He was treated with the utmost respect, and even affection. The vivacity of Mrs. Thrale's literary talk roused him to cheerfulness and exertion, even when they were alone. But this was not often the case; for he found here a constant succession of what gave him the highest enjoyment, the society of the learned, the witty, and the eminent in every way; who were assembled in numerous companies, called forth his wonderful powers, and gratified him with admiration, to which no man could be insensible.

In the October of this year he at length gave to the world his edition of "Shakspeare," which, if it had no other merit but that of producing his Preface, in which the excellences and defects of that immortal bard are displayed with a masterly hand, the nation would have had no reason to complain. A blind indiscriminate admiration of Shakspeare had exposed the British nation to the ridicule of foreigners. Johnson, by candidly admitting the faults of his poet, had the more credit in bestowing on him deserved and indisputable praise; and doubtless none of all his panegyrists have done him half so much honour. Their praise was like that of a counsel, upon his own side of the cause: Johnson's was like the grave, well considered, and impartial opinion of the judge, which falls from his lips with weight, and is received with reverence. What he did as a commentator has no small share of merit, though his researches were not so ample, and his investigations so acute, as they might have been, which we now certainly know from the labours of other able and ingenious critics who have followed him. He has enriched his edition with a concise account of each play, and of its characteristic excellence. Many of his notes have illustrated obscurities in the text, and placed passages eminent for beauty in a more conspicuous light; and he has, in general, exhibited such a mode of annotation, as may be beneficial to all subsequent editors.

His "Shakspeare" was virulently attacked by Mr. William Kendrick, who obtained the degree of LL.D. from a Scotch University, and wrote for the booksellers in a great variety of branches. Though he certainly was not without considerable merit, he wrote with so little regard to decency, and principles, and decorum, and in so hasty a manner, that his reputation was neither extensive nor lasting. I remember one evening, when some of his works were mentioned, Dr. Goldsmith said he had never heard of them; upon which Dr. Johnson observed, "Sir, he is one of the many who have made themselves *public,* without making themselves *known."*

In his Preface to "Shakspeare," Johnson treated Voltaire very contemptuously, observing, upon some of his remarks, "These are the petty cavils of petty minds." Voltaire, in revenge, made an attack upon Johnson, in one of his numerous literary sallies, which I remember to have read; but there being no general index to his voluminous works, I have searched in vain, and therefore cannot quote it.

Voltaire was an antagonist with whom I thought Johnson should not disdain to contend. I pressed him to answer. He said, he perhaps might; but he never did.

CHAPTER XVI—1766–1767

Table Talk

In 1764 and 1765 it should seem that Dr. Johnson was so busily employed with his edition of "Shakspeare" as to have had little leisure for any other literary exertion, or, indeed, even for private correspondence. He did not favour me with a single letter for more than two years, for which it will appear that he afterwards apologized.

He was, however, at all times ready to give assistance to his friends, and others, in revising their works, and in writing for them, or greatly improving, their Dedications. In that courtly species of composition no man excelled Dr. Johnson. Though the loftiness of his mind prevented him from ever dedicating in his own person, he wrote a very great number of Dedications for others. Some of these, the persons who were favoured with them are unwilling should be mentioned, from a too anxious apprehension, as I think, that they might be suspected of having received larger assistance; and some, after all the diligence I have bestowed, have escaped my inquiries. He told me a great many years ago, "he believed he had dedicated to all the Royal Family round"; and it was indifferent to him what was the subject of the work dedicated, provided it were innocent. He once dedicated some Music for the German Flute to Edward, Duke of York. In writing Dedications for others, he considered himself as by no means speaking his own sentiments.

Notwithstanding his long silence, I never omitted to write to him, when I had any thing worthy of communicating. I generally kept copies of my letters to him that I might have a full view of our correspondence, and never be at a loss to understand any reference in his letters. He kept the greater part of mine very carefully; and a short time before his death was attentive enough to seal them up in bundles, and order them to be delivered to me, which was accordingly done. Amongst them I found one, of which I had not made a copy, and which I own I read with pleasure at the distance of almost twenty years. It is dated November, 1765, at the palace of Pascal Paoli, in Corte, the capital of Corsica, and is full of generous enthusiasm. After giving a sketch of what I had seen and heard in that island, it proceeded thus: "I dare to call this a spirited tour. I dare to challenge your approbation."

This letter produced the following answer, which I found on my arrival at Paris.

"*A* Mr. Boswell, *chez* Mr. Waters, *Banquier, a Paris.*

"Dear Sir,—

"Apologies are seldom of any use. We will delay till your arrival the reasons, good or bad, which have made me such a sparing and ungrateful correspondent. Be assured, for the present, that nothing has lessened either the esteem or love with which I dismissed you at Harwich. Both have been increased by all that I have been told of you by yourself or others; and when you return you will return to an unaltered, and, I hope, unalterable friend.

"All that you have to fear from me is the vexation of disappointing me. No man loves to frustrate expectations which have been formed in his favour; and the pleasure which I promise myself from your journals and remarks is so great, that perhaps no degree of attention or discernment will be sufficient to afford it.

"Come home, however, and take your chance. I long to see you, and to hear you; and hope that we shall not be so long separated again. Come home, and expect such welcome as is due to him, whom a wise and noble curiosity has led, where perhaps no native of this country ever was before.

"I have no news to tell you that can deserve your notice; nor would

Gordon Ross del.

New York, 1945

An early morning frolic in Covent Garden.

I willingly lessen the pleasure that any novelty may give you at your return. I am afraid we shall find it difficult to keep among us a mind which has been so long feasted with variety. But let us try what esteem and kindness can effect.

"As your father's liberality has indulged you with so long a ramble, I doubt not but you will think his sickness, or even his desire to see you, a sufficient reason for hastening your return. The longer we live, and the more we think, the higher value we learn to put on the friendship and tenderness of parents and of friends. Parents we can have but once; and he promises himself too much who enters life with the expectation of finding many friends. Upon some motive, I hope, that you will be here soon; and am willing to think that it will be an inducement to your return, that it is sincerely desired by, dear Sir,

"Your affectionate humble servant,
"SAM. JOHNSON.

"*Johnson's Court, Fleet Street,*
"*January 14, 1766.*"

I returned to London in February, and found Dr. Johnson in a good house in Johnson's Court, Fleet Street, in which he had accommodated Miss Williams with an apartment on the ground-floor, while Mr. Levet occupied his post in the garret; his faithful Francis was still attending upon him. He received me with much kindness. The fragments of our first conversation, which I have preserved, are these; I told him that Voltaire, in a conversation with me, had distinguished Pope and Dryden thus:—"Pope drives a handsome chariot, with a couple of neat trim nags; Dryden a coach, and six stately horses!" JOHNSON: "Why, Sir, the truth is, they both drive coaches and six; but Dryden's horses are either galloping or stumbling: Pope's go at a steady even trot." He said of Goldsmith's "Traveller," which had been published in my absence, "There has not been so fine a poem since Pope's time."

At night I supped with him at the Mitre Tavern, that we might renew our social intimacy at the original place of meeting. But there was now a considerable difference in his way of living. Having had an illness, in which he was advised to leave off wine, he had, from that period, continued to abstain from it, and drank only water, or lemonade.

I told him that a foreign friend of his, whom I had met with abroad, was so wretchedly perverted to infidelity, that he treated the hopes of immortality with brutal levity; and said, "As man dies like a dog, let him lie like a dog." JOHNSON: *"If he dies like a dog, let him lie like a dog."* I added that this man said to me, "I hate mankind, for I think myself one of the best of them, and I know how bad I am." JOHNSON: "Sir, he must be very singular in his opinion, if he thinks himself one of the best of men; for none of his friends think him so."—He said, "No honest man could be a Deist; for no man could be so after a fair examination of the proofs of Christianity." I named Hume. JOHNSON: "No, Sir; Hume owned to a clergyman in the bishopric of Durham that he had never read the New Testament with attention."—I mentioned Hume's notion, that all who are happy are equally happy; a little miss with a new gown at a dancing-school ball, a general at the head of a victorious army, and an orator, after having made an eloquent speech in a great assembly. JOHNSON: "Sir, that all who are happy are equally happy is not true. A peasant and a philosopher may be equally *satisfied,* but not equally *happy.* Happiness consists in the multiplicity of agreeable consciousness. A peasant has not capacity for having equal happiness with a philosopher." I remember this very question very happily illustrated in opposition to Hume, by the Reverend Mr. Robert Brown, at Utrecht. "A small drinking-glass and a large one (said he) may be equally full; but the large one holds more than the small."

Dr. Johnson was very kind this evening, and said to me, "You have now lived five-and-twenty years, and you have employed them well." "Alas, Sir (said I), I fear not. Do I know history? Do I know mathematics? Do I know law?" JOHNSON: "Why, Sir, though you may know no science so well as to be able to teach it, and no profession so well as to be able to follow it, your general mass of knowledge of books and men renders you very capable to make yourself master of any science, or fit yourself for any profession." I mentioned that a gay friend had advised me against being a lawyer, because I should be excelled by plodding blockheads. JOHNSON: "Why, Sir, in the formulary and statutory part of law, a plodding blockhead may excel; but in the ingenious and rational part of it a plodding blockhead can never excel."

I talked of the mode adopted by some to rise in the world, by courting great men, and asked him whether he had ever submitted to it. JOHNSON: "Why, Sir, I never was near enough to great men to court them. You may be prudently attached to great men and yet independent. You are not to do what you think wrong; and, Sir, you are to calculate, and not pay too dear for what you get. You must not give a shilling's worth of court for sixpence worth of good. But if you can get a shilling's worth of good for sixpence worth of court, you are a fool if you do not pay court."

Our next meeting at the *Mitre* was on Saturday, the 15th of February, when I presented to him my old and most intimate friend, the Reverend Mr. Temple, then of Cambridge. I having mentioned that I had passed some time with Rousseau in his wild retreat, and having quoted some remark made by Mr. Wilkes, with whom I had spent many pleasant hours in Italy, Johnson said (sarcastically), "It seems, Sir, you have kept very good company abroad, Rousseau and Wilkes!" Thinking it enough to defend one at a time, I said nothing as to my gay friend, but answered with a smile, "My dear Sir, you don't call Rousseau bad company. Do you really think *him* a bad man?" JOHNSON: "Sir, if you are talking jestingly of this, I don't talk with you. If you mean to be serious, I think him one of the worst of men; a rascal, who ought to be hunted out of society, as he has been. Three or four nations have expelled him; and it is a shame that he is protected in this country." BOSWELL: "I don't deny, Sir, but that his novel may, perhaps, do harm; but I cannot think his intention was bad." JOHNSON: "Sir, that will not do. We cannot prove any man's intention to be bad You may shoot a man through the head, and say you intended to miss him; but the judge will order you to be hanged. An alleged want of intention, when evil is committed, will not be allowed in a court of justice. Rousseau, Sir, is a very bad man. I would sooner sign a sentence for his transportation than that of any felon who has gone from the Old Bailey these many years. Yes, I should like to have him work in the plantations." BOSWELL: "Sir, do you think him as bad a man as Voltaire?" JOHNSON: "Why, Sir, it is difficult to settle the proportion of iniquity between them."

This violence seemed very strange to me, who had read many of Rousseau's animated writings with great pleasure, and even edification; had been much pleased with his society, and was just come from the Continent, where he was very generally admired. Nor can I yet allow that he deserves the very severe censure which Johnson pronounced upon him. His absurd preference of savage to civilised life, and other singularities, are proofs rather of a defect in his understanding than of any depravity in his heart.

On his favourite subject of subordination, Johnson said, "So far is it from being true that men are naturally equal, that no two people can be half-an-hour together but one shall acquire an evident superiority over the other."

I mentioned the advice given us by philosophers, to console ourselves, when distressed or embarrassed, by thinking of those who are in a worse situation than ourselves. This, I observed, could not apply to all, for there must be some who have nobody worse than they are. JOHNSON: "Why, to be sure, Sir, there are; but they don't know it. There is no being so poor and so contemptible, who does not think there is somebody still poorer, and still more contemptible."

As my stay in London at this time was very short, I had not many opportunities of being with Dr. Johnson; but I felt my veneration for him in no degree lessened, by my having seen *multorum hominum mores et urbes*. On the contrary, by having it in my power to compare him with many of the most celebrated persons of other countries, my admiration of his extraordinary mind was increased and confirmed.

The roughness, indeed, which sometimes appeared in his manners was more striking to me now, from my having been accustomed to the studied smooth complying habits of the Continent; and I clearly recognised in him, not without respect for his honest conscientious zeal, the same indignant and sarcastical mode of treating every attempt to unhinge or weaken good principles.

Another evening Dr. Goldsmith and I called on him, with the hope of prevailing on him to sup with us at the *Mitre*. We found him indisposed, and resolved not to go abroad. "Come, then (said Goldsmith), we will not go to the *Mitre* to-night, since we cannot have the big man with us." Johnson then called for a bottle of port, of which Goldsmith and I partook, while our friend, now a water-drinker, sat by us. GOLDSMITH: "I think, Mr. Johnson, you don't go near the theatres now. You give yourself no more concern about a new play than if you never had anything to do with the stage." JOHNSON: "Why, Sir, our tastes greatly alter. The lad does not care for the child's rattle, and the old man does not care for the young man's whore." GOLDSMITH: "Nay, Sir; but your Muse was not a whore." JOHNSON: "Sir, I do not think she was. But as we advance in the journey of life we drop some of the things which have pleased us; whether it be that we are fatigued and don't choose to carry so many things any farther, or that we find other things which we like better." BOSWELL: "But, Sir, why don't you give us something in some other way?" GOLDSMITH: "Ay, Sir, we have a claim upon you." JOHNSON: "No, Sir, I am not obliged to do any more. No man is obliged to do as much as he can do. A man is to have part of his life to himself. If a soldier has fought a good many campaigns, he is not to be blamed if he retires to ease and tranquillity. A physician who has practised long in a great city may be excused if he retires to a small town and takes less practice. Now, Sir, the good that I can do by my conversation bears the same proportion to the good I can do by my writings, that the practice of a physician, retired to a small town, does to his practice in a great city." BOSWELL: "But I wonder, Sir, you have not more pleasure in writing than in not writing." JOHNSON: "Sir, you *may* wonder."

Such specimens of the easy and playful conversation of the great Samuel Johnson are, I think, to be prized, as exhibiting the little varieties of a mind so enlarged and so powerful when objects of consequence required its exertions, and as giving us a minute knowledge of his character and modes of thinking.

"TO BENNET LANGTON, ESQ., AT LANGTON, NEAR SPILSBY, LINCOLNSHIRE.

"DEAR SIR,—

"What your friends have done, that from your departure till now nothing has been heard of you, none of us are able to inform the rest; but as we are all neglected alike, no one thinks himself entitled to the privilege of complaint.

"I should have known nothing of you or of Langton, from the time that dear Miss Langton left us, had not I met Mr. Simpson, of Lincoln, one day in the street, by whom I was informed that Mr. Langton, your mamma, and yourself, had been all ill, but that you were all recovered.

"That sickness should suspend your correspondence, I did not wonder; but hoped that it would be renewed at your recovery.

"Since you will not inform us where you are, or how you live, I know not whether you desire to know anything of us. However, I will tell you that the Club subsists; but we have the loss of Burke's company since he has been engaged in public business, in which he has gained more reputation than perhaps any man at his [first] appearance ever gained before. He made two speeches in the House for repealing the Stamp Act, which were publicly commended by Mr. Pitt, and have filled the town with wonder.

"Burke is a great man by nature, and is expected soon to attain civil greatness. I am grown greater too, for I have maintained the newspapers these many weeks; and what is greater still, I have risen every morning since New Year's Day at about eight; when I was up, I have indeed done but little; yet it is no slight advancement to obtain for so many hours more, the consciousness of being.

"I wish you were in my new study; I am now writing the first letter in it. I think it looks very pretty about me.

"Dyer is constant at the Club; Hawkins is remiss; I am not over diligent. Dr. Nugent, Dr. Goldsmith, and Mr. Reynolds, are very constant. Mr. Lye is printing his Saxon and Gothic Dictionary; all the Club subscribes.

"You will pay my respects to all my Lincolnshire friends.

"I am, dear Sir,

"Most affectionately yours,

"SAM. JOHNSON.

"*March 9, 1766.*
"*Johnson's Court, Fleet Street.*"

It appears from Johnson's diary, that he was this year at Mr. Thrale's from before Midsummer till after Michaelmas, and that he afterwards passed a month at Oxford. He had then contracted a great intimacy with Mr. Chambers of that University, afterwards Sir Robert Chambers, one of the Judges in India.

He published nothing this year in his own name; but the noble dedication [*] to the King, of Gwyn's "London and Westminster Improved," was written by him; and he furnished the Preface, [†] and several of the pieces, which compose a volume of Miscellanies by Mrs. Anna Williams, the blind lady who had an asylum in his house. Of these, there are his "Epitaph on Philips"; [*] "Translation of a Latin Epitaph on Sir Thomas Hanmer"; [†] "Friendship, an Ode"; [*] and "The Ant," [*] a paraphrase from the Proverbs, of which I have a copy in his own handwriting; and, from internal evidence, I ascribe to him, "To Miss —— on her giving the Author a gold and silk network Purse of her own weaving"; [†] and "The Happy Life." [†] Most of the pieces of this volume have evidently received additions from his superior pen, particularly "Verses to Mr. Richardson, on his Sir Charles Grandison"; "The Excursion"; "Reflections on a Grave Digging in Westminster Abbey." There is in this collection a poem, "On the Death of Stephen Grey, the Electrician," [*] which, on reading it, appeared to me to be undoubtedly Johnson's. I asked Mrs. Williams whether it was not his. "Sir (said she, with some warmth), I wrote that poem before I had the honour of Dr. Johnson's acquaintance." I, however, was so much impressed with my first notion, that I mentioned it to Johnson, repeating, at the same time, what Mrs. Williams had said. His answer was, "It is true, Sir, that she wrote it before she was acquainted with me; but she has not told you that I wrote it all over again, except two lines." "The Fountains," [†] a beautiful little Fairy tale in prose, written with exquisite simplicity, is one of Johnson's productions; and I cannot withhold from Mrs. Thrale the praise of being the author of that admirable poem, "The Three Warnings."

He wrote this year a letter, not intended for publication, which has, perhaps, as strong marks of his sentiment and style, as any of his compositions. The original is in my possession. It is addressed to the late Mr. William Drummond, bookseller in Edinburgh, a gentleman of good family, but small estate, who took arms for the House of Stuart in 1745; and during his concealment in London till the act of general pardon came out, obtained the acquaintance of Dr. Johnson, who justly esteemed him as a very worthy man. It seems, some of the members of the society in Scotland for Propagating Christian Knowledge had opposed the scheme of translating the Holy Scriptures into the Erse or Gaelic language, from political considerations of the disadvantage of keeping up the distinction between the Highlanders and the other inhabitants of North-Britain. Dr. Johnson being informed of this, I suppose by Mr. Drummond, wrote with a generous indignation as follows:—

"TO MR. WILLIAM DRUMMOND.

"SIR,—
"I did not expect to hear that it could be, in an assembly convened for the propagation of Christian knowledge, a question whether any nation uninstructed in religion should receive instruction; or whether that instruction should be imparted to them by a translation of the holy books into their own language. If obedience to the will of God be necessary to happiness, and knowledge of his will be necessary to obedience, I know not how he that withholds this knowledge, or delays it, can be said to love his neighbour as himself. He that voluntarily continues in ignorance is guilty of all the crimes which ignorance produces; as to him that should extinguish the tapers of a lighthouse might justly be imputed the calamities of shipwrecks. Christianity is the highest perfection of humanity; and as no man is good but as he wishes the good of others, no man can be good in the highest degree who wishes

not to others the largest measures of the greatest good. To omit for a year, or for a day, the most efficacious method of advancing Christianity, in compliance with any purposes that terminate on this side of the grave, is a crime of which I know not that the world has yet had an example, except in the practice of the planters of America, a race of mortals whom, I suppose, no other man wishes to resemble.

"The Papists have, indeed, denied to the laity the use of the Bible; but this prohibition, in few places now very rigorously enforced, is defended by arguments which have for their foundation the care of souls. To obscure, upon motives merely political, the light of revelation, is a practice reserved for the reformed; and, surely, the blackest midnight of popery is meridian sunshine to such a reformation. I am not very willing that any language should be totally extinguished. The similitude and derivation of languages afford the most indubitable proof of the traduction of nations, and the genealogy of mankind. They add often physical certainty to historical evidence; and often supply the only evidence of ancient migrations, and of the revolutions of ages which left no written monuments behind them.

"Every man's opinions, at least his desires, are a little influenced by his favourite studies. My zeal for languages may seem, perhaps, rather over-heated, even to those by whom I desire to be well esteemed. To those who have nothing in their thoughts but trade or policy, present power, or present money, I should not think it necessary to defend my opinions; but with men of letters I would not unwillingly compound, by wishing the continuance of every language, however narrow in its extent, or however incommodious for common purposes, till it is reposited in some version of a known book, that it may be always hereafter examined and compared with other languages, and then permitting its disuse. For this purpose, the translation of the Bible is most to be desired. It is not certain that the same method will not preserve the Highland language, for the purposes of learning, and abolish it from daily use. When the Highlanders read the Bible they will naturally wish to have its obscurities cleared, and to know the history, collateral or appendant. Knowledge always desires increase; it is like fire, which must first be kindled by some external agent, but which will afterward propagate itself. When they once desire to learn, they will naturally have recourse to the nearest language by which that desire can be gratified; and one will tell another that if he would attain knowledge he must learn English.

"This speculation may, perhaps, be thought more subtle than the grossness of real life will easily admit. Let it, however, be remembered, that the efficacy of ignorance has long been tried, and has not produced the consequence expected. Let knowledge, therefore, take its turn; and let the patrons of privation stand awhile aside, and admit the operation of positive principles.

"You will be pleased, Sir, to assure the worthy man who is employed in the new translation, that he has my wishes for his success; and if here or at Oxford I can be of any use, that I shall think it more than honour to promote his undertaking.

"I am sorry that I delayed so long to write.

"I am, Sir,

"Your most humble servant,

"SAM. JOHNSON.

"*Johnson's Court, Fleet Street,*
"*Aug. 13, 1766.*"

The opponents of this pious scheme being made ashamed of their conduct, the benevolent undertaking was allowed to go on.

CHAPTER XVII—1767–1768

Johnson and the King

IN FEBRUARY, 1767, there happened one of the most remarkable incidents of Johnson's life, which gratified his monarchical enthusiasm, and which he loved to relate with all its circumstances, when requested by his friends. This was his being honoured by a private conversation with his Majesty, in the library of the Queen's house. He had frequently visited those splendid rooms and noble collection of books,[1] which he used to say was more numerous and curious than he supposed any person could have made in the time which the King had employed. Mr. Barnard, the librarian, took care that he should have every ac-

---

[1] Dr. Johnson had the honour of contributing his assistance towards the formation of this library; for I have read a long letter from him to Mr. Barnard, giving the most masterly instructions on the subject. I wished much to have gratified my readers with the perusal of this letter, and have reason to think that His Majesty would have been graciously pleased to permit its publication; but Mr. Barnard to whom I applied, declined it "on his own account."

commodation that could contribute to his ease and convenience, while indulging his literary taste in that place; so that he had here a very agreeable resource at leisure hours.

His Majesty, having been informed of his occasional visits, was pleased to signify a desire that he should be told when Dr. Johnson came next to the library. Accordingly, the next time that Johnson did come, as soon as he was fairly engaged with a book, on which, while he sat by the fire, he seemed quite intent, Mr. Barnard stole round to the apartment where the King was, and, in obedience to his Majesty's commands, mentioned that Dr. Johnson was then in the library. His Majesty said he was at leisure, and would go to him; upon which Mr. Barnard took one of the candles that stood on the King's table, and lighted his Majesty through a suite of rooms, till they came to a private door into the library, of which his Majesty had the key. Being entered, Mr. Barnard stepped forward hastily to Dr. Johnson, who was still in a profound study, and whispered him, "Sir, here is the King." Johnson started up, and stood still. His Majesty approached him, and at once was courteously easy.[2]

His Majesty began by observing that he understood he came sometimes to the library; and then mentioned his having heard that the Doctor had been lately at Oxford, and asked him if he was not fond of going thither. To which Johnson answered that he was indeed fond of going to Oxford sometimes, but was likewise glad to come back again. The King then asked him what they were doing at Oxford. Johnson answered he could not much commend their diligence, but that in some respects they were mended, for they had put their press under better regulations, and were at that time printing Polybius. He

[2]The particulars of this conversation I have been at great pains to collect with the utmost authenticity, from Dr. Johnson's own detail to myself; from Mr. Langton who was present when he gave an account of it to Dr. Joseph Warton, and several other friends at Sir Joshua Reynolds's; from Mr. Barnard; from the copy of a letter written by the late Mr. Strahan, the printer, to Bishop Warburton; and from a minute, the original of which is among the papers of the late Sir James Caldwell, and a copy of which was most obligingly obtained for me from his son, Sir John Caldwell, by Sir Francis Lumm. To all these gentlemen I beg leave to make my grateful acknowledgments, and particularly to Sir Francis Lumm, who was pleased to take a great deal of trouble, and even had the minute laid before the King by Lord Caermarthen, now Duke of Leeds, then one of his Majesty's Principal Secretaries of State, who announced to Sir Francis the royal pleasure concerning it by a letter, in these words: "I have the King's commands to assure you, Sir, how sensible his Majesty is of your attention in communicating the minute of conversation previous to its publication. As there appears no objection to your complying with Mr. Boswell's wishes on the subject, you are at full liberty to deliver it to that gentleman, to make such use of in his 'Life of Dr. Johnson' as he may think proper."

was then asked whether there were better libraries at Oxford or Cambridge. He answered, he believed the Bodleian was larger than any they had at Cambridge; at the same time adding, "I hope, whether we have more books or not than they have at Cambridge, we shall make as good use of them as they do." Being asked whether All Souls or Christ Church library was the largest, he answered, "All Souls library is the largest we have, except the Bodleian." "Aye (said the King), that is the public library."

His Majesty inquired if he was then writing anything. He answered he was not, for he had pretty well told the world what he knew, and must now read to acquire more knowledge. The King, as it should seem with a view to urge him to rely on his own stores as an original writer, and to continue his labours, then said, "I do not think you borrow much from any body." Johnson said he thought he had already done his part as a writer. "I should have thought so too (said the King), if you had not written so well."—Johnson observed to me, upon this, that "no man could have paid a handsomer compliment; and it was fit for a King to pay. It was decisive." When asked by another friend, at Sir Joshua Reynolds's, whether he made any reply to this high compliment, he answered, "No, Sir. When the King had said it, it was to be so. It was not for me to bandy civilities with my Sovereign." Perhaps no man who had spent his whole life in courts could have shown a more nice and dignified sense of true politeness than Johnson did in this instance.

His Majesty having observed to him that he supposed he must have read a great deal, Johnson answered that he thought more than he read; that he had read a great deal in the early part of his life, but, having fallen into ill-health, he had not been able to read much, compared with others; for instance, he said he had not read much, compared with Dr. Warburton. Upon which, the King said that he heard Dr. Warburton was a man of such general knowledge, that you could scarcely talk with him on any subject on which he was not qualified to speak; and that his learning resembled Garrick's acting in its universality.[3] His Majesty then talked of the controversy between Warburton and Lowth, which he seemed to have read, and asked Johnson what he thought of it. Johnson answered, "Warburton has most general,

[3] The Reverend Mr. Strahan clearly recollects having been told by Johnson that the King observed that Pope made Warburton a Bishop. "True, Sir (said Johnson), but Warburton did more for Pope; he made him a Christian"; alluding no doubt, to his ingenious comments on the "Essay on Man."

most scholastic, learning; Lowth is the more correct scholar. I do not know which of them calls names best." The King was pleased to say he was of the same opinion; adding, "You do not think then, Dr. Johnson, that there was much argument in the case." Johnson said he did not think there was. "Why, truly (said the King), when once it comes to calling names, argument is pretty well at an end."

His Majesty then asked him what he thought of Lord Lyttelton's history, which was then just published. Johnson said he thought his style pretty good, but that he had blamed Henry the Second rather too much. "Why (said the King), they seldom do these things by halves." "No, Sir (answered Johnson), not to Kings." But fearing to be misunderstood, he proceeded to explain himself; and immediately subjoined, "That for those who spoke worse of Kings than they deserved, he could find no excuse; but that he could more easily conceive how some might speak better of them than they deserved, without any ill intention; for, as Kings had much in their power to give, those who were favoured by them would frequently, from gratitude, exaggerate their praises; and as this proceeded from a good motive, it was certainly excusable, as far as error could be excusable."

The King asked him what he thought of Dr. Hill. Johnson answered that he was an ingenious man, but had no veracity; and immediately mentioned, as an instance of it, an assertion of that writer, that he had seen objects magnified to a much greater degree by using three or four microscopes at a time than by using one. "Now (added Johnson), every one acquainted with microscopes knows that the more of them he looks through the less the object will appear." "Why (replied the King), this is not only telling an untruth, but telling it clumsily; for, if that be the case, every one who can look through a microscope will be able to detect him."

"I now (said Johnson to his friends, when relating what had passed) began to consider that I was depreciating this man in the estimation of his Sovereign, and thought it was time for me to say something that might be more favourable." He added, therefore, that Dr. Hill was, notwithstanding, a very curious observer; and if he would have been contented to tell the world no more than he knew, he might have been a very considerable man, and needed not to have recourse to such mean expedients to raise his reputation.

The King then talked of literary journals, mentioned particularly the *Journal des Savans,* and asked Johnson if it was well done. Johnson said it was formerly very well done, and gave some account of the persons who began it, and carried it on for some years: enlarging, at the same time, on the nature and use of such works. The King asked him if it was well done now. Johnson answered he had no reason to think that it was. The King then asked him if there were any other literary journals published in this kingdom, except the *Monthly* and *Critical Reviews;* and on being answered there was no other, his Majesty asked which of them was the best; Johnson answered that the *Monthly Review* was done with most care, the *Critical* upon the best principles; adding that the authors of the *Monthly Review* were enemies to the Church. This, the King said, he was sorry to hear.

The conversation next turned on the "Philosophical Transactions," when Johnson observed that they had now a better method of arranging their materials than formerly. "Ay (said the King), they are obliged to Dr. Johnson for that"; for his Majesty had heard and remembered the circumstance which Johnson himself had forgot.

His Majesty expressed a desire to have the literary biography of this country ably executed, and proposed to Dr. Johnson to undertake it. Johnson signified his readiness to comply with his Majesty's wishes.

During the whole of this interview Johnson talked to his Majesty with profound respect, but still in his firm, manly manner, with a sonorous voice, and never in that subdued tone which is commonly used at the levée and in the drawing-room. After the King withdrew, Johnson showed himself highly pleased with his Majesty's conversation and gracious behaviour. He said to Mr. Barnard, "Sir, they may talk of the King as they will; but he is the finest gentleman I have ever seen." And he afterward observed to Mr. Langton, "Sir, his manners are those of as fine a gentleman as we may suppose Lewis the Fourteenth or Charles the Second."

At Sir Joshua Reynolds's, where a circle of Johnson's friends was collected round him to hear his account of this memorable conversation, Dr. Joseph Warton, in his frank and lively manner, was very active in pressing him to mention the particulars. "Come, now, Sir, this is an interesting matter; do favour us with it." Johnson, with great good humour, complied.

He told them, "I found his Majesty wished I should talk, and I made it my business to talk. I find it does a man good to be talked to by his Sovereign. In the first place, a man cannot be in a passion———." Here some question interrupted him, which is to be regretted, as he certainly would have pointed out and illustrated many circumstances of advantage, from being in a situation where the powers of the mind are at once excited to vigorous exertion, and tempered by reverential awe.

During all the time in which Dr. Johnson was employed in relating to the circle at Sir Joshua Reynolds's the particulars of what passed between the King and him, Dr. Goldsmith remained unmoved upon a sofa at some distance, affecting not to join in the least in the eager curiosity of the company. He assigned as a reason for his gloom and seeming inattention, that he apprehended Johnson had relinquished his purpose of furnishing him with a Prologue to his play, with the hopes of which he had been flattered; but it was strongly suspected that he was fretting with chagrin and envy at the singular honour Dr. Johnson had lately enjoyed. At length the frankness and simplicity of his natural character prevailed. He sprang from the sofa, advanced to Johnson, and in a kind of flutter, from imagining himself in the situation which he had just been hearing described, exclaimed, "Well you acquitted yourself in this conversation better than I should have done; for I should have bowed and stammered through the whole of it."

It appears from his notes of the state of his mind, that he suffered great perturbation and distraction in 1768. Nothing of his writing was given to the public this year, except the Prologue [*] to his friend Goldsmith's comedy of "The Good-natured Man." The first lines of this Prologue are strongly characteristical of the dismal gloom of his mind; which in his case, as in the case of all who are distressed with the same malady of imagination, transfers to others its own feelings. Who could suppose it was to introduce a comedy, when Mr. Bensley solemnly began—

> "Press'd with the load of life, the weary mind
> Surveys the general toil of human kind."

But this dark ground might make Goldsmith's humour shine the more.

In the spring of this year, having published my "Account of Corsica, with the Journal of a Tour to that Island," I returned to London, very desirous to see Dr. Johnson and hear him upon the subject. I found he was at Oxford, with his friend Mr. Chambers, who was now Vinerian Professor, and lived in New Inn Hall. I found that Dr. Johnson had sent a letter to me to Scotland, and that I had nothing to complain of but his being more indifferent to my anxiety than I wished him to be. Instead of giving, with the circumstances of time and place, such fragments of his conversation as I preserved during this visit to Oxford, I shall throw them together in continuation.

I asked him whether, as a moralist, he did not think that the practice of the law, in some degree, hurt the nice feeling of honesty. JOHNSON: "Why, no, Sir, if you act properly. You are not to deceive your clients with false representations of your opinion: you are not to tell lies to a judge." BOSWELL: "But what do you think of supporting a cause which you know to be bad?" JOHNSON: "Sir, you do not know it to be bad or good till the judge determines it. I have said that you are to state facts fairly; so that your thinking, or what you call knowing, a cause to be bad, must be from reasoning, must be from your supposing your arguments to be weak and inconclusive. But, Sir, that is not enough. An argument which does not convince yourself may convince the judge to whom you urge it; and if it does convince him, why, then, Sir, you are wrong, and he is right. It is his business to judge; and you are not to be confident in your own opinion that a cause is bad, but to say all you can for your client, and then hear the judge's opinion." BOSWELL: "But, Sir, does not affecting a warmth when you have no warmth, and appearing to be clearly of one opinion when you are in reality of another opinion, does not such dissimulation impair one's honesty? Is there not some danger that a lawyer may put on the same mask in common life, in the intercourse with his friends?" JOHNSON: "Why, no, Sir. Everybody knows you are paid for affecting warmth for your client; and it is, therefore, properly no dissimulation: the moment you come from the bar, you resume your usual behaviour. Sir, a man will no more carry the artifice of the bar into the common intercourse of society, than a man who is paid for tumbling upon his hands will continue to tumble upon his hands when he should walk on his feet."

He renewed his promise of coming to Scotland, and going with me to the Hebrides, but said he would now content himself with seeing one or two of the most curious of them. He said, "Macaulay, who writes the account of St. Kilda, set out with a prejudice against prejudice, and wanted to be a smart modern thinker; and yet he affirms for a truth that, when a ship arrives there, all the inhabitants are seized with a cold."

Dr. John Campbell, the celebrated writer, took a great deal of pains to ascertain this fact, and attempted to account for it on physical principles, from the effect of effluvia from human bodies. Johnson at another time praised Macaulay for his "*magnanimity*," in asserting this wonderful story, because it was well attested. A lady of Norfolk, by a letter to my friend Dr. Burney, has favoured me with the following solution: "Now for the explication of this seeming mystery, which is so very obvious, as, for that reason, to have escaped the penetration of

Dr. Johnson and his friend, as well as that of the author. Reading the book with my ingenious friend, the late Reverend Mr. Christian, of Docking—after ruminating a little, 'The cause (says he) is a natural one. The situation of St. Kilda renders a north-east wind indispensably necessary before a stranger can land. The wind, not the stranger, occasions an epidemic cold.' If I am not mistaken, Mr. Macaulay is dead; if living, this solution might please him, as I hope it will Mr. Boswell, in return for the many agreeable hours his works have afforded us."

He said he had lately been a long while at Lichfield, but had grown very weary before he left it. Boswell: "I wonder at that, Sir; it is your native place." Johnson: "Why so is Scotland *your* native place."

His prejudice against Scotland appeared remarkably strong at this time. When I talked of our advancement in literature, "Sir (said he), you have learnt a little from us, and you think yourselves very great men. Hume would never have written history, had not Voltaire written it before him. He is an echo of Voltaire." Boswell: "But, Sir, we have Lord Kames." Johnson: "You *have* Lord Kames. Keep him; ha, ha, ha! We don't envy you him. Do you ever see Dr. Robertson?" Boswell: "Yes, Sir." Johnson: "Does the dog talk of me?" Boswell: "Indeed, Sir, he does, and loves you." Thinking that I now had him in a corner, and being solicitous for the literary fame of my country, I pressed him for his opinion on the merit of Dr. Robertson's "History of Scotland." But, to my surprise, he escaped.—"Sir, I love Robertson, and I won't talk of his book."

An essay, written by Mr. Deane, a divine of the Church of England, maintaining the future life of brutes, by an explication of certain parts of the Scriptures, was mentioned, and the doctrine insisted on by a gentleman who seemed fond of curious speculation. Johnson, who did not like to hear of any thing concerning a future state which was not authorized by the regular canons of orthodoxy, discouraged this talk; and being offended at its continuation, he watched an opportunity to give the gentleman a blow of reprehension. So, when the poor speculatist, with a serious metaphysical pensive face, addressed him, "But really, Sir, when we see a very sensible dog, we don't know what to think of him," Johnson, rolling with joy at the thought which beamed in his eye, turned quickly round, and replied, "True, Sir; and when we see a very foolish *fellow,* we don't know what to think of *him*." He then rose up, strided to the fire, and stood for some time laughing and exulting.

I told him that I had several times, when in Italy, seen the experiment of placing a scorpion within a circle of burning coals; that it ran round and round in extreme pain; and finding no way of escape, retired to the centre, and, like a true Stoic philosopher, darted its sting into its head, and thus at once freed itself from its woes. *"This must end 'em."* I said this was a curious fact, as it showed deliberate suicide in a reptile. Johnson would not admit the fact. He said Maupertuis was of opinion that it does not kill itself, but dies of the heat; that it gets to the centre of the circle, as the coolest place; that its turning its tail in upon its head is merely a convulsion, and that it does not sting itself. He said he would be satisfied if the great anatomist Morgagni, after dissecting a scorpion on which the experiment had been tried, should certify that its sting had penetrated into its head.

He talked of the heinousness of the crime of adultery, by which the peace of families was destroyed. He said, "Confusion of progeny constitutes the essence of the crime; and therefore a woman who breaks her marriage vows is much more criminal than a man who does it. A man, to be sure, is criminal in the sight of God; but he does not do his wife a material injury, if he does not insult her; if, for instance, from mere wantonness of appetite, he steals privately to her chambermaid. Sir, a wife ought not greatly to resent this. I would not receive home a daughter who had run away from her husband on that account. A wife should study to reclaim her husband by more attention to please him. Sir, a man will not, once in a hundred instances, leave his wife and go to a harlot, if his wife has not been negligent of pleasing."

I asked him if it was not hard that one deviation from chastity should so absolutely ruin a young woman. JOHNSON: "Why, no, Sir; it is the great principle which she is taught. When she has given up that principle, she has given up every notion of female honour and virtue, which are all included in chastity."

A gentleman talked to him of a lady whom he greatly admired and wished to marry, but was afraid of her superiority of talents. "Sir (said he), you need not be afraid; marry her. Before a year goes about, you'll find that reason much weaker, and that wit not so bright." Yet the gentleman may be justified in his apprehension by one of Dr. Johnson's admirable sentences in his life of Waller: "He doubtless praised many whom he would have been afraid to marry; and, perhaps, married one whom he would have been ashamed to praise. Many qualities contribute to domestic happiness, upon which poetry has no colours to bestow; and many airs and sallies may delight imagination, which he who flatters them never can approve."

He praised Signor Baretti. "His account of Italy is a very entertaining book; and, Sir, I know no man who carries his head higher in conversation than Baretti. There are strong powers in his mind. He has not, indeed, many hooks; but with what hooks he has, he grapples very forcibly."

At this time I observed upon the dial-plate of his watch a short Greek inscription, taken from the New Testament, Νὺξ γὰρ ἔρχεται, being the first words of our Saviour's solemn admonition to the improvement of that time which is allowed us to prepare for eternity; "the night cometh when no man can work." He sometime afterwards laid aside this dial-plate; and when I asked him the reason, he said, "It might do very well upon a clock which a man keeps in his closet; but to have it upon his watch which he carries about with him, and which is often looked at by others, might be censured as ostentatious." Mr. Steevens is now possessed of the dial-plate inscribed as above.

He remained at Oxford a considerable time; I was obliged to go to London, where I received his letter, which had been returned from Scotland.

"TO JAMES BOSWELL, ESQ.

"My dear Boswell,—

"I have omitted a long time to write to you, without knowing very well why. I could not tell why I should not write; for who would write to men who publish the letters of their friends, without their leave? Yet I write to you in spite of my caution, to tell you that I shall be glad to see you, and that I wish you would empty your head of Corsica, which I think has filled it rather too long. But, at all events, I shall be glad, very glad, to see you.

"I am, Sir,
"Yours affectionately,
"Sam. Johnson.

"*Oxford, March 23, 1768.*"

I answered thus:

"TO MR. SAMUEL JOHNSON.

"*London, 26th April, 1768.*

"My dear Sir,—

"I have received your last letter, which, though very short, and by no means complimentary, yet gave me real pleasure, because it contains these words, 'I shall be glad, very glad, to see you.'—Surely you have no reason to complain of my publishing a single paragraph of one of your letters; the temptation to it was so strong. An irrevocable grant of your friendship, and your dignifying my desire of visiting Corsica with the epithet of 'a wise and noble curiosity,' are to me more valuable than many of the grants of kings.

"But how can you bid me 'empty my head of Corsica'? My noble-minded friend, do you not feel for an oppressed nation bravely struggling to be free? Consider fairly what is the case. The Corsicans never received any kindness from the Genoese. They never agreed to be subject to them. They owe them nothing; and, when reduced to an abject state of slavery, by force, shall they not rise in the great cause of liberty, and break the galling yoke? And shall not every liberal soul be warm for them? Empty my head of Corsica! Empty it of honour, empty it of humanity, empty it of friendship, empty it of piety. No! while I live, Corsica and the cause of the brave islanders shall ever employ much of my attention, shall ever interest me in the sincerest manner.

*   *   *

"I am, etc.,
"JAMES BOSWELL."

Upon his arrival in London in May, he surprised me one morning with a visit at my lodging in Half-Moon street, was quite satisfied with my explanation, and was in the kindest and most agreeable frame of mind. As he had objected to a part of one of his letters being published, I thought it right to take this opportunity of asking him explicitly whether it would be improper to publish his letters after his death. His answer was, "Nay, Sir, when I am dead, you may do as you will."

He talked in his usual style with a rough contempt of popular liberty. "They make a rout about *universal* liberty, without considering that all that is to be valued, or indeed can be enjoyed by individuals, is *private* liberty. Political liberty is good only so far as it produces private liberty. Now, Sir, there is the liberty of the press, which you know is a constant topic. Suppose you and I, and two hundred more, were restrained from printing our thoughts: What then? What proportion would that restraint upon us bear to the private happiness of the nation?"

This mode of representing the inconveniences of restraint as light and insignificant, was a kind of sophistry, in which he delighted to indulge himself, in opposition to the extreme laxity for which it has been fashionable for too many to argue, when it is evident, upon reflection, that the very essence of government is restraint; and certain it is, that as government produces rational happiness, too much restraint is better than too little. But when restraint is unnecessary, and so close as to gall those who are subject to it, the people may and ought to remonstrate; and, if relief is not granted, to resist. Of this manly and spirited principle, no man was more convinced than Johnson himself.

About this time, Dr. Kenrick attacked him, through my sides, in a pamphlet, entitled "An Epistle to James Boswell, Esq., occasioned by his having transmitted the moral Writings of Dr. Samuel Johnson to Pascal Paoli, General of the Corsicans." I was at first inclined to answer this pamphlet; but Johnson, who knew that my doing so would only gratify Kenrick, by keeping alive what would soon die away of itself, would not suffer me to take any notice of it.

His sincere regard for Francis Barber, his faithful negro servant, made him so desirous of his farther improvement that he now placed him at a school at Bishop Stortford, in Hertfordshire. This humane attention does Johnson's heart much honour.

Soon afterwards, he supped at the Crown and Anchor Tavern, in the Strand, with a company whom I collected to meet him. They were Dr. Percy, now Bishop of Dromore, Dr. Douglas, now Bishop of Salisbury, Mr. Langton, Dr. Robertson, the historian, Dr. Hugh Blair, and Mr. Thomas Davies, who wished much to be introduced to these eminent Scotch *literati;* but on the present occasion he had very little opportunity of hearing them talk, for with an excess of prudence, for which Johnson afterwards found fault with them, they hardly opened their lips, and that only to say something which they were certain would not expose them to the sword of Goliath; such was their anxiety for their fame when in the presence of Johnson. He was this evening in remarkable vigour of mind, and eager to exert himself in conversation, which he did with great readiness and fluency; but I am sorry to find that I have preserved but a small part of what passed.

He was vehement against old Dr. Mounsey, of Chelsea College, as "a fellow who swore and talked bawdy." "I have been often in his company (said Dr. Percy), and never heard him swear or talk bawdy." Mr. Davies, who sat next to Dr. Percy, having after this had some conversation aside with him, made a discovery, which, in his zeal to pay court to Dr. Johnson, he eagerly proclaimed aloud from the foot of the table: "O, Sir, I have found out a very good reason why Dr. Percy never heard Mounsey swear or talk bawdy, for he never saw him but at the Duke of Northumberland's table." "And so, Sir (said Dr. Johnson loudly to Dr. Percy), you would shield this man from the charge of swearing and talking bawdy, because he did not do so at the Duke of Northumberland's table. Sir, you might as well tell us that you had seen him hold up his hand at the Old Bailey, and he neither swore nor talked bawdy; or that you had seen him in the cart at Tyburn, and he neither swore nor talked bawdy. And is it thus, Sir, that you presume to controvert what I have related?" Dr. Johnson's animadversion was uttered in such a manner, that Dr. Percy seemed to be displeased, and soon afterwards left the company, of which Johnson did not at that time take any notice.

Swift having been mentioned, Johnson, as usual, treated him with little respect as an author. Some of us endeavoured to support the Dean of St. Patrick's, by various arguments. One in particular praised his "Conduct of the Allies." JOHNSON: "Sir, his 'Conduct of the Allies' is a performance of very little ability." "Surely, Sir (said Dr. Douglas), you must allow it has strong facts." JOHNSON: "Why, yes, Sir; but what is that to the merit of the composition? In the Sessions-paper of the Old Bailey there are strong facts. Housebreaking is a strong fact; robbery is a strong fact; and murder is a *mighty* strong fact; but is great praise due to the historian to those strong facts? No, Sir; Swift has told what he had to tell, distinctly enough, but that is all. He had to count ten, and he has counted it right."—Then recollecting that Mr. Davies, by acting as an *informer,* had been the occasion of his talking somewhat too harshly to his friend Dr. Percy, for which, probably, when the first ebullition was over, he felt some compunction, he took an opportunity to give him a hit: so added, with a preparatory laugh, "Why, Sir, Tom Davies might have written 'The Conduct of the Allies.' " Poor Tom being thus suddenly dragged into ludicrous notice in presence of the Scottish Doctors, to whom he was ambitious of appearing to advantage, was grievously mortified. Nor did his punishment rest here; for upon subsequent occasions, whenever he, "statesman all over," assumed a strutting importance, I used to hail him—*"the Author of the Conduct of the Allies."*

When I called upon Dr. Johnson next morning, I found him highly satisfied with his colloquial prowess the preceding evening. "Well (said he), we had good talk." BOSWELL: "Yes, Sir; you tossed and gored several persons."

The late Alexander Earl of Eglinton, who loved wit more than wine, and men of genius more than sycophants, had a great admiration of

Johnson; but from the remarkable elegance of his own manners, was, perhaps, too delicately sensible of the roughness which sometimes appeared in Johnson's behaviour. One evening about this time, when his Lordship did me the honour to sup at my lodgings with Dr. Robertson and several other men of literary distinction, he regretted that Johnson had not been educated with more refinement, and lived in more polished society. "No, no, my Lord (said Signor Baretti), do with him what you would, he would always have been a bear." "True (answered the Earl, with a smile), but he would have been a *dancing bear.*"

To obviate all the reflections which have gone round the world to Johnson's prejudice, by applying to him the epithet of a *bear,* let me impress upon my readers a just and happy saying of my friend Goldsmith, who knew him well: "Johnson, to be sure, has a roughness in his manner; but no man alive has a more tender heart. *He has nothing of the bear but his skin.*"

CHAPTER XVIII—1769

Baretti's Trial

IN 1769, so far as I can discover, the public was favoured with nothing of Johnson's composition, either for himself or any of his friends. His "Meditations" too strongly prove that he suffered much both in body and mind; yet was he perpetually striving against *evil,* and nobly endeavouring to advance his intellectual and devotional improvement. Every generous and grateful heart must feel for the distresses of so eminent a benefactor to mankind; and now that his unhappiness is certainly known, must respect that dignity of character which prevented him from complaining.

His Majesty having the preceding year instituted the Royal Academy of Arts in London, Johnson had now the honour of being appointed Professor in Ancient Literature. In the course of the year he wrote some letters to Mrs. Thrale, passed some part of the summer at Oxford and at Lichfield, and when at Oxford he wrote the following letter:

"TO THE REVEREND MR. THOMAS WARTON.

"DEAR SIR,—

"Many years ago, when I used to read in the library of your College, I promised to recompense the College for that permission, by adding to their books a Baskerville's Virgil. I have now sent it, and desire you to reposit it on the shelves in my name.

"If you will be pleased to let me know when you have an hour of leisure, I will drink tea with you. I am engaged for the afternoon, tomorrow and on Friday; all my mornings are my own.

"I am, etc.,

"SAM. JOHNSON.

"*May 31, 1769.*"

Stratford-on-Avon

I came to London in the autumn, and having informed him that I was going to be married in a few months, I wished to have as much of his conversation as I could before engaging in a state of life which would probably keep me more in Scotland, and prevent me seeing him so often as when I was a single man; but I found he was at Brighthelmstone with Mr. and Mrs. Thrale.

From Brighthelmstone Dr. Johnson wrote me the following letter, which they who may think that I ought to have suppressed, must have less ardent feelings than I have always avowed.

"TO JAMES BOSWELL, ESQ.

"DEAR SIR,—

"Why do you charge me with unkindness? I have omitted nothing that could do you good, or give you pleasure, unless it be that I have forborne to tell you my opinion of your 'Account of Corsica.' I believe my opinion, if you think well of my judgment, might have given you pleasure; but when it is considered how much vanity is excited by praise, I am not sure that it would have done you good. Your History is like other histories, but your Journal is in a very high degree curious and delightful. There is between the history and the journal that difference which there will always be found between notions borrowed from without, and notions generated within. Your history was copied from books; your journal rose out of your own experience and observation. You express images which operated strongly upon yourself, and you have impressed them with great force upon your readers. I know not whether I could name any narrative by which curiosity is better excited, or better gratified.

"I am glad that you are going to be married; and as I wish you well in things of less importance, wish you well with proportionate ardour in this crisis of your life. What I can contribute to your happiness, I should be very unwilling to withhold; for I have always loved and valued you, and shall love you and value you still more, as you become more regular and useful: effects which a happy marriage will hardly fail to produce.

"I do not find that I am likely to come back very soon from this place. I shall, perhaps, stay a fortnight longer; and a fortnight is a long time to a lover absent from his mistress. Would a fortnight ever have an end?

"I am, dear Sir,

"Your most affectionate humble servant,

"SAM. JOHNSON.

"*Brighthelmstone.*
"*Sept. 9, 1769.*"

After his return to town, we met frequently, and I continued the practice of making notes of his conversation, though not with so much assiduity as I wish I had done. At this time, indeed, I had a sufficient excuse for not being able to appropriate so much time to my journal; for General Paoli, after Corsica had been overpowered by the monarchy of France, was now no longer at the head of his brave country-men, but having with difficulty escaped from his native island, had sought an asylum in Great Britain; and it was my duty, as well as my pleasure, to attend much upon him. Such particulars of Johnson's con-versation at this period as I have committed to writing, I shall here introduce, without any strict attention to methodical arrangement. Sometimes short notes of different days shall be blended together, and sometimes a day may seem important enough to be separately dis-tinguished.

He said he would not have Sunday kept with rigid severity and gloom, but with a gravity and simplicity of behaviour.

He said, "The duration of Parliament, whether for seven years, or the life of the King, appears to me so immaterial, that I would not give half-a-crown to turn the scale one way or the other. The *habeas corpus* is the single advantage which our government has over that of other countries."

On the 30th of September we dined together at the *Mitre*. I at-tempted to argue for the superior happiness of the savage life, upon the usual fanciful topics. JOHNSON: "Sir, there can be nothing more false. The savages have no bodily advantages beyond those of civilized men. They have not better health; and as to care or mental uneasiness, they are not above it, but below it, like bears. No, Sir; you are not to talk such paradox; let me have no more on't. It cannot entertain, far less can it instruct. Lord Monboddo, one of your Scotch judges, talked a great deal of such nonsense. I suffered *him;* but I will not suffer *you.*" BOSWELL: "But, Sir, does not Rousseau talk such nonsense?" JOHN-SON: "True, Sir, but Rousseau *knows* he is talking nonsense, and laughs at the world for staring at him." BOSWELL: "How so, Sir?" JOHNSON: "Why, Sir, a man who talks nonsense so well must know that he is talking nonsense. But I am *afraid* (chuckling and laughing) Monboddo does *not* know that he is talking nonsense." BOSWELL: "Is it wrong then, Sir, to affect singularity, in order to make people stare?" JOHNSON: "Yes, if you do it by propagating error; and, indeed, it is wrong in any way. There is in human nature a general inclination to make people stare: and every wise man has himself to cure of it, and does cure himself. If you wish to make people stare by doing better than others, why, make them stare till they stare their eyes out. But consider how easy it is to make people stare, by being absurd. I may do it by going into a drawing-room without my shoes. You remember the gentleman in the *Spectator,* who had a commission of lunacy taken out against him for his extreme singularity, such as never wearing a wig, but a night-cap. Now, Sir, abstractedly, the night-cap was best; but, relatively, the advantage was overbalanced by his making the boys run after him."

Talking of a London life, he said, "The happiness of London is not to be conceived but by those who have been in it. I will venture to say there is more learning and science within the circumference of ten miles from where we now sit, than in all the rest of the kingdom." BOSWELL: "The only disadvantage is, the great distance at which people live from one another." JOHNSON: "Yes, Sir; but that is occasioned by the largeness of it, which is the cause of all the other advantages." BOSWELL: "Sometimes I have been in the humour of wishing to retire to a desert." JOHNSON: "Sir, you have desert enough in Scotland."

When I censured a gentleman of my acquaintance for marrying a second time, as it showed a disregard of his first wife, he said, "Not at all, Sir. On the contrary, were he not to marry again, it might be concluded that his first wife had given him a disgust to marriage; but by taking a second wife he pays the highest compliment to the first, by showing that she made him so happy as a married man, that he wishes to be so a second time." So ingenious a turn did he give to this delicate question. And yet, on another occasion, he owned that he once had almost asked a promise of Mrs. Johnson that she would not marry again, but had checked himself. Indeed I cannot help thinking that in his case the request would have been unreasonable; for if Mrs. Johnson forgot, or thought it no injury to the memory of her first love—the husband of her youth and the father of her children—to make a second marriage, why should she be precluded from a third, should she be so inclined? In Johnson's persevering fond appropriation of his *Tetty*, even after her decease, he seems totally to have overlooked the prior claim of the honest Birmingham trader. I presume that her having been married before had, at times, given him some uneasiness; for I remember his observing upon the marriage of one of our common friends: "He has done a very foolish thing, Sir; he has married a widow, when he might have had a maid."

We drank tea with Mrs. Williams. I had last year the pleasure of seeing Mrs. Thrale at Dr. Johnson's one morning, and had conversation enough with her to admire her talents; and to show her that I was as Johnsonian as herself. Dr. Johnson had probably been kind enough to speak well of me, for this evening he delivered me a very polite card from Mr. Thrale and her, inviting me to Streatham.

On the 6th of October I complied with this obliging invitation, and found, at an elegant villa, six miles from town, every circumstance that can make society pleasing. Johnson, though quite at home, was yet looked up to with an awe, tempered by affection, and seemed to be equally the care of his host and hostess. I rejoiced at seeing him so happy.

He played off his wit against Scotland with a good-humoured pleasantry, which gave me, though no bigot to national prejudices, an opportunity for a little contest with him. I having said that England was obliged to us for gardeners, almost all their good gardeners being Scotsmen. JOHNSON: "Why, Sir, that is because gardening is much more necessary amongst you than with us, which makes so many of your people learn it. It is *all* gardening with you. Things, which grow wild here, must be cultivated with great care in Scotland. Pray now (throwing himself back in his chair, and laughing), are you ever able to bring the *sloe* to perfection?"

Talking of history, Johnson said, "We may know historical facts to be true, as we may know facts in common life to be true. Motives are generally unknown. We cannot trust to the characters we find in history, unless when they are drawn by those who knew the persons; as those, for instance, by Sallust and by Lord Clarendon."

I know not from what spirit of contradiction he burst out into a violent declamation against the Corsicans, of whose heroism I talked in high terms. "Sir (said he), what is all this rout about the Corsicans? They have been at war with the Genoese for upwards of twenty years, and have never yet taken their fortified towns. They might have battered down their walls, and reduced them to powder in twenty years. They might have pulled the walls in pieces, and cracked the stones with their teeth in twenty years." It was in vain to argue with him upon the want of artillery; he was not to be resisted for the moment.

On the evening of October 10, I presented Dr. Johnson to General Paoli. I had greatly wished that two men, for whom I had the highest esteem, should meet. They met with a manly ease, mutually conscious of their own abilities, and of the abilities of each other. The General spoke Italian, and Dr. Johnson English, and understood one another very well, with a little aid of interpretation from me, in which I compared myself to an isthmus which joins two great continents. Upon Johnson's approach, the General said, "From what I have read of your works, Sir, and from what Mr. Boswell has told me of you, I have long held you in great veneration." The General talked of languages being formed on the particular notions and manners of a people, without knowing which we cannot know the language. We may know the direct signification of single words; but by these no beauty of expression, no sally of genius, no wit is conveyed to the mind. All this must be by allusion to other ideas. "Sir (said Johnson), you talk of language, as if you had never done anything else but study it, instead of governing a nation." The General said, *"Questo é un troppo gran complimento";* this is too great a compliment. Johnson answered, "I should have thought so, Sir, if I had not heard you talk."

He talked a few words of French to the General; but finding he did not do it with facility, he asked for pen, ink, and paper, and wrote the following note:

"J'ai lu dans la géographie de Lucas de Linda un Pater-noster écrit dans une langue tout-à-fait différente de l'Italienne, et de toutes autres lesquelles se dérivent du Latin. L'auteur l'appelle linguam Corsicæ rusticam; *elle a peut-être passé, peu à peu; mais elle a certainement prévalue autrefois dans les montagnes et dans la campagne. Le même auteur dit la même chose en parlant de Sardaigne; qu'il y a deux langues dans l'Isle, une des villes, l'autre de la campagne."*

The General immediately informed him that the *lingua rustica* was only in Sardinia.

Dr. Johnson went home with me, and drank tea till late in the night. He said, "General Paoli had the loftiest port of any man he had ever seen." He denied that military men were always the best bred men. "Perfect good breeding," he observed, "consists in having no particular mark of any profession, but a general elegance of manners; whereas, in a military man, you can commonly distinguish the *brand* of a soldier, *l'homme d'épée."*

He honoured me with his company at dinner on the 16th of October, at my lodgings in Old Bond Street, with Sir Joshua Reynolds, Mr. Garrick, Dr. Goldsmith, Mr. Murphy, Mr. Bickerstaff, and Mr. Thomas Davies. Garrick played round him with a fond vivacity, taking hold of the breasts of his coat, and looking up in his face with a lively archness, complimented him on the good health which he seemed then to enjoy; while the sage, shaking his head, beheld him with a gentle complacency. One of the company not being come at the appointed hour, I proposed, as usual upon such occasions, to order dinner to be served; adding, "Ought six people to be kept waiting for one?" "Why, yes (answered Johnson, with a delicate humanity), if the one will suffer more by your sitting down than the six will do by waiting."

After dinner our conversation first turned upon Pope. Johnson said his characters of men were admirably drawn, those of women not so well. He repeated to us, in his forcible melodious manner, the concluding lines of the Dunciad. While he was talking loudly in praise of those lines, one of the company ventured to say, "Too fine for such a poem: —a poem on what?" JOHNSON (with a disdainful look): "Why, on *dunces*. It was worth while being a dunce then. Ah, Sir, hadst *thou* lived in those days! It is not worth while being a dunce now, when there are no wits."

Talking of a Barrister who had a bad utterance, some one (to rouse Johnson) wickedly said that he was unfortunate in not having been taught oratory by Sheridan. JOHNSON: "Nay, Sir, if he had been taught by Sheridan, he would have cleared the room." GARRICK: "Sheridan has too much vanity to be a good man."—We shall now see Johnson's mode of *defending* a man; taking him into his own hands, and discriminating. JOHNSON: "No, Sir. There is, to be sure, in Sheridan something to reprehend, and everything to laugh at; but, Sir, he is not a bad man. No, Sir; were mankind to be divided into good and bad, he would stand considerably within the ranks of good. And, Sir, it must be allowed that Sheridan excels in plain declamation, though he can exhibit no character."

I should, perhaps, have suppressed this disquisition concerning a person of whose merit and worth I think with respect, had he not attacked Johnson so outrageously in his "Life of Swift," and, at the same time, treated us his admirers as a set of pigmies. He who has provoked the lash of wit cannot complain that he smarts from it.

On Thursday, October 19, I passed the evening with him at his house. He advised me to complete a Dictionary of words peculiar to Scotland, of which I showed him a specimen. "Sir (said he), Ray has made a collection of north-country words. By collecting those of your country, you will do a useful thing towards the history of the language." He bade me also go on with collections which I was making upon the antiquities of Scotland. "Make a large book; a folio." BOSWELL: "But of what use will it be, Sir?" JOHNSON: "Never mind the use; do it."

I complained that he had not mentioned Garrick in his Preface to "Shakspeare"; and asked him if he did not admire him. JOHNSON: "Yes, as 'a poor player, who frets and struts his hour upon the stage';— as a shadow." BOSWELL: "But has he not brought Shakspeare into notice?" JOHNSON: "Sir, to allow that would be to lampoon the age. Many of Shakspeare's plays are the worse for being acted; 'Macbeth,' for instance." BOSWELL: "What, Sir, is nothing gained by decoration and action? Indeed, I do wish that you had mentioned Garrick." JOHNSON: "My dear Sir, had I mentioned him, I must have mentioned many more: Mrs. Pritchard, Mrs. Cibber—nay, and Mr. Cibber too; he too altered Shakspeare." BOSWELL: "You have read his apology, Sir?" JOHNSON: "Yes, it is very entertaining. But as for Cibber himself, taking from his conversation all that he ought not to have said, he was a poor creature. I remember when he brought me one of his Odes to have my opinion of it, I could not bear such nonsense, and would not let him read it to the end; so little respect had I for *that great man!* (laughing). Yet I remember Richardson wondering that I could treat him with familiarity."

I mentioned to him that I had seen the execution of several convicts at Tyburn, two days before, and that none of them seemed to be under any concern. JOHNSON: "Most of them, Sir, have never thought at all." BOSWELL: "But is not the fear of death natural to man?" JOHNSON: "So much so, Sir, that the whole of life is but keeping away the thoughts of it." He then, in a low and earnest tone, talked of his meditating upon the awful hour of his own dissolution, and in what manner he should conduct himself upon that occasion: "I know not (said he) whether I should wish to have a friend by me, or have it all between God and myself."

Talking of our feeling for the distresses of others:—JOHNSON: "Why, Sir, there is much noise made about it, but it is greatly exaggerated. No, Sir; we have a certain degree of feeling to prompt us to do good; more than that, Providence does not intend. It would be misery to no purpose." BOSWELL: "But suppose now, Sir, that one of your intimate friends were apprehended for an offence for which he might be hanged." JOHNSON: "I should do what I could to bail him, and give him any other assistance; but if he were once fairly hanged I should not suffer." BOSWELL: "Would you eat your dinner that day, Sir?" JOHNSON: "Yes, Sir; and eat it as if he were eating with me. Why, there's Baretti, who is to be tried for his life to-morrow, friends that have risen up for him on every side; yet if he should be hanged, none of them will eat a slice of plum-pudding the less. Sir, that sympathetic feeling goes a very little way in depressing the mind."

I told him that I had dined lately at Foote's, who showed me a letter which he had received from Tom Davies, telling him that he had not been able to sleep from the concern he felt on account of *"This sad affair of Baretti,"* begging of him to try if he could suggest anything that might be of service; and, at the same time, recommending to him an industrious young man who kept a pickle-shop. JOHNSON: "Ay, Sir, here you have a specimen of human sympathy; a friend hanged and a cucumber pickled. We know not whether Baretti or the pickle-man has kept Davies from sleep; nor does he know himself. And as to his not sleeping, Sir; Tom Davies is a very great man; Tom has been upon the stage, and knows how to do those things; I have not been upon the stage, and cannot do those things." BOSWELL: "I have often blamed myself, Sir, for not feeling for others as sensibly as many say they do." JOHNSON: "Sir, don't be duped by them any more. You will find these very feeling people are not very ready to do you good. They *pay* you by *feeling*."

BOSWELL: "What do you think of Dr. Young's 'Night Thoughts,' Sir?" JOHNSON: "Why, Sir, there are very fine things in them." BOSWELL: "Is there not less religion in the nation now, Sir, than there was formerly?" JOHNSON: "I don't know, Sir, that there is." BOSWELL: "For instance, there used to be a chaplain in every great family, which we do not find now." JOHNSON: "Neither do you find any of the state servants which great families used formerly to have. There is a change of modes in the whole department of life."

Next day, October 20, he appeared for the only time I suppose in his life as a witness in a Court of Justice, being called to give evidence to the character of Mr. Baretti, who, having stabbed a man in the street, was arraigned at the Old Bailey for murder. Never did such a constellation of genius enlighten the awful Sessions House, emphatically called Justice Hall; Mr. Burke, Mr. Garrick, Mr. Beauclerk, and Dr. Johnson: and undoubtedly their favourable testimony had due weight with the Court and Jury. Johnson gave his evidence in a slow, deliberate, and distinct manner, which was uncommonly impressive. It is well known that Mr. Baretti was acquitted.

On the 26th of October we dined together at the Mitre Tavern. We went home to his house to tea. Mrs. Williams made it with sufficient dexterity, notwithstanding her blindness, though her manner of satisfying herself that the cups were full enough, appeared to me a little awkward; for I fancied she put her finger down a certain way, till she felt the tea touch it. In my first elation at being allowed the privilege of attending Dr. Johnson at his late visits to this lady, which was like being *e secretioribus consiliis*, I willingly drank cup after cup as if it had been the Heliconian spring. But as the charm of novelty went off, I grew more fastidious: and, besides, I discovered that she was of a peevish temper.

There was a pretty large circle this evening. Dr. Johnson was in very good humour, lively and ready to talk upon all subjects. Mr. Ferguson, the self-taught philosopher, told him of a new-invented machine which went without horses; a man who sat in it turned a handle, which worked a spring that drove it forward. "Then, Sir (said Johnson), what is gained is, the man has his choice whether he will move himself alone, or himself and the machine too." Dominicetti being mentioned, he would not allow him any merit. "There is nothing in all this boasted system. No, Sir; medicated baths can do no better than warm water; their only effect can be that of tepid moisture." One of the company took the other side, maintaining that medicines of various sorts, and some too of most powerful effect, are introduced into the human frame by the medium of the pores; and, therefore, when warm water is impregnated with salutiferous substances, it may produce great effects as a bath. This appeared to me very satisfactory. Johnson did not answer it; but talking for victory, and determined to be master of the field, he had recourse to the device which Goldsmith imputed to him in the witty words of one of Cibber's comedies: "There is no arguing with Johnson; for when his pistol misses fire, he knocks you down with the butt end of it." He turned to the gentleman; "Well, Sir, go to Dominicetti, and get thyself fumigated; but be sure that the steam be directed to thy *head*, for *that* is the *peccant part*." This produced a triumphant roar of laughter from the motley assembly of philosophers, printers, and dependents, male and female.

BOSWELL: "Do you think, Sir, that what is called natural affection is born with us? It seems to me to be the effect of habit, or of gratitude for kindness. No child has it for a parent whom it has not seen." JOHNSON: "Why, Sir, I think there is an instinctive natural affection in parents towards their children."

Russia being mentioned as likely to become a great empire, by the rapid increase of population: JOHNSON: "Why, Sir, I see no prospect of their propagating more. They can have no more children than they can get. I know of no way to make them breed more than they do. It is not from reason and prudence that people marry, but from inclination. A man is poor; he thinks, 'I cannot be worse, and so I'll e'en take Peggy.'" BOSWELL: "But have not nations been more populous at one period than another?" JOHNSON: "Yes, Sir; but that has been owing to the people being less thinned at one period than another, whether

Gordon Ross del   New York, 1945

Temple Bar.

by emigration, war, or pestilence, not by their being more or less prolific. Births at all times bear the same proportion to the same number of people." BOSWELL: "But, to consider the state of our own country; —does not throwing a number of farms into one hand hurt population?" JOHNSON: "Why, no, Sir; the same quantity of food being produced, will be consumed by the same number of mouths, though the people may be disposed of in different ways. We see, if corn be dear, and butchers' meat cheap, the farmers all apply themselves to the raising of corn, till it becomes plentiful and cheap, and then butchers' meat becomes dear; so that an equality is always preserved. No, Sir, let fanciful men do as they will, depend upon it, it is difficult to disturb the system of life." BOSWELL: "But, Sir, is it not a very bad thing for landlords to oppress their tenants by raising their rents?" JOHNSON: "Very bad. But, Sir, it never can have any general influence; it may distress some individuals. For, consider this: landlords cannot do without tenants. Now, tenants will not give more for land than land is worth. If they can make more of their money by keeping a shop, or any other way, they'll do it, and so oblige landlords to let land come back to a reasonable rent, in order that they might get tenants. Land, in England, is an article of commerce. A tenant who pays his landlord his rent thinks himself no more obliged to him than you think yourself obliged to a man in whose shop you buy a piece of goods. He knows the landlord does not let him have his land for less than he can get from others, in the same manner as the shopkeeper sells his goods. No shopkeeper sells a yard of riband for sixpence when sevenpence is the current price." BOSWELL: "But, Sir, is it not better that tenants should be dependent on landlords?" JOHNSON: "Why, Sir, as there are many more tenants than landlords, perhaps, strictly speaking, we should wish not. But if you please you may let your lands cheap, and so get the value, part in money and part in homage. I should agree with you in that." BOSWELL: "So, Sir, you laugh at schemes of political improvement." JOHNSON: "Why, Sir, most schemes of political improvement are very laughable things."

He observed, "Providence has wisely ordered that the more numerous men are, the more difficult it is for them to agree in any thing, and so they are governed. There is no doubt that if the poor should reason, 'We'll be the poor no longer, we'll make the rich take their turn,' they could easily do it, were it not that they can't agree. So the common soldiers, though so much more numerous than their officers, are governed by them for the same reason."

He said, "Mankind have a strong attachment to the habitations to which they have been accustomed. You see the inhabitants of Norway do not with one consent quit it, and go to some part of America, where there is a mild climate, and where they may have the same produce from land, with the tenth part of the labour. No, Sir; their affectation for their old dwellings, and the terror of a general change, keep them at home. Thus, we see many of the finest spots in the world thinly inhabited, and many rugged spots well inhabited."

When we were alone I introduced the subject of death, and endeavoured to maintain that the fear of it might be got over. I told him that David Hume said to me he was no more uneasy to think he should *not be* after his life, than that he *had not been* before he began to exist. JOHNSON: "Sir, if he really thinks so, his perceptions are disturbed; he is mad: if he does not think so, he lies. He may tell you he holds his finger in the flame of a candle without feeling pain; would you believe him? When he dies, he at least gives up all he has." BOSWELL: "Foote, Sir, told me that when he was very ill he was not afraid to die." JOHNSON: "It is not true, Sir. Hold a pistol to Foote's breast, or to Hume's breast, and threaten to kill them, and you'll see how they behave." BOSWELL: "But may we not fortify our minds for the approach of death?"—Here I am sensible I was in the wrong to bring before his view what he ever looked upon with horror; for although when in a celestial frame of mind in his "Vanity of Human Wishes," he has supposed death to be "kind Nature's signal for retreat," from this state of being to "a happier seat," his thoughts upon this awful change were in general full of dismal apprehensions. His mind resembled the vast amphitheatre, the Coliseum at Rome. In the centre stood his judgment, which, like a mighty gladiator, combated those apprehensions that, like the wild beasts of the *Arena,* were all around in cells, ready to be let out upon him. After a conflict he drives them back into their dens; but not killing them, they were still assailing him. To my question, whether we might not fortify our minds for the approach of death, he answered in a passion, "No, Sir, let it alone. It matters not how a man dies, but how he lives. The act of dying is not of importance, it lasts so short a time." He added (with an earnest look), "A man knows it must be so, and submits. It will do him no good to whine."

I attempted to continue the conversation. He was so provoked that he said: "Give us no more of this"; and was thrown into such a state of agitation that he expressed himself in a way that alarmed and distressed me; showed an impatience that I should leave him, and when I was going away, called to me sternly, "Don't let us meet to-morrow."

I went home exceedingly uneasy. All the harsh observations which I had ever heard made upon his character crowded into my mind; and I seemed to myself like the man who had put his head into the lion's mouth a great many times with perfect safety, but at last had it bit off.

Next morning I sent him a note, stating that I might have been in the wrong, but it was not intentionally; he was, therefore, I could not help thinking, too severe upon me. That notwithstanding our agreement not to meet that day, I would call on him in my way to the city, and stay five minutes by my watch. "You are (said I) in my mind, since last night, surrounded with cloud and storm. Let me have a glimpse of sunshine, and go about my affairs in serenity and cheerfulness."

Upon entering his study, I was glad that he was not alone, which would have made our meeting more awkward. There were with him Mr. Steevens and Mr. Tyers, both of whom I now saw for the first time. My note had, on his own reflection, softened him, for he received me very complacently; so that I unexpectedly found myself at ease; and joined in the conversation.

Johnson spoke unfavourably of a certain pretty voluminous author, saying, "He used to write anonymous books, and then other books commending those books, in which there was something of rascality.'

I whispered him, "Well, Sir, you are now in good humour." JOHNSON: "Yes, Sir." I was going to leave him, and had got as far as the staircase. He stopped me, and smiling, said, "Get you gone *in*"; a curious mode of inviting me to stay, which I accordingly did for some time longer.

This little incidental quarrel and reconciliation, which, perhaps, I may be thought to have detailed too minutely, must be esteemed as one of many proofs which his friends had that, though he might be charged with *bad humour* at times, he was always a *good-natured* man; and I have heard Sir Joshua Reynolds, a nice and delicate observer of manners, particularly remark that, when upon any occasion Johnson had been rough to any person in company, he took the first opportunity of reconciliation, by drinking to him, or addressing his discourse to him; but if he found his dignified indirect overtures sullenly neglected, he was quite indifferent, and considered himself as having done all that he ought to do, and the other as now in the wrong.

Being to set out for Scotland on the 10th of November, I wrote to him at Streatham, begging that he would meet me in town on the 9th; but if this should be very inconvenient to him, I would go thither. His answer was as follows:

"DEAR SIR,—

"Upon balancing the inconveniences of both parties, I find it will less incommode you to spend your night here than me to come to town. I wish to see you, and am ordered by the lady of this house to invite you hither. Whether you can come or not, I shall not have any occasion of writing to you again before your marriage, and therefore tell you now that with great sincerity I wish you happiness.

"I am, dear Sir,
"Your most affectionate humble servant,
"SAM. JOHNSON.

"*Nov. 9, 1769.*"

I was detained in town till it was too late on the ninth, so went to him early in the morning of the tenth of November. "Now (said he) that you are going to marry, do not expect more from life than life will afford. You may often find yourself out of humour, and you may often think your wife not studious enough to please you; and yet you may have reason to consider yourself as upon the whole very happily married."

Talking of marriage in general, he observed: "Our marriage service is too refined. It is calculated only for the best kind of marriages; whereas, we should have a form for matches of convenience, of which there are many." He agreed with me that there was no absolute necessity for having the marriage ceremony performed by a regular clergyman, for this was not commanded in Scripture.

I was volatile enough to repeat to him a little epigrammatic song of mine, on Matrimony, which Mr. Garrick had a few days before procured to be set to music by the very ingenious Mr. Dibdin.

A MATRIMONIAL THOUGHT

"IN the blithe days of honey-moon,
With Kate's allurements smitten,
I lov'd her late, I lov'd her soon,
And call'd her dearest kitten.

"But now my kitten's grown a cat,
And cross like other wives,
O! by my soul, my honest Mat,
I fear she has nine lives."

My illustrious friend said, "It is very well, Sir; but you should not swear." Upon which I altered, "O! by my soul," to "Alas, alas!"

He was so good as to accompany me to London, and see me into the post-chaise which was to carry me on my road to Scotland. And sure I am, that however inconsiderable many of the particulars recorded at this time may appear to some, they will be esteemed by the best part of my readers as genuine traits of his character, contributing together to give a full, fair, and distinct view of it.

CHAPTER XIX—1770–1771

"The False Alarm" and "Falkland Islands"

In 1770 he published a political pamphlet entitled, "The False Alarm," intended to justify the conduct of the Ministry and their majority in the House of Commons for having virtually assumed it as an axiom that the expulsion of a Member of Parliament was equivalent to exclusion, and thus having declared Colonel Lutterel to be duly elected for the county of Middlesex, notwithstanding Mr. Wilkes had a great majority of votes. This being justly considered as a gross violation of the right of election, an alarm for the Constitution extended itself all over the kingdom. To prove this alarm to be false was the purpose of Johnson's pamphlet; but even his vast powers were inadequate to cope with constitutional truth and reason, and his argument failed of effect; and the House of Commons have since expunged the offensive resolution from their Journals. That the House of Commons might have expelled Mr. Wilkes repeatedly, and as often as he should be re-chosen, was not denied; but incapacitation cannot be but by an act of the whole Legislature. It was wonderful to see how a prejudice in favour of government in general, and an aversion to popular clamour, could blind and contract such an understanding as Johnson's, in this particular case; yet the wit, the sarcasm, the eloquent vivacity which this pamphlet displayed, made it be read with great avidity at the time, and it will ever be read with pleasure, for the sake of its composition. That it endeavoured to infuse a narcotic indifference, as to public concerns, into the minds of the people, and that it broke out sometimes into an extreme coarseness of contemptuous abuse, is but too evident.

During this year there was a total cessation of all correspondence between Dr. Johnson and me, without any coldness on either side, but merely from procrastination, continued from day to day; and as I was not in London, I had no opportunity of enjoying his company and recording his conversation. To supply this blank, I shall present my readers with some *Collectanea*, obligingly furnished to me by the Rev. Dr. Maxwell, of Falkland, in Ireland, some time assistant preacher at the Temple, and for many years the social friend of Johnson, who spoke of him with a very kind regard.

"My acquaintance with that great and venerable character commenced in the year 1754. Though I can hope to add but little to the celebrity of so exalted a character, by any communications I can furnish, yet, out of pure respect to his memory, I will venture to transmit to you some anecdotes concerning him, which fell under my own observation. The very *minutiæ* of such a character must be interesting and may be compared to the filings of diamonds.

"In politics he was deemed a Tory, but certainly was not so in the obnoxious or party sense of the term: for while he asserted the legal and salutary prerogatives of the crown, he no less respected the constitutional liberties of the people. Whiggism, at the time of the Revolution, he said, was accompanied with certain principles; but latterly, as a mere party distinction under Walpole and the Pelhams, was no better than the politics of stock-jobbers, and the religion of infidels.

"His general mode of life, during my acquaintance, seemed to be pretty uniform. About twelve o'clock I commonly visited him, and frequently found him in bed, or declaiming over his tea, which he drank very plentifully. He generally had a *levée* of morning visitors, chiefly men of letters: Hawkesworth, Goldsmith, Murphy, Langton, Steevens, Beauclerk, etc., etc., and sometimes learned ladies; particularly, I remember a French lady of wit and fashion doing him the honour of a visit. He seemed to me to be considered as a kind of public oracle, whom everybody thought they had a right to visit and consult; and doubtless they were well rewarded. I never could discover how he found time for his compositions. He declaimed all the morning, then went to dinner at a tavern, where he commonly stayed late, and then drank his tea at some friend's house, over which he loitered a great while, but seldom took supper. I fancy he must have read and wrote chiefly in the night, for I can scarcely recollect that he ever refused going with me to a tavern, and he often went to Ranelagh, which he deemed a place of innocent recreation.

"He frequently gave all the silver in his pocket to the poor, who watched him, between his house and the tavern where he dined. He walked the streets at all hours, and said he was never robbed, for the rogues knew he had little money, nor had the appearance of having much.

"Though the most accessible and communicative man alive, yet when he suspected he was invited to be exhibited, he constantly spurned the invitation.

"Two young women from Staffordshire visited him when I was present, to consult him on the subject of Methodism, to which they were inclined. 'Come (said he), you pretty fools, dine with Maxwell and me at the *Mitre,* and we will talk over that subject'; which they did, and after dinner he took one of them upon his knee, and fondled her for half-an-hour together.

"Upon a visit to me at a country lodging near Twickenham, he asked what sort of society I had there. I told him, but indifferent; as they chiefly consisted of opulent traders, retired from business. He said he never much liked that class of people; 'For, Sir (said he), they have lost the civility of tradesmen, without acquiring the manners of gentlemen.'

"Johnson was much attached to London: he observed that a man stored his mind better there than anywhere else; and that in remote situations a man's body might be feasted, but his mind was starved, and his faculties apt to degenerate, from want of exercise and competition. No place (he said) cured a man's vanity or arrogance so well as London; for as no man was either great or good *per se,* but as compared with others not so good or great, he was sure to find in the metropolis many his equals, and some his superiors. He observed that a man in London was in less danger of falling in love indiscreetly than anywhere else; for there the difficulty of deciding between the conflicting pretensions of a vast variety of objects, kept him safe. He told me that he had frequently been offered country preferment, if he would consent to take orders; but he could not leave the improved society of the capital, or consent to exchange the exhilarating joys and splendid decorations of public life, for the obscurity, insipidity, and uniformity of remote situations.

"He loved, he said, the old black-letter books; they were rich in matter, though their style was inelegant; wonderfully so, considering how conversant the writers were with the best models of antiquity.

"Burton's 'Anatomy of Melancholy,' he said, was the only book that ever took him out of bed two hours sooner than he wished to rise.

"He frequently exhorted me to set about writing a History of Ireland, and archly remarked there had been some good Irish writers, and that one Irishman might at least aspire to be equal to another. He had great compassion for the miseries and distresses of the Irish nation, particularly the Papists; and severely reprobated the barbarous debilitating policy of the British government, which, he said, was the most detestable mode of persecution. To a gentleman who hinted such policy might be necessary to support the authority of the English government, he replied by saying, 'Let the authority of the English government perish, rather than be maintained by iniquity. Better would it be to restrain the turbulence of the natives by the authority of the sword, and to make them amenable to law and justice by an effectual and vigorous police, than to grind them to powder by all manner of disabilities and incapacities. Better (said he) to hang or drown people at once, than by an unrelenting persecution to beggar and starve them.' The moderation and humanity of the present times have, in some measure, justified the wisdom of his observations.

"When exasperated by contradiction, he was apt to treat his opponents with too much acrimony: as, 'Sir, you don't see your way through that question':—'Sir, you talk the language of ignorance.' On my observing to him that a certain gentleman had remained silent the whole evening, in the midst of a very brilliant and learned society, 'Sir (said he), the conversation overflowed, and drowned him.'

"His philosophy, though austere and solemn, was by no means morose and cynical, and never blunted the laudable sensibilities of his character, or exempted him from the influence of the tender passions. Want of tenderness, he always alleged, was want of parts, and was no less a proof of stupidity than depravity.

"Speaking of Mr. Hanway, who published 'An Eight Days' Journey from London to Portsmouth,' 'Jonas (said he) acquired some reputation by travelling abroad, but lost it all by travelling at home.'

"Of the passion of love, he remarked that its violence and ill-effects were much exaggerated; for who knows any real sufferings on that head, more than from the exorbitancy of any other passion?

"He was much affected by the death of his mother, and wrote to me to come and assist him to compose his mind, which, indeed, I found extremely agitated. He lamented that all serious and religious conversation was banished from the society of men, and yet great advantages might be derived from it. All acknowledged, he said, what hardly anybody practised, the obligations we were under of making the concerns of eternity the governing principles of our lives. Every man, he observed, at last wishes for retreat; he sees his expectations frustrated in the world, and begins to wean himself from it, and to prepare for everlasting separation.

"He reproved me once for saying grace without mentioning the name of our Lord Jesus Christ, and hoped in future I would be more mindful of the apostolical injunction.

"He refused to go out of a room before me at Mr. Langton's house, saying he hoped he knew his rank better than to presume to take place of a Doctor in Divinity. I mention such little anecdotes merely to show the peculiar turn and habit of his mind.

"He was of opinion that the English nation cultivated both their soil and their reason better than any other people; but admitted that the French, though not the highest, perhaps, in any department of literature, yet in every department were very high. Intellectual preeminence, he observed, was the highest superiority; and that every nation derived their highest reputation from the splendour and dignity of their writers. Voltaire, he said, was a good narrator, and that his principal merit consisted in a happy selection and arrangement of circumstances.

"Speaking of the French novels, compared with Richardson's, he said they might be pretty baubles, but a wren was not an eagle.

"In a Latin conversation with the Père Boscovitch, at the house of Mrs. Cholmondeley, I heard him maintain the superiority of Sir Isaac Newton, over all foreign philosophers, with a dignity and eloquence that surprised that learned foreigner. It being observed to him that a rage for everything English prevailed much in France after Lord Chatham's glorious war, he said he did not wonder at it, for that we had drubbed those fellows into a proper reverence for us, and that their national petulance required periodical chastisement.

"Being asked by a young nobleman what was become of the gallantry and military spirit of the old English nobility, he replied, 'Why, my Lord, I'll tell you what has become of it; it is gone into the city to look for a fortune.'

"Speaking of a dull, tiresome fellow, whom he chanced to meet, he said, 'That fellow seems to me to possess but one idea, and that is a wrong one.'

"Much inquiry having been made concerning a gentleman, who had quitted a company where Johnson was, and no information being obtained; at last Johnson observed that 'he did not care to speak ill of any man behind his back, but he believed the gentleman was an *attorney.*'

"Speaking of the national debt, he said it was an idle dream to suppose that the country could sink under it. Let the public creditors be ever so clamorous, the interest of millions must ever prevail over that of thousands.

"A gentleman who had been very unhappy in marriage, married immediately after his wife died; Johnson said it was the triumph of hope over experience.

"He observed that a man of sense and education should meet a suitable companion in a wife. It was a miserable thing when the conversation could only be such as whether the mutton should be boiled or roasted, and probably a dispute about that.

"He did not approve of late marriages, observing that more was lost in point of time than compensated for by any possible advantages. Even ill-assorted marriages were preferable to cheerless celibacy.

"Of old Sheridan he remarked that he neither wanted parts nor literature; but that his vanity and Quixotism obscured his merits.

"He said foppery was never cured; it was the bad stamina of the mind which, like those of the body, were never rectified; once a coxcomb, and always a coxcomb.

"Being told that Gilbert Cowper called him the Caliban of literature: 'Well (said he), I must dub him the Punchinello.'

"Speaking of the old Earl of Cork and Orrery, he said, 'that man spent his life in catching at an object (literary eminence), which he had not power to grasp.'

"To find a substitution for violated morality, he said, was the leading feature in all perversions of religion.

"He observed, 'it was a most mortifying reflection for any man to consider *what he had done,* compared with what *he might have done.*'

"He said, few people had intellectual resources sufficient to forego the pleasures of wine. They could not otherwise contrive how to fill the interval between dinner and supper.

"He went with me one Sunday to hear my old Master, Gregory Sharpe, preach at the Temple.—In the prefatory prayer, Sharpe ranted about *Liberty,* as a blessing most fervently to be implored, and its continuance prayed for. Johnson observed that our *liberty* was in no sort of danger:—he would have done much better to pray against our *licentiousness.*

"One evening at Mrs. Montague's, where a splendid company was assembled, consisting of the most eminent literary characters, I thought he seemed highly pleased with the respect and attention that were shown him, and asked him, on our return home, if he was not highly *gratified* by his visit: 'No, Sir (said he), not highly *gratified;* yet I do not recollect to have passed many evenings *with fewer objections.'*

"Though of no high extraction himself, he had much respect for birth and family, especially among ladies. He said, 'adventitious accomplishments may be possessed by all ranks; but one may easily distinguish the *born gentleman.'*

"He said, 'the poor in England were better provided for than in any other country of the same extent: he did not mean little Cantons, or petty Republics. Where a great proportion of the people (said he) are suffered to languish in helpless misery, that country must be ill-policed and wretchedly governed: a decent provision for the poor is the true test of civilization.—Gentlemen of education, he observed, were pretty much the same in all countries; the condition of the lower orders, the poor especially, was the true mark of national discrimination.'

"When the corn-laws were in agitation in Ireland, by which that country has been enabled not only to feed itself, but to export corn to a large amount, Sir Thomas Robinson observed that those laws might be prejudicial to the corn-trade of England. 'Sir Thomas (said he), you talk the language of a savage: what, Sir, would you prevent any people from feeding themselves, if by any honest means they can do it?'

"Speaking of Burke, he said, 'It was commonly observed he spoke too often in Parliament; but nobody could say he did not speak well, though too frequently and too familiarly.'

"Speaking of economy, he remarked it was hardly worth while to save anxiously twenty pounds a year. If a man could save to that degree, so as to enable him to assume a different rank in society, then, indeed, it might answer some purpose.

"He observed, a principal source of erroneous judgment was, viewing things partially and only on *one side:* as, for instance, *fortune-hunters,* when they contemplated the fortunes *singly* and *separately,* it was a dazzling and tempting object; but when they came to possess the wives and their fortunes *together,* they began to suspect they had not made quite so good a bargain.

"Talking of the Irish clergy, he said Swift was a man of great parts and the instrument of much good to his country.—Berkeley was a profound scholar, as well as a man of fine imagination; but Usher, he said, was the great luminary of the Irish church; and a greater, he added, no church could boast of; at least in modern times.

"We dined *tête-à-tête* at the *Mitre*, as I was preparing to return to Ireland, after an absence of many years. I regretted much leaving London, where I had formed many agreeable connexions. 'Sir (said he), I don't wonder at it; no man fond of letters, leaves London without regret. But remember, Sir, you have seen and enjoyed a great deal; —you have seen life in its highest decorations, and the world has nothing new to exhibit.—No man is so well qualified to leave public life as he who has long tried it and known it well. We are always hankering after untried situations, and imagining greater felicity from them than they can afford. No, Sir; knowledge and virtue may be acquired in all countries, and your local consequence will make you some amends for the intellectual gratifications you relinquish.'

"He then took a most affecting leave of me; said he knew it was a point of *duty* that called me away.—'We shall all be sorry to lose you,' said he: *'laudo tamen.'*"

In 1771 he published another political pamphlet, entitled, "Thoughts on the late Transactions respecting Falkland's Islands," in which, upon materials furnished to him by the Ministry, and upon general topics expanded in his rich style, he successfully endeavoured to persuade the nation that it was wise and laudable to suffer the question of right to remain undecided, rather than involve our country in another war. It has been suggested by some, with what truth I shall not take upon me to decide, that he rated the consequence of those islands to Great Britain too low. But, however this may be, every humane mind must surely applaud the earnestness with which he averted the calamity of war; a calamity so dreadful, that it is astonishing how civilized, nay, Christian nations, can deliberately continue to renew it. His description of its miseries in this pamphlet is one of the finest pieces of eloquence in the English language. Upon this occasion, too, we find Johnson lashing the party in opposition with unbounded severity, and making the fullest use of what he ever reckoned a most effectual argumentative instrument—contempt. His character of their very able mysterious champion, Junius, is executed with all the force of his genius, and finished with the highest care. He seems to have exulted in sallying forth to single combat against the boasted and formidable hero, who bade defiance to "principalities and powers, and the rulers of this world."

"TO BENNET LANGTON, ESQ.

"DEAR SIR,—

"After much lingering of my own, and much of the Ministry, I have at length got out my paper. But delay is not yet at an end: Not many had been dispersed, before Lord North ordered the sale to stop. His reasons I do not distinctly know. You may try to find them in the perusal. Before his order, a sufficient number were dispersed to do all the mischief, though, perhaps, not to make all the sport that might be expected from it.

"Soon after your departure, I had the pleasure of finding all the danger past with which your navigation was threatened. I hope nothing happens at home to abate your satisfaction; but that Lady Rothes, and Mrs. Langton, and the young ladies, are all well.

"I was last night at the Club. Dr. Percy has written a long ballad in many *fits;* it is pretty enough. He has printed, and will soon publish it. Goldsmith is at Bath, with Lord Clare. At Mr. Thrale's, where I am now writing, all are well.

" I am, dear Sir,
"Your most humble servant,
"SAM. JOHNSON.

"*March 20, 1771.*"

Mr. Strahan, the printer, who had been long in intimacy with Johnson, in the course of his literary labours; who was at once his friendly agent in receiving his pension for him, and his banker in supplying him with money when he wanted it; who was himself now a Member of Parliament, and who loved much to be employed in political negotiation; thought he should do eminent service, both to government and Johnson, if he could be the means of getting a seat in the House of Commons. With this view, he wrote a letter to one of the Secretaries of the Treasury, of which he gave me a copy in his own handwriting, which is as follows:

"SIR,—

"You will easily recollect, when I had the honour of waiting upon you some time ago, I took the liberty to observe to you that Dr. Johnson would make an excellent figure in the House of Commons, and heartily wished he had a seat there. My reasons are briefly these:

"I know his perfect good affection to his Majesty, and his Government, which I am certain he wishes to support by every means in his power.

"He possesses a great share of manly, nervous, and ready eloquence; is quick in discerning the strength and weakness of an argument; can express himself with clearness and precision, and fears the face of no man alive.

"His known character, as a man of extraordinary sense and unimpeached virtue, would secure him the attention of the House, and could not fail to give him a proper weight there.

"He is capable of the greatest application, and can undergo any degree of labour, where he sees it necessary, and where his heart and affections are strongly engaged. His Majesty's ministers might, therefore, securely depend on his doing, upon every proper occasion, the utmost that could be expected from him. They would find him ready to vindicate such measures as tended to promote the stability of Government, and resolute and steady in carrying them into execution. Nor is anything to be apprehended from the supposed impetuosity of his temper. To the friends of the King, you will find him a lamb; to his enemies, a lion.

"For these reasons I humbly apprehend that he would be a very able and useful member. And I will venture to say the employment would not be disagreeable to him; and knowing, as I do, his strong affection to the King, his ability to serve him in that capacity, and the extreme ardour with which I am convinced he would engage in that service, I must repeat that I wish most heartily to see him in the House.

"If you think this worthy of attention, you will be pleased to take a convenient opportunity of mentioning it to Lord North. If his lordship should happily approve of it, I shall have the satisfaction of having been, in some degree, the humble instrument of doing my country, in my opinion, a very essential service. I know your good-nature, and your zeal for the public welfare, will plead my excuse for giving you this trouble. I am with the greatest respect, Sir,

"Your most obedient and humble servant,
"WILLIAM STRAHAN.

"*New Street,*
"*March 30, 1771.*"

This recommendation, we know, was not effectual; but, how, or for what reason, can only be conjectured. It is not to be believed that Mr.

Strahan would have applied, unless Johnson had approved of it. I never heard him mention the subject; but at a later period of his life, when Sir Joshua Reynolds told him that Mr. Edmund Burke had said that if he had come early into Parliament he certainly would have been the greatest speaker that ever was there, Johnson exclaimed, "I should like to try my hand now."

I at length renewed a correspondence which had been too long discontinued:

"TO DR. JOHNSON.

"*Edinburgh, April 18, 1771.*

"MY DEAR SIR,—

"I can now fully understand those intervals of silence in your correspondence with me, which have often given me anxiety and uneasiness; for although I am conscious that my veneration and love for Mr. Johnson have never in the least abated, yet I have deferred for almost a year and a half to write to him." * * *

In the subsequent part of this letter, I gave him an account of my comfortable life as a married man, and a lawyer in practice at the Scotch bar; invited him to Scotland, and promised to attend him to the Highlands, and Hebrides.

"TO JAMES BOSWELL, ESQ.

"DEAR SIR,—

"If you are now able to comprehend that I might neglect to write without diminution of affection, you have taught me, likewise, how that neglect may be uneasily felt without resentment. I wished for your letter a long time, and, when it came, it amply recompensed the delay. I never was so much pleased as now, with your account of yourself; and sincerely hope that between public business, improving studies, and domestic pleasures, neither melancholy nor caprice will find any place for entrance. Whatever philosophy may determine of material nature, it is certainly true of intellectual nature that it *abhors a vacuum:* our minds cannot be empty; and evil will break in upon them, if they are not pre-occupied by good. My dear Sir, mind your studies, mind your business, make your lady happy, and be a good Christian. After this,—

'————————*tristitiam et metus*
Trades protervis in mare Creticum
Portare ventis.'

[231]

"If we perform our duty, we shall be safe and steady, '*Sive per*,' etc., whether we climb the Highlands, or are tost among the Hebrides; and I hope the time will come when we may try our powers both with cliffs and water. I see but little of Lord Elibank, I know not why; perhaps by my own fault. I am this day going into Staffordshire and Derbyshire for six weeks.

"I am, dear Sir,

"Your most affectionate

"And most humble servant,

"SAM. JOHNSON.

"*London, June 20, 1771.*"

"TO SIR JOSHUA REYNOLDS, IN LEICESTER-FIELDS.

"DEAR SIR,—

"When I came to Lichfield, I found that my portrait had been much visited, and much admired. Every man has a lurking wish to appear considerable in his native place; and I was pleased with the dignity conferred by such a testimony of your regard.

"Be pleased, therefore, to accept the thanks of, Sir, your most obliged, and most humble servant,

"SAM. JOHNSON.

"*Ashbourne in Derbyshire,*
   "*July 17, 1771.*
"*Compliments to Miss Reynolds.*"

"TO BENNET LANGTON, ESQ., AT LANGTON, NEAR SPILSBY, LINCOLNSHIRE.

"DEAR SIR,—

"I am lately returned from Staffordshire and Derbyshire. The last letter mentions two others which you have written to me since you received my pamphlet. Of these two I never had but one, in which you mentioned a design of visiting Scotland, and, by consequence, put my journey to Langton out of my thoughts. My summer wanderings are now over, and I am engaging in a very great work, the revision of my Dictionary; from which I know not, at present, how to get loose.

"If you have observed, or been told, any errors or omissions, you will do me a great favour by letting me know them.

"Lady Rothes, I find, has disappointed you and herself. Ladies will have these tricks. The Queen and Mrs. Thrale, both ladies of experience, yet both missed their reckoning this summer. I hope a few months will recompense your uneasiness.

"Please to tell Lady Rothes how highly I value the honour of her invitation, which it is my purpose to obey as soon as I have disengaged myself. In the meantime, I shall hope to hear often of her ladyship, and every day better news and better, till I hear that you have both the happiness which to both is very sincerely wished by, Sir,

"Your most affectionate and
"Most humble servant,
"SAM. JOHNSON.

"August 29, 1771."

CHAPTER XX—1772

Samuel Foote

IN 1772 he was altogether quiescent as an author; but it will be found, from the various evidences which I shall bring together, that his mind was acute, lively, and vigorous.

"TO DR. JOHNSON.

"MY DEAR SIR,—

"It is hard that I cannot prevail on you to write to me oftener. But I am convinced that it is in vain to expect from you a private correspondence with any regularity. I must, therefore, look upon you as a fountain of wisdom, from whence few rills are communicated to a distance, and which must be approached at its source to partake fully of its virtues.

*   *   *

"I am coming to London soon, and am to appear in an appeal from the Court of Session in the House of Lords. A schoolmaster in Scotland was, by a court of inferior jurisdiction, deprived of his office, for being somewhat severe in the chastisement of his scholars. The Court of Session considering it to be dangerous to the interest of learning and education to lessen the dignity of teachers, and make them afraid of too indulgent parents, instigated by the complaints of their children, restored him. His enemies have appealed to the House of Lords, though the salary is only twenty pounds a year. I was Counsel for him here. I hope there will be little fear of a reversal; but I must beg to have your aid in my plan of supporting the decree. It is a general question, and not a point of particular law.

*   *   *

"I am, etc.,
"JAMES BOSWELL."

"TO JAMES BOSWELL, ESQ.

"DEAR SIR,—

"That you are coming so soon to town, I am very glad; and still more glad that you are coming as an advocate. I think nothing more likely to make your life pass happily away than the consciousness of your own value, which eminence in your profession will certainly confer. If I can give you any collateral help, I hope you do not suspect that it will be wanting. My kindness for you has neither the merit of singular virtue, nor the reproach of singular prejudice. Whether to love you be right or wrong, I have many on my side: Mrs. Thrale loves you, and Mrs. Williams loves you, and what would have inclined me to love you, if I had been neutral before, you are a great favourite of Dr. Beattie.

"Of Dr. Beattie, I should have thought much, but that his lady puts him out of my head; she is a very lovely woman.

"The ejection which you come hither to oppose appears very cruel, unreasonable, and oppressive. I should think there could not be much doubt of your success.

"My health grows better, yet I am not fully recovered. I believe it is held that men do not recover very fast after three score. I hope yet to see Beattie's College: and have not given up the western voyage. But however all this may be, or not, let us try to make each other happy when we meet, and not refer our pleasure to distant times or distant places.

"How comes it that you tell me nothing of your lady? I hope to see her, some time, and till then shall be glad to hear of her.

"I am, dear Sir, etc.,
"SAM. JOHNSON.

"*March 15, 1772.*"

[234]

On the 21st of March, I was happy to find myself again in my friend's study, and was glad to see my old acquaintance, Mr. Francis Barber, who was now returned home. Dr. Johnson received me with a hearty welcome, saying: "I am glad you are come, and glad you are come upon such an errand" (alluding to the cause of the schoolmaster). BOSWELL: "I hope, Sir, he will be in no danger. It is a very delicate matter to interfere between a master and his scholar; nor do I see how you can fix the degree of severity that a master may use." JOHNSON: "Why, Sir, till you can fix the degree of obstinacy and negligence of the scholars, you cannot fix the degree of severity of the master. Severity must be continued until obstinacy be subdued, and negligence be cured." He mentioned the severity of Hunter, his own master. "Sir (said I), Hunter is a Scotch name; so it should seem this schoolmaster, who beat you so severely, was a Scotchman. I can now account for your prejudice against the Scotch." JOHNSON: "Sir, he was not Scotch; and, abating his brutality, he was a very good master."

We talked of his two political pamphlets, "The False Alarm," and "Thoughts concerning Falkland's Islands." JOHNSON: "Well, Sir, which of them did you think the best?" BOSWELL: "I liked the second best." JOHNSON: "Why, Sir, I liked the first best; and Beattie liked the first best. Sir, there is a subtlety of disquisition in the first, that is worth all the fire of the second!" BOSWELL: "Pray, Sir, is it true, that Lord North paid you a visit, and that you got two hundred a year in addition to your pension?" JOHNSON: "No, Sir. Except what I had from the bookseller, I did not get a farthing by them. And, between you and me, I believe Lord North is no friend to me." BOSWELL: "How so, Sir?" JOHNSON: "Why, Sir, you cannot account for the fancies of men.—Well, how does Lord Elibank? and how does Lord Monboddo?" BOSWELL: "Very well, Sir. Lord Monboddo still maintains the superiority of the savage life." JOHNSON: "What strange narrowness of mind now is that, to think the things we have not known are better than the things which we have known." BOSWELL: "Why, Sir, that is a common prejudice." JOHNSON: "Yes, Sir, but a common prejudice should not be found in one whose trade it is to rectify error."

He then spoke of St. Kilda, the most remote of the Hebrides. I told him I thought of buying it. JOHNSON: "Pray do, Sir. We will go and pass a winter amid the blasts there. We shall have fine fish, and we will take some dried tongues with us, and some books. We will have a strong-built vessel, and some Orkney men to navigate her. We must build a tolerable house: but we may carry with us a wooden house ready made, and requiring nothing but to put up. Consider, Sir, by buying St. Kilda, you may keep the people from falling into worse hands. We must give them a clergyman, and he shall be one of Beattie's choosing. He shall be educated at Marischal College. I'll be your Lord Chancellor, or what you please." BOSWELL: "Are you serious, Sir, in advising me to buy St. Kilda? for, if you should advise me to go to Japan, I believe I should do it." JOHNSON: "Why, yes, Sir, I am serious." BOSWELL: "Why, then, I'll see what can be done."

He was engaged to dine abroad, and asked me to return to him in the evening, at nine, which I accordingly did.

We drank tea with Mrs. Williams, who told us a story of second sight, which happened in Wales, where she was born.—He listened to it very attentively; and said he should be glad to have some instances of that faculty well authenticated. His elevated wish for more and more evidence for spirit, in opposition to the grovelling belief of materialism, led him to a love of such mysterious disquisitions. He again justly observed that we could have no certainty of the truth of supernatural appearances, unless something was told us which we could not know by ordinary means, or something done which could not be done but by supernatural power: that Pharaoh in reason and justice required such evidence from Moses; nay, that our Saviour said, "If I had not done among them the works which none other man did, they had not had sin." He had said in the morning that "Macaulay's History of St. Kilda" was very well written, except some foppery about liberty and slavery. I mentioned to him that Macaulay told me he was advised to leave out of his book the wonderful story that, upon the approach of a stranger, all the inhabitants catch cold; but that it had been so well authenticated, he determined to retain it. JOHNSON: "Sir, to leave things out of a book merely because people tell you they will not be believed, is meanness. Macaulay acted with more magnanimity."

In the morning we had talked of old families, and the respect due to them. JOHNSON: "Sir, you have a right to that kind of respect, and are arguing for yourself. I am for supporting the principle, and am disinterested in doing it, as I have no such right." BOSWELL: "Why, Sir, it is one more incitement to a man to do well." JOHNSON: "Yes, Sir; and it is a matter of opinion, very necessary to keep society together. What is it but opinion, by which we have a respect for authority, that prevents us, who are the rabble, from rising up and pulling down you who are gentlemen from your places, and saying, 'We will be gentlemen in our turn'? Now, Sir, that respect for authority is much more easily granted to a man whose father has had it, than to an upstart, and so society is more easily supported." BOSWELL: "Perhaps, Sir, it might be done by the respect belonging to office, as among the Romans, where the dress, the *toga,* inspired reverence." JOHNSON: "Why, we know very little about the Romans. But, surely, it is much easier to respect a man who has always had respect, than to respect a man who we know was last year no better than ourselves, and will be no better next year. In republics, there is no respect for authority, but a fear of power." BOSWELL: "At present, Sir, I think riches seem to gain most respect." JOHNSON: "No, Sir, riches do not gain hearty respect; they only procure external attention. A very rich man, from low beginnings, may buy his election in a borough; but, *cæteris paribus,* a man of family will be preferred. People will prefer a man for whose father their fathers have voted, though they should get no money more, or even less. That shows that the respect for family is not merely fanciful, but has an actual operation. If gentlemen of family would allow the rich upstarts to spend their money profusely, which they are ready enough to do, and not vie with them in expense, the upstarts would soon be at an end, and the gentlemen would remain; but if the gentlemen will vie in expense with the upstarts, which is very foolish, they must be ruined."

On Monday, March 23, I found him busy, preparing a fourth edition of his folio Dictionary. Mr. Peyton, one of his original amanuenses, was writing for him. I put him in mind of a meaning of the word *side* which he had omitted, viz., relationship; as father's side, mother's side. He inserted it. I asked him if *humiliating* was a good word. He said he had seen it frequently used, but he did not know it to be legitimate English. He would not admit *civilization,* but only *civility.* With great deference to him, I thought *civilization,* from *to civilize,* better, in the sense opposed to *barbarity,* than *civility;* as it is better to have a distinct word for each sense than one word with two senses, which *civility* is, in his way of using it.

He seemed also to be intent on some sort of chemical operation. I was entertained by observing how he contrived to send Mr. Peyton on an errand, without seeming to degrade him; "Mr. Peyton—Mr. Peyton, will you be so good as to take a walk to Temple Bar? You will there see a chemist's shop, at which you will be pleased to buy for me an ounce of oil of vitriol; not spirit of vitriol, but oil of vitriol. It will cost three half-pence." Peyton immediately went, and returned with it, and told him it cost but a penny.

We went to the *Mitre,* and dined in the room where he and I first supped together. He gave me great hopes of my cause. "Sir (said he), the government of a schoolmaster is somewhat of the nature of military government; that is to say, it must be arbitrary, it must be exercised by the will of one man, according to particular circumstances. You must show some learning upon this occasion. You must show that a schoolmaster has a prescriptive right to beat; and that an action of assault and battery cannot be admitted against him unless there is some great excess, some barbarity. This man has maimed none of his boys. They are all left with the full exercise of their corporeal faculties. In our schools in England, many boys have been maimed; yet I never heard of an action against a schoolmaster on that account. Puffendorff, I think, maintains the right of a schoolmaster to beat his scholars."

On Saturday, March 27, I introduced to him Sir Alexander Macdonald, with whom he had expressed a wish to be acquainted. He received him very courteously.

Sir A.: "I have been correcting several Scotch accents in my friend Boswell. I doubt, Sir, if any Scotchman ever attains to a perfect English pronunciation." Johnson: "Why, Sir, few of them do, because they do not persevere after acquiring a certain degree of it. But, Sir, there can be no doubt that they may attain to a perfect English pronunciation if they will. We find how near they come to it; and certainly a man who conquers nineteen parts of the Scottish accent may conquer the twentieth. But, Sir, when a man has got the better of nine-tenths he grows weary, he relaxes his diligence, he finds he has corrected his accent so far as not to be disagreeable, and he no longer desires his friends to tell him when he is wrong; nor does he choose to be told. Sir, when people watch me narrowly, and I do not watch myself, they will find me out to be of a particular county. In the same manner, Dunning may be found out to be a Devonshire man. So most Scotchmen may be found out. But, Sir, little aberrations are of no disadvantage. I never catched Mallet in a Scotch accent; and yet Mallet, I suppose, was past five-and-twenty before he came to London."

Upon another occasion I talked to him on this subject, having myself taken some pains to improve my pronunciation, by the aid of the late Mr. Love, Drury-lane Theatre, when he was a player at Edinburgh, and also of old Mr. Sheridan. Johnson said to me, "Sir, your pronunciation is not offensive." With this concession I was pretty well satisfied; and let me give my countrymen of North Britain an advice, not to aim at absolute perfection in this respect; not to speak *High*

English, as we are apt to call what is far removed from the *Scotch,* but which is by no means *good English,* and makes "the fools who use it" truly ridiculous. Good English is plain, easy, and smooth, in the mouth of an unaffected English gentleman. A studied and factitious pronunciation, which requires perpetual attention, and imposes perpetual constraint, is exceedingly disgusting. A small intermixture of provincial peculiarities may, perhaps, have an agreeable effect, as the notes of different birds concur in the harmony of the grove, and please more than if they were all exactly alike. I could name some gentlemen of Ireland to whom a slight proportion of the accent and recitative of that country is an advantage. The same observation will apply to the gentlemen of Scotland. I do not mean that we should speak as broad as a certain prosperous member of Parliament from that country; though it has been well observed that "it has been of no small use to him; as it rouses the attention of the House by its uncommonness; and is equal to tropes and figures in a good English speaker." I would give as an instance of what I mean to recommend to my countrymen the pronunciation of the late Sir Gilbert Elliot: and may I presume to add that of the present Earl of Marchmont, who told me, with great good humour, that a master of a shop in London, where he was not known, said to him "I suppose, Sir, you are an American." "Why so, Sir?" (said his Lordship). "Because, Sir (replied the shopkeeper), you speak neither English nor Scotch but something different from both, which I conclude is the language of America."

BOSWELL: "It may be of use, Sir, to have a Dictionary to ascertain the pronunciation." JOHNSON: "Why, Sir, my Dictionary shows you the accent of words, if you can but remember them." BOSWELL: "But, Sir, we want marks to ascertain the pronunciation of the vowels. Sheridan, I believe, has finished such a work." JOHNSON: "Why, Sir, consider how much easier it is to learn a language by the ear than by any marks. Sheridan's Dictionary may do very well; but you cannot always carry it about with you; and, when you want the word, you have not the Dictionary. It is like a man who has a sword that will not draw. It is an admirable sword, to be sure: but while your enemy is cutting your throat, you are unable to use it. Besides, Sir, what entitles Sheridan to fix the pronunciation of English? He has, in the first place, the disadvantage of being an Irishman; and if he says he will fix it after the example of the best company, why they differ among themselves. I remember an instance: when I published the Plan for my Dictionary, Lord Chesterfield told me that the word *great* should be pronounced so as to rhyme to *state;* and Sir William Yonge sent me word that it should be pronounced so as to rhyme to *seat,* and that none but an Irishman would pronounce it *grait.* Now here were two men of the highest rank, the one the best speaker in the House of Lords, the other the best speaker in the House of Commons, differing entirely."

On Tuesday, March 31, he and I dined at General Paoli's. A question was started, whether the state of marriage was natural to man. JOHNSON: "Sir, it is so far from being natural for a man and woman to live in a state of marriage, that we find all the motives which they have for remaining in that connexion, and the restraints which civilized society imposes to prevent separation, are hardly sufficient to keep them together." The General said that in a state of nature a man and woman uniting together would form a strong and constant affection by the mutual pleasure each would receive; and that the same causes of dissension would not arise between them as occur between husband and wife in a civilized state. JOHNSON: "Sir, they would have dissensions enough, though of another kind. One would choose to go a hunting in this wood, the other in that; one would choose to go a fishing in this lake, the other in that; or, perhaps, one would choose to go a hunting, when the other would choose to go a fishing; and so they would part. Besides, Sir, a savage man and a savage woman meet by chance; and when the man sees another woman that pleases him better, he will leave the first."

We then fell into a disquisition whether there is any beauty independent of utility. The General maintained there was not. Dr. Johnson maintained that there was; and he instanced a coffee-cup which he held in his hand, the painting of which was of no real use, as the cup would hold the coffee equally well if plain; yet the painting was beautiful.

We talked of the strange custom of swearing in conversation. The General said that all barbarous nations swore from a certain violence of temper, that could not be confined to earth, but was always reaching at the powers above. He said, too, that there was greater variety of swearing, in proportion as there was a greater variety of religious ceremonies.

Dr. Johnson went home with me to my lodgings in Conduit-street, and drank tea, previous to our going to the Pantheon, which neither of us had seen before.

He said, "Goldsmith's 'Life of Parnell' is poor; not that it is poorly written, but that he had poor materials; for nobody can write the life

of a man, but those who have eat and drunk and lived in social intercourse with him."

I said that if it was not troublesome and presuming too much, I
would request him to tell me all the little circumstances of his life; what
schools he attended, when he came to Oxford, when he came to
London, etc., etc. He did not disapprove of my curiosity as to these
particulars; but said, "They'll come out by degrees, as we talk together."

We talked of the proper use of riches. JOHNSON: "If I were a man
of great estate, I would drive all the rascals whom I did not like out of
the country, at an election."

I asked him how far he thought wealth should be employed in hospitality. JOHNSON: "You are to consider that ancient hospitality, of
which we hear so much, was in an uncommercial country, when men,
being idle, were glad to be entertained at rich men's tables. But in a
commercial country, a busy country, time becomes precious, and therefore hospitality is not so much valued. No doubt there is still room for
a certain degree of it; and a man has a satisfaction in seeing his friends
eating and drinking around him. But promiscuous hospitality is not
the way to gain real influence. You must help some people at table
before others; you must ask some people how they like their wine
oftener than others. You therefore offend more people than you please.
You are like the French statesman, who said, when he granted a favour,
'*J'ai fait dix mécontents et un ingrat.*' Besides, Sir, being entertained
ever so well at a man's table impresses no lasting regard or esteem. No,
Sir; the way to make sure of power and influence is, by lending money
confidentially to your neighbours at a small interest, or perhaps at no
interest at all, and having their bonds in your possession." BOSWELL:
"May not a man, Sir, employ his riches to advantage, in educating
young men of merit?" JOHNSON: "Yes, Sir, if they fall in your way;
but if it be understood that you patronise young men of merit, you will
be harassed with solicitations. You will have numbers forced upon you,
who have no merit; some will force them upon you from mistaken
partiality; and some from downright interested motives, without
scruple; and you will be disgraced."

We then walked to the Pantheon. The first view of it did not strike
us so much as Ranelagh, of which he said the "*coup d'œil* was the finest
thing he had ever seen." The truth is, Ranelagh is of a more beautiful
form; more of it, or rather indeed the whole *rotunda,* appears at once,
and it is better lighted. However, as Johnson observed, we saw the

Pantheon in time of mourning, when there was a dull uniformity; whereas we had seen Ranelagh when the view was enlivened with a gay profusion of colours. Mrs. Bosville, of Gunthwait, in Yorkshire, joined us, and entered into conversation with us. Johnson said to me afterwards, "Sir, this is a mighty intelligent lady."

I said there was not half a guinea's worth of pleasure in seeing this place. JOHNSON: "But, Sir, there is half a guinea's worth of inferiority to other people in not having seen it." BOSWELL: "I doubt, Sir, whether there are many happy people here." JOHNSON: "Yes, Sir, there are many happy people here. There are many people here who are watching hundreds, and who think hundreds are watching them."

Happening to meet Sir Adam Ferguson, I presented him to Dr. Johnson. Sir Adam expressed some apprehension that the Pantheon would encourage luxury. "Sir (said Johnson), I am a great friend to public amusements; for they keep people from vice. You now (addressing himself to me) would have been with a wench, had you not been here.—O! I forgot you were married."

Sir Adam suggested that luxury corrupts a people, and destroys the spirit of liberty. JOHNSON: "Sir, that is all visionary. I would not give half a guinea to live under one form of government rather than another. It is of no moment to the happiness of an individual. Sir, the danger of the abuse of power is nothing to a private man. What Frenchman is prevented from passing his life as he pleases?" SIR ADAM: "But, Sir, in the British Constitution, it is surely of importance to keep up a spirit in the people, so as to preserve a balance against the crown." JOHNSON: "Sir, I perceive you are a vile Whig.—Why all this childish jealousy of the power of the crown? The crown has not power enough. When I say that all governments are alike, I consider that in no government power can be abused long. Mankind will not bear it. If a sovereign oppresses his people to a great degree, they will rise and cut off his head. There is a remedy in human nature against tyranny that will keep us safe under every form of government. Had not the people of France thought themselves honoured in sharing in the brilliant actions of Louis XIV they would not have endured him; and we may say the same of the King of Prussia's people." Sir Adam introduced the ancient Greeks and Romans. JOHNSON: "Sir, the mass of both of them were barbarians. The mass of every people must be barbarous where there is no printing, and consequently knowledge is not generally diffused. Knowledge is diffused among our people by the newspapers." Sir Adam mentioned the orators, poets, and artists of

Greece. JOHNSON: "Sir, I am talking of the mass of the people. We see even what the boasted Athenians were. The little effect which Demosthenes' orations had upon them shows that they were barbarians."

Sir Adam was unlucky in his topics; for he suggested a doubt of the propriety of bishops having seats in the House of Lords. JOHNSON: "How so, Sir? Who is more proper for having the dignity of a peer than a bishop, provided a bishop be what he ought to be; and if improper bishops be made, that is not the fault of the bishops, but of those who make them."

I mentioned a cause in which I had appeared as counsel at the bar of the General Assembly of the Church of Scotland, where a *Probationer* (as one licensed to preach, but not yet ordained, is called) was opposed in his application to be inducted, because it was alleged that he had been guilty of fornication five years before. JOHNSON: "Why, Sir, if he has repented, it is not a sufficient objection. A man who is good enough to go to heaven, is good enough to be a clergyman." This was a humane and liberal sentiment. But the character of a clergyman is more sacred than that of an ordinary Christian. I told him, that by the rules of the Church of Scotland, in their "Book of Discipline," if a *scandal,* as it is called, is not prosecuted for five years, it cannot afterwards be proceeded upon, "unless it be *of a heinous nature,* or again become flagrant"; and that hence a question arose whether fornication was a sin of a heinous nature; and that I had maintained that it did not deserve that epithet, inasmuch as it was not one of those sins which argue very great depravity of heart: in short, was not, in the general acceptation of mankind, a heinous sin. JOHNSON: "No, Sir, it is not a heinous sin. A heinous sin is that for which a man is punished with death or banishment." BOSWELL: "But, Sir, after I had argued that it was not a heinous sin, an old clergyman rose up, and repeating the text of Scripture denouncing judgment against whoremongers, asked whether, considering this, there could be any doubt of fornication being a heinous sin." JOHNSON: "Why, Sir, observe the word *whoremonger.* Every sin, if persisted in, will become heinous. Whoremonger is a dealer in whores, as ironmonger is a dealer in iron. But as you don't call a man an ironmonger for buying and selling a penknife, so you don't call a man a whoremonger for getting one wench with child."

CHAPTER XXI—1772

General Oglethorpe

ON MONDAY, APRIL 6, I dined with him at Sir Alexander Macdonald's, where was a young officer in the regimentals of the Scots Royals, who talked with a vivacity, fluency, and precision so uncommon, that he attracted particular attention. He proved to be the Honourable Thomas Erskine, youngest brother to the Earl of Buchan, who has since risen into such brilliant reputation at the bar in Westminster Hall.

Fielding being mentioned, Johnson exclaimed, "he was a blockhead"; and upon my expressing my astonishment at so strange an assertion, he said, "What I mean by his being a blockhead is, that he was a barren rascal." BOSWELL: "Will you not allow, Sir, that he draws very natural pictures of human life?" JOHNSON: "Why, Sir, it is of very low life. Richardson used to say, that had he not known who Fielding was, he should have believed he was an ostler. Sir, there is more knowledge of the heart in one letter of Richardson's than in all 'Tom Jones.' I, indeed, never read 'Joseph Andrews.'" ERSKINE: "Surely, Sir, Richardson is very tedious." JOHNSON: "Why, Sir, if you were to read Richardson for the story, your impatience would be so much fretted that you would hang yourself. But you must read him for the sentiment, and consider the story as only giving occasion to the sentiment."—I have already given my opinion of Fielding; but I cannot refrain from repeating here my wonder at Johnson's excessive and unaccountable depreciation of one of the best writers that England has produced. "Tom Jones" has stood the test of public opinion with such success as to have established its great merit, both for the story, the sentiments, and the manners, and also the varieties of diction, so as to leave no doubt of its having an animated truth of execution throughout.

We talked of gaming, and animadverted on it with severity. JOHNSON: "Nay, gentlemen, let us not aggravate the matter. It is not roguery to play with a man who is ignorant of the game, while you are master of it, and so win his money; for he thinks he can play better than you, as you think you can play better than he; and the superior skill carries it." ERSKINE: "He is a fool, but you are not a rogue." JOHN-SON: "That's much about the truth, Sir. It must be considered that a man who only does what everyone of the society to which he belongs would do, is not a dishonest man. In the republic of Sparta, it was agreed that stealing was not dishonourable if not discovered. I do not commend a society where there is an agreement that what would not otherwise be fair, shall be fair; but I maintain that an individual of any society, who practises what is allowed, is not a dishonest man." BOSWELL: "So, then, Sir, you do not think ill of a man who wins, perhaps, forty thousand pounds in a winter?" JOHNSON: "Sir, I do not call a gamester a dishonest man; but I call him an unsocial man, an unprofitable man. Gaming is a mode of transferring property without producing any intermediate good. Trade gives employment to numbers, and so produces intermediate good."

Mr. Erskine told us that when he was in the island of Minorca, he not only read prayers, but preached two sermons to the regiment. He seemed to object to the passage in Scripture where we are told that the angel of the Lord smote in one night forty thousand Assyrians. "Sir (said Johnson), you should recollect that there was a supernatural interposition; they were destroyed by pestilence. You are not to suppose that the angel of the Lord went about and stabbed each of them with a dagger, or knocked them on the head, man by man."

After Mr. Erskine was gone, a discussion took place whether the present Earl of Buchan, when Lord Cardross, did right to refuse to go Secretary of the Embassy to Spain, when Sir James Gray, a man of inferior rank, went Ambassador. Dr. Johnson said that perhaps in point of interest he did wrong; but in point of dignity he did well. Sir Alexander insisted that he was wrong: and said that Mr. Pitt intended it as an advantageous thing for him. "Why, Sir (said Johnson), Mr. Pitt might think it an advantageous thing for him to make him a vintner, and get him all the Portugal trade: but he would have demeaned himself strangely had he accepted of such a situation. Sir, had he gone Secretary, while his inferior was Ambassador, he would have been a traitor to his rank and family."

On Friday, April 10, I dined with him at General Oglethorpe's, where we found Dr. Goldsmith.

I started the question whether duelling was consistent with moral duty. The brave old General fired at this, and said, with a lofty air, "Undoubtedly a man has a right to defend his honour." GOLDSMITH (turning to me): "I ask you first, Sir, what would you do if you were affronted?" I answered I should think it necessary to fight. "Why, then (replied Goldsmith), that solves the question." JOHNSON: "No, Sir, it does not solve the question. It does not follow that what a man would do is therefore right." I said I wished to have it settled whether duelling was contrary to the laws of Christianity. Johnson immediately entered on the subject, and treated it in a masterly manner; and so far as I have been able to recollect, his thoughts were these: "Sir, as men become in a high degree refined, various causes of offence arise; which are considered to be of such importance that life must be staked to atone for them, though in reality they are not so. A body that has received a very fine polish may be easily hurt. Before men arrive at this artificial refinement, if one tells his neighbour—he lies, his neighbour tells him—he lies; if one gives his neighbour a blow, his neighbour gives him a blow; but in a state of highly polished society, an affront is held to be a serious injury. It must, therefore, be resented, or rather a duel must be fought upon it; as men have agreed to banish from their society one who puts up with an affront without fighting a duel. Now, Sir, it is never unlawful to fight in self-defence. He, then, who fights a duel, does not fight from passion against his antagonist, but out of self-defence; to avert the stigma of the world, and to prevent himself from being driven out of society. I could wish there was not that superfluity of refinement; but while such notions prevail, no doubt a man may lawfully fight a duel."

Let it be remembered that this justification is applicable only to the person who *receives* an affront. All mankind must condemn the aggressor.

The General told us that when he was a very young man, I think only fifteen, serving under Prince Eugene of Savoy, he was sitting in a company at table with a Prince of Wirtemberg. The Prince took up a glass of wine, and, by a fillip, made some of it fly in Oglethorpe's face. Here was a nice dilemma. To have challenged him instantly, might have fixed a quarrelsome character upon the young soldier; to have taken no notice of it might have been considered as cowardice. Oglethorpe therefore, keeping his eye upon the Prince, and smiling all the time, as if he took what his Highness had done in jest, said, *"Mon Prince—"* (I forget the French words he used, the purport, however, was), "That's a good joke; but we do it much better in England"; and threw a whole glass of wine in the Prince's face. An old General, who sat by, said, *"Il a bien fait, mon Prince, vous l'avez commencé"*: and thus all ended in good humour.

General Oglethorpe. From a caricature by Ireland

A question was started how far people who disagreed in a capital point can live in friendship together. Johnson said they might. Goldsmith said they could not, as they had not the *idem velle atque idem nolle*—the same likings and the same aversions. JOHNSON: "Why, Sir, you must shun the subject as to which you disagree. For instance, I can live very well with Burke: I love his knowledge, his genius, his diffusion, and affluence of conversation; but I would not talk to him of the Rockingham party." GOLDSMITH: "But, Sir, when people live together who have something as to which they disagree, and which they want to shun, they will be in the situation mentioned in the story of Bluebeard: 'You may look into all the chambers but one.' But we should have the greatest inclination to look into that chamber, to talk of that subject." JOHNSON (with a loud voice): "Sir, I am not saying that *you* could live in friendship with a man from whom you differ as to some point: I am only saying that *I* could do it. You put me in mind of Sappho in Ovid."

On Saturday, April 11, he appointed me to come to him in the evening, when he should be at leisure to give me some assistance for the defence of Hastie, the schoolmaster of Campbelltown, for whom I was to appear in the House of Lords. When I came, I found him unwilling to exert himself. I pressed him to write down his thoughts upon the subject. He said, "There's no occasion for my writing. I'll talk to you." He was, however, at last prevailed on to dictate to me, while I wrote as follows:

"The charge is that he has used immoderate and cruel correction. Correction, in itself, is not cruel; children, being not reasonable, can be governed only by fear. To impress this fear is, therefore, one of the first duties of those who have the care of children. It is the duty of a parent; and has never been thought inconsistent with parental tenderness. It is the duty of a master, who is in his highest exaltation when he is *loco parentis*. Yet, as good things become evil by excess, correction, by being immoderate, may become cruel. But when is correction immoderate? When it is more frequent or more severe than is required *ad monendum et docendum,* for reformation and instruction. No severity is cruel which obstinacy makes necessary; for the greatest cruelty would be to desist, and leave the scholar too careless for instruction, and too much hardened for reproof. Locke, in his treatise of Education, mentions a mother, with applause, who whipped an infant eight times before she had subdued it; for had she stopped at the seventh act of correction, her daughter, says he, would have been ruined. The degrees of obstinacy in young minds are very different: as different must be the degrees of persevering severity. A stubborn scholar must be corrected till he is subdued. The discipline of a school is military. There must be either unbounded licence or absolute authority. The master, who punishes, not only consults the future happiness of him who is the immediate subject of correction, but he propagates obedience through the whole school; and establishes regularity by exemplary justice. The victorious obstinacy of a single boy would make his future endeavours of reformation or instruction totally ineffectual. Obstinacy, therefore, must never be victorious. Yet it is well known that there sometimes occurs a sullen and hardy resolution, that laughs at all common punishment, and bids defiance to all common

Gordon Ross del.

New York, 1945

Blackfriar's Bridge which Johnson criticised severely.

degrees of pain. Correction must be proportioned to occasions. The flexible will be reformed by gentle discipline, and the refractory must be subdued by harsher methods. The degrees of scholastic, as of military punishment, no stated rules can ascertain. It must be enforced till it overpowers temptation; till stubbornness becomes flexible, and perverseness regular. Custom and reason have, indeed, set some bounds to scholastic penalties. The schoolmaster inflicts no capital punishments; nor enforces his edicts by either death or mutilation. The civil law has wisely determined that a master who strikes at a scholar's eye shall be considered as criminal. But punishments, however severe, that produce no lasting evil, may be just and reasonable, because they may be necessary. Such have been the punishments used by the respondent. No scholar has gone from him either blind or lame, or with any of his limbs or powers injured or impaired. They were irregular, and he punished them; they were obstinate, and he enforced his punishment. But however provoked, he never exceeded the limits of moderation, for he inflicted nothing beyond present pain; and how much of that was required, no man is so little able to determine as those who have determined against him—the parents of the offenders.—It has been said that he used unprecedented and improper instruments of correction. Of this accusation the meaning is not very easy to be found. No instrument of correction is more proper than another, but as it is better adapted to produce present pain without lasting mischief. Whatever were his instruments, no lasting mischief has ensued; and therefore, however unusual, in hands so cautious they were proper.—It has been objected that the respondent admits the charge of cruelty, by producing no evidence to confute it. Let it be considered, that his scholars are either dispersed at large in the world, or continue to inhabit the place in which they were bred. Those who are dispersed cannot be found; those who remain are the sons of his prosecutors, and are not likely to support a man to whom their fathers are enemies. If it be supposed that the enmity of their fathers proves the justness of the charge, it must be considered how often experience shows us that men who are angry on one ground will accuse on another; with how little kindness, in a town of low trade, a man who lives by learning is regarded; and how implicitly, where the inhabitants are not very rich, a rich man is hearkened to and followed. In a place like Campbelltown it is easy for one of the principal inhabitants to make a party. It is easy for that party to heat themselves with imaginary grievances. It is easy for them to oppress a man poorer than themselves; and natural to assert the dignity of riches by persisting in oppression. The argument which attempts to prove the impropriety of restoring him to the school by alleging that he has lost the confidence of the people, is not the subject of juridical consideration; for he is to suffer, if he must suffer, not for their judgment, but for his own actions. It may be convenient for them to have another master; but it is a convenience of their own making. It would be likewise convenient for him to find another school; but this convenience he cannot obtain.—The question is not what is now convenient, but what is generally right. If the people of Campbelltown be distressed by the restoration of the respondent, they are distressed only by their own fault; by turbulent passions and unreasonable desires; by tyranny, which law has defeated, and by malice, which virtue has surmounted.

"This, Sir (said he), you are to turn in your mind, and make the best use of it you can in your speech."

On Tuesday, April 14, the decree of the Court of Session in the Schoolmaster's cause was reversed in the House of Lords, after a very eloquent speech by Lord Mansfield, who showed himself an adept in school discipline, but I thought was too rigorous towards my client. On the evening of the next day I supped with Dr. Johnson, at the Crown and Anchor Tavern in the Strand, in company with Mr. Langton and his brother-in-law, Lord Binning. I repeated a sentence of Lord Mansfield's speech, of which, by the aid of Mr. Longlands, the solicitor on the other side, who obligingly allowed me to compare his note with my own, I have a full copy: "My Lords, severity is not the way to govern either boys or men." "Nay (said Johnson), it is the way to *govern* them. I know not whether it be the way to *mend* them."

I talked of the recent expulsion of six students from the University of Oxford, who were Methodists, and would not desist from publicly praying and exhorting. JOHNSON: "Sir, that expulsion was extremely just and proper. What have they to do at a University, who are not willing to be taught, but will presume to teach? Where is religion to be learnt, but at a University? Sir, they were examined, and found to be mighty ignorant fellows." BOSWELL: "But, was it not hard, Sir, to expel them, for I am told they were good beings?" JOHNSON: "I believe they might be good beings; but they were not fit to be in the University of Oxford. A cow is a very good animal in the field; but we turn her out of a garden." Lord Elibank used to repeat this as an illustration uncommonly happy.

Desirous of calling Johnson forth to talk, and exercise his wit, though

I should myself be the object of it, I resolutely ventured to undertake the defence of convivial indulgence in wine, though he was not to-night in the most genial humour. After urging the common plausible topics, I at last had recourse to the maxim, *in vino veritas*, a man who is well warmed with wine will speak truth. JOHNSON: "Why, Sir, that may be an argument for drinking, if you suppose men in general to be liars. But, Sir, I would not keep company with a fellow who lies as long as he is sober, and whom you must make drunk before you can get a word of truth out of him."

Mr. Langton told us he was about to establish a school upon his estate, but it had been suggested to him that it might have a tendency to make the people less industrious. JOHNSON: "No, Sir. While learning to read and write is a distinction, the few who have that distinction may be the less inclined to work; but when everybody learns to read and write, it is no longer a distinction. A man who has a laced waistcoat is too fine a man to work; but if everybody had laced waistcoats, we should have people working in laced waistcoats. There are no people whatever more industrious, none who work more, than our manufacturers; yet they have all learnt to read and write. Sir, you must not neglect doing a thing immediately good, from fear of remote evil;— from fear of its being abused. A man who has candles may sit up too late, which he would not do if he had not candles; but nobody will deny that the art of making candles, by which light is continued to us beyond the time that the sun gives us light, is a valuable art, and ought to be preserved." BOSWELL: "But, Sir, would it not be better to follow nature; and go to bed and rise just as nature gives us light or withholds it?" JOHNSON: "No, Sir; for then we should have no kind of equality in the partition of our time between sleeping and waking. It would be very different in different seasons and in different places. In some of the northern parts of Scotland, how little light is there in the depth of winter!"

On Sunday, April 19, being Easter Day, General Paoli and I paid him a visit before dinner. Talking on the subject of taste in the arts, he said that difference of taste was in truth difference of skill. BOSWELL: "But, Sir, is there not a quality called taste, which consists merely in perception or in liking? For instance, we find people differ much as to what is the best style of English composition. Some think Swift's the best; others prefer a fuller and grander way of writing." JOHNSON: "Sir, you must first define what you mean by style, before you can judge who has a good taste in style, and who has a bad. The two classes of persons whom you have mentioned don't differ as to good and bad. They both agree that Swift has a good neat style; but one loves a neat style, another loves a style of more splendour. In like manner, one loves a plain coat, another loves a laced coat; but neither will deny that each is good in its kind."

While I remained in London this spring, I was with him at several other times, both by himself and in company. I dined with him one day at the Crown and Anchor Tavern, in the Strand, with Lord Elibank, Mr. Langton, and Dr. Vansittart, of Oxford. Without specifying each particular day, I have preserved the following memorable things.

I regretted the reflection in his preface to "Shakspeare" against Garrick, to whom we cannot but apply the following passage: "I collated such copies as I could procure, and wished for more, but have not found the collectors of these rarities very communicative." I told him that Garrick had complained to me of it, and had vindicated himself by assuring me that Johnson was made welcome to the full use of his collection, and that he left the key of it with a servant, with orders to have a fire and every convenience for him. I found Johnson's notion was that Garrick wanted to be courted for them, and that, on the contrary, Garrick should have courted him, and sent him the plays of his own accord. But, indeed, considering the slovenly and careless manner in which books were treated by Johnson, it could not be expected that scarce and valuable editions should have been lent to him.

A gentleman having to some of the usual arguments for drinking added this: "You know, Sir, drinking drives away care, and makes us forget whatever is disagreeable. Would not you allow a man to drink for that reason?" JOHNSON: "Yes, Sir, if he sat next *you.*"

A learned gentleman who in the course of conversation wished to inform us of this simple fact, that the Counsel upon the Circuit at Shrewsbury were much bitten by fleas, took, I suppose, seven or eight minutes in relating it circumstantially. He in a plenitude of phrase told us that large bales of woollen cloth were lodged in the town hall; —that by reason of this, fleas nestled there in prodigious numbers; that the lodgings of the Counsel were near the town hall;—and that those little animals moved from place to place with wonderful agility. Johnson sat in great impatience till the gentleman had finished his tedious narrative, and then burst out (playfully, however), "It is a pity, Sir, that you have not seen a lion; for a flea has taken you such a time, that a lion must have served you a twelvemonth."

He would not allow Scotland to derive any credit from Lord Mansfield; for he was educated in England. "Much (said he) may be made of a Scotchman, if he be *caught* young."

I mentioned a friend of mine who had resided long in Spain, and was unwilling to return to Britain. JOHNSON: "Sir, he is attached to some woman." BOSWELL: "I rather believe, Sir, it is the fine climate which keeps him there." JOHNSON: "Nay, Sir, how can you talk so? What is *climate* to happiness? Place me in the heart of Asia, should I not be exiled? What proportion does climate bear to the complex system of human life? You may advise me to go to live at Bologna to eat sausages. The sausages there are the best in the world; they lose much by being carried."

On Saturday, May 9, Mr. Dempster and I had agreed to dine by ourselves at the British Coffee House. Johnson, on whom I happened to call in the morning, said he would join us, which he did, and we spent a very agreeable day, though I recollect but little of what passed.

He said, "Walpole was a minister given by the King to the people; Pitt was a minister given by the people to the King—as an adjunct."

"The misfortune of Goldsmith in conversation is this: he goes on without knowing how he is to get off. His genius is great, but his knowledge is small. As they say of a generous man, it is a pity he is not rich, we may say of Goldsmith it is a pity he is not knowing. He would not keep his knowledge to himself."

CHAPTER XXII—1773

"She Stoops to Conquer"

IN 1773 his only publication was an edition of his folio Dictionary, with additions and corrections; nor did he, so far as is known, furnish any productions of his fertile pen to any of his numerous friends or dependants, except the Preface [*] to his old amanuensis Macbean's "Dictionary of Ancient Geography." His Shakspeare, indeed, which had been received with high approbation by the public, and gone through several editions, was this year re-published by George Steevens, Esq., a gentleman not only deeply skilled in ancient learning, and of very extensive reading in English literature, especially the early writers, but at the same time of acute discernment and elegant taste. It is almost unnecessary to say that by his great and valuable additions to Dr. Johnson's work, he justly obtained considerable reputation:

"Divisum imperium cum Jove Cæsar habet."

"TO JAMES BOSWELL, ESQ.

"DEAR SIR,—

"I have read your kind letter much more than the elegant Pindar which it accompanied. I am always glad to find myself not forgotten; and to be forgotten by you would give me great uneasiness. My northern friends have never been unkind to me: I have from you, dear Sir, testimonies of affection which I have not often been able to excite; and Dr. Beattie rates the testimony which I was desirous of paying to his merit much higher than I should have thought it reasonable to expect.

"I have heard of your masquerade. What says your synod to such innovations? I am not studiously scrupulous, nor do I think a masquerade either evil in itself, or very likely to be the occasion of evil; yet as the world thinks it a very licentious relaxation of manners, I would not have been one of the *first* masquers in a country where no masquerade had ever been before.

"A new edition of my great Dictionary is printed, from a copy which I was persuaded to revise; but having made no preparation, I was able to do very little. Some superfluities I have expunged, and some faults I have corrected, and here and there have scattered a remark; but the main fabric of the work remains as it was. I had looked very little into it since I wrote it, and I think I found it full as often better, as worse, than I expected.

"Baretti and Davies have had a furious quarrel; a quarrel, I think, irreconcilable. Dr. Goldsmith has a new comedy, which is expected in the spring. No name is yet given it. The chief diversion arises from a stratagem by which a lover is made to mistake his future father-in-law's house for an inn. This, you see, borders upon farce. The dialogue is quick and gay, and the incidents are so prepared as not to seem improbable.

"I am sorry that you lost your cause of Intromission, because I yet think the arguments on your side unanswerable. But you seem, I think, to say that you gained reputation even by your defeat; and reputation you will daily gain, if you keep Lord Auchinleck's precept in your mind, and endeavour to consolidate in your mind a firm and regular system of law, instead of picking up occasional fragments.

"My health seems in general to improve; but I have been troubled for many weeks with a vexatious catarrh, which is sometimes sufficiently distressful. I have not found any great effects from bleeding and physic; and am afraid that I must expect help from brighter days and softer air.

"Write to me now and then; and whenever any good befalls you, make haste to let me know it, for no one will rejoice at it more than, dear Sir,

> "Your most humble servant,
> "SAM. JOHNSON.

"London, Feb. 22, 1773."

While a former edition of my work was passing through the press, I was unexpectedly favoured with a packet from Philadelphia, from Mr. James Abercrombie, a gentleman of that country, who is pleased to honour me with very high praise of my "Life of Dr. Johnson." To have the fame of my illustrious friend and his faithful biographer echoed from the New World is extremely flattering; and my grateful acknowledgments shall be wafted across the Atlantic. Mr. Abercrombie has politely conferred on me a considerable additional obligation by transmitting to me copies of two letters from Dr. Johnson to American gentlemen. "Gladly, Sir (says he), would I have sent you the originals; but being the only relics of the kind in America, they are considered by the possessors of such inestimable value that no possible consideration would induce them to part with them. In some future publication of yours relative to that great and good man, they may perhaps be thought worthy of insertion."

"TO MR. B——D.

"SIR,—

"That in the hurry of a sudden departure you should yet find leisure to consult my convenience, is a degree of kindness, and an instance of regard, not only beyond my claims, but above my expectation. You are not mistaken in supposing that I set a high value on my American friends, and that you should confer a very valuable favour upon me by giving me an opportunity of keeping myself in their memory.

"I have taken the liberty of troubling you with a packet, to which I wish a safe and speedy conveyance, because I wish a safe and speedy voyage to him that conveys it.

"I am, Sir,

"Your most humble servant,

"SAM. JOHNSON.

"*London, Johnson's Court,*

"*Fleet Street, March 4, 1773.*"

"TO THE REVEREND MR. WHITE.

"DEAR SIR,—

"Your kindness for your friends accompanies you across the Atlantic. It was long since observed by Horace that no ship could leave care behind; you have been attended in your voyage by other powers —by benevolence and constancy; and I hope care did not often show her face in their company.

"I received the copy of 'Rasselas.' The impression is not magnificent, but it flatters an author, because the printer seems to have expected that it would be scattered among the people. The little book has been well received, and is translated into Italian, French, German, and Dutch. It has now one honour more by an American edition.

"I know not that much has happened since your departure that can engage your curiosity. Of all public transactions the whole world is now informed by the newspapers. Opposition seems to despond; and the dissenters, though they have taken advantage of unsettled times, and a government much enfeebled, seem not likely to gain any immunities.

"Dr. Goldsmith has a new comedy in rehearsal at Covent Garden, to which the manager predicts ill-success. I hope he will be mistaken. I think it deserves a very kind reception.

"I shall soon publish a new edition of my large Dictionary; I have been persuaded to revise it, and have mended some faults, but added little to its usefulness.

"No book has been published since your departure, of which much notice is taken. Faction only fills the town with pamphlets, and greater subjects are forgotten in the noise of discord.

"Thus have I written, only to tell you how little I have to tell. Of myself I can only add, that having been afflicted many weeks with a very troublesome cough, I am now recovered.

"I take the liberty which you give me of troubling you with a letter, cf which you will please to fill up the direction.

"I am, Sir,

"Your most humble servant,

"SAM. JOHNSON.

"Johnson's Court, Fleet Street,
"London, March 4, 1773."

On Saturday, April 3, the day after my arrival in London this year, I went to his house late in the evening, and sat with Mrs. Williams till he came home. I found in the *London Chronicle* Dr. Goldsmith's apology to the public for beating Evans, a bookseller, on account of a paragraph in a newspaper published by him, which Goldsmith thought impertinent to him and to a lady of his acquaintance. The apology was written so much in Dr. Johnson's manner, that both Mrs. Williams and I supposed it to be his; but when he came home, he soon undeceived us. When he said to Mrs. Williams, "Well, Dr. Goldsmith's *manifesto* has got into your paper"; I asked him if Dr. Goldsmith had written it, with an air that made him see I suspected it was his, though subscribed by Goldsmith. JOHNSON: "Sir, Dr. Goldsmith would no more have asked me to write such a thing as that for him than he would have asked me to feed him with a spoon, or to do anything else that denoted his imbecility. I as much believe that he wrote it as if I had seen him do it. Sir, had he shown it to any one friend, he would not have been allowed to publish it. He has, indeed, done it very well; but it is a foolish thing well done. I suppose he has been so much elated with the success of his new comedy, that he has thought every thing that concerned him must be of importance to the public." BOSWELL: "I fancy, Sir, this is the first time that he has been engaged in such an adventure." JOHNSON: "Why, Sir, I believe it is the first time he has *beat;* he may have *been beaten* before. This, Sir, is a new plume to him."

At Mr. Thrale's, in the evening, he repeated his usual paradoxical declamation against action in public speaking. "Action can have no effect upon reasonable minds. It may augment noise, but it never can enforce argument. If you speak to a dog, you use action; you hold up your hand thus, because he is a brute; and in proportion as men are removed from brutes, action will have the less influence upon them." MRS. THRALE: "What, then, Sir, becomes of Demosthenes's saying?

'Action, action, action!'" JOHNSON: "Demosthenes, Madam, spoke to an assembly of brutes; to a barbarous people."

Lord Chesterfield being mentioned, Johnson remarked that almost all of that celebrated nobleman's witty sayings were puns. He, however, allowed the merit of good wit to his Lordship's saying of Lord Tyrawley and himself, when both very old and infirm: "Tyrawley and I have been dead these two years; but we don't choose to have it known."

On Thursday, April 8, I sat a good part of the evening with him, but he was very silent. He said, "Burnet's 'History of his Own Times' is very entertaining. The style, indeed, is mere chit-chat. I do not believe that Burnet intentionally lied; but he was so much prejudiced, that he took no pains to find out the truth. He was like a man who resolves to regulate his time by a certain watch; but he will not inquire whether the watch is right or not."

Though he was not disposed to talk, he was unwilling that I should leave him; and when I looked at my watch, and told him it was twelve o'clock, he cried, "What's that to you and me?" and ordered Frank to tell Mrs. Williams that we were coming to drink tea with her, which we did. It was settled that we should go to church together next day.

On the 9th of April, being Good Friday, I breakfasted with him on tea and crossbuns; *Doctor* Levett, as Frank called him, making the tea. He carried me with him to the church of St. Clement Danes, where he had his seat; and his behaviour was, as I had imaged to myself, solemnly devout. I never shall forget the tremulous earnestness with which he pronounced the awful petition in the Litany: "In the hour of death, and in the day of judgment, good Lord deliver us."

We went to church both in the morning and evening. In the interval between the two services we did not dine; but he read in the Greek New Testament, and I turned over several of his books.

To my great surprise he asked me to dine with him on Easter-Day. I never supposed that he had a dinner at his house; for I had not then heard of any one of his friends having been entertained at his table. He told me, "I generally have a meat-pie on Sunday: it is baked at a public oven, which is very properly allowed, because one man can attend it; and thus the advantage is obtained of not keeping servants from church to dress dinners."

April 11, being Easter Sunday, after having attended Divine Service at St. Paul's, I repaired to Dr. Johnson's. I had gratified my curiosity much in dining with Jean Jacques Rousseau, while he lived in the wilds of Neufchatel: I had as great a curiosity to dine with Dr. Samuel Johnson, in the dusky recess of a court in Fleet-street. I supposed we should scarcely have knives and forks, and only some strange, uncouth, ill-drest dish: but I found everything in very good order. We had no other company but Mrs. Williams and a young woman whom I did not know. As a dinner here was considered as a singular phenomenon, and as I was frequently interrogated on the subject, my readers may perhaps be desirous to know our bill of fare. Foote, I remember, in allusion to Francis, the *negro,* was willing to suppose that our repast was *black broth.* But the fact was that we had a very good soup, a boiled leg of lamb and spinach, a veal pie, and a rice pudding.

He owned that he thought Hawkesworth was one of his imitators, but he did not think Goldsmith was. Goldsmith, he said, had great merit. Boswell: "But, Sir, he is much indebted to you for his getting so high in the public estimation." Johnson: "Why, Sir, he has perhaps got *sooner* to it by his intimacy with me."

Goldsmith, though his vanity often excited him to occasional competition, had a very high regard for Johnson, which he had at this time expressed in the strongest manner in the Dedication of his Comedy, entitled, "She Stoops to Conquer."

He told me that he had twelve or fourteen times attempted to keep a journal of his life, but never could persevere. He advised me to do it. "The great thing to be recorded (said he) is the state of your own mind; and you should write down every thing that you remember, for you cannot judge at first what is good or bad; and write immediately while the impression is fresh, for it will not be the same a week afterwards."

I again solicited him to communicate to me the particulars of his early life. He said, "You shall have them all for two-pence. I hope you shall know a great deal more of me before you write my Life." He mentioned to me this day many circumstances, which I wrote down when I went home, and have interwoven in the former part of this narrative.

On Tuesday, April 13, he and Dr. Goldsmith and I dined at General Oglethorpe's. Goldsmith expatiated on the common topic, that the race of our people was degenerated, and that this was owing to luxury. Johnson: "Sir, in the first place, I doubt the fact. I believe there are as many tall men in England now as ever there were. But, secondly, supposing the stature of our people to be diminished, that is not owing to luxury; for, Sir, consider to how very small a proportion of our people luxury can reach. Our soldiery, surely, are not luxurious, who live on sixpence a day; and the same remark will apply to almost all the other classes. Luxury, so far as it reaches the poor, will do good to the race of people; it will strengthen and multiply them. Sir, no nation was ever hurt by luxury; for, as I said before, it can reach but to a very few. I admit that the great increase of commerce and manufactures hurts the military spirit of a people; because it produces a competition for something else than martial honours—a competition for riches. It also hurts the bodies of the people; for you will observe, there is no man who works at any particular trade, but you may know him from his appearance to do so. One part or the other of his body being more used than the rest, he is in some degree deformed: but, Sir, that is not luxury. A tailor sits cross-legged; but that is not luxury." GOLDSMITH: "Come, you're just going to the same place by another road." JOHNSON: "Nay, Sir, I say that is not *luxury*. Let us take a walk from Charing Cross to Whitechapel, through, I suppose, the greatest series of shops in the world, what is there in any of these shops (if you except gin-shops) that can do any human being any harm?" GOLDSMITH: "Well, Sir, I'll accept your challenge. The very next shop to Northumberland House is a pickle shop." JOHNSON: "Well, Sir: do we not know that a maid can in one afternoon make pickles sufficient to serve a whole family for a year? Nay, that five pickle shops can serve all the kingdom? Besides, Sir, there is no harm done to anybody by the making of pickles, or the eating of pickles."

We drank tea with the ladies; and Goldsmith sung Tony Lumpkin's song in his comedy, "She Stoops to Conquer," and a very pretty one, to an Irish tune, which he had designed for Miss Hardcastle! but as Mrs. Bulkeley, who played the part, could not sing, it was left out. He afterwards wrote it down for me, by which means it was preserved, and now appears amongst his poems. Dr. Johnson, on his way home, stopped at my lodgings in Piccadilly, and sat with me, drinking tea a second time, till a late hour.

Talking of law cases, he said, "The English reports, in general, are very poor: only the half of what has been said is taken down; and of that half much is mistaken. Whereas, in Scotland, the arguments on each side are deliberately put in writing, to be considered by the court. I think a collection of your cases upon subjects of importance, with the opinions of the Judges upon them, would be valuable."

On Thursday, April 15, I dined with him and Dr. Goldsmith, at

General Paoli's. We found here Signor Martinelli, of Florence, author of a History of England in Italian, printed at London.

The General observed that Martinelli was a Whig. JOHNSON: "I am sorry for it. It shows the spirit of the times: he is obliged to temporize." BOSWELL: "I rather think, Sir, that Toryism prevails in this reign." JOHNSON: "I know not why you should think so, Sir. You see your friend Lord Lyttelton, a nobleman, is obliged in his History to write the most vulgar Whiggism."

An animated debate took place whether Martinelli should continue his History of England to the present day. GOLDSMITH: "To be sure he should." JOHNSON: "No, Sir; he would give great offence. He would have to tell of almost all the living great what they do not wish told." GOLDSMITH: "It may, perhaps, be necessary for a native to be more cautious; but a foreigner who comes among us without prejudice, may be considered as holding the place of a judge, and may speak his mind freely." JOHNSON: "Sir, a foreigner, when he sends a work from the press, ought to be on his guard against catching the error and mistaken enthusiasm of the people among whom he happens to be." GOLDSMITH: "Sir, he wants only to sell his history, and to tell truth; one an honest, the other a laudable motive." JOHNSON: "Sir, they are both laudable motives. It is laudable in a man to wish to live by his labours; but he should write so as he may *live* by them, not so as he may be knocked on the head. I would advise him to be at Calais before he publishes his history of the present age. A foreigner who attaches himself to a political party in this country, is in the worst state that can be imagined: he is looked upon as a mere intermeddler. A native may do it from interest." BOSWELL: "Or principle." GOLDSMITH: "There are people who tell a hundred political lies every day, and are not hurt by it. Surely, then, one may tell truth with safety." JOHNSON: "Why, Sir, in the first place, he who tells a hundred lies has disarmed the force of his lies. But besides; a man had rather have a hundred lies told of him than one truth which he does not wish should be told." GOLDSMITH: "For my part, I'd tell truth, and shame the devil." JOHNSON: "Yes, Sir; but the devil will be angry. I wish to shame the devil as much as you do, but I should choose to be out of the reach of his claws." GOLDSMITH: "His claws can do you no harm, when you have the shield of truth."

It having been observed that there was little hospitality in London; JOHNSON: "Nay, Sir, any man who has a name, or who has the power of pleasing, will be very generally invited in London. The man, Sterne,

I have been told, has had engagements for three months." GOLD-SMITH: "And a very dull fellow." JOHNSON: "Why, no, Sir."

We talked of the King's coming to see Goldsmith's new play.—"I wish he would," said Goldsmith, adding, however, with an affected indifference, "Not that it would do me the least good." JOHNSON: "Well, then, Sir, let us say it would do *him* good (laughing). No, Sir, this affectation will not pass;—it is mighty idle. In such a state as ours, who would not wish to please the Chief Magistrate?" GOLDSMITH: "I *do* wish to please him. I remember a line in Dryden.

> 'And every poet is the monarch's friend.'

It ought to be reversed." JOHNSON: "Nay, there are finer lines in Dryden on this subject:

> 'For colleges on bounteous Kings depend,
> And never rebel was to arts a friend.' "

A person was mentioned who, it was said, could take down in shorthand the speeches in Parliament with perfect exactness.—JOHNSON: "Sir, it is impossible. I remember one Angel, who came to me to write for him a Preface or Dedication to a book upon shorthand, and he professed to write as fast as any man could speak. In order to try him, I took down a book, and read while he wrote; and I favoured him, for I read more deliberately than usual. I had proceeded but a very little way, when he begged I would desist, for he could not follow me." Hearing now for the first time of this Preface or Dedication, I said, "What an expense, Sir, do you put us to in buying books, to which you have written Prefaces or Dedications." JOHNSON: "Why, I have dedicated to the Royal Family all round; that is to say, to the last generation of the Royal Family." GOLDSMITH: "And perhaps, Sir, not one sentence of wit in a whole Dedication." JOHNSON: "Perhaps not, Sir." BOSWELL: "What then is the reason for applying to a particular person to do that which anyone may do as well?" JOHNSON: "Why, Sir, one man has greater readiness at doing it than another."

I spoke of Mr. Harris, of Salisbury, as being a very learned man, and in particular an eminent Grecian. JOHNSON: "I am not sure of that. His friends give him out as such, but I know not who of his friends are able to judge of it." GOLDSMITH: "He is what is much better: he is a worthy humane man." JOHNSON: "Nay, Sir, that is not to the purpose of our argument; that will as much prove that he can play upon the fiddle as well as Giardini, as that he is an eminent Grecian." GOLDSMITH: "The greatest musical performers have but small emoluments. Giardini, I am told, does not get above seven hundred a year." JOHNSON: "That is indeed but little for a man to get who does best that which so many endeavour to do. There is nothing, I think, in which the power of art is shown so much as in playing on the fiddle. In all other things we can do something at first. Any man will forge a bar of iron, if you give him a hammer; not so well as a smith, but tolerably. A man will saw a piece of wood, and make a box, though a clumsy one; but give him a fiddle and a fiddle-stick, and he can do nothing."

On Wednesday, April 21, I dined with him at Mr. Thrale's. A gentleman attacked Garrick for being vain. JOHNSON: "No wonder, Sir, that he is vain; a man who is perpetually flattered in every mode that can be conceived. So many bellows have blown the fire, that one wonders he is not by this time become a cinder." BOSWELL: "And such bellows too. Lord Mansfield with his cheeks like to burst: Lord Chatham like an Æolus. I have read such notes from them to him, as were enough to turn his head." JOHNSON: "True. When he whom everybody else flatters, flatters me, I then am truly happy." MRS. THRALE: "The sentiment is in Congreve, I think." JOHNSON: "Yes, Madam, in 'The Way of the World':

> 'If there's delight in love, 'tis when I see
> That heart which others bleed for, bleed for me.'

No, Sir, I should not be surprised though Garrick chained the ocean and lashed the winds." BOSWELL: "Should it not be, Sir, lashed the ocean and chained the winds?" JOHNSON: "No, Sir; recollect the original:

> 'In Corum atque Eurum solitus sævire flagellis
> Barbarus, Æolio nunquam hoc in carcere passos,
> Ipsum compedibus qui vinxerat Ennosigæum.'

This does very well, when both the winds and the sea are personified, and mentioned by their mythological names, as in Juvenal; but when they are mentioned in plain language, the application of the epithets suggested by me is the most obvious; and accordingly my friend himself, in his imitation of the passage which describes Xerxes, has—

> 'The waves he lashes, and enchains the wind.' "

On Tuesday, April 27, Mr. Beauclerk and I called on him in the morning. He said, "Goldsmith should not be for ever attempting to shine in conversation: he has not temper for it, he is so much mortified when he fails. Sir, a game of jokes is composed partly of skill, partly of chance; a man may be beat at times by one who has not the tenth part of his wit. Now Goldsmith's putting himself against another, is like a man laying a hundred to one who cannot spare the hundred. It is not worth a man's while. A man should not lay a hundred to one, unless he can easily spare it, though he has a hundred chances for him: he can get but a guinea, and he may lose a hundred. Goldsmith is in this state. When he contends, if he gets the better, it is a very little addition to a man of his literary reputation: if he does not get the better, he is miserably vexed."

Johnson's own superlative powers of wit set him above any risk of such uneasiness. Garrick had remarked to me of him, a few days before: "Rabelais and all other wits are nothing compared with him. You may be diverted by them; but Johnson gives you a forcible hug, and shakes laughter out of you, whether you will or no."

Goldsmith, however, was often very fortunate in his witty contests, even when he entered the lists with Johnson himself. Sir Joshua Reynolds was in company with them one day, when Goldsmith said that he thought he could write a good fable, mentioned the simplicity which that kind of composition requires, and observed that in most fables the animals introduced seldom talk in character. "For instance (said he), the fable of the little fishes, who saw birds fly over their heads, and envying them, petitioned Jupiter to be changed into birds. The skill (continued he) consists in making them talk like little fishes." While he indulged himself in this fanciful reverie, he observed Johnson shaking his sides, and laughing. Upon which he smartly proceeded, "Why, Dr. Johnson, this is not so easy as you seem to think; for if you were to make little fishes talk, they would talk like whales."

On Thursday, April 29, I dined with him at General Oglethorpe's, where were Sir Joshua Reynolds, Mr. Langton, Dr. Goldsmith, and Mr. Thrale. I was very desirous to get Dr. Johnson absolutely fixed in his resolution to go with me to the Hebrides this year; and I told him that I had received a letter from Dr. Robertson the historian, upon the subject, with which he was much pleased, and now talked in such a manner of his long intended tour, that I was satisfied he meant to fulfil his engagement.

Dr. Goldsmith's new play, "She Stoops to Conquer," being mentioned; JOHNSON: "I know of no comedy for many years that has so much exhilarated an audience, that has answered so much the great end of comedy—making an audience merry."

Goldsmith having said that Garrick's compliment to the Queen, which he introduced into the play of "The Chances," which he had altered and revised this year, was mean and gross flattery;—JOHNSON: "Why, Sir, I would not *write,* I would not give solemnly under my hand, a character beyond what I thought really true; but a speech on the stage, let it flatter ever so extravagantly, is formular. It has always been formular to flatter kings and queens; so much so, that even in our church-service we have 'our most religious King,' used indiscriminately, whoever is king. Nay, they even flatter themselves;—'we have been graciously pleased to grant.'—No modern flattery, however, is so gross as that of the Augustan age, where the Emperor was deified. *'Præsens Divus habebitur Augustus.'* And as to meanness (rising into warmth), how is it mean in a player—a showman—a fellow who exhibits himself for a shilling, to flatter his Queen? The attempt, indeed, was dangerous; for if it had missed, what became of Garrick, and what became of the Queen? As Sir William Temple says of a great general, it is necessary not only that his designs be formed in a masterly manner, but that they should be attended with success. Sir, it is right, at a time when the Royal Family is not generally liked, to let it be seen that the people like at least one of them." SIR JOSHUA REYNOLDS: "I do not perceive why the profession of a player should be despised; for the great and ultimate end of all the employments of mankind is to produce amusement. Garrick produces more amusement than any body." BOSWELL: "You say, Dr. Johnson, that Garrick exhibits himself for a shilling. In this respect he is only on a footing with a lawyer, who exhibits himself for his fee, and even will maintain any nonsense or absurdity, if the case require it. Garrick refuses a play or a part which he does not like: a lawyer never refuses." JOHNSON: "Why, Sir, what does this prove? Only that a lawyer is worse. Boswell is now like Jack in 'The Tale of a Tub,' who, when he is puzzled by an argument, hangs himself. He thinks I shall cut him down, but I'll let him hang" (laughing vociferously). SIR JOSHUA REYNOLDS: "Mr. Boswell thinks, that the profession of a lawyer being unquestionably honourable, if he can show the profession of a player to be more honourable, he proves his argument."

CHAPTER XXIII—1773

Johnson and Goldsmith

ON FRIDAY, APRIL 30, I dined with him at Mr. Beauclerk's, where were Lord Charlemont, Sir Joshua Reynolds, and some more members of the Literary Club, whom he had obligingly invited to meet me, as I was this evening to be balloted for as candidate for admission into that distinguished society. Johnson had done me the honour to propose me, and Beauclerk was very zealous for me.

Johnson praised John Bunyan highly. "His 'Pilgrim's Progress' has great merit, both for invention, imagination, and the conduct of the story: and it has had the best evidence of its merit, the general and continued approbation of mankind. Few books, I believe, have had a more extensive sale. It is remarkable that it begins very much like the poem of Dante; yet there was no translation of Dante when Bunyan wrote. There is reason to think that he had read Spenser."

A proposition which had been agitated that monuments to eminent persons should, for the time to come, be erected in St. Paul's Church as well as in Westminster Abbey, was mentioned; and it was asked who should be honoured by having his monument first erected there. Somebody suggested Pope. JOHNSON: "Why, Sir, as Pope was a Roman Catholic, I would not have his to be first. I think Milton's rather should have the precedence. I think more highly of him now than I did at twenty. There is more thinking in him and in Butler than in any of our poets."

The gentlemen went away to their club, and I was left at Beauclerk's till the fate of my election should be announced to me. I sat in a state of anxiety which even the charming conversation of Lady Di Beauclerk could not entirely dissipate. In a short time I received the agreeable intelligence that I was chosen. I hastened to the place of meeting, and was introduced to such a society as can seldom be found. Mr. Edmund Burke, whom I then saw for the first time, and whose splendid talents had long made me ardently wish for his acquaintance; Dr. Nugent, Mr. Garrick, Dr. Goldsmith, Mr. (afterwards Sir William)

Jones, and the company with whom I had dined. Upon my entrance, Johnson placed himself behind a chair, on which he leaned as on a desk or pulpit, and with humorous formality gave me a *charge,* pointing out the conduct expected from me as a good member of this club.

Talking of puns, Johnson, who had a great contempt for that species of wit, deigned to allow that there was one good pun in "Menagiana," I think on the word *corps.*

Much pleasant conversation passed, which Johnson relished with great good humour. But his conversation alone, or what led to it, or was interwoven with it, is the business of this work.

On Saturday, May 1, we dined by ourselves at our old rendezvous, the Mitre Tavern. He was placid, but not much disposed to talk. He observed that "The Irish mix better with the English than the Scotch do; their language is nearer to English; as a proof of which, they succeed very well as players, which Scotchmen do not. Then, Sir, they have not that extreme nationality which we find in the Scotch. I will do you, Boswell, the justice to say that you are the most *unscottified* of your countrymen. You are almost the only instance of a Scotchman that I have known who did not at every other sentence bring in some other Scotchman."

On Friday, May 7, I breakfasted with him at Mr. Thrale's, in the Borough. While we were alone, I endeavoured as well as I could to apologise for a lady who had been divorced from her husband by Act of Parliament. I said that he had used her very ill, had behaved brutally to her, and that she could not continue to live with him without having her delicacy contaminated: that all affection for him was thus destroyed; that the essence of conjugal union being gone, there remained only a cold form, a mere civil obligation: that she was in the prime of life, with qualities to produce happiness; that these ought not to be lost; and that the gentleman on whose account she was divorced had gained her heart while thus unhappily situated. Seduced, perhaps, by the charms of the lady in question, I thus attempted to palliate what I was sensible could not be justified; for when I had finished my harangue, my venerable friend gave me a proper check: "My dear Sir, never accustom your mind to mingle virtue and vice. The woman's a whore, and there's an end on't."

I dined with him this day at the house of my friends, Messieurs Edward and Charles Dilly, booksellers in the Poultry: there were present, their elder brother, Mr. Dilly of Bedfordshire, Dr. Goldsmith, Mr. Langton, Mr. Claxton, Reverend Dr. Mayo, a dissenting minister, the Reverend Mr. Toplady, and my friend, the Reverend Mr. Temple.

Hawkesworth's compilation of the voyages to the South Sea being mentioned;—JOHNSON: "Sir, if you talk of it as a subject of commerce, it will be gainful; if as a book that is to increase human knowledge, I believe there will not be much of that. Hawkesworth can tell only what the voyagers have told him; and they have found very little, only one new animal, I think." BOSWELL: "But many insects, Sir." JOHNSON: "Why, Sir, as to insects, Ray reckons of British insects twenty thousand species. They might have stayed at home and discovered enough in that way."

BOSWELL: "I am well assured that the people of Otaheite who have the bread tree, the fruit of which serves them for bread, laughed heartily when they were informed of the tedious process necessary with us to have bread;—ploughing, sowing, harrowing, reaping, threshing, grinding, baking." JOHNSON: "Why, Sir, all ignorant savages will laugh when they are told of the advantages of civilised life. Were you to tell men who live without houses how we pile brick upon brick, and rafter upon rafter, and that after a house is raised to a certain height, a man tumbles off a scaffold, and breaks his neck; he would laugh heartily at our folly in building; but it does not follow that men are better without houses. No, Sir (holding up a slice of a good loaf), this is better than the bread-tree."

I introduced the subject of toleration. JOHNSON: "Every society has a right to preserve public peace and order, and therefore has a good right to prohibit the propagation of opinions which have a dangerous tendency. To say the *magistrate* has this right, is using an inadequate word: it is the *society* for which the magistrate is agent. He may be morally or theologically wrong in restraining the propagation of opinions which he thinks dangerous, but he is politically right." MAYO: "I am of opinion, Sir, that every man is entitled to liberty of conscience in religion; and that the magistrate cannot restrain that right." JOHNSON: "Sir, I agree with you. Every man has a right to liberty of conscience, and with that the magistrate cannot interfere. People confound liberty of thinking with liberty of talking; nay, with liberty of preaching. Every man has a physical right to think as he pleases; for it cannot be discovered how he thinks. He has not a moral right, for he ought to inform himself, and think justly. But, Sir, no member of a society has a right to *teach* any doctrine contrary to what the society holds to be true. The magistrate, I say, may be wrong in what he thinks: but while he thinks himself right, he may and ought to enforce what he thinks."

MAYO: "Then, Sir, we are to remain always in error, and truth never can prevail; and the magistrate was right in persecuting the first Christians." JOHNSON: "Sir, the only method by which religious truth can be established is by martyrdom. The magistrate has a right to enforce what he thinks; and he who is conscious of the truth has a right to suffer. I am afraid there is no other way of ascertaining the truth, but by persecution on the one hand, and enduring it on the other." GOLDSMITH: "But how is a man to act, Sir? Though firmly convinced of the truth of his doctrine, may he not think it wrong to expose himself to persecution? Has he a right to do so? Is it not as it were, committing voluntary suicide?" JOHNSON: "Sir, as to voluntary suicide, as you call it, there are twenty thousand men in an army who will go without scruple to be shot at, and mount a breach for fivepence a day." GOLDSMITH: "But have they a moral right to do this?" JOHNSON: "Nay, Sir, if you will not take the universal opinion of mankind, I have nothing to say. If mankind cannot defend their own way of thinking, I cannot defend it. Sir, if a man is in doubt whether it would be better for him to expose himself to martyrdom or not, he should not do it. He must be convinced that he has a delegation from heaven." GOLDSMITH: "I would consider whether there is the greater chance of good or evil upon the whole. If I see a man who has fallen into a well, I would wish to help him out; but if there is a greater probability that he shall pull me in than that I shall pull him out, I would not attempt it. So were I to go to Turkey, I might wish to convert the Grand Signor to the Christian faith; but when I considered that I should probably be put to death without effectuating my purpose in any degree, I should keep myself quiet." JOHNSON: "Sir, you must consider that we have perfect and imperfect obligations. Perfect obligations, which are generally not to do something, are clear and positive; as, 'thou shalt not kill.' But charity, for instance, is not definable by limits. It is a duty to give to the poor; but no man can say how much another should give to the poor, or when a man has given too little to save his soul. In the same manner, it is a duty to instruct the ignorant, and of consequence to convert infidels to Christianity; but no man in the common course of things is obliged to carry this to such a degree as to incur the danger of martyrdom, as no man is obliged to strip himself to the shirt in order to give charity. I have said that a man must be persuaded that he has a particular delegation from heaven." GOLDSMITH: "How is this to be known? Our first reformers, who were burnt for not believing bread and wine to be Christ——" JOHNSON (interrupting him): "Sir, they were not burnt for not believing bread and wine to be Christ, but for insulting those who did believe it. And, Sir, when the first reformers began, they did not intend to be martyred: as many of them ran away as could." MAYO: "But, Sir, is it not very hard that I should not be allowed to teach my children what I really believe to be the truth?" JOHNSON: "Why, Sir, you might contrive to teach your children *extra scandalum;* but, Sir, the magistrate, if he knows it, has a right to restrain you. Suppose you teach your children to be thieves?" MAYO: "This is making a joke of the subject." JOHNSON: "Nay, Sir, take it thus:—that you teach them the community of goods; for which there are as many plausible arguments as for most erroneous doctrines. You teach them that all things at first were in common, and that no man had a right to anything but as he laid his hands upon it; and that this still is, or ought to be, the rule amongst mankind. Here, Sir, you sap a great principle in society—property. And don't you think the magistrate would have a right to prevent you? Or, suppose you should teach your children the notion of the Adamites, and they should run naked into the streets, would not the magistrate have a right to flog 'em into their doublets?" MAYO: "I think the magistrate has no right to interfere till there is some overt act." BOSWELL: "So, Sir, though he sees an enemy to the state charging a blunderbuss, he is not to interfere till it is fired off!" MAYO: "He must be sure of its direction against the state." JOHNSON: "The magistrate is to judge of that.—He has no right to restrain your thinking, because the evil centres in yourself. If a man were sitting at his table, and chopping off his fingers, the magistrate, as guardian of the community, has no authority to restrain him, however he might do it from kindness as a parent.—Though, indeed, upon more consideration, I think he may; as it is probable, that he who is chopping off his own fingers, may soon proceed to chop off those of other people. If I think it right to steal Mr. Dilly's plate, I am a bad man; but he can say nothing to me. If I make an open declaration that I think so, he will keep me out of his house. If I put forth my hand, I shall be sent to Newgate. This is the gradation of thinking, preaching, and acting: if a man thinks erroneously, he may keep his thoughts to himself, and nobody will trouble him: if he preaches erroneous doctrine, society may expel him; if he acts in consequence of it, the law takes place, and he is hanged." MAYO: "But, Sir, ought not Christians to have liberty of conscience?" JOHNSON: "I have already told you so, Sir. You are coming back to where you were." BOSWELL: "Dr. Mayo is always taking a return post-chaise, and going the stage over again. He has it at half-price." JOHNSON: "Dr. Mayo, like other champions for unlimited toleration, has got a set of words. Sir, it is no matter, politically, whether the magistrate be right or wrong. Suppose a club were to be formed, to drink confusion to King George the Third, and a happy restoration to Charles the Third; this would be very bad with respect to the state; but every member of that club must either conform to its rules, or be turned out of it. Old Baxter, I remember, maintains that the magistrate should 'tolerate all things that are tolerable.' This is no good definition of toleration upon any principle; but it shows that he thought some things were not tolerable." TOPLADY: "Sir, you have untwisted this difficult subject with great dexterity."

During this argument, Goldsmith sat in restless agitation, from a wish to get in and *shine*. Finding himself excluded, he had taken his hat to go away, but remained for some time with it in his hand, like a gamester, who, at the close of a long night, lingers for a little while, to see if he can have a favourable opening to finish with success. Once when he was beginning to speak, he found himself overpowered by the loud voice of Johnson, who was at the opposite end of the table, and did not perceive Goldsmith's attempt. Thus disappointed of his wish to obtain the attention of the company, Goldsmith, in a passion, threw down his hat, looking angrily at Johnson, and exclaiming in a bitter tone, *"Take it."* When Toplady was going to speak, Johnson uttered some sound, which led Goldsmith to think that he was beginning again, and taking the words from Toplady. Upon which, he seized this opportunity of venting his own envy and spleen, under the pretext of supporting another person: "Sir (said he to Johnson), the gentleman has heard you patiently for an hour: pray allow us now to hear him." JOHNSON (sternly): "Sir, I was not interrupting the gentleman. I was only giving him a signal of my attention. Sir, you are impertinent." Goldsmith made no reply, but continued in the company for some time.

BOSWELL: "Pray, Mr. Dilly, how does Dr. Leland's 'History of Ireland' sell?" JOHNSON (bursting forth with a generous indignation): "The Irish are in a most unnatural state; for we see there the minority prevailing over the majority. There is no instance, even in the ten persecutions, of such severity as that which the Protestants of Ireland have exercised against the Catholics. Did we tell them we have conquered them it would be above board: to punish them by confiscation and other penalties, as rebels, was monstrous injustice. King William was not their lawful sovereign: he had not been acknowledged by the Parliament of Ireland, when they appeared in arms against him."

He and Mr. Langton and I went together to the Club, where we found Mr. Burke, Mr. Garrick, and some other members, and amongst them our friend Goldsmith, who sat silently brooding over Johnson's reprimand to him after dinner. Johnson perceived this, and said aside to some of us: "I'll make Goldsmith forgive me"; and then called to him in a loud voice, "Dr. Goldsmith—something passed to-day where you and I dined; I ask your pardon." Goldsmith answered placidly, "It must be much from you, Sir, that I take ill." And so at once the difference was over, and they were on as easy terms as ever, and Goldsmith rattled away as usual.

In our way to the club to-night, when I regretted that Goldsmith would, upon every occasion, endeavour to shine, by which he often exposed himself, Mr. Langton observed that he was not like Addison, who was content with the fame of his writings, and did not aim also at excellency in conversation, for which he found himself unfit; and that he said to a lady who complained of his having talked little in company, "Madam, I have but ninepence in ready money, but I can draw for a thousand pounds." I observed that Goldsmith had a great deal of gold in his cabinet, but, not content with that, was always taking out his purse. JOHNSON: "Yes, Sir, and that so often an empty purse!"

Goldsmith's incessant desire of being conspicuous in company was the occasion of his sometimes appearing to such disadvantage as one should hardly have supposed possible in a man of his genius. When his literary reputation had risen deservedly high, and his society was much courted, he became very jealous of the extraordinary attention which was everywhere paid to Johnson. One evening, in a circle of wits, he found fault with me for talking of Johnson as entitled to the honour of unquestionable superiority. "Sir (said he), you are for making a monarchy of what should be a republic."

It may also be observed that Goldsmith was sometimes content to be treated with an easy familiarity, but, upon occasions, would be consequential and important. An instance of this occurred in a small particular. Johnson had a way of contracting the names of his friends: as Beauclerk, Beau; Boswell, Bozzy; Langton, Lanky; Murphy, Mur; Sheridan, Sherry. I remember one day, when Tom Davies was telling that Dr. Johnson said, "We are all in labour for a name to *Goldy's* play," Goldsmith seemed displeased that such a liberty should be taken with his name, and said, "I have often desired him not to call me

Goldy." Tom was remarkably attentive to the most minute circumstance about Johnson. I recollect his telling me once, on my arrival in London, "Sir, our great friend has made an improvement on his appellation of old Mr. Sheridan. He calls him now *Sherry derry.*"

On Monday, May 9, as I was to set out on my return to Scotland next morning, I was desirous to see as much of Dr. Johnson as I could. But I first called on Goldsmith to take leave of him. The jealousy and envy which, though possessed of many most amiable qualities, he frankly avowed, broke out violently at this interview. Upon another occasion, when Goldsmith confessed himself to be of an envious disposition, I contended with Johnson that we ought not to be angry with him, he was so candid in owning it. "Nay, Sir (said Johnson), we must be angry that a man has such a super-abundance of an odious quality, that he cannot keep it within his own breast, but it boils over." In my opinion, however, Goldsmith had not more of it than other people have, but only talked of it freely.

He now seemed very angry that Johnson was going to be a traveller; said, "he would be a dead weight for me to carry, and that I should never be able to lug him along through the Highlands and Hebrides." Nor would he patiently allow me to enlarge upon Johnson's wonderful abilities; but exclaimed, "Is he like Burke, who winds into a subject like a serpent?" "But (said I) Johnson is the Hercules who strangled serpents in his cradle."

I dined with Dr. Johnson at General Paoli's. He was obliged, by indisposition, to leave the company early; he appointed me, however, to meet him in the evening at Mr. (now Sir Robert) Chambers's, in the Temple, where he accordingly came, though he continued to be very ill. Chambers, as is common on such occasions, prescribed various remedies to him. JOHNSON (fretted by pain): "Pr'ythee don't tease me. Stay till I am well, and then you shall tell me how to cure myself." He grew better, and talked with a noble enthusiasm of keeping up the representation of respectable families. His zeal on this subject was a circumstance in his character exceedingly remarkable, when it is considered that he himself had no pretensions to blood. I heard him once say, "I have great merit in being zealous for subordination and the honours of birth; for I can hardly tell who was my grandfather." He maintained the dignity and propriety of male succession, in opposition to the opinion of one of our friends, who had that day employed Mr. Chambers to draw his will, devising his estate to his three sisters, in preference to a remote heir male. Johnson called them "three *dowdies,*" and said, with as high a spirit as the boldest Baron in the most perfect days of the feudal system, "An ancient estate should always go to males. It is mighty foolish to let a stranger have it because he marries your daughter and takes your name. As for an estate newly acquired by trade, you may give it, if you will, to the dog *Towser,* and let him keep his *own* name."

I have known him at times exceedingly diverted at what seemed to others a very small sport. He now laughed immoderately, without any reason that we could perceive, at our friend's making his will; called him the *testator,* and added, "I dare say he thinks he has done a mighty thing. He won't stay till he gets home to his seat in the country, to produce this wonderful deed: he'll call up the landlord of the first inn on the road; and after a suitable preface upon mortality and the uncertainty of life, will tell him that he should not delay making his will; and here, Sir, will he say, is my will, which I have just made, with the assistance of one of the ablest lawyers in the kingdom; and he will read it to him (laughing all the time). He believes he has made this will; but he did not make it; you, Chambers, made it for him. I trust you have had more conscience than to make him say, 'being of sound understanding'; ha, ha, ha! I hope he has left me a legacy. I'd have his will turned into verse, like a ballad."

Mr. Chambers did not by any means relish this jocularity upon a matter of which *pars magna fuit,* and seemed impatient till he got rid of us. Johnson could not stop his merriment, but continued it all the way till he got without the Temple-gate. He then burst into such a fit of laughter, that he appeared to be almost in a convulsion; and, in order to support himself, laid hold of one of the posts at the side of the foot pavement, and sent forth peals so loud, that in the silence of the night his voice seemed to resound from Temple-bar to Fleet-ditch.

This most ludicrous exhibition of the awful, melancholy, and venerable Johnson, happened well to counteract the feelings of sadness which I used to experience when parting with him for a considerable time. I accompanied him to his door, where he gave me his blessing.

CHAPTER XXIV—1773

The Tour to the Hebrides

IN A LETTER FROM EDINBURGH, dated the 29th of May, I pressed him to persevere in his resolution to make this year the projected visit to the Hebrides, of which he and I had talked for many years, and which I was confident would afford us much entertainment.

"TO JAMES BOSWELL, ESQ.

"DEAR SIR,—

"When your letter came to me, I was so darkened by an inflammation in my eye that I could not for some time read it. I can now write without trouble, and can read large prints. My eye is gradually growing stronger; and I hope will be able to take some delight in the survey of a Caledonian loch.

"Chambers is going a judge, with six thousand a year, to Bengal. He and I shall come down together as far as Newcastle, and thence I shall easily get to Edinburgh. Let me know the exact time when your courts intermit. I must conform a little to Chambers's occasions, and he must conform a little to mine. The time which you shall fix, must be the common point to which we will come as near as we can. Except this eye, I am very well.

"Beattie is so caressed, and invited, and treated, and liked, and flattered, by the great, that I can see nothing of him. I am in great hope that he will be well provided for, and then we will live upon him at the Marischal College, without pity or modesty.

"[Langton] left the town without taking leave of me, and is gone in deep dudgeon to [Langton]. Is not this very childish? Where is now my legacy?

"I hope your dear lady and her dear baby are both well. I shall see them too when I come; and I have that opinion of your choice, as to suspect that when I have seen Mrs. Boswell, I shall be less willing to go away. I am, dear Sir,

"Your affectionate humble servant,

"SAM. JOHNSON.

"*Johnson's-court, Fleet-street,*
    "*July 5, 1773.*

"Write to me as soon as you can. Chambers is now at Oxford."

I again wrote to him, informing him that the Court of Session rose on the twelfth of August, hoping to see him before that time, and expressing, perhaps in too extravagant terms, my admiration of him, and my expectation of pleasure from our intended tour.

"TO JAMES BOSWELL, ESQ.

"DEAR SIR,—

"I shall set out from London on Friday the sixth of this month, and purpose not to loiter much by the way. Which day I shall be at Edinburgh, I cannot exactly tell. I suppose I must drive to an inn, and send a porter to find you.

"I am afraid Beattie will not be at his College soon enough for us, and I shall be sorry to miss him; but there is no staying for the concurrence of all conveniences. We will do as well as we can.

"I am, Sir,

"Your most humble servant,

"SAM. JOHNSON.

"*August 3, 1773.*"

"TO THE SAME.

"DEAR SIR,—

"Not being at Mr. Thrale's when your letter came, I had written the enclosed paper and sealed it; bringing it hither for a frank, I found yours. If any thing could repress my ardour, it would be such a letter as yours. To disappoint a friend is unpleasing: and he that forms expectations like yours, must be disappointed. Think only when you see me that you see a man who loves you, and is proud and glad that you love him.

"I am, Sir,

"Your most affectionate,

"SAM. JOHNSON.

"*August 3, 1773.*"

"TO THE SAME.

"DEAR SIR,—

"I came hither last night, and hope, but do not absolutely promise, to be in Edinburgh on Saturday. Beattie will not come so soon.

"I am, Sir,

"Your most humble servant,

"SAM. JOHNSON.

"My compliments to your lady."

"TO THE SAME.

"Mr. Johnson sends his compliments to Mr. Boswell, being just arrived at Boyd's.

"Saturday night."

His stay in Scotland was from the 18th of August, on which day he arrived, till the 22nd of November, when he set out on his return to London; and I believe ninety-four days were never passed by any man in a more vigorous exertion.

He came by the way of Berwick-upon-Tweed to Edinburgh, where he remained a few days, and then went by St. Andrews, Aberdeen, Inverness, and Fort Augustus, to the Hebrides, to visit which was the principal object he had in view. He visited the isles of Sky, Rasay, Col, Mull, Inchkenneth, and Icolmkill. He travelled through Argyleshire by Inverary, and from thence by Lochlomond and Dunbarton to Glasgow, then by Loudon to Auchinleck in Ayrshire, the seat of my family, and then by Hamilton, back to Edinburgh, where he again spent some time. He thus saw the four Universities of Scotland, its three principal cities, and as much of the Highland and insular life as was sufficient for his philosophical contemplation. I had the pleasure of accompanying him during the whole of his journey. He was respectfully entertained by the great, the learned, and the elegant, wherever he went; nor was he less delighted with the hospitality which he experienced in humbler life.

His various adventures, and the force and vivacity of his mind, as exercised during this peregrination, upon innumerable topics, have been faithfully, and to the best of my abilities, displayed in my "Journal of a Tour to the Hebrides," to which, as the public has been pleased to honour it by a very extensive circulation, I beg leave to refer, as to a separate and remarkable portion of his life, which may be there seen

[277]

in detail, and which exhibits as striking a view of his powers in conversation as his works do of his excellence in writing.

During his stay at Edinburgh, after his return from the Hebrides, he was at great pains to obtain information concerning Scotland; and it will appear from his subsequent letters that he was not less solicitous for intelligence on this subject after his return to London.

"TO JAMES BOSWELL, ESQ.

"DEAR SIR,—

"I came home last night, without any incommodity, danger, or weariness, and am ready to begin a new journey. I shall go to Oxford on Monday. I know Mrs. Boswell wished me well to go;[1] her wishes have not been disappointed. Mrs. Williams has received Sir A.'s letter.

"Make my compliments to all those to whom my compliments may be welcome.

"Let the box be sent as soon as it can, and let me know when to expect it.

"Inquire, if you can, the order of the Clans: Macdonald is first, Maclean is second; farther I cannot go. Quicken Dr. Webster.

"I am, Sir,
"Yours affectionately,
SAM. JOHNSON.

"*Nov. 27, 1773.*"

His humane forgiving disposition was put to a pretty strong test on his return to London by a liberty which Mr. Thomas Davies had taken with him in his absence, which was to publish two volumes entitled, "Miscellaneous and Fugitive Pieces," which he advertised in the newspapers, "By the Author of the *Rambler*." In this collection, several of Dr. Johnson's acknowledged writings, several of his anonymous performances, and some which he had written for others, were inserted; but there were also some in which he had no concern whatever. He

---

[1]In this he showed acute penetration. My wife paid him the most assiduous and respectful attention, while he was our guest: so that I wonder how he discovered her wishing for his departure. The truth is, that his irregular hours and uncouth habits, such as turning the candles with their heads downwards, when they did not burn bright enough, and letting the wax drop upon the carpet, could not but be disagreeable to a lady. Besides, she had not that high admiration of him which was felt by most of those who knew him; and what was very natural to a female mind, she thought he had too much influence over her husband. She once, in a little warmth, made, with more point than justice, this remark upon that subject: "I have seen many a bear led by a man; but I never before saw a man led by a bear."

was at first very angry, as he had good reason to be. But, upon consideration of his poor friend's narrow circumstances, and that he had only a little profit in view, and meant no harm, he soon relented, and continued his kindness to him as formerly.

He was now seriously engaged in writing an account of our travels in the Hebrides, in consequence of which I had the pleasure of a more frequent correspondence with him.

"TO JAMES BOSWELL, ESQ.

"DEAR SIR,—

"My operations have been hindered by a cough; at least I flatter myself that if my cough had not come I should have been farther advanced. But I have had no intelligence from Dr. W.——, [Webster] nor from the Excise-office, nor from you. No account of the little borough. Nothing of the Erse language. I have yet heard nothing of my box.

"You must make haste and gather me all you can, and do it quickly, or I will and shall do without it.

"Make my compliments to Mrs. Boswell, and tell her that I do not love her the less for wishing me away. I gave her trouble enough, and shall be glad, in recompense, to give her any pleasure.

"I would send some porter into the Hebrides if I knew which way it could be got to my kind friends there. Inquire, and let me know.

"Make my compliments to all the Doctors of Edinburgh, and to all my friends, from one end of Scotland to the other.

"Write to me, and send me what intelligence you can: and if any thing is too bulky for the post, let me have it by the carrier. I do not like trusting winds and waves.

"I am, dear Sir,

"Your most, etc.,

"SAM. JOHNSON.

"*Jan. 29, 1774.*"

"TO THE SAME.

"DEAR SIR,—

"In a. day or two after I had written the last discontented letter, I received my box, which was very welcome. But still I must entreat you to hasten Dr. Webster, and continue to pick up what you can, that may be useful.

"Mr. Oglethorpe was with me this morning; you know his errand. He was not unwelcome.

"Tell Mrs. Boswell that my good intentions towards her still continue. I should be glad to do anything that would either benefit or please her.

"Chambers is not yet gone, but so hurried, or so negligent, or so proud, that I rarely see him. I have indeed, for some weeks past, been very ill of a cold and cough, and have been at Mrs. Thrale's, that I might be taken care of. I am much better; *novæ redeunt in prælia vires;* but I am yet tender, and easily disordered. How happy it was that neither of us were ill in the Hebrides.

"The question of Literary Property is this day before the Lords. Murphy drew up the Appellants' case, that is, the plea against the perpetual right. I have not seen it, nor heard the decision. I would not have the right perpetual.

"I will write to you as anything occurs, and do you send me something about my Scottish friends. I have very great kindness for them. Let me know likewise how fees come in, and when we are to see you.

"I am, Sir,
"Yours affectionately,
"Sam. Johnson.

"*London, Feb. 7, 1774.*"

"TO JAMES BOSWELL, ESQ.

"Dear Sir,—

"Dr. Webster's informations were much less exact and much less determinate than I expected: they are, indeed, much less positive than, if he can trust his own book which he laid before me, he is able to give. But I believe it will always be found that he who calls much for information will advance his work but slowly.

"I am, however, obliged to you, dear Sir, for your endeavours to help me, and hope that between us something will some time be done; if not on this, on some occasion.

"Chambers is either married, or almost married, to Miss Wilton, a girl of sixteen, exquisitely beautiful, whom he has with his lawyer's tongue, persuaded to take her chance with him in the East.

"We have added to the club, Charles Fox, Sir Charles Bunbury, Dr. Fordyce, and Mr. Steevens.

"Return my thanks to Dr. Webster. Tell Dr. Robertson I have not much to reply to his censure of my negligence; and tell Dr. Blair that

[280]

Oliver Goldsmith.

since he has written hither what I said to him, we must now consider ourselves as even, forgive one another, and begin again. I care not how soon, for he is a very pleasing man. Pay my compliments to all my friends, and remind Lord Elibank of his promise to give me all his works.

"I hope Mrs. Boswell and little Miss are well.—When shall I see them again? She is a sweet lady, only she was so glad to see me go that I have almost a mind to come again that she may again have the same pleasure.

"Inquire if it be practicable to send a small present of a cask of porter to Dunvegan, Rasay, and Col. I would not wish to be thought forgetful of civilities.

"I am, Sir,
"Your humble servant,
"Sam. Johnson.

"*March 5, 1774.*"

On the 5th of March I wrote to him, requesting his counsel whether I should this spring come to London. I stated to him on the one hand some pecuniary embarrassments, which, together with my wife's situation at that time, made me hesitate; and, on the other, the pleasure and improvement which my annual visit to the metropolis always afforded me; and particularly mentioned a peculiar satisfaction which I experienced in celebrating the festival of Easter in St. Paul's Cathedral; that, to my fancy, it appeared like going up to Jerusalem at the feast of the Passover; and that the strong devotion which I felt on that occasion diffused its influence on my mind through the rest of the year.

"to james boswell, esq.

[*Not dated, but written about the 15th of March.*]

"Dear Sir,—

"I am ashamed to think that since I received your letter I have passed so many days without answering it.

"I think there is no great difficulty in resolving your doubts. The reasons for which you are inclined to visit London are, I think, not of sufficient strength to answer the objections. That you should delight to come once a year to the fountain of intelligence and pleasure is very natural; but both information and pleasure must be regulated by propriety. Pleasure, which cannot be obtained but by unseasonable or unsuitable expense, must always end in pain; and pleasure, which must be enjoyed at the expense of another's pain, can never be such as a worthy mind can fully delight in.

"What improvement you might gain by coming to London, you may easily supply or easily compensate by enjoining yourself some particular study at home, or opening some new avenue to information. Edinburgh is not yet exhausted; and I am sure you will find no pleasure here which can deserve either that you should anticipate any part of your future fortune, or that you should condemn yourself and your lady to penurious frugality for the rest of the year.

"I need not tell you what regard you owe to Mrs. Boswell's entreaties; or how much you ought to study the happiness of her who studies yours with so much diligence, and of whose kindness you enjoy such good effects. Life cannot subsist in society but by reciprocal concessions. She permitted you to ramble last year, you must permit her now to keep you at home.

"Your last reason is so serious that I am unwilling to oppose it. Yet you must remember that your image of worshipping once a year in a certain place, in imitation of the Jews, is but a comparison; and *simile non est idem;* if the annual resort to Jerusalem was a duty to the Jews, it was a duty because it was commanded; and you have no such command, therefore no such duty. It may be dangerous to receive too readily, and indulge too fondly, opinions from which, perhaps, no pious mind is wholly disengaged, of local sanctity and local devotion. You know what strange effects they have produced over a great part of the Christian world. I am now writing, and you, when you read this, are reading, under the Eye of Omnipresence.

"To what degree fancy is to be admitted into religious offices, it would require much deliberation to determine. I am far from intending totally to exclude it. Fancy is a faculty bestowed by our Creator, and it is reasonable that all his gifts should be used to his glory, that all our faculties should co-operate in his worship; but they are to co-operate according to the will of him that gave them, according to the order which his wisdom has established. As ceremonies prudential or convenient are less obligatory than positive ordinances, as bodily worship is only the token to others or ourselves of mental adoration, so Fancy is always to act in subordination to Reason. We may take fancy for a companion, but must follow Reason as our guide. We may allow Fancy to suggest certain ideas in certain places; but Reason must always be heard when she tells us that those ideas and those places have no natural or necessary relation. When we enter a church, we habitually recall to mind the duty of adoration, but we must not omit adoration for want of a temple; because we know, and ought to remember, that the Universal Lord is everywhere present; and that, therefore, to come to Iona, or to Jerusalem, though it may be useful, cannot be necessary.

"Thus I have answered your letter, and have not answered it negligently. I love you too well to be careless when you are serious.

"I think I shall be very diligent next week about our travels, which I have too long neglected.

"I am, dear Sir,

"Your most, etc.,

"SAM. JOHNSON.

"Compliments to Madam and Miss."

"TO THE SAME.

"*Streatham, June 12, 1774.*

"DEAR SIR,—

"Yesterday I put the first sheets of the 'Journey to the Hebrides' to the Press. I have endeavoured to do you some justice in the first paragraph. It will be one volume in octavo, not thick.

"It will be proper to make some presents in Scotland. You shall tell me to whom I shall give; and I have stipulated twenty-five for you to give in your own name. Some will take the present better from me, others better from you. In this, you, who are to live in the place, ought to direct. Consider it. Whatever you can get for my purpose, send me: and make my compliments to your lady and both the young ones.

"I am, Sir, yours, etc.,

"SAM. JOHNSON.

"MR. BOSWELL TO DR. JOHNSON.

"*Edinburgh, June 24, 1774.*

"You do not acknowledge the receipt of the various packets which I have sent to you. Neither can I prevail with you to *answer* my letters, though you honour me with *returns*. You have said nothing to me about poor Goldsmith, nothing about Langton.

"I have received for you, from the Society for Propagating Christian Knowledge in Scotland, the following Erse books:—'The New Testament';—'Baxter's Call';—'The Confession of Faith of the Assembly of Divines at Westminster';—'The Mother's Catechism';—'A Gaelic and English Vocabulary.' "

"TO JAMES BOSWELL, ESQ.

"DEAR SIR,—

"I wish you could have looked over my book before the printer, but it could not easily be. I suspect some mistakes; but as I deal, perhaps, more in notions than in facts, the matter is not great, and the second edition will be mended, if any such there be. The press will go on slowly for a time, because I am going into Wales to-morrow.

"I should be very sorry if I appeared to treat such a character as Lord Hailes otherwise than with high respect. I return the sheets, to which I have done what mischief I could; and finding it so little, thought not much of sending them. The narrative is clear, lively, and short.

"I have done worse to Lord Hailes than by neglecting his sheets: I have run him in debt. Dr. Horne, the President of Magdalen College in Oxford, wrote to me about three months ago that he purposed to reprint Walton's 'Lives,' and desired me to contribute to the work: my answer was, that Lord Hailes intended the same publication; and Dr. Horne has resigned it to him. His Lordship must now think seriously about it.

"Of poor dear Dr. Goldsmith there is little to be told more than the papers have made public. He died of a fever, made, I am afraid, more violent by uneasiness of mind. His debts began to be heavy, and all his resources were exhausted. Sir Joshua is of opinion that he owed not less than two thousand pounds. Was ever poet so trusted before?

"You may, if you please, put the inscription thus:

" '*Maria Scotorum Regina nata 15—, a suis in exilium acta 15—, a bhospitâ neci data 15—.*' You must find the years.

"Of your second daughter you certainly gave the account yourself, though you have forgotten it. While Mrs. Boswell is well, never doubt of a boy. Mrs. Thrale brought, I think, five girls running, but while I was with you she had a boy.

"I am obliged to you for all your pamphlets, and of the last I hope to make some use. I made some of the former.

"I am, dear Sir,

"Your most affectionate servant,

"SAM. JOHNSON.

"*July 4, 1774.*

"My compliments to all the three ladies."

"MR. BOSWELL TO DR. JOHNSON.

"*Edinburgh, Aug. 30, 1774.*

"You have given me an inscription for a portrait of Mary Queen of Scots, in which you, in a short and striking manner, point out her hard fate. But you will be pleased to keep in mind that my picture is a representation of a particular scene in her history; her being forced to resign her crown, while she was imprisoned in the castle of Lochleven. I must, therefore, beg that you will be kind enough to give me an inscription suited to that particular scene; or determine which of the two formerly transmitted to you is the best; and, at any rate, favour me with an English translation. It will be doubly kind if you comply with my request speedily.

"Your critical notes on the specimen of Lord Hailes's 'Annals of Scotland' are excellent. I agreed with you on every one of them. He himself objected only to the alteration of *free* to *brave,* in the passage where he says that Edward 'departed with the glory due to the conqueror of a free people.' He says, to call the Scots brave would only add to the glory of their conqueror. You will make allowance for the national zeal of our annalist. I now send a few more leaves of the Annals, which I hope you will peruse, and return with observations, as you did upon the former occasion. Lord Hailes writes to me thus: 'Mr. Boswell will be pleased to express the grateful sense which Sir David Dalrymple has of Dr. Johnson's attention to his little specimen. The farther specimen will show that

'Even in an *Edward* he can see desert.'

"It gives me much pleasure to hear that a republication of Isaac Walton's 'Lives' is intended. You have been in a mistake in thinking that Lord Hailes had it in view. I remember one morning, while he sat with you in my house, he said that there should be a new edition of Walton's 'Lives'; and you said that 'they should be be-noted a little.' This was all that passed on that subject. You must, therefore, inform Dr. Horne that he may resume his plan. I enclose a note concerning it; and if Dr. Horne will write to me, all the attention that I can give shall be cheerfully bestowed upon what I think a pious work, the preservation and elucidation of Walton, by whose writings I have been most pleasingly edified."

*   *   *

Dr. Johnson disliked Scotch scenery, and Scotchmen even more

"MR. BOSWELL TO DR. JOHNSON.

"Edinburgh, Sept. 16, 1774.

"Wales has probably detained you longer than I supposed. You will have become quite a mountaineer, by visiting Scotland one year and Wales another. You must next go to Switzerland. Cambria will complain if you do not honour her also with some remarks. And I find *concessere columnæ*, the booksellers expect another book. I am impatient to see your 'Tour to Scotland and the Hebrides.' Might you not send me a copy by the post as soon as it is printed off?"

*   *   *

"TO JAMES BOSWELL, ESQ.

"DEAR SIR,—

"Yesterday I returned from my Welsh journey. I was sorry to leave my book suspended so long; but having an opportunity of seeing, with so much convenience, a new part of the island, I could not reject it. I have been in five of the six counties of North Wales; and have seen St. Asaph and Bangor, the two seats of their bishops; have been upon Penmanmaur and Snowdon, and passed over into Anglesea. But Wales is so little different from England, that it offers nothing to the speculation of the traveller.

"When I came home, I found several of your papers, with some pages of Lord Hailes's 'Annals,' which I will consider. I am in haste to give you some account of myself, lest you should suspect me of negligence in the pressing business which I find recommended to my care, and which I knew nothing of till now, when all care is vain.

"In the distribution of my books I purpose to follow your advice, adding such as shall occur to me. I am not pleased with your notes of remembrance added to your names, for I hope I shall not easily forget them.

"I have received four Erse books, without any direction, and suspect that they are intended for the Oxford library. If that is the intention, I think it will be proper to add the metrical Psalms, and whatever else is printed in Erse, that the present may be complete. The donor's name should be told.

"I wish you could have read the book before it was printed, but our distance does not easily permit it.

"I am sorry Lord Hailes does not intend to publish Walton; I am afraid it will not be done so well, if it be done at all.

"I purpose now to drive the book forward. Make my compliments to Mrs. Boswell, and let me hear often from you.

> "I am, dear Sir,
> > "Your affectionate humble servant,
> > > "SAM. JOHNSON.

"*London, October 1, 1774.*"

This tour to Wales, which was made in company with Mr. and Mrs. Thrale, though it no doubt contributed to his health and amusement, did not give an occasion to such a discursive exercise of his mind as our tour to the Hebrides. I do not find that he kept any journal or notes of what he saw there. All that I heard him say of it was that "instead of bleak and barren mountains, there were green and fertile ones; and that one of the castles in Wales would contain all the castles that he had seen in Scotland."

Parliament having been dissolved, and his friend Mr. Thrale, who was a steady supporter of Government, having again to encounter the storm of a contested election, he wrote a short political pamphlet, entitled "The Patriot," [*] addressed to the electors of Great Britain; a title which, to factious men who consider a patriot only as an opposer of the measures of government, will appear strangely misapplied. It was, however, written with energetic vivacity; and, except those passages in which it endeavours to vindicate the glaring outrage of the House of Commons in the case of the Middlesex election, and to justify the attempt to reduce our fellow-subjects in America to unconditional submission, it contained an admirable display of the properties of a real patriot, in the original and genuine sense;—a sincere, steady, rational, and unbiased friend in the interests and prosperity of his king and country. It must be acknowledged, however, that both in this and his two former pamphlets, there was, amidst many powerful arguments, not only a considerable portion of sophistry, but a contemptuous ridicule of his opponents, which was very provoking.

CHAPTER XXV—1775

Johnson and Macpherson

THE FIRST EFFORT OF HIS PEN, in 1775, was "Proposals for publishing the Works of Mrs. Charlotte Lennox," [†] in three volumes quarto. In his diary, January 2, I find this entry: "Wrote Charlotte's 'Proposals.' " But, indeed, the internal evidence would have been quite sufficient.

He this year also wrote the Preface to Baretti's "Easy Lessons in Italian and English." [†]

"TO JAMES BOSWELL, ESQ.

"DEAR SIR,—

"You never did ask for a book by the post till now, and I did not think on it. You see now it is done. I sent one to the King, and I hear he likes it.

"I shall send a parcel into Scotland for presents, and intend to give to many of my friends. In your catalogue, you left out Lord Auchinleck.

"Let me know, as fast as you read it, how you like it; and let me know if any mistake is committed, or anything important left out. I wish you could have seen the sheets. My compliments to Mrs. Boswell, and to Veronica, and to all my friends.

"I am, Sir,

"Your most humble servant,

"SAM. JOHNSON.

"*January 14, 1775.*"

"MR. BOSWELL TO DR. JOHNSON.

"*Edinburgh, Jan. 19, 1775.*

"Be pleased to accept of my best thanks for your 'Journey to the Hebrides,' which came to me by last night's post. I did really ask the favour twice; but you have been even with me by granting it so speedily. Bis *dat qui cito dat.* Though ill of a bad cold, you kept me up the greatest part of the last night: for I did not stop till I had read every word of your book. I looked back to our first talking of a visit to the Hebrides, which was many years ago, when sitting by ourselves in the Mitre Tavern, in London, I think about *witching time o' night:* and then exulted in contemplating our scheme fulfilled, and a *monumentium perenne* of it erected by your superior abilities. I shall only say that your book has afforded me a high gratification. I shall afterwards give you my thoughts on particular passages. In the meantime, I hasten to tell you of your having mistaken two names, which you will correct in London, as I shall do here, that the gentlemen who deserve the valuable compliments which you have paid them, may enjoy their honours. In page 106, for *Gordon* read *Murchison;* and in page 357, for *Maclean* read *Macleod.*"

"TO JAMES BOSWELL, ESQ.

"DEAR SIR,—

"I long to hear how you like the book; it is, I think, much liked here. But Macpherson is very furious: can you give me any more intelligence about him, or his Fingal? Do what you can, and do it quickly. Is Lord Hailes on our side?

"Pray let me know what I owed you when I left you, that I may send it to you.

"I am going to write about the Americans. If you have picked up any hints among your lawyers, who are great masters of the law of

[289]

nations, or if your own mind suggest anything, let me know. But mum, it is a secret.

"I will send your parcel of books as soon as I can, but I cannot do as I wish. However, you will find everything mentioned in the book which you recommended.

"Langton is here; we are all that ever we were. He is a worthy fellow, without malice, though not without resentment.

"Poor Beauclerk is so ill, that his life is thought to be in danger. Lady Di nurses him with very great assiduity.

"Reynolds has taken too much to strong liquor, and seems to delight in his new character.

"This is all the news that I have; but as you love verses, I will send you a few which I made upon Inchkenneth; but remember the condition, you shall not show them, except to Lord Hailes, whom I love better than any man whom I know so little. If he asks you to transcribe them for him, you may do it, but I think he must promise not to let them be copied again, nor to show them as mine.

"I have at last sent back Lord Hailes's sheets. I never think about returning them, because I alter nothing. You will see that I might as well have kept them. However, I am ashamed of my delay: and if I have the honour of receiving any more, promise punctually to return them by the next post. Make my compliments to dear Mrs. Boswell, and to Miss Veronica.

> "I am, dear Sir,
> "Yours most faithfully,
> "SAM. JOHNSON.

"*Jan. 1, 1775.*"

"MR. BOSWELL TO DR. JOHNSON.

> "*Edinburgh, Jan. 27, 1775.*

*   *   *

"You rate our lawyers here too high, when you call them great masters of the law of nations.

*   *   *

"As for myself, I am ashamed to say I have read little and thought little on the subject of America. I will be much obliged to you if you will direct me where I shall find the best information of what is to be said on both sides. It is a subject vast in its present extent and future consequences. The imperfect hints which now float in my mind tend rather to the formation of an opinion that our Government has been precipitant and severe in the resolutions taken against the Bostonians. Well do you know that I have no kindness for that race. But nations, or bodies of men, should, as well as individuals, have a fair trial, and not be condemned on character alone. Have we not express contracts with our colonies, which afford a more certain foundation of judgment, than general political speculations on the mutual rights of States and their provinces or colonies? Pray let me know immediately what to read, and I shall diligently endeavour to gather for you anything that I can find. Is Burke's speech on American taxation published by himself? Is it authentic? I remember to have heard you say that you had never considered East India affairs: though, surely, they are of much importance to Great Britain. Under the recollection of this, I shelter myself from the reproach of ignorance about the Americans. If you write upon the subject, I shall certainly understand it. But, since you seem to expect that I should know something of it, without your instruction and that my own mind should suggest something, I trust you will put me in the way.

* * *

"What does Becket mean by the *Originals* of Fingal, and other poems of Ossian, which he advertises to have lain in his shop?"

"MR. BOSWELL TO DR. JOHNSON.

"*Edinburgh, Feb. 2, 1775.*

* * *

"As to Macpherson, I am anxious to have from yourself a full and pointed account of what has passed between you and him. It is confidently told here that before your book came out he sent to you to let you know that he understood you meant to deny the authenticity of Ossian's poems; that the originals were in his possession; that you might have inspection of them, and might take the evidence of people skilled in the Erse language; and that he hoped, after this fair offer, you would not be so uncandid as to assert that he had refused reasonable proof. That you paid no regard to his message, but published your strong attack upon him; and then he wrote a letter to you in such terms as he thought suited to one who had not acted as a man of veracity.

You may believe it gives me pain to hear your conduct represented as unfavourable, while I can only deny what is said, on the ground that your character refutes it, without having any information to oppose. Let me, I beg it of you, be furnished with a sufficient answer to any calumny upon this occasion.

"Lord Hailes writes to me (for we correspond more than we talk together): 'As to Fingal, I see a controversy arising, and purpose to keep out of its way. There is no doubt that I might mention some circumstances; but I do not choose to commit them to paper.' What his opinion is, I do not know. He says, 'I am singularly obliged to Dr. Johnson for his accurate and useful criticisms. Had he given some strictures on the general plan of the work, it would have added much to his favours.' He is charmed with your verses in Inchkenneth, says they are very elegant, but bids me tell you he doubts whether

'Legitimas faciunt pectora pura preces'

be according to the rubric: but that is your concern; for, you know, he is a Presbyterian."

"TO JAMES BOSWELL, ESQ.

"My dear Boswell,—

"I am surprised that, knowing as you do the disposition of your countrymen to tell lies in favour of each other, you can be at all affected by any reports that circulate among them. Macpherson never in his life offered me a sight of any original, or of any evidence of any kind; but thought only of intimidating me by noise and threats, till my last answer—that I would not be deterred from detecting what I thought a cheat, by the menaces of a ruffian—put an end to our correspondence.

"The state of the question is this. He, and Dr. Blair, whom I consider as deceived, say that he copied the poem from old manuscripts. His copies, if he had them, and I believe him to have none, are nothing. Where are the manuscripts? They can be shown if they exist, but they were never shown. *De non existentibus et non apparentibus*, says our law, *eadem est ratio*. No man has a claim to credit upon his own word, when better evidence, if he had it, may be easily produced. But so far as we can find, the Erse language was never written till very lately for the purposes of religion. A nation that cannot write, or a language that was never written, has no manuscripts.

"But whatever he has he never offered to show. If old manuscripts should now be mentioned, I should, unless there were more evidence than can be easily had, suppose them another proof of Scotch conspiracy in national falsehood.

"Do not censure the expression; you know it to be true.

"I am now engaged, but in a little time I hope to do all you would have. My compliments to Madam and Veronica.

"I am, Sir,

"Your most humble servant,

"SAM. JOHNSON.

"Feb. 7, 1775."

What words were used by Mr. Macpherson, in his letter to the venerable Sage, I have never heard; but they are generally said to have been of a nature very different from the language of literary contest. Dr. Johnson's answer appeared in the newspapers of the day, and has since been frequently re-published; but not with perfect accuracy. I give it as dictated to me by himself, written down in his presence and authenticated by a note in his own handwriting. *"This, I think, is a true copy."*

"MR. JAMES MACPHERSON,—

"I received your foolish and impudent letter. Any violence offered me I shall do my best to repel; and what I cannot do for myself, the law shall do for me. I hope I shall not be deterred from detecting what I think a cheat by the menaces of a ruffian.

"What would you have me retract? I thought your book an imposture; I think it an imposture still. For this opinion I have given my reasons to the public, which I here dare you to refute. Your rage I defy. Your abilities, since your Homer, are not so formidable: and what I hear of your morals inclines me to pay regard, not to what you shall say, but to what you shall prove. You may print this if you will.

"SAM. JOHNSON."

Mr. Macpherson little knew the character of Dr. Johnson if he supposed that he could be easily intimidated; for no man was ever more remarkable for personal courage. He had, indeed, an awful dread of death, or rather, "of something after death"; and what rational man, who seriously thinks of quitting all that he has ever known, and going into a new and unknown state of being, can be without that dread? But his fear was from reflection; his courage natural. His fear, in that

one instance, was the result of philosophical and religious consideration. He feared death, but he feared nothing else, not even what might
occasion death. Many instances of his resolution may be mentioned.
One day, at Mr. Beauclerk's house in the country, when two large dogs
were fighting, he went up to them and beat them till they separated;
and at another time, when told of the danger there was that a gun
might burst if charged with many balls, he put in six or seven, and
fired it off against a wall. Mr. Langton told me that when they were
swimming together near Oxford, he cautioned Dr. Johnson against a
pool, which was reckoned particularly dangerous; upon which Johnson
directly swam into it. He told me himself that one night he was attacked in the street by four men, to whom he would not yield, but
kept them all at bay, till the watch came up, and carried both him
and them to the round-house. In the play-house at Lichfield, as Mr
Garrick informed me, Johnson having for a moment quitted a chair
which was placed for him between the side-scenes, a gentleman took
possession of it, and when Johnson on his return civilly demanded his
seat, rudely refused to give it up; upon which Johnson laid hold of it,
and tossed him and the chair into the pit. Foote, who so successfully
revived the old comedy, by exhibiting living characters, had resolved to
imitate Johnson on the stage, expecting great profits from his ridicule
of so celebrated a man. Johnson being informed of his intention, and
being at dinner at Mr. Thomas Davies's the bookseller, from whom I
had the story, he asked Mr. Davies, "what was the common price of an
oak stick"; and being answered sixpence, "Why then, Sir (said he),
give me leave to send your servant to purchase me a shilling one. I'll
have a double quantity; for I am told Foote means to *take me off*, as
he calls it, and I am determined the fellow shall not do it with impunity." Davies took care to acquaint Foote of this, which effectually
checked the wantonness of the mimic. Mr. Macpherson's menaces made
Johnson provide himself with the same implement of defence; and
had he been attacked, I have no doubt that, old as he was, he would
have made his corporal prowess be felt as much as his intellectual.

Johnson's grateful acknowledgments of kindness received in the
course of this tour, completely refute the brutal reflections which have
been thrown out against him, as if he had made an ungrateful return;
and his delicacy in sparing in his book those who we find, from his
letters to Mrs. Thrale, were just objects of censure, is much to be
admired.

He expressed to his friend, Mr. Windham of Norfolk, his wonder at the extreme jealousy of the Scotch, and their resentment at having their country described by him as it really was; when to say that it was a country as good as England would have been a gross falsehood. "None of us (said he) would be offended if a foreigner who has travelled here should say that vines and olives don't grow in England." And as to his prejudice against the Scotch, which I always ascribed to that nationality which he observed in *them,* he said to the same gentleman, "When I find a Scotchman, to whom an Englishman is as a Scotchman, that Scotchman shall be as an Englishman to me." His intimacy with many gentlemen of Scotland, and his employing so many natives of that country as his amanuenses, prove that his prejudice was not virulent; and I have deposited in the British Museum, amongst other pieces of his writing, the following note in answer to one from me, asking if he would meet me at dinner at the *Mitre,* though a friend of mine, a Scotchman, was to be there:—"Mr. Johnson does not see why Mr. Boswell should suppose a Scotchman less acceptable than any other man. He will be at the *Mitre.*"

My much-valued friend Dr. Barnard, now Bishop of Killaloe, having once expressed to him an apprehension that if he should visit Ireland he might treat the people of that country more unfavourably than he had done the Scotch, he answered, with strong pointed double-edged wit, "Sir, you have no reason to be afraid of me. The Irish are not in a conspiracy to cheat the world by false representations of the merits of their countrymen. No, Sir; the Irish are a *fair people;*—they never speak well of one another."

"MR. BOSWELL TO DR. JOHNSON.

"*Edinburgh, Feb. 18, 1775.*

"You would have been very well pleased if you had dined with me to-day. I had for my guests, Macquharrie, young Maclean of Col, the successor of our friend, a very amiable man, though not marked with such active qualities as his brother; Mr. Maclean of Torloisk in Mull, a gentleman of Sir Allan's family; and two of the clan Grant; so that the Highland and Hebridean genius reigned. We had a great deal of conversation about you, and drank your health in a bumper. The toast was not proposed by me, which is a circumstance to be remarked, for I am now so connected with you that anything I can say or do to your honour has not the value of an additional compliment. It is only giving you a guinea out of that treasure of admiration which already belongs to you, and which is no hidden treasure; for I suppose my admiration of you is co-existent with the knowledge of my character.

"I find that the Highlanders and Hebrideans in general are much fonder of your 'Journey' than the low country or *hither* Scots. One of the Grants said to-day that he was sure you were a man of a good heart, and a candid man, and seemed to hope he should be able to convince you of the antiquity of a good proportion of the poems of Ossian. After all that has passed, I think the matter is capable of being proved to a certain degree. I am told that Macpherson got one old Erse MS. from Clanranald, for the restitution of which he executed a formal obligation; and it is affirmed that the Gaelic (call it Erse, or call it Irish) has been written in the Highlands and Hebrides for many centuries. It is reasonable to suppose that such of the inhabitants as acquired any learning possessed the art of writing as well as their Irish neighbours and Celtic cousins; and the question is, can sufficient evidence be shown of this?

"Those who are skilled in ancient writings can determine the age of MSS., or at least can ascertain the century in which they were written; and if men of veracity, who are so skilful, shall tell us that MSS. in the possession of families in the Highlands and isles are the works of a remote age, I think we should be convinced by their testimony.

"There is now come to this city Ranald Macdonald from the Isle of Egg, who has several MSS. of Erse poetry, which he wishes to publish by subscription. I have engaged to take three copies of the book, the price of which is to be six shillings, as I would subscribe for all the Erse that can be printed, be it old or new, that the language may be preserved. This man says that some of his manuscripts are ancient: and, to be sure, one of them which was shown to me does appear to have the duskiness of antiquity.

* * *

"The inquiry is not yet quite hopeless, and I should think that the exact truth may be discovered, if proper means be used.

"I am, etc.,

"JAMES BOSWELL."

"TO JAMES BOSWELL, ESQ.

"DEAR SIR,—

"I am sorry that I could get no books for my friends in Scotland. Mr. Strahan has at last promised to send two dozen to you. If they come, put the names of my friends into them; you may cut them out, and paste them with a little starch in the book.

"You then are going wild about Ossian. Why do you think any part can be proved? The dusky manuscript of Egg is probably not fifty years old; if it be a hundred, it proves nothing. The tale of Clanranald is no proof. Has Clanranald told it? Can he prove it? There are, I believe, no Erse manuscripts. None of the old families had a single letter in Erse that we heard of. You say it is likely that they could write. The learned, if any learned there were, could; but knowing by that learning, some written language, in that language they wrote, as letters had never been applied to their own. If there are manuscripts, let them be shown, with some proof that they are not forged for the occasion. You say, many can remember parts of Ossian. I believe all those parts are versions of the English; at least there is no proof of their antiquity.

"Macpherson is said to have made some translations himself: and having taught a boy to write it, ordered him to say that he had learnt it of his grandmother. The boy, when he grew up, told the story. This Mrs. Williams heard at Mr. Strahan's table. Don't be credulous; you know how little a Highlander can be trusted. Macpherson is, so far as I know, very quiet. Is not that proof enough? Every thing is against him. No visible manuscript: no inscription in the language: no correspondence among friends: no transaction of business, of which a single scrap remains in the ancient families. Macpherson's pretence is that the character was Saxon. If he had not talked unskilfully of *manuscripts*, he might have fought with oral tradition much longer. As to Mr. Grant's information, I suppose he knows much less of the matter than ourselves.

"In the meantime, the bookseller says that the sale is sufficiently quick. They printed four thousand. Correct your copy wherever it is wrong, and bring it up. Your friends will all be glad to see you. I think of going myself into the country about May.

"I am sorry that I have not managed to send the book sooner. I have left four for you, and do not restrict you absolutely to follow my directions in the distribution. You must use your own discretion.

"Make my compliments to Mrs. Boswell: I suppose she is now beginning to forgive me.

"I am, dear Sir,

"Your humble servant,

"SAM. JOHNSON.

"*Feb. 25, 1775.*"

CHAPTER XXVI—1775

Mrs. Abington

ON TUESDAY, MARCH 21, I arrived in London; and on repairing to Dr. Johnson's before dinner, found him in his study, sitting with Mr. Peter Garrick, the elder brother of David, strongly resembling him in countenance and voice, but of more sedate and placid manners. Both at this interview, and in the evening at Mr. Thrale's, where he and Mr. Peter Garrick and I met again, he was vehement on the subject of the Ossian controversy; observing, "We do not know that there are any ancient Erse manuscripts; and we have no other reason to disbelieve that there are men with three heads, but that we do not know that there are any such men." He also was outrageous, upon his supposition that my countrymen "loved Scotland better than truth," saying, "All of them—nay, not all—but *droves* of them, would come up and attest any thing for the honour of Scotland." He also persevered in his wild allegation that he questioned if there was a tree between Edinburgh and the English border older than himself. I assured him he was mistaken, and suggested that the proper punishment would be that he should receive a stripe at every tree above a hundred years old that was found within that space. He laughed, and said, "I believe I might submit to it for a *baubee.*"

The doubts which, in my correspondence with him, I had ventured to state as to the justice and wisdom of the conduct of Great Britain towards the American colonies, while I at the same time requested that he would enable me to inform myself upon that momentous subject, he had altogether disregarded; and had recently published a pamphlet, entitled, "Taxation no Tyranny; an answer to the Resolutions and Address of the American Congress." [*]

He had long before indulged most unfavourable sentiments of our fellow-subjects in America. For, as early as 1769, I was told by Dr. John Campbell that he had said of them, "Sir, they are a race of convicts, and ought to be thankful for any thing we allow them short of hanging."

Of this performance I avoided to talk with him; for I had now formed a clear and settled opinion that the people of America were well warranted to resist a claim that their fellow-subjects in the mother-country should have the entire command of their fortunes, by taxing them without their own consent; and the extreme violence which it breathed appeared to me so unsuitable to the mildness of a Christian philosopher, and so directly opposite to the principles of peace which he had so beautifully recommended in his pamphlet respecting Falkland's Islands, that I was sorry to see him appear in so unfavourable a light. Besides, I could not perceive in it that ability of argument, or that felicity of expression, for which he was, upon other occasions, so eminent. Positive assertion, sarcastical severity, and extravagant ridicule, which he himself reprobated as a test of truth, were united in this rhapsody.

That this pamphlet was written at the desire of those who were then in power, I have no doubt; and, indeed, he owned to me that it had been revised and curtailed by some of them. He told me that they had struck out one passage, which was to this effect: "That the Colonists could with no solidity argue, from their not having been taxed while in their infancy, that they should not now be taxed. We do not put a calf into the plough: we wait till he is an ox." He said, "They struck it out either critically as too ludicrous, or politically as too exasperating. I care not which. It was their business. If an architect says, I will build five stories, and the man who employs him says, I will have only three, the employer is to decide." "Yes, Sir (said I), in ordinary cases. But should it be so when the architect gives his skill and labour *gratis?*"

He complained to a Right Honourable friend of distinguished talents and very elegant manners, with whom he maintained a long intimacy, and whose generosity towards him will afterwards appear, that his pension having been given to him as a literary character, he had been applied to by Administration to write political pamphlets; and he was even so much irritated that he declared his resolution to resign his pension. His friend showed him the impropriety of such a measure, and he afterwards expressed his gratitude, and said he had received good advice. To that friend he once signified a wish to have his pension secured to him for his life; but he neither asked nor received from Government any reward whatsoever for his political labours.

On Friday, March 24, I met him at the Literary Club, where were Mr. Beauclerk, Mr. Langton, Mr. Colman, Dr. Percy, Mr. Vesey, Sir Charles Bunbury, Dr. George Fordyce, Mr. Steevens, and Mr. Charles Fox.

I found his "Journey" the common topic of conversation in London at this time, wherever I happened to be. At one of Lord Mansfield's formal Sunday evening conversations, strangely called *levées,* his Lordship addressed me, "We have all been reading your travels, Mr. Boswell." I answered, "I was but the humble attendant of Dr. Johnson." The Chief Justice replied, with that air and manner which none who ever saw and heard him can forget, "He speaks ill of nobody but Ossian."

Johnson was in high spirits this evening at the club, and talked with great animation and success. JOHNSON: "Sheridan is a wonderful admirer of the tragedy of Douglas, and presented its author with a gold medal. Some years ago, at a coffee-house in Oxford, I called to him, 'Mr. Sheridan, Mr. Sheridan, how came you to give a gold medal to Home, for writing that foolish play?' This, you see, was wanton and insolent; but I *meant* to be wanton and insolent. A medal has no value but as a stamp of merit. And was Sheridan to assume to himself the right of giving that stamp? If Sheridan was magnificent enough to bestow a gold medal as an honorary reward of dramatic excellence, he should have requested one of the Universities to choose the person on whom it should be conferred. Sheridan had no right to give a stamp of merit: it was counterfeiting Apollo's coin."

On Monday, March 27, I breakfasted with him at Mr. Strahan's. He told us that he was engaged to go that evening to Mrs. Abington's benefit. "She was visiting some ladies whom I was visiting, and begged that I would come to her benefit. I told her I could not hear: but she insisted so much on my coming that it would have been brutal to have refused her." This was a speech quite characteristical. He loved to bring forward his having been in the gay circles of life; and he was, perhaps, a little vain of the solicitations of this elegant and fashionable actress. He told us the play was to be "The Hypocrite," altered from Cibber's "Nonjuror," so as to satirize the Methodists.

Mr. Strahan had taken a poor boy from the country as an apprentice, upon Johnson's recommendation. Johnson having inquired after him, said, "Mr. Strahan, let me have five guineas on account, and I'll give this boy one. Nay, if a man recommends a boy, and does nothing for him, it is sad work. Call him down."

I followed him into the court-yard, behind Mr. Strahan's house; and there I had a proof of what I had heard him profess, that he talked alike to all. "Some people tell you that they let themselves down to the capacity of their hearers. I never do that. I speak uniformly, in as intelligible a manner as I can."

"Well, my boy, how do you go on?"—"Pretty well, Sir; but they are afraid I ain't strong enough for some parts of the business." JOHNSON: "Why, I shall be sorry for it; for when you consider with how little mental power and corporeal labour a printer can get a guinea a week, it is a very desirable occupation for you. Do you hear—take all the pains you can; and if this does not do, we must think of some other way of life for you. There's a guinea."

Here was one of the many, many instances of his active benevolence. At the same time, the slow and sonorous solemnity with which, while he bent himself down, he addressed a little thick short-legged boy, contrasted with the boy's awkwardness and awe, could not but excite some ludicrous emotions.

I met him at Drury-lane playhouse in the evening. Sir Joshua Reynolds, at Mrs. Abington's request, had promised to bring a body of wits to her benefit; and having secured forty places in the front boxes, had done me the honour to put me in the group. Johnson sat on the seat directly behind me; and as he could neither see nor hear at such a distance from the stage, he was wrapped up in grave abstraction, and seemed quite a cloud, amidst all the sunshine of glitter and gaiety. I wondered at his patience in sitting out a play of five acts, and a farce of two. He said very little; but after the prologue to "Bon Ton" had been spoken, which he could hear pretty well from the more slow and distinct utterance, he talked on prologue-writing, and observed, "Dryden has written prologues superior to any that David Garrick has written, but David Garrick has written more good prologues than Dryden has done. It is wonderful that he has been able to write such variety of them."

At Mr. Beauclerk's, where I supped, was Mr. Garrick, whom I made happy with Johnson's praise of his prologues; and I suppose, in gratitude to him, he took up one of his favourite topics, the nationality of the Scotch, which he maintained in a pleasant manner, with the aid of a little poetical fiction.

Garrick, when he pleased, could imitate Johnson very exactly; for that great actor, with his distinguished powers of expression, which were so universally admired, possessed also an admirable talent of mimicry. He was always jealous that Johnson spoke lightly of him. I recollect his exhibiting him to me one day, as if saying, "Davy has some convivial pleasantry about him, but 'tis a futile fellow"; which he uttered perfectly with the tone and air of Johnson.

I cannot too frequently request of my readers, while they peruse my account of Johnson's conversation, to endeavour to keep in mind his deliberate and strong utterance. His mode of speaking was indeed very impressive, and I wish it could be preserved as music is written, according to the very ingenious method of Mr. Steele, who has shown how the recitation of Mr. Garrick, and other eminent speakers, might be transmitted to posterity *in score*."

Next day I dined with Johnson at Mr. Thrale's. He attacked Gray, calling him "a dull fellow." BOSWELL: "I understand he was reserved, and might appear dull in company; but surely he was not dull in poetry." JOHNSON: "Sir, he was dull in company, dull in his closet, dull everywhere. He was dull in a new way, and that made many people think him *great*. He was a mechanical poet." He then repeated some ludicrous lines, which have escaped my memory, and said, "Is not that *great*, like his Odes?" Mrs. Thrale maintained that his odes were melodious; upon which he exclaimed,

> "Weave the warp, and weave the woof";—

I added, in a solemn tone,

> " 'The winding-sheet of Edward's race.'

There is a good line."—"Ay (said he), and the next line is a good **one**" (pronouncing it contemptuously),

> " 'Give ample verge and room enough,'—

No, Sir, there are but two stanzas in Gray's poetry, which are in his 'Elegy in a Country Church-yard.' " He then repeated the stanza,

> "For who, to dumb forgetfulness a prey," etc.

mistaking one word; for instead of *precincts* he said *confines*. He added, "The other stanza I forget."

A young lady, who had married a man much her inferior in rank, being mentioned, a question arose, how a woman's relations should behave to her in such a situation; and, while I recapitulate the debate, and recollect what has since happened, I cannot but be struck in a manner that delicacy forbids me to express. While I contended that she ought to be treated with an inflexible steadiness of displeasure, Mrs. Thrale was all for mildness and forgiveness, and, according to the vulgar phrase, "making the best of a bad bargain." JOHNSON: "Madam, we must distinguish. Were I a man of rank, I would not let a daughter starve who had made a mean marriage; but having voluntarily degraded herself from the station which she was originally entitled to hold, I would support her only in that which she herself had chosen; and would not put her on a level with my other daughters. You are to consider, Madam, that it is our duty to maintain the subordination of civilized society; and when there is a gross and shameful deviation from rank, it should be punished so as to deter others from the same perversion."

Lord Chesterfield's letters being mentioned, Johnson said, "It was not to be wondered at that they had so great a sale, considering that they were the letters of a statesman, a wit, one who had been so much in the mouths of mankind, one long accustomed *virûm volitare per ora.*"

On Friday, March 31, I supped with him and some friends at a tavern. One of the company attempted, with too much forwardness, to rally him on his late appearance at the theatre; but had reason to repent of his temerity. "Why, Sir, did you go to Mrs. Abington's benefit? Did you see?" JOHNSON: "No, Sir." "Did you hear?" JOHNSON: "No, Sir." "Why, then, Sir, did you go?" JOHNSON: "Because, Sir, she is a favourite of the public; and when the public cares the thousandth part for you that it does for her, I will go to your benefit too."

Next morning I won a small bet from Lady Diana Beauclerk, by asking him as to one of his particularities, which her Ladyship laid I durst not do. It seems he had been frequently observed at the Club to put into his pocket the Seville oranges, after he had squeezed the juice of them into the drink which he made for himself. Beauclerk and Garrick talked of it to me, and seemed to think that he had a strange unwillingness to be discovered. We could not divine what he did with them; and this was the bold question to be put. I saw on his table the spoils of the preceding night, some fresh peels nicely scraped and cut into pieces. "O, Sir (said I), I now partly see what you do with the squeezed oranges which you put into your pocket at the Club." JOHNSON: "I have a great love for them." BOSWELL: "And pray, Sir, what do you do with them? You scrape them, it seems, very neatly, and what next?" JOHNSON: "Let them dry, Sir." BOSWELL: "And what next?" JOHNSON: "Nay, Sir, you shall know their fate no farther." BOSWELL: "Then the world must be left in the dark. It must be said (assuming a mock solemnity) he scraped them, and let them dry, but what he did with them next, he never could be prevailed upon to tell." JOHNSON: "Nay, Sir, you should say it more emphatically:—he could not be prevailed upon, even by his dearest friends, to tell."

He had this morning received his Diploma as Doctor of Laws, from the University of Oxford. He did not vaunt of his new dignity, but I understood he was highly pleased with it.[1]

He revised some sheets of Lord Hailes's "Annals of Scotland," and wrote a few notes on the margin with red ink, which he bade me tell his Lordship did not sink into the paper, and might be wiped off with a wet sponge, so that he did not spoil his manuscript.—I observed to him that there were very few of his friends so accurate as that I could venture to put down in writing what they told me as his sayings. JOHNSON: "Why should you write down *my* sayings?" BOSWELL: "I write them when they are good." JOHNSON: "Nay, you may as well write down the sayings of anyone else that are good." But, *where,* I might with great propriety have added, can I find such?

On Thursday, April 6, I dined with him at Mr. Thomas Davies's, with Mr. Hicky, the painter, and my old acquaintance, Mr. Moody, the player.

Dr. Johnson, as usual, spoke contemptuously of Colley Cibber. "It is wonderful that a man, who for forty years had lived with the great and witty, should have acquired so ill the talents of conversation: and he had but half to furnish; for one half of what he said was oaths." He, however, allowed considerable merit to some of his comedies, and said there was no reason to believe that the "Careless Husband" was not written by himself. Davies said he was the first dramatic writer who introduced genteel ladies upon the stage. Johnson refuted his observation by instancing several such characters in comedies before his time. DAVIES (trying to defend himself from a charge of ignorance): "I mean genteel moral characters." "I think (said Hicky) gentility and morality are inseparable." BOSWELL: "By no means, Sir. The genteel-

---

[1]The original is in my possession. He showed me the Diploma, and allowed me to read it, but would not consent to my taking a copy of it, fearing perhaps that I should blaze it abroad in his lifetime. His objection to this appears from his 99th letter to Mrs. Thrale, whom in his letter he thus scolds for the grossness of her flattery of him.—"The other Oxford news is that they have sent me a degree of Doctor of Laws, with such praises in the Diploma as perhaps ought to make me ashamed: they are very like your praises. I wonder whether I shall ever show it to you."

It is remarkable that he never, so far as I know, assumed his title of *Doctor,* but called himself *Mr.* Johnson, as appears from many of his cards or notes to myself, and I have seen many from him to other persons, in which he uniformly takes that designation.—I once observed on his table a letter directed to him with the addition of *Esquire,* and objected to it as being a designation inferior to that of Doctor; but he checked me, and seemed pleased with it, because, as I conjectured, he liked to be sometimes taken out of the class of literary men, and to be merely *genteel—un gentilhomme comme un autre.*

est characters are often the most immoral. Does not Lord Chesterfield give precepts for uniting wickedness and the graces? A man, indeed, is not genteel when he gets drunk; but most vices may be committed very genteelly: a man may debauch his friend's wife genteelly; he may cheat at cards genteelly." HICKY: "I do not think *that* is genteel." BOSWELL: "Sir, it may not be like a gentleman, but it may be genteel." JOHNSON: "You are meaning two different things. One means exterior grace; the other, honour. It is certain that a man may be very immoral with exterior grace. Lovelace, in 'Clarissa,' is a very genteel and a very wicked character, Tom Hervey, who died t'other day, though a vicious man, was one of the genteelest men that ever lived." Tom Davies instanced Charles the Second. JOHNSON (taking fire at any attack upon that Prince, for whom he had an extraordinary partiality): "Charles the Second was licentious in his practice; but he always had a reverence for what was good. Charles the Second knew his people, and rewarded merit. The Church was at no time better filled than in his reign. He was the best king we have had from his time till the reign of his present Majesty, except James the Second, who was a very good king, but unhappily believed that it was necessary for the salvation of his subjects that they should be Roman Catholics. *He* had the merit of endeavouring to do what he thought was for the salvation of the souls of his subjects, till he lost a great empire. *We,* who thought that we should *not* be saved if we were Roman Catholics, had the merit of maintaining our religion at the expense of submitting ourselves to the government of King William, for it could not be done otherwise—to the government of one of the most worthless scoundrels that ever existed."

I mentioned that Dr. Thomas Campbell had come from Ireland to London, principally to see Dr. Johnson. He seemed angry at this observation. DAVIES: "Why, you know, Sir, there came a man from Spain to see Livy; and Corelli came to England to see Purcell, and, when he heard he was dead, went directly back again to Italy." JOHNSON: "I should not have wished to be dead to disappoint Campbell, had he been so foolish as you represent him; but I should have wished to have been a hundred miles off." This was apparently perverse; and I do believe it was not his real way of thinking; he could not but like a man who came so far to see him. He laughed with some complacency when I told him Campbell's odd expression to me concerning him: "That having seen such a man was a thing to talk of a century hence"—as if he could live so long.

We got into an argument whether the judges who went to India might with propriety engage in trade. Johnson warmly maintained that they might, "For why (he urged) should not judges get riches, as well as those who deserve them less?" I said they should have sufficient salaries, and have nothing to take off their attention from the affairs of the public. JOHNSON: "No judge, Sir, can give his whole attention to his office; and it is very proper that he should employ what time he has to himself, to his own advantage, in the most profitable manner." "Then, Sir (said Davies, who enlivened the dispute by making it somewhat dramatic), he may become an insurer; and when he is going to the bench, he may be stopped—'Your Lordship cannot go yet; here is a bunch of invoices; several ships are about to sail.' " JOHNSON: "Sir, you may as well say a judge should not have a house; for they may come and tell him, 'Your Lordship's house is on fire'; and so, instead of minding the business of his court, he is to be occupied in getting the engine with the greatest speed. There is no end of this. Every judge who has land, trades to a certain extent in corn or in cattle; and in the land itself undoubtedly his steward acts for him, and so do clerks for a great merchant. A judge may be a farmer; but he is not to geld his own pigs. A judge may play a little at cards for his amusement; but he is not to play at marbles or chuck farthing in the Piazza. No, Sir; there is no profession to which a man gives a very great proportion of his time. It is wonderful, when a calculation is made, how little the mind is actually employed in the discharge of any profession. No man would be a judge, upon the condition of being totally a judge. The best employed lawyer has his mind at work but for a small proportion of his time: a great deal of his occupation is merely mechanical.—I once wrote for a magazine; I made a calculation that if I should write but a page a day, at the same rate I should, in ten years, write nine volumes in folio, of an ordinary size and print." BOSWELL: "Such as Carte's History?" JOHNSON: "Yes, Sir; when a man writes from his own mind, he writes very rapidly. The greatest part of a writer's time is spent in reading, in order to write; a man will turn over half a library to make one book."

Friday, April 7, I dined with him at a tavern, with a numerous company.

One of the company suggested an internal objection to the antiquity of the poetry said to be Ossian's, that we do not find the wolf in it, which must have been the case had it been of that age.

The mention of the wolf had led Johnson to think of other wild beasts; and while Sir Joshua Reynolds and Mr. Langton were carrying on a dialogue about something which engaged them earnestly, he, in the midst of it, broke out, "Pennant tells of Bears——" [what he added, I have forgotten]. They went on, which he being dull of hearing did not perceive, or, if he did, was not willing to break off his talk; so he continued to vociferate his remarks, and *Bear* ("like a word in a catch," as Beauclerk said) was repeatedly heard at intervals, which, coming from him who, by those who did not know him, had been so often assimilated to that ferocious animal, while we who were sitting around could hardly stifle laughter, produced a very ludicrous effect. Silence having ensued, he proceeded: "We are told that the black bear is innocent; but I should not like to trust myself with him." Mr. Gibbon muttered, in a low tone of voice, "I should not like to trust myself with *you*." This piece of sarcastic pleasantry was a prudent resolution, if applied to a competition of abilities.

Patriotism having become one of our topics, Johnson suddenly uttered, in a strong determined tone, an apophthegm, at which many will start: "Patriotism is the last refuge of a scoundrel." But let it be considered that he did not mean a real and generous love of our country, but that pretended patriotism which so many, in all ages and countries, have made a cloak for self-interest. I maintained that, certainly, all patriots were not scoundrels. Being urged (not by Johnson) to name one exception, I mentioned an eminent person, whom we all greatly admired. JOHNSON: "Sir, I do not say that he is *not* honest; but we have no reason to conclude, from his political conduct, that he *is* honest. Were he to accept a place from this Ministry, he would lose that character of firmness which he has, and might be turned out of his place in a year. This Ministry is neither stable, nor grateful to their friends, as Sir Robert Walpole was: so that he may think it more for his interest to take his chance of his party coming in."

On Saturday, May 8, I dined with him at Mr. Thrale's, where we met the Irish Dr. Campbell. Johnson had supped the night before at Mrs. Abington's, with some fashionable people whom he named; and he seemed much pleased with having made one in so elegant a circle. Nor did he omit to pique his *mistress* a little with jealousy of her housewifery; for he said (with a smile), "Mrs. Abington's jelly, my dear lady, was better than yours."

Mrs. Thrale, who frequently practised a coarse mode of flattery, by repeating his *bon-mots* in his hearing, told us that he had said a certain celebrated actor was just fit to stand at the door of an auction-room with a long pole, and cry, "Pray, gentlemen, walk in"; and that a certain author, upon hearing this, had said that another still more celebrated actor was fit for nothing better than that, and would pick your pocket after you came out. JOHNSON: "Nay, my dear lady, there is no wit in what our friend added: there is only abuse. You may as well say of any man that he will pick a pocket. Besides, the man who is stationed at the door does not pick people's pockets; that is done within by the auctioneer."

On Monday, April 10, I dined with him at General Oglethorpe's, with Mr. Langton and the Irish Dr. Campbell, whom the General had obligingly given me leave to bring with me. This learned gentleman was thus gratified with a very high intellectual feast, by not only being in company with Dr. Johnson, but with General Oglethorpe, who had been so long a celebrated name both at home and abroad.

I must, again and again, entreat of my readers not to suppose that my imperfect record of conversation contains the whole of what was said by Johnson, or other eminent persons who lived with him. What I have preserved, however, has the value of the most perfect authenticity.

He urged General Oglethorpe to give the world his Life. He said, "I know no man whose Life would be more interesting. If I were furnished with materials, I should be very glad to write it."

No more of his conversation for some days appears in my journal, except that when a gentleman told him he had bought a suit of lace for his lady, he said, "Well, Sir, you have done a good thing and a wise thing." "I have done a good thing (said the gentleman), but I do not know that I have done a wise thing." JOHNSON: "Yes, Sir; no money is better spent than what is laid out for domestic satisfaction. A man is pleased that his wife is dressed as well as other people, and a wife is pleased that she is dressed."

CHAPTER XXVII—1775

Dinner at Mr. Cambridge's

ON FRIDAY, APRIL 14, being Good Friday, I repaired to him in the morning, according to my usual custom on that day, and breakfasted with him. I observed that he fasted so very strictly that he did not even taste bread, and took no milk with his tea; I suppose, because it is a kind of animal food.

He entered upon the state of the nation, and thus discoursed: "Sir, the great misfortune now is that Government has too little power. All that it has to bestow must of necessity be given to support itself; so that it cannot reward merit. No man, for instance, can now be made a Bishop for his learning and piety; his only chance for promotion is his being connected with somebody who has parliamentary interest. Our several ministers in this reign have out-bid each other in concessions to the people. Lord Bute, though a very honourable man—a man who meant well—a man who had his blood full of prerogative—was a theoretical statesman—a book-minister—and thought this country could be governed by the influence of the Crown alone. Then, Sir, he gave up a great deal. He advised the King to agree that the judges should hold their places for life, instead of losing them at the accession of a new king. Lord Bute, I suppose, thought to make the King popular by his concession; but the people never minded it; and it was a most impolitic measure. There is no reason why a judge should hold his office for life more than any other person in public trust. A judge may be partial otherwise than to the Crown: we have seen judges partial to the populace. A judge may become corrupt, and yet there may not be legal evidence against him. A judge may become froward from age. A judge may grow unfit for his office in many ways. It was desirable that there should be a possibility of being delivered from him by a new King. That is now gone by an Act of Parliament *ex gratiâ* of the Crown. Lord Bute advised the King to give up a very large sum of money, for which nobody thanked him. It was of consequence to the King, but nothing to the public, among whom it was divided. When I say Lord Bute advised, I mean that such acts were done when he was Minister, and we are to suppose that he advised them.—Lord Bute showed an undue partiality to Scotchmen. He turned out Dr. Nichols, a very eminent man, from being physician to the King, to make room for one of his countrymen, a man very low in his profession.

"Lord Bute (he added) took down too fast, without building up something new." BOSWELL: "Because, Sir, he found a rotten building. The political coach was drawn by a set of bad horses; it was necessary to change them." JOHNSON: "But he should have changed them one by one."

I told him that I had been informed by Mr. Orme that many parts of the East Indies were better mapped than the Highlands of Scotland. JOHNSON: "That a country may be mapped, it must be travelled over." "Nay (said I, meaning to laugh with him at one of his prejudices), can't you say it is not *worth* mapping?"

As we walked to St. Clement's Church, and saw several shops open upon this most solemn fast-day of the Christian world, I remarked that one disadvantage arising from the immensity of London was that nobody was heeded by his neighbour; there was no fear of censure for not observing Good Friday as it ought to be kept, and as it is kept in country towns. He said it was, upon the whole, very well observed even in London. He, however, owned that London was too large; but added, "It is nonsense to say the head is too big for the body. It would be as much too big, though the body were ever so large; that is to say, though the country were ever so extensive. It has no similarity to a head connected with a body."

We went again to St. Clement's in the afternoon. He had found fault with the preacher in the morning, for not choosing a text adapted to the day. The preacher in the afternoon had chosen one extremely proper: "It is finished."

After the evening service he said, "Come, you shall go home with me, and sit just an hour." But he was better than his word; for after we had drunk tea with Mrs. Williams, he asked me to go up to his study with him, where we sat a long while together, in a serene undisturbed frame of mind, sometimes in silence and sometimes conversing, as we felt ourselves inclined, or, more properly speaking, as *he* was inclined; for, during all the course of my long intimacy with him, my respectful attention never abated, and my wish to hear him was such that I constantly watched every dawning of communication from that great and illuminated mind.

He observed, "All knowledge is of itself of some value. There is nothing so minute or inconsiderable that I would not rather know it than not. In the same manner, all power, of whatsoever sort, is of itself desirable. A man would not submit to learn to hem a ruffle, of his wife, or his wife's maid; but if a mere wish could attain it, he would rather wish to be able to hem a ruffle."

I told him that our friend Goldsmith had said to me that he had come too late into the world, for that Pope and other poets had taken up the places in the Temple of Fame; so that, as but a few at any period can possess poetical reputation, a man of genius can now hardly acquire it. JOHNSON: "That is one of the most sensible things I have ever heard of Goldsmith. It is difficult to get literary fame, and it is every day growing more difficult. Ah, Sir, that should make a man think of securing happiness in another world, which all who try sincerely for it may attain. In comparison of that, how little are all other things! The belief of immortality is impressed upon all men, and all men act under an impression of it, however they may talk, and though, perhaps, they may be scarcely sensible of it." I said it appeared to me that some people had not the least notion of immortality; and I mentioned a distinguished gentleman of our acquaintance. JOHNSON: "Sir, if it were not for the notion of immortality, he would cut a throat to fill his pockets."

On Sunday, April 16, being Easter Day, after having attended the solemn service at St. Paul's, I dined with Dr. Johnson and Mrs. Williams. I maintained that Horace was wrong in placing happiness in *Nil admirari,* for that I thought admiration one of the most agreeable of all our feelings; and I regretted that I had lost much of my disposition to admire, which people generally do as they advance in life. JOHNSON: "Sir, as a man advances in life, he gets what is better than admiration—judgment, to estimate things at their true value." I still insisted that admiration was more pleasing than judgment, as love is more pleasing than friendship. The feeling of friendship is like that of being comfortably filled with roast beef; love, like being enlivened with champagne. JOHNSON: "No, Sir; admiration and love are like being intoxicated with champagne; judgment and friendship like being enlivened. Waller has hit upon the same thought with you: but I don't believe you have borrowed from Waller. I wish you would enable yourself to borrow more."

He then took occasion to enlarge on the advantages of reading, and combated the idle superficial notion, that knowledge enough may be acquired in conversation. "The foundation (said he) must be laid by reading. General principles must be had from books, which, however, must be brought to the test of real life. In conversation you never get a system. What is said upon a subject is to be gathered from a hundred people. The parts of a truth which a man gets thus are at such a distance from each other, that he never attains to a full view."

On Tuesday, April 11, he and I were engaged to go with Sir Joshua Reynolds to dine with Mr. Cambridge, at his beautiful villa on the banks of the Thames, near Twickenham. Dr. Johnson's tardiness was such that Sir Joshua, who had an appointment at Richmond early in the day, was obliged to go by himself on horseback, leaving his coach to Johnson and me. Johnson was in such good spirits, that everything seemed to please him as we drove along.

Our conversation turned on a variety of subjects. He thought portrait-painting an improper employment for a woman. "Public practice of any art (he observed), and staring in men's faces, is very indelicate in a female." I happened to start a question, whether, when a man knows that some of his intimate friends are invited to the house of another friend, with whom they are all equally intimate, he may join them without an invitation. JOHNSON: "No, Sir, he is not to go when he is not invited. They may be invited on purpose to abuse him" (smiling).

As a curious instance how little a man knows, or wishes to know, his own character in the world, or, rather, as a convincing proof that Johnson's roughness was only external, and did not proceed from his heart, I insert the following dialogue. JOHNSON: "It is wonderful, Sir, how rare a quality good humour is, in life. We meet with very few good-humoured men." I mentioned four of our friends, none of whom he would allow to be good-humoured. One was *acid,* another was *muddy,* and to the others he had objections which have escaped me. Then, shaking his head and stretching himself at ease in the coach, and smiling with much complacency, he turned to me and said, "I look upon *myself* as a good-humoured fellow." The epithet *fellow,* applied to the great Lexicographer, the stately Moralist, the masterly Critic, as if he had been *Sam* Johnson, a mere pleasant companion, was highly diverting; and this light notion of himself struck me with wonder. I answered, also smiling, "No, no, Sir; that will *not* do. You are good-natured, but not good-humoured: you are irascible. You have not patience with folly and absurdity. I believe you would pardon them if there were time to deprecate your vengeance; but punishment follows so quick after sentence, that they cannot escape."

No sooner had we made our bow to Mr. Cambridge, in his library, than Johnson ran eagerly to one side of the room, intent on poring over the backs of the books. Sir Joshua observed (aside), "He runs to the books as I do to the pictures: but I have the advantage. I can see much more of the pictures than he can of the books." Mr. Cambridge, upon this, politely said, "Dr. Johnson, I am going, with your pardon, to accuse myself, for I have the same custom which I perceive you have. But it seems odd that one should have such a desire to look at the backs of books." Johnson, ever ready for contest, instantly started from his reverie, wheeled about and answered, "Sir, the reason is very

When Johnson declined, Boswell visited Voltaire and liked him.

plain. Knowledge is of two kinds. We know a subject ourselves, or we know where we can find information upon it. When we inquire into any subject, the first thing we have to do is to know what books have treated of it. This leads us to look at catalogues, and the backs of books in libraries." Sir Joshua observed to me the extraordinary promptitude with which Johnson flew upon an argument. "Yes (said I), he has no formal preparation, no flourishing with his sword; he is through your body in an instant."

"The Beggar's Opera," and the common question, whether it was pernicious in its effects, having been introduced;—JOHNSON: "As to this matter, which has been very much contested, I myself am of opinion, that more influence has been ascribed to 'The Beggar's Opera' than it in reality ever had; for I do not believe that any man was ever made a rogue by being present at its representation. At the same time, I do not deny that it may have some influence, by making the character of a rogue familiar, and in some degree pleasing." Then, collecting himself, as it were, to give a heavy stroke: "There is in it such a *labefactation* of all principles, as may be injurious to morality."

While he pronounced this response, we sat in a comical sort of restraint, smothering a laugh, which we were afraid might burst out. In his life of Gay, he has been still more decisive as to the inefficiency of "The Beggar's Opera" in corrupting society.

We talked of a young gentleman's marriage with an eminent singer, and his determination that she should no longer sing in public, though his father was very earnest she should, because her talents would be liberally rewarded, so as to make her a good fortune. It was questioned whether the young gentleman, who had not a shilling in the world, but was blest with very uncommon talents, was not foolishly delicate, or foolishly proud, and his father truly rational without being mean. Johnson, with all the high spirit of a Roman senator, exclaimed, "He resolved wisely and nobly, to be sure. He is a brave man. Would not a gentleman be disgraced by having his wife singing publicly for hire? No, Sir, there can be no doubt here. I know not if I should not *prepare* myself for a public singer, as readily as let my wife be one."

Having set out next day on a visit to the Earl of Pembroke, at Wilton, and to my friend, Mr. Temple, at Mamhead, in Devonshire, and not having returned to town till the second of May, I did not see Dr. Johnson for a considerable time, and, during the remaining part of my stay in London, kept very imperfect notes of his conversation, which had I, according to my usual custom, written out at large soon after the time, much might have been preserved, which is now irretrievably lost. I can now only record some particular scenes, and a few fragments of his *memorabilia*.

On Friday, May 12, as he has been so good as to assign me a room in his house, where I might sleep occasionally, when I happened to sit with him to a late hour, I took possession of it this night, found everything in excellent order, and was attended by honest Francis with a most civil assiduity. I asked Johnson whether I might go to a consultation with another lawyer upon Sunday, as that appeared to me to be doing work as much in my way, as if an artisan should work on the day appropriated for religious rest. JOHNSON: "Why, Sir, when you are of consequence enough to oppose the practice of consulting upon Sunday, you should do it: but you may go now. It is not criminal, though it is not what one should do who is anxious for the preservation and increase of piety, to which a peculiar observance of Sunday is a great help. The distinction is clear between what is of moral and what is of ritual obligation."

On Saturday, May 13, I breakfasted with him by invitation, accompanied by Mr. Andrew Crosbie, a Scotch advocate, whom he had seen at Edinburgh, and the Hon. Colonel (now General) Edward Stopford, brother to Lord Courtown, who was desirous of being introduced to him. His tea and rolls and butter, and whole breakfast-apparatus, were all in such decorum, and his behaviour so courteous, that Colonel Stopford was quite surprised, and wondered at his having heard so much said of Johnson's slovenliness and roughness.

I passed many hours with him on the 17th, of which I find all my memorial is, "much laughing." It should seem he had that day been in a humour for jocularity and merriment, and upon such occasions I never knew a man laugh more heartily. We may suppose that the high relish of a state so different from his habitual gloom produced more than ordinary exertions of that distinguishing faculty of man, which has puzzled philosophers so much to explain. Johnson's laugh was as remarkable as any circumstance in his manner. It was a kind of good humoured growl. Tom Davies described it drolly enough: "He laughs like a rhinoceros."

"TO JAMES BOSWELL, ESQ.

"DEAR SIR,—

"I make no doubt but you are now safely lodged in your own habitation, and have told all your adventures to Mrs. Boswell and Miss

Veronica. Pray teach Veronica to love me. Bid her not mind mamma.

"Make my compliments to Mrs. Boswell, though she does not love me. You see what perverse things ladies are, and how little to be trusted with feudal estates. When she mends and loves me, there may be more hope of her daughters.

"I will not send compliments to my friends by name, because I would be loth to leave out any in the enumeration. Tell them, as you see them, how well I speak of Scotch politeness, and Scotch hospitality, and Scotch beauty, and of everything Scotch but Scotch oat-cakes and Scotch prejudices.

"Let me know the answer of Rasay, and the decision relating to Sir Allan.

> "I am, my dearest Sir, with great affection,
> "Your most obliged, and
> "Most humble servant,
> "Sam. Johnson.

"*May 27, 1775.*"

"to the same.

"Dear Sir,—

"I am returned from the annual ramble into the middle counties. Having seen nothing I had not seen before, I have nothing to relate. Time has left that part of the island few antiquities; and commerce has left the people no singularities. I was glad to go abroad, and, perhaps, glad to come home; which is, in other words, I was, I am afraid, weary of being at home, and weary of being abroad. Is not this the state of life? But, if we confess this weariness, let us not lament it; for all the wise and all the good say that we may cure it.

For the black fumes which rise in your mind, I can prescribe nothing but that you disperse them by honest business or innocent pleasure, and by reading, sometimes easy and sometimes serious. Change of place is useful; and I hope that your residence at Auchinleck will have many good effects.

"I have now three parcels of Lord Hailes's history, which I purpose to return all the next week: that his respect for my little observations should keep his work in suspense, makes one of the evils of my journey. It is in our language, I think, a new mode of history which tells all that is wanted, and, I suppose, all that is known, without laboured splendour of language, or affected subtilty of conjecture. The exactness of his dates raises my wonder. He seems to have the closeness of Henault without his constraint.

"Mrs. Thrale was so entertained with your 'Journal,' that she almost read herself blind. She has a great regard for you.

"Of Mrs. Boswell, though she knows in her heart that she does not love me, I am always glad to hear any good, and hope that she and the little dear ladies will have neither sickness nor any other affliction. But she knows that she does not care what becomes of me, and for that she may be sure that I think her very much to blame.

"Never, my dear Sir, do you take it into your head to think that I do not love you; you may settle yourself in full confidence both of my love and my esteem; I love you as a kind man, I value you as a worthy man, and hope in time to reverence you as a man of exemplary piety. I hold you, as Hamlet has it, 'in my heart of hearts,' and therefore, it is little to say, that I am, Sir,

"Your affectionate humble servant,

"SAM. JOHNSON.

"London, August 27, 1775."

"TO THE SAME.

"MY DEAR SIR,—

"I now write to you, lest in some of your freaks and humours you should fancy yourself neglected. Such fancies I must entreat you never to admit, at least never to indulge; for my regard for you is so radicated and fixed, that it is become part of my mind and cannot be effaced but by some cause uncommonly violent; therefore whether I write or not, set your thoughts at rest. I now write to tell you that I shall not very soon write again, for I am to set out to-morrow on another journey.

*   *   *

"Your friends are all well at Streatham, and in Leicester-fields. Make my compliments to Mrs. Boswell, if she is in good humour with me.

"I am, Sir, etc.,

"SAM. JOHNSON.

"Sep. 14, 1775."

CHAPTER XXVIII—1775

The Tour to France

WHAT HE MENTIONS in such light terms as, "I am to set out to-morrow on another journey," I soon afterwards discovered was no less than a tour to France with Mr. and Mrs. Thrale. This was the only time in his life that he went upon the Continent.

"TO MR. ROBERT LEVETT.

"*Calais, Sept. 18, 1775.*

"DEAR SIR,—

"We are here in France, after a very pleasing passage of no more than six hours. I know not when I shall write again, and therefore I write now, though you cannot suppose that I have much to say. You have seen France yourself. From this place we are going to Rouen, and from Rouen to Paris, where Mr. Thrale designs to stay about five or six weeks. We have a regular recommendation to the English resident, so we shall not be taken for vagabonds. We think to go one way and return another, and see as much as we can. I will try to speak a little French; I tried hitherto but little, but I spoke sometimes. If I heard better, I suppose I should learn faster.

"I am, Sir,
"Your humble servant,
"SAM. JOHNSON."

"TO THE SAME.

"*Paris, Oct. 22, 1775.*

"DEAR SIR,—

"We are still here, commonly very busy in looking about us. We have been to-day at Versailles. You have seen it, and I shall not describe it. We came yesterday from Fontainebleau, where the Court is now. We went to see the King and Queen at dinner, and the Queen was so impressed by Miss,[1] that she sent one of the Gentlemen to inquire who she

[1]Miss Thrale.

was. I find all true that you have ever told me at Paris. Mr. Thrale is very liberal, and keeps us two coaches, and a very fine table; but I think our cookery very bad. Mrs. Thrale got into a convent of English nuns, and I talked with her through the grate, and I am very kindly used by the English Benedictine friars. But upon the whole I cannot make much acquaintance here; and though the churches, palaces, and some private houses are very magnificent, there is no very great pleasure, after having seen many, in seeing more; at least the pleasure, whatever it be, must some time have an end, and we are beginning to think when we shall come home. Mr. Thrale calculates that as we left Streatham on the fifteenth of September, we shall see it again about the fifteenth of November.

"I think I had not been on this side of the sea five days, before I found a sensible improvement in my health. I ran a race in the rain this day, and beat Baretti. Baretti is a fine fellow, and speaks French, I think, quite as well as English.

"Make my compliments to Mrs. Williams; and give my love to Francis; and tell my friends that I am not lost.

"I am, dear Sir,

"Your affectionate humble, etc.,

"SAM. JOHNSON."

"TO DR. SAMUEL JOHNSON.

"*Edinburgh, Oct. 24, 1775.*

"MY DEAR SIR,—

"If I had not been informed that you were at Paris, you should have had a letter from me by the earliest opportunity, announcing the birth of my son, on the 9th instant; I have named him Alexander, after my father. I now write, as I suppose your fellow-traveller, Mr. Thrale, will return to London this week, to attend his duty in Parliament, and that you will not stay behind him.

"I send another parcel of Lord Hailes's 'Annals.' I have undertaken to solicit you for a favour to him, which he thus requests in a letter to me: 'I intend soon to give you "The Life of Robert Bruce," which you will be pleased to transmit to Dr. Johnson. I wish that you could assist me in a fancy which I have taken, of getting Dr. Johnson to draw a character of Robert Bruce, from the account that I give of that prince. If he finds materials for it in my work, it will be a proof that I have been fortunate in selecting the most striking incidents.'

"I suppose by 'The Life of Robert Bruce,' his Lordship means that part of his 'Annals' which relates to the history of that prince, and not a separate work.

"Shall we have 'A Journey to Paris' from you in the winter? You will, I hope, at any rate be kind enough to give me some account of your French travels very soon, for I am very impatient. What a different scene have you viewed this autumn, from that which you viewed in autumn, 1773! I ever am, my dear Sir,

"Your much obliged and

"Affectionate humble servant,

"JAMES BOSWELL."

"TO JAMES BOSWELL, ESQ.

"DEAR SIR,—

"I am glad that the young Laird is born, and an end, I hope, put to the only difference that you can ever have with Mrs. Boswell. I know that she does not love me; but I intend to persist in wishing her well till I get the better of her.

"Paris is, indeed, a place very different from the Hebrides, but it is to a hasty traveller not so fertile of novelty, nor affords so many opportunities of remark. I cannot pretend to tell the public any thing of a place better known to many of my readers than to myself. We can talk of it when we meet.

"I shall go next week to Streatham, from whence I purpose to send a parcel of the 'History' every post. Concerning the character of Bruce, I can only say that I do not see any great reason for writing it; but I shall not easily deny what Lord Hailes and you concur in desiring.

"I have been remarkably healthy all the journey, and hope you and your family have known only that trouble and danger which has so happily terminated. Among all the congratulations that you may receive, I hope you believe none more warm or sincere, than those of, dear Sir,

"Your most affectionate,

"SAM. JOHNSON.

"*November 16, 1775.*"

It is to be regretted that he did not write an account of his travels in France; for as he is reported to have once said, that "he could write the Life of a Broomstick," so, notwithstanding so many former travellers have exhausted almost every subject for remark in that kingdom, his very accurate observation, and peculiar vigour of thought and illustration, would have produced a valuable work. During his visit to it, which lasted but two months, he wrote notes or minutes of what he saw. He promised to show me them, but I neglected to put him in mind of it; and the greatest part of them has been lost, or perhaps destroyed in a precipitate burning of his papers a few days before his death, which must ever be lamented: one small paper-book, however, entitled 'France II,' has been preserved, and is in my possession. It is a diurnal register of his life and observations, from the 10th of October to the 4th of November, inclusive, being twenty-six days, and shows an extraordinary attention to various minute particulars. Being the only memorial of this tour that remains, my readers, I am confident, will peruse it with pleasure, though his notes are very short, and evidently written only to assist his own recollection.

"Oct. 10. Tuesday. We saw the *École Militaire,* in which one hundred and fifty young boys are educated for the army. They have arms of different sizes, according to the age;—flints of wood. The building is very large, but nothing fine except the council-room. The French have large squares in the windows;—they make good iron palisades. Their meals are gross.

"Oct. 11. Wednesday. We went to see *Hôtel de Chatlois,* a house not very large, but very elegant. One of the rooms was gilt to a degree that I never saw before. The upper part for servants and their masters was pretty.

"Thence we went to Mr. Monville's, a house divided into small apartments, furnished with effeminate and minute elegance.—Porphyry.

"Thence we went to St. Roque's Church, which is very large;—the lower part of the pillars incrusted with marble.—Three chapels behind the high altar;—the last a mass of low arches.—Altars, I believe all round.

"We passed through *Place de Vendôme,* a fine square, about as big as Hanover-square.—Inhabited by the high families.—Lewis XIV on horse-back in the middle.

"Monville is the son of a farmer-general. In the house of Chatlois is a room furnished with japan, fitted up in Europe.

"We dined with Bocage, the Marquis Blanchetti, and his lady. The sweetmeats taken by the Marchioness Blanchetti, after observing that they were dear. Mr. Le Roy, Count Manucci, the Abbé, the Prior, and Father Wilson, who stayed with me, till I took him home in the coach.

"Bathiani is gone.

"The French have no laws for the maintenance of their poor.—Monk not necessarily a priest.—Benedictines rise at four;—are at church an hour and half; at church again half an hour before, half an hour after, dinner; and again from half an hour after seven to eight. They may sleep eight hours.—Bodily labour wanted in monasteries.

"The poor taken to hospitals, and miserably kept.—Monks in the convent fifteen;—accounted poor.

"Oct. 12. Thursday. We went to the Gobelins.—Tapestry makes a good picture;—imitates flesh exactly.—One piece with a gold ground;—the birds not exactly coloured;—thence we went to the King's cabinet;—very neat, not, perhaps, perfect.—Gold ore.—Candles, of the candle-tree.—Seeds.—Woods. Thence to Gagnier's house, where I saw rooms nine, furnished with a profusion of wealth and elegance which I never had seen before.—Vases.—Pictures.—The dragon china.—The lustre said to be of crystal, and to have cost £3,500.—The whole furniture said to have cost £125,000.—Damask hangings covered with pictures.—Porphyry.—This house struck me.

"Oct. 14. Saturday. We went to the house of Mr. Argenson, which was almost wainscoted with looking-glasses, and covered with gold.—The ladies' closet wainscoted with large squares of glass over painted paper. They always place mirrors to reflect their rooms.

"Then we went to Julien's, the Treasurer of the Clergy:—£30,000 a year.—The house has no very large room, but is set with mirrors, and covered with gold.—Books of wood here, and in another library.

"At D[argenson]'s I looked into the books in the lady's closet, and, in contempt, showed them to Mr. T.—'Prince Titi'; 'Bibl. des Fées,' and other books.—She was offended, and shut up, as we heard afterwards, her apartment.

"Then we went to Julien Le Roy, the King's watchmaker, a man of character in his business, who showed a small clock made to find the longitude.—A decent man.

"Much disturbed; hope no ill will be.

"Oct. 16. Monday. The Palais Royal very grand, large, and lofty.—A very great collection of pictures.—Three of Raphael.—Two Holy Family.—One small piece of M. Angelo.—One room of Rubens.—I thought the pictures of Raphael fine.

"The Tuilleries.—Statues.—Venus.—Æn. and Anchises in his arms.

—Nilus.—Many more. The walks not open to mean persons.—Chairs at night hired for two sous a piece.—Pont tournant.

"We heard the lawyers plead.—N. As many killed at Paris as there are days in the year.—*Chambre de question.*—Tournelle at the Palais Marchand.—An old venerable building.

"The Palais Bourbon, belonging to the Prince of Condé. Only one small wing shown;—lofty;—splendid;—gold and glass.—The battles of the great Condé are painted in one of the rooms. The present Prince a grandsire at thirty-nine.

"The sight of palaces, and other great buildings, leaves no very distinct images, unless to those who talk of them. As I entered, my wife was in my mind:[2] she would have been pleased. Having now nobody to please, I am little pleased.

"N. In France there is no middle rank.

"So many shops open, that Sunday is little distinguished at Paris.—The palaces of Louvre and Tuilleries granted out in lodgings.

"Oct. 18. Wednesday. We went to Fontainebleau, which we found a large mean town, crowded with people. The forest thick with woods, very extensive.—Manucci secured us lodgings.—The appearance of the country pleasant.—No hills, few streams, only one hedge.—I remember no chapels nor crosses on the road.—Pavement still, and rows of trees.

"N. Nobody but mean people walk in Paris.

"Oct. 19. Thursday. At Court, we saw the apartments; the King's bed-chamber and council-chamber extremely splendid.—Persons of all ranks in the external rooms through which the family passes;—servants and masters.—Brunet with us the second time.

"The introducer came to us;—civil to me.—Presenting.—I had scruples.—Not necessary. We went and saw the King and Queen at dinner.—We saw the other ladies at dinner.—Madame Elizabeth, with the Princess of Guimené.—At night we went to a comedy. I neither saw nor heard.—Drunken women.—Mrs. Th. preferred one to the other.

"Oct. 20. Friday. We saw the Queen mount in the forest.—Brown habit; rode aside: one lady rode aside.—The Queen's horse light gray;—martingale.—She galloped.—We then went to the apartments, and admired them.—Then wandered through the palace.—In the passages, stalls, and shops.—Painting in Fresco by a great master, worn out.—

[2]His tender affection for his departed wife, of which there are many evidences in his "Prayers and Meditations," appears very feelingly in this passage.

We saw the King's horses and dogs.—The dogs almost all English.—Degenerate.

"The horses not much commended.—The stables cool; the kennel filthy.

"At night the ladies went to the opera. I refused, but should have been welcome.

"The King fed himself with his left hand as we.

"Saturday, 21. In the night I got round.—We came home to Paris. I think we did not see the chapel.—Tree broken by the wind.—The French chairs made all of boards painted.

"Faggots in the palace.—Everything slovenly, except in the chief rooms.—Trees in the road, some tall, none old, many very young and small.

"Women's saddles seem ill made.—Queen's bridle woven with silver.—Tags to strike the horse.

"Sunday, Oct. 22. To Versailles, a mean town. Carriages of business passing. Mean shops against the wall.—Our way lay through Sèvres, where is the China manufacture.—Wooden bridge at Sèvres, in the way to Versailles.—The palace of great extent.—The front long; I saw it not perfectly.

"Trianon is a kind of retreat appendant to Versailles. It has an open portico; the pavement, and I think, the pillars, of marble.—There are many rooms, which I do not distinctly remember.—A table of porphyry, about five feet long, and between two and three broad, given to Louis XIV by the Venetian State.—In the council-room, almost all that was not door or window was, I think, looking-glass. Little Trianon is a small palace like a gentleman's house.—The upper floor paved with brick.—Little Vienne.—The court is ill paved.—The rooms at the top are small, fit to soothe the imagination with privacy. In the front of Versailles are small basons of water on the terrace, and other basons, I think, below them. There are little courts.—The great gallery is wainscoted with mirrors, not very large, but joined by frames. I suppose the large plates were not yet made.—The playhouse was very large.—The chapel I do not remember if we saw. We saw one chapel, but I am not certain whether there or at Trianon.—The foreign office paved with bricks.—The dinner half a Louis each, and, I think, a Louis over.—Money given at Menagerie, three livres; at palace, six livres.

"Oct. 23. Monday. Last night I wrote to Levett.—We went to see the looking-glasses wrought. They come from Normandy in cast plates, perhaps the third of an inch thick. At Paris they are ground upon a marble table, by rubbing one plate upon another with grit between them. The various sands, of which there are said to be five, I could not learn. The handle, by which the upper glass is moved, has the form of a wheel, which may be moved in all directions. The plates are sent up with their surfaces ground, but not polished, and so continue till they are bespoken, lest time should spoil the surface, as we were told. Those that are to be polished are laid on a table covered with several thick cloths, hard strained, that the resistance may be equal; they are then rubbed with a hand-rubber, held down hard by a contrivance which I did not well understand. The powder which is used last seemed to me to be iron dissolved in aqua fortis: they called it, as Baretti said, *marc de l'eau forte,* which he thought was dregs. They mentioned vitriol and saltpetre. The cannon ball swam in the quicksilver. To silver them, a leaf of beaten tin is laid, and rubbed with quicksilver, to which it unites. Then more quicksilver is poured upon it, which, by its mutual [attraction] rises very high. Then a paper is laid at the nearest end of the plate, over which the glass is slided till it lies upon the plate, having driven much of the quicksilver before it. It is then, I think, pressed upon cloth, and then set sloping to drop the superfluous mercury; the slope is daily heightened towards a perpendicular.

"Saturday, Oct. 28. I visited the Grand Chartreux, built by St. Louis.—It is built for forty, but contains only twenty-four, and will not maintain more. The friar that spoke to us had a pretty apartment.—Mr. Baretti says four rooms, I remember but three.—His books seemed to be French.—His garden was neat; he gave me grapes. We saw the Place de Victoire, with the statues of the King, and the captive nations.

"We saw the palace and gardens of Luxembourg, but the gallery was shut.—We climbed to the top stairs. I dined with Colbrooke, who had much company:—Foote, Sir George Rodney, Motteux, Udson, Taaf:—Called on the Prior, and found him in bed.—Hotel—a guinea a day.—Coach three guineas a week.—Valet de place three l. a day.—*Avant coureur,* a guinea a week.—Ordinary dinner, six l. a head.—Our ordinary seems to be about five guineas a day.—Our extraordinary expenses, as diversions, gratuities, clothes, I cannot reckon.—Our travelling is ten guineas a day.

"White stockings, 18 liv. Wig.—Hat.

"Oct. 31. Tuesday. I lived at the Benedictines; meagre day; soup meagre, herrings, eels, both with sauce; fried fish; lentils, tasteless in themselves. In the library; where I found Maffeus's 'De Historia Indica: Promontorium flectere, to double the Cape.' I parted very tenderly from the Prior and Friar Wilkes.

"Nov. 2. Thursday. We came this day to Chantilly, a seat belonging to the Prince of Condé.—This place is eminently beautified by all varieties of waters starting up in fountains, falling in cascades, running in streams, and spread in lakes.—The water seems to be too near the house.—All this water is brought from a source or river three leagues off, by an artificial canal, which for one league is carried underground.—The house is magnificent.—The cabinet seems well stocked; what I remember, was the jaws of a hippopotamus, and a young hippopotamus preserved, which, however, is so small, that I doubt its reality.—It seems too hairy for an abortion, and too small for a mature birth.—Nothing was in spirits; all was dry.—The dog; the deer; the ant-bear with long snout.—The toucan, long broad beak.—The stables were of very great length.—The kennel had no scents.—There was a mockery of a village.—The Menagerie had few animals.—Two faussans, or Brazilian weasels, spotted, very wild.—There is a forest, and, I think, a park.—I walked till I was very weary, and next morning felt my feet battered, and with pains in the toes.

"Nov. 4. Saturday we rose very early, and came through St. Quintin to Cambray, not long after three. We went to an English nunnery, to give a letter to Father Welch, the confessor, who came to visit us in the evening.

"Nov. 5. Sunday. We saw the Cathedral. It is very beautiful, with chapels on each side.—The choir splendid.—The balustrade on one part brass.—The Neff very high and grand.—The altar silver, as far as it is seen.—The vestments very splendid.—At the Benedictines' church——."

Here his Journal ends abruptly. Whether he wrote any more after this time, I know not; but probably not much, as he arrived in England about the 12th of November. These short notes of his tour, though they may seem minute taken singly, make together a considerable mass of information, and exhibit such an ardour of inquiry and acuteness of examination, as, I believe, are found in but few travellers, especially at an advanced age. They completely refute the idle notion which has been propagated, *that he could not see:* and, if he had taken the trouble to revise and digest them, he undoubtedly could have expanded them into a very entertaining narrative.

CHAPTER XXIX—1775–1776

French Impressions

WHEN I MET HIM IN LONDON the following year, the account which he gave me of his French tour was, "Sir, I have seen all the visibilities of Paris, and around it; but to have formed an acquaintance with the people there would have required more time than I could stay. I was just beginning to creep into acquaintance by means of Colonel Drumgold, a very high man, Sir, head of *L'Ecole Militaire,* a most complete character, for he had first been a professor of rhetoric, and then became a soldier. And, Sir, I was very kindly treated by the English Benedictines, and have a cell appropriated to me in their convent."

He observed, "The great in France live very magnificently, but the rest very miserably. There is no happy middle state, as in England. The shops of Paris are mean: the meat in the markets is such as would be sent to a gaol in England; and Mr. Thrale justly observed that the cookery of the French was forced upon them by necessity; for they could not eat their meat unless they added some taste to it. The French are an indelicate people; they will spit upon any place. At Madame [Du Bocage]'s, a literary lady of rank, the footman took the sugar in his fingers, and threw it into my coffee. I was going to put it aside: but hearing it was made on purpose for me, I e'en tasted Tom's fingers. The same lady would needs make tea *à l'Anglaise.* The spout of the tea-pot did not pour freely; she bade the footman blow into it. France is worse than Scotland in everything but climate. Nature has done more for the French; but they have done less for themselves than the Scotch have done."

It happened that Foote was at Paris at the same time with Dr. Johnson, and his description of my friend, while there, was abundantly ludicrous. He told me that the French were quite astonished at his figure and manner, and at his dress, which he obstinately continued exactly as in London;—his brown clothes, black stockings and plain shirt. He mentioned that an Irish gentleman said to Johnson, "Sir, you have not seen the best French players." JOHNSON: "Players, Sir! I look on them as no better than creatures set upon tables and joint stools to make faces and produce laughter, like dancing dogs."—"But, Sir, you will allow that some players are better than others?" JOHNSON: "Yes, Sir, as some dogs dance better than others."

While Johnson was in France, he was generally very resolute in speaking Latin. It was a maxim with him that a man should not let himself down, by speaking a language which he speaks imperfectly. Indeed, we must have often observed how inferior, how much like a child a man appears, who speaks a broken tongue. When Sir Joshua Reynolds, at one of the dinners of the Royal Academy, presented him to a Frenchman of great distinction, he would not deign to speak French, but talked Latin, though his Excellency did not understand it, owing, perhaps, to Johnson's English pronunciation: yet upon another occasion he was observed to speak French to a Frenchman of high rank, who spoke English; and being asked the reason, with some expression of surprise,—he answered, "Because I think my French is as good as his English."

He spoke Latin with wonderful fluency and elegance. When Père Boscovich was in England, Johnson dined in company with him at Sir Joshua Reynolds's, and at Dr. Douglas's, now Bishop of Salisbury. Upon both occasions that celebrated foreigner expressed his astonishment at Johnson's Latin conversation.

In the course of this year, Dr. Burney informs me that "he very frequently met Dr. Johnson at Mr. Thrale's, at Streatham, where they had many long conversations, often sitting up as long as the fire and candles lasted, and much longer than the patience of the servants subsisted."

A few of Johnson's sayings, which that gentleman recollects, shall here be inserted.

"I never take a nap after dinner but when I have had a bad night, and then the nap takes me."

"The writer of an epitaph should not be considered as saying nothing but what is strictly true. Allowance must be made for some degree of exaggerated praise. In lapidary inscriptions a man is not upon oath."

"There is now less flogging in our great schools than formerly, but then less is learned there; so that what the boys get at one end they lose at the other."

"After having talked slightingly of music, he was observed to listen very attentively while Miss Thrale played on the harpsichord, and with eagerness he called to her, 'Why don't you dash away like Burney?' Dr.

Burney upon this said to him, 'I believe, Sir, we shall make a musician of you at last.' Johnson with candid complacency replied, 'Sir, I shall be glad to have a new sense given to me.' "

"He had come down one morning to the breakfast-room, and been a considerable time by himself before anybody appeared. When on a subsequent day he was twitted by Mrs. Thrale for being very late, which he generally was, he defended himself by alluding to the extraordinary morning when he had been too early. 'Madam, I do not like to come down to *vacuity*.' "

"Dr. Burney having remarked that Mr. Garrick was beginning to look old, he said, 'Why, Sir, you are not to wonder at that; no man's face has had more wear and tear.' "

At this time was in agitation a matter of great consequence to me and my family, which I should not obtrude upon the world, were it not that the part which Dr. Johnson's friendship for me made him take in it was the occasion of an exertion of his abilities which it would be injustice to conceal. That what he wrote upon the subject may be understood, it is necessary to give a state of the question, which I shall do as briefly as I can.

In the year 1504, the barony or manor of Auchinleck (pronounced *Affléck*), in Ayrshire, which belonged to a family of the same name with the lands, having fallen to the Crown by forfeiture, James the Fourth, King of Scotland, granted it to Thomas Boswell, a branch of an ancient family in the county of Fife, styling him in the charter, "*dilecto familiari nostro*"; and assigning as the cause of the grant, "*pro bono et fideli servitio nobis præstito*." Thomas Boswell was slain in battle, fighting along with his Sovereign, at the fatal field of Flodden, in 1513.

From this very honourable founder of our family, the estate was transmitted, in a direct series of heirs male, to David Boswell, my father's great-grand-uncle, who had no sons, but four daughters, who were all respectably married, the eldest to Lord Cathcart.

David Boswell, being resolute in the military feudal principle of continuing the male succession, passed by his daughters, and settled the estate on his nephew by his next brother, who approved of the deed, and renounced any pretensions which he might possibly have, in preference to his son. But the estate having been burdened with large portions to the daughters, and other debts, it was necessary for the nephew to sell a considerable part of it, and what remained was still much encumbered.

The frugality of the nephew preserved, and, in some degree, relieved the estate. His son, my grandfather, an eminent lawyer, not only re-purchased a great part of what had been sold, but acquired other lands; and my father, who was one of the judges of Scotland, and had added considerably to the estate, now signified his inclination to take the privilege allowed by our law, to secure it to his family in perpetuity by an entail, which, on account of his marriage articles, could not be done without my consent.

In the plan of entailing the estate, I heartily concurred with him, though I was the first to be restrained by it; but we unhappily differed as to the series of heirs which should be established, or, in the language of our law, called to the succession. My father had declared a predilection for heirs general, that is, males and females indiscriminately. He was willing, however, that all males, descending from his grandfather, should be preferred to females; but would not extend that privilege to males deriving their descent from a higher source. I, on the other hand, had a zealous partiality for heirs male, however remote, which I maintained by arguments which appeared to me to have considerable weight. And in the particular case of our family, I apprehended that we were under an implied obligation, in honour and good faith, to transmit the estate by the same tenure which we held it, which was as heirs male, excluding nearer females. I therefore, as I thought conscientiously, objected to my father's scheme.

My opposition was very displeasing to my father, who was entitled to great respect and deference; and I had reason to apprehend disagreeable consequences from my non-compliance with his wishes. After much perplexity and uneasiness, I wrote to Dr. Johnson, stating the case, with all its difficulties, at full length, and earnestly requesting that he would consider it at leisure, and favour me with his friendly opinion and advice.

"TO JAMES BOSWELL, ESQ.

"Dear Sir,—

"I was much impressed by your letter, and if I can form upon your case any resolution satisfactory to myself, will very gladly impart it: but whether I am equal to it, I do not know. It is a case compounded of law and justice, and requires a mind versed in juridical disquisitions. Could not you tell your whole mind to Lord Hailes? He is, you know, both a Christian and a Lawyer. I suppose he is above partiality, and above loquacity: and, I believe, he will not think the time lost in which he may quiet a disturbed or settle a wavering mind. Write to me, as any thing occurs to you; and if I find myself stopped by want of facts necessary to be known, I will make inquiries of you as my doubts arise.

"If your former resolutions should be found only fanciful, you decide rightly in judging that your father's fancies may claim the preference; but whether they are fanciful or rational, is the question. I really think Lord Hailes could help us.

"Make my compliments to dear Mrs. Boswell; and tell her, that I hope to be wanting in nothing that I can contribute to bring you all out of your troubles.

"I am, dear Sir, most affectionately,
"Your humble servant,
"SAM. JOHNSON.

"*London, Jan. 15, 1776.*"

"TO THE SAME.

"DEAR SIR,—

"I am going to write upon a question which requires more knowledge of local law, and more acquaintance with the general rules of inheritance, than I can claim; but I write because you request it.

"Land is, like any other possession, by natural right wholly in the power of its present owner; and may be sold, given, or bequeathed, absolutely or conditionally, as judgment shall direct, or passion incite.

"But natural right would avail little without the protection of law; and the primary notion of law is, restraint in the exercise of natural right. A man is therefore, in society, not fully master of what he calls his own, but he still retains all the power which law does not take from him.

"In the exercise of the right which law either leaves or gives, regard is to be paid to moral obligations.

"Of the estate which we are now considering, your father still retains such possession, with such power over it, that he can sell it, and do with the money what he will, without any legal impediment. But when he extends his power beyond his own life, by settling the order of succession, the law makes your consent necessary.

"Let us suppose that he sells the land to risk the money in some specious adventure, and in that adventure loses the whole; his posterity would be disappointed; but they could not think themselves injured or robbed. If he spent it upon vice or pleasure, his successors could only

[330]

call him vicious and voluptuous; they could not say that he was injurious or unjust.

"He that may do more may do less. He that, by selling or squandering, may disinherit a whole family, may certainly disinherit part, by a partial settlement.

"Laws are formed by the manners and exigencies of particular times, and it is but accidental that they last longer than their causes; the limitation of feudal succession to the male arose from the obligation of the tenant to attend his chief in war.

"As times and opinions are always changing, I know not whether it be not usurpation to prescribe rules to posterity, by presuming to judge of what we cannot know; and I know not whether I fully approve either your design or your father's, to limit that succession which descended to you unlimited. If we are to leave *sartum tectum* to posterity, what we have without any merit of our own received from our ancestors, should not choice and free-will be kept unviolated? Is land to be treated with more reverence than liberty?—If this consideration should restrain your father from disinheriting some of the males, does it leave you the power of disinheriting all the females?

"Can the possessor of a feudal estate make any will? Can he appoint, out of the inheritance, any portions to his daughter? There seems to be a very shadowy difference between the power of leaving land, and of leaving money to be raised from land; between leaving an estate to females, and leaving the male heir, in effect, only their steward.

"Suppose at one time a law that allowed only males to inherit, and during the continuance of this law many estates to have descended, passing by the females, to remoter heirs. Suppose afterwards the law repealed in correspondence with a change of manners, and women made capable of inheritance; would not then the tenure of estates be changed? Could the women have no benefit from a law made in their favour? Must they be passed by upon moral principles for ever, because they were once excluded by a legal prohibition? Or may that which passed only to males by one law, pass likewise to females by another?

"You mention your resolution to maintain the right of your brother; I do not see how any of their rights are invaded.

"As your whole difficulty arises from the act of your ancestor, who diverted the succession from the females, you inquire, very properly, what were his motives, and what was his intention; for you certainly are not bound by his act more than he intended to bind you, nor hold your land on harder or stricter terms than those on which it was granted.

"Intentions must be gathered from acts. When he left the estate to his nephew, by excluding his daughters, was it, or was it not, in his power to have perpetuated the succession to the males? If he could have done it, he seems to have shown, by omitting it, that he did not desire it to be done; and upon your own principles, you will not easily prove your right to destroy that capacity of succession which your ancestors have left.

"If your ancestor had not the power of making a perpetual settlement; and if, therefore, we cannot judge distinctly of his intentions, yet his act can only be considered as an example; it makes not an obligation. And, as you observe, he set no example of rigorous adherence to the line of succession. He that overlooked a brother would not wonder that little regard is shown to remote relations.

"As the rules of succession are, in a great part, purely legal, no man can be supposed to bequeath anything, but upon legal terms; he can grant no power which the law denies; and if he makes no special and definite limitation, he confers all the power which the law allows.

"Your ancestor, for some reason, disinherited his daughters; but it no more follows that he intended this act as a rule for posterity, than the disinheriting of his brother.

"If therefore, you ask by what right your father admits daughters to inheritance, ask yourself, first, by what right you require them to be excluded?

"It appears, upon reflection, that your father excludes nobody; he only admits nearer females to inherit before males more remote: and the exclusion is purely consequential.

"These, dear Sir, are my thoughts, immethodical and deliberative; but, perhaps, you may find in them some glimmering of evidence.

"I cannot, however, but again recommend to you a conference with Lord Hailes whom you know to be both a Lawyer and a Christian.

"Make my compliments to Mrs. Boswell, though she does not love me.

"I am, Sir,

"Your affectionate servant,

"SAM. JOHNSON.

"Feb. 3, 1776."

I had followed his recommendation, and consulted Lord Hailes, who upon this subject had a firm opinion contrary to mine. His Lordship obligingly took the trouble to write me a letter, in which he discussed, with legal and historical learning, the points in which I saw much difficulty, maintaining that "the succession of heirs general was the succession, by the law of Scotland, from the throne to the cottage, as far as we can learn it by record"; observing that the estate of our family had not been limited to heirs male: and that, though an heir male had in one instance been chosen in preference to nearer females, that had been an arbitrary act, which had seemed to be best in the embarrassed state of affairs at that time; and the fact was, that upon a fair computation of the value of land and money at the time, applied to the estate and the burdens upon it, there was nothing given to the heir male but the skeleton of an estate. "The plea of conscience (said his Lordship), which you put, is a most respectable one, especially when *conscience* and *self* are on different sides. But I think that conscience is not well informed, and that *self* and *she* ought, on this occasion, to be of a side."

This letter, which had considerable influence upon my mind, I sent to Dr. Johnson, begging to hear from him again, upon this interesting question.

"TO JAMES BOSWELL, ESQ.

"Dear Sir,—

"To the letters which I have written about your great question, I have nothing to add. If your conscience is satisfied, you have now only your prudence to consult. I long for a letter that I may know how this troublesome and vexatious question is at last decided.[1] I hope that it will at last end well. Lord Hailes's letter was very friendly, and very seasonable, but I think his aversion from entails has something in it like superstition. Providence is not counteracted by any means which Providence puts into our power. The continuance and propagation of families makes a great part of the Jewish law, and is by no means prohibited in the Christian institution, though the necessity of it continues no longer. Hereditary tenures are established in all civilised countries, and are accompanied in most with hereditary authority. Sir William

---

[1]The entail framed by my father with various judicious clauses was settled by him and me, settling the estate upon the heirs male of his grandfather, which I found had been already done by my grandfather, imperfectly, but so as to be defeated only by selling the lands. I was freed by Dr. Johnson from scruples of conscientious obligation, and could, therefore, gratify my father. But my opinion and partiality for male succession, in its full extent, remained unshaken. Yet, let me not be thought harsh or unkind to daughters; for my notion is that they should be treated with great affection and tenderness, and always participate of the prosperity of the family.

Temple considers our constitution as defective; that there is not an unalienable estate in land connected with a peerage; and Lord Bacon mentions, as a proof that the Turks are Barbarians, their want of *Stirpes,* as he calls them, or hereditary rank. Do not let your mind, when it is freed from the supposed necessity of a rigorous entail, be entangled with contrary objections, and think all entails unlawful, till you have cogent arguments, which I believe you will never find. I am afraid of scruples.

"I have now sent all Lord Hailes's papers; part I found hidden in a drawer in which I had laid them for security, and had forgotten them. Part of these are written twice; I have returned both the copies. Part I had read before.

"Be so kind as to return Lord Hailes my most respectful thanks for his first volume: his accuracy strikes me with wonder; his narrative is far superior to that of Henault, as I have formerly mentioned.

"I am afraid that the trouble which my irregularity and delay have cost him is greater, far greater, than any good that I can do him will ever recompense; but if I have any more copy, I will try to do better.

"Pray let me know if Mrs. Boswell is friends with me, and pay my respects to Veronica, and Euphemia, and Alexander.

"I am, Sir,

"Your most humble servant,

"SAM. JOHNSON.

"Feb. 15, 1776."

"MR. BOSWELL TO DR. JOHNSON.

"Edinburgh, Feb. 20, 1776.

*　　　*　　　*

"You have illuminated my mind, and relieved me from imaginary shackles of conscientious obligation. Were it necessary, I could immediately join in an entail upon the series of heirs approved by my father; but it is better not to act too suddenly."

Having communicated to Lord Hailes what Dr. Johnson wrote concerning the question which perplexed me so much, his Lordship wrote to me; "Your scruples have produced more fruit than I ever expected from them; an excellent dissertation on general principles of morals and law."

I wrote to Dr. Johnson on the 20th of February, complaining of melancholy, and expressing a strong desire to be with him; informing him that the ten packets came all safe; that Lord Hailes was much obliged to him, and said he had almost wholly removed his scruples against entails.

"TO JAMES BOSWELL, ESQ.

"DEAR SIR,—

"I have not had your letter half an hour: as you lay so much weight upon my notions, I should think it not just to delay my answer.

"I am very sorry that your melancholy should return, and should be sorry likewise if it could have no relief but from my company. My counsel you may have when you are pleased to require it; but of my company you cannot in the next month have much, for Mr. Thrale will take me to Italy, he says, on the 1st of April.

"Let me warn you very earnestly against scruples. I am glad that you are reconciled to your settlement, and think it a great honour to have shaken Lord Hailes's opinion of entails. Do not, however, hope wholly to reason away your troubles; do not feed them with attention, and they will die imperceptibly away. Fix your thoughts upon your business, fill your intervals with company, and sunshine will again break in upon your mind. If you will come to me, you must come very quickly; and even then I know not but we may scour the country together, for I have a mind to see Oxford and Lichfield, before I set out on this long journey. To this I can only add that I am, dear Sir,

"Your most affectionate humble servant,

"SAM. JOHNSON.

"*March 5, 1776.*"

"TO THE SAME.

"DEAR SIR,—

"Very early in April we leave England, and in the beginning of the next week I shall leave London for a short time; of this I think it necessary to inform you that you may not be disappointed in any of your enterprises. I had not fully resolved to go into the country before this day.

"Please to make my compliments to Lord Hailes; and mention very particularly to Mrs. Boswell my hope that she is reconciled to, Sir, your faithful servant,

"SAM. JOHNSON.

"*March 12, 1776.*"

[335]

CHAPTER XXX—1776

Bolt Court

HAVING ARRIVED IN LONDON late on Friday, the 15th of March, I hastened next morning to wait on Dr. Johnson, at his house; but found he was removed from Johnson's Court, No. 7, to Bolt Court, No. 8, still keeping to his favourite Fleet-street. My reflection at the time upon this change as marked in my Journal, is as follows: "I felt a foolish regret that he had left a court which bore his name; but it was not foolish to be affected with some tenderness of regard for a place in which I had seen him a great deal, from whence I had often issued a better and a happier man than when I went in, and which had often appeared to my imagination while I trod its pavement, in the solemn darkness of the night, to be sacred to wisdom and piety." Being informed that he was at Mr. Thrale's, in the Borough, I hastened thither, and found Mrs. Thrale and him at breakfast. I was kindly welcomed. In a moment he was in a full glow of conversation, and I felt myself elevated as if brought into another state of being. Mrs. Thrale and I looked to each other while he talked, and our looks expressed our congenial admiration and affection for him. I shall ever recollect this scene with great pleasure. I exclaimed to her, "I am now, intellectually, *Hermippus redivivus,* I am quite restored by him, by transfusion of *mind.*" "There are many (she replied) who admire and respect Mr. Johnson; but you and I *love* him."

He seemed very happy in the near prospect of going to Italy with Mr. and Mrs. Thrale. "But (said he), before leaving England I am to take a jaunt to Oxford, Birmingham, my native city Lichfield, and my old friend, Dr. Taylor's, at Ashbourne, in Derbyshire. I shall go in a few days, and you, Boswell, shall go with me." I was ready to accompany him; being willing even to leave London to have the pleasure of his conversation.

I mentioned Dr. Adam Smith's book on "The Wealth of Nations," which was just published, and that Sir John Pringle had observed to me that Dr. Smith, who had never been in trade, could not be expected to write well on that subject any more than a lawyer upon physic. JOHNSON: "He is mistaken, Sir: a man who has never been engaged in trade himself may undoubtedly write well upon trade, and there is nothing which requires more to be illustrated by philosophy than trade does. As to mere wealth, that is to say, money, it is clear that one nation or one individual cannot increase its store but by making another poorer: but trade procures what is more valuable, the reciprocation of the peculiar advantages of different countries. A merchant seldom thinks but of his own particular trade. To write a good book upon it, a man must have extensive views. It is not necessary to have practised, to write well upon a subject." I mentioned law as a subject on which no man could write well without practice. JOHNSON: "Why, Sir, in England where so much money is to be got by the practice of the law, most of our writers upon it have been in practice; though Blackstone had not been much in practice when he published his 'Commentaries.' But upon the Continent the great writers on law have not all been in practice: Grotius, indeed, was; but Puffendorf was not; Burlamaqui was not."

When we had talked of the great consequence which a man acquired by being employed in his profession, I suggested a doubt of the justice of the general opinion that it is improper in a lawyer to solicit employment; for why, I urged, should it not be equally allowable to solicit that as the means of consequence, as it is to solicit votes to be elected a member of Parliament? Mr. Strahan had told me that a countryman of his and mine, who had risen to eminence in the law, had, when first making his way, solicited him to get him employed in city causes. JOHNSON: "Sir, it is wrong to stir up law-suits; but when once it is certain that a law-suit is to go on, there is nothing wrong in a lawyer's endeavouring that he shall have the benefit rather than another." BOSWELL: "You would not solicit employment, Sir, if you were a lawyer." JOHNSON: "No, Sir; but not because I should think it wrong, but because I should disdain it." This was a good distinction, which will be felt by men of just pride. He proceeded: "However, I would not have a lawyer to be wanting to himself in using fair means. I would have him to inject a little hint now and then, to prevent his being overlooked."

We got into a boat to cross over to Blackfriars; and as we moved along the Thames I talked to him of a little volume, which, altogether unknown to him, was advertised to be published in a few days, under the title of "*Johnsoniana, or Bon-Mots* of Dr. Johnson." JOHNSON: "Sir, it is a mighty impudent thing." BOSWELL: "Pray, Sir, could you have no redress if you were to prosecute a publisher for bringing out, under your name, what you never said, and ascribing to you dull, stupid nonsense, or making you swear profanely, as many ignorant relaters of your *bon-mots* do?" JOHNSON: "No, Sir, there will always be some truth mixed with the falsehood, and how can it be ascertained how much is true and how much is false? Besides, Sir, what damages would a jury give me for having been represented as swearing?" BOSWELL: "I think, Sir, you should at least disavow such a publication, because the world and posterity might, with much plausible foundation, say, 'Here is a volume which was publicly advertised and came out in Dr. Johnson's own time, and, by his silence, was admitted by him to be genuine.'" JOHNSON: "I shall give myself no trouble about the matter."

The importance of strict and scrupulous veracity cannot be too often inculcated. Johnson was known to be so rigidly attentive to it, that even in his common conversation the slightest circumstance was mentioned with exact precision. The knowledge of his having such a principle and habit made his friends have a perfect reliance on the truth of everything that he told, however it might have been doubted if told by many others. As an instance of this, I may mention an odd incident which he related as having happened to him one night in Fleet-street. "A gentlewoman (said he) begged I would give her my arm to assist her in crossing the street, which I accordingly did; upon which she offered me a shilling, supposing me to be the watchman. I perceived that she was somewhat in liquor." This, if told by most people, would have been thought an invention; when told by Johnson, it was believed by his friends as much as if they had seen what passed.

We landed at the Temple-stairs, where we parted.

I found him in the evening in Mrs. Williams's room. We talked of religious orders. He said, "It is as unreasonable for a man to go into a Carthusian convent for fear of being immoral, as for a man to cut off his hands for fear he should steal. There is, indeed, great resolution in the immediate act of dismembering himself: but when that is once done, he has no longer any merit: for though it is out of his power to steal, yet he may all his life be a thief in his heart. So when a man has once become a Carthusian he is obliged to continue so, whether he chooses it or not. Their silence, too, is absurd. We read in the Gospel of the Apostles being sent to preach, but not to hold their tongues. All severity that does not tend to increase good, or prevent evil, is idle. I said to the Lady Abbess of a convent, 'Madam, you are here not for the love of virtue, but the fear of vice.' She said, 'She should remember this as long as she lived.' " I thought it hard to give her this view of her situation, when she could not help it; and, indeed, I wondered at the whole of what he now said; because both in his *Rambler* and *Idler*, he treats religious austerities with much solemnity of respect.

Finding him still persevering in his abstinence from wine, I ventured to speak to him of it.—JOHNSON: "Sir, I have no objection to a man's drinking wine if he can do it in moderation. I found myself apt to go to excess in it, and therefore, after having been for some time without it, on account of illness, I thought it better not to return to it. Every man is to judge for himself, according to the effects which he experiences. One of the fathers tells us he found fasting made him so peevish that he did not practise it."

Though he often enlarged upon the evil of intoxication, he was by no means harsh and unforgiving to those who indulged in occasional excess of wine. One of his friends, I well remember, came to sup at a tavern with him and some other gentlemen, and too plainly discovered that he had drunk too much at dinner. When one who loved mischief, thinking to produce a severe censure, asked Johnson, a few days afterwards, "Well, Sir, what did your friend say to you, as an apology for being in such a situation?" Johnson answered, "Sir, he said all that a man *should* say; he said he was sorry for it."

I heard him once give a very judicious practical advice upon this subject: "A man who has been drinking wine at all freely, should never go into a new company. With those who have partaken wine with him, he may be pretty well in unison; but he will, probably, be offensive, or appear ridiculous, to other people."

CHAPTER XXXI—1776

A Tour in the Midlands

ON TUESDAY, MARCH 19, which was fixed for our proposed jaunt, we met in the morning at the Somerset coffee-house in the Strand, where we were taken up by the Oxford Coach. He was accompanied by Mr. Gwyn, the architect; and a gentleman of Merton College, whom we did not know, had the fourth seat. We soon got into conversation; for it was very remarkable of Johnson that the presence of a stranger had no restraint upon his talk. I observed that Garrick, who was about to quit the stage, would soon have an easier life. JOHNSON: "I doubt that, Sir." BOSWELL: "Why, Sir, he will be Atlas with the burden off his back." JOHNSON: "But I know not, Sir, if he will be so steady without his load. However, he should never play any more, but be entirely the gentleman, and not partly the player: he should no longer subject himself to be hissed by a mob, or to be insolently treated by performers, whom he used to rule with a high hand, and who would gladly retaliate." BOSWELL: "I think he should play once a year for the benefit of decayed actors, as it has been said he means to do." JOHNSON: "Alas, Sir! he will soon be a decayed actor himself."

Gwyn was a fine, lively, rattling fellow. Dr. Johnson kept him in subjection, but with a kindly authority. The spirit of the artist, however, rose against what he thought a Gothic attack, and he made a brisk defence. "What, Sir! will you allow no value to beauty in architecture or in statuary? Why should we allow it then in writing? Why do you take the trouble to give us so many fine allusions, and bright images, and elegant phrases? You might convey all your instruction without these ornaments." Johnson smiled with complacency; but said, "Why, Sir, all these ornaments are useful, because they obtain an easier reception for truth; but a building is not at all more convenient for being decorated with superfluous carved work."

Gwyn at last was lucky enough to make one reply to Dr. Johnson which he allowed to be excellent. Johnson censured him for taking down a church which might have stood many years, and building a new one at a different place, for no other reason but that there might be a direct road to a new bridge; and his expression was, "You are taking a church out of the way, that the people may go in a straight line to the bridge."—"No, Sir (said Gwyn), I am putting the church *in* the way that the people may not *go out of the way.*" JOHNSON (with a hearty loud laugh of approbation): "Speak no more. Rest your colloquial fame upon this."

We then went to Pembroke College, and waited on his old friend Dr. Adams, the Master of it, whom I found to be a most polite, pleasing, communicative man. Before his advancement to the headship of his college, I had intended to go and visit him at Shrewsbury, where he was rector of St. Chad's, in order to get from him what particulars he could recollect of Johnson's academical life. He now obligingly gave me part of that authentic information which, with what I afterwards owed to his kindness, will be found incorporated in its proper place in this work.

Dr. Adams told us that in some of the Colleges at Oxford, the Fellows had excluded the students from social intercourse with them in the common room. JOHNSON: "They are in the right, Sir: there can be no real conversation, no fair exertion of mind amongst them, if the young men are by; for a man who has a character does not choose to stake it in their presence." BOSWELL: "But, Sir, may there not be very good conversation without a contest for superiority?" JOHNSON: "No animated conversation, Sir, for it cannot be but one or other will come off superior. I do not mean that the victor must have the better of the argument, for he may take the weak side; but his superiority of parts and knowledge will necessarily appear: and he to whom he thus shows himself superior is lessened in the eyes of the young men. You know it was said, '*Mallem cum Scaligero errare quam cum Clavio recte sapere.*' In the same manner take Bentley's and Jason de Nores' 'Comments upon Horace,' you will admire Bentley more when wrong, than Jason when right."

We walked with Dr. Adams into the Master's garden, and into the common room. JOHNSON (after a reverie of meditation): "Ay! here I used to play at draughts with Phil. Jones and Fludyer. Jones loved beer, and did not get very forward in the Church. Fludyer turned out a scoundrel, a Whig, and said he was ashamed of having been bred at Oxford. He had a living at Putney, and got under the eye of some retainers to the Court at that time, and so became a violent Whig: but he had been a scoundrel all along, to be sure." BOSWELL: "Was he a scoundrel, Sir, in any other way than that of being a political scoundrel? Did he cheat at draughts?" JOHNSON: "Sir, we never played for *money*."

We then went to Trinity College, where he introduced me to Mr. Thomas Warton, with whom we passed a part of the evening. We talked of biography.—JOHNSON: "It is rarely well executed. They only who live with a man can write his life with any genuine exactness and discrimination; and few people who have lived with a man know what to remark about him. The chaplain of a late Bishop, whom I was to assist in writing some memoirs of his Lordship, could tell me scarcely anything."[1]

[1]It has been mentioned to me by an accurate English friend that Dr. Johnson could never have used the phrase *almost nothing,* as not being English; and therefore I have put another in its place. At the same time I am not quite convinced it is not good English. For the best writers use this phrase *"little or nothing"; i.e.,* almost so little as to be nothing.

I said Mr. Robert Dodsley's life should be written, as he had been so much connected with the wits of his time, and by his literary merit had raised himself from the station of a footman. Mr. Warton said he had published a little volume under the title of "The Muse in Livery." JOHNSON: "I doubt whether Dodsley's brother would thank a man who should write his life; yet Dodsley himself was not unwilling that his original low condition should be recollected. When Lord Lyttelton's 'Dialogues of the Dead,' came out, one of which is between Apicius, an ancient epicure, and Dartineuf, a modern epicure, Dodsley said to me, 'I knew Dartineuf well, for I was once his footman.' "

I mentioned Sir Richard Steele having published his "Christian Hero," with the avowed purpose of obliging himself to lead a religious life; yet, that his conduct was by no means strictly suitable. JOHNSON: "Steele, I believe, practised the lighter vices."

I censured some ludicrous fantastic dialogues between two coach-horses and other such stuff, which Baretti had lately published. He joined with me, and said, "Nothing odd will do long. 'Tristram Shandy' did not last." I mentioned Mr. Burke. JOHNSON: "Yes; Burke *is* an extraordinary man. His stream of mind is perpetual." It is very pleasing to me to record that Johnson's high estimation of the talents of this gentleman was uniform from their early acquaintance. Sir Joshua Reynolds informs me that when Mr. Burke was first elected a Member of Parliament, and Sir John Hawkins expressed a wonder at his attaining a seat, Johnson said, "Now we who know Mr. Burke, know that he will be one of the first men in the country." And once, when Johnson was ill, and unable to exert himself as much as usual without fatigue, Mr. Burke having been mentioned, he said, "That fellow calls forth all my powers. Were I to see Burke now it would kill me." So much was he accustomed to consider conversation as a contest, and such was his notion of Burke as an opponent.

Next morning, Thursday, March 21, we set out in a post-chaise to pursue our ramble. It was a delightful day, and we rode through Blenheim Park. When I looked at the magnificent bridge built by John Duke of Marlborough, over a small rivulet, and recollected the Epigram made upon it—

> "The lofty arch his high ambition shows,
> The stream, an emblem of his bounty flows:"

and saw that now, by the genius of Brown, a magnificent body of water was collected, I said, "They have *drowned* the Epigram." I observed to him, while in the midst of the noble scene around us, "You and I, Sir, have, I think, seen together the extremes of what can be seen in Britain—the wild rough island of Mull, and Blenheim Park."

We dined at an excellent inn at Chapel House, where he expatiated on the felicity of England in its taverns and inns, and triumphed over the French for not having, in any perfection, the tavern life. "There is no private house (said he) in which people can enjoy themselves so well as in a capital tavern. Let there be ever so great plenty of good things, ever so much grandeur, ever so much elegance, ever so much desire that everybody should be easy; in the nature of things it cannot be: there must always be some degree of care and anxiety. The master of the house is anxious to entertain his guests; the guests are anxious to be agreeable to him: and no man, but a very impudent dog indeed, can as freely command what is in another man's house as if it were his own. Whereas, at a tavern, there is a general freedom from anxiety. You are sure you are welcome: and the more noise you make, the more trouble you give, the more good things you call for, the welcomer you are. No servants will attend you with the alacrity which waiters do, who are incited by the prospect of an immediate reward in proportion as they please. No, Sir; there is nothing which has yet been contrived by man by which so much happiness is produced as by a good tavern or inn."

We stopped at Stratford-upon-Avon, and drank tea and coffee; and it pleased me to be with him upon the classic ground of Shakspeare's native place.

On Friday, March 22, having set out early from Henley, where we had lain the preceding night, we arrived at Birmingham about nine o'clock, and after breakfast went to call on his old schoolfellow, Mr. Hector. A very stupid maid, who opened the door, told us that "her master was gone out; he was gone to the country; she could not tell when he would return." In short, she gave us a miserable reception; and Johnson observed, "She would have behaved no better to people who wanted him in the way of his profession." He said to her, "My name is Johnson; tell him I called. Will you remember the name?" She answered, with rustic simplicity, in the Warwickshire pronunciation, "I don't understand you, Sir."—"Blockhead (said he), I'll write." I never heard the word *blockhead* applied to a woman before, though I do not see why it should not, when there is evident occasion for it. He, however, made another attempt to make her understand him, and roared loud in her ear, "*Johnson*," and then she catched the sound.

We next called on Mr. Lloyd, one of the people called Quakers. He too was not at home, but Mrs. Lloyd was, and received us courteously, and asked us to dinner. Johnson said to me, "After the uncertainty of all human things at Hector's, this invitation came very well." We walked about the town, and he was pleased to see it increasing.

I talked of legitimation by subsequent marriage, which obtained in the Roman law, and still obtains in the law of Scotland. JOHNSON: "I think it a bad thing; because the chastity of women being of the utmost importance, as all property depends upon it, they who forfeit it should not have any possibility of being restored to good character; nor should the children, by an illicit connexion, attain the full right of lawful children, by the posterior consent of the offending parties." His opinion upon this subject deserves consideration. Upon his principle, there may, at times, be a hardship, and seemingly a strange one, upon individuals; but the general good of society is better secured. And, after all, it is unreasonable in an individual to repine that he has not the advantage of a state which is made different from his own by the social institution under which he is born. A woman does not complain that her brother, who is younger than her, gets their common father's estate. Why then should a natural son complain that a younger brother, by the same parents lawfully begotten, gets it? The operation of law is similar in both cases. Besides, an illegitimate son, who has a younger legitimate brother by the same father and mother, has no stronger claim to the father's estate, than if that legitimate brother had only the same father, from whom alone the estate descends.

Mr. Lloyd joined us in the street; and in a little while we met *Friend Hector,* as Mr. Lloyd called him. It gave me great pleasure to observe the joy which Johnson and he expressed at seeing each other again. Mr. Lloyd and I left them together, while he obligingly showed me some of the manufactures of this very curious assemblage of artificers. We all met at dinner at Mr. Lloyd's, where we were entertained with great hospitality. Mr. and Mrs. Lloyd had been married the same year with their Majesties, and like them had been blessed with a numerous family of fine children, their numbers being exactly the same. Johnson said, "Marriage is the best state for man in general; and every man is a worse man, in proportion as he is unfit for the married state."

I have always loved the simplicity of manners and the spiritual-mindedness of the Quakers; and talking with Mr. Lloyd, I observed that the essential part of religion was piety, a devout intercourse with the Divinity; and that many a man was a Quaker without knowing it.

New York, 1945

The burning of Newgate Prison.

As Dr. Johnson had said to me in the morning, while we walked together, that he liked individuals among the Quakers, but not the sect; when we were at Mr. Lloyd's, I kept clear of introducing any questions concerning the peculiarities of their faith. But I having asked to look at Baskerville's edition of "Barclay's Apology," Johnson laid hold of it; and the chapter on baptism happening to open, Johnson remarked, "He says there is neither precept nor practice for baptism, in the Scriptures; that is false." Here he was the aggressor, by no means in a gentle manner; and the good Quakers had the advantage of him; for he had read negligently, and had not observed that Barclay speaks of *infant* baptism; which they calmly made him perceive. Mr. Lloyd, however, was in a great mistake; for when insisting that the rite of baptism by water was to cease, when the *spiritual* administration of Christ began, he maintained that John the Baptist said, *"My baptism* shall decrease, but *his* shall increase." Whereas the words are, *"He* must increase, but I *must* decrease."

From Mr. Hector I now learnt many particulars of Dr. Johnson's early life, which, with others that he gave me at different times since, have contributed to the formation of this work.

Dr. Johnson said to me in the morning, "You will see, Sir, at Mr. Hector's, his sister, Mrs. Careless, a clergyman's widow. She was the first woman with whom I was in love. It dropt out of my head imperceptibly; but she and I shall always have a kindness for each other." He laughed at the notion that a man can never be really in love but once, and considered it as a mere romantic fancy.

On our return from Mr. Bolton's, Mr. Hector took me to his house, where we found Johnson sitting placidly at tea, with his *first love;* who, though now advanced in years, was a genteel woman, very agreeable and well-bred.

When he again talked of Mrs. Careless to-night, he seemed to have had his affection revived; for he said, "If I had married her, it might have been as happy for me." BOSWELL: "Pray, Sir, do you not suppose that there are fifty women in the world, with any one of whom a man may be as happy as with any one woman in particular?" JOHNSON: "Aye, Sir, fifty thousand." BOSWELL: "Then, Sir, you are not of opinion with some who imagine that certain men and certain women are made for each other; and that they cannot be happy if they miss their counterparts." JOHNSON: "To be sure not, Sir. I believe marriages would in general be as happy, and often more so, if they were all made by the Lord Chancellor, upon a due consideration of the characters and circumstances without the parties having any choice in the matter."

I wished to have stayed at Birmingham to-night, to have talked more with Mr. Hector; but my friend was impatient to reach his native city; so we drove on that stage in the dark, and were long pensive and silent. When we came within the focus of the Lichfield lamps, "Now (said he), we are getting out of a state of death." We put up at the *Three Crowns,* not one of the great inns, but a good old-fashioned one, which was kept by Mr. Wilkins, and was the very next house to that in which Johnson was born and brought up, and which was still his own property. We had a comfortable supper, and got into high spirits. I felt all my Toryism glow in this old capital of Staffordshire. I could have offered incense *genio loci;* and I indulged in libations of that ale which Boniface, in the "Beaux Stratagem," recommends with such an eloquent jollity.

Next morning he introduced me to Mrs. Lucy Porter, his stepdaughter. She was now an old maid, with much simplicity of manner. She had never been in London. Her brother, a captain in the Navy, had left her a fortune of ten thousand pounds; about a third of which she had laid out in building a stately house, and making a handsome garden, in an elevated situation in Lichfield. Johnson, when here by himself, used to live at her house. She reverenced him, and he had a parental tenderness for her.

We dined at our inn, and had with us a Mr. Jackson, one of Johnson's school-fellows, whom he treated with much kindness, though he seemed to be a low man, dull and untaught. He had a coarse gray coat, black waistcoat, greasy leather breeches, and yellow uncurled wig; and his countenance had the ruddiness which betokens one who is in no haste to "leave his can." He drank only ale. He had tried to be a cutler at Birmingham, but had not succeeded: and now he lived poorly at home, and had some scheme of dressing leather in a better manner than common: to his indistinct account of which Dr. Johnson listened with patient attention, that he might assist him with his advice. Here was an instance of genuine humanity and real kindness in this great man, who has been most unjustly represented as altogether harsh and destitute of tenderness.

I saw here, for the first time, *oat-ale;* and oat-cakes, not hard as in Scotland, but soft like a Yorkshire cake, were served at breakfast. It was pleasant to me to find that *"oats,"* the *"food of horses,"* were so much used as the *food of the people* in Dr. Johnson's own town. He expatiated in praise of Lichfield and its inhabitants, who, he said, were "the most sober, decent people in England, the genteelest in proportion to their wealth, and spoke the purest English." I doubted as to the last article of this eulogy: for they had several provincial sounds; as, *there* pronounced like *fear,* instead of like *fair; once* pronounced *woonse,* instead of *wunse* or *wonse.* Johnson himself never got entirely free of those provincial accents. Garrick sometimes used to take him off, squeezing a lemon into a punch-bowl, with uncouth gesticulations, looking round the company, and calling out, "Who's for *poonsh?*"

Three Crowns Inn. Lichfield

Very little business appeared to be going forward in Lichfield. I found, however, two strange manufactures for so inland a place, sail-cloth and streamers for ships; and I observed them making some saddle-cloths, and dressing sheep-skins: but upon the whole the busy hand of industry seemed to be quite slackened. "Surely, Sir (said I), you are an idle set of people." "Sir (said Johnson), we are a city of philosophers, we work with our heads, and make the boobies of Birmingham work for us with their hands."

There was at this time a company of players performing at Lichfield. The manager, Mr. Stanton, sent his compliments, and begged leave to wait on Dr. Johnson. Johnson received him very courteously, and he drank a glass of wine with us. He was a plain, decent, well-behaved man, and expressed his gratitude to Dr. Johnson for having once got him permission from Dr. Taylor, at Ashbourne, to play there upon moderate terms.

We had promised Mr. Stanton to be at his theatre on Monday. Dr. Johnson jocularly proposed me to write a Prologue for the occasion: "A Prologue, by James Boswell, Esq., from the Hebrides." I was really inclined to take the hint. Methought, "Prologue, spoken before Dr. Samuel Johnson, at Lichfield, 1776," would have sounded as well as, "Prologue, spoken before the Duke of York, at Oxford," in Charles the Second's time. Much might have been said of what Lichfield had done for Shakspeare, by producing Johnson and Garrick. But I found he was averse to it.

We went and viewed the museum of Mr. Richard Green, apothecary here, who told me he was proud of being a relation of Dr. Johnson's. It was, truly, a wonderful collection, both of antiquities and natural curiosities, and ingenious works of art. He had all the articles accurately arranged, with their names upon labels, printed at his own little press; and on the staircase leading to it was a board, with the names of contributors marked in gold letters. A printed catalogue of the collection was to be had at a bookseller's. Johnson expressed his admiration of the activity and diligence and good fortune of Mr. Green, in getting together, in his situation, so great a variety of things: and Mr. Green told me that Johnson once said to him, "Sir, I should as soon have thought of building a man-of-war, as of collecting such a museum." Mr. Green's obliging alacrity in showing it was very pleasing. His engraved portrait, with which he has favoured me, has a motto truly characteristical of his disposition, *"Nemo sibi vivat."*

A physician being mentioned who had lost his practice, because his whimsically changing his religion had made people distrustful of him, I maintained that this was unreasonable, as religion is unconnected with medical skill. JOHNSON: "Sir, it is not unreasonable; for when people see a man absurd in what they understand, they may conclude the same of him in what they do not understand. If a physician were to take to eating of horseflesh, nobody would employ him; though one may eat horseflesh, and be a very skilful physician. If a man were educated in an absurd religion, his continuing to profess it would not hurt him, though his changing to it would."

We dined at Mr. Peter Garrick's, who was in a very lively humour, and verified Johnson's saying, that if he had cultivated gaiety as much as his brother David, he might have equally excelled in it. He was today quite a London narrator, telling us a variety of anecdotes with that earnestness and attempt at mimicry which we usually find in the wits of the metropolis. Dr. Johnson went with me to the Cathedral in the afternoon. It was grand and pleasing to contemplate this illustrious writer, now full of fame, worshipping in "the solemn temple" of his native city.

On Monday, March 25, we breakfasted at Mrs. Lucy Porter's. Johnson had sent an express to Dr. Taylor's, acquainting him of our being at Lichfield, and Taylor had returned an answer that his post-chaise should come for us this day. While we sat at breakfast, Dr. Johnson received a letter by the post, which seemed to agitate him very much. When he had read it, he exclaimed, "One of the most dreadful things that has happened in my time." The phrase *my time,* like the word *age,* is usually understood to refer to an event of a public or general nature. I imagined something like an assassination of the King—like a gunpowder plot carried into execution—or like another fire of London. When asked, "What is it, Sir?" he answered, "Mr. Thrale has lost his only son!" This was, no doubt, a very great affliction to Mr. and Mrs. Thrale, which their friends would consider accordingly; but from the manner in which the intelligence of it was communicated by Johnson, it appeared for the moment to be comparatively small. I, however, soon felt a sincere concern, and was curious to observe how Dr. Johnson would be affected. He said, "This is a total extinction to their family, as much as if they were sold into captivity." Upon my mentioning that Mr. Thrale had daughters, who might inherit his wealth;—"Daughters (said Johnson warmly), he'll no more value his daughters than——" I was going to speak,—"Sir (said he), don't you know how you yourself think? Sir, he wishes to propagate his name." In short, I saw male succession strong in his mind, even where there was no name, no family of any long standing. I said it was lucky he was not present when this misfortune happened. JOHNSON: "It is lucky for *me.* People in distress never think that you feel enough." BOSWELL: "And, Sir, they will have the hope of seeing you, which will be a relief in the meantime; and when you get to them, the pain will be so far abated, that they will be capable of being consoled by you, which, in the first violence of it, I believe, would not be the case." JOHNSON: "No, Sir; violent pain of mind, like violent pain of body, *must* be severely felt." BOSWELL: "I own, Sir, I have not so much feeling for the distress of others as some people have, or pretend to have; but I know this, that I would do all in my power to relieve them." JOHNSON: "Sir, it is affectation to pretend to feel the distress of others, as much as they do themselves. It is equally so, as if one should pretend to feel as much pain while a friend's leg is cutting off, as he does. No, Sir: you have expressed the rational and just nature of sympathy. I would have gone to the extremity of the earth to have preserved this boy."

He was soon quite calm. The letter was from Mr. Thrale's clerk, and concluded, "I need not say how much they wish to see you in London." He said, "We shall hasten back from Taylor's."

Mrs. Lucy Porter and some other ladies of the place talked a great deal of him when he was out of the room, not only with veneration but affection. It pleased me to find that he was so much *beloved* in his native city.

After dinner Dr. Johnson wrote a letter to Mrs. Thrale on the death of her son. I said it would be very distressing to Thrale, but she would soon forget it, as she had so many things to think of. JOHNSON: "No, Sir, Thrale will forget it first. *She* has many things that she *may* think of. *He* has many things that he *must* think of." This was a very just remark upon the different effects of those light pursuits which occupy a vacant and easy mind, and those serious engagements which arrest attention, and keep us from brooding over grief.

In the evening we went to the Town Hall, which was converted into a temporary theatre, and saw "Theodosius," with "The Stratford Jubilee." I was happy to see Dr. Johnson sitting in a conspicuous part of the pit, and receiving affectionate homage from all his acquaintance. We were quite gay and merry. I afterwards mentioned to him that I condemned myself for being so, when poor Mr. and Mrs. Thrale were in such distress. JOHNSON: "You are wrong, Sir; twenty years hence Mr. and Mrs. Thrale will not suffer much pain from the death of their son. Now, Sir, you are to consider that distance of place, as well as distance of time, operates upon the human feelings. I would not have you be gay in the presence of the distressed, because it would shock them; but you may be gay at a distance. Pain for the loss of a friend, or of a relation whom we love, is occasioned by the want which we feel. In time, the vacuity is filled with something else; or sometimes the vacuity closes up of itself."

Mr. Seward and Mr. Pearson, another clergyman here, supped with us at our inn, and after they left us, we sat up late as we used to do in London.

Here I shall record some fragments of my friend's conversation during this jaunt.

"Never speak of a man in his own presence. It is always indelicate, and may be offensive."

"Questioning is not the mode of conversation among gentlemen. It is assuming a superiority, and it is particularly wrong to question a man concerning himself. There may be parts of his former life which he may not wish to be made known to other persons, or even brought to his own recollection."

"A man should be careful never to tell tales of himself to his own disadvantage. People may be amused and laugh at the time, but they will be remembered and brought out against him upon some subsequent occasion."

CHAPTER XXXII—1776

Johnson Returns to London

ON TUESDAY, MARCH 26, there came for us an equipage properly suited to a wealthy well-beneficed clergyman: Dr. Taylor's large, roomy post-chaise, drawn by four stout plump horses, and driven by two steady jolly postillions, which conveyed us to Ashbourne; where I found my friend's schoolfellow living upon an establishment perfectly corresponding with his substantial creditable equipage; his house, garden, pleasure-grounds, table, in short everything good, and no scantiness appearing. Every man should form such a plan of living as he can execute completely. Let him not draw an outline wider than he can fill up. I have seen many skeletons of show and magnificence which excite at once ridicule and pity. Dr. Taylor had a good estate of his own, and good preferment in the Church, being a prebendary of Westminster, and rector of Bosworth. He was a diligent justice of the peace, and presided over the town of Ashbourne, to the inhabitants of which I was told he was very liberal; and as a proof of this it was mentioned to me he had, the preceding winter, distributed two hundred pounds among such of them as stood in need of his assistance. He had consequently a considerable political interest in the county of Derby, which he employed to support the Devonshire family; for, though the schoolfellow and friend of Johnson, he was a Whig. I could not perceive in his character much congeniality of any sort with that of Johnson, who, however, said to me, "Sir, he has a very strong understanding." His size, and figure, and countenance, and manner, were that of a hearty English squire, with the parson superinduced: and I took particular notice of his upper-servant, Mr. Peters, a decent grave man, in purple clothes, and a large white wig, like the butler or *major domo* of a bishop.

Dr. Taylor commended a physician who was known to him and Dr. Johnson, and said, "I fight many battles for him, as many people in the country dislike him." JOHNSON: "But you should consider, Sir, that by every one of your victories he is a loser; for, every man of whom you get the better will be very angry, and resolve not to employ him: whereas if people get the better of you in argument about him, they'll think, 'We'll send for Dr. [Butter] nevertheless.' " This was an observation deep and sure in human nature.

Next day, as Dr. Johnson had acquainted Dr. Taylor of the reason for his returning speedily to London, it was resolved that we should set out after dinner. A few of Dr. Taylor's neighbours were his guests that day.

Dr. Johnson talked with approbation of one who had attained to the state of the philosophical wise man, that is, to have no want of anything. "Then, Sir (said I), the savage is a wise man." "Sir (said he), I do not mean simply being without—but not having a want." I maintained, against this proposition, that it was better to have fine clothes, for instance, than not to feel the want of them. JOHNSON: "No, Sir; fine clothes are good only as they supply the want of other means of procuring respect. Was Charles the Twelfth, think you, less respected for his coarse blue coat and black stock? And you find the King of Prussia dresses plain, because the dignity of his character is sufficient." I here brought myself into a scrape, for I heedlessly said, "Would not *you,* Sir, be the better for velvet embroidery?" JOHNSON: "Sir, you put an end to all argument when you introduce your opponent yourself. Have you no better manners? There is *your want.*" I apologised by saying I had mentioned him as an instance of one who wanted as little as any man in the world, and yet, perhaps, might receive some additional lustre from dress.

Having left Ashbourne in the evening, we stopped to change horses at Derby, and availed ourselves of a moment to enjoy the conversation of my countryman, Dr. Butter, then physician there. He was in great indignation because Lord Mountstuart's bill for a Scotch militia had been lost. Dr. Johnson was as violent against it. "I am glad (said he) that Parliament has had the spirit to throw it out. You wanted to take advantage of the timidity of our scoundrels" (meaning, I suppose, the Ministry). It may be observed that he used the epithet scoundrel, very commonly, not quite in the sense in which it is generally understood, but as a strong term of disapprobation; as when he abruptly answered Mrs. Thrale, who had asked him how he did, "Ready to become a scoundrel, Madam; with a little more spoiling, you will, I think, make me a complete rascal":—he meant, easy to become a capricious and self-indulgent valetudinarian; a character for which I have heard him express great disgust.

He said, "It is commonly a weak man who marries for love." We then talked of marrying women of fortune; and I mentioned a common remark that a man may be, upon the whole, richer by marrying a woman with a very small portion, because a woman of fortune will be proportionately expensive; whereas a woman who brings none will be very moderate in expenses. JOHNSON: "Depend upon it, Sir, this is not true. A woman of fortune, being used to the handling of money, spends it judiciously: but a woman who gets the command of money for the first time upon her marriage has such a gust in spending it, that she throws it away with great profusion."

He praised the ladies of the present age, insisting that they were more faithful to their husbands, and more virtuous in every respect, than in former times, because their understandings were better cultivated. It was an undoubted proof of his good sense and good disposition that he was never querulous, never prone to inveigh against the present times, as is so common when superficial minds are on the fret. On the contrary, he was willing to speak favourably of his own age; and, indeed, maintained its superiority in every respect, except in its reverence for government; the relaxation of which he imputed, as its grand cause, to the shock which our monarchy received at the Revolution, though necessary; and secondly, to the timid concessions made to faction by successive Administrations in the reign of his present Majesty. I am happy to think that he lived to see the crown at last recover its just influence.

Having lain at St. Albans, on Thursday, March 28, we breakfasted the next morning at Barnet. I expressed to him a weakness of mind which I could not help; an uneasy apprehension that my wife and children, who were at a great distance from me, might, perhaps, be ill. "Sir (said he), consider how foolish you would think it in *them* to be apprehensive that *you* are ill." This sudden turn relieved me for the moment; but I afterwards perceived it to be an ingenious fallacy. I might, to be sure, be satisfied that they had no reason to be apprehensive about me, because I *knew* that I myself was well: but we might have mutual anxiety, without the charge of folly; because each was, in some degree, uncertain as to the condition of the other.

I enjoyed the luxury of our approach to London, that metropolis which we both loved so much, for the high and varied intellectual pleasure which it furnishes. I experienced immediate happiness while whirled along with such a companion, and said to him, "Sir, you observed one day at General Oglethorpe's that a man is never happy for the present but when he is drunk. Will you not add—or when driving rapidly in a post-chaise?" JOHNSON: "No, Sir, you are driving rapidly *from* something, or *to* something."

We stopped at Messieurs Dilly's, booksellers in the Poultry; from whence he hurried away, in a hackney coach, to Mr. Thrale's in the Borough. I called at his house in the evening, having promised to acquaint Mrs. Williams of his safe return; when, to my surprise, I found him sitting with her at tea, and, as I thought, not in a very good humour: for, it seems, when he had got to Mr. Thrale's, he found the coach was at the door waiting to carry Mrs. and Miss Thrale, and Signor Baretti, their Italian master, to Bath. This was not showing the attention which might have been expected to the "Guide, Philosopher, and Friend"! the *Imlac* who had hastened from the country to console a distressed mother, who he understood was very anxious for his return. They had, I found, without ceremony, proceeded on their intended journey. I was glad to understand from him that it was still resolved that his tour to Italy with Mr. and Mrs. Thrale should take place, of which he had entertained some doubt, on account of the loss which they had suffered; and his doubts afterwards appeared to be well founded. He observed, indeed, very justly, that "their loss was an additional reason for their going abroad; and if it had not been fixed that he should have been one of the party, he would force them out, but he would not advise them unless his advice was asked, lest they might suspect that he recommended what he wished on his own account." I was not pleased that his intimacy with Mr. Thrale's family, though it no doubt contributed much to his comfort and enjoyment, was not without some degree of restraint: not, as has been grossly suggested, that it was required of him as a task to talk for the entertainment of them and their company; but that he was not quite at his ease; which, however, might partly be owing to his own honest pride—that dignity of mind which is always jealous of appearing too compliant.

On Sunday, March 31, I called on him, and showed him as a curiosity which I had discovered his "Translation of Lobo's Account of Abyssinia," which Sir John Pringle had lent me, it being then little known as one of his works. He said, "Take no notice of it," or "don't talk of it." He seemed to think it beneath him, though done at six-and-twenty. I said to him, "Your style, Sir, is much improved since you translated this." He answered, with a sort of triumphant smile, "Sir, I hope it is."

On Wednesday, April 3, in the morning I found him very busy putting his books in order, and as they were generally very old ones, clouds of dust were flying around him. He had on a pair of large gloves, such as hedgers use. His present appearance put me in mind of my uncle Dr. Boswell's description of him, "A robust genius, born to grapple with whole libraries."

I gave him an account of a conversation which had passed between me and Captain Cook, the day before, at dinner at Sir John Pringle's; and he was much pleased with the conscientious accuracy of that celebrated circumnavigator, who set me right as to many of the exaggerated accounts given by Dr. Hawkesworth of his Voyages. I told him that while I was with the Captain, I catched the enthusiasm of curiosity and adventure, and felt a strong inclination to go with him on his next voyage. JOHNSON: "Why, Sir, a man *does* feel so, till he considers how very little he can learn from such voyages." BOSWELL: "But one is carried away with the general grand and indistinct notion of a Voyage Round the World." JOHNSON: "Yes, Sir, but a man is to guard himself against taking a thing in general." I said I was certain that a great part of what we are told by the travellers to the South Sea must be conjecture, because they had not enough of the language of those countries to understand so much as they have related. Objects falling under the observation of the senses might be clearly known; but everything intellectual, everything abstract—politics, morals, and religion, must be darkly guessed. Dr. Johnson was of the same opinion. He upon another occasion, when a friend mentioned to him several extraordinary facts as communicated to him by the circumnavigators, slily observed, "Sir, I never before knew how much I was respected by these gentlemen; they told *me* none of these things."

He had been in company with Omai, a native of one of the South Sea Islands, after he had been some time in this country. He was struck with the elegance of his behaviour, and accounted for it thus: "Sir, he had passed his time, while in England, only in the best company; so that all that he had acquired of our manners was genteel. As a proof of this, Sir, Lord Mulgrave and he dined one day at Streatham; they sat with their backs to the light fronting me, so that I could not see distinctly: and there was so little of the savage in Omai, that I was afraid to speak to either, lest I should mistake one for the other."

We talked of education at great schools; the advantages and disadvantages of which Johnson displayed in a luminous manner; but his arguments preponderate so much in favour of the benefit which a boy of good parts might receive at one of them, that I have reason to believe Mr. Murray was very much influenced by what he had heard to-day, in his determination to send his own son to Westminster School—I have acted in the same manner with regard to my own two sons; having placed the eldest at Eton, and the second at Westminster. I cannot say which is best. But in justice to both those noble seminaries, I with high satisfaction declare that my boys have derived from them a great deal of good, and no evil: and I trust they will, like Horace, be grateful to their father for giving them so valuable an education.

On Thursday, April 4, having called on Dr. Johnson, I said it was a pity that truth was not so firm as to bid defiance to all attacks, so that it might be shot at as much as people chose to attempt, and yet remain unhurt. JOHNSON: "Then, Sir, it would not be shot at. Nobody attempts to dispute that two and two make four: but with contests concerning moral truth, human passions are generally mixed, and therefore it must ever be liable to assault and misrepresentation."

On Friday, April 5, being Good Friday, after having attended the morning service at St. Clement's Church, I walked home with Johnson. We talked of the Roman Catholic religion. JOHNSON: "In the barbarous ages, Sir, priests and people were equally deceived; but afterwards there were gross corruptions introduced by the clergy, such as indulgences to priests to have concubines, and the worship of images, not, indeed, inculcated, but knowingly permitted." He strongly censured the licensed stews at Rome. BOSWELL: "So, then, Sir, you would allow no irregular intercourse whatever between the sexes?" JOHNSON: "To be sure I would not, Sir. I would punish it much more than it is done, and so restrain it. In all countries there has been fornication, as in all countries there has been theft; but there may be more or less of the one, as well as of the other, in proportion to the force of law. All men will naturally commit fornication, as all men will naturally steal. And, Sir, it is very absurd to argue, as has been often done, that prostitutes are necessary to prevent the violent effects of appetite from violating the decent order of life; nay, should be permitted in order to preserve the chastity of our wives and daughters. Depend upon it, Sir, severe laws, steadily enforced, would be sufficient against those evils, and would promote marriage."

I stated to him this case:—"Suppose a man has a daughter, who he knows has been seduced, but her misfortune is concealed from the world; should he keep her in his house? Would he not, by doing so, be accessory to imposition? And, perhaps, a worthy, unsuspecting man might come and marry this woman, unless the father inform him of the truth." JOHNSON: "Sir, he is accessory to no imposition. His daughter is in his house; and if a man courts her, he takes his chance. If a friend, or indeed, if any man, asks his opinion whether he should marry her, he ought to advise him against it, without telling why, because his real opinion is then required. Or, if he has other daughters who know of her frailty, he ought not to keep her in his house. You are to consider the state of life is this; we are to judge of one another's characters as well as we can; and a man is not bound, in honesty or honour, to tell us the faults of his daughter or of himself. A man who has debauched his friend's daughter is not obliged to say to everybody —'Take care of me; don't let me enter your house without suspicion. I once debauched a friend's daughter. I may debauch yours.'"

Mr. Thrale called upon him, and appeared to bear the loss of his son with a manly composure. There was no affectation about him; and he talked, as usual, upon indifferent subjects. He seemed to me to hesitate as to the intended Italian tour, on which, I flattered myself, he and Mrs. Thrale and Dr. Johnson were soon to set out; and, therefore, I pressed it as much as I could. I mentioned that Mr. Beauclerk had said that Baretti, whom they were to carry with them, would keep them so long in the little towns of his own district that they would not have time to see Rome. I mentioned this to put them on their guard. JOHNSON: "Sir, we do not thank Mr. Beauclerk for supposing that we are to be directed by Baretti. No, Sir; Mr. Thrale is to go, by my advice, to Mr. Jackson (the all-knowing), and get from him a plan for seeing the most that can be seen in the time that we have to travel. We must, to be sure, see Rome, Naples, Florence, and Venice, and as much more as we can" (speaking with a tone of animation).

When I expressed an earnest wish for his remarks on Italy, he said, "I do not see that I could make a book upon Italy; yet I should be glad to get £200 or £500 by such a work." This showed both that a journal of his Tour upon the Continent was not wholly out of his contemplation, and that he uniformly adhered to that strange opinion which his indolent disposition made him utter: "No man but a block-head ever wrote, except for money." Numerous instances to refute this will occur to all who are versed in the history of literature.

He gave us one of the many sketches of character which were treasured in his mind, and which he was wont to produce quite un-expectedly in a very entertaining manner. "I lately (said he) received a letter from the East Indies, from a gentleman whom I formerly knew very well; he had returned from that country with a handsome fortune, as it was reckoned, before means were found to acquire those immense sums which have been brought from thence of late: he was a scholar, and an agreeable man, and lived very prettily in London, till his wife died. After her death, he took to dissipation and gaming, and lost all he had. One evening, he lost £1,000 to a gentleman whose name I am sorry I have forgotten. Next morning, he sent the gentle-man £500 with an apology that it was all he had in the world. The gentleman sent the money back to him, declaring he would not accept of it; and adding that if Mr. [Fowke] had occasion for £500 more, he would lend it to him. He resolved to go out again to the East Indies, and make his fortune anew. He got a considerable appoint-ment, and I had some intention of accompanying him. Had I thought then as I do now, I should have gone: but, at that time, I had ob-jections to quitting England."

It was a very remarkable circumstance about Johnson, whom shal-low observers have supposed to have been ignorant of the world, that very few men had seen greater variety of characters; and none could observe them better, as was evident from the strong, yet nice portraits which he often drew. I have frequently thought that if he had made out what the French call *une catalogue raisonnée* of all the people who had passed under his observation, it would have afforded a very rich fund of instruction and entertainment. The suddenness with which his accounts of some of them started out in conversation was not less pleasing than surprising. I remember he once observed to me, "It is wonderful, Sir, what is to be found in London. The most literary conversation that I ever enjoyed was at the table of Jack Ellis, a money-scrivener behind the Royal Exchange, with whom I at one period used to dine generally once a week."

Volumes would be required to contain a list of his numerous and various acquaintance, none of whom he ever forgot; and could describe and discriminate them all with precision and vivacity. He associated with persons the most widely different in manners, abilities, rank, and accomplishments. He was at once the companion of the brilliant Colonel Forrester of the Guards, who wrote "The Polite Philosopher," and of the awkward and uncouth Robert Levett; of Lord Thurlow, and Mr. Sastres, the Italian master; and has dined one day with the beautiful, gay, and fascinating Lady Craven, and the next with good Mrs. Gardiner, the tallow-chandler, on Snowhill.

I mentioned a new gaming-club, of which Mr. Beauclerk had given me an account, where the members played to a desperate extent. JOHNSON: "Depend upon it, Sir, this is mere talk. *Who* is ruined by gaming? You will not find six instances in an age. There is a strange rout made about deep play: whereas you have many more people ruined by adventurous trade, and yet we do not hear such an outcry against it." THRALE: "There may be few people absolutely ruined by deep play; but very many are much hurt in their circumstances by it." JOHNSON: "Yes, Sir, and so are very many by other kinds of expense." I had heard him talk once before in the same manner; and at Oxford, he said, he wished he had learned to play at cards. The truth, however, is that he loved to display his ingenuity in argument; and therefore would sometimes in conversation maintain opinions which he was sensible were wrong, but in supporting which, his reasoning and wit would be most conspicuous. He would begin thus: "Why, Sir, as to the good or evil of card-playing——" "Now (said Garrick) he is thinking which side he shall take." He appeared to have a pleasure in contradiction, especially when any opinion whatever was delivered with an air of confidence; so that there was hardly any topic, if not one of the great truths of Religion and Morality, that he might not have been incited to argue, either for or against. Lord Elibank had the highest admiration of his powers. He once observed to me: "Whatever opinion Johnson maintains, I will not say that he convinces me; but he never fails to show me that he has good reasons for it." I have heard Johnson pay his Lordship this high compliment: "I never was in Lord Elibank's company without learning something."

We sat together till it was too late for the afternoon service. Thrale said he had come with intention to go to church with us. We went at seven to evening prayers at St. Clement's Church, after having drunk coffee; an indulgence which I understood Johnson yielded to on this occasion in compliment to Thrale.

On Sunday, April 7, Easter Day, after having been at St. Paul's Cathedral, I came to Dr. Johnson, according to my usual custom.

I repeated to him an argument of a lady of my acquaintance, who maintained that her husband's having been guilty of numberless infidelities released her from conjugal obligations, because they were reciprocal. JOHNSON: "This is miserable stuff, Sir. To the contract of marriage, besides the man and wife, there is a third party—Society; and if it be considered as a vow—God: and, therefore, it cannot be dissolved by their consent alone. Laws are not made for particular cases, but for men in general. A woman may be unhappy with her husband; but she cannot be freed from him without the approbation of the civil and ecclesiastical power. A man may be unhappy, because he is not so rich as another; but he is not to seize upon another's property with his own hand." BOSWELL: "But, Sir, this lady does not want that the contract should be dissolved; she only argues that she may indulge herself in gallantries with equal freedom as her husband does, provided she takes care not to introduce a spurious issue into his family. You know, Sir, what Macrobius has told of Julia." JOHNSON: "This lady of yours, Sir, I think, is very fit for a brothel."

Mr. Macbean, author of the "Dictionary of Ancient Geography," came in. He mentioned that he had been forty years absent from Scotland. "Ah, Boswell (said Johnson, smiling), what would you give to be forty years from Scotland?" I said, "I should not like to be so long absent from the seat of my ancestors." This gentleman, Mrs. Williams, and Mr. Levett, dined with us.

Mrs. Williams was very peevish; and I wondered at Johnson's patience with her now, as I had often done on similar occasions. The truth is that his humane consideration of the forlorn and indigent state in which this lady was left by her father, induced him to treat her with the utmost tenderness, and even to be desirous of procuring her amusement, so as sometimes to incommode many of his friends, by carrying her with him to their houses, where, from her manner of eating, in consequence of her blindness, she could not but offend the delicacy of persons of nice sensations.

On Wednesday, April 10, I dined with him at Mr. Thrale's, where were Mr. Murphy and some other company. Before dinner, Dr. Johnson and I passed some time by ourselves. I was sorry to find it was now resolved that the proposed journey to Italy should not take place this year. He said, "I am disappointed, to be sure; but it is not a great disappointment." I wondered to see him bear, with a philosophical calmness, what would have made most people peevish and fretful. I perceived, however, that he had so warmly cherished the hope of enjoying classical scenes, that he could not easily part with the scheme; for he said, "I shall probably contrive to get to Italy some other way. But I won't mention it to Mr. and Mrs. Thrale, as it might vex them." I suggested that going to Italy might have done Mr. and Mrs. Thrale good. JOHNSON: "I rather believe not, Sir. While grief is fresh, every attempt to divert only irritates. You must wait till grief be *digested*, and then amusement will dissipate the remains of it."

I said I disliked the custom which some people had of bringing their children into company, because it in a manner forced us to pay foolish compliments to please their parents. JOHNSON: "You are right, Sir. We may be excused for not caring much about other people's children, for there are many who care very little about their own children. It may be observed that men, who from being engaged in business, or from their course of life in whatever way, seldom see their children, do not care much about them. I myself should not have had much fondness for a child of my own." MRS. THRALE: "Nay, Sir, how can you talk so?" JOHNSON: "At least, I never wished to have a child."

Talking of the *Reviews,* Johnson said, "I think them very impartial: I do not know an instance of partiality." He mentioned what had passed upon the subject of the *Monthly* and *Critical Reviews,* in the conversation with which his Majesty had honoured him. He expatiated a little more on them this evening. "The Monthly Reviewers (said he) are not Deists; but they are Christians with as little Christianity as may be; and are for pulling down all establishments. The Critical Reviewers are for supporting the Constitution both in Church and State. The Critical Reviewers, I believe, often review without reading the books through; but lay hold of a topic, and write chiefly from their own minds. The Monthly Reviewers are duller men, and are glad to read the books through."

He talked of Lord Lyttelton's extreme anxiety as an author; observing that "he was thirty years in preparing his 'History,' and that he employed a man to point it for him; as if (laughing) another man could point his sense better than himself." Mr. Murphy said he understood his "History" was kept back several years for fear of Smollet. JOHNSON: "This seems strange to Murphy and me, who never felt that anxiety, but sent what we wrote to the press, and let it take its chance." MRS. THRALE: "The time has been, Sir, when you felt it." JOHNSON: "Why, really, Madam, I do not recollect a time when that was the case."

CHAPTER XXXIII—1776

A Visit to Bath

ON THURSDAY, APRIL 11, I dined with him at General Paoli's, in whose house I now resided, and where I had ever afterwards the honour of being entertained with the kindest attention as his constant guest, while I was in London, till I had a house of my own there. I mentioned my having that morning introduced to Mr. Garrick Count Neni, a Flemish nobleman of great rank and fortune, to whom Garrick talked of *Abel Drugger* as *a small part;* and related, with pleasant vanity, that a Frenchman who had seen him in one of his low characters, exclaimed, *"Comment! je ne le crois pas. Ce n'est pas Monsieur Garrick, ce grand homme!"* Garrick added, with an appearance of grave recollection, "If I were to begin life again, I think I should not play these low characters." Upon which I observed, "Sir, you would be in the wrong; for your great excellence is your variety of playing, your representing, so well, characters so very different." JOHNSON: "Garrick, Sir, was not in earnest in what he said; for, to be sure, his peculiar excellence is his variety; and, perhaps there is not any one character which has not been as well acted by somebody else, as he could do it." BOSWELL: "Why, then, Sir, did he talk so?" JOHNSON: "Why, Sir, to make you answer as you did." BOSWELL: "I don't know, Sir; he seemed to dip deep into his mind for the reflection." JOHNSON: "He had not far to dip, Sir: he had said the same thing, probably, twenty times before."

A journey to Italy was still in his thoughts. He said, "A man who has not been in Italy is always conscious of an inferiority, from his not having seen what it is expected a man should see. The grand object of travelling is to see the shores of the Mediterranean. On those shores were the four great Empires of the world; the Assyrian, the Persian, the Grecian, and the Roman. All our religion, almost all our law, almost all our arts, almost all that sets us above savages, has come to us from the shores of the Mediterranean." The General observed that "The Mediterranean would be a noble subject for a poem."

We talked of translation. I said I could not define it, nor could I think of a similitude to illustrate it; but that it appeared to me the translation of poetry could be only imitation. JOHNSON: "You may translate books of science exactly. You may also translate history, in so far as it is not embellished with oratory, which is poetical. Poetry, indeed, cannot be translated; and, therefore, it is the poets that preserve the languages; for we would not be at the trouble to learn a language if we could have all that is written in it just as well as a translation. But as the beauties of poetry cannot be preserved in any language except that in which it was originally written, we learn the language."

"Goldsmith (he said) referred every thing to vanity; his virtues, and his vices too, were from that motive. He was not a social man. He never exchanged mind with you."

We spent the evening at Mr. Hoole's. Mr. Mickle, the excellent translator of "The Lusiad," was there. I have preserved little of the conversation of this evening. Dr. Johnson said, "Thomson had a true poetical genius, the power of viewing everything in a poetical light. His fault is such a cloud of words sometimes, that the sense can hardly peep through. Shiels, who compiled 'Cibber's Lives of the Poets,' was one day sitting with me. I took down Thomson, and read aloud a large portion of him, and then asked,—'Is not this fine?' Shiels having expressed the highest admiration, 'Well, Sir (said I), I have omitted every other line.'"

I introduced Aristotle's doctrine in his "Art of Poetry," of, "the κάθαρσις τῶν παθημάτων, the purging of the passions," as the purpose of tragedy. "But how are the passions to be purged by terror and pity?" (said I, with an assumed air of ignorance, to incite him to talk, for which it was often necessary to employ some address). JOHNSON: "Why, Sir, you are to consider what is the meaning of purging in the original sense. It is to expel impurities from the human body. The mind is subject to the same imperfection. The passions are the greatest movers of human actions; but they are mixed with such impurities that it is necessary they should be purged or refined by means of terror and pity. For instance, ambition is a noble passion; but by seeing, upon the stage, that a man who is so excessively ambitious as to raise himself by injustice, is punished, we are terrified at the fatal consequences of such a passion. In the same manner a certain degree of resentment is necessary; but if we see that a man carries it too far, we pity the object of it, and are taught to moderate that passion." My record upon this occasion does great injustice to Johnson's expression, which was so forcible and brilliant that Mr. Cradock whispered me, "O that his words were written in a book!"

I observed the great defect of the tragedy of "Othello" was that it had not a moral; for that no man could resist the circumstances of suspicion which were artfully suggested to Othello's mind. JOHNSON: "In the first place, Sir, we learn from Othello this very useful moral, not to make an unequal match: in the second place, we learn not to yield too readily to suspicion. The handkerchief is merely a trick, though a very pretty trick; but there are no other circumstances of reasonable suspicion, except what is related by *Iago* of *Cassio's* warm expressions concerning *Desdemona* in his sleep; and that depended entirely upon the assertion of one man. No, Sir, I think *Othello* has more moral than almost any play."

Talking of a penurious gentleman of our acquaintance, Johnson said, "Sir, he is narrow, not so much from avarice, as from impotence to spend his money. He cannot find in his heart to pour out a bottle of wine; but he would not much care if it should sour."

Johnson and I supped this evening at the Crown and Anchor Tavern, in company with Sir Joshua Reynolds, Mr. Langton, Mr. Nairne, now one of the Scotch Judges, with the title of Lord Dunsinan, and my very worthy friend, Sir William Forbes, of Pitsligo.

We discussed the question whether drinking improved conversation and benevolence. Sir Joshua maintained it did. JOHNSON: "No, Sir; before dinner, men meet with great inequality of understanding; and those who are conscious of their inferiority, have the modesty not to talk. When they have drunk wine, every man feels himself happy, and loses that modesty, and grows impudent and vociferous: but he is not improved: he is only sensible of his defects." Sir Joshua said the Doctor was talking of the effects of excess in wine; but that a moderate glass enlivened the mind, by giving a proper circulation to the blood. "I am (said he) in very good spirits when I get up in the morning. By dinner-time I am exhausted; wine puts me in the same state as when I got up; and I am sure that moderate drinking makes people talk better." JOHNSON: "No, Sir; wine gives not light, gay, ideal hilarity; but tumultuous, noisy, clamorous merriment. I have heard none of those drunken—nay, drunken is a coarse word—none of those *vinous* flights." SIR JOSHUA: "Because you have sat by, quite sober, and felt an envy of the happiness of those who were drinking." JOHNSON: "Perhaps, contempt.—And, Sir, it is not necessary to be drunk one's self to relish the wit of drunkenness. Do we not judge of the drunken wit of the dialogue between Iago and Cassio, the most excellent in its kind, when we are quite sober? Wit is wit, by whatever means it is produced; and, if good, will appear so at all times. I admit that the spirits are raised by drinking, as by the common participation of any pleasure: cock-fighting, or bear-baiting, will raise the spirits of a company, as drinking does, though surely they will not improve conversation. I also admit that there are some sluggish men who are improved by drinking; as there are fruits which are not good till they are rotten. There are such men, but they are medlars. I indeed allow that there have been a very few men of talents who were improved by drinking; but I maintain that I am right as to the effects of drinking in general: and let it be considered, that there is no position, however false in its universality, which is not true of some particular man." Sir William Forbes said, "Might not a man warmed with wine be like a bottle of beer, which is made brisker by being set before the fire?"—"Nay (said Johnson, laughing), I cannot answer that: that is too much for me."

I observed that wine did some people harm, by inflaming, confusing, and irritating their minds; but that the experience of mankind had declared in favour of moderate drinking. JOHNSON: "Sir, I do not say it is wrong to produce self-complacency by drinking; I only deny that it improves the mind. When I drank wine, I scorned to drink it when in company. I have drunk many a bottle by myself; in the first place, because I had need of it to raise my spirits; in the second place, because I would have nobody to witness its effects upon me."

He told us "almost all his *Ramblers* were written just as they were wanted for the press; that he sent a certain portion of the copy of an essay, and wrote the remainder while the former part of it was printing. When it was wanted, and he had fairly sat down to it, he was sure it would be done."

He said that, for general improvement, a man should read whatever his immediate inclination prompts him to; though to be sure, if a man has a science to learn, he must regularly and resolutely advance. He added, "What we read with inclination makes a much stronger impression. If we read without inclination, half the mind is employed in fixing the attention; so there is but one half to be employed on what we read." He told us he read Fielding's "Amelia" through without stopping.[1] He said, "If a man begins to read in the middle of a book, and feels an inclination to go on, let him not quit it to go to the beginning. He may perhaps not feel again the inclination."

We talked of the *Reviews,* and Dr. Johnson spoke of them as he did

---

[1] We have here an involuntary testimony to the excellence of this admirable writer, to whom we have seen that Dr. Johnson *directly* allowed so little merit.

at Thrale's. Sir Joshua said, what I have often thought, that he wondered to find so much good writing employed in them, when the
authors were to remain unknown, and so could not have the motive of
fame. JOHNSON: "Nay, Sir, those who write in them, write well in
order to be paid well."

Soon after this day he went to Bath with Mr. and Mrs. Thrale. I had
never seen that beautiful city, and wished to take the opportunity of
visiting it, while Johnson was there.

Dr. Johnson and Mr. Boswell visit Bath

On the 26th of April, I went to Bath; and on my arrival at the
Pelican Inn, found lying for me an obliging invitation from Mr. and
Mrs. Thrale, by whom I was agreeably entertained almost constantly
during my stay. They were gone to the Rooms; but there was a kind
note from Dr. Johnson, that he should sit at home all the evening. I
went to him directly, and before Mr. and Mrs. Thrale returned, we
had by ourselves some hours of tea-drinking and talk.

I shall group together such of his sayings as I preserved during the
few days that I was at Bath.

Of a person [Burke] who differed from him in politics, he said, "In
private life he is a very honest gentleman; but I will not allow him to
be so in public life. People *may* be honest, though they are doing
wrong: that is, between their Maker and them. But *we*, who are suffering by their pernicious conduct, are to destroy them. We are sure that
[Burke] acts from interest. We know what his genuine principles were.

They who allow their passions to confound the distinctions between right and wrong, are criminal. They may be convinced; but they have not come honestly by their conviction."

It having been mentioned, I know not with what truth, that a certain female political writer [Mrs. Macaulay] whose doctrines he disliked had of late become very fond of dress, sat hours together at her toilet and even put on rouge:—JOHNSON: "She is better employed at her toilet than using her pen. It is better she should be reddening her own cheeks than blackening other people's characters."

A literary lady of large fortune [Mrs. Montagu] was mentioned, as one who did good to many, but by no means "by stealth," and instead of "blushing to find it fame," acted evidently from vanity. JOHNSON: "I have seen no beings who do as much good from benevolence, as she does from whatever motive. If there are such under the earth, or in the clouds, I wish they would come up, or come down. What Soame Jenyns says upon this subject is not to be minded; he is a wit. No, Sir; to act from pure benevolence is not possible for finite beings. Human benevolence is mingled with vanity, interest, or some other motive."

He would not allow me to praise a lady [Hannah More] then at Bath; observing, "She does not gain upon me, Sir; I think her empty-headed." He was, indeed, a stern critic upon character and manners. Even Mrs. Thrale did not escape his friendly animadversion at times. When he and I were one day endeavouring to ascertain, article by article, how one of our friends [Langton] could possibly spend as much money in his family as he told us he did, she interrupted us by a lively extravagant sally on the expense of clothing his children, describing it in a very ludicrous and fanciful manner. Johnson looked a little angry, and said, "Nay, Madam, when you are declaiming, declaim; and when you are calculating, calculate." At another time, when she said, perhaps affectedly, "I don't like to fly":—JOHNSON: "With *your* wings, Madam, you *must* fly: but have a care, there are *clippers* abroad." How very well was this said, and how fully has experience proved the truth of it! But have they not *clipped* rather *rudely*, and gone a great deal *closer* than was necessary?

On Monday, April 29, he and I made an excursion to Bristol, where I was entertained with seeing him inquire, upon the spot, into the authenticity of *Rowley's* poetry, as I had seen him inquire, upon the spot, into the authenticity of *Ossian's* poetry. George Catcot, the pewterer, who was as zealous for Rowley as Hugh Blair was for *Ossian* (I trust my Reverend friend will excuse the comparison), attended us at our inn, and with a triumphant air of lively simplicity called out, "I'll make Dr. Johnson a convert." Dr. Johnson, at his desire, read aloud some of Chatterton's fabricated verses, while Catcot stood at the back of his chair, moving himself like a pendulum, and beating time with his feet, and now and then looking into Dr. Johnson's face, wondering that he was not yet convinced. We called on Mr. Barret, the surgeon, and saw some of the *originals,* as they were called, which were executed very artificially; but from a careful inspection of them, and a consideration of the circumstances with which they were attended, we were quite satisfied of the imposture, which, indeed, has been clearly demonstrated from internal evidence, by several able critics.

Honest Catcot seemed to pay no attention whatever to any objections, but insisted, as an end of all controversy, that we should go with him to the tower of the church of St. Mary, Redcliff, and *view with our own eyes* the ancient chest in which the manuscripts were found. To this Dr. Johnson good-naturedly agreed; and, though troubled with a shortness of breathing, laboured up a long flight of steps, till we came to the place where the wondrous chest stood. *"There* (said Catcot, with a bouncing confident credulity), *there* is the very chest itself." After this *ocular demonstration,* there was no more to be said. He brought to my recollection a Scotch Highlander, a man of learning too, and who had seen the world, attesting, and at the same time giving his reasons for, the authenticity of Fingal:—"I have heard all that poem when I was young."—"Have you, Sir? Pray, what have you heard?"—"I have heard Ossian, Oscar, and *every one of them.*"

Johnson said of Chatterton, "This is the most extraordinary young man that has encountered my knowledge. It is wonderful how the whelp has written such things."

We were by no means pleased with our inn at Bristol. "Let us see now (said I), how we should describe it." Johnson was ready with his raillery. "Describe it, Sir?—Why, it was so bad that Boswell wished to be in Scotland!"

After Dr. Johnson's return to London, I was several times with him at his house, where I occasionally slept in the room that had been assigned for me. I dined with him at Dr. Taylor's, at General Oglethorpe's, and at General Paoli's. To avoid a tedious minuteness, I shall group together what I have preserved of his conversation during this period also, without specifying each scene where it passed, except one, which will be found so remarkable as certainly to deserve a very particular relation.

"Garrick (he observed) does not play the part of *Archer,* in 'The Beaux Stratagem,' well. The gentleman should break out through the footman, which is not the case as he does it."

"Where there is no education, as in savage countries, men will have the upper hand of women. Bodily strength, no doubt, contributes to this: but it would be so, exclusive of that; for it is mind that always governs. When it comes to dry understanding, man has the better."

"That man is never happy for the present, is so true, that all his relief from unhappiness is only forgetting himself for a little while. Life is a progress from want to want, not from enjoyment to enjoyment."

"Though many men are nominally intrusted with the administration of hospitals and other public institutions, almost all the good is done by one man, by whom the rest are driven on: owing to confidence in him, and indolence in them."

"Lord Chesterfield's Letters to his son, I think, might be made a very pretty book. Take out the immorality, and it should be put in the hands of every young gentleman. An elegant manner and easiness of behaviour are acquired gradually and imperceptibly. No man can say 'I'll be genteel.' There are ten genteel women for one genteel man, because they are more restrained. A man without some degree of restraint is insufferable; but we are all less restrained than women. Were a woman sitting in company to put out her legs before her as most men do, we should be tempted to kick them in." No man was a more attentive and nice observer of behaviour in those in whose company he happened to be, than Johnson; or, however strange it may seem to many, had a higher estimation of its refinements. Lord Eliot informs me that one day when Johnson and he were at dinner in a gentleman's house in London, upon Lord Chesterfield's Letters being mentioned, Johnson surprised the company by this sentence: "Every man of any education would rather be called a rascal than accused of deficiency in *the graces.*" Mr. Gibbon, who was present, turned to a lady who knew Johnson well, and lived much with him, and in his quaint manner, tapping his box, addressed her thus: "Don't you think, Madam (looking towards Johnson), that among *all* your acquaintance you could find *one* exception?" The lady smiled, and seemed to acquiesce.

"Mrs. Williams was angry that Thrale's family did not send regularly to her every time they heard from me while I was in the Hebrides. Little people are apt to be jealous; but they should not be jealous; for they ought to consider that superior attention will necessarily be paid to superior fortune or rank. Two persons may have equal merit, and on that account may have an equal claim to attention; but one of them may have also fortune and rank, and so may have a double claim."

A gentleman, whom I found sitting with him one morning, said that in his opinion the character of an infidel was more detestable than that of a man notoriously guilty of an atrocious crime. I differed from him, because we are surer of the odiousness of the one than of the error of the other. JOHNSON: "Sir, I agree with him; for the infidel would be guilty of any crime if he were inclined to it."

"Many things which are false are transmitted from book to book, and gain credit in the world. One of these is the cry against the evil of luxury. Now the truth is, that luxury produces much good. Take the luxury of buildings in London. Does it not produce real advantage in the conveniency and elegance of accommodation, and this all from the exertion of industry? People will tell you, with a melancholy face, how many builders are in jail. It is plain they are in jail, not for building; for rents are not fallen.—A man gives half-a-guinea for a dish of green peas. How much gardening does this occasion? How many labourers must the competition to have such things early in the market keep in employment? You will hear it said very gravely, 'Why was not the half-guinea, thus spent in luxury, given to the poor? To how many might it have afforded a good meal.' Alas! has it not gone to the *industrious* poor, whom it is better to support than the *idle* poor? You are much surer that you are doing good when you *pay* money to those who work, as the recompense of their labour, than when you *give* money merely in charity. Suppose the ancient luxury of a dish of peacocks' brains were to be revived, how many carcases would be left to the poor at a cheap rate: and as to the rout that is made about people who are ruined by extravagance, it is no matter to the nation that some individuals suffer. When so much general productive exertion is the consequence of luxury, the nation does not care though there are debtors in jail: nay, they would not care though their creditors were there too."

The uncommon vivacity of General Oglethorpe's mind, and variety of knowledge, having sometimes made his conversation seem too desultory, Johnson observed, "Oglethorpe, Sir, never *completes* what he has to say."

Being irritated by hearing a gentleman ask Mr. Levett a variety of questions concerning him when he was sitting by, he broke out, "Sir, you have but two topics, yourself and me. I am sick of both." "A man (said he) should not talk of himself, nor much of any particular person. He should take care not to be made a proverb; and therefore should avoid having any one topic, of which people can say, 'We shall hear him upon it.' There was a Dr. Oldfield, who was always talking of the Duke of Marlborough. He came into a coffee-house one day, and told that his Grace had spoken in the House of Lords for half an hour. 'Did he indeed speak for half an hour?' (said Belchier, the surgeon).—'Yes.'—'And what did he say of Dr. Oldfield?'—'Nothing.'— 'Why, then, Sir, he was very ungrateful; for Dr. Oldfield could not have spoken for a quarter of an hour, without saying something of him.' "

"Every man is to take existence on the terms on which it is given to him. To some men it is given on condition of not taking liberties, which other men may take without much harm. One may drink wine, and be nothing the worse for it; on another, wine may have effects so inflammatory as to injure him both in body and mind, and perhaps make him commit something for which he may deserve to be hanged."

CHAPTER XXXIV—1776

The Dinner at Dilly's

I AM NOW TO RECORD a very curious incident in Dr. Johnson's Life, which fell under my own observation; of which *pars magna fui*, and which, I am persuaded, will, with the liberal minded, be much to his credit.

My desire of being acquainted with celebrated men of every description, had made me, much about the same time, obtain an introduction to Dr. Samuel Johnson and to John Wilkes, Esq. Two men more different could perhaps not be selected out of all mankind. They had even attacked one another with some asperity in their writings; yet I lived in habits of friendship with both. I could fully relish the excellence of each; for I have ever delighted in that intellectual chemistry, which can separate good qualities from evil in the same person.

Sir John Pringle, "mine own friend and my father's friend," between whom and Dr. Johnson I in vain wished to establish an acquaintance, as I respected and lived in intimacy with both of them, observed to me once, very ingeniously, "It is not in friendship as in mathematics, where two things, each equal to a third, are equal between themselves. You agree with Johnson as a middle quality, and you agree with me as a middle quality; but Johnson and I should not agree." Sir John was not sufficiently flexible; so I desisted; knowing, indeed, that the repulsion was equally strong on the part of Johnson; who, I know not from what cause, unless his being a Scotchman, had formed a very erroneous opinion of Sir John. But I conceived an irresistible wish, if possible, to bring Dr. Johnson and Mr. Wilkes together. How to manage it, was a nice and difficult matter.

My worthy booksellers and friends, Messieurs Dilly in the Poultry, at whose hospitable and well-covered table I have seen a greater number of literary men than at any other, except that of Sir Joshua Reynolds, had invited me to meet Mr. Wilkes and some more gentlemen, on Wednesday, May 15. "Pray (said I), let us have Dr. Johnson."—"What, with Mr. Wilkes? Not for the world (said Mr. Edward Dilly); Dr. Johnson would never forgive me."—"Come (said I), if you'll let me negotiate for you, I will be answerable that all shall go well." DILLY: "Nay, if you will take it upon you, I am sure I shall be very happy to see them both here."

Notwithstanding the high veneration which I entertained for Dr. Johnson, I was sensible that he was sometimes a little actuated by the spirit of contradiction, and by means of that I hoped I should gain my point. I was persuaded that if I had come upon him with a direct proposal, "Sir, will you dine in company with Jack Wilkes?" he would have flown into a passion, and would probably have answered, "Dine with Jack Wilkes, Sir! I'd as soon dine with Jack Ketch." I therefore, while we were sitting quietly by ourselves at his house in an evening, took occasion to open my plan thus:—"Mr. Dilly, Sir, sends his respectful compliments to you, and would be happy if you would do him the honour to dine with him on Wednesday next, along with me, as I must soon go to Scotland." JOHNSON: "Sir, I am obliged to Mr. Dilly. I will wait upon him——" BOSWELL: "Provided, Sir, I suppose, that the company which he is to have, is agreeable to you." JOHNSON: "What do you mean, Sir? What do you take me for? Do you think I am so ignorant of the world, as to imagine that I am to prescribe to a gentleman what company he is to have at his table?" BOSWELL: "I beg your pardon, Sir, for wishing to prevent you from meeting people whom you might not like. Perhaps he may have some of what he calls his patriotic friends with him." JOHNSON: "Well, Sir, and what then?

What care *I* for his *patriotic friends?* Poh!" BOSWELL: "I should not be surprised to find Jack Wilkes there." JOHNSON: "And if Jack Wilkes *should* be there, what is that to *me*, Sir? My dear friend, let us have no more of this. I am sorry to be angry with you; but really it is treating me strangely, to talk to me as if I could not meet any company whatever, occasionally." BOSWELL: "Pray forgive me, Sir; I meant well. But you shall meet whoever comes, for me." Thus I secured him, and told Dilly that he would find him very well pleased to be one of his guests, on the day appointed.

Upon the much-expected Wednesday, I called on him about half-an-hour before dinner, as I often did when we were to dine out together, to see that he was ready in time, and to accompany him. I found him buffeting his books, as upon a former occasion, covered with dust, and making no preparation for going abroad. "How is this, Sir? (said I). Don't you recollect that you are to dine at Mr. Dilly's?" JOHNSON: "Sir, I did not think of going to Dilly's: it went out of my head. I have ordered dinner at home with Mrs. Williams." BOSWELL: "But, my dear Sir, you know you were engaged to Mr. Dilly, and I told him so. He will expect you, and will be much disappointed if you don't come." JOHNSON: "You must talk to Mrs. Williams about this."

Here was a sad dilemma. I feared that what I was so confident I had secured, would yet be frustrated. He had accustomed himself to show Mrs. Williams such a degree of humane attention, as frequently imposed some restraint upon him; and I knew that if she should be obstinate, he would not stir. I hastened down stairs to the blind lady's room, and told her I was in great uneasiness, for Dr. Johnson had engaged to me to dine this day at Mr. Dilly's, but that he had told me he had forgotten his engagement, and had ordered dinner at home. "Yes, Sir (said she, pretty peevishly), Dr. Johnson is to dine at home." —"Madam (said I), his respect for you is such that I know he will not leave you, unless you absolutely desire it. But as you have so much of his company, I hope you will be good enough to forego it for a day, as Mr. Dilly is a very worthy man, has frequently had agreeable parties at his house for Dr. Johnson, and will be vexed if the Doctor neglects him to-day. And then, Madam, be pleased to consider my situation; I carried the message, and I assured Mr. Dilly that Dr. Johnson was to come; and no doubt he has made a dinner, and invited a company, and boasted of the honour he expected to have. I shall be quite disgraced if the Doctor is not there." She gradually softened to my solicitations, which were certainly as earnest as most entreaties to ladies upon any occasion, and was graciously pleased to empower me to tell Dr. Johnson, "That, all things considered, she thought he should certainly go." I flew back to him, still in dust, and careless of what should be the event, "indifferent in his choice to go or stay"; but as soon as I had announced to him Mrs. Williams's consent, he roared, "Frank, a clean shirt!" and was very soon dressed. When I had him fairly seated in a hackney-coach with me, I exulted as much as a fortune-hunter, who has got an heiress into a post-chaise with him, to set out for Gretna-Green.

When we entered Mr. Dilly's drawing-room, he found himself in the midst of a company he did not know. I kept myself snug and silent, watching how he would conduct himself. I observed him whispering to Mr. Dilly, "Who is that gentleman, Sir?"—"Mr. Arthur Lee."— JOHNSON: "Too, too, too" (under his breath), which was one of his habitual mutterings. Mr. Arthur Lee could not but be very obnoxious to Johnson, for he was not only a *patriot*, but an *American*. He was afterwards minister from the United States at the Court of Madrid. "And who is the gentleman in lace?" "Mr. Wilkes, Sir." This information confounded him still more; he had some difficulty to restrain himself, and taking up a book, sat down upon a window-seat and read, or at least kept his eye upon it intently for some time, till he composed himself. His feelings, I dare say, were awkward enough. But he no doubt recollected his having rated me, for supposing that he could be at all disconcerted by any company, and he, therefore, resolutely set himself to behave quite as an easy man of the world, who could adapt himself at once to the disposition and manners of those whom he might chance to meet.

The cheering sound of "Dinner is upon the table," dissolved his reverie, and we *all* sat down without any symptom of ill humour. There were present, beside Mr. Wilkes, and Mr. Arthur Lee, who was an old companion of mine when he studied physic at Edinburgh, Mr. (now Sir John) Miller, Dr. Lettsom, and Mr. Slater the druggist. Mr. Wilkes placed himself next to Dr. Johnson, and behaved to him with so much attention and politeness, that he gained upon him insensibly. No man ate more heartily than Johnson, or loved better what was nice and delicate. Mr. Wilkes was very assiduous in helping him to some fine veal. "Pray give me leave, Sir;—It is better here—A little of the brown—Some fat, Sir—A little of the stuffing—Some gravy—Let me have the pleasure of giving you some butter—Allow me to recommend a squeeze of this orange;—or the lemon, perhaps, may have more zest."

—"Sir, Sir, I am obliged to you, Sir," cried Johnson, bowing, and turning his head to him with a look for some time, of "surly virtue," but, in a short while, of complacency.

Foote being mentioned, Johnson said, "He is not a good mimic." One of the company added, "A merry-Andrew, a buffoon." JOHNSON: "But he has wit, too, and is not deficient in ideas, or in fertility and variety of imagery, and not empty of reading; he has knowledge enough to fill up his part. One species of wit he has in an eminent degree, that of escape. You drive him into a corner with both hands; but he's gone, Sir, when you think you have got him—like an animal that jumps over your head. Then he has a great range for wit; he never lets truth stand between him and a jest, and is sometimes mighty coarse. Garrick is under many restraints from which Foote is free." WILKES: "Garrick's wit is more like Lord Chesterfield's." JOHNSON: "The first time I was in company with Foote, was at Fitzherbert's. Having no good opinion of the fellow, I was resolved not to be pleased; and it is very difficult to please a man against his will. I went on eating my dinner pretty sullenly, affecting not to mind him. But the dog was so very comical, that I was obliged to lay down my knife and fork, throw myself back upon my chair, and fairly laugh it out. No, Sir, he was irresistible. He upon one occasion experienced, in an extraordinary degree, the efficacy of his powers of entertaining. Amongst the many and various modes which he tried of getting money, he became a partner with a small-beer brewer, and he was to have a share of the profits for procuring customers amongst his numerous acquaintance. Fitzherbert was one who took his small-beer; but it was so bad that the servants resolved not to drink it. They were at some loss how to notify their resolution, being afraid of offending their master, who they knew liked Foote much as a companion. At last they fixed upon a little black boy, who was rather a favourite, to be their deputy, and deliver their remonstrance; and having invested him with the whole authority of the kitchen, he was to inform Mr. Fitzherbert, in all their names, upon a certain day, that they would drink Foote's small-beer no longer. On that day, Foote happened to dine at Fitzherbert's, and this boy served at table; he was so delighted with Foote's stories, and merriment, and grimace, that when he went down stairs, he told them, 'This is the finest man I have ever seen. I will not deliver your message. I will drink his small-beer.'"

Mr. Wilkes remarked, that, "among all the bold flights of Shakspeare's imagination, the boldest was making Birnam-wood march to

Dunsinane; creating a wood where there never was a shrub; a wood in Scotland! ha! ha! ha!" And he also observed that "the clannish slavery of the Highlands of Scotland was the single exception to Milton's remark of 'The Mountain Nymph,' sweet Liberty,' being worshipped in all hilly countries."—"When I was at Inverary (said he), on a visit to my old friend, Archibald Duke of Argyle, his dependents congratulated me on being such a favourite of his Grace. I said, 'It is then, gentlemen, truly lucky for me; for if I had displeased the Duke, and he had wished it, there is not a Campbell among you but would have been ready to bring John Wilkes's head to him in a charger. It would have been only

> 'Off with his head! So much for *Aylesbury.*'

I was then Member for Aylesbury."

Dr. Johnson and Mr. Wilkes talked of the contested passage in Horace's "Art of Poetry," *"Difficile est proprie communia dicere."* Mr. Wilkes, according to my note, gave the interpretation thus: "It is difficult to speak with propriety of common things; as, if a poet had to speak of Queen Caroline drinking tea, he must endeavour to avoid the vulgarity of cups and saucers. You will easier make a tragedy out of the 'Iliad' than on any subject not handled before." JOHNSON: "He means that it is difficult to appropriate to particular persons qualities which are common to all mankind, as Homer has done."

WILKES: "We have no City-Poet now: that is an office which has gone into disuse. The last was Elkanah Settle. There is something in *names* which one cannot help feeling. Now, *Elkanah Settle* sounds so *queer*, who can expect much from that name? We should have no hesitation to give it for John Dryden, in preference to Elkanah Settle, from the names only, without knowing their different merits." JOHNSON: "I suppose, Sir, Settle did as well for Aldermen in his time, as John Home could do now. Where did Beckford and Trecothick learn English?"

Mr. Arthur Lee mentioned some Scotch who had taken possession of a barren part of America, and wondered why they should choose it. JOHNSON: "Why, Sir, all barrenness is comparative. The *Scotch* would not know it to be barren." BOSWELL: "Come, come, he is flattering the English. You have now been in Scotland, Sir, and say if you did not see meat and drink enough there." JOHNSON: "Why, yes, Sir; meat and drink enough to give the inhabitants sufficient strength to run away from home." All these quick and lively sallies were said sportively, quite

Gordon Ross del.

New York, 1945

The debate at Sir Joshua's

in jest, and with a smile, which showed that he meant only wit. Upon this topic, he and Mr. Wilkes could perfectly assimilate; here was a bond of union between them and I was conscious that, as both of them had visited Caledonia, both were fully satisfied of the strange narrow ignorance of those who imagined that it is a land of famine. But they amused themselves with persevering in the old jokes. When I claimed a superiority for Scotland over England in one respect, that no man can be arrested there for a debt, merely because another swears it against him; but there must first be the judgment of a court of law ascertaining its justice; and that a seizure of the person, before judgment is obtained, can take place only if his creditor could swear that he is about to fly from the country, or, as it is technically expressed, is *in meditatione fugæ:* WILKES: "That, I should think, may be safely sworn of all the Scotch nation." JOHNSON (to Mr. Wilkes): "You must know, Sir, I lately took my friend Boswell, and showed him genuine civilised life in an English provincial town. I turned him loose at Lichfield, my native city, that he might see for once real civility: for you know he lives among savages in Scotland, and among rakes in London." WILKES: "Except when he is with grave, sober, decent people, like you and me." JOHNSON (smiling): "And we ashamed of him."

They were quite frank and easy. Johnson told the story of his asking Mrs. Macaulay to allow her footman to sit down with them, to prove the ridiculousness of the argument for the equality of mankind; and he said to me afterwards, with a nod of satisfaction, "You saw Mr. Wilkes acquiesced." Wilkes talked with all imaginable freedom of the ludicrous title given to the Attorney-General, *Diabolus Regis;* adding, "I have reason to know something about that officer; for I was prosecuted for a libel." Johnson, who many people would have supposed must have been furiously angry at hearing this talked of so lightly, said not a word. He was now, *indeed,* "a good-humoured fellow."

After dinner, we had an accession of Mrs. Knowles, the Quaker lady, well known for her various talents, and of Mr. Alderman Lee. Amidst some patriotic groans somebody (I think the Alderman) said, "Poor old England is lost!" JOHNSON: "Sir, it is not so much to be lamented that Old England is lost, as that the Scotch have found it." WILKES: "Had Lord Bute governed Scotland only, I should not have taken the trouble to write his eulogy, and dedicate 'Mortimer' to him."

Mr. Wilkes held a candle to show a face print of a beautiful female figure which hung in the room, and pointed out the elegant contour of the bosom, with the finger of an arch connoisseur. He afterwards, in a conversation with me, waggishly insisted that all the time Johnson showed visible signs of a fervent admiration of the corresponding charms of the fair Quaker.

This record, though by no means so perfect as I could wish, will serve to give a notion of a very curious interview, which was not only pleasing at the time, but had the agreeable and benignant effect of reconciling any animosity, and sweetening any acidity, which, in the various bustle of political contest, had been produced in the minds of two men, who, though widely different, had so many things in common —classical learning, modern literature, wit and humour, and ready repartee—that it would have been much to be regretted if they had been for ever at a distance from each other.

Mr. Burke gave me much credit for this successful *negotiation;* and pleasantly said, "that there was nothing equal to it in the whole history of the *Corps Diplomatique.*"

I attended Dr. Johnson home, and had the satisfaction to hear him tell Mrs. Williams how much he had been pleased with Mr. Wilkes's company, and what an agreeable day he had passed.

I talked a good deal to him of the celebrated Margaret Caroline Rudd, whom I had visited, induced by the fame of her talents, address, and irresistible power of fascination. To a lady who disapproved of my visiting her, he said, on a former occasion, "Nay, Madam, Boswell is in the right; I should have visited her myself, were it not that they have now a trick of putting everything into the newspapers." This evening he exclaimed, "I envy him his acquaintance with Mrs. Rudd."

I mentioned a scheme which I had, of making a tour of the Isle of Man, and giving a full account of it; and that Mr. Burke had playfully suggested as a motto,

"The proper study of mankind is Man."

JOHNSON: "Sir, you will get more by the book than the jaunt will cost you; so you will have your diversion for nothing, and add to your reputation."

On the evening of the next day, I took leave of him, being to set out for Scotland. I thanked him with great warmth for all his kindness. "Sir (said he), you are very welcome. Nobody repays it with more."

"DR. JOHNSON TO MRS. BOSWELL.

"MADAM,—

"You must not think me uncivil in omitting to answer the letter with which you favoured me some time ago. I imagined it to have been written without Mr. Boswell's knowledge, and therefore supposed the answer to require, what I could not find, a private conveyance.

"The difference with Lord Auchinleck is now over; and since young Alexander has appeared, I hope no more difficulties will arise among you; for I sincerely wish you all happy. Do not teach the young ones to dislike me, as you dislike me yourself; but let me at least have Veronica's kindness, because she is my acquaintance.

"You will now have Mr. Boswell home: it is well that you have him; he has led a wild life. I have taken him to Lichfield, and he has followed Mr. Thrale to Bath. Pray take care of him, and tame him. The only thing in which I have the honour to agree with you is, in loving him; and while we are so much of a mind in a matter of so much importance, our other quarrels will, I hope, produce no great bitterness.

"I am, Madam,
"Your most humble servant,
"SAM. JOHNSON.

"*May 16, 1776.*"

"MR. BOSWELL TO DR. JOHNSON.

"*Edinburgh, June 25, 1776.*

"You have formerly complained that my letters were too long. There is no danger of that complaint being made at present; for I find it difficult for me to write to you at all. [Here an account of having been afflicted with a return of melancholy or bad spirits.]

"The boxes of books[1] which you sent to me, are arrived; but I have not yet examined the contents."

"DR. JOHNSON TO MR. BOSWELL.

"DEAR SIR,—

"These black fits, of which you complain, perhaps hurt your memory as well as your imagination. When did I complain that your letters were

[1] Upon a settlement of our account of expenses on a Tour to the Hebrides, there was a balance due to me, which Dr. Johnson chose to discharge by sending books.

too long?[2] Your last letter, after a very long delay, brought very bad news. [Here a series of reflections upon melancholy, and—what I could not help thinking strangely unreasonable in him who had suffered so much from it himself—a good deal of severity and reproof, as if it were owing to my own fault, or that I was perhaps affecting it from a desire of distinction.]

"Read Cheyne's 'English Malady'; but do not let him teach you a foolish notion, that melancholy is a proof of acuteness. * * * * *

"To hear that you have not opened your boxes of books, is very offensive. The examination and arrangement of so many volumes might have afforded you an amusement very seasonable at present, and useful for the whole of life. I am, I confess, very angry that you manage yourself so ill. * * * * *

"I do not now say any more, than that I am, with great kindness and sincerity, dear Sir,

"Your humble servant,
"SAM JOHNSON.

"*July 2, 1776.*"

"DR. JOHNSON TO MR. BOSWELL.

"DEAR SIR,—

"I make haste to write again, lest my last letter should give you too much pain. If you are really oppressed with overwhelming and involuntary melancholy, you are to be pitied rather than reproached.

*   *   *

"Now, my dear Bozzy, let us have done with quarrels and with censure. Let me know whether I have not sent you a pretty library. There are, perhaps, many books among them which you never need read through; but there are none which it is not proper for you to know, and sometimes to consult. Of these books, of which the use is only occasional, it is often sufficient to know the contents, that, when any question arises, you may know where to look for information.

"It vexes me to tell you, that on the evening of the 29th of May, I was seized by the gout, and am not quite well. The pain has not been violent, but the weakness and tenderness were very troublesome; and what is said to be very uncommon, it has not alleviated my other

---

[2] Baretti told me that Johnson complained of my writing very long letters to him when I was upon the continent; which was most certainly true; but it seems my friend did not remember it.

disorders. Make use of youth and health while you have them; make my compliments to Mrs. Boswell.

"I am, my dear Sir,
"Your most affectionate,
"SAM. JOHNSON.
"*July 6, 1776.*"

"MR. BOSWELL TO DR. JOHNSON.

"*Edinburgh, July 18, 1776.*

"MY DEAR SIR,—

"Your letter of the second of this month was rather a harsh medicine, but I was delighted with that spontaneous tenderness, which, a few days afterwards, sent forth such balsam as your next brought me. I found myself for some time so ill that all I could do was to preserve a decent appearance, while all within was weakness and distress. Like a reduced garrison that has some spirit left, I hung out flags, and planted all the force I could muster, upon the walls. I am now much better, and I sincerely thank you for your kind attention and friendly counsel."

"MR. BOSWELL TO DR. JOHNSON.

"*Edinburgh, August 30, 1776.*

[After giving him an account of my having examined the chest of books which he had sent to me, and which contained what may be truly called a numerous and miscellaneous *Stall Library,* thrown together at random:—]

"I have, since I saw you, read every word of Granger's 'Biographical History.' It has entertained me exceedingly, and I do not think him the *Whig* that you supposed. Horace Walpole's being his patron is, indeed, no good sign of his political principles. But he denied to Lord Mountstuart that he was a Whig, and said he had been accused by both parties of partiality. It seems he was like Pope,

'While Tories call me Whig, and Whigs a Tory.'

I wish you would look more into his book: and as Lord Mountstuart wishes much to find a proper person to continue the work upon Granger's plan, and has desired I would mention it to you; if such a man occurs, please to let me know. His Lordship will give him generous encouragement."

I again wrote to Dr. Johnson on the 21st of October, informing him that my father had, in the most liberal manner, paid a large debt for me, and that I had now the happiness of being upon very good terms with him; to which he returned the following answer.

"TO JAMES BOSWELL, ESQ.

"DEAR SIR,—

"I had great pleasure in hearing that you are at last on good terms with your father. Cultivate his kindness by all honest and manly means. Life is but short; no time can be afforded but for the indulgence of real sorrow, or contests upon questions seriously momentous. Let us not throw away any of our days upon useless resentment, or contend who shall hold out longest in stubborn malignity. It is best not to be angry; and best, in the next place, to be quickly reconciled. May you and your father pass the remainder of your time in reciprocal benevolence!

*   *   *

"Do you ever hear from Mr. Langton? I visit him sometimes, but he does not talk. I do not like his scheme of life; but as I am not permitted to understand it, I cannot set any thing right that is wrong. His children are sweet babies.

"I hope my irreconcilable enemy, Mrs. Boswell, is well. Desire her not to transmit her malevolence to the young people. Let me have Alexander, and Veronica, and Euphemia, for my friends.

"Mrs. Williams, whom you may reckon as one of your well-wishers, is in a feeble and languishing state, with little hopes of growing better. She went for some part of the autumn into the country, but is little benefited; and Dr. Lawrence confesses that his art is at end. Death is, however, at a distance: and what more than that can we say of ourselves? I am sorry for her pain, and more sorry for her decay. Mr. Levett is sound, wind and limb.

"I was some weeks this autumn at Brighthelmstone. The place was very dull, and I was not well; the expedition to the Hebrides was the most pleasant journey that I ever made. Such an effort annually would give the world a little diversification.

"Every year, however, we cannot wander, and must therefore endeavour to spend our time at home as well as we can. I believe it is best to throw life into a method, that every hour may bring its employment, and every employment have its hour. Xenophon observes, in his 'Treatise of Economy,' that if everything be kept in a certain place, when anything is worn out or consumed, the vacuity which it leaves will show what is wanting; so if every part of time has its duty, the hour will call into remembrance its proper engagement.

"I have not practised all this prudence myself, but I have suffered much for want of it; and I would have you, by timely recollection and steady resolution, escape from those evils which have lain heavy upon me.

"I am, my dearest Boswell,

"Your most humble servant,

"SAM. JOHNSON.

"Bolt Court, Nov. 16, 1776."

On the 16th of November, I informed him that Mr. Strahan had sent me *twelve* copies of the "Journey to the Western Islands," handsomely bound, instead of the *twenty* copies which were stipulated; but which, I supposed, were to be only in sheets; requested to know how they should be distributed: and mentioned that I had another son born to me, who was named David, and was a sickly infant.

"TO JAMES BOSWELL, ESQ.

"DEAR SIR,—

"I have been for some time ill of a cold, which, perhaps, I made an excuse to myself for not writing, when in reality I knew not what to say.

"The books you must at last distribute as you think best, in my name, or your own, as you are inclined, or as you judge most proper. Everybody cannot be obliged, but I wish that nobody may be offended. Do the best you can.

"I congratulate you on the increase of your family, and hope that little David is by this time well, and his mamma perfectly recovered. I am much pleased to hear of the re-establishment of kindness between you and your father. Cultivate his paternal tenderness as much as you can. To live at variance at all is uncomfortable; and variance with a father is still more uncomfortable. Besides that, in the whole dispute, you have the wrong side; at least you gave the first provocations, and some of them very offensive. Let it now be all over. As you have no reason to think that your new mother has shown you any foul play, treat her with respect, and with some degree of confidence; this will secure your father. When once a discordant family has felt the pleasure of peace they will not willingly lose it. If Mrs. Boswell would but be friends with me, we might now shut the temple of Janus.

[383]

"Mrs. Williams has been much out of order; and though she is something better, is likely, in her physician's opinion, to endure her malady for life, though she may, perhaps, die of some other. Mrs. Thrale is big, and fancies that she carries a boy; if it were very reasonable to wish much about it, I should wish her not to be disappointed. The desire of male heirs is not appended only to feudal tenures. A son is almost necessary to the continuance of Thrale's fortune; for what can misses do with a brew-house? Lands are fitter for daughters than trades.

"Baretti went away from Thrale's in some whimsical fit of disgust, or ill-nature, without taking any leave. It is well if he finds in any other place as good an habitation, and as many conveniences. He has got five-and-twenty guineas by translating Sir Joshua's 'Discourses' into Italian, and Mr. Thrale gave him an hundred in the spring; so that he is yet in no difficulties.

"I am, dear Sir,

"Your humble servant,

"SAM. JOHNSON.

"*Dec. 21, 1776.*"

CHAPTER XXXV—1777

The Lives of the Poets

IN 1777, it appears, from his "Prayers and Meditations," that Johnson suffered much from a state of mind "unsettled and perplexed," and from that constitutional gloom, which, together with his extreme humility and anxiety with regard to his religious state, made him contemplate himself through too dark and unfavourable a medium. It may be said of him that he "saw God in clouds."

"MR. BOSWELL TO DR. JOHNSON.

"*Edinburgh, Feb. 14, 1777.*

"MY DEAR SIR,—

"My state of epistolary accounts with you at present is extraordinary. The balance, as to number, is on your side. I am indebted to you for two letters; one dated the 16th November, upon which very day I wrote to you, so that our letters were exactly exchanged, and one dated the 21st of December last.

"My heart was warmed with gratitude by the truly kind contents of both of them; and it is amazing and vexing that I have allowed so much time to elapse without writing to you. But delay is inherent in me, by nature, or by bad habit. I waited till I should have an opportunity of paying you my compliments on a new year. I have procrastinated till the new year is no longer new.

"I have not yet distributed all your books. Lord Hailes and Lord Monboddo have each received one, and return you thanks. Monboddo dined with me lately, and having drank tea, we were a good while by ourselves, and as I knew that he had read the 'Journey' superficially, he did not talk of it as I wished, I brought it to him, and read aloud several passages; and then he talked so that I told him he was to have a copy *from the author*. He begged *that* might be marked on it.

* * *

"I ever am, my dear Sir,
"Your most faithful
"And affectionate humble servant,
"JAMES BOSWELL."

"SIR ALEXANDER DICK TO DR. SAMUEL JOHNSON.

"Prestonfield, Feb. 17, 1777.

"SIR,—

"I had yesterday the honour of receiving your book of your 'Journey to the Western Islands of Scotland,' which you were so good as to send me by the hands of our mutual friend, Mr. Boswell, of Auchinleck; for which I return you my most hearty thanks; and after carefully reading it over again, shall deposit it in my little collection of choice books, next our worthy friend's 'Journey to Corsica.' As there are many things to admire in both performances, I have often wished that no Travels or Journey should be published but those undertaken by persons of integrity and capacity, to judge well, and describe faithfully, and in good language, the situation, condition, and manners of the countries passed through. Indeed, our country of Scotland, in spite of the union of the crowns, is still in most places so devoid of clothing, or cover from hedges and plantations, that it was well you gave your readers a sound *Monitoire* with respect to that circumstance. The truths you have told, and the purity of the language in which they are expressed, as your 'Journey' is universally read, may, and already appear to, have a very good effect. For a man of my acquaintance, who has the largest nursery for trees and hedges in the country, tells me that of late the demand upon him for these articles is doubled, and sometimes tripled. I have, therefore, listed Dr. Samuel Johnson, in some of my memorandums of the principal planters and favourers of the enclosures, under a name which I took the liberty to invent from the Greek, *Papadendrion*. Lord Auchinleck and some few more are of the list. I am told that one gentleman in the shire of Aberdeen, *viz.*, Sir Archibald Grant, has planted above fifty millions of trees on a piece of very wild ground at Monimusk: I must inquire if he has fenced them well, before he enters my list; for that is the soul of enclosing. I began myself to plant a little, our ground being too valuable for much, and that is now fifty years ago; and the trees, now in my seventy-fourth year, I look up to with reverence, and show them to my eldest son, now in his fifteenth year, and they are full the height of my country-house here, where I had the pleasure of receiving you, and hope again to have that satisfaction with our mutual friend, Mr. Boswell. I shall always continue, with the truest esteem, dear Doctor, your most obliged

"And obedient humble servant,
"ALEXANDER DICK."

"TO JAMES BOSWELL, ESQ.

"DEAR SIR,—

"It is so long since I heard anything from you, that I am not easy about it; write something to me next post. When you sent your last letter, every thing seemed to be mending; I hope nothing has lately grown worse. I suppose young Alexander continues to thrive, and Veronica is now very pretty company. I do not suppose the lady is yet reconciled to me, yet let her know that I love her very well, and value her very much.

"Dr. Blair is printing some sermons. If they are all like the first, which I have read, they are *sermones aurei, ac auro magis aurei*. It is excellently written, both as to doctrine and language. Mr. Watson's book seems to be much esteemed.

*   *   *

"Poor Beauclerk still continues very ill. Langton lives on as he used to do. His children are very pretty, and, I think, his lady loses her Scotch. Paoli I never see.

"I have been so distressed by difficulty of breathing, that I lost, as was computed, six-and-thirty ounces of blood in a few days. I am better, but not well.

"I wish you would be vigilant and get me Graham's 'Telemachus' that was printed at Glasgow, a very little book; and '*Johnstoni Poemata,*' another little book, printed at Middleburgh.

"Mrs. Williams sends her compliments, and promises that when you come hither, she will accommodate you as well as ever she can in the old room. She wishes to know whether you sent her book to Sir Alexander Gordon.

"My dear Boswell, do not neglect to write to me, for your kindness is one of the pleasures of my life, which I should be sorry to lose.

"I am, Sir,

"Your humble servant,

"Sam. Johnson.

"*February 18, 1777.*"

"to dr. samuel johnson.

"*Edinburgh, Feb. 24, 1777.*

"Dear Sir,—

"Your letter dated the 18th instant, I had the pleasure to receive last post. Although my late long neglect, or rather delay, was truly culpable, I am tempted not to regret it, since it has produced me so valuable a proof of your regard. I did, indeed, during that inexcusable silence, sometimes divert the reproaches of my own mind, by fancying that I should hear again from you, inquiring with some anxiety about me, because, for aught you knew, I might have been ill.

"You are pleased to show me, that my kindness is of some consequence to you. My heart is elated at the thought. Be assured, my dear Sir, that my affection and reverence for you are exalted and steady. I do not believe that a more perfect attachment ever existed in the history of mankind. And it is a noble attachment; for the attractions are Genius, Learning, and Piety.

"Your difficulty of breathing alarms me, and brings into my imagi-

[387]

nation an event, which, although in the natural course of things I must expect at some period, I cannot view with composure.

*   *   *

"My wife is much honoured by what you say of her. She begs you may accept of her best compliments. She is to send you some marmalade of oranges, of her own making.

*   *   *

"I ever am, my dear Sir, your most obliged
    "And faithful humble servant,
        "JAMES BOSWELL."

"TO JAMES BOSWELL, ESQ.

"DEAR SIR,—

"I have been much pleased with your late letter, and am glad that my old enemy, Mrs. Boswell, begins to feel some remorse. As to Miss Veronica's Scotch, I think it cannot be helped. An English maid you might easily have; but she would still imitate the greater number, as they would be likewise those whom she must most respect. Her dialect will not be gross. Her mamma has not much Scotch, and you have yourself very little. I hope she knows my name, and does not call me *Johnston*.[1]

"The immediate cause of my writing is this:—One Shaw, who seems a modest and a decent man, has written an Erse Grammar, which a very learned Highlander, Macbean, has, at my request, examined and approved.

"The book is very little, but Mr. Shaw has been persuaded by his friends to set it at half-a-guinea, though I advised only a crown, and thought myself, liberal. You whom the author considers as a great encourager of ingenious men, will receive a parcel of his proposals and receipts. I have undertaken to give you notice of them, and to solicit your countenance. You must ask no poor man, because the price is really too high. Yet such a work deserves patronage.

"It is proposed to augment our club from twenty to thirty, of which I am glad; for as we have several in it whom I do not much like to

---

[1] *John*son is the most common English formation of the surname from *John;* *John*ston, the Scotch. My illustrious friend observed, that many North Britons pronounced his name in their own way.

consort with, I am for reducing it to a mere miscellaneous collection
of conspicuous men, without any determinate character. * * * * * *
"I am, dear Sir,
"Most affectionately yours,
"SAM. JOHNSON.

"March 14, 1777.
"My respects to Madam, to Veronica, to Alexander, to Euphemia,
to David."

"MR. BOSWELL TO DR. JOHNSON.

"Edinburgh, April 4, 1777.

[After informing him of the death of my little son David, and that
I could not come to London this spring:—]

"I think it hard that I should be a whole year without seeing you.
May I presume to petition for a meeting with you in the autumn?
You have, I believe, seen all the cathedrals in England, except that
of Carlisle. If you are to be with Dr. Taylor, at Ashbourne, it would
not be a great journey to come thither. We may pass a few most agreeable days there by ourselves, and I will accompany you a good part
of the way to the southward again. Pray think of this.

"You forget that Mr. Shaw's Erse Grammar was put into your
hands by myself last year. Lord Eglinton put it into mine. I am glad
that Mr. Macbean approves of it. I have received Mr. Shaw's proposals for its publication, which I can perceive are written *by the hand
of a Master.*"

"TO DR. SAMUEL JOHNSON.

"Glasgow, April 24, 1777.

"MY DEAR SIR,—
"Our worthy friend Thrale's death having appeared in the newspapers, and been afterwards contradicted, I have been placed in a
state of very uneasy uncertainty, from which I hoped to be relieved
by you: but my hopes have as yet been in vain. How could you omit
to write to me on such an occasion? I shall wait with anxiety.

"I am going to Auchinleck to stay a fortnight with my father. It is
better not to be there very long at one time. But frequent renewals of
attention are agreeable to him.

"Pray tell me about this edition of 'The English Poets, with a Preface, biographical and critical, to each Author, by Samuel Johnson,

LL.D.' which I see advertised. I am delighted with the prospect of it. Indeed I am happy to feel that I am capable of being so much delighted with literature. But is not the charm of this publication chiefly owing to the *magnum nomen* in the front of it?

"What do you say of Lord Chesterfield's Memoirs and last Letters?

"My wife has made marmalade of oranges for you. I left her and my daughters and Alexander all well yesterday. I have taught Veronica to speak of you thus: Dr. John*son*, not John*ston*.

"I remain, my dear Sir,

"Your most affectionate,

"And obliged humble servant,

"James Boswell."

"TO JAMES BOSWELL, ESQ.

"Dear Sir,—

"The story of Mr. Thrale's death, as he had neither been sick nor in any other danger, made so little impression upon me, that I never thought about obviating its effects on anybody else. It is supposed to have been produced by the English custom of making April fools, that is, of sending one another on some foolish errand on the first of April.

"Tell Mrs. Boswell that I shall taste her marmalade cautiously at first. *Timeo Danaos et dona ferentes.* Beware, says the Italian proverb, of a reconciled enemy. But when I find it does me no harm, I shall then receive it and be thankful for it, as a pledge of firm, and, I hope, unalterable kindness. She is, after all, a dear, dear lady.

"Please to return Dr. Blair thanks for his sermons. The Scotch write English wonderfully well.

*　　　*　　　*

"Your frequent visits to Auchinleck, and your short stay there, are very laudable and very judicious. Your present concord with your father gives me great pleasure: it was all that you seemed to want.

"My health is very bad, and my nights are very unquiet. What can I do to mend them? I have for this summer nothing better in prospect than a journey into Staffordshire and Derbyshire, perhaps with Oxford and Birmingham in my way.

"Make my compliments to Miss Veronica; I must leave it to *her* philosophy to comfort you for the loss of little David. You must remember that to keep three out of four is more than your share. Mrs. Thrale has but four out of eleven.

"I am engaged to write little Lives and little Prefaces to a little edition of the English Poets. I think I have persuaded the booksellers to insert something of Thomson; and if you could give me some information about him, for the life which we have is very scanty, I should be glad.

"I am, dear Sir,
"Your most affectionate humble servant,
"SAM. JOHNSON.

"*May 3, 1777.*"

To those who delight in tracing the progress of works of literature, it will be an entertainment to compare the limited design with the ample execution of that admirable performance, "The Lives of the English Poets," which is the richest, most beautiful, and indeed most perfect, production of Johnson's pen. His notion of it at this time appears in the preceding letter. He has a memorandum in this year, "29 May, Easter Eve, I treated with booksellers on a bargain, but the time was not long." The bargain was concerning that undertaking; but his tender conscience seems alarmed, lest it should have intruded too much on his devout preparation for the solemnity of the ensuing day. But, indeed, very little time was necessary for Johnson's concluding a treaty with the booksellers; as he had, I believe, less attention to profit from his labours than any man to whom literature has been a profession. I shall here insert from a letter to me from my late worthy friend Mr. Edward Dilly, though of a later date, an account of this plan so happily conceived; since it was the occasion of procuring for us an elegant collection of the best biography and criticism of which our language can boast.

"TO JAMES BOSWELL, ESQ.

"*Southill, Sept. 26, 1777.*

"DEAR SIR,—
"You will find, by this letter, that I am still in the same calm retreat from the noise and bustle of London, as when I wrote to you last. I am happy to find you had such an agreeable meeting with your old friend Dr. Johnson; I have no doubt your stock is much increased by the interview; few men, nay, I may say, scarcely any man, has got that fund of knowledge and entertainment as Dr. Johnson in conversation. When he opens freely, every one is attentive to what he says, and cannot fail of improvement as well as pleasure.

[391]

"The edition of the Poets, now printing, will do honour to the English press; and a concise account of the life of each author, by Dr. Johnson, will be a very valuable addition, and stamp the reputation of this edition superior to anything that is gone before. The first cause that gave rise to this undertaking, I believe, was owing to the little trifling edition of the Poets, printing by the Martins at Edinburgh, and to be sold by Bell, in London. Upon examining the volumes which were printed, the type was found so extremely small, that many persons could not read them; not only this inconvenience attended it, but the inaccuracy of the press was very conspicuous. These reasons, as well as the idea of an invasion of what we call our Literary Property, induced the London booksellers to print an elegant and accurate edition of all the English poets of reputation, from Chaucer to the present time.

"Accordingly, a select number of the most respectable booksellers met on the occasion; and, on consulting together, agreed, that all the proprietors of copyright in the various poets should be summoned together; and when their opinions were given, to proceed immediately on the business. Accordingly, a meeting was held, consisting of about forty of the most respectable booksellers of London, when it was agreed that an elegant and uniform edition of 'The English Poets' should be immediately printed, with a concise account of the life of each author, by Dr. Samuel Johnson; and that three persons should be deputed to wait upon Dr. Johnson, to solicit him to undertake the Lives, *viz.,* T. Davies, Strahan, and Cadell. The Doctor very politely undertook it, and seemed exceedingly pleased with the proposal. As to the terms, it was left entirely to the Doctor to name his own; he mentioned two hundred guineas: it was immediately agreed to; and a farther compliment, I believe, will be made him. A committee was likewise appointed to engage the best engravers, *viz.,* Bartolozzi, Sherwin, Hall, etc. Likewise, another committee for giving directions about the paper, printing, etc., so that the whole will be conducted with spirit, and in the best manner, with respect to authorship, editorship, engravings, etc., etc. My brother will give you a list of the Poets we mean to give, many of which are within the time of the Act of Queen Anne, which Martin and Bell cannot give, as they have no property in them; the proprietors are almost all the booksellers in London, of consequence.

"I am, dear Sir, ever yours,

"Edward Dilly."

I shall afterwards have occasion to consider the extensive and varied range which Johnson took, when he was once led upon ground which he trod with a peculiar delight, having long been intimately acquainted with all the circumstances of it that could interest and please.

In the summer he wrote a Prologue [*] which was spoken before "A Word to the Wise," a comedy by Mr. Hugh Kelly, which had been brought upon the stage in 1770; but, he being a writer for the Ministry in one of the newspapers, it fell a sacrifice to popular fury, and, in the playhouse phrase, was *damned*. By the generosity of Mr. Harris, the proprietor of Covent Garden Theatre, it was now exhibited for one night, for the benefit of the author's widow and children. To conciliate the favour of the audience was the intention of Johnson's Prologue, which, as it is not long, I shall here insert, as a proof that his poetical talents were in no degree impaired.

"This night presents a play, which public rage,
Or right or wrong, once hooted from the stage:
From zeal or malice, now no more we dread,
For English vengeance *wars not with the dead*.
A generous foe regards with pitying eye
The man whom Fate has laid where all must lie.
To wit, reviving from its author's dust,
Be kind, ye judges, or at least be just;
Let no renewed hostilities invade
Th' oblivious grave's inviolable shade.
Let one great payment every claim appease,
And him who cannot hurt, allow to please;
To please by scenes, unconscious of offence,
By harmless merriment, or useful sense.
Where aught of bright or fair the piece displays,
Approve it only;—'tis too late to praise.
If want of skill or want of care appear,
Forbear to hiss;—the poet cannot hear.
By all, like him, must praise and blame be found,
At last, a fleeting gleam, or empty sound;
Yet then shall calm reflection bless the night,
When liberal pity dignified delight;
When pleasure fir'd her torch at virtue's flame,
And mirth was bounty with an humbler name."

A circumstance which could not fail to be very pleasing to Johnson, occurred this year. The tragedy of "Sir Thomas Overbury," written by his early companion in London, Richard Savage, was brought up with alterations at Drury Lane Theatre. The Prologue to it was written by Mr. Richard Brinsley Sheridan; in which, after describing very pathetically the wretchedness of

> "Ill-fated Savage, at whose birth was giv'n
> No parent but the Muse, no friend but Heav'n":

he introduced an elegant compliment to Johnson on his Dictionary, that wonderful performance which cannot be too often or too highly praised; of which Mr. Harris, in his "Philological Inquiries," justly and liberally observes, "Such is its merit, that our language does not possess a more copious, learned, and valuable work." The concluding lines of this Prologue were these:

> "So pleads the tale that gives to future times
> The son's misfortunes and the parent's crimes;
> There shall his fame (if own'd to night) survive,
> Fix'd by THE HAND THAT BIDS OUR LANGUAGE LIVE."

Mr. Sheridan here at once did honour to his taste and to his liberality of sentiment, by showing that he was not prejudiced from the unlucky difference which had taken place between his worthy father and Dr. Johnson. I have already mentioned that Johnson was very desirous of reconciliation with old Mr. Sheridan. It will, therefore, not seem at all surprising that he was zealous in acknowledging the brilliant merit of his son. While it had as yet been displayed only in the drama, Johnson proposed him as a member of the Literary Club, observing that "He who has written the two best comedies of his age is surely a considerable man." And he had, accordingly, the honour to be elected; for an honour it undoubtedly must be allowed to be, when it is considered of whom that society consists, and that a single black ball excludes a candidate.

"MR. BOSWELL TO DR. JOHNSON.

"July 9, 1777.

"My dear Sir,—

"For the health of my wife and children, I have taken the little country-house at which you visited my uncle, Dr. Boswell, who, having lost his wife, is gone to live with his son. We took possession of our villa about a week ago; we have a garden of three quarters of an acre, well stocked with fruit-trees and flowers, and gooseberries and currants, and peas and beans, and cabbages, etc., etc., and my children are quite happy. I now write to you in a little study, from the window of which I see around me a verdant grove, and beyond it the lofty mountain called Arthur's Seat.

"Most sincerely do I regret the bad health and bad rest with which you have been afflicted; and I hope you are better. I cannot believe that the prologue which you generously gave to Mr. Kelly's widow and children the other day is the effusion of one in sickness and in disquietude: but external circumstances are never sure indications of the state of man. I send you a letter which I wrote to you two years ago at Wilton; and did not send it at the time, for fear of being reproved as indulging too much tenderness: and one written to you at the tomb of Melancthon, which I kept back, lest I should appear at once too superstitious and too enthusiastic. I now imagine that perhaps they may please you.

"You do not take the least notice of my proposal for our meeting at Carlisle. Though I have meritoriously refrained from visiting London this year, I ask you if it would not be wrong that I should be two years without having the benefit of your conversation, when, if you come down as far as Derbyshire, we may meet at the expense of a few days' journeying, and not many pounds. I wish you to see Carlisle, which made me mention that place. But if you have not a desire to complete your tour of the English cathedrals, I will take a larger share of the road between this place and Ashbourne. So tell me *where* you will fix for our passing a few days by ourselves. Now, don't cry 'foolish fellow,' or 'idle dog.' Chain your humour, and let your kindness play.

"Without doubt you have read what is called 'The *Life* of David Hume,' written by himself, with the letter from Dr. Adam Smith subjoined to it. Is not this an age of daring effrontery? My friend Mr. Anderson, Professor of Natural Philosophy at Glasgow, at whose house you and I supped, and to whose care Mr. Windham, of Norfolk, was intrusted at that University, paid me a visit lately; and after we had talked with indignation and contempt of the poisonous productions with which this age is infested, he said there was now an excellent opportunity for Dr. Johnson to step forth. I agreed with him that you might knock Hume's and Smith's heads together, and make vain and ostentatious infidelity exceedingly ridiculous. Would it not be worth your while to crush such noxious weeds in the moral garden?

"You have said nothing to me of Dr. Dodd. I know not how you think on that subject; though the newspapers give us a saying of yours in favour of mercy to him. But I own I am very desirous that the royal prerogative of remission of punishment should be employed to exhibit an illustrious instance of the regard which God's Vicegerent will ever show to piety and virtue. If for ten righteous men the Almighty would have spared Sodom, shall not a thousand acts of goodness done by Dr. Dodd counterbalance one crime? Such an instance would do more to encourage goodness, than his execution would do to deter from vice. I am not afraid of any bad consequence to society; for who will persevere for a long course of years in a distinguished discharge of religious duties, with a view to commit a forgery with impunity?

"Pray make my best compliments acceptable to Mr. and Mrs. Thrale, by assuring them of my hearty joy that the *Master,* as you call him, is alive. I hope I shall often taste his Champagne—*soberly.*

"I have not heard from Langton for a long time; I suppose he is, as usual,

> 'Studious the busy moments to deceive.'

*　　*　　*

> "I remain, my dear Sir,
>> "Your most affectionate
>>> "And faithful humble servant,
>>>> "JAMES BOSWELL."

On the 23rd of June, I again wrote to Dr. Johnson, enclosing a ship-master's receipt for a jar of orange-marmalade, and a large packet of Lord Hailes's "Annals of Scotland."

"TO JAMES BOSWELL, ESQ.

"DEAR SIR,—

"I have just received your packet from Mr. Thrale's, but have not daylight enough to look much into it. I am glad that I have credit enough with Lord Hailes to be trusted with more copy. I hope to take more care of it than of the last. I return Mrs. Boswell my affectionate thanks for her present, which I value as a token of reconciliation.

"Poor Dodd was put to death yesterday, in opposition to the recommendation of the jury—the petition of the City of London—and a subsequent petition signed by three-and-twenty thousand hands. Surely the voice of the public, when it calls so loudly, and only for mercy, ought to be heard.

"The saying that was given me in the papers I never spoke; but I wrote many of his petitions, and some of his letters. He applied to me very often. He was, I am afraid, long flattered with hopes of life; but I had no part in the dreadful delusion, for as soon as the King had signed his sentence, I obtained from Mr. Chamier an account of the disposition of the Court towards him, with a declaration that there *was no hope even of a respite*. This letter was immediately laid before Dodd; but he believed those whom he wished to be right, as it is thought, till within three days of his end. He died with pious composure and resolution. I have just seen the Ordinary that attended him. His address to his fellow-convicts offended the Methodists; but he had a Moravian with him much of his time. His moral character is very bad: I hope all is not true that is charged upon him. Of his behaviour in prison an account will be published.

"I hope to meet you somewhere towards the north, but am loth to come quite to Carlisle. Can we not meet at Manchester? But we will settle it in some other letters.

"Langton has been exercising the militia. Mrs. Williams is, I fear, declining. Dr. Lawrence says, he can do no more. She is gone to summer in the country, with as many conveniences about her as she can expect; but I have no great hope. We must all die: may we all be prepared!

"I suppose Miss Boswell reads her book, and young Alexander takes to his learning. Let me hear about them, for everything that belongs to you, belongs in a more remote degree, and not, I hope, very remote, to, dear Sir, yours affectionately,

"Sam. Johnson.

"June 28, 1777."

CHAPTER XXXVI—1777

Dr. Dodd

Johnson's benevolence to the unfortunate was, I am confident, as steady and active as that of any of those who have been most eminently distinguished for that virtue. Innumerable proofs of it I have no doubt will be for ever concealed from mortal eyes. We may, however, form some judgment of it, from the many and very various instances which have been discovered. One, which happened in the course of this summer, is remarkable from the name and connection of the person who was the object of it.

"TO THE REVEREND DR. VYSE, AT LAMBETH.

"SIR,—

"I doubt not but you will readily forgive me for taking the liberty of requesting your assistance in recommending an old friend to his Grace the Archbishop as Governor of the Charter-house.

"His name is De Groot; he was born at Gloucester; I have known him many years. He has all the common claims to charity, being old, poor, and infirm in a great degree. He has likewise another claim, to which no scholar can refuse attention; he is by several descents the nephew of Hugo Grotius; of him, from whom perhaps every man of learning has learnt something. Let it not be said that in any lettered country a nephew of Grotius asked a charity and was refused.

"I am, reverend Sir,
"Your most humble servant,
"SAM. JOHNSON.

"July 9, 1777."

"TO THE REVEREND DR. VYSE, AT LAMBETH.

"If any notice should be taken of the recommendation which I took the liberty of sending you, it will be necessary to know that Mr. De Groot is to be found at No. 8 in Pye Street, Westminster. This information, when I wrote, I could not give you; and being going soon to Lichfield, think it necessary to be left behind me.

"More I will not say. You will want no persuasion to succour the nephew of Grotius.

"I am, Sir,
"Your most humble servant,
"SAM. JOHNSON.

"July 22, 1777."

"THE REVEREND DR. VYSE TO MR. BOSWELL.

"Lambeth, June 9, 1787.

"SIR,—

"I have searched in vain for the letter which I spoke of, and which I wished, at your desire, to communicate to you. It was from Dr. Johnson, to return me thanks for my application to Archbishop Cornwallis in favour of poor De Groot. He rejoices at the success it met with, and is lavish in the praise he bestows upon his favourite, Hugo Grotius. I am really sorry that I cannot find this letter, as it is worthy of the writer. That which I send you enclosed, is at your service. It is very short, and will not perhaps be thought of any consequence, unless you should judge proper to consider it as a proof of the very humane part which Dr. Johnson took in behalf of a distressed and deserving person.

"I am, Sir,
"Your most obedient humble servant,
"W. Vyse."

"TO JAMES BOSWELL, ESQ.

"DEAR SIR,—

"Your notion of the necessity of an yearly interview is very pleasing to both my vanity and tenderness. I shall, perhaps, come to Carlisle another year; but my money has not held out so well as it used to do. I shall go to Ashbourne, and I purpose to make Dr. Taylor invite you. If you live awhile with me at his house, we shall have much time to ourselves, and our stay will be no expense to us or him. I shall leave London the 28th; and after some stay at Oxford and Lichfield, shall probably come to Ashbourne about the end of your Session; but of all this you shall have notice. Be satisfied we will meet somewhere.

"What passed between me and poor Dr. Dodd, you shall know more fully when we meet.

"Of law-suits there is no end; poor Sir Allan must have another trial, for which, however, his antagonist cannot be much blamed, having two judges on his side. I am more afraid of the debts than of the House of Lords. It is scarcely to be imagined to what debts will swell, that are daily increasing by small additions, and how carelessly in a state of desperation debts are contracted. Poor Macquarry was far from thinking that when he sold his islands he should receive nothing. For what were they sold? And what was their yearly value? The admission of money into the Highlands will soon put an end to the feudal modes of life, by making these men landlords who were not chiefs. I do not know that the people will suffer by the change; but there was in the patriarchal authority something venerable and pleasing. Every eye must look with pain on a *Campbell* turning the *Macquarries* at will out of their *sedes avitæ*, their hereditary island.

"Sir Alexander Dick is the only Scotsman liberal enough not to be angry that I could not find trees, where trees were not. I was much delighted by his kind letter.

"You have done right in taking your uncle's house. Some change in the form of life gives from time to time a new epocha of existence. In a new place there is something new to be done, and a different system of thoughts arises in the mind. I wish I could gather currants in your garden. Now fit up a little study, and have your books ready at hand; do not spare a little money, to make your habitation pleasing to yourself.

"I have dined lately with poor dear [Langton]. I do not think he goes on well. His table is rather coarse, and he has his children too much about him.[1] But he is a very good man.

"Mrs. Williams is in the country, to try if she can improve her health; she is very ill. Matters have come so about, that she is in the country with very good accommodation; but age, and sickness, and pride, have made her so peevish, that I was forced to bribe the maid to stay with her, by a secret stipulation of half-a-crown a week over her wages.

"Our Club ended its session about six weeks ago. We now only meet to dine once a fortnight. Mr. Dunning, the great lawyer, is one of our members. The Thrales are well.

> "I am, dear Sir,
> "Your most affectionate, etc.,
> "SAM. JOHNSON.

"*July 22, 1777.*"

"DR. JOHNSON TO MRS. BOSWELL.

"MADAM,—

"Though I am well enough pleased with the taste of sweetmeats, very little of the pleasure which I received at the arrival of your jar of marmalade arose from eating it. I received it as a token of friendship, as a proof of reconciliation, things much sweeter than sweetmeats, and upon this consideration I return you, dear madam, my

---

[1] This very just remark I hope will be constantly held in remembrance by parents, who are in general too apt to indulge their own fond feelings for their children at the expense of their friends. The common custom of introducing them after dinner is highly injudicious. It is agreeable enough that they should appear at any other time; but they should not be suffered to poison the moments of festivity by attracting the attention of the company, and in a manner compelling them from politeness to say what they do not think.

sincerest thanks. By having your kindness I think I have a double
security for the continuance of Mr. Boswell's, which it is not to be
expected that any man can long keep, when the influence of a lady
so highly and so justly valued operates against him. Mr. Boswell will
tell you that I was always faithful to your interest, and always endeavoured to exalt you in his estimation. You must now do the same
for me. We must all help one another, and you must now consider
me as, dear Madam,

"Your most obliged

"And most humble servant,

"SAM. JOHNSON.

"*July 22, 1777.*"

"MR. BOSWELL TO DR. JOHNSON.

"*Edinburgh, July 28, 1777.*

"MY DEAR SIR,—

"This is the day on which you were to leave London, and I have
been amusing myself, in the intervals of my law-drudgery, with figuring you in the Oxford post-coach. I doubt, however, if you have had
so merry a journey as you and I had in that vehicle last year, when you
made so much sport with Gwyn, the architect. Incidents upon a
journey are recollected with peculiar pleasure; they are preserved in
brisk spirits, and come up again in our minds, tinctured with that
gaiety, or at least that animation, with which we first perceived them."

*   *   *

[I added that something had occurred, which I was afraid might
prevent me from meeting him; and that my wife had been affected
with complaints which threatened a consumption, but was now better.]

"TO JAMES BOSWELL, ESQ.

"DEAR SIR,—

"Do not disturb yourself about our interviews; I hope we shall have
many; nor think it anything hard or unusual, that your design of
meeting me is interrupted. We have both endured greater evils, and
have greater evils to expect.

"Mrs. Boswell's illness makes a more serious distress. Does the
blood rise from her lungs or from her stomach? From little vessels
broken in the stomach there is no danger. Blood from the lungs is, I

believe, always frothy, as mixed with wind. Your physicians know very well what is to be done. The loss of such a lady would, indeed, be very afflictive, and I hope she is in no danger. Take care to keep her mind as easy as is possible.

"I have left Langton in London. He has been down with the militia, and is again quiet at home, talking to his little people, as, I suppose, you do sometimes. Make my compliments to Miss Veronica. The rest are too young for ceremony.

"I cannot but hope that you have taken your country house at a very seasonable time, and that it may conduce to restore or establish Mrs. Boswell's health, as well as provide room and exercise for the young ones. That you and your lady may both be happy, and long enjoy your happiness, is the sincere and earnest wish of,

"Dear Sir, your most, etc.,

"SAM. JOHNSON.

"*Oxford, Aug. 4, 1777.*"

"MR. BOSWELL TO DR. JOHNSON.

[Informing him that my wife had continued to grow better, so that my alarming apprehensions were relieved; and that I hoped to disengage myself from the other embarrassment which had occurred, and therefore requesting to know particularly when he intended to be at Ashbourne.]

"TO JAMES BOSWELL, ESQ.

"DEAR SIR,—

"On Saturday I wrote a very short letter, immediately upon my arrival hither, to show you that I am not less desirous of the interview than yourself. Life admits not of delays; when pleasure can be had, it is fit to catch it: Every hour takes away part of the things that please us, and perhaps part of our disposition to be pleased. When I came to Lichfield, I found my old friend Harry Jackson dead. It was a loss, and a loss not to be repaired, as he was one of the companions of my childhood. I hope we may long continue to gain friends; but the friends which merit or usefulness can procure us are not able to supply the place of old acquaintance with whom the days of youth may be retraced, and those images revived which gave the earliest delight. If you and I live to be much older, we shall take great delight in talking over the Hebridean Journey.

"In the mean time it may not be amiss to contrive some other little adventure; but what it can be I know not; leave it, as Sidney says,

'To virtue, fortune, time, and woman's breast;'

for I believe Mrs. Boswell must have some part in the consultation.

"One thing you will like. The Doctor, so far as I can judge, is likely to leave us enough to ourselves. He was out to-day before I came down, and I fancy will stay out to dinner. I have brought the papers about poor Dodd, to show you, but you will soon have dispatched them.

"Write to me, and let us know when we may expect you.

"I am, dear Sir,

"Your most humble servant,

"SAM. JOHNSON.

"*Ashbourne, Sept. 1, 1777.*"

"*Edinburgh, Sept. 9, 1777.*

[After informing him that I was to set out next day in order to meet him at Ashbourne:—]

"I have a present for you from Lord Hailes; 'the fifth book of Lactantius,' which he has published with Latin notes. He is also to give you a few anecdotes for your 'Life of Thomson,' who I find was private tutor to the present Earl of Hadington, Lord Hailes's cousin, a circumstance not mentioned by Dr. Murdoch. I have keen expectations of delight from your edition of the English Poets.

"Let us, by all means, have another expedition. I shrink a little from our scheme of going up the Baltic.[2] I am sorry you have already been

[2]It appears that Johnson, now in his sixty-eighth year, was seriously inclined to realise the project of our going up the Baltic, which I had started when we were in the Isle of Sky; for he thus writes to Mrs. Thrale; Letters, vol. i, p. 366:—

"*Ashbourne, Sept. 13, 1777.*

"Boswell, I believe, is coming. He talks of being here to-day: I shall be glad to see him: but he shrinks from the Baltic expedition, which, I think, is the best scheme in our power: what we shall substitute, I know not. He wants to see Wales; but, except the woods of *Bachycraigh,* what is there in Wales that can fill the hunger of ignorance, or quench the thirst of curiosity? We may, perhaps, form some scheme or other: but, in the phrase of *Hockley in the Hole,* it is pity he has not a *better bottom.*"

Such an ardour of mind and vigour of enterprise is admirable at any age: but more particularly so at the advanced period at which Johnson was then arrived. I am sorry now that I did not insist on our executing that scheme. Besides the other objects of curiosity and observation, to have seen my illustrious friend received, as he probably would have been, by a prince so eminently distinguished for in Wales, for I wish to see it. Shall we go to Ireland, of which I have seen but little? We shall try to strike out a plan when we are at Ashbourne.

"I am ever,

"Your most faithful humble servant,

"James Boswell."

On Sunday evening, Sept. 14, I arrived at Ashbourne, and drove directly up to Dr. Taylor's door. Dr. Johnson and he appeared before I had got out of the post-chaise, and welcomed me cordially.

I was somewhat disappointed in finding that the edition of the English Poets, for which he was to write Prefaces and Lives, was not an undertaking directed by him: but that he was to furnish a Preface and Life to any poet the booksellers pleased. I asked him if he would do this to any dunce's works, if they asked him. Johnson: "Yes, Sir; and *say* he was a dunce." My friend seemed now not much to relish talking of this edition.

On Monday, September 15, Dr. Johnson observed that everybody commended such parts of his "Journey to the Western Islands" as were in their own way. "For instance (said he), Mr. Jackson (the all-knowing) told me there was more good sense upon trade in it, than he should hear in the House of Commons in a year, except from Burke. Jones commended the part which treats of language; Burke that which describes the inhabitants of mountainous countries."

After breakfast, Johnson carried me to see the garden belonging to the school of Ashbourne, which is very prettily formed upon a bank, rising gradually behind the house. The Reverend Mr. Langley, the headmaster, accompanied us.

We had with us at dinner several of Dr. Taylor's neighbours, good civil gentlemen, who seemed to understand Dr. Johnson very well, and not to consider him in the light that a certain person [George Garrick] did, who being struck, or rather stunned, by his voice and manner, when he was afterwards asked what he thought of him, answered, "He's a tremendous companion."

And here is a proper place to give an account of Johnson's humane

his variety of talents and acquisitions as the late King of Sweden: and by the Empress of Russia, whose extraordinary abilities, information, and magnanimity, astonish the world, would have afforded a noble subject for contemplation and record. This reflection may possibly be thought too visionary by the more sedate and cold-blooded part of my readers; yet I own, I frequently indulge it, with an earnest unavailing regret.

and zealous interference in behalf of the Reverend Dr. William Dodd, formerly Prebendary of Brecon, and chaplain in ordinary to his Majesty; celebrated as a very popular preacher, an encourager of charitable institutions, and author of a variety of works, chiefly theological. Having unhappily contracted expensive habits of living, partly occasioned by licentiousness of manners, he in an evil hour, when pressed by want of money, and dreading an exposure of his circumstances, forged a bond, of which he attempted to avail himself to support his credit, flattering himself with hopes that he might be able to repay its amount without being detected. The person, whose name he thus rashly and criminally presumed to falsify, was the Earl of Chesterfield, to whom he had been tutor, and who he, perhaps, in the warmth of his feelings, flattered himself would have generously paid the money in case of an alarm being taken, rather than suffer him to fall a victim to the dreadful consequences of violating the law against forgery, the most dangerous crime in a commercial country; but the unfortunate divine had the mortification to find that he was mistaken. His noble pupil appeared against him, and he was capitally convicted.

Johnson told me, that Dr. Dodd was very little acquainted with him, having been but once in his company, many years previous to this period (which was precisely the state of my own acquaintance with Dodd); but in his distress he bethought himself of Johnson's persuasive powers of writing, if haply it might avail to obtain for him the Royal Mercy. He did not apply to him directly, but, extraordinary as it may seem, through the late Countess of Harrington, who wrote a letter to Johnson, asking him to employ his pen in favour of Dodd. Mr. Allen, the printer, who was Johnson's landlord and next neighbour in Bolt Court, and for whom he had much kindness, was one of Dodd's friends, of whom, to the credit of humanity be it recorded, that he had many who did not desert him, even after his infringement of the law had reduced him to the state of a man under sentence of death. Mr. Allen told me that he carried Lady Harrington's letter to Johnson, that Johnson read it walking up and down his chamber, and seemed much agitated, after which he said, "I will do what I can";—and certainly he did make extraordinary exertions.

He this evening, as he had obligingly promised in one of his letters, put into my hands the whole series of his writings upon this melancholy occasion.

I found a letter to Dr. Johnson from Dr. Dodd, May 23, 1777, in which "The Convict's Address" seems clearly to be meant:

"I am so penetrated, my ever dear Sir, with a sense of your extreme benevolence towards me, that I cannot find words equal to the sentiments of my heart.*****

"You are too conversant in the world to need the slightest hint from me, of what infinite utility the Speech[3] on the awful day has been to me. I experience, every hour, some good effect from it. I am sure that effects still more salutary and important must follow from *your kind and intended favour*. I will labour——God being my helper——to do justice to it from the pulpit. I am sure, had I your sentiments constantly to deliver from thence, in all their mighty force and power, not a soul could be left unconvinced and unpersuaded."********

He added, "May God Almighty bless and reward, with his chiefest comforts, your philanthropic actions, and enable me at all times to express what I feel of the high and uncommon obligation which I owe to the *first man* in our times."

On Sunday, June 22, he writes, begging Dr. Johnson's assistance in framing a supplicatory letter to his Majesty:

"If his Majesty would be pleased of his royal clemency to spare me and my family the horrors and ignominy of a *public death*, which the *public* itself is solicitous to waive, and to grant me in some silent distant corner of the globe to pass the remainder of my days in penitence and prayer, I would bless his clemency and be humbled."

This letter was brought to Dr. Johnson when in church. He stooped down and read it, and wrote, when he went home, the following letter for Dr. Dodd to the King:

"SIR,——

"May it not offend your Majesty, that the most miserable of men applies himself to your clemency, as his last hope and his last refuge; that your mercy is most earnestly and humbly implored by a clergyman, whom your Laws and Judges have condemned to the horror and ignominy of a public execution.

"I confess the crime, and own the enormity of its consequences, and the danger of its example. Nor have I the confidence to petition for impunity; but humbly hope, that public security may be established, without the spectacle of a clergyman dragged through the streets, to a death of infamy, amidst the derision of the profligate and profane; and that justice may be satisfied with irrevocable exile, perpetual disgrace, and hopeless penury.

[3]His speech at the Old Bailey, when found guilty.

Dr. Dodd

"My life, Sir, has not been useless to mankind. I have benefited many. But my offences against God are numberless, and I have had little time for repentance. Preserve me, Sir, by your prerogative of mercy, from the necessity of appearing unprepared at that tribunal, before which Kings and Subjects must stand at last together. Permit me to hide my guilt in some obscure corner of a foreign country, where, if I can ever attain confidence to hope that my prayers will be heard, they shall be poured with all the fervour of gratitude for the life and happiness of your Majesty.

"I am, Sir,

"Your Majesty's, etc."

Subjoined to it was written as follows:

"TO DR. DODD.

"SIR,—
"I most seriously enjoin you not to let it be at all known that I have written this letter, and to return the copy to Mr. Allen in a cover to me. I hope I need not tell you that I wish it success.—But do not indulge hope.—Tell nobody."

It happened luckily that Mr. Allen was pitched on to assist in this melancholy office, for he was a great friend of Mr. Akerman, the keeper of Newgate. Dr. Johnson never went to see Dr. Dodd. He said to me, "it would have done *him* more harm, than good to Dodd, who once expressed a desire to see him, but not earnestly."

All applications for the Royal Mercy having failed, Dr. Dodd prepared himself for death; and, with a warmth of gratitude, wrote to Dr. Johnson as follows:—

"*June 25, Midnight.*

"Accept, thou *great* and *good* heart, my earnest and fervent thanks and prayers for all thy benevolent and kind efforts in my behalf.—Oh! Dr. Johnson! as I sought your knowledge at an early hour in life, would to heaven I had cultivated the love and acquaintance of so excellent a man!—I pray God most sincerely to bless you with the highest transports—the infelt satisfaction of *humane* and benevolent exertions! —And admitted, as I trust I shall be, to the realms of bliss before you, I shall hail *your* arrival there with transports, and rejoice to acknowledge that you were my Comforter, my Advocate, and my *Friend!* God *be ever* with *you!*"

Dr. Johnson lastly wrote to Dr. Dodd this solemn and soothing letter:

"TO THE REVEREND DR. DODD.

"DEAR SIR,—

"That which is appointed to all men is now coming upon you. Outward circumstances, the eyes and the thoughts of men, are below the notice of an immortal being about to stand the trial for eternity, before the Supreme Judge of heaven and earth. Be comforted: your crime, morally and religiously considered, has no very deep dye of turpitude. It corrupted no man's principles; it attacked no man's life. It involved only a temporary and repairable injury. Of this, and of all other sins, you are earnestly to repent; and may God, who knoweth our frailty, and desireth not our death, accept your repentance, for the sake of His Son Jesus Christ our Lord.

"In requital of those well intended offices which you are pleased so emphatically to acknowledge, let me beg that you make in your devotions one petition for my eternal welfare.

"I am, dear Sir,
"Your most affectionate servant,
"SAM. JOHNSON.

"*June 26, 1777.*"

Under the copy of this letter I found written, in Johnson's own hand, "Next day, June 27, he was executed."

Tuesday, September 16, Dr. Johnson having mentioned to me the extraordinary size and price of some cattle reared by Dr. Taylor, I rode out with our host, surveyed his farm, and was shown one cow which he had sold for a hundred and twenty guineas, and another for which he had been offered a hundred and thirty. Taylor thus described to me his old schoolfellow and friend, Johnson: "He is a man of a very clear head, great power of words, and a very gay imagination; but there is no disputing with him. He will not hear you, and having a louder voice than you, must roar you down."

In the evening the Reverend Mr. Seward, of Lichfield, who was passing through Ashbourne on his way home, drank tea with us. Johnson described him thus:—"Sir, his ambition is to be a fine talker; so he goes to Buxton, and such places, where he may find companies to listen to him. And, Sir, he is a valetudinarian, one of those who are always mending themselves. I do not know a more disagreeable character than valetudinarian, who thinks he may do anything that is for his ease, and indulges himself in the grossest freedoms: Sir, he brings himself to the state of a hog in a stye."

Dr. Taylor's nose happening to bleed, he said it was because he had omitted to have himself blooded four days after a quarter of a year's interval. Dr. Johnson, who was a great dabbler in physic, disapproved much of periodical bleeding. For (said he) you accustom yourself to an evacuation which Nature cannot perform of herself, and therefore she cannot help you, should you from forgetfulness or any other cause omit it; so you may be suddenly suffocated. You may accustom yourself to other periodical evacuations, because, should you omit them, Nature can supply the omission; but Nature cannot open a vein to blood you."—"I do not like to take an emetic (said Taylor), for fear of breaking some small vessels."—"Poh! (said Johnson), if you have so many things that will break, you had better break your neck at once, and there's an end on't. You will break no small vessels": (blowing with high derision).

I mentioned to Dr. Johnson, that David Hume's persisting in his infidelity, when he was dying, shocked me much. JOHNSON: "Why should it shock you, Sir? Hume owned he had never read the New Testament with attention. Here then was a man who had been at no pains to inquire into the truth of religion, and had continually turned his mind the other way. It was not to be expected that the prospect of death would alter his way of thinking, unless God should send an angel to set him right." I said I had reason to believe that the thought of annihilation gave Hume no pain. JOHNSON: "It was not so, Sir. He had a vanity in being thought easy. It is more probable that he should assume an appearance of ease, than so very improbable a thing should be, as a man not afraid of going (as, in spite of his delusive theory, he cannot be sure but he may go) into an unknown state, and not being uneasy at leaving all he knew. And you are to consider that upon his own principle of annihilation he had no motive to speak the truth." The horror of death, which I had always observed in Dr. Johnson, appeared strong to-night. I ventured to tell him that I had been, for moments in my life, not afraid of death; therefore I could suppose another man in that state of mind for a considerable space of time. He said, "he never had a moment in which death was not terrible to him." He added that it had been observed that scarce any man dies in public, but with apparent resolution; from that desire of praise which never quits us. I said, Dr. Dodd seemed to be willing to die, and full of hopes of happiness. "Sir (said he), Dr. Dodd would have given both his hands and both his legs to have lived. The better a man is, the more afraid is he of death, having a clearer view of infinite purity." He owned that our being in an unhappy uncertainty as to our salvation, was mysterious; and said, "Ah! we must wait till we are in another state of being, to have many things explained to us." Even the powerful mind of Johnson seemed foiled by futurity. But I thought, that the gloom of uncertainty in solemn religious speculation, being mingled with hope, was yet more consolatory than the emptiness of infidelity. A man can live in thick air, but perishes in an exhausted receiver.

CHAPTER XXXVII—1777

Derby

On WEDNESDAY, SEPTEMBER 17, Dr. Butter, physician at Derby, drank tea with us; and it was settled that Dr. Johnson and I should go on Friday and dine with him. Johnson said, "I'm glad of this." He seemed weary of the uniformity of life at Dr. Taylor's.

Talking of biography, I said, in writing a life, a man's peculiarities should be mentioned, because they mark his character. JOHNSON: "Sir, there is no doubt as to peculiarities: the question is, whether a man's vices should be mentioned; for instance, whether it should be mentioned that Addison and Parnell drank too freely; for people will, probably, more easily indulge in drinking from knowing this; so that more ill may be done by the example, than good by telling the whole truth." Here was an instance of his varying from himself in talk; for when Lord Hailes and he sat one morning calmly conversing in my house at Edinburgh, I well remember that Dr. Johnson maintained that "If a man is to write *A Panegyric,* he may keep vices out of sight; but if he professes to write *A Life,* he must represent it really as it was": and when I objected to the danger of telling that Parnell drank to excess, he said that "it would produce an instructive caution to avoid drinking, when it was seen that even the learning and genius of Parnell could be debased by it." And in the Hebrides he maintained, as appears from my "Journal," that a man's intimate friend should mention his faults, if he writes his life.

Thursday, September 18. Last night, Dr. Johnson had proposed that the crystal lustre, or chandelier, in Dr. Taylor's large room, should be lighted up some time or other. Taylor said it should be lighted up next night. "That will do very well (said I), for it is Dr. Johnson's birthday." When we were in the Isle of Sky, Johnson had desired me not to mention his birthday. He did not seem pleased at this time that I mentioned it, and said (somewhat sternly), "he would *not* have the lustre lighted the next day."

Some ladies, who had been present yesterday when I mentioned his birthday, came to dinner to-day, and plagued him unintentionally, by wishing him joy. I know not why he disliked having his birthday mentioned, unless it were that it reminded him of his approaching nearer to death, of which he had a constant dread.

Friday, September 19, after breakfast, Johnson and I set out in Dr. Taylor's chaise to go to Derby. The day was fine, and we resolved to go by Keddlestone, the seat of Lord Scarsdale, that I might see his Lordship's fine house. I was struck with the magnificence of the building; and the extensive park, with the finest verdure, covered with deer, and cattle, and sheep, delighted me. The number of old oaks, of an immense size, filled me with a sort of respectful admiration: for one of them, £60 was offered. The excellent smooth gravel roads; the large piece of water, formed by his Lordship from some small brooks, with a handsome barge upon it; the venerable Gothic church, now the family chapel, just by the house; in short, the grand group of objects agitated and distended my mind in a most agreeable manner. "One should think (said I) that the proprietor of all this *must* be happy."— "Nay, Sir (said Johnson), all this excludes but one evil—poverty."[1]

Dr. Manningham, physician in London, who was visiting at Lord Scarsdale's, accompanied us through many of the rooms, and soon afterwards my Lord himself, to whom Dr. Johnson was known, appeared, and did the honours of the house. We talked of Mr. Langton. Johnson, with a warm vehemence of affectionate regard, exclaimed,

[1]When I mentioned Dr. Johnson's remark to a lady of admirable good sense and quickness of understanding, she observed, "It is true, all this excludes only one evil; but how much good does it let in?"—To this observation much praise has been justly given. Let me then now do myself the honour to mention that the lady who made it was the late Margaret Montgomerie, my very valuable wife, and the very affectionate mother of my children, who, if they inherit her good qualities, will have no reason to complain of their lot. *Dos magna parentum virtus.*

"The earth does not bear a worthier man than Bennet Langton." We saw a good many fine pictures, which I think are described in one of "Young's Tours." There is a printed catalogue of them, which the housekeeper put into my hand; I should like to view them at leisure. I was much struck with Daniel interpreting Nebuchadnezzar's dream, by Rembrandt.—We were shown a pretty large library. In his Lordship's dressing-room lay Johnson's small Dictionary: he showed it to me, with some eagerness, saying, "Look'ye! *Quæ regio in terris nostri non plena laboris?*" He observed, also, Goldsmith's "Animated Nature"; and said, "Here's our friend! The poor Doctor would have been happy to hear of this."

When we arrived at Derby, Dr. Butter accompanied us to see the manufactory of china there. I admired the ingenuity and delicate art with which a man fashioned clay into a cup, a saucer, or a tea-pot, while a boy turned round a wheel to give the mass rotundity. I thought this as excellent in its species of power as making good verses in its species. Yet I had no respect for this potter. Neither, indeed, has a man of any extent of thinking for a mere verse-maker, in whose numbers, however perfect, there is no poetry, no mind. The china was beautiful, but Dr. Johnson justly observed it was too dear; for that he could have vessels of silver, of the same size, as cheap as what were here made of porcelain.

We dined with Dr. Butter, whose lady is daughter of my cousin Sir John Douglas, whose grandson is now presumptive heir to the noble family of Queensberry. Johnson and he had a good deal of medical conversation. Johnson said he had somewhere or other given an account of Dr. Nichols's discourse *"De Animâ Medicâ."* He told us, "that whatever a man's distemper was, Dr. Nichols would not attend him as a physician, if his mind was not at ease; for he believed that no medicines would have any influence. He once attended a man in trade, upon whom he found none of the medicines he prescribed had any effect; he asked the man's wife privately whether his affairs were not in a bad way. She said no. He continued his attendance some time, still without success. At length the man's wife told him she had discovered that her husband's affairs *were* in a bad way. When Goldsmith was dying, Dr. Turton said to him, 'Your pulse is in greater disorder than it should be, from the degree of fever which you have: is your mind at ease?' Goldsmith answered it was not."

Dr. Johnson told us at tea that when some of Dr. Dodd's pious friends were trying to console him by saying that he was going to leave

"a wretched world," he had honesty enough not to join in the cant:—
"No, no (said he), it has been a very agreeable world to me." Johnson
added, "I respect Dodd for thus speaking the truth; for, to be sure, he
had for several years enjoyed a life of great voluptuousness."

He told us that Dodd's city friends stood by him so that a thousand
pounds were ready to be given to the jailer if he would let him escape.
He added that he knew a friend of Dodd's who walked about Newgate
for some time on the evening before the day of his execution, with five
hundred pounds in his pocket, ready to be paid to any of the turnkeys
who could get him out: but it was too late; for he was watched with
much circumspection. He said Dodd's friends had an image of him
made of wax, which was to have been left in his place; and he believed
it was carried into the prison.

Johnson disapproved of Dr. Dodd's leaving the world persuaded that
"The Convict's Address to his unhappy Brethren" was of his own
writing. "But, Sir (said I), you contributed to the deception; for when
Mr. Seward expressed a doubt to you that it was not Dodd's own,
because it had a great deal more force of mind in it than anything
known to be his, you answered—'Why should you think so? Depend
upon it, Sir, when a man knows he is to be hanged in a fortnight, it
concentrates his mind wonderfully.'" JOHNSON: "Sir, as Dodd got it
from me to pass as his own, while that could do him any good, that was
an *implied promise* that I should not own it. To own it, therefore,
would have been telling a lie, with the addition of breach of promise,
which was worse than simply telling a lie to make it be believed it was
Dodd's. Besides, Sir, I did not *directly* tell a lie: I left the matter uncertain. Perhaps I thought that Seward would not believe it the less
to be mine for what I said; but I would not put it in his power to say
I had owned it."

He said, "Goldsmith was a plant that flowered late. There appeared
nothing remarkable about him when he was young; though when he
had got high in fame, one of his friends began to recollect something
of his being distinguished at College. Goldsmith in the same manner
recollected more of that friend's early years, as he grew a greater man."

I mentioned that Lord Monboddo told me he awakened every morning at four, and then for his health got up and walked in his room
naked, with the window open, which he called taking *an air bath;*
after which he went to bed again, and slept two hours more. Johnson,
who was always ready to beat down anything that seemed to be exhibited with disproportionate importance, thus observed: "I suppose,

Sir, there is no more in it than this, he wakes at four, and cannot sleep till he chills himself, and makes the warmth of the bed a grateful sensation."

I talked of the difficulty of rising in the morning. Dr. Johnson told me "that the learned Mrs. Carter, at that period when she was eager in study, did not awake as early as she wished, and she therefore had a contrivance that, at a certain hour, her chamber-light should burn a string, to which a heavy weight was suspended, which then fell with a strong, sudden noise: this roused her from her sleep, and then she had no difficulty in getting up." But I said *that* was my difficulty; and wished there could be some medicine invented which would make one rise without pain, which I never did, unless after lying in bed a very long time. Perhaps there may be something in the stores of Nature which could do this.

Johnson observed that "a man should take a sufficient quantity of sleep, which Dr. Mead says is between seven and nine hours." I told him that Dr. Cullen said to me that a man should not take more sleep than he can take at once. JOHNSON: "This rule, Sir, cannot hold in all cases; for many people have their sleep broken by sickness; and surely Cullen would not have a man to get up after having slept but an hour. Such a regimen would soon end in a *long sleep*." Dr. Taylor remarked, I think very justly, that "a man who does not feel an inclination to sleep at the ordinary times, instead of being stronger than other people, must not be well; for a man in health has all the natural inclinations to eat, drink, and sleep in a strong degree."

Johnson advised me to-night not to *refine* in the education of my children. "Life (said he) will not bear refinement; you must do as other people do."

I ventured to mention a person who was as violent a Scotchman as he was an Englishman; and literally had the same contempt for an Englishman compared with a Scotchman, that he had for a Scotchman compared with an Englishman; and that he would say of Dr. Johnson, "Damned rascal! to talk as he does of the Scotch." This seemed, for a moment, "to give him pause." It, perhaps, presented his extreme prejudice against the Scotch in a point of view somewhat new to him, by the effect of *contrast*.

By the time when we returned to Ashbourne, Dr. Taylor was gone to bed. Johnson and I sat up a long time by ourselves.

I mentioned to him that Dr. Hugh Blair, in his lectures on Rhetoric and Belles Lettres, which I heard him deliver at Edinburgh, had animadverted on the Johnsonian style as too pompous; and attempted to imitate it, by giving a sentence of Addison in the *Spectator,* No. 411, in the manner of Johnson. When treating of the utility of the pleasures of imagination in preserving us from vice, it is observed of those "who know not how to be idle and innocent," that "their very first step out of business is into vice or folly"; which Dr. Blair supposed would have been expressed in the *Rambler* thus: "their very first step out of the regions of business is into the perturbation of vice, or the vacuity of folly." JOHNSON: "Sir, these are not the words I should have used. No, Sir; the imitators of my style have not hit it. Miss Aikin has done it the best; for she has imitated the sentiment as well as the diction."

I intend, before this work is concluded, to exhibit specimens of imitation of my friend's style in various modes; some caricaturing or mimicking it, and some formed upon it, whether intentionally or with a degree of similarity to it, of which, perhaps, the writers were not conscious.

I read to him a letter which Lord Monboddo had written to me, containing some critical remarks upon the style of his "Journey to the Western Islands of Scotland." His Lordship praised the very fine passage upon landing at Icolmkill; but his own style being exceedingly dry and hard, he disapproved of the richness of Johnson's language, and of his frequent use of metaphorical expressions. JOHNSON: "Why, Sir, this criticism would be just, if in my style, superfluous words, or words too big for the thoughts, could be pointed out; but this I do not believe can be done. For instance; in the passage which Lord Monboddo admires, 'We were now treading that illustrious region,' the word *illustrious* contributes nothing to the mere narration; for the fact might be told without it: but it is not, therefore, superfluous; for it wakes the mind to peculiar attention, where something of more than usual importance is to be presented. 'Illustrious!'—for what?—and then the sentence proceeds to expand the circumstances connected with Iona. And, Sir, as to metaphorical expression, that is a great excellence in style, when it is used with propriety, for it gives you two ideas for one; —conveys the meaning more luminously, and generally with a perception of delight."

On Saturday, September 20, after breakfast, when Taylor was gone out to his farm, Dr. Johnson and I had a serious conversation, by ourselves, on melancholy and madness; which he was, I always thought, erroneously inclined to confound together. Melancholy, like "great wit," may be "near allied to madness"; but there is, in my opinion, a distinct separation between them. When he talked of madness, he was to be understood as speaking of those who were in any great degree disturbed, or, as it is commonly expressed, "troubled in mind." Some of the ancient philosophers held that all deviations from right reason were madness; and whoever wishes to see the opinions both of ancients and moderns upon this subject, collected and illustrated with a variety of curious facts, may read Dr. Arnold's very entertaining work.

We entered seriously upon a question of much importance to me, which Johnson was pleased to consider with friendly attention. I had long complained to him that I felt discontented in Scotland, as too narrow a sphere, and that I wished to make my chief residence in London, the great scene of ambition, instruction, and amusement: a scene, which was to me, comparatively speaking, a heaven upon earth. JOHNSON: "Why, Sir, I never knew anyone who had such a *gust* for London as you have: and I cannot blame you for your wish to live there: yet, Sir, were I in your father's place, I should not consent to your settling there; for I have the old feudal notions, and I should be afraid that Auchinleck would be deserted, as you would soon find it more desirable to have a country-seat in a better climate. I own, however, that to consider it as a *duty* to reside on a family estate is a prejudice; for we must consider, that working-people get employment equally, and the produce of the land is sold equally, whether a great family resides at home or not; and if the rents of an estate be carried to London, they return again in the circulation of commerce; nay, Sir, we must perhaps allow that carrying the rents to a distance is a good, because it contributes to that circulation. We must, however, allow that a well-regulated great family may improve a neighbourhood in civility and elegance, and give an example of good order, virtue, and piety; and so its residence at home may be of much advantage. But if a great family be disorderly and vicious, its residence at home is very pernicious to a neighbourhood. There is not now the same inducement to live in the country as formerly; the pleasures of social life are much better enjoyed in town; and there is no longer in the country that power and influence in proprietors of land which they had in old times, and which made the country so agreeable to them. The Laird of Auchinleck now is not near so great a man as the Laird of Auchinleck was a hundred years ago."

I suggested a doubt, that if I were to reside in London, the exquisite zest with which I relished it in occasional visits might go off, and I might grow tired of it. JOHNSON: "Why, Sir, you find no man, at all intellectual, who is willing to leave London. No, Sir, when a man is tired of London, he is tired of life; for there is in London all that life can afford."

To obviate his apprehension that by settling in London I might desert the seat of my ancestors, I assured him that I had old feudal principles to a degree of enthusiasm; and that I felt all the *dulcedo* of the *natale solum*. I reminded him that the Laird of Auchinleck had an elegant house, in front of which he could ride ten miles forward upon his own territories, upon which he had upwards of six hundred people attached to him; that the family seat was rich in natural romantic beauties of rock, wood, and water; and that in my "morn of life" I had appropriated the finest descriptions in the ancient Classics to certain scenes there, which were thus associated in my mind. That when all this was considered, I should certainly pass a part of the year at home, and enjoy it the more from variety, and from bringing with me a share of the intellectual stores of the metropolis. He listened to all this, and kindly "hoped it might be as I now supposed."

He said a country gentleman should bring his lady to visit London as soon as he can, that they may have agreeable topics for conversation when they are by themselves.

As I meditated trying my fortune in Westminster Hall, our conversation turned upon the profession of the law in England. JOHNSON: "You must not indulge too sanguine hopes, should you be called to our bar. I was told, by a very sensible lawyer, that there are a great many chances against any man's success in the profession of the law; the candidates are so numerous, and those who get large practice so few. He said it was by no means true that any man of good parts and application is sure of having business, though he indeed allowed that if such a man could but appear in a few causes, his merit would be known, and he would get forward; but that the great risk was that a man might pass half a life-time in the Courts, and never have an opportunity of showing his abilities."

We talked of employment being absolutely necessary to preserve the mind from wearying and growing fretful, especially in those who have a tendency to melancholy; and I mentioned to him a saying which somebody had related of an American savage, who, when a European was expatiating on all the advantages of money, put this question: "Will it purchase *occupation?*" JOHNSON: "Depend upon it, Sir, this saying is too refined for a savage. And, Sir, money *will* purchase occupation; it will purchase all the conveniences of life; it will purchase variety of company; it will purchase all sorts of entertainment."

CHAPTER XXXVIII—1777

Ashbourne

ON SUNDAY, SEPTEMBER 21, we went to the church of Ashbourne, which is one of the largest and most luminous that I have seen in any town of the same size. I felt great satisfaction in considering that I was supported in my fondness for solemn public worship by the general concurrence and munificence of mankind.

Johnson and Taylor were so different from each other, that I wondered at their preserving an intimacy. Their having been at school and college together, might, in some degree, account for this; but Sir Joshua Reynolds has furnished me with a stronger reason; for Johnson mentioned to him that he had been told by Taylor he was to be his heir. I shall not take upon me to animadvert upon this; but certain it is that Johnson paid great attention to Taylor. He now, however, said to me, "Sir, I love him; but I do not love him more; my regard for him does not increase. As it is said in the Apocrypha, 'his talk is of bullocks.' I do not suppose he is very fond of my company. His habits are by no means sufficiently clerical: this he knows that I see; and no man likes to live under the eye of perpetual disapprobation."

I have no doubt that a good many sermons were composed for Taylor by Johnson. At this time I found, upon his table, a part of one which he had newly begun to write: and *Concio pro Tayloro* appears in one of his diaries. When to these circumstances we add the internal evidence from the power of thinking and style in the collection which the Reverend Mr. Hayes had published, with the *significant* title of "Sermons *left for publication* by the Reverend John Taylor, LL.D.," our conviction will be complete.

I, however, would not have it thought that Dr. Taylor, though he could not write like Johnson (as, indeed, who could?), did not sometimes compose sermons as good as those which we generally have from very respectable divines. He showed me one with notes on the margin in Johnson's handwriting; and I was present when he read another to Johnson, that he might have his opinion of it, and Johnson said it was "very well." These, we may be sure, were not Johnson's; for he was above little arts, or tricks of deception.

In the evening, Johnson, being in very good spirits, entertained us with several characteristical portraits; I regret that any of them escaped my retention and diligence. I found from experience that to collect my friend's conversation, so as to exhibit it with any degree of its original flavour, it was necessary to write it down without delay. To record his sayings, after some distance of time, was like preserving or pickling long-kept and faded fruits, or other vegetables, which, when in that state, have little or nothing of their taste when fresh.

I shall present my readers with a series of what I gathered this evening from the Johnsonian garden.

"My friend, the late Earl of Cork, had a great desire to maintain the literary character of his family; he was a genteel man, but did not keep up the dignity of his rank. He was so generally civil, that nobody thanked him for it."

"Did we not hear so much said of Jack Wilkes, we should think more highly of his conversation. Jack has a great variety of talk, Jack is a scholar, and Jack has the manners of a gentleman. But after hearing his name sounded from pole to pole, as the phœnix of convivial felicity, we are disappointed in his company. He has always been *at me:* but I would do Jack a kindness, rather than not. The contest is now over."

On Monday, September 22, when at breakfast, I unguardedly said to Dr. Johnson, "I wish I saw you and Mrs. Macaulay together." He grew very angry; and, after a pause, while a cloud gathered on his brow, he burst out, "No, Sir; you would not see us quarrel, to make you sport. Don't you know that it is very uncivil to *pit* two people against one another?" Then, checking himself, and wishing to be more gentle, he added, "I do not say you should be hanged or drowned for this; but it *is* very uncivil." Dr. Taylor thought him in the wrong, and spoke to him privately of it; but I afterwards acknowledged to Johnson that I was to blame, for I candidly owned that I meant to express a desire to see a contest between Mrs. Macaulay and him; but then I knew how the contest would end; so that I was to see him triumph. JOHNSON: "Sir, you cannot be sure how a contest will end; and no man has a right to engage two people in a dispute by which their passions may be inflamed, and they may part with bitter resentment against each other. I would sooner keep company with a man from whom I must guard my pockets, than with a man who contrives to bring me into a dispute with somebody that he may hear it. This is the great fault of ———— (naming one of our friends), endeavouring to introduce a subject upon which he knows two people in the company differ." BOSWELL: "But he told me, Sir, he does it for instruction." JOHNSON: "Whatever the motive be, Sir, the man who does so, does very wrong. He has no more right to instruct himself at such risk than he has to make two people fight a duel, that he may learn how to defend himself."

He found great fault with a gentleman of our acquaintance for keeping a bad table. "Sir (said he), when a man is invited to dinner, he is disappointed if he does not get something good. I advised Mrs. Thrale, who has no card-parties at her house, to give sweetmeats, and such good things, in an evening, as are not commonly given, so she would find company enough come to her: for everybody loves to have things which please the palate put in their way, without trouble or preparation." Such was his attention to the *minutiæ* of life and manners.

In the evening, a gentleman-farmer, who was on a visit at Dr. Taylor's, attempted to dispute with Johnson in favour of Mungo Campbell, who shot Alexander, Earl of Eglinton, upon his having fallen, when retreating from his Lordship, who he believed was about to seize his gun, as he had threatened to do. He said he should have done just as Campbell did. JOHNSON: "Whoever would do as Campbell did deserves to be hanged; not that I could, as a juryman, have found him legally guilty of murder; but I am glad they found means to convict him." The gentleman-farmer said, "A poor man has as much honour as a rich man: and Campbell had *that* to defend." Johnson exclaimed, "A poor man has no honour." The English yeoman, not dismayed, proceeded: "Lord Eglinton was a damned fool to run on upon Campbell, after being warned that Campbell would shoot him *if* he did." Johnson, who could not bear anything like swearing, angrily replied, "He was *not a damned* fool: he only thought too well of Campbell. He did not believe Campbell would be such a *damned* scoundrel, as to do so *damned* a thing." His emphasis on *damned*, accompanied with frowning looks, reproved his opponent's want of decorum in *his* presence.

During this interview at Ashbourne, Johnson seemed to be more uniformly social, cheerful, and alert, than I had almost ever seen him. He was prompt on great occasions and on small. Taylor, who praised everything of his own to excess, in short, "whose geese were all swans," as the proverb says, expatiated on the excellence of his bull-dog, which, he told us, was "perfectly well shaped." Johnson, after examining the animal attentively, thus repressed the vain-glory of our host:—"No,

Sir, he is *not* well shaped; for there is not the quick transition from the thickness of the forepart to the *tenuity*—the thin part—behind—which a bull-dog ought to have." This *tenuity* was the only *hard word* that I heard him use during this interview, and, it will be observed, he instantly put another expression in its place. Taylor said a small bull-dog was as good as a large one. JOHNSON: "No, Sir; for, in proportion to his size, he has strength: and your argument would prove that a good bull-dog may be as small as a mouse." It was amazing how he entered with perspicuity and keenness upon everything that occurred in conversation. Most men, whom I know, would no more think of discussing a question about a bull-dog than of attacking a bull.

One morning, after breakfast, when the sun shone bright, we walked out together, and "pored" for some time with placid indolence upon an artificial water-fall, which Dr. Taylor had made by building a strong dyke of stone across the river behind the garden. It was now somewhat obstructed by branches of trees and other rubbish, which had come down the river, and settled close to it. Johnson, partly from a desire to see it play more freely, and partly from that inclination to activity which will animate, at times, the most inert and sluggish mortal, took a long pole which was lying on a bank, and pushed down several parcels of this wreck with painful assiduity, while I stood quietly by, wondering to behold the Sage thus curiously employed, and smiling with a humorous satisfaction each time when he carried his point. He worked till he was quite out of breath; and having found a large dead cat, so heavy that he could not move it after several efforts, "Come," said he (throwing down the pole), "*you* shall take it now"; which I accordingly did, and, being a fresh man, soon made the cat tumble over the cascade. This may be laughed at as too trifling to record; but it is a small characteristic trait in the Flemish picture which I give of my friend, and in which, therefore, I mark the most minute particulars. And let it be remembered that "Æsop at play" is one of the instructive apologues of antiquity.

I mentioned an old gentleman of our acquaintance whose memory was beginning to fail. JOHNSON: "There must be a diseased mind, where there is a failure of memory at seventy. A man's head, Sir, must be morbid, if he fails so soon." My friend, being now himself sixty-eight, might think thus: but I imagine that *threescore and ten,* the Psalmist's period of sound human life in later ages, may have a failure, though there be no disease in the constitution.

Talking of Rochester's Poems, he said he had given them to Mr.

Steevens to castrate for the edition of the poets, to which he was to write Prefaces. Dr. Taylor (the only time I ever heard him say anything witty) observed that "If Rochester had been castrated himself, his exceptionable poems would not have been written." I asked if Burnet had not given a good "Life of Rochester." JOHNSON: "We have a good *Death:* there is not much *Life.*" I asked whether "Prior's Poems" were to be printed entire: Johnson said they were. I mentioned Lord Hailes's censure of Prior, in his Preface to a collection of "Sacred Poems," by various hands, published by him at Edinburgh a great many years ago, where he mentions "those impure tales which will be the eternal opprobrium of their ingenious author." JOHNSON: "Sir, Lord Hailes has forgot. There is nothing in Prior that will excite to lewdness. If Lord Hailes thinks there is, he must be more combustible than other people." I instanced the tale of "Paulo Purganti and his Wife." JOHNSON: "Sir, there is nothing there, but that his wife wanted to be kissed, when poor Paulo was out of pocket. No, Sir, Prior is a lady's book. No lady is ashamed to have it standing in her library."

Wishing to be satisfied what degree of truth there was in a story which a friend of Johnson's and mine had told me to his disadvantage, I mentioned it to him in direct terms; and it was to this effect: that a gentleman who had lived in great intimacy with him, shown him much kindness, and even relieved him from a spunging house, having afterwards fallen into bad circumstances, was one day, when Johnson was at dinner with him, seized for debt, and carried to prison; that Johnson sat still undisturbed, and went on eating and drinking; upon which the gentleman's sister, who was present, could not repress her indignation; "What, Sir (said she), are you so unfeeling as not even to offer to go to my brother in his distress; you who have been so much obliged to him?" And that Johnson answered, "Madam, I owe him no obligation; what he did for me he would have done for a dog."

Johnson assured me that the story was absolutely false: but like a man conscious of being in the right, and desirous of completely vindicating himself from such a charge, he did not arrogantly rest on a mere denial, and on his general character, but proceeded thus:—"Sir, I was very intimate with that gentleman, and was once relieved by him from an arrest; but I never was present when he was arrested, never knew that he was arrested, and I believe he never was in difficulties after the time when he relieved me. I loved him much: yet, in talking of his general character, I may have said, though I do not remember that I ever did say so, that as his generosity proceeded from no principle, but was a part of his profusion, he would do for a dog what he would do for a friend: but I never applied this remark to any particular instance, and certainly not to his kindness to me. If a profuse man, who does not value his money, and gives a large sum to a whore, gives half as much, or an equally large sum to relieve a friend, it cannot be esteemed as virtue. This was all that I could say of that gentleman; and, if said at all, it must have been said after his death. Sir, I would have gone to the world's end to relieve him. The remark about the dog, if made by me, was such a sally as might escape one when painting a man highly."

On Tuesday, September 23, Johnson was remarkably cordial to me. It being necessary for me to return to Scotland soon, I had fixed on the next day for my setting out, and I felt a tender concern at the thought of parting with him. He had, at this time, frankly communicated to me many particulars, which are inserted in this work in their proper places; and once, when I happened to mention that the expense of my jaunt would come to much more than I had computed, he said, "Why, Sir, if the expense were to be an inconvenience, you would have reason to regret it; but, if you have had the money to spend, I know not that you could have purchased as much pleasure with it in any other way."

During this interview at Ashbourne, Johnson and I frequently talked with wonderful pleasure of mere trifles which had occurred in our tour to the Hebrides; for it had left a most agreeable and lasting impression upon his mind.

He found fault with me for using the phrase to *make* money. "Don't you see (said he) the impropriety of it? To *make* money is to *coin* it; you should say *get* money." The phrase, however, is, I think, pretty current. But Johnson was at all times jealous of infractions upon the genuine English Language, and prompt to repress colloquial barbarisms; such as *pledging myself*, for *undertaking; line*, for *department*, or *branch*, as, the *civil line*, the *banking line*. He was particularly indignant against the almost universal use of the word *idea* in the sense of *notion* or *opinion*, when it is clear that *idea* can only signify something of which an image can be formed in the mind. We may have an *idea* or *image* of a mountain, a tree, a building; but we cannot surely have an *idea* or *image* of an *argument* or *proposition*. Yet we hear the sages of the law "delivering their *ideas* upon the question under consideration"; and the first speakers in parliament "entirely coinciding in the *idea* which has been ably stated by an honourable member";—or "reprobating an *idea* unconstitutional, and fraught with the most dangerous consequences to a great and free country." Johnson called this "modern cant."

In the evening our gentleman-farmer, and two others, entertained themselves and the company with a great number of tunes on the fiddle. Johnson desired to have "Let ambition fire thy mind" played over again, and appeared to give a patient attention to it; though he owned to me that he was very insensible to the power of music. I told him that it affected me to such a degree as often to agitate my nerves painfully, producing in my mind alternate sensations of pathetic dejection, so that I was ready to shed tears; and of daring resolution, so that I was inclined to rush into the thickest part of the battle. "Sir (said he), I should never hear it, if it made me such a fool."

Much of the effect of music, I am satisfied, is owing to the association of ideas. That air which instantly and irresistibly excites in the Swiss, when in a foreign land, the *maladie du pais,* has, I am told, no intrinsic power of sound. And I know from my own experience that Scotch reels, though brisk, make me melancholy, because I used to hear them in my early years, at a time when Mr. Pitt called for soldiers "from the mountains of the north," and numbers of brave Highlanders were going abroad, never to return. Whereas the airs in "The Beggar's Opera," many of which are very soft, never fail to render me gay, because they are associated with the warm sensations and high spirits of London.—This evening, while some of the tunes of ordinary composition were played with no great skill, my frame was agitated, and I was conscious of a generous attachment to Dr. Johnson, as my preceptor and friend, mixed with an affectionate regret that he was an old man, whom I should probably lose in a short time. I thought I could defend him at the point of my sword. My reverence and affection for him were in full glow. I said to him, "My dear Sir, we must meet every year, if you don't quarrel with me." JOHNSON: "Nay, Sir, you are more likely to quarrel with me, than I with you. My regard for you is greater almost than I have words to express; but I do not choose to be always repeating it; write it down in the first leaf of your pocketbook, and never doubt of it again."

While Johnson and I stood in calm conference by ourselves in Dr. Taylor's garden, at a pretty late hour in a serene autumn night, looking up to the heavens, I directed the discourse to the subject of a future state. My friend was in a placid and most benignant frame of mind. "Sir (said he), I do not imagine that all things will be made clear to us immediately after death, but that the ways of Providence will be explained to us very gradually." I ventured to ask him whether, although the words of some texts of Scripture seemed strong in support of the dreadful doctrine of an eternity of punishment, we might not hope that the denunciation was figurative, and would not literally be executed. JOHNSON: "Sir, you are to consider the intention of punishment in a future state. We have no reason to be sure that we shall then be no longer liable to offend against God. We do not know that even the angels are quite in a state of security; nay, we know that some of them have fallen. It may therefore, perhaps, be necessary, in order to preserve both men and angels in a state of rectitude, that they should have continually before them the punishment of those who have deviated from it; but we may hope that by some other means a fall from rectitude may be prevented. Some of the texts of Scripture, upon this subject, are, as you observe, indeed strong; but they may admit of a mitigated interpretation." He talked to me upon this awful and delicate question in a gentle tone, and as if afraid to be decisive.

After supper I accompanied him to his apartment, and at my request he dictated to me an argument in favour of the negro who was then claiming his liberty, in an action in the Court of Session in Scotland. He had always been very zealous against slavery in every form, in which I with all deference thought that he discovered "a zeal without knowledge." Upon one occasion, when in company with some very grave men at Oxford, his toast was, "Here's to the next insurrection of the negroes in the West Indies." His violent prejudice against our West Indian and American settlers appeared whenever there was an opportunity. Towards the conclusion of his "Taxation no Tyranny," he says, "How is it that we hear the loudest *yelps* for liberty among the drivers of negroes?"

The argument dictated by Dr. Johnson was as follows:

"It must be agreed that in most ages many countries have had part of their inhabitants in a state of slavery; yet it may be doubted whether slavery can ever be supposed the natural condition of man. It is impossible not to conceive that men in their original state were equal; and very difficult to imagine how one would be subjected to another but by violent compulsion. An individual may, indeed, forfeit his liberty by a crime; but he cannot by that crime forfeit the liberty of his children. What is true of a criminal seems true likewise of a captive. A man may accept life from a conquering enemy, on condition of perpetual servitude; but it is very doubtful whether he can entail that servitude on his descendants; for no man can stipulate without commission for another. The condition which he himself accepts, his son or grandson perhaps would have rejected. If we should admit, what perhaps may with more reason be denied, that there are certain relations between man and man which may make slavery necessary and just, yet it can never be proved that he who is now suing for his freedom ever stood in any of these relations. He is certainly subject by no law, but that of violence, to his present master; who pretends no claim to his obedience, but that he bought him from a merchant of slaves, whose right to sell him never was examined. It is said that according to the constitutions of Jamaica he was legally enslaved; these constitutions are merely positive; and apparently injurious to the rights of mankind, because whoever is exposed to sale is condemned to slavery without appeal; by whatever fraud or violence he might have been originally brought into the merchant's power. In our own time Princes have been sold, by wretches to whose care they were intrusted, that they might have a European education; but when once they were brought to a market in the plantations, little would avail either their dignity or their wrongs. The laws of Jamaica afford a negro no redress. His colour is considered as a sufficient testimony against him. It is to be lamented that moral right should ever give way to political convenience. But if temptations of interest are sometimes too strong for human virtue, let us at least retain a virtue where there is no temptation to quit it. In the present case there is apparent right on one side, and no convenience on the other. Inhabitants of this island can neither gain riches nor power by taking away the liberty of any part of the human species. The sum of the argument is this: No man is by nature the property of another: The defendant is, therefore, by nature free: The rights of nature must be some way forfeited before they can be justly taken away: That the defendant has by any act forfeited the rights of nature, we require to be proved; and if no proof of such forfeiture can be given, we doubt not but the justice of the court will declare him free."

I record Dr. Johnson's argument fairly upon this particular case; where, perhaps, he was in the right. But I beg leave to enter my most solemn protest against his general doctrine with respect to the *Slave Trade*. For I will resolutely say—that his unfavourable notion of it was owing to prejudice and imperfect or false information. The wild and dangerous attempt which has for some time been persisted in to obtain an act of our Legislature, to abolish so very important and necessary a branch of commercial interest, must have been crushed at once, had not the insignificance of the zealots, who vainly took the lead in it, made the vast body of planters, merchants, and others, whose immense properties are involved in that trade, reasonably enough suppose that there could be no danger.

When I said now to Johnson that I was afraid I kept him too late up, "No, Sir (said he), I don't care though I sit all night with you." This was an animated speech from a man in his sixty-ninth year.

Had I been as attentive not to displease him as I ought to have been, I know not but this vigil might have been fulfilled; but I unluckily entered upon the controversy concerning the right of Great Britain to tax America, and attempted to argue in favour of our fellow-subjects on the other side of the Atlantic. I insisted that America might be very well governed, and made to yield sufficient revenue by the means of *influence,* as exemplified in Ireland, while the people might be pleased with the imagination of their participating of the British Constitution, by having a body of representatives, without whose consent money could not be exacted from them. Johnson could not bear my thus opposing his avowed opinion, which he had exerted himself with an extreme degree of heat to enforce; and the violent agitation into which he was thrown, while answering, or rather reprimanding me, alarmed me so, that I heartily repented of my having unthinkingly introduced the subject. I myself, however, grew warm, and the change was great, from the calm state of philosophical discussion in which we had a little before been pleasingly employed.

We were fatigued by the contest, which was produced by my want of caution; and he was not then in the humour to slide into easy and cheerful talk. It therefore so happened that we were, after an hour or two, very willing to separate and go to bed.

On Wednesday, September 24, I went into Dr. Johnson's room before he got up, and finding that the storm of the preceding night was quite laid, I sat down upon his bed-side, and he talked with as much readiness and good humour as ever. He recommended me to plant a considerable part of a large moorish farm which I had purchased, and he made several calculations of the expense and profit; for he delighted in exercising his mind on the science of numbers. He pressed upon me the importance of planting at the first in a very sufficient manner, quoting the saying, *"In bello non licet bis errare"*: and adding, "This is equally true in planting."

I spoke with gratitude of Dr. Taylor's hospitality; and as evidence that it was not on account of his good table alone that Johnson visited him often, I mentioned a little anecdote which had escaped my friend's recollection, and at hearing which repeated, he smiled. One evening, when I was sitting with him, Frank delivered this message: "Sir, Dr. Taylor sends his compliments to you, and begs you will dine with him to-morrow. He has got a hare." "My compliments (said Johnson), and I'll dine with him—hare or rabbit."

After breakfast I departed, and pursued my journey northwards. I cannot omit a curious circumstance which occurred at Edensor Inn, close by Chatsworth, to survey the magnificence of which I had gone a considerable way out of my road to Scotland. The inn was then kept by a very jolly landlord, whose name, I think, was Malton. He happened to mention that "the celebrated Dr. Johnson had been in his house." I inquired *who* this Dr. Johnson was, that I might hear my host's notion of him. "Sir (said he), Johnson, the great writer; *Oddity,* as they call him. He's the greatest writer in England; he writes for the Ministry; he has a correspondence abroad, and lets them know what's going on."

My friend, who had a thorough dependance upon the authenticity of my relation without any *embellishment,* as *falsehood* or *fiction* is too gently called, laughed a good deal at this representation of himself.

"MR. BOSWELL TO DR. JOHNSON.

"*Edinburgh, Sep. 29, 1777.*

"MY DEAR SIR,—

"By the first post I inform you of my safe arrival at my own house, and that I had the comfort of finding my wife and children all in good health.

"When I look back upon our late interview, it appears to me to have answered expectation better than almost any scheme of happiness that I ever put in execution. My journal is stored with wisdom and wit; and my memory is filled with the recollection of lively and affectionate feelings, which now, I think, yield me more satisfaction than at the time when they were first excited. I have experienced this upon other occasions. I shall be obliged to you if you will explain it to me; for it seems wonderful that pleasure should be more vivid at a distance than when near. I wish you may find yourself in a humour to do me this favour; but I flatter myself with no strong hope of it; for I have observed that, unless upon very serious occasions, your letters to me are not *answers* to those which I write."

[I then expressed much uneasiness that I had mentioned to him the name of the gentleman who had told me the story so much to his disadvantage, the truth of which he had completely refuted; for that my having done so might be interpreted as a breach of confidence, and offend one whose society I valued:—therefore earnestly requesting that no notice might be taken of it to any body, till I should be in London, and have an opportunity to talk it over with the gentleman.]

"TO JAMES BOSWELL, ESQ.

"DEAR SIR,—

"You will wonder, or you have wondered, why no letter has come from me. What you wrote at your return, had in it such a strain of cowardly caution as gave me no pleasure. I could not well do what you wished; I had no need to vex you with a refusal. I have seen Mr. ———, and, as to him have set all right, without any inconvenience, so far as I know, to you. Mrs. Thrale had forgot the story. You may now be at ease.

"And at ease I certainly wish you, for the kindness that you showed in coming so long a journey to see me. It was pity to keep you so long in pain, but, upon reviewing the matter, I do not see what I could have done better than I did.

"I hope you found at your return my dear enemy, and all her little people, quite well, and had no reason to repent of your journey. I think on it with great gratitude.

"I was not well when you left me at the Doctor's, and I grew worse; yet I stayed on, and at Lichfield was very ill. Travelling, however, did not make me worse; and when I came to London, I complied with a summons to go to Brighthelmstone, where I saw Beauclerk, and stayed three days.

"My dear Friend, let me thank you once more for your visit; you did me great honour, and I hope met with nothing that displeased you. I stayed long at Ashbourne, not much pleased, yet awkward at departing. I then went to Lichfield, where I found my friend at Stow Hill very dangerously diseased. Such is life. Let us try to pass it well, whatever it be, for there is surely something beyond it.

"Well, now, I hope all is well. Write as soon as you can, to, dear Sir,

"Your affectionate servant,
"SAM. JOHNSON.

"*London, Nov. 26, 1777.*"

"Edinburgh, Nov. 29, 1777.

"MY DEAR SIR,—

"This day's post has at length relieved me from much uneasiness, by bringing me a letter from you. I was, indeed, doubly uneasy;— on my own account and yours. I was very anxious to be secured against any bad consequences from my imprudence in mentioning the gentleman's name who had told me a story to your disadvantage; and as I could hardly suppose it possible that you would delay so long to make me easy, unless you were ill, I was not a little apprehensive about you. You must not be offended when I venture to tell you that you appear to me to have been too rigid upon this occasion. The *'cowardly caution which gave you no pleasure,'* was suggested to me by a friend here, to whom I mentioned the strange story and the detection of its falsity, as an instance how one may be deceived by what is apparently very good authority. But, as I am still persuaded that, as I might have obtained the truth without mentioning the gentleman's name, it was wrong in me to do it, I cannot see that you are just in blaming my caution. But if you were ever so just in your disapprobation, might you not have dealt more tenderly with me?

"I went to Auchinleck about the middle of October, and passed some time with my father very comfortably.

"I ever am, my dear Sir,

"Your faithful humble servant,

"JAMES BOSWELL."

About this time I wrote to Johnson, giving him an account of the decision of the *Negro cause* by the Court of Session, which by those who hold even the mildest and best regulated slavery in abomination (of which number I do not hesitate to declare that I am none), should be remembered with high respect, and to the credit of Scotland; for it went upon a much broader ground than the case of *Somerset,* which was decided in England; being truly the general question, whether a perpetual obligation of service to one master in any mode should be sanctified by the law of a free country. A negro, then called *Joseph Knight,* a native of Africa, who having been brought to Jamaica in the usual course of the slave-trade, and purchased by a Scotch gentleman in that island, had attended his master to Scotland, where it was officiously suggested to him that he would be found entitled to his liberty without any limitation. He accordingly brought his action, in the course of which the advocates on both sides did themselves great honour. A great majority of the Lords of Session decided for the negro. But four of their number, the Lord President, Lord Elliock, Lord Monboddo, and Lord Covington, resolutely maintained the lawfulness of a *status* which has been acknowledged in all ages and countries, and that when freedom flourished, as in old Greece and Rome.

CHAPTER XXXIX—1778

Talk at the Club

"TO DR. SAMUEL JOHNSON.

"Edinburgh, Jan. 8, 1778.

"DEAR SIR,—

"Your congratulations upon a new year are mixed with complaint: mine must be so too. My wife has for some time been very ill, having been confined to the house these three months by a severe cold, attended with alarming symptoms.

[Here I gave a particular account of the distress which the person upon every account most dear to me suffered; and of the dismal state of apprehension in which I now was: adding that I never stood more in need of his consoling philosophy.]

"I am, dear Sir,
"Your most affectionate humble servant,
"JAMES BOSWELL."

"TO JAMES BOSWELL, ESQ.

"DEAR SIR,—

"To a letter so interesting as your last, it is proper to return some answer, however little I may be disposed to write.

"Your alarm at your lady's illness was reasonable, and not disproportionate to the appearance of the disorder. I hope your physical friend's conjecture is now verified, and all fear of a consumption at an end: a little care and exercise will then restore her. London is a good air for ladies; and if you bring her hither, I will do for her what she did for me—I will retire from my apartments for her accommodation. Behave kindly to her, and keep her cheerful.

"You always seem to call for tenderness. Know, then, that in the first month of the present year I very highly esteem and very cordially love you. I hope to tell you this at the beginning of every year as long as we live; and why should we trouble ourselves to tell or hear it oftener?

"I am, dear Sir, yours affectionately,
"SAM. JOHNSON.

"*January 24, 1778.*"

Johnson maintained a long and intimate friendship with Mr. Welch, who succeeded the celebrated Henry Fielding as one of his Majesty's Justices of the Peace for Westminster; kept a regular office for the police of that great district; and discharged his important trust, for many years, faithfully and ably. Johnson, who had an eager and unceasing curiosity to know human life in all its variety, told me that he attended Mr. Welch in his office for a whole winter, to hear the examinations of the culprits; but that he found an almost uniform tenor of misfortune, wretchedness, and profligacy. Mr. Welch's health being impaired, he was advised to try the effect of a warm climate; and Johnson, by his interest with Mr. Chamier, procured him leave of absence to go to Italy, and a promise that the pension or salary of two hundred pounds a year, which Government allowed him, should not be discontinued. Mr. Welch accordingly went abroad, accompanied by his daughter Anne, a young lady of uncommon talents and literature.

"TO SAUNDERS WELCH, ESQ., AT THE ENGLISH COFFEE-HOUSE, ROME.

"DEAR SIR,—

"To have suffered one of my best and dearest friends to pass almost two years in foreign countries without a letter, has a very shameful appearance of inattention. But the truth is that there was no particular time in which I had anything particular to say; and general expressions of goodwill, I hope, our long friendship is grown too solid to want.

"Of public affairs you have information from the newspapers wherever you go, for the English keep no secret; and of other things, Mrs. Nollekens informs you. My intelligence could therefore be of no use; and Miss Nancy's letters made it unnecessary to write to you for information: I was likewise for some time out of humour, to find that motion, and nearer approaches to the sun, did not restore your health so fast as I expected. Of your health, the accounts have lately been more pleasing; and I have the gratification of imagining to myself a length of years which I hope you have gained, and of which the enjoyment will be improved by a vast accession of images and observations which your journeys and various residence have enabled you to make and accumulate. You have travelled with this felicity, almost peculiar to yourself, that your companion is not to part from you at your journey's end; but you are to live on together, to help each other's recollection, and to supply each other's omissions. The world has few greater pleasures than that which two friends enjoy, in tracing back, at some distant time, those transactions and events through which they have passed together. One of the old man's miseries is that he cannot easily find a companion able to partake with him of the past. You and your fellow-traveller have this comfort in store, that your conversation will be not easily exhausted; one will always be glad to say what the other will always be willing to hear.

"That you may enjoy this pleasure long, your health must have your constant attention. I suppose you propose to return this year. There is no need of haste: do not come hither before the height of summer, that you may fall gradually into the inconveniences of your native clime. July seems to be the proper month. August and September will prepare you for the winter. After having travelled so far to find health, you must take care not to lose it at home; and I hope a little care will effectually preserve it.

"Miss Nancy has doubtless kept a constant and copious journal. She must not expect to be welcome when she returns, without a great mass of information. Let her review her journal often, and set down what she finds herself to have omitted, that she may trust to memory as little as possible, for memory is soon confused by a quick succession of things; and she will grow every day less confident of the truth of her own narratives, unless she can recur to some written memorials. If she has satisfied herself with hints, instead of full representations, let her supply the deficiencies now while her memory is yet fresh, and while her father's memory may help her. If she observes this direction, she will not have travelled in vain: for she will bring home a book with which she may entertain herself to the end of life. If it were not now too late, I would advise her to note the impression which the first sight of anything new and wonderful made upon her mind.

[433]

Let her now set her thoughts down as she can recollect them; for, faint as they may already be, they will grow every day fainter.

"Perhaps I do not flatter myself unreasonably when I imagine that you may wish to know something of me. I can gratify your benevolence with no account of health. The hand of time or of disease is very heavy upon me. I pass restless and uneasy nights, harassed with convulsions of my breast, and flatulences at my stomach; and restless nights make heavy days. But nothing will be mended by complaints, and therefore I will make an end. When we meet, we will try to forget our cares and our maladies, and contribute, as we can, to the cheerfulness of each other. If I had gone with you, I believe I should have been better; but I do not know that it was in my power.

"I am, dear Sir,

"Your most humble servant,

"SAM. JOHNSON.

"*Feb. 3, 1778.*"

"TO DR. SAMUEL JOHNSON.

"*Edinburgh, Feb. 26, 1778.*

"MY DEAR SIR,—

"Why I have delayed, for near a month, to thank you for your last affectionate letter, I cannot say; for my mind has been in better health these three weeks than for some years past.

"My wife, who is, thank God, a good deal better, is much obliged to you for your very polite and courteous offer of your apartment: but, if she goes to London, it will be best for her to have lodgings in the more airy vicinity of Hyde Park. I, however, doubt much if I shall be able to prevail with her to accompany me to the metropolis; for she is so different from you and me that she dislikes travelling; and she is so anxious about her children, that she thinks she should be unhappy if at a distance from them. She therefore wishes rather to go to some country place in Scotland, where she can have them with her.

"I purpose being in London about the 20th of next month, as I think it creditable to appear in the House of Lords as one of Douglas's Counsel, in the great and last competition between Duke Hamilton and him.

"I ever am, my dear Sir,

"Your affectionate humble servant,

"JAMES BOSWELL."

"TO THE SAME.

"*Edinburgh, Feb. 28, 1778.*

"MY DEAR SIR,—

"What do you say to 'Taxation no Tyranny,' now, after Lord North's declaration, or confession, or whatever else his conciliatory speech should be called? I never differed from you in politics but upon two points—the Middlesex Election, and the Taxation of the Americans by the British *Houses of Representatives.* There is a *charm* in the word *Parliament,* so I avoid it. As I am a steady and a warm Tory, I regret that the King does not see it to be better for him to receive constitutional supplies from his American subjects by the voice of their own assemblies, where his Royal Person is represented, than through the medium of his British subjects. I am persuaded that the power of the Crown, which I wish to increase, would be greater when in contact with all its dominions, than if 'the rays of regal bounty' were 'to shine' upon America, through that dense troubled body, a modern British Parliament. But, enough of this subject; for your angry voice at Ashbourne upon it still sounds awful 'in my mind's *ears.*' "

"I ever am, my dear Sir,
"Your most affectionate humble servant,
"JAMES BOSWELL."

"TO THE SAME.

"*Edinburgh, March 12, 1778.*

"MY DEAR SIR,—

"The alarm of your late illness distressed me but a few hours; for on the evening of the day that it reached me, I found it contradicted in the *London Chronicle,* which I could depend upon as authentic concerning you, Mr. Strahan being the printer of it. I did not see the paper in which 'the approaching extinction of a bright luminary' was announced. Sir William Forbes told me of it; and he says he saw me so uneasy that he did not give me the report in such strong terms as he read it. He afterwards sent me a letter from Mr. Langton to him, which relieved me much. I am, however, not quite easy, as I have not heard from you; and now I shall not have that comfort before I see you, for I set out for London to-morrow before the post comes in. I hope to be with you on Wednesday morning; and I ever am, with the highest veneration,

"My dear Sir, your most obliged,
"Faithful, and affectionate humble servant,
"JAMES BOSWELL."

On Wednesday, March 18, I arrived in London, and was informed by good Mr. Francis that his master was better, and was gone to Mr. Thrale's at Streatham, to which place I wrote to him, begging to know when he would be in town. He was not expected for some time, but next day having called on Dr. Taylor, in Dean's Yard, Westminster, I found him there, and was told he had come to town for a few hours. He met me with his usual kindness, but instantly returned to the writing of something on which he was employed when I came in, and on which he seemed much intent. Finding him thus engaged, I made my visit very short, and had no more of his conversation, except his expressing a serious regret that a friend of ours was living at too much expense, considering how poor an appearance he made: "If (said he) a man has splendour from his expense, if he spends his money in pride or in pleasure, he has value: but if he lets others spend it for him, which is most commonly the case, he has no advantage from it."

On Friday, March 20, I found him at his own house, sitting with Mrs. Williams, and was informed that the room formerly allotted to me was now appropriated to a charitable purpose; Mrs. Desmoulins, and I think her daughter, and a Miss Carmichael, being all lodged in it. Such was his humanity, and such his generosity, that Mrs. Desmoulins herself told me he allowed her half-a-guinea a week. Let it be remembered that this was above a twelfth part of his pension.

We retired from Mrs. Williams to another room. Tom Davies soon after joined us. He had now unfortunately failed in his circumstances, and was much indebted to Dr. Johnson's kindness for obtaining for him many alleviations of his distress. After he went away, Johnson blamed his folly in quitting the stage, by which he and his wife got £500 a year. I said I believed it was owing to Churchill's attack upon him,

"He mouths a sentence, as curs mouth a bone."

JOHNSON: "I believe so too, Sir. But what a man is he, who is to be driven from the stage by a line? Another line would have driven him from his shop."

I told him that I was engaged as Counsel at the bar of the House of Commons to oppose a road-bill in the county of Stirling, and asked him what mode he would advise me to follow in addressing such an audience. JOHNSON: "Why, Sir, you must provide yourself with a good deal of extraneous matter, which you are to produce occasionally, so as to fill up the time; for you must consider that they do not listen much. If you begin with the strength of your cause, it may be lost before they begin to listen. When you catch a moment of attention, press the merits of the question upon them." He said, as to one point of the merits, that he thought "it would be a wrong thing to deprive the small landowners of the privilege of assessing themselves for making and repairing the high roads; *it was destroying a certain portion of liberty, without a good reason, which was always a bad thing.*" When I mentioned this observation next day to Mr. Wilkes, he pleasantly said, "What! does he talk of liberty? *Liberty* is as ridiculous in *his* mouth as *Religion* in *mine.*"

In my interview with Dr. Johnson this evening I was quite easy, quite as his companion; upon which I find in my Journal the following reflection: "So ready is my mind to suggest matter for dissatisfaction, that I felt a sort of regret that I was so easy. I missed that awful reverence with which I used to contemplate Mr. Samuel Johnson, in the complex magnitude of his literary, moral, and religious character. I have a wonderful superstitious love of *mystery;* when, perhaps, the truth is, that it is owing to the cloudy darkness of my own mind. I should be glad that I am more advanced in my progress of being, so that I can view Dr. Johnson with a steadier and clearer eye. My dissatisfaction to-night was foolish. Would it not be foolish to regret that we shall have less mystery in a future state? That 'we now see in a glass darkly,' but shall 'then see face to face?' "—This reflection, which I thus freely communicate, will be valued by the thinking part of my readers, who may have themselves experienced a similar state of mind.

He returned next day to Streatham, to Mr. Thrale's; where, as Mr. Strahan once complained to me, "he was in a great measure absorbed from the society of his old friends." I was kept in London by business, and wrote to him on the 27th that a separation from him for a week, when we were so near, was equal to a separation for a year, when we were at four hundred miles distance. I went to Streatham on Monday, March 30. Before he appeared, Mrs. Thrale made a very characteristical remark:—"I do not know for certain what will please Dr. Johnson: but I know for certain that it will displease him to praise any thing, even what he likes, extravagantly."

Next morning, while we were at breakfast, Johnson gave a very earnest recommendation of what he himself practised with the utmost conscientiousness: I mean a strict attention to truth, even in the most minute particulars. "Accustom your children (said he) constantly to this; if a thing happened at one window, and they, when relating it, say that it happened at another, do not let it pass, but instantly check them; you do not know where deviation from truth will end." BOSWELL: "It may come to the door: and when once an account is at all varied in one circumstance, it may by degrees be varied so as to be totally different from what really happened." Our lively hostess, whose fancy was impatient of the rein, fidgeted at this, and ventured to say, "Nay, this is too much. If Mr. Johnson should forbid me to drink tea, I would comply, as I should feel the restraint only twice a day; but little variations in narrative must happen a thousand times a day, if one is not perpetually watching." JOHNSON: "Well, Madam, and you *ought* to be perpetually watching. It is more from carelessness about truth than from intentional lying, that there is so much falsehood in the world."

In his review of Dr. Warton's "Essay on the Writings and Genius of Pope," Johnson has given the following salutary caution upon this subject: "Nothing but experience could evince the frequency of false information, or enable any man to conceive that so many groundless reports should be propagated, as every man of eminence may hear of himself. Some men relate what they think, as what they know; some men of confused memories and habitual inaccuracy, ascribe to one man what belongs to another; and some talk on, without thought or care. A few men are sufficient to broach falsehoods, which are afterwards innocently diffused by successive relators." Had he lived to read what Sir John Hawkins and Mrs. Piozzi have related concerning himself, how much would he have found his observation illustrated. He was indeed so much impressed with the prevalence of falsehood, voluntary or unintentional, that I never knew any person who, upon hearing an extraordinary circumstance told, discovered more of the *incredulus odi*. He would say, with a significant look and decisive tone, "It is not so. Do not tell this again."

On Friday, April 3, I dined with him in London, in a company where were present several eminent men, whom I shall not name, but distinguish their parts in the conversation by different letters.

R.: "Mr. E., I don't mean to flatter, but when posterity reads one of your speeches in Parliament, it will be difficult to believe that you took so much pains, knowing with certainty that it could produce no effect, that not one vote would be gained by it." E.: "Waiving your compliment to me, I shall say in general that it is very well worth while for a man to take pains to speak well in Parliament. A man, who has vanity, speaks to display his talents; and if a man speaks well he gradually establishes a certain reputation and consequence in the general opinion, which sooner or later will have its political reward. Besides, though not one vote is gained, a good speech has its effect. Though an act which has been ably opposed passes into a law, yet in its progress it is modelled, it is softened in such a manner, that we see plainly the Minister has been told that the members attached to him are so sensible of its injustice or absurdity from what they have heard, that it must be altered." JOHNSON: "And, Sir, there is a gratification of pride. Though we cannot out-vote them, we will out-argue them. They shall not do wrong without its being shown, both to themselves and to the world." E.: "The House of Commons is a mixed body (I except the minority, which I hold to be pure [smiling], but I take the whole House). It is a mass by no means pure; but neither is it wholly corrupt, though there is a large proportion of corruption in it. There are many honest, well-meaning country gentlemen who are in Parliament only to keep up the consequence of their families. Upon most of these a good speech will have influence." JOHNSON: "We are all, more or less, governed by interest. But interest will not make us do everything. In a case which admits of doubt, we try to think on the side which is for our interest, and generally bring ourselves to act accordingly. But the subject must admit of diversity of colouring; it must receive a colour on that side. In the House of Commons there are members enough who will not vote what is grossly unjust or absurd. No, Sir, there must always be right enough, or appearance of right, to keep wrong in countenance." BOSWELL: "There is surely always a majority in Parliament who have places, or who want to have them, and who therefore will be generally ready to support government, without requiring any pretext."

E.: "From the experience which I have had—and I have had a great deal—I have learnt to think *better* of mankind. JOHNSON: "From my experience I have found them worse in commercial dealings, more disposed to cheat, than I had any notion of; but more disposed to do one another good than I had conceived." J.: "Less just and more beneficent." JOHNSON: "And really it is wonderful, considering how much attention is necessary for men to take care of themselves, and ward off immediate evils which press upon them, it is wonderful how much they do for others. As it is said of the greatest liar, that he tells more truth than falsehood; so it may be said of the worst man, that he does more good than evil." BOSWELL: "Perhaps from experience men may be found *happier* than we suppose." JOHN-SON: "No, Sir; the more we inquire we shall find men less happy." P.: "As to thinking better or worse of mankind from experience, some cunning people will not be satisfied unless they have put men to the test, as they think. There is a very good story told of Sir Godfrey Kneller, in his character of a justice of the peace. A gentleman brought his servant before him, upon an accusation of having stolen some money from him; but it having come out that he had laid it purposely in the servant's way, in order to try his honesty, Sir Godfrey sent the master to prison." JOHNSON: "To resist temptation once, is not a sufficient proof of honesty. If a servant, indeed, were to resist the con-tinued temptation of silver lying in a window, as some people let it lie, when he is sure his master does not know how much there is of it he would give a strong proof of honesty. But this is a proof to which you have no right to put a man. You know, humanly speaking, there is a certain degree of temptation, which will overcome any virtue. Now, in so far as you approach temptation to a man, you do him an injury; and, if he is overcome, you share his guilt." P.: "And, when once overcome, it is easier for him to be got the better of again." BOSWELL: "Yes, you are his seducer; you have debauched him. I have known a man resolved to put friendship to the test, by asking a friend to lend him money, merely with that view, when he did not want it." JOHNSON: "That is very wrong, Sir. Your friend may be a narrow man, and yet have many good qualities: narrowness may be his only fault. Now you are trying his general character as a friend, by one particular singly, in which he happens to be defective, when, in truth, his character is composed of many particulars."

E.: "I understand the hogshead of claret, which this society was favoured with by our friend the Dean, is nearly out; I think he should be written to, to send another of the same kind. Let the request be made with a happy ambiguity of expression, so that we may have the chance of his sending *it* also as a present." JOHNSON: "I am willing to offer my services as secretary on this occasion." P.: "As many as are for Dr. Johnson being secretary hold up your hands.—Carried unanimously." BOSWELL: "He will be our dictator." JOHNSON: "No, the company is to dictate to me. I am only to write for wine; and I am quite disinterested, as I drink none: I shall not be suspected of having forged the application. I am no more than humble *scribe*." E.: "Then you shall *pre*scribe." BOSWELL: "Very well. The first play of words to-day." J.: "No, no; the *bulls* in Ireland." JOHNSON: "Were

New York, 1945

Dr. Johnson tidies his library once in awhile.

I your dictator you should have no wine. It would be my business *cavere ne quid detrimenti Respublica caperet,* and wine is dangerous. Rome was ruined by luxury" (smiling). E.: "If you allow no wine as Dictator, you shall not have me for your Master of Horse."

On Saturday, April 4, I drank tea with Johnson at Dr. Taylor's, where he had dined. He was very silent this evening; and read in a variety of books: suddenly throwing down one, and taking up another.

He talked of going to Streatham that night. TAYLOR: "You'll be robbed, if you do: or you must shoot a highwayman. Now I would rather be robbed than do that; I would not shoot a highwayman." JOHNSON: "But I would rather shoot him in the instant when he is attempting to rob me, than afterwards swear against him at the Old Bailey, to take away his life, after he has robbed me. I am surer I am right in the one case, than in the other. I may be mistaken as to the man when I swear: I cannot be mistaken if I shoot him in the act. Besides, we feel less reluctance to take away a man's life, when we are heated by the injury, than to do it at a distance of time by an oath, after we have cooled." BOSWELL: "So, Sir, you would rather act from the motive of private passion than that of public advantage." JOHNSON: "Nay, Sir, when I shoot the highwayman, I act from both." BOSWELL: "Very well, very well.—There is no catching him." JOHNSON: "At the same time, one does not know what to say. For perhaps one may, a year after, hang himself from uneasiness for having shot a highwayman. Few minds are fit to be trusted with so great a thing." BOSWELL: "Then, Sir, you would not shoot him." JOHNSON: "But I might be vexed afterwards for that too."

Thrale's carriage not having come for him as he expected, I accompanied him some part of the way home to his own house. I told him that I had talked of him to Mr. Dunning a few days before, and had said that in his company we did not so much interchange conversation, as listen to him; and that Dunning observed, upon this, "One is always willing to listen to Dr. Johnson"; to which I answered, "That is a great deal from you, Sir"—"Yes, Sir (said Johnson), a great deal indeed. Here is a man willing to listen, to whom the world is listening all the rest of the year." BOSWELL: "I think, Sir, it is right to tell one man of such a handsome thing, which has been said of him by another. It tends to increase benevolence." JOHNSON: "Undoubtedly it is right, Sir."

On Tuesday, April 7, I breakfasted with him at his house. He said, "nobody was content." I mentioned to him a respectable person in

Scotland whom he knew; and I asserted that I really believed he was always content. JOHNSON: "No, Sir, he is not content with the present; he has always some new scheme, some new plantation, something which is future. You know he was not content as a widower; for he married again." BOSWELL: "But he is not restless." JOHNSON: "Sir, he is only locally at rest. A chemist is locally at rest; but his mind is hard at work. This gentleman has done with external exertions. It is too late for him to engage in distant projects." BOSWELL: "He seems to amuse himself quite well; to have his attention fixed, and his tranquillity preserved by very small matters. I have tried this; but it would not do with me." JOHNSON (laughing): "No, Sir; it must be born with a man to be contented to take up with little things. Women have a great advantage that they may take up with little things, without disgracing themselves; a man cannot, except with fiddling. Had I learnt to fiddle, I should have done nothing else." BOSWELL: "Pray, Sir, did you ever play on any musical instrument?" JOHNSON: "No, Sir. I once bought me a flageolet; but I never made out a tune." BOSWELL: "A flageolet, Sir!—so small an instrument? I should have liked to hear you play on the violoncello. *That* should have been *your* instrument." JOHNSON: "Sir, I might as well have played on the violoncello as another; but I should have done nothing else. No, Sir; a man would never undertake great things, could he be amused with small. I once tried knotting. Dempster's sister undertook to teach me; but I could not learn it." BOSWELL: "So, Sir; it will be related in pompous narrative, 'Once for his amusement he tried knotting; nor did this Hercules disdain the distaff.'" JOHNSON: "Knitting of stockings is a good amusement. As a freeman of Aberdeen I should be a knitter of stockings." He asked me to go down with him and dine at Mr. Thrale's at Streatham, to which I agreed.

BOSWELL: "Was not Dr. John Campbell a very inaccurate man in his narrative, Sir? He once told me that he drank thirteen bottles of port at a sitting." JOHNSON: "Why, Sir, I do not know that Campbell ever lied with pen and ink; but you could not entirely depend on any thing that he told you in conversation, there was fact mixed with it. However, I loved Campbell: he was a solid orthodox man: he had a reverence for religion. Though defective in practice, he was religious in principle; and he did nothing grossly wrong that I have heard."

Talking of drinking wine, he said, "I did not leave off wine, because I could not bear it! I have drunk three bottles of port without being the worse for it. University College has witnessed this." Bos-

WELL: "Why, then, Sir, did you leave it off?" JOHNSON: "Why, Sir, because it is so much better for a man to be sure that he is never to be intoxicated, never to lose the power over himself. I shall not begin to drink wine till I grow old and want it." BOSWELL: "I think, Sir, you once said to me that not to drink wine was a great deduction from life." JOHNSON: "It is a diminution of pleasure, to be sure: but I do not say a diminution of happiness. There is more happiness in being rational." BOSWELL: "But if we could have pleasure always, should not we be happy? The greatest part of men would compound for pleasure." JOHNSON: "Supposing we could have pleasure always, an intellectual man would not compound for it. The greatest part of men would compound, because the greatest part of men are gross." BOSWELL: "I allow there may be greater pleasure than from wine. I have had more pleasure from your conversation. I have indeed; I assure you I have." JOHNSON: "When we talk of pleasure, we mean sensual pleasure. When a man says he had pleasure with a woman, he does not mean conversation, but something of a very different nature. Philosophers tell you that pleasure is *contrary* to happiness. Gross men prefer animal pleasure. So there are men who have preferred living among savages. Now, what a wretch must he be, who is content with such conversation as can be had among savages! You may remember an officer at Fort Augustus, who had served in America, told us of a woman whom they were obliged to *bind,* in order to get her back from savage life." BOSWELL: "She must have been an animal, a beast." JOHNSON: "She was a speaking cat."

Soon after our arrival at Thrale's, I heard one of the maids calling eagerly on another to go to Dr. Johnson. I wondered what this could mean. I afterwards learnt that it was to give her a Bible, which he had brought from London as a present to her.

He was for a considerable time occupied in reading, *"Mémoires de Fontenelle,"* leaning and swinging upon the low gate into the court, without his hat.

At dinner Mrs. Thrale expressed a wish to go and see Scotland. JOHNSON: "Seeing Scotland, Madam, is only seeing a worse England. It is seeing the flower gradually fade away to the naked stalk. Seeing the Hebrides, indeed, is seeing quite a different scene."

He and I returned to town in the evening. Upon the road, I endeavoured to maintain, in argument, that a landed gentleman is not under any obligation to reside upon his estate; and that by living in London he does no injury to his country. JOHNSON: "Why, Sir, he does no injury to his country in general, because the money which he draws from it gets back again in circulation; but to his particular district, his particular parish, he does an injury. All that he has to give away is not given to those who have the first claim to it. And though I have said that the money circulates back, it is a long time before that happens. Then, Sir, a man of family and estate ought to consider himself as having the charge of a district, over which he is to diffuse civility and happiness."

CHAPTER XL—1778

Dr. Johnson and Dr. Percy

ON THURSDAY, APRIL 9, I dined with him at Sir Joshua Reynolds's, with the Bishop of St. Asaph (Dr. Shipley), Mr. Allan Ramsay, Mr. Gibbon, Mr. Cambridge, and Mr. Langton. Mr. Ramsay had lately returned from Italy, and entertained us with his observations upon Horace's villa, which he had examined with great care. I relished this much, as it brought fresh into my mind what I had viewed with great pleasure thirteen years before. The Bishop, Dr. Johnson, and Mr. Cambridge, joined with Mr. Ramsay, in recollecting the various lines in Horace relating to the subject.

Goldsmith being mentioned, Johnson observed that it was long before his merit came to be acknowledged: that he once complained to him, in ludicrous terms of distress, "Whenever I write anything, the public *make a point* to know nothing about it": but that his "Traveller" brought him into high reputation. LANGTON: "There is not one bad line in that poem; no one of Dryden's careless verses." SIR JOSHUA: "I was glad to hear Charles Fox say it was one of the finest poems in the English language." LANGTON: "Why were you glad? You surely had no doubt of this before." JOHNSON: "No; the merit of 'The Traveller' is so well established that Mr. Fox's praise cannot augment it, nor his censure diminish it." SIR JOSHUA: "But his friends may suspect they had too great a partiality for him." JOHNSON: "Nay, Sir, the partiality of his friends was always against him. It was with difficulty we could give him a hearing. Goldsmith had no settled notions upon any subject; so he talked always at random. It seemed to be his intention to blurt out whatever was in his mind, and see what would become of it. He was angry, too, when catched in an absurdity; but it did not prevent him from falling into another the next minute. I remember Chamier, after talking with him some time, said, 'Well, I do believe he wrote this poem himself: and, let me tell you, that is believing a great deal.' Chamier once asked him what he meant by *slow,* the last word in the first line of 'The Traveller,'

'Remote, unfriended, melancholy, slow,'—

Did he mean tardiness of locomotion? Goldsmith, who would say something without consideration, answered, 'Yes.' I was sitting by, and said, 'No, Sir; you do not mean tardiness of locomotion; you mean that sluggishness of mind which comes upon a man in solitude.' Chamier believed then that I had written the line, as much as if he had seen me write it. Goldsmith, however, was a man who, whatever he wrote, did it better than any other man could do. He deserved a place in Westminster Abbey; and every year he lived would have deserved it better. He had, indeed, been at no pains to fill his mind with knowledge. He transplanted it from one place to another; and it did not settle in his mind; so he could not tell what was in his own books."

We talked of living in the country. JOHNSON: "No wise man will go to live in the country, unless he has something to do which can be better done in the country. For instance: if he is to shut himself up for a year to study a science, it is better to look out to the fields, than to an opposite wall. Then, if a man walks out in the country, there is nobody to keep him from walking in again; but if a man walks out in London, he is not sure when he shall walk in again. A great city is, to be sure, the school for studying life; and 'The proper study of mankind is man,' as Pope observes." BOSWELL: "I fancy London is the best place for society; though I have heard that the very first society of Paris is still beyond anything that we have here." JOHNSON: "Sir, I question if in Paris such a company as is sitting round this table could be got together in less than half a year. They talk in France of the felicity of men and women living together: the truth is that there the men are not higher than the women, they know no more than the women do, and they are not held down in their conversation by the presence of women." RAMSAY: "Literature is upon the growth, it is in its spring in France; here it is rather *passée.*" JOHNSON: "Literature was in France long before we had it. Paris was the second city for the revival of letters: Italy had it first, to be sure. What have we done for literature, equal to what was done by the Stephani and others in France? Our literature came to us through France. Caxton printed only two books, Chaucer, and Gower, that were not translations from the French; and Chaucer, we know, took much from the Italians. No, Sir, if literature be in its spring in France, it is a second spring; it is after a winter. We are now before the French in literature; but we had it long after them. In England, any man who wears a sword and a powdered wig, is ashamed to be illiterate. I believe it is not so in France. Yet there is, probably, a great deal of learning in France, because they have such a number of religious establishments; so many men who have nothing else to do but to study. I do not know this; but I take it upon the common principles of chance. Where there are many shooters, some will hit."

This season, there was a whimsical fashion in the newspapers of applying Shakspeare's words to describe living persons well known in the world; which was done under the title of "Modern Characters from Shakspeare"; many of which were admirably adapted. The fancy took so much, that they were afterwards collected into a pamphlet. Somebody said to Johnson, across the table, that he had not been in those characters. "Yes (said he), I have. I should have been sorry to be left out." He then repeated what had been applied to him,

> "You must borrow me Garagantua's mouth."
> ["As You Like It," iii, 2.]

Miss Reynolds not perceiving at once the meaning of this, he was obliged to explain it to her, which had something of an awkward and ludicrous effect. "Why, Madam, it has a reference to me, as using big words, which require the mouth of a giant to pronounce them. Garagantua is the name of a giant in 'Rabelais.' " BOSWELL: "But, Sir, there is another amongst them for you.

> 'He would not flatter Neptune for his trident,
> Or Jove for his power to thunder.' "

JOHNSON: "There is nothing marked in that. No, Sir; Garagantua is the best." Notwithstanding this ease and good humour, when I, a little while afterwards, repeated his sarcasm on Kenrick, which was received with applause, he asked, *"Who* said that?" and on my suddenly answering *Garagantua,* he looked serious, which was a sufficient indication that he did not wish it to be kept up.

When we went to the drawing-room, there was a rich assemblage.

Besides the company who had been at dinner, there were Mr. Garrick, Mr. Harris of Salisbury, Dr. Percy, Dr. Burney, the Honourable Mrs. Cholmondeley, Miss Hannah More, etc., etc.

After wandering about in a kind of pleasing distraction for some time, I got into a corner, with Johnson, Garrick, and Harris. GARRICK (to Harris): "Pray, Sir, have you read Potter's 'Æschylus?'" HARRIS: "Yes; and think it pretty." GARRICK (to Johnson): "And what think you, Sir, of it?" JOHNSON: "I thought what I read of it *verbiage:* but, upon Mr. Harris's recommendation, I will read a play. (To Mr. Harris.) Don't prescribe two." Mr. Harris suggested one, I do not remember which. JOHNSON: "We must try its effect as an English poem; that is the way to judge of the merit of a translation: translations are, in general, for people who cannot read the original." GARRICK: "Of all the translations that ever were attempted, I think Elphinston's 'Martial' the most extraordinary. He consulted me upon it, who am a little of an epigrammatist myself, you know. I told him freely, 'You don't seem to have that turn.' I asked him if he was serious; and finding he was, I advised him against publishing. Why, his translation is more difficult to understand than the original. I thought him a man of some talents; but he seems crazy in this." JOHNSON: "Sir, you have done what I had not courage to do. But he did not ask my advice, and I did not force it upon him, to make him angry with me." GARRICK: "But as a friend, Sir——." JOHNSON: "Why, such a friend as I am with him—no." GARRICK: "But if you see a friend going to tumble over a precipice?" JOHNSON: "That is an extravagant case, Sir. You are sure a friend will thank you for hindering him from tumbling over a precipice: but, in the other case, I should hurt his vanity and do him no good. He would not take my advice. His brother-in-law, Strahan, sent him a subscription of £50, and said he would send him £50 more, if he would not publish." GARRICK: "What! eh! is Strahan a good judge of an epigram? Is not he rather an *obtuse* man, eh?" JOHNSON: "Why, Sir, he may not be a judge of an epigram: but you see he is a judge of what is *not* an epigram." BOSWELL: "It is easy for you, Mr. Garrick, to talk to an author as you talked to Elphinston; you, who have been so long the manager of a theatre, rejecting the plays of poor authors. You are an old judge, who have often pronounced sentence of death. You are a practised surgeon, who have often amputated limbs; and though this may have been for the good of your patients, they cannot like you. Those who have undergone a dreadful operation, are not very fond of seeing the operator again."

GARRICK: "Yes, I know enough of that. There was a reverend gentleman (Mr. Hawkins) who wrote a tragedy, the *siege* of something, which I refused." HARRIS: "So, the siege was raised." JOHNSON: "Ay, he came to me and complained; and told me that Garrick said his play was wrong in the *concoction*. Now, what is the concoction of a play?" (Here Garrick started, and twisted himself, and seemed sorely vexed; for Johnson told me he believed the story was true.) GARRICK: "I—I—I—said, *first* concoction." JOHNSON (smiling): "Well, he left out *first*. And Rich, he said, refused him *in false English:* he could show it under his hand." GARRICK: "He wrote to me in violent wrath for having refused his play: 'Sir, this is growing a very serious and terrible affair; I am resolved to publish my play, I will appeal to the world; and how will your judgment appear!' I answered, 'Sir, notwithstanding all the seriousness, and all the terrors, I have no objection to your publishing your play; and as you live at a great distance (Devonshire, I believe), if you will send it to me, I will convey it to the press.' I never heard more of it, ha! ha! ha!"

On Friday, April 10, I found Johnson at home in the morning. We resumed the conversation of yesterday.

He found fault with our friend Langton for having been too silent. "Sir (said I), you will recollect that he very properly took up Sir Joshua for being glad that Charles Fox had praised Goldsmith's 'Traveller,' and you joined him." JOHNSON: "Yes, Sir, I knocked Fox on the head without ceremony. Reynolds is too much under Fox and Burke at present. He is under the *Fox star,* and the *Irish constellation.* He is always under some planet." BOSWELL: "There is no Fox star." JOHNSON: "But there is a Dog star." BOSWELL: "They say, indeed, a fox and a dog are the same animal."

We dined together with Mr. Scott (now Sir William Scott, his Majesty's Advocate General), at his chambers in the Temple, nobody else there. The company being small, Johnson was not in such spirits as he had been the preceding day, and for a considerable time little was said.

Talking of fame, for which there is so great a desire, I observed how little there is of it in reality, compared with the other objects of human attention. "Let every man recollect, and he will be sensible how small a part of his time is employed in talking or thinking of Shakspeare, Voltaire, or any of the most celebrated men that have ever lived, or are now supposed to occupy the attention and admiration of the world. Let this be extracted and compressed; into what a narrow space will it go!" I then slily introduced Mr. Garrick's fame, and his assuming the airs of a great man. JOHNSON: "Sir, it is wonderful how *little* Garrick assumes. No, Sir, Garrick *fortunam reverenter habet.* Consider, Sir; celebrated men, such as you have mentioned, have had their applause at a distance; but Garrick had it dashed in his face, sounded in his ears, and went home every night with the plaudits of a thousand in his *cranium.* Then, Sir, Garrick did not *find,* but *made* his way to the tables, the *levées,* and almost the bedchambers of the great. Then, Sir, Garrick had under him a numerous body of people; who, from fear of his power and hopes of his favour, and admiration of his talents, were constantly submissive to him. And here is a man who has advanced the dignity of his profession. Garrick has made a player a higher character." SCOTT: "And he is a very sprightly writer too." JOHNSON: "Yes, Sir; and all this supported by great wealth, of his own acquisition. If all this had happened to me, I should have had a couple of fellows with long poles walking before me, to knock down everybody that stood in the way. Consider if all this had happened to Cibber or Quin, they'd have jumped over the moon.—Yet Garrick speaks to *us*" (smiling). BOSWELL: "And Garrick is a very good man, a charitable man." JOHNSON: "Sir, a liberal man. He has given away more money than any man in England. There may be a little vanity mixed: but he has shown that money is not his first object."

On the subject of wealth, the proper use of it, and the effects of that art which is called economy, he observed, "It is wonderful to think how men of very large estates not only spend their yearly incomes, but are often actually in want of money. It is clear they have not value for what they spend. Lord Shelburne told me that a man of high rank, who looks into his own affairs, may have all that he ought to have, all that can be of any use, or appear with any advantage, for £5,000 a year. Therefore a great proportion must go in waste; and, indeed, this is the case with most people, whatever their fortune is." BOSWELL: "I have no doubt, Sir, of this. But how is it? What is waste?" JOHNSON: "Why, Sir, breaking bottles, and a thousand other things. Waste cannot be accurately told, though we are sensible how destructive it is. Economy on the one hand, by which a certain income is made to maintain a man genteelly, and waste on the other, by which, on the same income, another man lives shabbily, cannot be defined. It is a very nice thing; as one man wears his coat out much sooner than another, we cannot tell how."

We talked of war. JOHNSON: "Every man thinks meanly of himself for not having been a soldier, or not having been at sea." BOSWELL: "Lord Mansfield does not." JOHNSON: "Sir, if Lord Mansfield were in a company of general officers and admirals who have been in service, he would shrink; he'd wish to creep under the table." BOSWELL: "No; he'd think he could *try* them all." JOHNSON: "Yes, if he could catch them: but they'd try him much sooner. No, Sir; were Socrates and Charles the Twelfth of Sweden both present in any company, and Socrates to say, 'Follow me, and hear a lecture in philosophy'; and Charles, laying his hand on his sword, to say, 'Follow me, and dethrone the Czar'; a man would be ashamed to follow Socrates. Sir, the impression is universal; yet it is strange. As to the sailor, when you look down from the quarter-deck to the space below, you see the utmost extremity of human misery: such crowding, such filth, such stench!" BOSWELL: "Yet sailors are happy." JOHNSON: "They are happy as brutes are happy, with a piece of fresh meat—with the grossest sensuality. But, Sir, the profession of soldiers and sailors has the dignity of danger. Mankind reverence those who have got over fear, which is so general a weakness." SCOTT: "But is not courage mechanical, and to be acquired?" JOHNSON: "Why, yes, Sir, in a collective sense. Soldiers consider themselves only as part of a great machine." SCOTT: "We find people fond of being sailors." JOHNSON: "I cannot account for that, any more than I can account for other strange perversions of imagination."

He expressed great indignation at the imposture of the Cock-lane Ghost, and related, with much satisfaction, how he had assisted in detecting the cheat, and had published an account of it in the newspapers. Upon this subject I incautiously offended him by pressing him with too many questions, and he showed his displeasure. I apologised, saying, "That I asked questions in order to be instructed and entertained; I repaired eagerly to the fountain; but that the moment he gave me a hint, the moment he put a lock upon the well, I desisted."— "But, Sir (said he), that is forcing one to do a disagreeable thing": and he continued to rate me. "Nay, Sir (said I), when you have put a lock upon the well, so that I can no longer drink, do not make the fountain of your wit play upon me and wet me."

He sometimes could not bear being teased with questions. I was once present when a gentleman asked so many, as, "What did you do, Sir?"—"What did you say, Sir?" that he at last grew enraged, and said, "I will not be put to the *question*. Don't you consider, Sir, that these are not the manners of a gentleman? I will not be baited with *what* and *why;* what is this? what is that? why is a cow's tail long? why is a fox's tail bushy?" The gentleman, who was a good deal out of countenance, said, "Why, Sir, you are so good, that I venture to trouble you." JOHNSON: "Sir, my being so *good* is no reason why you should be so *ill*."

He talked, with an uncommon animation, of travelling into distant countries; that the mind was enlarged by it, and that an acquisition of dignity of character was derived from it. He expressed a particular enthusiasm with respect to visiting the wall of China. I catched it for the moment, and said I really believed I should go and see the wall of China had I not children, of whom it was my duty to take care. "Sir (said he), by doing so, you would do what would be of importance in raising your children to eminence. There would be a lustre reflected upon them from your spirit and curiosity. They would be at all times regarded as the children of a man who had gone to view the wall of China. I am serious, Sir."

When we had left Mr. Scott's, he said, "Will you go home with me?" —"Sir (said I), it is late; but I'll go with you for three minutes." JOHNSON: "Or *four*." We went to Mrs. Williams's room, where we found Mr. Allen, the printer, who was the landlord of his house in Bolt-court, a worthy obliging man, and his very old acquaintance; and what was exceedingly amusing, though he was of a very diminutive size, he used, even in Johnson's presence, to imitate the stately periods and slow and solemn utterance of the great man.—I this evening boasted that although I did not write what is called stenography, or shorthand, in appropriated characters devised for the purpose, I had a method of my own of writing half-words, and leaving out some altogether, so as yet to keep the substance and language of any discourse which I had heard so much in view, that I could give it very completely soon after I had taken it down. He defied me, as he had once defied an actual shorthand writer; and he made the experiment by reading slowly and distinctly a part of Robertson's "History of America," while I endeavoured to write it in my way of taking notes. It was found that I had it very imperfectly; the conclusion from which was that its excellence was principally owing to a studied arrangement of words, which could not be varied or abridged without an essential injury.

On Sunday, April 12, I found him at home before dinner; Dr. Dodd's poem, entitled "Thoughts in Prison," was lying upon his table. This appearing to me an extraordinary effort by a man who was in Newgate for a capital crime, I was desirous to hear Johnson's opinion of it: to my surprise, he told me he had not read a line of it. I took up the book, and read a passage to him. JOHNSON: "Pretty well, if you are previously disposed to like them." I read another passage, with which he was better pleased. He then took the book into his own hands, and having looked at the prayer at the end of it, he said, "What *evidence* is there that this was composed the night before he suffered? *I* do not believe it." He then read aloud where he prays for the King, etc., and observed, "Sir, do you think that a man, the night before he is to be hanged, cares for the succession of a royal family?—Though he *may* have composed this prayer, then. A man who has been canting all his life may cant to the last.—And yet, a man who has been refused a pardon after so much petitioning would hardly be praying thus fervently for the King."

He and I, and Mrs. Williams, went to dine with the Reverend Dr. Percy. And here I shall record a scene of too much heat between Dr. Johnson and Dr. Percy, which I should have suppressed, were it not that it gave occasion to display the truly tender and benevolent heart of Johnson, who, as soon as he found a friend was at all hurt by anything which he had "said in his wrath," was not only prompt and desirous to be reconciled, but exerted himself to make ample reparation.

Books of Travels having been mentioned, Johnson praised Pennant very highly, as he did at Dunvegan, in the Isle of Sky. Dr. Percy, knowing himself to be the heir male of the ancient Percies, and having the warmest and most dutiful attachment to the noble House of Northumberland, could not sit quietly and hear a man praised who had spoken disrespectfully of Alnwick-castle and the Duke's pleasure-grounds, especially as he thought meanly of his travels. He therefore opposed Johnson eagerly. JOHNSON: "Pennant, in what he has said of Alnwick, has done what he intended; he has made you very angry." PERCY: "He has said the garden is trim, which is representing it like a citizen's parterre, when the truth is, there is a very large extent of fine turf and gravel walks." JOHNSON: "According to your own account, Sir, Pennant is right. It *is* trim. Here is grass cut close, and gravel rolled smooth. Is not that trim? The extent is nothing against that; a mile may be as trim as a square yard. Your extent puts me in mind of the citizen's enlarged dinner, two pieces of roast beef and two puddings. There is no variety, no mind exerted in laying out the ground, no trees." PERCY: "He pretends to give the natural history of Northumberland, and yet takes no notice of the immense number of trees planted there of late." JOHNSON: "That, Sir, has nothing to do with the *natural* history; that is *civil* history. A man who gives the natural history of the oak is not to tell how many oaks have been planted in this place or that. A man who gives the natural history of the cow is not to tell how many cows are milked at Islington. The animal is the same, whether milked in the Park or at Islington." PERCY: "Pennant does not describe well; a carrier who goes along the side of Lochlomond would describe it better." JOHNSON: "I think he describes very well." PERCY: "I travelled after him." JOHNSON: "And *I* travelled after him." PERCY: "But, my good friend, you are short-sighted, and do not see so well as I do." I wondered at Dr. Percy's venturing thus. Dr. Johnson said nothing at the time: but inflammable particles were collecting for a cloud to burst. In a little while, Dr. Percy said something more in disparagement of Pennant. JOHNSON (pointedly): "This is the resentment of a narrow mind, because he did not find everything in Northumberland." PERCY (feeling the stroke): "Sir, you may be as rude as you please." JOHNSON: "Hold, Sir! Don't talk of rudeness; remember, Sir, you told me (puffing hard with passion struggling for a vent), I was short-sighted. We have done with civility. We are to be as rude as we please." PERCY: "Upon my honour, Sir, I did not mean to be uncivil." JOHNSON: "I cannot say so, Sir; for I *did* mean to be uncivil, thinking *you* had been uncivil." Dr. Percy rose, ran up to him, and taking him by the hand, assured him affectionately that his meaning had been misunderstood; upon which a reconcilation instantly took place. JOHNSON: "My dear Sir, I am willing you shall *hang* Pennant." PERCY (resuming the former subject): "Pennant complains that the helmet is not hung out to invite to the hall of hospitality. Now I never heard that it was a custom to hang out a *helmet*." JOHNSON: "Hang him up, hang him up." BOSWELL (humouring the joke): "Hang out his skull instead of a helmet, and you may drink ale out of it in your hall of Odin, as he is your enemy; that will be truly ancient. *There* will be 'Northern Antiquities.'" JOHNSON: "He's a *Whig*, Sir; a *sad dog* (smiling at his own violent expressions, merely for *political* difference of opinion). But he's the best traveller I ever read; he observes more things than any one else does."

We had a calm after the storm, stayed the evening and supped, and were pleasant and gay. But Dr. Percy told me he was very uneasy at what had passed; for there was a gentleman there who was acquainted with the Northumberland family, to whom he hoped to have appeared more respectable, by showing how intimate he was with Dr. Johnson, and who might now, on the contrary, go away with an opinion to his disadvantage. He begged I would mention this to Dr. Johnson, which I afterwards did. His observation upon it was, "This comes of a *stratagem;* had he told me that he wished to appear to advantage before that gentleman, he should have been at the top of the House all the time." He spoke of Dr. Percy in the handsomest manner. "Then, Sir (said I), may I be allowed to suggest a mode by which you may effectually counteract any unfavourable report of what passed? I will write a letter to you upon the subject of the unlucky contest of that day, and you will be kind enough to put in writing, as an answer to that letter, what you have now said, and as Lord Percy is to dine with us at General Paoli's soon, I will take an opportunity to read the correspondence in his Lordship's presence." This friendly scheme was accordingly carried into execution without Dr. Percy's knowledge. I breakfasted the day after with him, and informed him of my scheme, and its happy completion, for which he thanked me in the warmest terms, and was highly delighted with Dr. Johnson's letter in his praise, of which I gave him a copy. He said, "I would rather have this than degrees from all the Universities in Europe. It will be for me, and my children and grandchildren." Dr. Johnson having afterwards asked me if I had given him a copy of it, and being told I had, was offended, and insisted that I should get it back, which I did. As, however, he did not desire me to destroy either the original or the copy, or forbid me to let it be seen, I think myself at liberty to apply to it his general declaration to me concerning his own letters. "That he did not choose they should be published in his lifetime; but had no objection to their appearing after his death." I shall therefore insert this kindly correspondence, having faithfully narrated the circumstances accompanying it.

"TO JAMES BOSWELL, ESQ.

"Sir,—

"The debate between Dr. Percy and me is one of those foolish controversies which begin upon a question of which neither party cares how it is decided, and which is, nevertheless, continued to acrimony, by the vanity with which every man resists confutation. Dr. Percy's warmth proceeded from a cause which, perhaps, does him more honour than he could have derived from juster criticism. His abhorrence of Pennant proceeded from his opinion that Pennant had wantonly and indecently censured his patron. His anger made him resolve that, for having been once wrong, he never should be right. Pennant has much in his notions that I do not like; but still I think him a very intelligent traveller. If Percy is really offended, I am sorry; for he is a man whom I never knew to offend any one. He is a man very willing to learn, and very able to teach; a man, out of whose company I never go without having learned something. It is sure that he vexes me sometimes, but I am afraid it is by making me feel my own ignorance. So much extension of mind, and so much minute accuracy of inquiry, if you survey your whole circle of acquaintance, you will find so scarce, if you find it at all, that you will value Percy by comparison. Lord Hailes is somewhat like him: but Lord Hailes does not, perhaps, go beyond him in research; and I do not know that he equals him in elegance. Percy's attention to poetry has given grace and splendour to his studies of antiquity. A mere antiquarian is a rugged being.

"Upon the whole, you see that what I might say in sport or petulance to him, is very consistent with full conviction of his merit.

"I am, dear Sir,

"Your most, etc.,

"SAM. JOHNSON.

"April 23, 1778."

"TO THE REVEREND DOCTOR PERCY, NORTHUMBERLAND-HOUSE.

"DEAR SIR,—

"I wrote to Dr. Johnson on the subject of the *Pennantian* controversy: and have received from him an answer which will delight you. I read it yesterday to Dr. Robertson, at the exhibition; and at dinner to Lord Percy, General Oglethorpe, etc., who dined with us at General Paoli's; who was also a witness to the high *testimony* to your honour.

"General Paoli desires the favour of your company next Tuesday to dinner, to meet Dr. Johnson. If I can, I will call on you to-day. I am, with sincere regard,

"Your most obedient humble servant,

"JAMES BOSWELL.

"South Audley-street, April 25."

On Monday, April 13, I dined with Johnson at Mr. Langton's, where were Dr. Porteus, then Bishop of Chester, now of London, and Dr. Stinton. He was at first in a very silent mood. Before dinner he said nothing but "Pretty Baby," to one of the children.

Mr. Topham Beauclerk came in the evening, and he and Dr. Johnson and I stayed to supper. It was mentioned that Dr. Dodd had once wished to be a member of the Literary Club. JOHNSON: "I should be sorry if any of our Club were hanged. I will not say but some of them deserve it." Beauclerk (supposing this to be aimed at persons for whom he had at that time a wonderful fancy, which, however, did not last long) was irritated, and eagerly said: "You, Sir, have a friend (naming him) who deserves to be hanged; for he speaks behind their backs against those with whom he lives on the best terms, and attacks them in the newspapers. *He* certainly ought to be *kicked*." JOHNSON: "Sir, we all do this in some degree: *'Veniam petimus damusque vicissim.'* To be sure it may be done so much, that a man may deserve to be kicked." BEAUCLERK: "He is very malignant." JOHNSON: "No, Sir; he is not malignant. He is mischievous, if you will. He would do no man an essential injury; he may, indeed, love to make sport of people by vexing their vanity. I, however, once knew an old gentleman who was absolutely malignant. He really wished evil to others, and rejoiced at it." BOSWELL: "The gentleman, Mr. Beauclerk, against whom you are so violent, is, I know, a man of good principles." BEAUCLERK: "Then he does not wear them out in practice."

CHAPTER XLI—1778

Johnson and Edwards

ON WEDNESDAY, APRIL 15, I dined with Dr. Johnson at Mr. Dilly's, and was in high spirits, for I had been a good part of the morning with Mr. Orme, the able and eloquent historian of Hindostan, who expressed a great admiration of Johnson. "I do not care (said he) on what subject Johnson talks; but I love better to hear him talk than anybody. He either gives you new thoughts, or a new colouring. It is a shame to the nation that he has not been more liberally rewarded. Had I been George the Third, and thought as he did about America, I would have given Johnson three hundred a year for his

'Taxation no Tyranny,' alone." I repeated this, and Johnson was much pleased with such praise from such a man as Orme.

At Mr. Dilly's to-day were Mrs. Knowles, the ingenious Quaker lady, Miss Seward, the poetess of Lichfield, the Reverend Dr. Mayo, and the Rev. Mr. Beresford, tutor to the Duke of Bedford. Before dinner, Dr. Johnson seized upon Mr. Charles Sheridan's "Account of the late Revolution in Sweden," and seemed to read it ravenously, as if he devoured it, which was to all appearance his method of studying. "He knows how to read better than any one (said Mrs. Knowles); he gets at the substance of a book directly; he tears out the heart of it." He kept it wrapt up in the tablecloth in his lap during the time of dinner, from an avidity to have one entertainment in readiness, when he should have finished another; resembling (if I may use so coarse a simile) a dog who holds a bone in his paws in reserve, while he eats something else which has been thrown to him.

The subject of cookery having been very naturally introduced at a table where Johnson, who boasted of the niceness of his palate, owned that "he always found a good dinner," he said, "I could write a better book of cookery than has ever yet been written; it should be a book upon philosophical principles. Pharmacy is now made much more simple. Cookery may be made so too. A prescription which is now compounded of five ingredients, had formerly fifty in it. So in cookery, if the nature of the ingredients be well known, much fewer will do. Then, as you cannot make bad meat good, I would tell what is the best butcher's meat, the best beef, the best pieces; how to choose young fowls; the proper seasons of different vegetables; and then how to roast, and boil, and compound." DILLY: "Mrs. Glasse's 'Cookery,' which is the best, was written by Dr. Hill. Half the *trade* know this." JOHNSON: "Well, Sir. This shows how much better the subject of cookery may be treated by a philosopher. I doubt if the book be written by Dr. Hill; for, in Mrs. Glasse's 'Cookery,' which I have looked into, saltpetre and sal-prunella are spoken of as different substances, whereas sal-prunella is only saltpetre burnt on charcoal; and Hill could not be ignorant of this. However, as the greatest part of such a book is made by transcription, this mistake may have been carelessly adopted. But you shall see what a book of cookery I shall make. I shall agree with Mr. Dilly for the copyright." MISS SEWARD: "That would be Hercules with the distaff indeed." JOHNSON: "No, Madam. Women can spin very well; but they cannot make a good book of cookery."

Mrs. Knowles affected to complain that men had much more liberty allowed them than women. JOHNSON: "Why, Madam, women have all the liberty they should wish to have. We have all the labour and the danger, and the women all the advantage. We go to sea, we build houses, we do everything, in short, to pay our court to the women." MRS. KNOWLES: "The Doctor reasons very wittily, but not convincingly. Now, take the instance of building; the mason's wife, if she is ever seen in liquor, is ruined; the mason may get himself drunk as often as he pleases, with little loss of character; nay, may let his wife and children starve." JOHNSON: "Madam, you must consider, if the mason does get himself drunk, and let his wife and children starve, the parish will oblige him to find security for their maintenance. We have different modes of restraining evil. Stocks for the men, a ducking-stool for women, and a pound for beasts. If we require more perfection from women than from ourselves, it is doing them honour. And women have not the same temptations that we have; they may always live in virtuous company: men must mix in the world indiscriminately. If a woman has no inclination to do what is wrong, being secured from it is no restraint to her. I am at liberty to walk into the Thames; but if I were to try it, my friends would restrain me in Bedlam, and I should be obliged to them." MRS. KNOWLES: "Still, Doctor, I cannot help thinking it a hardship that more indulgence is allowed to men than to women. It gives a superiority to men, to which I do not see how they are entitled." JOHNSON: "It is plain, Madam, one or other must have the superiority. As Shakspeare says, 'If two men ride on a horse, one must ride behind.'" DILLY: "I suppose, Sir, Mrs. Knowles would have them ride in panniers, one on each side." JOHNSON: "Then, Sir, the horse would throw them both."

Dr. Mayo having asked Johnson's opinion of Soame Jenyns's "View of the Internal Evidence of the Christian Religion";—JOHNSON: "I think it a pretty book; not very theological, indeed; and there seems to be an affectation of ease and carelessness, as if it were not suitable to his character to be very serious about the matter." BOSWELL: "He may have intended this to introduce his book the better among genteel people, who might be unwilling to read too grave a treatise. There is a general levity in the age. We have physicians, now, with bag-wigs; may we not have airy divines, at least somewhat less solemn in their appearance than they used to be?" JOHNSON: "Jenyns might mean as you say." BOSWELL: "*You* should like his book, Mrs. Knowles, as it maintains, as you *friends* do, that

[458]

courage is not a Christian virtue." MRS. KNOWLES: "Yes, indeed, I like him there; but I cannot agree with him that friendship is not a Christian virtue." JOHNSON: "Why, Madam, strictly speaking, he is right. All friendship is preferring the interest of a friend to the neglect, or, perhaps, against the interest of others; so that an old Greek said, 'He that has *friends* has *no friend.*' Now Christianity recommends universal benevolence—to consider all men as our brethren; which is contrary to the virtue of friendship, as described by the ancient philosophers. Surely, Madam, your sect must approve of this; for, you call all men *friends.*" MRS. KNOWLES: "We are commanded to do good to all men, 'but especially to them who are of the household of Faith.' " JOHNSON: "Well, Madam. The household of Faith is wide enough." MRS. KNOWLES: "But, Doctor, our Saviour had twelve Apostles, yet there was *one* whom he *loved.* John was called 'the disciple whom Jesus loved.' " JOHNSON (with eyes sparkling benignantly): "Very well, indeed, Madam. You have said very well." BOSWELL: "A fine application. Pray, Sir, had you ever thought of it?" JOHNSON: "I had not, Sir."

From this pleasing subject, he, I know not how or why, made a sudden transition to one upon which he was a violent aggressor; for he said, "I am willing to love all mankind, *except an American*"; and his inflammable corruption bursting into horrid fire, he "breathed out threatenings and slaughter"; calling them, "rascals—robbers—pirates"; and exclaiming, he'd "burn and destroy them." Miss Seward, looking to him with mild but steady astonishment, said, "Sir, this is an instance that we are always most violent against those whom we have injured."—He was irritated still more by this delicate and keen reproach; and roared out another tremendous volley, which one might fancy could be heard across the Atlantic. During this tempest, I sat in great uneasiness, lamenting his heat of temper; till, by degrees, I diverted his attention to other topics.

Talking of Miss [Hannah More], a literary lady, he said, "I was obliged to speak to Miss Reynolds, to let her know that I desired she would not flatter me so much." Somebody now observed, "She flatters Garrick." JOHNSON: "She is in the right to flatter Garrick. She is in the right for two reasons; first, because she has the world with her, who have been praising Garrick these thirty years; and, secondly, because she is rewarded for it by Garrick. Why should she flatter *me?* I can do nothing for her. Let her carry her praise to a better market. (Then turning to Mrs. Knowles): You, Madam, have been flattering me all the evening; I wish you would give Boswell a little now. If you knew his merit as well as I do, you would say a great deal; he is the best travelling companion in the world."

Somebody mentioned the Reverend Mr. Mason's prosecution of Mr. Murray, the bookseller, for having inserted a collection of "Gray's Poems," only fifty lines, of which Mr. Mason had still the exclusive property, under the statute of Queen Anne; and that Mr. Mason had persevered, notwithstanding his being requested to name his own terms of compensation. Johnson signified his displeasure at Mr. Mason's conduct very strongly; but added, by way of showing that he was not surprised at it, "Mason's a Whig." MRS. KNOWLES (not hearing distinctly): "What! a Prig, Sir?" JOHNSON: "Worse, Madam; a Whig! But he is both."

We remained together till it was pretty late. Notwithstanding occasional explosions of violence, we were all delighted upon the whole with Johnson. I compared him at this time to a warm West-Indian climate, where you have a bright sun, quick vegetation, luxuriant foliage, luscious fruits; but where the same heat sometimes produces thunder, lightning, earthquakes, in a terrible degree.

April 17, being Good-Friday, I waited on Johnson, as usual. I observed at breakfast that although it was a part of his abstemious discipline, on this most solemn fast, to take no milk in his tea, when Mrs. Desmoulins inadvertently poured it in, he did not reject it. I talked of the strange indecision of mind, and imbecility in the common occurrences of life, which we may observe in some people. JOHNSON: "Why, Sir, I am in the habit of getting others to do things for me." BOSWELL: "What, Sir, have you that weakness?" JOHNSON: "Yes, Sir. But I always think afterwards I should have done better for myself."

I expressed some inclination to publish an account of my travels upon the continent of Europe, for which I had a variety of materials collected. JOHNSON: "I do not say, Sir, you may not publish your travels; but I give you my opinion, that you would lessen yourself by it. What can you tell of countries so well known as those upon the continent of Europe, which you have visited?" BOSWELL: "But I can give an entertaining narrative, with many incidents, anecdotes, *jeux d'esprit*, and remarks, so as to make very pleasant reading." JOHNSON: "Why, Sir, most modern travellers in Europe, who have published their travels, have been laughed at: I would not have you added to the number. The world is now not contented to be merely entertained by a traveller's narrative; they want to learn something. Now, some of my friends asked me why I did not give some account of my travels in France. The reason is plain; intelligent readers had seen more of France than I had. *You* might have liked my travels in France, and the Club might have liked them; but, upon the whole, there would have been more ridicule than good produced by them." BOSWELL: "I cannot agree with you, Sir. People would like to read what you say of anything. Suppose a face has been painted by fifty painters before; still we love to see it done by Sir Joshua." JOHNSON: "True, Sir; but Sir Joshua cannot paint a face when he has not time to look on it." BOSWELL: "Sir, a sketch of any sort by him is valuable. And, Sir, to talk to you in your own style (raising my voice, and shaking my head), you *should* have given us your Travels in France. I am *sure* I am right, and *there's an end on't.*"

There was a very numerous congregation to-day at St. Clement's Church, which Dr. Johnson said he observed with pleasure.

And now I am to give a pretty full account of one of the most curious incidents in Johnson's life, of which he himself has made the following minute on this day: "In my return from church, I was accosted by Edwards, an old fellow-collegian, who had not seen me since 1729. He knew me, and asked if I remembered one Edwards; I did not at first recollect the name, but gradually, as we walked along, recovered it, and told him a conversation that had passed at an ale-house between us. My purpose is to continue our acquaintance."

It was in Butcher-row that this meeting happened. Mr. Edwards, who was a decent-looking elderly man in gray clothes, and a wig of many curls, accosted Johnson with familiar confidence, knowing who he was, while Johnson returned his salutation with a courteous formality, as to a stranger. But as soon as Edwards had brought to his recollection their having been at Pembroke College together nine-and-forty years ago, he seemed much pleased, asked where he lived, and said he should be glad to see him at Bolt-court. EDWARDS: "Ah, Sir! we are old men now." JOHNSON (who never liked to think of being old): "Don't let us discourage one another." EDWARDS: "Why, Doctor, you look stout and hearty. I am happy to see you so; for the newspapers told us you were very ill." JOHNSON: "Ay, Sir, they are always telling lies of *us old fellows.*"

Wishing to be present at more of so singular a conversation as that between two fellow-collegians, who had lived forty years in London without ever having chanced to meet, I whispered to Mr. Edwards that Dr. Johnson was going home, and that he had better accompany him now. So Edwards walked along with us, I eagerly assisting to keep up the conversation. Mr. Edwards informed Dr. Johnson that he had practised long as a solicitor in Chancery, but that he now lived in the country upon a little farm, about sixty acres, just by Stevenage in Hertfordshire, and that he came to London (to Barnard's-inn, No. 6) generally twice a week. Johnson appearing to be in a reverie, Mr. Edwards addressed himself to me, and expatiated on the pleasure of living in the country. BOSWELL: "I have no notion of this, Sir. What you have to entertain you, is, I think, exhausted in half-an-hour." EDWARDS: "What! don't you love to have hope realised? I see my grass, and my corn, and my trees growing. Now, for instance, I am curious to see if this frost has not nipped my fruit-trees." JOHNSON (who we did not imagine was attending): "You find, Sir, you have fears as well as hopes."

So well did he see the whole, when another saw but the half of a subject.

When we got to Dr. Johnson's house, and were seated in his library, the dialogue went on admirably. EDWARDS: "Sir, I remember you would not let us say *prodigious* at College. For, even then, Sir (turning to me), he was delicate in language, and we all feared him." JOHNSON (to Edwards): "From your having practised the law long, Sir, I presume you must be rich." EDWARDS: "No, Sir; I got a good deal of money; but I had a number of poor relations, to whom I gave great part of it." JOHNSON: "Sir, you have been rich in the most valuable sense of the word." EDWARDS: "But I shall not die rich." JOHNSON: "Nay, sure, Sir, it is better to *live* rich, than to *die* rich." EDWARDS: "I wish I had continued at college." JOHNSON: "Why do you wish that, Sir?" EDWARDS: "Because I think I should have had a much easier life than mine has been. I should have been a parson, and had a good living, like Bloxham and several others, and lived comfortably." JOHNSON: "Sir, the life of a parson, of a conscientious clergyman, is not easy. I have always considered a clergyman as the father of a larger family than he is able to maintain. I would rather have Chancery suits upon my hands than the cure of souls. No, Sir, I do not envy a clergyman's life as an easy life, nor do I envy the clergyman who makes it an easy life."

EDWARDS: "I have been twice married, Doctor. You, I suppose, have never known what it was to have a wife." JOHNSON: "Sir, I have known what it was to have a wife, and (in a solemn, tender, faltering tone) I have known what it was to *lose a wife.*—It had almost broke my heart."

This interview confirmed my opinion of Johnson's most humane and benevolent heart. His cordial and placid behaviour to an old fellow-collegian, a man so different from himself, and his telling him that he would go down to his farm and visit him, showed a kindness of disposition very rare at an advanced age. He observed "how wonderful it was that they had both been in London forty years, without having ever once met, and both walkers in the street, too!" Mr. Edwards, when going away, again recurred to his consciousness of senility, and looking full in Johnson's face, said to him, "You'll find in Dr. Young,

'O, my coevals! remnants of yourselves.' "

Johnson did not relish this at all; but shook his head with impatience. Edwards walked off, seemingly highly pleased with the honour of having been thus noticed by Dr. Johnson. When he was gone, I said to Johnson, I thought him but a weak man. JOHNSON: "Why, yes, Sir. Here is a man who has passed through life without experience; yet I would rather have him with me than a more sensible man who will not talk readily. This man is always willing to say what he has to say."

Mr. Edwards had said to me aside that Dr. Johnson should have been of a profession. I repeated the remark to Johnson that I might have his own thoughts on the subject. JOHNSON: "Sir, it *would* have been better that I had been of a profession. I ought to have been a lawyer." BOSWELL: "I do not think, Sir, it would have been better, for we should not have had the English Dictionary." JOHNSON: "But you would have had Reports." BOSWELL: "Ay; but there would not have been another who could have written the Dictionary. There would have been many very good judges. Suppose you had been Lord Chancellor; you would have delivered opinions with more extent of mind, and in a more ornamented manner, than perhaps any Chancellor ever did, or ever will do. But, I believe, causes have been as judiciously decided as you could have done." JOHNSON: "Yes, Sir. Property has been well settled."

Johnson, however, had a noble ambition floating in his mind, and had, undoubtedly, often speculated on the possibility of his supereminent powers being rewarded in this great and liberal country by the highest honours of the state. Sir William Scott informed me that, upon the death of the late Lord Lichfield, who was Chancellor of the University of Oxford, he said to Johnson, "What a pity it is, Sir, that you did not follow the profession of the law. You might have been Lord Chancellor of Great Britain, and attained to the dignity of the peerage; and now that the title of Lichfield, your native city, is extinct, you might have had it." Johnson, upon this, seemed much agitated; and, in an angry tone, exclaimed, "Why will you vex me by suggesting this, when it is too late?"

Yet no man had a higher notion of the dignity of literature than Johnson, or was more determined in maintaining the respect which he justly considered as due to it. Of this, besides the general tenour of his conduct in society, some characteristical instances may be mentioned.

He told Sir Joshua Reynolds that once when he dined in a numerous company of booksellers, where, the room being small, the head of the table, at which he sat, was almost close to the fire, he persevered in suffering a great deal of inconvenience from the heat, rather than quit his place, and let one of them sit above him.

Goldsmith, in his diverting simplicity, complained one day, in a mixed company, of Lord Camden. "I met him (said he) at Lord Clare's house, in the country, and he took no more notice of me than if I had been an ordinary man." The company having laughed heartily, Johnson stood forth in defence of his friend. "Nay, gentlemen (said he), Dr. Goldsmith is in the right. Noblemen ought to have made up to such a man as Goldsmith; and I think it is much against Lord Camden that he neglected him."

We went to St. Clement's Church again in the afternoon, and then returned and drank tea and coffee in Mrs. Williams's room; Mrs. Desmoulins doing the honours of the tea-table. I observed that he would not even look at a proof-sheet of his "Life of Waller" on Good Friday.

The gentlemen who had dined with us at Dr. Percy's came in. Johnson attacked the Americans with intemperate vehemence of abuse. I said something in their favour; and added that I was always sorry when he talked on that subject. This, it seems, exasperated him; though he said nothing at the time. The cloud was charged with sulphureous vapour, which was afterwards to burst in thunder.— We talked of a gentleman [Langton] who was running out his fortune in London; and I said, "We must get him out of it. All his friends must quarrel with him, and that will soon drive him away."

JOHNSON: "Nay, Sir, we'll send *you* to him. If your company does not drive a man out of his house, nothing will." This was a horrible shock, for which there was no visible cause. I afterwards asked him why he had said so harsh a thing. JOHNSON: "Because, Sir, you made me angry about the Americans." BOSWELL: "But why did you not take your revenge directly?" JOHNSON (smiling): "Because, Sir, I had nothing ready. A man cannot strike till he has weapons." This was a candid and pleasant confession.

He showed me to-night his drawing-room, very genteelly fitted up; and said, "Mrs. Thrale sneered when I talked of my having asked you and your lady to live at my house. I was obliged to tell her that you would be in as respectable a situation in my house as in hers. Sir, the insolence of wealth will creep out." BOSWELL: "She has a little both of the insolence of wealth and the conceit of parts." JOHNSON: "The insolence of wealth is a wretched thing; but the conceit of parts has some foundation. To be sure, it should not be. But who is without it?" BOSWELL: "Yourself, Sir." JOHNSON: "Why, I play no tricks: I lay no traps." BOSWELL: "No, Sir. You are six feet high, and you only do not stoop."

CHAPTER XLII—1778

Dinner at Allan Ramsay's

ON MONDAY, APRIL 20, I found him at home in the morning. We talked of a gentleman [Langton] who we apprehended was gradually involving his circumstances by bad management. JOHNSON: "Wasting a fortune is evaporation by a thousand imperceptible means. If it were a stream, they'd stop it. You must speak to him. It is really miserable. Were he a gamester, it could be said he had hopes of winning. Were he a bankrupt in trade, he might have grown rich; but he has neither spirit to spend, nor resolution to spare. He does not spend fast enough to have pleasure from it. He has the crime of prodigality, and the wretchedness of parsimony. If a man is killed in a duel, he is killed as many a one has been killed; but it is a sad thing for a man to lie down and die; to bleed to death, because he has not fortitude enough to sear the wound, or even to stitch it up."

On Saturday, April 25, I dined with him at Sir Joshua Reynolds's, with the learned Dr. Musgrave, Counsellor Leyland of Ireland, son to the historian, Mrs. Cholmondeley, and some more ladies.

Mrs. Cholmondeley, in a high flow of spirits, exhibited some lively sallies of hyperbolical compliment to Johnson, with whom she had been long acquainted, and was very easy. He was quick in catching the *manner* of the moment, and answered her somewhat in the style of the hero of a romance, "Madam, you crown me with unfading laurels."

We went to the drawing-room, where was a considerable increase of company. Several of us got round Dr. Johnson, and complained that he would not give us an exact catalogue of his works, that there might be a complete edition. He smiled, and evaded our entreaties. That he intended to do it, I have no doubt, because I have heard him say so; and I have in my possession an imperfect list, fairly written out, which he entitles *Historia Studorium*. I once got from one of his friends a list, which there was pretty good reason to suppose was accurate, for it was written down in his presence by this friend, who enumerated each article aloud, and had some of them mentioned to him by Mr. Levett, in concert with whom it was made out; and Johnson, who heard all this, did not contradict it. But when I showed a copy of this list to him, and mentioned the evidence for its exactness, he laughed and said, "I was willing to let them go on as they pleased, and never interfered." Upon which I read it to him, article by article, and got him positively to own or refuse; and then, having obtained certainty so far, I got some other articles confirmed by him directly, and afterwards, from time to time, made additions under his sanction.

He observed, "A man cannot with propriety speak of himself, except he relates simple facts; as, 'I was at Richmond': or what depends on mensuration; as, 'I am six feet high.' He is sure he has been at Richmond; he is sure he is six feet high; but he cannot be sure he is wise, or that he has any other excellence. Then, all censure of a man's self is oblique praise. It is in order to show how much he can spare. It has all the invidiousness of self-praise, and all the reproach of falsehood." BOSWELL: "Sometimes it may proceed from a man's strong consciousness of his faults being observed. He knows that others would throw him down, and therefore he had better lie down softly of his own accord."

On Tuesday, April 28, he was engaged to dine at General Paoli's, where, as I have already observed, I was still entertained in elegant hospitality, and with all the ease and comfort of a home. I called on him, and accompanied him in a hackney-coach. We stopped first at the bottom of Hedge-lane, into which he went to leave a letter, "with good news for a poor man in distress," as he told me. I did not question him particularly as to this. He himself often resembled Lady Boling-broke's lively description of Pope: that "he was *un politique aux chous et aux raves.*" He would say, "I dine to-day in Grosvenor-square"; this might be with a Duke; or, perhaps, "I dine to-day at the other end of the town": or, "A gentleman of great eminence called on me yester-day."—He loved thus to keep things floating in conjecture: *Omne ignotum pro magnifico est.* I believe I ventured to dissipate the cloud, to unveil the mystery, more freely and frequently than any of his friends. We stopped again at Wirgman's, the well-known *toy-shop,* in St. James's-street, at the corner of St. James's-place, to which he had been directed, but not clearly, for he searched about some time, and could not find it at first; and said, "To direct one only to a corner shop, is *toying* with one." I suppose he meant this as a play upon the word *toy;* it was the first time that I knew him stoop to such sport. After he had been some time in the shop, he sent to me to come out of the coach, and help him to choose a pair of silver buckles, as those he had were too small. Probably this alteration in dress had been suggested by Mrs. Thrale, by associating with whom, his external appearance was much improved. He got better clothes; and the dark colour from which he never deviated was enlivened by metal buttons. His wigs, too, were much better; and, during their travels in France, he was furnished with a Paris-made wig, of handsome construction. This choosing of silver buckles was a negotiation: "Sir (said he), I will not have the ridiculous large ones now in fashion; and I will give no more than a guinea for a pair." Such were the *principles* of the business; and, after some examination, he was fitted. As we drove along, I found him in a talking humour, of which I availed myself. BOSWELL: "I was this morning in Ridley's shop, Sir, and was told that the collection called '*Johnsoniana*' has sold very much." JOHNSON: "Yet the 'Journey to the Hebrides' has not had a great sale." BOSWELL: "That is strange." JOHNSON: "Yes, Sir; for in that book I have told the world a great deal that they did not know before."

At General Paoli's were Sir Joshua Reynolds, Mr. Langton, Mar-chese Gherardi of Lombardy, and Mr. John Spottiswoode the younger, of Spottiswoode, the solicitor. At this time fears of invasion were cir-culated; to obviate which, Mr. Spottiswoode observed that Mr. Fraser, the engineer, who had lately come from Dunkirk, said that the French had the same fears of us. JOHNSON: "It is thus that mutual cowardice keeps us in peace. Were one half of mankind brave, and one half cowards, the brave would be always beating the cowards. Were all brave, they would lead a very uneasy life; all would be continually fighting: but being all cowards we go on very well."

We talked of drinking wine. JOHNSON: "I require wine only when I am alone. I have then often wished for it, and often taken it." SPOTTISWOODE: "What, by way of a companion, Sir?" JOHNSON: "To get rid of myself, to send myself away. Wine gives great pleasure; and every pleasure is of itself a good. It is a good, unless counterbalanced by evil. A man may have a strong reason not to drink wine; and that may be greater than the pleasure. Wine makes a man better pleased with himself. I do not say that it makes him more pleasing to others. Sometimes it does. But the danger is, that while a man grows better pleased with himself, he may be growing less pleasing to others. Wine gives a man nothing. It neither gives him knowledge nor wit; it only animates a man, and enables him to bring out what a dread of the company has repressed. It only puts in motion what has been locked up in frost. But this may be good, or it may be bad." SPOTTISWOODE: "So, Sir, wine is a key which opens a box; but this box may be either full or empty?" JOHNSON: "Nay, Sir, conversation is the key: wine is a pick-lock, which forces open the box, and injures it. A man should cultivate his mind, so as to have that confidence and readiness without wine, which wine gives." BOSWELL: "The great difficulty of resisting wine is from benevolence. For instance, a good, worthy man asks you to taste his wine, which he has had twenty years in his cellar." JOHNSON: "Sir, all this notion about benevolence arises from a man's imagining himself to be of more importance to others than he really is. They don't care a farthing whether he drinks wine or not." SIR JOSHUA REYNOLDS: "Yes, they do for the time." JOHNSON: "For the time!—if they care this minute they forget it the next. And as for the good, worthy man; how do you know he is good and worthy? No good and worthy man will insist upon another man's drinking wine. As to the wine twenty years in the cellar—of ten men, three say this, merely because they must say something; three are telling a lie, when they say they have had the wine twenty years;—three would rather save the wine;—one, perhaps, cares. I allow it is something to please one's company; and people are always pleased with those who partake pleasure with them. But after a man has brought himself to relinquish the great personal pleasure which arises from drinking wine, any other consideration is a trifle. To please others by drinking wine, is something only, if there be nothing against it."

I was at this time myself a water-drinker, upon trial, by Johnson's recommendation. JOHNSON: "Boswell is a bolder combatant than Sir Joshua: he argues for wine without the help of wine; but Sir Joshua with it." SIR JOSHUA REYNOLDS: "But to please one's company is a strong motive." JOHNSON (who, from drinking only water, supposed everybody who drunk wine to be elevated): "I won't argue any more with you, Sir. You are too far gone." SIR JOSHUA: "I should have thought so indeed, Sir, had I made such a speech as you have now done." JOHNSON (drawing himself in, and I really thought blushing): "Nay, don't be angry. I did not mean to offend you." SIR JOSHUA: "At first the taste of wine was disagreeable to me; but I brought myself to drink it, that I might be like other people. The pleasure of drinking wine is so connected with pleasing your company, that altogether there is something of social goodness in it." JOHNSON: "Sir, this is only saying the same thing over again." SIR JOSHUA: "No, this is new." JOHNSON: "You put it in new words, but it is an old thought. This is one of the disadvantages of wine, it makes a man mistake words for thoughts." BOSWELL: "I think it is a new thought; at least, it is in a new *attitude*." JOHNSON: "Nay, Sir, it is only in a new coat; or an old coat with a new facing. (Then, laughing heartily), It is the old dog in a new doublet.—An extraordinary instance, however, may occur where a man's patron will do nothing for him, unless he will drink; *there* may be a good reason for drinking."

On Wednesday, April 29, I dined with him at Mr. Allan Ramsay's, where were Lord Binning, Dr. Robertson the historian, Sir Joshua Reynolds, and the Honourable Mrs. Boscawen, widow of the Admiral, and mother of the present Viscount Falmouth; of whom, if it be not presumptuous in me to praise her, I would say that her manners are the most agreeable, and her conversation the best, of any lady with whom I ever had the happiness to be acquainted. Before Johnson came, we talked a good deal of him; Ramsay said he had always found him a very polite man, and that he treated him with great respect, which he did very sincerely. I said I worshipped him. ROBERTSON: "But some of you spoil him: you should not worship him; you should worship no man." BOSWELL: "I cannot help worshipping him, he is so much superior to other men." ROBERTSON: "In criticism, and in wit and conversation, he is no doubt very excellent; but in other respects

he is not above other men; he will believe anything, and will strenuously defend the most minute circumstances connected with the Church
of England." Boswell: "Believe me, Doctor, you are much mistaken
as to this; for when you talk with him calmly in private, he is very
liberal in his way of thinking." Robertson: "He and I have been
always very gracious; the first time I met him was one evening at
Strahan's, when he had just had an unlucky altercation with Adam
Smith, to whom he had been so rough, that Strahan, after Smith was
gone, had remonstrated with him, and told him that I was coming
soon, and that he was uneasy to think that he might behave in the
same manner to me. 'No, no, Sir (said Johnson), I warrant you,
Robertson and I shall do very well.' Accordingly, he was gentle and
good-humoured and courteous with me, the whole evening; and he
has been so upon every occasion that we have met since. I have often
said (laughing) that I have been in a great measure indebted to Smith
for my good reception." Boswell: "His power of reasoning is very
strong, and he has a peculiar art of drawing characters, which is as
rare as good portrait-painting." Sir Joshua Reynolds: "He is undoubtedly admirable in this; but, in order to mark the characters
which he draws, he overcharges them, and gives people more than they
really have, whether of good or bad."

No sooner did he, of whom we had been thus talking so easily, arrive,
than we were all as quiet as a school upon the entrance of the head
master; and were very soon sat down to a table covered with such
variety of good things, as contributed not a little to dispose him to be
pleased.

Dr. Robertson expatiated on the character of a certain nobleman
[Lord Clive]; that he was one of the strongest minded men that ever
lived; that he would sit in company quite sluggish, while there was
nothing to call forth his intellectual vigour; but the moment that any
important subject was started, for instance, how this country is to be
defended against a French invasion, he would rouse himself, and show
his extraordinary talents with the most powerful ability and animation.
Johnson: "Yet this man cut his own throat. The true strong and
sound mind is the mind that can embrace equally great things and
small. Now I am told the King of Prussia will say to a servant, 'Bring
me a bottle of such a wine, which came in such a year; it lies in such a
corner of the cellars.' I would have a man great in great things, and
elegant in little things." He said to me afterwards, when we were by
ourselves, "Robertson was in a mighty romantic humour; he talked

of one whom he did not know; but I *downed* him with the King of Prussia." "Yes, Sir (said I), you threw a *bottle* at his head."

An ingenious gentleman was mentioned, concerning whom both Robertson and Ramsay agreed that he had a constant firmness of mind; for after a laborious day, and amidst a multiplicity of cares and anxieties, he would sit down with his sisters, and be quite cheerful and good-humoured. Such a disposition, it was observed, was a happy gift of nature. JOHNSON: "I do not think so; a man has from nature a certain portion of mind; the use he makes of it depends upon his own free will. That a man has always the same firmness of mind, I do not say; because every man feels his mind less firm at one time than another; but I think a man's being in a good or bad humour depends upon his will."—I, however, could not help thinking that a man's humour is often uncontrollable by his will.

Johnson harangued against drinking wine. "A man (said he) may choose whether he will have abstemiousness and knowledge, or claret and ignorance." Dr. Robertson (who is very companionable) was beginning to dissent as to the proscription of claret. JOHNSON (with a placid smile): "Nay, Sir, you shall not differ with me; as I have said that the man is most perfect who takes in the most things, I am for knowledge and claret." ROBERTSON (holding a glass of generous claret in his hand): "Sir, I can only drink your health." JOHNSON: "Sir, I should be sorry if *you* should be ever in such a state as to be able to do nothing more." ROBERTSON: "Dr. Johnson, allow me to say that in one respect I have the advantage of you; when you were in Scotland, you would not come to hear any of our preachers; whereas, when I am here, I attend your public worship without scruple, and, indeed, with great satisfaction." JOHNSON: "Why, Sir, that is not so extraordinary: the King of Siam sent ambassadors to Louis the Fourteenth; but Louis the Fourteenth sent none to the King of Siam."

Here my friend for once discovered a want of knowledge or forgetfulness; for Louis the Fourteenth did send an embassy to the King of Siam, and the Abbé Choisi, who was employed in it, published an account of it in two volumes.

Next day, Thursday, April 30, I found him at home by himself. JOHNSON: "Well, Sir, Ramsay gave us a splendid dinner. I love Ramsay. You will not find a man in whose conversation there is more instruction, more information, and more elegance, than in Ramsay's." BOSWELL: "What I admire in Ramsay, is his continuing to be so young." JOHNSON: "Why, yes, Sir, it is to be admired. I value myself upon this, that there is nothing of the old man in my conversation. I am now sixty-eight, and I have no more of it than at twenty-eight." BOSWELL: "But, Sir, would not you wish to know old age? He who is never an old man does not know the whole of human life; for old age is one of the divisions of it." JOHNSON: "Nay, Sir, what talk is this?" BOSWELL: "I mean, Sir, the Sphinx's description of it;—morning, noon, and night. I would know night, as well as morning and noon." JOHNSON: "What, Sir, would you know what it is to feel the evils of old age? Would you have the gout? Would you have decrepitude?" —Seeing him heated, I would not argue any farther; but I was confident that I was in the right. I would, in due time, be a Nestor, an elder of the people; and there *should* be some difference between the conversation of twenty-eight and sixty-eight.

On Saturday, May 2, I dined with him at Sir Joshua Reynolds's, where there was a very large company, and a great deal of conversation; but owing to some circumstances which I cannot now recollect, I have no record of any part of it, except that there were several people there by no means of the Johnsonian school; so that less attention was paid to him than usual, which put him out of humour; and upon some imaginary offence from me, he attacked me with such rudeness that I was vexed and angry, because it gave those persons an opportunity of enlarging upon his supposed ferocity, and ill treatment of his best friends. I was so much hurt, and had my pride so much aroused, that I kept away from him for a week, and perhaps might have kept away much longer, nay, gone to Scotland without seeing him again, had not we fortunately met and been reconciled. To such unhappy chances are human friendships liable.

On Friday, May 8, I dined with him at Mr. Langton's. I was reserved and silent, which I suppose he perceived, and might recollect the cause. After dinner, when Mr. Langton was called out of the room, and we were by ourselves, he drew his chair near to mine, and said, in a tone of conciliating courtesy, "Well, how have you done?" BOSWELL: "Sir, you have made me very uneasy by your behaviour to me when we were last at Sir Joshua Reynolds's. You know, my dear Sir, no man has a greater respect and affection for you, or would sooner go to the end of the world to serve you. Now to treat me so——" He insisted that I had interrupted him, which I assured him was not the case; and proceeded—"But why treat me so before people who neither love you nor me?" JOHNSON: "Well, I am sorry for it. I'll make it up to you twenty different ways, as you please." BOSWELL: "I said to-day to Sir

Gordon Ross del.

New York, 1945

James Boswell, Esq.

Joshua, when he observed that you *tossed* me sometimes—'I don't care how often, or how high he tosses me, when only friends are present, for then I fall upon soft ground: but I do not like falling on stones, which is the case when enemies are present.'—I think this is a pretty good image, Sir." JOHNSON: "Sir, it is one of the happiest I have ever heard."

The truth is, there was no venom in the wounds which he inflicted at any time, unless they were irritated by some malignant infusion by other hands. We were instantly as cordial again as ever, and joined in hearty laugh at some ludicrous but innocent peculiarities of one of our friends. BOSWELL: "Do you think, Sir, it is always culpable to laugh at a man to his face?" JOHNSON: "Why, Sir, that depends upon the man and the thing. If it is a slight man, and a slight thing, you may; for you take nothing valuable from him."

When Mr. Langton returned to us, the "flow of talk" went on. An eminent author being mentioned;—JOHNSON: "He is not a pleasant man. His conversation is neither instructive nor brilliant. He does not talk as if impelled by any fulness of knowledge or vivacity of imagination. His conversation is like that of any other sensible man. He talks with no wish either to inform or to hear, but only because he thinks it does not become [Dr. Robertson] to sit in a company and say nothing."

Mr. Langton having repeated the anecdote of Addison having distinguished between his powers in conversation and in writing, by saying, "I have only ninepence in my pocket; but I can draw for a thousand pounds";—JOHNSON: "He had not that retort ready, Sir; he had prepared it beforehand." LANGTON (turning to me): "A fine surmise. Set a thief to catch a thief."

Johnson called the East-Indians barbarians. BOSWELL: "You will except the Chinese, Sir?" JOHNSON: "No, Sir." BOSWELL: "Have they not arts?" JOHNSON: "They have no pottery." BOSWELL: "What do you say to the written characters of their language?" JOHNSON: "Sir, they have not an alphabet. They have not been able to form what all other nations have formed." BOSWELL: "There is more learning in their language than in any other, from the immense number of their characters." JOHNSON: "It is only more difficult from its rudeness; as there is more labour in hewing down a tree with a stone than with an axe.—— I shall be at home to-morrow." BOSWELL: "Then let us dine by ourselves at the *Mitre,* to keep up the old custom, 'the custom of the manor,' custom of the *Mitre.*" JOHNSON: "Sir, so it shall be."

On Saturday, May 9, we fulfilled our purpose of dining by ourselves at the *Mitre,* according to old custom. There was, on these occasions, a little circumstance of kind attention to Mrs. Williams, which must not be omitted. Before coming out, and leaving her to dine alone, he gave her her choice of a chicken, a sweetbread, or any other little nice thing, which was carefully sent to her from the tavern, ready-dressed.

Our conversation to-day, I know not how, turned, I think for the only time at any length during our long acquaintance, upon the sensual intercourse between the sexes, the delight of which he ascribed chiefly to imagination. "Were it not for imagination, Sir (said he), a man would be as happy in the arms of a Chambermaid as of a Duchess. But such is the adventitious charm of fancy, that we find men who have violated the best principles of society, and ruined their fame and their fortune, that they might possess a woman of rank." It would not be proper to record the particulars of such a conversation in moments of unreserved frankness, when nobody was present on whom it could have any hurtful effect. That subject when philosophically treated, may surely employ the mind in a curious discussion, and as innocently, as anatomy; provided that those who do treat it, keep clear of inflammatory incentives.

CHAPTER XLIII—1778

Dr. Johnson and Lord Marchmont

ON SUNDAY, MAY 10, I supped with him at Mr. Hoole's, with Sir Joshua Reynolds. I have neglected the memorial of this evening, so as to remember no more of it than two particulars; one that he strenuously opposed an argument by Sir Joshua, that virtue was preferable to vice, considering this life only; and that a man would be virtuous were it only to preserve his character: and that he expressed much wonder at the curious formation of the bat, a mouse with wings; saying that it was almost as strange a thing in physiology as if the fabulous dragon could be seen.

On Tuesday, May 12, I waited on the Earl of Marchmont, to know if his Lordship would favour Dr. Johnson with information concerning Pope, whose life he was about to write. Johnson had not flattered himself with the hopes of receiving any civility from this nobleman; for he said to me, when I mentioned Lord Marchmont as one who could tell him a great deal about Pope—"Sir, he will tell *me* nothing." I had the honour of being known to his Lordship, and applied to him of myself, without being commissioned by Johnson. His Lordship behaved in the most polite and obliging manner, promised to tell all he recollected about Pope, and was so very courteous as to say, "Tell Dr. Johnson I have a great respect for him, and am ready to show it in any way I can. I am to be in the city to-morrow, and will call at his house as I return." His Lordship however asked, "Will he write 'The Lives of the Poets' impartially? He was the first that brought Whig and Tory into a Dictionary. And what do you think of his definition of excise? Do you know the history of his aversion to the word *transpire?*" Then taking down the folio Dictionary, he showed it with this censure on its secondary sense: " 'To escape from secrecy to notice; a sense lately innovated from France, without necessity.' The truth was, Lord Bolingbroke, who left the Jacobites, first used it; therefore, it was to be condemned. He should have shown what word would do for it, if it was unnecessary."

I proposed to Lord Marchmont that he should revise Johnson's "Life of Pope": "So (said his Lordship), you would put me in a dangerous situation. You know he knocked down Osborne, the bookseller."

Elated with the success of my spontaneous exertion to procure material and respectable aid to Johnson for his very favourite work, "The Lives of the Poets," I hastened down to Mr. Thrale's at Streatham, where he now was, that I might ensure his being at home next day; and after dinner, when I thought he would receive the good news in the best humour, I announced it eagerly: "I have been at work for you to-day, Sir. I have been with Lord Marchmont. He bade me tell you he has a great respect for you, and will call on you to-morrow, at one o'clock, and communicate all he knows about Pope."—Here I paused, in full expectation that he would be pleased with this intelligence, would praise my active merit, and would be alert to embrace such an offer from a nobleman. But whether I had shown an over-exaltation, which provoked his spleen; or whether he was seized with a suspicion that I had obtruded him on Lord Marchmont, and humbled him too much; or whether there was anything more than an unlucky fit of ill-humour, I know not; but to my surprise, the result was—JOHNSON: "I shall not be in town to-morrow. I don't care to know about Pope." MRS. THRALE (surprised as I was, and a little angry): "I suppose, Sir, Mr. Boswell thought that as you are to write Pope's 'Life,' you would wish to know about him." JOHNSON: "Wish! why, yes. If it rained knowledge, I'd hold out my hand; but I would not give myself the trouble to go in quest of it." There was no arguing with him at the moment. Some time afterwards he said, "Lord Marchmont will call on me, and then I shall call on Lord Marchmont." Mrs. Thrale was uneasy at his unaccountable caprice; and told me that if I did not take care to bring about a meeting between Lord Marchmont and him, it would never take place, which would be a great pity. I sent a card to his Lordship, to be left at Johnson's house, acquainting him that Dr. Johnson could not be in town next day, but would do himself the honour of waiting on him at another time.—I give this account fairly, as a specimen of that unhappy temper with which this great and good man had occasionally to struggle, from something morbid in his constitution. But it must not be erroneously supposed that he was, in the smallest degree, careless concerning any work which he undertook, or that he was generally thus peevish. It will be seen that in the following year he had a very agreeable interview with Lord Marchmont, at his Lordship's house; and this very afternoon he soon forgot any fretfulness, and fell into conversation as usual.

Mrs. Thrale told us that a curious clergyman of our acquaintance had discovered a licentious stanza, which Pope had originally in his "Universal Prayer," before the stanza,

> "What conscience dictates to be done,
> Or warns us not to do," etc.

It was this:

> "Can sins of moment claim the rod
> Of everlasting fires?
> And that offend great Nature's God,
> Which Nature's self inspires?"

and that Dr. Johnson observed, "it had been borrowed from *Guarini*."

BOSWELL: "In that stanza of Pope's, *'rod of fires'* is certainly a bad metaphor." MRS. THRALE: "And 'sins of *moment*' is a faulty expression; for its true import is *momentous*, which cannot be intended." JOHNSON: "It must have been written of *'moments.'* Of moment, is *momentous;* of moments, momentary. I warrant you, however, Pope wrote this stanza, and some friend struck it out. Boileau wrote some such thing, and Arnaud struck it out, saying, *'Vous gagnerez deux ou trois impies, et perdrez je ne sçais combien des honnêtes gens.'* These fellows want to say a daring thing, and don't know how to go about it. Mere poets know no more of fundamental principles than——." Here he was interrupted somehow.

Talking of divorces, I asked if Othello's doctrine was not plausible;

> "He that is robb'd, not wanting what is stolen,
> Let him not know't, and he's not robb'd at all."

Dr. Johnson and Mrs. Thrale joined against this. JOHNSON: "Ask any man if he'd wish not to know of such an injury." BOSWELL: "Would you tell your friend to make him unhappy?" JOHNSON: "Perhaps, Sir, I should not; but that would be from prudence on my own account. A man would tell his father." BOSWELL: "Yes; because he would not have spurious children to get any share of the family inheritance." MRS. THRALE: "Or he would tell his brother." BOSWELL: "Certainly his *elder* brother." JOHNSON: "You would tell your friend of a woman's infamy, to prevent his marrying a whore: there is the same reason to tell him of his wife's infidelity, when he is married, to prevent the consequences of imposition. It is a breach of confidence not to tell a friend." BOSWELL: "Would you tell Mr. ———?" (naming a gentleman who assuredly was not in the least danger of such a miserable disgrace, though married to a fine woman). JOHNSON: "No, Sir; because it would do no good: he is so sluggish, he'd never go to Parliament and get through a divorce."

After Mrs. Thrale was gone to bed, Johnson and I sat up late. We resumed Sir Joshua Reynolds's argument on the preceding Sunday, that a man would be virtuous, though he had no other motive than to preserve his character. JOHNSON: "Sir, it is not true: for, as to this world, vice does not hurt a man's character." BOSWELL: "Yes, Sir, debauching a friend's wife will." JOHNSON: "No, Sir. Who thinks the worse of [Beauclerk] for it?" BOSWELL: "Lord [Bolingbroke] was not his friend." JOHNSON: "That is only a circumstance, Sir, a slight distinction. He could not get into the house but by Lord [Bolingbroke]. A man is chosen Knight of the Shire not the less for having debauched ladies." BOSWELL: "What, Sir, if he debauched the ladies of gentlemen in the county, will not there be a general resentment against him?" JOHNSON: "No, Sir, he will lose those particular gentlemen; but the rest will not trouble their heads about it" (warmly). BOSWELL: "Well, Sir, I cannot think so." JOHNSON: "Nay, Sir, there is no talking with a man who will dispute what everybody knows (angrily). Don't you know this?" BOSWELL: "No, Sir; and I wish to think better of your country than you represent it. I knew in Scotland a gentleman obliged to leave it for debauching a lady; and in one of our counties an earl's brother lost his election, because he had debauched the lady of another earl in that county, and destroyed the peace of a noble family."

Still he would not yield. He proceeded: "Will you not allow, Sir, that vice does not hurt a man's character so as to obstruct his prosperity in life, when you know that [Lord Clive] was loaded with wealth and honours; a man who had acquired his fortune by such crimes, that his consciousness of them impelled him to cut his own throat?" BOSWELL: "You will recollect, Sir, that Dr. Robertson said he cut his throat because he was weary of still life; little things not being sufficient to move his great mind." JOHNSON (very angry): "Nay, Sir, what stuff is this? You had no more this opinion after Robertson said it, than before. I know nothing more offensive than repeating what one knows to be foolish things, by way of continuing a dispute, to see what a man will answer—to make him your butt!" (angrier still). BOSWELL: "My dear Sir, I had no such intention as you seem to suspect: I had not indeed. Might not this nobleman have felt everything 'weary, stale, flat, and unprofitable,' as Hamlet says!" JOHNSON: "Nay, if you are to bring in gabble, I'll talk no more. I will not, upon my honour."—My readers will decide upon this dispute.

Next morning I stated to Mrs. Thrale at breakfast, before he came down, the dispute of last night as to the influence of character upon success in life. She said he was certainly wrong; and told me that a baronet lost an election in Wales because he had debauched the sister of a gentleman in the country whom he made one of his daughters invite as her companion at his seat in the country, when his lady and his other children were in London. But she would not encounter Johnson upon the subject.

I stayed all this day with him at Streatham. He talked a great deal in very good humour.

Looking at Messrs. Dilly's splendid edition of Lord Chesterfield's miscellaneous works, he laughed, and said, "Here are now two speeches ascribed to him, both of which were written by me: and the best of it is, they have found out that one is like Demosthenes, and the other like Cicero."

As he was a zealous friend of subordination, he was at all times watchful to repress the vulgar cant against the manners of the great; "High people, Sir (said he), are the best; take a hundred ladies of quality, you'll find them better wives, better mothers, more willing to sacrifice their own pleasure to their children, than a hundred other women. Tradeswomen (I mean the wives of tradesmen) in the City, who are worth from 10 to £15,000 are the worst creatures upon the earth, grossly ignorant, and thinking viciousness fashionable. Farmers, I think, are often worthless fellows. Few lords will cheat; and, if they do, they'll be ashamed of it; farmers cheat and are not ashamed of it: they have all the sensual vices too of the nobility, with cheating into the bargain. There is as much fornication and adultery amongst farmers as amongst noblemen." BOSWELL: "The notion of the world, Sir, however, is, that the morals of women of quality are worse than those in lower stations." JOHNSON: "Yes, Sir, the licentiousness of one woman of quality makes more noise than that of a number of women in lower stations; then, Sir, you are to consider the malignity of women in the City against women of quality, which will make them believe anything of them such as that they call their coachmen to bed. No, Sir, so far as I have observed, the higher in rank the richer ladies are, they are the better instructed and the more virtuous."

On Tuesday, May 19, I was to set out for Scotland in the evening. Johnson was engaged to dine with me at Mr. Dilly's; I waited upon him to remind him of his appointment and attend him thither; he gave me some salutary counsel, and recommended vigorous resolution against any deviation from moral duty. BOSWELL: "But you would not have me to bind myself by a solemn obligation?" JOHNSON (much agitated): "What! a vow—O, no, Sir, a vow is a horrible thing, it is a snare for sin. The man who cannot go to heaven without a vow—may—go——" Here standing erect, in the middle of his library, and rolling grand, his pause was truly a curious compound of the solemn and the ludicrous; he half-whistled in his usual way, when pleasant, and he paused, as if checked by religious awe.—Methought he would have added—to Hell—but was restrained. I humoured the dilemma. "What! Sir (said I), *'In cœlum jusseris ibit.'*" alluding to his imitation of it,

"And bid him go to Hell, to Hell he goes."

We had a quiet comfortable meeting at Mr. Dilly's, nobody there but ourselves. Mr. Dilly mentioned somebody having wished that Milton's "Tractate on Education" should be printed along with his Poems in the edition of the English Poets then going on. JOHNSON: "It would be breaking in upon the plan; but would be of no great consequence

So far as it would be anything it would be wrong. Education in England has been in danger of being hurt by two of its greatest men, Milton and Locke. Milton's plan is impracticable, and I suppose has never been tried. Locke's, I fancy, has been tried often enough, but is very imperfect; it gives too much to one side, and too little to the other; it gives too little to literature—I shall do what I can for Dr. Watts; but my materials are very scanty. His poems are by no means his best works; I cannot praise his poetry itself highly; but I can praise its design."

My illustrious friend and I parted with assurances of affectionate regard.

"TO DR. SAMUEL JOHNSON.

"*Edinburgh, June 18, 1778.*

"MY DEAR SIR,—

*   *   *

"Since my return to Scotland, I have been again at Lanark, and have had more conversation with Thomson's sister. It is strange that Murdoch, who was his intimate friend, should have mistaken his mother's maiden name, which he says was Hume, whereas Hume was the name of his grandmother by the mother's side. His mother's name was Beatrix Trotter,[1] a daughter of Mr. Trotter, of Fogo, a small proprietor of land. Thomson had one brother, whom he had with him in England as his amanuensis; but he was seized with a consumption and having returned to Scotland, to try what his native air would do for him, died young. He had three sisters, one married to Mr. Bell, minister of the parish of Strathaven; one to Mr. Craig, father of the ingenious architect, who gave the plan of the New Town of Edinburgh; and one to Mr. Thomson, master of the grammar-school at Lanark. He was of a humane and benevolent disposition; not only sent valuable presents to his sisters, but a yearly allowance in money, and was always wishing to have it in his power to do them more good. Lord Lyttelton's observation, that 'he loathed much to write,' was very true. His letters to his sister, Mrs. Thomson, were not frequent, and in one of them he says, 'All my friends who know me, know how backward I am to write letters; and never impute the negligence of my hand to the coldness of my heart.' I send you a copy of the last letter which she had from him; she never heard that he had any in-

---

[1] Dr. Johnson was by no means attentive to minute accuracy in his "Lives of the Poets"; for notwithstanding my having detected this mistake, he has continued it.

tention of going into holy orders. From this late interview with his sister, I think much more favourably of him, as I hope you will. I am eager to see more of your Prefaces to the Poets: I solace myself with the few proof-sheets which I have.

"I send another parcel of Lord Hailes's 'Annals,' which you will please to return to me as soon as you conveniently can. He says, 'he wishes you would cut a little deeper'; but he may be proud that there is so little occasion to use the critical knife. I ever am, my dear Sir, your faithful and affectionate,

"Humble servant,
"JAMES BOSWELL."

Mr. Langton has been pleased, at my request, to favour me with some particulars of Dr. Johnson's visit to Warley Camp, where this gentleman was at the time stationed as a captain in the Lincolnshire Militia. I shall give them in his own words in a letter to me.

"It was in the summer of the year 1778 that he complied with my invitation to come down to the Camp at Warley, and he stayed with me about a week; the scene appeared, notwithstanding a great degree of ill-health that he seemed to labour under, to interest and amuse him, as agreeing with the disposition that I believe you know he constantly manifested towards inquiring into subjects of the military kind. He sat, with a patient degree of attention, to observe the proceedings of a regimental court-martial, that happened to be called in the time of his stay with us; and one night, as late as at eleven o'clock, he accompanied the Major of the regiment in going what are styled the *Rounds,* where he might observe the forms of visiting the guards, for the seeing that they and their sentries are ready in their duty on their several posts. He took occasion to converse at times on military topics, one in particular, that I see the mention of, in your 'Journal of a Tour to the Hebrides,' which lies open before me, as to gunpowder; which he spoke of to the same effect, in part, that you relate.

"On one occasion, when the regiment were going through their exercise, he went quite close to the men at one of the extremities of it, and watched all their practices attentively; and, when he came away, his remark was, 'The men indeed do load their muskets and fire with wonderful celerity.' He was likewise particular in requiring to know what was the weight of the musket balls in use, and within what distance they might be expected to take effect when fired off.

"In walking among the tents, and observing the difference between those of the officers and private men, he said that the superiority of accommodation of the better conditions of life, to that of the inferior ones, was never exhibited to him in so distinct a view. The civilities paid to him in the camp were from the gentlemen of the Lincolnshire Regiment, one of the officers of which accommodated him with a tent in which he slept; and from General Hall, who very courteously invited him to dine with him, where he appeared to be very well pleased with his entertainment, and the civilities he received on the part of the General; the attention likewise of the General's aide-de-camp, Captain Smith, seemed to be very welcome to him, as appeared by their engaging in a great deal of discourse together. The gentlemen of the East York Regiment likewise, on being informed of his coming, solicited his company at dinner, but by that time he had fixed his departure, so that he could not comply with the invitation."

"TO JAMES BOSWELL, ESQ.

"SIR,—

"I have received two letters from you, of which the second complains of the neglect shown to the first. You must not tie your friends to such punctual correspondence. You have all possible assurances of my affection and esteem; and there ought to be no need of reiterated professions. When it may happen that I can give you either counsel or comfort, I hope it will never happen to me that I should neglect you; but you must not think me criminal or cold, if I say nothing when I have nothing to say.

"You are now happy enough. Mrs. Boswell is recovered; and I congratulate you upon the probability of her long life. If general approbation will add anything to your enjoyment, I can tell you that I have heard you mentioned as *a man whom everybody likes*. I think life has little more to give.

"[Langton] has gone to his regiment. He has laid down his coach, and talks of making more contractions of his expense: how he will succeed, I know not. It is difficult to reform a household gradually; it may be better done by a system totally new. I am afraid he has always something to hide. When we pressed him to go to [Langton], he objected the necessity of attending his navigation; yet he could talk of going to Aberdeen, a place not much nearer his navigation. I believe he cannot bear the thought of living at [Langton] in a state of diminution; and of appearing among the gentlemen of the neighbourhood, *shorn of his beams*. This is natural, but it is cowardly. What I told him of the increasing expense of a growing family, seems to have struck him. He certainly had gone on with very confused views, and we have, I think, shown him that he is wrong; though, with the common deficience of advisers, we have not shown him how to do right.

"I wish you would a little correct or restrain your imagination, and imagine that happiness, such as life admits, may be had at other places as well as London. Without asserting stoicism, it may be said that it is our business to exempt ourselves as much as we can from the power of external things. There is but one solid basis of happiness; and that is, the reasonable hope of a happy futurity. This may be had everywhere.

"I do not blame your preference of London to other places, for it is really to be preferred, if the choice is free; but few have the choice of their place, or their manner of life; and mere pleasure ought not to be the prime motive of action.

"Mrs. Thrale, poor thing, has a daughter. Mr. Thrale dislikes the times, like the rest of us. Mrs. Williams is sick; Mrs. Desmoulins is poor. I have miserable nights. Nobody is well but Mr. Levett.

"I am, dear Sir, your most, etc.,

"SAM. JOHNSON.

"*London, July 3, 1778.*"

I wrote to him on the 18th of August, the 18th of September, and the 6th of November; informing him of my having had another son born, whom I had called James; that I had passed some time at Auchinleck; that the Countess of Loudoun, now in her ninety-ninth year, was as fresh as when he saw her, and remembered him with respect; and that his mother by adoption, the Countess of Eglinton, had said to me, "Tell Mr. Johnson I love him exceedingly"; that I had again suffered much from bad spirits; and that, as it was very long since I heard from him, I was not a little uneasy.

"TO JAMES BOSWELL, ESQ.

"DEAR SIR,—

"It is indeed a long time since I wrote, and think you must have some reason to complain; however, you must not let small things disturb you, when you have such a fine addition to your happiness as a new boy, and I hope your lady's health is restored by bringing him. It seems very probable that a little care will now restore her, if any remains of her complaints are left.

"You seem, if I understand your letter, to be gaining ground at Auchinleck, an incident that would give me great delight.

*   *   *

"When any fit of anxiety, or gloominess, or perversion of mind, lays hold upon you, make it a rule not to publish it by complaints, but exert your whole care to hide it: by endeavouring to hide it, you will drive it away. Be always busy.

"The Club is to meet with the Parliament; we talk of electing Banks, the traveller; he will be a reputable member.

"Langton has been encamped with his company of militia on Warley Common; I spent five days amongst them; he signalized himself as a diligent officer, and has very high respect in the regiment. He presided when I was there at a court-martial; he is now quartered in Hertfordshire; his lady and little ones are in Scotland. Paoli came to the camp, and commended the soldiers.

"Of myself, I have no great matters to say; my health is not restored, my nights are restless and tedious. The best night that I have had these twenty years was at Fort Augustus.

"I hope soon to send you a few Lives to read.

"I am, dear Sir, your most affectionate,

"SAM. JOHNSON.

"*November 21, 1778.*"

CHAPTER XLIV—1779

Death of Garrick

THIS YEAR Johnson gave the world a luminous proof that the vigour of his mind in all its faculties, whether memory, judgment, or imagination, was not in the least abated; for this year came out the first four volumes of his "Prefaces, Biographical and Critical, to the most Eminent of the English Poets," [*] published by the booksellers of

London. The remaining volumes came out in the year 1780. The Poets were selected by the several booksellers who had the honorary copyright which is still preserved among them by mutual compact, notwithstanding the decision of the House of Lords against the perpetuity of literary property.

On the 22nd of January, I wrote to him on several topics, and mentioned that as he had been so good as to permit me to have the proof sheets of his "Lives of the Poets," I had written to his servant Francis, to take care of them for me.

"MR. BOSWELL TO DR. JOHNSON.

"*Edinburgh, Feb. 2, 1779.*

"MY DEAR SIR,—

"Garrick's death is a striking event: not that we should be surprised with the death of any man who has lived sixty-two years; but because there was a *vivacity* in our late celebrated friend, which drove away the thoughts of *death* from any association with *him*. I am sure you will be tenderly affected with his departure; and I would wish to hear from you upon the subject. I was obliged to him in my days of effervescence in London, when poor Derrick was my governor; and since that time I received many civilities from him. Do you remember how pleasing it was, when I received a letter from him, at Inverary, upon our first return to civilized living after our Hebridean journey? I shall always remember him with affection as well as admiration.

"On Saturday last, being the 30th of January, I drank coffee and old port, and had solemn conversation with the Reverend Mr. Falconer, a nonjuring bishop, a very learned and worthy man. He gave two toasts, which you will believe I drank with cordiality, Dr. Samuel Johnson, and Flora Macdonald. I sat about four hours with him; and it was really as if I had been living in the last century. The Episcopal Church of Scotland, though faithful to the Royal House of Stuart, has never accepted of any *congé d'élire* since the Revolution; it is the only true Episcopal Church in Scotland, as it has its own succession of bishops. For as to the episcopal clergy who take the oaths to the present Government, they indeed follow the rites of the Church of England, but, as Bishop Falconer observed, 'they are not *Episcopals;* for they are under no bishop, as a bishop cannot have authority beyond his diocese.' This venerable gentleman did me the honour to dine with me yesterday, and he laid his hands upon the heads of my little ones. We had a good deal of curious literary conversation, particularly about Mr. Thomas Ruddiman, with whom he lived in great friendship.

"Any fresh instance of the uncertainty of life makes one embrace more closely a valuable friend. My dear and much respected Sir, may God preserve you long in this world while I am in it.

"I am, ever, your much obliged,

"And affectionate humble servant,

"JAMES BOSWELL."

On the 23rd of February I wrote to him again, complaining of his silence, as I had heard he was ill, and had written to Mr. Thrale for information concerning him; and I announced my intention of soon being again in London.

"TO JAMES BOSWELL, ESQ.

"DEAR SIR,—

"Why should you take such delight to make a bustle, to write to Mr. Thrale that I am negligent, and to Francis to do what is so very unnecessary. Thrale, you may be sure, cared not about it; and I shall spare Francis the trouble, by ordering a set both of the 'Lives' and 'Poets' to dear Mrs. Boswell, in acknowledgment of her marmalade. Persuade her to accept them, and accept them kindly. If I thought she would receive them scornfully, I would send them to Miss Boswell, who, I hope, has yet none of her mamma's ill-will to me.

"I would send sets of 'Lives,' four volumes, to some other friends, to Lord Hailes first. His second volume lies by my bedside; a book surely of great labour, and, to every just thinker, of great delight. Write me word to whom I shall send besides; would it please Lord Auchinleck? Mrs. Thrale waits in the coach.

"I am, dear Sir, etc.,

"SAM. JOHNSON.

"March 13, 1779."

This letter crossed me on the road to London, where I arrived on Monday, March 15; and next morning, at a late hour, found Dr. Johnson sitting over his tea, attended by Mrs. Desmoulins, Mr. Levett, and a clergyman, who had come to submit some poetical pieces to his revision. It is wonderful what a number and variety of writers, some of them even unknown to him, prevailed on his good-nature to look over their works, and suggest corrections and improvements. My arrival interrupted, for a little while, the important business of this true representative of Bayes; upon its being resumed, I found that the subject under immediate consideration was a translation, yet in manuscript, of the *"Carmen Seculare"* of Horace, which had this year been set to music, and performed as a public entertainment in London, for the joint benefit of Monsieur Philidor and Signor Baretti. When Johnson had done reading, the author asked him bluntly, "If upon the whole it was a good translation?" Johnson, whose regard for truth was uncommonly strict, seemed to be puzzled for a moment, what answer to make; as he certainly could not honestly commend the performance, with exquisite address he evaded the question thus, "Sir, I do not say that it may not be made a very good translation." Here nothing whatever in favour of the performance was affirmed, and yet the writer was not shocked. A printed "Ode to the Warlike Genius of Britain," came next in review; the bard was a lank, bony figure, with short black hair; he was writhing himself in agitation, while Johnson read, and showing his teeth in a grin of earnestness, exclaimed in broken sentences, and in a keen sharp tone, "Is that poetry, Sir?—Is it Pindar?" JOHNSON: "Why, Sir, there is here a great deal of what is called poetry." Then turning to me, the poet cried, "My muse has not been long upon the town, and (pointing to the Ode) it trembles under the hand of the great critic."

Although I was several times with him in the course of the following days, such it seems were my occupations, or such my negligence, that I have preserved no memorial of his conversation till Friday, March 26, when I visited him. He said he expected to be attacked on account of his "Lives of the Poets." "However (said he), I would rather be attacked than unnoticed. For the worst thing you can do to an author is to be silent as to his works. An assault upon a town is a bad thing; but starving it is still worse; an assault may be unsuccessful; you may have more men killed than you kill; but if you starve the town, you are sure of victory."

During my stay in London this spring, I find I was unaccountably negligent in preserving Johnson's sayings, more so than at any time when I was happy enough to have an opportunity of hearing his wisdom and wit. There is no help for it now. I must content myself with presenting such scraps as I have. But I am nevertheless ashamed and vexed to think how much has been lost. It is not that there was a bad crop this year; but that I was not sufficiently careful in gathering it in. I, therefore, in some instances, can only exhibit a few detached fragments.

At Streatham on Monday, March 29, at breakfast, he maintained that a father had no right to control the inclinations of his daughters in marriage.

On Friday, April 2, being Good-Friday, I visited him in the morning as usual; and finding that we insensibly fell into a train of ridicule upon the foibles of one of our friends, a very worthy man, I, by way of a check, quoted some good admonition from "The Government of the Tongue," that very pious book. It happened also remarkably enough that the subject of the sermon preached to us to-day by Dr. Burrows, the rector of St. Clement Danes, was the certainty that at the last day we must give an account of "the deeds done in the body"; and amongst various acts of culpability he mentioned evil-speaking. As we were moving slowly along in the crowd from church, Johnson jogged my elbow, and said, "Did you attend to the sermon?"—"Yes, Sir (said I), it was very applicable to *us.*" He, however, stood upon the defensive. "Why, Sir, the sense of ridicule is given us, and may be lawfully used. The author of 'The Government of the Tongue' would have us treat all men alike."

On Saturday, April 3, I visited him at night, and found him sitting in Mrs. Williams's room, with her, and one, who he afterwards told me was a natural son of the second Lord Southwell. The table had a singular appearance, being covered with a heterogeneous assemblage of oysters and porter for his company, and tea for himself. I mentioned my having heard an eminent physician, who was himself a Christian, argue in favour of universal toleration, and maintain that no man could be hurt by another man's differing from him in opinion. JOHNSON: "Sir, you are to a certain degree hurt by knowing that even one man does not believe."

On Easter Day, after solemn service at St. Paul's, I dined with him. Mr. Allen, the printer, was also his guest. He was uncommonly silent; and I have not written down anything, except a single curious fact, which, having the sanction of his inflexible veracity, may be received as a striking instance of human insensibility and inconsideration. As he was passing by a fishmonger who was skinning an eel alive, he heard him "curse it, because it would not lie still."

On Wednesday, April 7, I dined with him at Sir Joshua Reynolds's. I have not marked what company was there. Johnson harangued upon the qualities of different liquors, and spoke with great contempt of claret, as so weak, that "a man would be drowned by it before it made him drunk." He was persuaded to drink one glass of it, that he might judge, not from recollection, which might be dim, but from immediate sensation. He shook his head, and said, "Poor stuff! No, Sir; claret is the liquor for boys; port for men; but he who aspires to be a hero (smiling) must drink brandy. In the first place, the flavour of brandy is most grateful to the palate; and then brandy will do soonest for a man what drinking *can* do for him. There are, indeed, few who are able to drink brandy. That is a power rather to be wished for than attained. And yet (proceeded he), as in all pleasure hope is a considerable part, I know not but fruition comes too quick by brandy. Florence wine I think the worst; it is wine only to the eye; it is wine neither while you are drinking it, nor after you have drunk it; it neither pleases the taste, nor exhilarates the spirits." I reminded him how heartily he and I used to drink wine together, when we were first acquainted; and how I used to have a headache after sitting up with him. He did not like to have this recalled, or, perhaps, thinking that I boasted improperly, resolved to have a witty stroke at me; "Nay, Sir, it was not the *wine* that made your head ache, but the *sense* that I put into it." Boswell: "What, Sir! will sense make the head ache?" Johnson: "Yes, Sir (with a smile), when it is not used to it."—No man who has a true relish of pleasantry could be offended at this; especially if Johnson in a long intimacy had given him repeated proofs of his regard and good estimation. I used to say that as he had given me £1,000 in praise, he had a good right now and then to take a guinea from me.

On Thursday, April 8, I dined with him at Mr. Allan Ramsay's, with Lord Graham and some other company. Lord Graham, while he praised the beauty of Loch Lomond, on the banks of which is his family seat, complained of the climate, and said he could not bear it. Johnson: "Nay, my Lord, don't talk so: you may bear it well enough. Your ancestors have borne it more years than I can tell." This was a handsome compliment to the antiquity of the House of Montrose. His Lordship told me afterwards that he had only affected to complain of the climate; lest, if he had spoken as favourably of his country as he really thought, Dr. Johnson might have attacked it. Johnson was very courteous to Lady Margaret Macdonald. "Madam (said he), when I was in the Isle of Sky, I heard of the people running to take the stones off the road, lest Lady Margaret's horse should stumble."

On Friday, April 16, I had been present at the trial of the unfortunate Mr. Hackman, who, in a fit of frantic jealous love, had shot Miss Ray, the favourite of a nobleman. Johnson, in whose company I had dined to-day with some other friends, was much interested by my account of what passed, and particularly with his prayer for the mercy of heaven. He said, in a solemn fervid tone, "I hope he *shall* find mercy."

This day, a violent altercation arose between Johnson and Beauclerk, which having made much noise at the time, I think it proper, in order to prevent any future misrepresentation, to give a minute account of it.

In talking of Hackman, Johnson argued, as Judge Blackstone had done, that his being furnished with two pistols was a proof that he meant to shoot two persons. Mr. Beauclerk said, "No, for that every wise man who intended to shoot himself took two pistols, that he might be sure of doing it at once. Lord ———'s cook shot himself with one pistol, and lived ten days in great agony. Mr. ———, who loved buttered muffins, but durst not eat them because they disagreed with his stomach, resolved to shoot himself; and then he ate three buttered muffins for breakfast, before shooting himself, knowing that he should not be troubled with indigestion: *he* had two charged pistols; one was found lying charged upon the table by him, after he had shot himself with the other."—"Well (said Johnson, with an air of triumph), you see here one pistol was sufficient." Beauclerk replied smartly, "Because it happened to kill him." And either then, or very little afterwards, being piqued at Johnson's triumphant remark, added, "This is what you don't know, and I do." There was then a cessation of the dispute; and some minutes intervened, during which, dinner and the glass went on cheerfully; when Johnson suddenly and abruptly exclaimed, "Mr. Beauclerk, how came you to talk so petulantly to me, as 'This is what you don't know, but what I know'? One thing *I* know, which *you* don't seem to know, that you are very uncivil." Beauclerk: "Because *you* began by being uncivil (which you always are)." The words in parentheses were, I believe, not heard by Dr. Johnson. Here again there was a cessation of arms. Johnson told me that the reason why he waited at first some time without taking any notice of what Mr. Beauclerk said, was because he was thinking whether he should resent it. But when he considered that there were present a young Lord and an eminent traveller, two men of the world, with whom he had never dined before, he was apprehensive that they might think they had a right to take such liberties with him as Beauclerk did, and therefore resolved he would not let it pass; adding, "that he would not appear a coward." A little while after this, the conversation turned on the violence of Hackman's temper. Johnson then said, "It was his business to *command* his temper, as my friend, Mr. Beauclerk, should have done some time ago." BEAUCLERK: "I should learn of *you*, Sir." JOHNSON: "Sir, you have given *me* opportunities enough of learning, when I have been in *your* company. No man loves to be treated with contempt." BEAUCLERK (with a polite inclination towards Johnson): "Sir, you have known me twenty years, and however I may have treated others, you may be sure I could never treat you with contempt." JOHNSON: "Sir, you have said more than was necessary." Thus it ended; and Beauclerk's coach not having come for him till very late, Dr. Johnson and another gentleman sat with him a long time after the rest of the company were gone; and he and I dined at Beauclerk's on the Saturday se'nnight following.

After this tempest had subsided, I recollect the following particulars of his conversation.

"I am always for getting a boy forward in his learning; for that is a sure good. I would let him at first read *any* English book which happens to engage his attention; because you have done a great deal, when you have brought him to have entertainment from a book. He'll get better books afterwards."

"Mallet, I believe, never wrote a single line of his projected life of the Duke of Marlborough. He groped for materials; and thought of it, till he had exhausted his mind. Thus it sometimes happens that men entangle themselves in their own schemes."

"To be contradicted in order to force you to talk, is mighty unpleasing. You *shine,* indeed; but it is by being *ground.*"

On Saturday, April 24, I dined with him at Mr. Beauclerk's, with Sir Joshua Reynolds, Mr. Jones (afterwards Sir William), Mr. Langton, Mr. Stevens, Mr. Paradise, and Dr. Higgins. I mentioned that Mr. Wilkes had attacked Garrick to me, as a man who had no friend. JOHNSON: "I believe he is right, Sir. Οἱ φίλοι, οὐ φίλος——He had friends but no friend. Garrick was so diffused, he had no man to whom he wished to unbosom himself. He found people always ready to applaud him, and that always for the same thing; so he saw life with great uniformity." I took upon me, for once, to fight with Goliath's weapons, and play the sophist.——"Garrick did not need a friend, as he got from everybody all that he wanted. What is a friend? One who supports you and comforts you, while others do not. Friendship, you know, Sir, is the cordial drop, 'to make the nauseous draught of life go down': but if the draught be not nauseous, if it be all sweet, there is no occasion for that drop." JOHNSON: "Many men would not be content to live so. I hope I should not. They would wish to have an intimate friend, with whom they might compare minds, and cherish private virtues." One of the company mentioned Lord Chesterfield, as a man who had no friend. JOHNSON: "There were more materials to make friendship in Garrick, had he not been so diffused." BOSWELL: "Garrick was pure gold, but beat out to thin leaf. Lord Chesterfield was tinsel." JOHNSON: "Garrick was a very good man, the cheerfulest man of his age; a decent liver in a profession which is supposed to give indulgence to licentiousness; and a man who gave away, freely, money acquired by himself. He began the world with a great hunger for money; the son of a half-pay officer, bred in a family whose study was to make fourpence do as much as others made fourpence halfpenny do. But when he had got money, he was very liberal." I presumed to animadvert on his eulogy on Garrick, in his "Lives of the Poets." "You say, Sir, his death eclipsed the gaiety of nations." JOHNSON: "I could not have said more nor less. It is the truth; *eclipsed* not *extinguished;* and his death *did* eclipse; it was like a storm." BOSWELL: "But why nations? Did his gaiety extend farther than his own nation?" JOHNSON: "Why, Sir, some exaggeration must be allowed. Besides, nations may be said—if we allow the Scotch to be a nation, and to have gaiety—which they have not. *You* are an exception, though. Come, gentlemen, let us candidly admit that there is one Scotchman who is cheerful." BEAUCLERK: "But he is a very unnatural Scotchman." I, however, continued to think the compliment to Garrick hyperbolically untrue. His acting had ceased some time before his death; at any rate he had acted in Ireland but a short time, at an early period of his life, and never in Scotland. I objected also to what appears an anticlimax of praise, when contrasted with the preceding panegyric—"and diminished the public stock of harmless pleasure!"—"Is not *harmless pleasure* very tame?" JOHNSON: "Nay, Sir, harmless pleasure is the highest praise. Pleasure is a word of dubious import; pleasure is in general dangerous, and pernicious to virtue; to be able therefore to furnish pleasure that is harmless, pleasure pure and unalloyed, is as great a power as man can possess." This was, perhaps, as ingenious a defence as could be made; still, however, I was not satisfied.

Mr. Beauclerk was very entertaining this day, and told us a

number of short stories in a lively elegant manner, and with that air of *the world* which has I know not what impressive effect, as if there were something more than is expressed, or than perhaps we could perfectly understand. As Johnson and I accompanied Sir Joshua Reynolds in his coach, Johnson said, "There is in Beauclerk a predominance over his company, that one does not like. But he is a man who has lived so much in the world, that he has a short story on every occasion; he is always ready to talk, and is never exhausted."

Johnson being now better disposed to obtain information concerning Pope than he was last year, sent by me to my Lord Marchmont, a present of those volumes of his "Lives of the Poets," which were at this time published, with a request to have permission to wait on him; and his Lordship, who had called on him twice, obligingly appointed Saturday, the first of May, for receiving us.

On that morning Johnson came to me from Streatham, and after drinking chocolate at General Paoli's in South Audley-street, we proceeded to Lord Marchmont's in Curzon-street. His Lordship met us at the door of his library, and with great politeness said to Johnson, "I am not going to make an encomium upon *myself*, by telling you the high respect I have for *you*, Sir." Johnson was exceedingly courteous; and the interview, which lasted about two hours, during which the Earl communicated his anecdotes of Pope, was as agreeable as I could have wished. When we came out, I said to Johnson that, considering his Lordship's civility, I should have been vexed if he had again failed to come. "Sir (said he), I would rather have given twenty pounds than not have come." I accompanied him to Streatham, where we dined, and returned to town in the evening.

On Monday, May 3, I dined with him at Mr. Dilly's. This evening I set out for Scotland. I did not write to Johnson, as usual, upon my return to my family; but tried how he would be affected by my silence. Mr. Dilly sent me a copy of a note which he received from him on the 13th of July, in these words:

"TO MR. DILLY.

"SIR,—

"Since Mr. Boswell's departure I have never heard from him; please to send word what you know of him, and whether you have sent my books to his lady.

"I am, etc.,
"SAM. JOHNSON."

My readers will not doubt that his solicitude about me was very flattering.

"TO JAMES BOSWELL, ESQ.

"DEAR SIR,—

"What can possibly have happened, that keeps us two such strangers to each other? I expected to have heard from you when you came home; I expected afterwards. I went into the country and returned, and yet there was no letter from Mr. Boswell. No ill I hope has happened; and if ill should happen, why should it be concealed from him who loves you? Is it a fit of humour, that has disposed you to try who can hold out longest without writing? If it be, you have the victory. But I am afraid of something bad; set me free from my suspicions.

"My thoughts are at present employed in guessing the reason of your silence: you must not expect that I should tell you anything, if I had anything to tell. Write, pray write to me, and let me know what is, or what has been the cause of this long interruption.

"I am, dear Sir,

"Your most affectionate humble servant,

"SAM. JOHNSON.

"*July 13, 1779.*"

"TO DR. SAMUEL JOHNSON.

"*Edinburgh, July 17, 1779.*

"MY DEAR SIR,—

"What may be justly denominated a supine indolence of mind has been my state of existence since I last returned to Scotland. In a livelier state I had often suffered severely from long intervals of silence on your part; and I had even been chid by you for expressing my uneasiness. I was willing to take advantage of my insensibility, and while I could bear the experiment, to try whether your affection for me would, after an unusual silence on my part, make you write first. This afternoon I have had very high satisfaction by receiving your kind letter of inquiry, for which I most gratefully thank you. I am doubtful if it was right to make the experiment; though I have gained by it. I was beginning to grow tender, and to upbraid myself, especially after having dreamt two nights ago that I was with you. I and my wife, and my four children, are all well. I would not delay one post to answer your letter; but as it is late, I have not time to do more. You

shall soon hear from me, upon many and various particulars; and I
shall never again put you to any test.

> "I am, with veneration, my dear Sir,
>> "Your much obliged,
>>> "And faithful humble servant,
>>>> "JAMES BOSWELL."

On the 22nd of July, I wrote to him again; and gave him an
account of my last interview with my worthy friend Mr. Edward
Dilly, at his brother's house at Southill in Bedfordshire, where he
died soon after I parted from him, leaving me a very kind remembrance of his regard.

My letter was a pretty long one, and contained a variety of particulars; but he, it should seem, had not attended to it; for his next to
me, was as follows:

> "TO JAMES BOSWELL, ESQ.

"MY DEAR SIR,—

"Are you playing the same trick again, and trying who can keep
silence longest? Remember that all tricks are either knavish or childish: and that it is as foolish to make experiments upon the constancy
of a friend, as upon the chastity of a wife.

"What can be the cause of this second fit of silence, I cannot conjecture; but after one trick, I will not be cheated by another, nor will
harass my thoughts with conjectures about the motives of a man who,
probably, acts only by caprice. I therefore suppose you are well, and
that Mrs. Boswell is well too: and that the fine summer has restored
Lord Auchinleck. I am much better than you left me; I think I am
better than when I was in Scotland.

"Mr. Thrale goes to Brighthelmstone, about Michaelmas, to be
jolly and ride a-hunting. I shall go to town, or perhaps to Oxford.
Exercise and gaiety, or rather carelessness, will, I hope, dissipate all
remains of his malady; and I likewise hope by the change of place,
to find some opportunities of growing yet better myself.

> "I am, dear Sir,
>> "Your humble servant,
>>> "SAM. JOHNSON.

"*Streatham, Sept. 9, 1779.*"

CHAPTER XLV—1779

The Gordon Riots

MY FRIEND, Colonel James Stuart, second son of the Earl of Bute, who had distinguished himself as a good officer of the Bedfordshire militia, had taken a public spirited resolution to serve his country in its difficulties, by raising a regular regiment, and taking the command of it himself. This, in the heir of the immense property of Wortley, was highly honourable. Having been in Scotland recruiting, he obligingly asked me to accompany him to Leeds, then the head-quarters of his corps; from thence to London for a short time, and afterwards to other places to which the regiment might be ordered. Such an offer, at a time of the year when I had full leisure, was very pleasing; especially as I was to accompany a man of sterling good sense, information, discernment, and conviviality; and was to have a second crop, in one year, of London and Johnson. Of this I informed my illustrious friend, in characteristical warm terms, in a letter dated the 30th of September, from Leeds.

On Monday, October 4, I called at his house before he was up. He sent for me to his bedside, and expressed his satisfaction at this incidental meeting, with as much vivacity as if he had been in the gaiety of youth. He called briskly, "Frank, go and get coffee, and let us breakfast *in splendour*."

During this visit to London, I had several interviews with him, which it is unnecessary to distinguish particularly. I consulted him as to the appointment of guardians to my children, in case of my death. "Sir (said he), do not appoint a number of guardians. When there are many, they trust one to another, and the business is neglected. I would advise you to choose only one; let him be a man of respectable character, who, for his own credit, will do what is right; let him be a rich man, so that he may be under no temptation to take advantage; and let him be a man of business, who is used to conduct affairs with ability and expertness, to whom, therefore, the execution of the trust will not be burdensome."

On Sunday, October 10, we dined together at Mr. Strahan's. We talked of the state of the poor in London.—JOHNSON: "Saunders Welch, the Justice, who was once high-constable of Holborn, and had the best opportunities of knowing the state of the poor, told me that I under-rated the number, when I computed that twenty a week, that is above a thousand a year, died of hunger, not absolutely of immediate hunger, but of the wasting and other diseases which are the consequences of hunger. This happens only in so large a place as London, where people are not known. What we are told about the great sums got by begging, is not true: the trade is overstocked. And, you may depend upon it, there are many who cannot get work. A particular kind of manufacture fails; those who have been used to work at it can, for some time, work at nothing else. You meet a man begging; you charge him with idleness: he says, 'I am willing to labour. Will you give me work?'—'I cannot.'—'Why then you have no right to charge me with idleness.'"

We left Mr. Strahan's at seven, as Johnson had said he intended to go to evening prayers. As we walked along he complained of a little gout in his toe, and said, "I shan't go to prayers to-night; I shall go to-morrow: Whenever I miss church on a Sunday, I resolve to go another day. But I do not always do it."

I went home with him, and we had a long quiet conversation.

BOSWELL: "Why, Sir, do people play this trick which I observe now, when I look at your grate, putting the shovel against it to make the fire burn." JOHNSON: "They play the trick, but it does not make the fire burn. *There* is a better (setting the poker perpendicularly up at right angles with the grate). In days of superstition they thought, as it made a cross with the bars, it would drive away the witch."

BOSWELL: "By associating with you, Sir, I am always getting an accession of wisdom. But perhaps a man, after knowing his own character—the limited strength of his own mind, should not be desirous of having too much wisdom, considering, *quid valeant humeri*, how little he can carry." JOHNSON: "Sir, be as wise as you can; let a man be *aliis lætus, sapiens sibi*:

'Though pleas'd to see the dolphins play,
I mind my compass and my way.'

You may be as wise in your study in the morning, and gay in company at a tavern in the evening. Every man is to take care of his own wisdom and his own virtue, without minding too much what others think."

I mentioned to him a dispute between a friend of mine and his lady, concerning conjugal infidelity, which my friend had maintained was by no means so bad in the husband as in the wife. JOHNSON: "Your friend was in the right, Sir. Between a man and his Maker it is a different question: but between a man and his wife, a husband's infidelity is nothing. They are connected by children, by fortune, by serious considerations of community. Wise married women don't trouble themselves about infidelity in their husbands." BOSWELL: "To be sure there is a great difference between the offence of infidelity in a man and that of his wife." JOHNSON: "The difference is boundless. The man imposes no bastards upon his wife."

Here it may be questioned whether Johnson was entirely in the right. I suppose it will not be controverted, that the difference in the degree of criminality is very great, on account of consequences: but still it may be maintained that, independent of moral obligation, infidelity is by no means a light offence in a husband; because it must hurt a delicate attachment in which a mutual constancy is implied, with such refined sentiments as Massinger has exhibited in his play of "The Picture."—Johnson probably at another time would have admitted this opinion. And let it be kept in remembrance that he was very careful not to give any encouragement to irregular conduct. A gentleman not advertising to the distinction made by him upon this subject, supposed a case of singular perverseness in a wife, and heedlessly said, "That then he thought a husband might do as he pleased with a safe conscience." JOHNSON: "Nay, Sir, this is wild indeed (smiling); you must consider that fornication is a crime in a single man; and you cannot have more liberty by being married."

He this evening expressed himself strongly against the Roman Catholics; observing, "In everything in which they differ from us, they are wrong." He was even against the invocation of saints; in short, he was in the humour of opposition.

On Tuesday, October 12, I dined with him at Mr. Ramsay's, with Lord Newhaven, and some other company, none of whom I recollect, but a beautiful Miss Graham, a relation of his Lordship's, who asked Dr. Johnson to hob or nob with her. He was flattered by such pleasing attention, and politely told her he never drank wine; but if she would drink a glass of water, he was much at her service. She accepted. "Oho, Sir! (said Lord Newhaven) you are caught." JOHNSON: "Nay, I do not see *how* I am *caught;* but if I am caught, I don't want to get free again. If I am caught I hope to be kept." Then, when the two glasses of water were brought, smiling placidly to the young lady, he said, "Madam, let us *reciprocate.*"

Lord Newhaven and Johnson carried on an argument for some time concerning the Middlesex election. Johnson said, "Parliament may be considered as bound by law, as a man is bound where there is nobody to tie the knot. As it is clear that the House of Commons may expel, and expel again and again, why not allow of the power to incapacitate for that Parliament, rather than have a perpetual contest kept up between Parliament and the people." Lord Newhaven took the opposite side; but respectfully said, "I speak with great deference to you, Dr. Johnson; I speak to be instructed." This had its full effect on my friend. He bowed his head almost as low as the table, to a complimenting nobleman; and called out, "My Lord, my Lord, I do not desire all this ceremony; let us tell our minds to one another quietly." After the debate was over, he said, "I have got lights on the subject to-day, which I had not before." This was a great deal from him, especially as he had written a pamphlet upon it.

What I have preserved of his conversation during the remainder of my stay in London at this time, is only what follows: I told him that when I objected to keeping company with a notorious infidel, a celebrated friend of ours said to me: "I do not think that men who live laxly in the world, as you and I do, can with propriety assume such an authority: Dr. Johnson may, who is uniformly exemplary in his conduct. But it is not very consistent to shun an infidel to-day, and get drunk to-morrow." JOHNSON: "Nay, Sir, this is sad reasoning. Because a man cannot be right in all things, is he to be right in nothing? Because a man sometimes gets drunk, is he therefore to steal? This doctrine would very soon bring a man to the gallows."

He, I know not why, showed upon all occasions an aversion to go to Ireland, where I proposed to him that we should make a tour. JOHNSON: "It is the last place where I should wish to travel." BOSWELL: "Should you not like to see Dublin, Sir?" JOHNSON: "No, Sir; Dublin is only a worse capital." BOSWELL: "Is not the Giant's Causeway worth seeing?" JOHNSON: "Worth seeing? Yes; but not worth going to see."

Yet he had a kindness for the Irish nation, and thus generously expressed himself to a gentleman from that country, on the subject of an *union* which artful Politicians have often had in view—"Do not make an union with us, Sir; we should unite with you, only to rob you. We should have robbed the Scotch, if they had anything of which we could have robbed them."

A foreign minister of no very high talents, who had been in his company for a considerable time quite overlooked, happened luckily to mention that he had read some of his *Rambler* in Italian, and admired it much. This pleased him greatly; he observed that the title had been translated, *"Il Genio errante,"* though I have been told it was rendered more ludicrously, *"Il Vagabondo";* and finding that this minister gave such a proof of his taste, he was all attention to him, and on the first remark which he made, however simple, exclaimed, "The Ambassador says well:—His Excellency observes—"; And then he expanded and enriched the little that had been said in so strong a manner that it appeared something of consequence. This was exceedingly entertaining to the company who were present, and many a time afterwards it furnished a pleasant topic of merriment: *"The Ambassador says well"* became a laughable term of applause, when no mighty matter had been expressed.

I left London on Monday, October 18, and accompanied Colonel Stuart to Chester, where his regiment was to lie for some time.

"MR. BOSWELL TO DR. JOHNSON.

"Chester, Oct. 22, 1779.

"MY DEAR SIR,—

"It was not till one o'clock on Monday morning that Colonel Stuart and I left London; for we chose to bid a cordial adieu to Lord Mount-stuart, who was to set out on that day on his embassy to Turin. We drove on excellently, and reached Lichfield in good time enough that night. Next morning it rained very hard; and as I had much to do in a little time, I ordered a post-chaise, and between eight and nine sallied forth to make a round of visits. I first went to Mr. Green, hoping to have had him to accompany me to all my other friends, but he was engaged to attend the Bishop of Sodor and Man, who was then lying at Lichfield very ill of the gout. Having taken a hasty glance at the additions to Green's Museum, from which it was not so easy to break away, I next went to the Friary, where I at first occasioned some tumult in the ladies, who were not prepared to receive *company* so early; but my *name,* which has by wonderful felicity come to be closely associated with yours, soon made all easy; and Mrs. Cobb and Miss Adey re-assumed their seats at the breakfast table, which they had quitted with some precipitation. They received me with the kindness of an old acquaintance; and after we had joined in a cordial chorus to *your* praise, Mrs. Cobb gave *me* the high satisfaction of hearing that you said, 'Boswell is a man who I believe never left a house without leaving a wish for his return.' And she afterwards added that she bid you tell me that if ever I came to Lichfield, she hoped I would take a bed at the Friary. From thence I drove to Peter Garrick's, where I also found a very flattering welcome. He appeared to me to enjoy his usual cheerfulness; and he very kindly asked me to come when I could, and pass a week with him. From Mr. Garrick's I went to the Palace to wait on Mr. Seward. I was first entertained by his lady and daughter, he himself being in bed with a cold, according to his valetudinary custom. But he desired to see me; and I found him dressed in his black gown, with a white flannel nightgown above it; so that he looked like a Dominican friar. He was good-humoured and polite; and under his roof too my reception was very pleasing. I then proceeded to Stow-hill, and first paid my respects to Mrs. Gastrell, whose conversation I was not willing to quit. But my sand-glass was now beginning to run low, as I could not trespass too long on the Colonel's kindness, who obligingly waited for me; so I hastened to Mrs. Aston's, whom I found much better than I feared I should; and there I met a brother-in-law of these ladies, who talked much of you, and very well too, as it appeared to me. It then only remained to visit Mrs. Lucy Porter, which I did, I really believe, with sincere satisfaction on both sides. I am sure I was glad to see her again; and, as I take her to be very honest, I trust she was glad to see me again; for she expressed herself so that I could not doubt of her being in earnest.

"We got to Chester about midnight on Tuesday; and here again I am in a state of much enjoyment. Colonel Stuart and his officers treat me with all the civility I could wish; and I play my part admirably. The Bishop, to whom I had the honour to be known several years ago, shows me much attention; and I am edified by his conversation. I must not omit to tell you that his Lordship admires, very highly, your Prefaces to the Poets. I am daily obtaining an extension of agreeable acquaintance, so that I am kept in animated variety; and the study of the place itself, by the assistance of books, and of the Bishop, is sufficient occupation. Chester pleases my fancy, more than any town I ever saw. But I will not enter upon it at all in this letter.

"How long I shall stay here I cannot yet say. I told a very pleasing young lady, niece to one of the Prebendaries, at whose house I saw her, 'I have come to Chester, Madam, I cannot tell how; and far less can I tell how I am to get away from it. Do not think me too juvenile.' I beg it of you, my dear Sir, to favour me with a letter while I am here, and add to the happiness of a happy friend, who is ever, with affectionate veneration, most sincerely yours,

"JAMES BOSWELL."

"TO JAMES BOSWELL, ESQ.

"DEAR SIR,—

"Why should you importune me so earnestly to write? Of what importance can it be to hear of distant friends, to a man who finds himself welcome wherever he goes, and makes new friends faster than he can want them? If to the delight of such universal kindness of reception, anything can be added by knowing that you retain my good-will, you may indulge yourself in the full enjoyment of that small addition.

"I am glad that you made the round of Lichfield with so much success: the oftener you are seen, the more you will be liked. It was pleasing to me to read that Mrs. Aston was so well and that Lucy Porter was so glad to see you.

"There is a letter for you, from
"Your humble servant,
"SAM. JOHNSON.
"*London, October 27, 1779.*"

"TO DR. SAMUEL JOHNSON.

"*Carlisle, Nov. 7, 1779.*

"MY DEAR SIR,—

"That I should importune you to write to me at Chester, is not wonderful, when you consider what an avidity I have for delight; and that the *amor* of pleasure, like the *amor nummi,* increases in proportion with the quantity which we possess of it.

"I arrived here late last night. Our friend the Dean has been gone from hence some months; but I am told at my inn, that he is very *populous* (popular). However, I found Mr. Law, the Archdeacon, son to the Bishop, and with him I have breakfasted and dined very agreeably. I got acquainted with him at the Assizes here about a year and a half ago; he is a man of great variety of knowledge, uncommon genius, and, I believe, sincere religion. I received the holy sacrament in the Cathedral in the morning, this being the first Sunday in the month; and was at prayers there in the morning. It is divinely cheering to me to think that there is a Cathedral so near Auchinleck; and I now leave Old England in such a state of mind as I am thankful to God for granting me.

"Colonel Stuart did me the honour to escort me in his carriage to show me Liverpool, and from thence back again to Warrington, where we parted. In justice to my valuable wife, I must inform you she wrote to me that, as I was so happy, she would not be so selfish as to wish me to return sooner than business absolutely required my presence. She made my clerk write to me a post or two after to the same purpose, by commission from her; and this day a kind letter from her met me at the Post Office here, acquainting me that she and the little ones were well, and expressing all their wishes for my return home. I am, more and more, my dear Sir,
                    "Your affectionate,
                         "And obliged humble servant,
                                   "JAMES BOSWELL."

              "TO JAMES BOSWELL, ESQ.

"DEAR SIR,—
    "Your last letter was not only kind but fond. But I wish you to get rid of all intellectual excesses, and neither to exalt your pleasures, nor aggravate your vexations beyond their real and natural state. Why should you not be as happy at Edinburgh as at Chester? *In culpa est animus, qui se non effugit usquam.* Please yourself with your wife and children, and studies, and practice.
    "How near is the Cathedral to Auchinleck that you are so much delighted with it? It is, I suppose, at least an hundred and fifty miles off. However, if you are pleased, it is so far well.
    "Make my compliments to Mrs. Boswell, etc. I am, Sir, your humble servant,
                                   "SAM. JOHNSON.
    "*London, Nov. 13, 1779.*"

                    CHAPTER XLVI—1780

                    # Death of Beauclerk

IN 1780, the world was kept in impatience for the completion of his "Lives of the Poets," upon which he was employed so far as his indolence allowed him to labour.
    I wrote to him on January 1 and March 13, sending him my notes

[503]

of Lord Marchmont's information concerning Pope;—complaining that I had not heard from him for almost four months, though he was two letters in my debt;—that I had suffered again from melancholy;—hoping that he had been in so much better company (the Poets), that he had not time to think of his distant friends; for, if that were the case, I should have some recompense for my uneasiness;—that the state of my affairs did not admit of my coming to London this year; and begging he would return me Goldsmith's two poems, with his lines marked.

"TO JAMES BOSWELL, ESQ.

"DEAR SIR,—

"Well, I had resolved to send you the Chesterfield letter; but I will write once again without it. Never impose tasks upon mortals. To require two things is the way to have them both undone.

"For the difficulties which you mention in your affairs, I am sorry; but difficulty is now very general: it is not therefore less grievous, for there is less hope of help. I pretend not to give you advice, not knowing the state of your affairs: and general counsels about prudence and frugality would do you little good. You are, however, in the right not to increase your own perplexity by a journey hither; and I hope that by staying at home you will please your father.

"Poor dear Beauclerk—*nec, ut soles, dabis joca.* His wit and his folly, his acuteness and his maliciousness, his merriment and reasoning, are now over. Such another will not often be found among mankind. He directed himself to be buried by the side of his mother, an instance of tenderness which I hardly expected. He has left his children to the care of Lady Di, and if she dies, of Mr. Langton, and of Mr. Leicester, his relation, and a man of good character. His library has been offered to sale to the Russian ambassador.

"Poor Mr. Thrale has been in extreme danger from an apoplectical disorder, and recovered beyond the expectation of his physicians; he is now at Bath, that his mind may be quiet, and Mrs. Thrale and Miss are with him.

"Having told you what has happened to your friends, let me say something to you of yourself. You are always complaining of melancholy, and I conclude from those complaints that you are fond of it. No man talks of that which he is desirous to conceal, and every man desires to conceal that of which he is ashamed. Do not pretend to deny it; *manifestum habemus furem;* make it an invariable and obligatory law to yourself never to mention your own mental diseases; if you are never to speak of them you will think on them but little, and if you think little of them, they will molest you rarely. When you talk of them, it is plain that you want either praise or pity; for praise there is no room, and pity will do you no good; therefore, from this hour speak no more, think no more, about them.

"Please to make my compliments to your lady and to the young ladies. I should like to see them, pretty loves. I am, dear Sir, yours affectionately,

"SAM. JOHNSON.

"*April 8, 1780.*"

On the second of May I wrote to him, and requested that we might have another meeting somewhere in the North of England, in the autumn of this year.

While Johnson was thus engaged in preparing a delightful literary entertainment for the world, the tranquillity of the metropolis of Great Britain was unexpectedly disturbed by the most horrid series of outrages that ever disgraced a civilized country. A relaxation of some of the severe penal provisions against our fellow-subjects of the Catholic communion had been granted by the legislature, with an opposition so inconsiderable, that the genuine mildness of Christianity, united with liberal policy, seemed to have become general in this island. But a dark and malignant spirit of persecution soon showed itself, in an unworthy petition for the repeal of the wise and humane statute. That petition was brought forward by a mob, with the evident purpose of intimidation, and was justly rejected. But the attempt was accompanied and followed by such daring violence as is unexampled in history.

"TO JAMES BOSWELL, ESQ.

"DEAR SIR,—

"I find you have taken one of your fits of taciturnity, and have resolved not to write till you are written to; it is but a peevish humour, but you shall have your way.

"I have sat at home in Bolt-court, all the summer, thinking to write the 'Lives,' and a great part of the time only thinking. Several of them, however, are done, and I still think to do the rest.

"Mr. Thrale and his family have, since his illness, passed their time first at Bath, and then at Brighthelmstone; but I have been at neither place. I would have gone to Lichfield if I could have had time, and I might have had time if I had been active; but I have missed much, and done little.

"In the late disturbances, Mr. Thrale's house and stock were in great danger; the mob was pacified, at their first invasion, with about £50 in drink and meat; and at their second, were driven away by the soldiers. Mr. Strahan got a garrison into his house, and maintained them a fortnight; he was so frightened that he removed part of his goods. Mrs. Williams took shelter in the country.

"I know not whether I shall get a ramble this autumn; it is now about the time when we were travelling. I have, however, better health than I had then, and hope you and I may yet show ourselves on some part of Europe, Asia, or Africa. In the meantime, let us play no trick, but keep each other's kindness by all means in our power.

> "I am, Sir,
> > "Yours most affectionately,
> > > "SAM. JOHNSON.

"*London, Aug. 21, 1780.*"

My next letters to him were dated August 24, September 6, and October 1, and from them I extract the following passages:

"My brother David and I find the long-indulged fancy of our comfortable meeting again at Auchinleck so well realized, that it in some degree confirms the pleasing hope of *O! preclarum diem!* in a future state.

"I beg that you may never again harbour a suspicion of my indulging a peevish humour, or playing tricks; you will recollect that when I confessed to you that I had once been intentionally silent to try your regard, I gave you my word and honour that I would not do so again.

"I rejoice to hear of your good state of health; I pray God to continue it long. I have often said that I would willingly have ten years added to my life, to have ten taken from yours; I mean that I would be ten years older to have you ten years younger. But let me be thankful for the years during which I have enjoyed your friendship, and please myself with the hopes of enjoying it many years to come in this state of being, trusting always that, in another state, we shall meet never to be separated. Of this we can form no notion; but the thought, though indistinct, is delightful, when the mind is calm and clear.

"The riots in London were certainly horrible; but you give me no account of your own situation during the barbarous anarchy. A description of it by Dr. Johnson would be a great painting; you might write another 'London, a Poem.'

"I am charmed with your condescending affectionate expression, 'Let us keep each other's kindness by all the means in our power': my revered Friend! how elevating it is to my mind that I am found worthy to be a companion to Dr. Samuel Johnson! All that you have said in grateful praise of Mr. Walmsley, I have long thought of you; but we are both Tories, which has a very general influence upon our sentiments. I hope that you will agree to meet me at York, about the end of this month; or if you will come to Carlisle, that would be better still, in case the Dean be there.

"Please to consider that to keep each other's kindness, we should every year have that free and intimate communication of mind which can be had only when we are together. We should have both our solemn and our pleasant talk.

"I write now, for the third time, to tell you that my desire for our meeting this autumn is much increased. I wrote to Squire Godfrey Bosville, my Yorkshire chief, that I should, perhaps, pay him a visit, as I was to hold a conference with Dr. Johnson at York. I give you my word and honour that I said not a word of his inviting you; but he wrote to me as follows:

" 'I need not tell you I shall be happy to see you here the latter end of this month, as you propose; and I shall likewise be in hopes that you will persuade Dr. Johnson to finish the conference here. It will add to the favour of your own company, if you prevail upon such an associate to assist your observations. I have often been entertained with his writings, and I once belonged to a club of which he was a member, and I never spent an evening there, but I heard something from him well worth remembering.'

"We have thus, my dear Sir, good comfortable quarters in the neighbourhood of York, where you may be assured we shall be heartily welcome. I pray you then resolve to set out; and let not the year 1780 be a blank in our social calendar, and in that record of wisdom and wit, which I keep with so much diligence, to your honour, and the instruction and delight of others."

"TO THE RIGHT HONOURABLE LADY SOUTHWELL, DUBLIN.

"MADAM,—

"Among the numerous addresses of condolence which your great loss must have occasioned, be pleased to receive this from one whose name perhaps you have never heard, and to whom your Ladyship is known only by the reputation of your virtue, and to whom your Lord was known only by his kindness and beneficence.

"Your Ladyship is now again summoned to exert that piety of which you once gave, in a state of pain and danger, so illustrious an example; and your Lord's beneficence may still be continued by those, who with his fortune inherit his virtues.

"I hope to be forgiven the liberty which I shall take of informing your Ladyship that Mr. Mauritius Lowe, a son of your late Lord's father, had, by recommendation to your Lord, a quarterly allowance of £10 the last of which, due July 26, he has not received: he was in hourly hope of his remittance, and flattered himself that on October 26 he should have received the whole half year's bounty, when he was struck with the dreadful news of his benefactor's death.

"May I presume to hope that his want, his relation, and his merit, which excited his Lordship's charity, will continue to have the same effect upon those whom he has left behind; and that, though he has lost one friend, he may not yet be destitute. Your Ladyship's charity cannot easily be exerted where it is wanted more; and to a mind like yours, distress is a sufficient recommendation.

"I hope to be allowed the honour of being,

"Madam, your Ladyship's

"Most humble servant,

"SAM. JOHNSON.

"*Bolt-court, Fleet-street, London,*
"*Sept. 9, 1780.*"

On his birthday, Johnson has this note: "I am now beginning the seventy-second year of my life, with more strength of body, and greater vigour of mind, than I think is common at that age." But still he complains of sleepless nights and idle days, and forgetfulness, or neglect of resolutions. He thus pathetically expresses himself: "Surely I shall not spend my whole life with my own total disapprobation."

"TO JAMES BOSWELL, ESQ.

"DEAR SIR,—

"I am sorry to write you a letter that will not please you, and yet it is at last what I resolve to do. This year must pass without an interview; the summer has been foolishly lost, like many other of my summers and winters. I hardly saw a green field, but staid in town to work, without working much.

"Mr. Thrale's loss of health has lost him the election; he is now going to Brighthelmstone, and expects me to go with him; and how long I shall stay, I cannot tell. I do not much like the place, but yet I shall go, and stay while my stay is desired. We must, therefore, content ourselves with knowing, what we know as well as man can know the mind of man, that we love one another, and that we wish each other's happiness, and that the lapse of a year cannot lessen our mutual kindness.

"I was pleased to be told that I accused Mrs. Boswell unjustly, in supposing that she bears me ill-will. I love you so much that I would be glad to love all that love you, and that you love; and I have love very ready for Mrs. Boswell, if she thinks it worthy of acceptance. I hope all the young ladies and gentlemen are well.

"I take a great liking to your brother. He tells me that his father received him kindly, but not fondly; however, you seemed to have lived well enough at Auchinleck, while you staid. Make your father as happy as you can.

"You lately told me of your health: I can tell you in return that my health has been, for more than a year past, better than it has been for many years before. Perhaps it may please God to give us some time together before we are parted.

"I am, dear Sir,
"Yours, most affectionately,
"SAM. JOHNSON.

"*Oct. 17, 1780.*"

CHAPTER XLVII—1780

Langton's Johnsoniana

BEING DISAPPOINTED in my hopes of meeting Johnson this year, so that I could hear none of his admirable sayings, I shall compensate for this want by inserting a collection of them, for which I am indebted to my worthy friend Mr. Langton, whose kind communications have been separately interwoven in many parts of this work. Very few articles of this collection were committed to writing by himself, he not having that habit; which he regrets, and which those who know the numerous opportunities he had of gathering the rich fruits of *Johnsonian* wit and wisdom, must ever regret. I however found, in conversation with him, that a good store of *Johnsoniana* was treasured in his mind; and I compared it to Herculaneum, or some old Roman field, which, when dug, fully rewards the labour employed. The authenticity of every article is unquestionable. For the expression, I, who wrote them down in his presence, am partly responsible.

"There is nothing more likely to betray a man into absurdity, than *condescension;* when he seems to suppose his understanding too powerful for his company."

"John Gilbert Cooper related that, soon after the publication of his Dictionary, Garrick, being asked by Johnson what people said of it, told him that among other animadversions, it was objected that he cited authorities which were beneath the dignity of such a work, and mentioned Richardson. 'Nay (said Johnson), I have done worse than that: I have cited *thee,* David.'"

"Talking of expense, he observed with what munificence a great merchant will spend his money, both from his having it at command, and from his enlarged views by calculation of a good effect upon the whole. 'Whereas (said he), you will hardly ever find a country gentleman who is not a good deal disconcerted at an unexpected occasion for his being obliged to lay out ten pounds.'"

"When in good humour, he would talk of his own writings with a wonderful frankness and candour, and would even criticise them with the closest severity. One day, having read over one of his *Ramblers,* Mr. Langton asked him how he liked that paper; he shook his head, and answered, 'Too wordy.' At another time, when one was reading his tragedy of 'Irene,' to a company at a house in the country, he left the room: and somebody having asked him the reason of this, he replied, 'Sir, I thought it had been better.'"

"He related that he had once in a dream a contest of wit with some other person, and that he was very much mortified by imagining that his opponent had the better of him. 'Now (said he), one may mark here the effect of sleep in weakening the power of reflection; for had not my judgment failed me, I should have seen that the wit of this supposed antagonist, by whose superiority I felt myself depressed, was as much furnished by me, as that which I thought I had been uttering in my own character.'"

"He thus defined the difference between physical and moral truth:

'Physical truth is, when you tell a thing as it actually is. Moral truth is, when you tell a thing sincerely and precisely as it appears to you. I say such a one walked across the street; if he really did so, I told a physical truth. If I thought so, though I should have been mistaken, I told a moral truth.' "

"His affection for Topham Beauclerk was so great, that when Beauclerk was labouring under that severe illness which at last occasioned his death, Johnson said (with a voice faltering with emotion), 'Sir, I would walk to the extent of the diameter of the earth to save Beauclerk.' "

"Johnson was well acquainted with Mr. Dossie, author of a treatise on Agriculture; and said of him, 'Sir, of the objects which the Society of Arts have chiefly in view, the chemical effects of bodies operating upon other bodies, he knows more than almost any man.' Johnson, in order to give Mr. Dossie his vote to be a member of this Society, paid up an arrear which had run on for two years. On this occasion he mentioned a circumstance, as characteristic of the Scotch. 'One of that nation (said he), who had been a candidate, against whom I had voted, came up to me with a civil salutation. Now, Sir, this is their way. An Englishman would have stomached it, and been sulky, and never have taken farther notice of you; but a Scotchman, Sir, though you vote nineteen times against him, will accost you with equal complaisance after each time, and the twentieth time, Sir, he will get your vote.' "

"A man, he observed, should begin to write soon; for, if he waits till his judgment is matured, his inability, through want of practice to express his conceptions, will make the disproportion so great between what he sees and what he can attain, that he will probably be discouraged from writing at all. As a proof of the justness of this remark, we may instance what is related of the great Lord Granville; that after he had written his letter giving an account of the battle of Dettingen, he said, 'Here is a letter, expressed in terms not good enough for a tallow-chandler to have used.' "

"His distinction of the different degrees of attainment of learning was thus marked upon two occasions. Of Queen Elizabeth he said, 'She had learning enough to have given dignity to a bishop'; and of Mr. Thomas Davies he said, 'Sir, Davies has learning enough to give credit to a clergyman.' "

"An eminent foreigner, when he was shown the British Museum, was very troublesome with many absurd inquiries. 'Now there, Sir (said he), is the difference between an Englishman and a Frenchman. A Frenchman must be always talking, whether he knows anything of the matter or not; an Englishman is content to say nothing, when he has nothing to say.' "

"His unjust contempt for foreigners was, indeed, extreme. One evening, at Old Slaughter's coffee-house, when a number of them were talking loud about little matters, he said, 'Does not this confirm old Meynell's observation—*For anything I see, foreigners are fools'?*"

"Hospitality to strangers and foreigners in our country is now almost at an end, since, from the increase of them that come to us, there have been a sufficient number of people that have found an interest in providing inns and proper accommodations, which is in general a more expedient method for the entertainment of travellers. Where the travellers and strangers are few, more of that hospitality subsists, as it has not been worth while to provide places of accommodation. In Ireland there is still hospitality to strangers, in some degree; in Hungary and Poland probably more."

" 'Snatches of reading (said he) will not make a Bentley or a Clarke. They are, however, in a certain degree advantageous. I would put a child into a library (where no unfit books are) and let him read at his choice. A child should not be discouraged from reading anything that he takes a liking to, from a notion that it is above his reach. If that be the case, the child will soon find it out and desist; if not, he of course gains the instruction; which is so much the more likely to come, from the inclination with which he takes up the study.' "

"Though he used to censure carelessness with great vehemence, he owned that he once, to avoid the trouble of locking up five guineas, hid them, he forgot where, so that he could not find them."

"A gentleman who introduced his brother to Dr. Johnson was earnest to recommend him to the Doctor's notice, which he did by saying, 'When we have sat together some time, you'll find my brother grow very entertaining.'—'Sir (said Johnson), I can wait.' "

"When the rumour was strong that we should have a war, because the French would assist the Americans, he rebuked a friend with some asperity for supposing it, saying, 'No, Sir, national faith is not yet sunk so low.' "

"In the latter part of his life, in order to satisfy himself whether his mental faculties were impaired, he resolved that he would try to learn a new language, and fixed upon the Low Dutch for that purpose, and this he continued till he had read about one half of 'Thomas à Kempis';

and finding that there appeared no abatement of his power of acquisition, he then desisted, as thinking the experiment had been duly tried. Mr. Burke justly observed that this was not the most vigorous trial, Low Dutch being a language so near to our own; had it been one of the languages entirely different, he might have been very soon satisfied."

" 'Greek, Sir (said he), is like lace; every man gets as much of it as he can.' "

"Drinking tea one day at Garrick's with Mr. Langton, he was questioned if he was not somewhat of a heretic as to Shakspeare; said Garrick, 'I doubt he is a little of an infidel.'—'Sir (said Johnson), I will stand by the lines I have written on Shakspeare in my Prologue at the opening of your Theatre.' Mr. Langton suggested that in the line—

> 'And panting Time toil'd after him in vain;'

Johnson might have had in his eye the passage in the 'Tempest,' where *Prospero* says of *Miranda*—

> '———She will outstrip all praise,
> And make it halt behind her.'

Johnson said nothing. Garrick then ventured to observe, 'I do not think that the happiest line in the praise of Shakspeare.' Johnson exclaimed (smiling), 'Prosaical rogues! next time I write, I'll make both time and space pant.' "

"It is well known that there was formerly a rude custom for those who were sailing upon the Thames to accost each other as they passed in the most abusive language they could invent, generally, however, with as much satirical humour as they were capable of producing. Addison gives a specimen of this ribaldry, in Number 383 of the *Spectator,* when Sir Roger de Coverley and he are going to Spring Garden. Johnson was once eminently successful in this species of contest; a fellow having attacked him with some coarse raillery, Johnson answered him thus, 'Sir, your wife, *under pretence of keeping a bawdy-house,* is a receiver of stolen goods.' One evening when he and Mr. Burke and Mr. Langton were in company together, and the admirable scolding of Timon of Athens was mentioned, this instance of Johnson's was quoted, and thought to have at least equal excellence."

"As Johnson always allowed the extraordinary talents of Mr. Burke, so Mr. Burke was fully sensible of the wonderful powers of Johnson. Mr. Langton recollects having passed an evening with both of them, when Mr. Burke repeatedly entered upon topics which it was evident he would have illustrated with extensive knowledge and richness of expression; but Johnson always seized upon the conversation, in which, however, he acquitted himself in a most masterly manner. As Mr. Burke and Mr. Langton were walking home, Mr. Burke observed that Johnson had been very great that night; Mr. Langton joined in this, but added, he could have wished to hear more from another person (plainly intimating that he meant Mr. Burke); 'O, no (said Mr. Burke), it is enough for me to have rung the bell to him.' "

"Beauclerk having observed to him of one of their friends that he was awkward at counting money, 'Why, Sir,' said Johnson, 'I am likewise awkward at counting money. But then, Sir, the reason is plain; I have had very little money to count.' "

"Being in company with a gentleman who thought fit to maintain Dr. Berkeley's ingenious philosophy that nothing exists but as perceived by some mind; when the gentleman was going away, Johnson said to him, 'Pray, Sir, don't leave us; for we may perhaps forget to think of you, and then you will cease to exist.' "

"When Mr. Vesey was proposed as a member of the Literary Club, Mr. Burke began by saying that he was a man of gentle manners. 'Sir,' said Johnson, 'you need say no more. When you have said a man of gentle manners, you have said enough.' "

"The late Mr. Fitzherbert told Mr. Langton that Johnson said to him, 'Sir, a man has no more right to *say* an uncivil thing, than to *act* one; no more right to say a rude thing to another, than to knock him down.' "

"Once when somebody produced a newspaper in which there was a letter of stupid abuse of Sir Joshua Reynolds, of which Johnson himself came in for a share,—'Pray (said he), let us have it read aloud from beginning to end'; which being done, he, with a ludicrous earnestness, and not directing his look to any particular person, called out, 'Are we alive after all this satire!' "

"Of a certain noble Lord, he said, 'Respect him, you could not; for he had no mind of his own. Love him you could not; for that which you could do with him, everyone else could.' "

" 'Depend upon it,' said he, 'that if a man *talks* of his misfortunes, there is something in them that is not disagreeable to him; for where there is nothing but pure misery, there never is any recourse to the mention of it.' "

"A man must be a poor beast, that should *read* no more in quantity than he could *utter* aloud."

"Imlac in 'Rasselas,' I spelt with a *c* at the end, because it is less like English, which should always have the Saxon *k* added to the *c*."

" 'The applause of a single human being is of great consequence.' This he said to me with great earnestness of manner, very near the time of his decease, on occasion of having desired me to read a letter addressed to him from some person in the North of England; which when I had done, and he asked me what the contents were, as I thought being particular upon it might fatigue him, it being of great length, I only told him in general that it was highly in his praise;— and then he expressed himself as above."

CHAPTER XLVIII—1781

"Lives of the Poets"

IN 1781, Johnson at last completed his "Lives of the Poets," of which he gives this account: "Some time in March I finished the 'Lives of the Poets,' which I wrote in my usual way, dilatorily and hastily, unwilling to work, and working with vigour and haste." In a memorandum previous to this, he says of them: "Written, I hope, in such a manner as may tend to the promotion of piety."

This is the work which, of all Dr. Johnson's writings, will perhaps be read most generally, and with most pleasure. Philology and biography were his favourite pursuits, and those who lived most in intimacy with him, heard him upon all occasions, when there was a proper opportunity, take delight in expatiating upon the various merits of the English Poets: upon the niceties of their characters, and the events of their progress through the world which they contribute to illuminate. His mind was so full of that kind of information, and it was so well arranged in his memory, that in performing what he had undertaken in this way, he had little more to do than to put his thoughts upon paper; exhibiting first each Poet's life, and then subjoining a critical examination of his genius and works. But when he began to write, the subject swelled in such a manner, that instead of prefaces to each poet, of no more than a few pages, as he had originally intended, he pro- duced an ample, rich, and most entertaining view of them in every respect. The booksellers, justly sensible of the great additional value of the copyright, presented him with another hundred pounds, over and above two hundred, for which his agreement was to furnish such prefaces as he thought fit.

This was, however, but a small recompense for such a collection of biography, and such principles and illustrations of criticism, as, if digested and arranged in one system, by some modern Aristotle or Longinus, might form a code upon that subject, such as no other nation can show. As he was so good as to make me a present of the greatest part of the original and indeed only manuscript of this admirable work, I have an opportunity of observing with wonder the correctness with which he rapidly struck off such glowing composition.

So easy is his style in these "Lives" that I do not recollect more than three uncommon or learned words; one, when giving an account of the approach of Waller's mortal disease, he says, "he found his legs grow *tumid*"; by using the expression his legs *swelled,* he would have avoided this; and there would have been no impropriety in its being followed by the interesting question to his physician, "What that *swelling* meant?" Another, when he mentions that Pope had *emitted* proposals; when *published,* or *issued,* would have been more readily understood; and a third, when he calls Orrery and Dr. Delany, writers both undoubtedly *veracious;* when *true, honest,* or *faithful,* might have been used. Yet, it must be owned, that none of these are *hard* or *too big* words: that custom would make them seem as easy as any others; and that a language is richer and capable of more beauty of expression, by having a greater variety of synonyms.

His dissertation upon the unfitness of poetry for the awful subjects of our holy religion, though I do not entirely agree with him, has all the merit of originality, with uncommon force and reasoning.

That a man who venerated the Church and monarchy as Johnson did should speak with a just abhorrence of Milton as a politician, or rather as a daring foe to good polity, was surely to be expected; and to those who censure him, I would recommend his commentary on Milton's celebrated complaint of his situation, when by the lenity of Charles the Second, "a lenity of which (as Johnson well observes) the world has had perhaps no other example, he, who had written in justification of the murder of his Sovereign, was safe under an *Act of Oblivion.*" "No sooner is he safe than he finds himself in danger, *fallen on evil days and evil tongues, with darkness and with dangers compassed round.* This darkness, had his eyes been better employed, had undoubtedly deserved compassion; but to add the mention of danger, was ungrateful and unjust. He was fallen, indeed, on *evil days;* the time was come in which regicides could no longer boast their wickedness. But of *evil tongues* for Milton to complain, required impudence at least equal to his other powers; Milton, whose warmest advocates must allow that he never spared any asperity of reproach, or brutality of insolence."

In the "Life of Milton," Johnson took occasion to maintain his own and the general opinion of the excellence of rhyme over blank verse in English poetry; and quotes this apposite illustration of it by "an ingenious critic," that *it seems to be verse only to the eye.*[1]

The "Life of Pope" was written by Johnson *con amore,* both from the early possession which that writer had taken of his mind, and from the pleasure which he must have felt in for ever silencing all attempts to lessen his poetical fame, by demonstrating his excellence, and pronouncing the following triumphant eulogium:—"After all this, it is surely superfluous to answer the question that has once been asked, Whether Pope was a poet? otherwise than by asking in return, if Pope be not a poet, where is poetry to be found? To circumscribe poetry by a definition will only show the narrownesss of the definer; though a definition which shall exclude Pope, will not easily be made. Let us look round upon the present time, and back upon the past; let us inquire to whom the voice of mankind has decreed the wreath of poetry; let their productions be examined, and their claims stated, and the pretensions of Pope will be no more disputed."

I remember once to have heard Johnson say, "Sir, a thousand years may elapse before there shall appear another man with a power of versification equal to that of Pope." That power must undoubtedly be allowed its due share in enhancing the value of his captivating composition.

Speaking of Pope's not having been known to excel in conversation, Johnson observes that "traditional memory retains no sallies of raillery, or sentences of observation; nothing either pointed or solid, wise or merry; and that one apophthegm only is recorded." In this respect, Pope differed widely from Johnson, whose conversation was, perhaps, more admirable than even his writings, however excellent.

[1]One of the most natural instances of the effect of blank verse occurred to the late Earl of Hopeton. His Lordship observed one of his shepherds poring in the fields upon Milton's "Paradise Lost"; and having asked him what book it was, the man answered, "An't please your Lordship, this is a very odd sort of an author: he would fain rhyme, but cannot get at it."

Mr. Wilkes has, however, favoured me with one repartee of Pope, of which Johnson was not informed. Johnson, after justly censuring him for having "nursed in his mind a foolish disesteem of Kings," tells us, "yet a little regard shown him by the Prince of Wales melted his obduracy; and he had not much to say when he was asked by his Royal Highness, *how he could love a prince, while he disliked kings?*" The answer which Pope made was, "The young lion is harmless, and even playful; but when his claws are full grown he becomes cruel, dreadful, and mischievous."

But although we have no collection of Pope's sayings, it is not therefore to be concluded that he was not agreeable in social intercourse; for Johnson has been heard to say that "the happiest conversation is that of which nothing is distinctly remembered but a general effect of pleasing impression." The late Lord Somerville, who saw much of great and brilliant life, told me that he had dined in company with Pope, and that after dinner the *little man,* as he called him, drank his bottle of Burgundy, and was exceedingly gay and entertaining.

I cannot withhold from my great friend a censure of at least culpable inattention to a nobleman, who, it has been shown, behaved to him with uncommon politeness. He says, "Except Lord Bathurst, none of Pope's noble friends were such as that a good man would wish to have his intimacy with them known to posterity." This will not apply to Lord Mansfield, who was not ennobled in Pope's lifetime; but Johnson should have recollected that Lord Marchmont was one of those noble friends. He includes his Lordship along with Lord Bolingbroke, in a charge of neglect of the papers which Pope left by his will; when, in truth, as I myself pointed out to him, before he wrote that poet's life, the papers were "committed to *the sole care and judgment* of Lord Bolingbroke, unless he (Lord Bolingbroke) shall not survive me"; so that Lord Marchmont had no concern whatever with them. After the first edition of the "Lives," Mr. Malone, whose love of justice is equal to his accuracy, made, in my hearing, the same remark to Johnson; yet he omitted to correct the erroneous statement. These particulars I mention, in the belief that there was only forgetfulness in my friend; but I owe this much to the Earl of Marchmont's reputation, who, were there no other memorials, will be immortalized by that line of Pope, in the Verses on his Grotto:

"And the bright flame was shot through Marchmont's soul."

In the Life of Addison we find an unpleasing account of his having lent Steele a hundred pounds, and "reclaimed his loan by an execution." In the new edition of the *"Biographia Britannica,"* the authenticity of this anecdote is denied. But Mr. Malone has obliged me with the following note concerning it:—

"Many persons having doubts concerning this fact, I applied to Dr. Johnson, to learn on what authority he asserted it. He told me he had it from Savage, who lived in intimacy with Steele, and who mentioned that Steele told him the story with tears in his eyes.—Ben Victor, Dr. Johnson said, likewise informed him of this remarkable transaction, from the relation of Mr. Wilkes the comedian, who was also an intimate of Steele's.—Some, in defence of Addison, have said that 'the act was done with the good-natured view of rousing Steele, and correcting that profusion which always made him necessitous'— 'If that were the case (said Johnson), and that he only wanted to alarm Steele, he would afterwards have *returned* the money to his friend, which it is not pretended he did.'—'This, too (he added), might be retorted by an advocate for Steele, who might allege that he did not repay the loan *intentionally,* merely to see whether Addison would be mean and ungenerous enough to make use of legal process to recover it. But of such speculations there is no end: we cannot dive into the hearts of men; but their actions are open to observation.'

"I then mentioned to him that some people thought that Mr. Addison's character was so pure that the fact, *though true,* ought to have been suppressed. He saw no reason for this. 'If nothing but the bright side of characters should be shown, we should sit down in despondency, and think it utterly impossible to imitate them in *anything.* The sacred writers (he observed) related the vicious as well as the virtuous actions of men; which has this moral effect, that it kept mankind from *despair,* into which otherwise they would naturally fall, were they not supported by the recollection that others had offended like themselves, and by penitence and amendment of life had been restored to the favour of Heaven.

"E. M.

"March 15, 1782."

The last paragraph of this note is of great importance; and I request that my readers may consider it with particular attention. It will be afterwards referred to in this work.

In the Life of Blackmore, we find that writer's reputation generously cleared by Johnson from the cloud of prejudice which the malignity of contemporary wits had raised round it. In this spirited exertion of justice, he has been imitated by Sir Joshua Reynolds, in his praise of the architecture of Vanbrugh.

We trace Johnson's own character in his observations on Blackmore's "magnanimity as an author."—"The incessant attacks of his enemies, whether serious or merry, are never discovered to have disturbed his quiet, or to have lessened his confidence in himself." Johnson, I recollect, once told me, laughing heartily, that he understood it had been said of him, "He *appears* not to feel; but when he is *alone,* depend upon it, he *suffers sadly.*" I am as certain as I can be of any man's real sentiments, that he *enjoyed* the perpetual shower of little hostile arrows as evidences of his fame.

In the Life of Lyttelton, Johnson seems to have been not favourably disposed towards that nobleman. Mrs. Thrale suggests that he was offended by *Molly Aston's* preference of his Lordship to him. I can by no means join in the censure bestowed by Johnson on his Lordship, whom he calls "poor Lyttelton," for returning thanks to the Critical Reviewers, for having "kindly commended" his "Dialogues of the Dead." Such "acknowledgments (says my friend) never can be proper, since they must be paid either for flattery or for justice." In my opinion, the most upright man, who has been tried on a false accusation, may, when he is acquitted, make a bow to his jury. And when those who are so much the arbiters of literary merit, as in a considerable degree to influence the public opinion, review an author's work *placido lumine,* when I am afraid mankind in general are better pleased with severity, he may surely express a grateful sense of their civility.

As the introduction to his critical examination of the genius and writings of Young, he did Mr. Herbert Croft, then a Barrister of Lincoln's Inn, now a clergyman, the honour to adopt a Life of Young written by that gentleman, who was the friend of Dr. Young's son, and wished to vindicate him from some very erroneous remarks to his prejudice. Mr. Croft's performance was subjected to the revision of Dr. Johnson, as appears from the following note to Mr. John Nichols:

"This Life of Dr. Young was written by a friend of his son. What is crossed with black is expunged by the author, what is crossed with red is expunged by me. If you find anything more that can be well omitted, I shall not be sorry to see it yet shorter."

It has always appeared to me to have a considerable share of merit, and to display a pretty successful imitation of Johnson's style. When I mentioned this to a very eminent literary character, he opposed me vehemently, exclaiming, "No, no; it is *not* a good imitation of Johnson; it has all his pomp without his force; it has all the nodosities of the oak without its strength." This was an image so happy, that one might have thought he would have been satisfied with it: but he was not. And setting his mind again to work, he added, with exquisite felicity, "It has all the contortions of the sibyl, without the inspiration."

It gives me much pleasure to observe, that however Johnson may have casually talked, yet when he sits, as "an ardent judge zealous to his trust, giving sentence" upon the excellent works of Young, he allows them the high praise to which they are justly entitled. " 'The Universal Passion' (says he) is indeed a very great performance;— his distichs have the weight of solid sentiment, and his points the sharpness of resistless truth."

While the world in general was filled with admiration of Johnson's "Lives of the Poets," there were narrow circles in which prejudice and resentment were fostered, and from which attacks of different sorts issued against him. By some violent Whigs, he was arraigned of injustice to Milton; by some Cambridge men, of depreciating Gray; and his expressing with a dignified freedom what he really thought of George Lord Lyttelton, gave offence to some of the friends of that nobleman, and particularly produced a declaration of war against him from Mrs. Montague, the ingenious Essayist on Shakspeare, between whom and his Lordship a commerce of reciprocal compliments had long been carried on. In this war the smallest powers in alliance with him were of course led to engage, at least on the defensive; and thus I, for one, was excluded from the enjoyment of "A feast for Reason," such as Mr. Cumberland has described, with a keen, yet just and delicate pen, in his *Observer*. These minute inconveniences gave not the least disturbance to Johnson. He nobly said, when I talked to him of the feeble, though shrill outcry which had been raised, "Sir, I considered myself as entrusted with a certain portion of truth. I have given my opinion sincerely; let them show where they think me wrong."

CHAPTER XLIX—1781

Death of Thrale

WHILE MY FRIEND is thus contemplated in the splendour derived from his last and perhaps most admirable work, I introduce him with peculiar propriety as the correspondent of Warren Hastings; a man whose regard reflects dignity even upon Johnson; a man, the extent of whose abilities was equal to that of his power; and who, by those who are fortunate enough to know him in private life, is admired for his literature and taste, and beloved for the candour, moderation, and mildness of his character.

"TO JAMES BOSWELL, ESQ.

"*Park-lane, Dec. 2, 1790.*

"SIR,—

"I have been fortunately spared the troublesome suspense of a long search, to which, in performance of my promise, I had devoted this morning, by lighting upon the objects of it among the first papers that I laid my hands on: my veneration for your great and good friend, Dr. Johnson, and the pride, or I hope something of a better sentiment, which I indulge in possessing such memorials of his goodwill towards me, having induced me to bind them in a parcel containing other select papers, and labelled with the titles appertaining to them. They consist but of three letters, which I believe were all that I ever received from Dr. Johnson. Of these, one, which was written in quadruplicate, under the different dates of its respective dispatches, has already been made public, but not from any communication of mine. This, however, I have joined to the rest; and have now the pleasure of sending them to you for the use to which you informed me it was your desire to destine them.

"My promise was pledged with the condition that if the letters were found to contain anything which should render them improper for the public eye, you would dispense with the performance of it. You will have the goodness, I am sure, to pardon my recalling this stipulation to your recollection, as I shall be loath to appear negligent of that obligation which is always implied in an epistolary confidence. In the reservation of that right I have read them over with the most scrupulous attention, but have not seen in them the slightest cause on that ground to withhold them from you. But, though not on that, yet on another ground, I own I feel a little, yet but a little, reluctance to part with them; I mean on that of my own credit, which I fear will suffer by the information conveyed by them, that I was early in the possession of such valuable instructions for the beneficial employment of the influence of my late station, and (as it may seem) have so little availed myself of them. Whether I could, if it were necessary, defend myself against such an imputation, it little concerns the world to know. I look only to the effect which these relics may produce, considered as evidences of the virtues of their author; and believing that they will be found to display an uncommon warmth of private friendship, and a mind ever attentive to the improvement and extension of useful knowledge, and solicitous for the interests of mankind, I can cheerfully submit to the little sacrifice of my own fame, to contribute to the illustration of so great and venerable a character. They cannot be better applied, for that end, than by being entrusted to your hands. Allow me, with this offering, to infer from it a proof of the very great esteem with which I have the honour to profess myself, Sir,

"Your most obedient
"And most humble servant,
"WARREN HASTINGS.

"*P.S.*—At some future time, and when you have no farther occasion for these papers, I shall be obliged to you if you will return them."

The last of the three letters thus graciously put into my hands, and which has already appeared in public, belongs to this year, but I shall previously insert the first two, in order of their dates. They altogether form a group grand in my biographical picture.

"TO THE HONOURABLE WARREN HASTINGS, ESQ.

"SIR,—
"Though I have had but little personal knowledge of you, I have had enough to make me wish for more; and though it be now a long time since I was honoured by your visit, I had too much pleasure from it to forget it. By those whom we delight to remember, we are

unwilling to be forgotten; and therefore I cannot omit this opportunity of reviving myself in your memory by a letter which you will receive from the hands of my friend Mr. Chambers; a man whose purity of manners and vigour of mind are sufficient to make everything welcome that he brings.

"That this is my only reason for writing, will be too apparent by the uselessness of my letter to any other purpose. I have no questions to ask; not that I want curiosity after either the ancient or present state of regions, in which have been seen all the power and splendour of wide-extended empire; and which, as by some grant of natural superiority, supply the rest of the world with almost all that pride desires, and luxury enjoys. But my knowledge of them is too scanty to furnish me with proper topics of inquiry; I can only wish for information; and hope that a mind comprehensive like yours will find leisure, amidst the cares of your important station, to inquire into many subjects of which the European world either thinks not at all, or thinks with deficient intelligence and uncertain conjecture. I shall hope that he who once intended to increase the learning of his country by the introduction of the Persian language, will examine nicely the traditions and histories of the East; that he will survey the wonders of its ancient edifices, and trace the vestiges of its ruined cities; and that, at his return we shall know the arts and opinions of a race of men, from whom very little has been hitherto derived.

"You, Sir, have no need of being told by me how much may be added, by your attention and patronage, to experimental knowledge and natural history. There are arts of manufacture practised in the countries in which you preside, which are yet very imperfectly known here, either to artificers or philosophers. Of the natural productions, animate and inanimate, we yet have so little intelligence, that our books are filled, I fear, with conjectures about things which an Indian peasant knows by his senses.

"Many of those things my first wish is to see; my second to know, by such accounts as a man like you will be able to give.

"As I have not skill to ask proper questions, I have likewise no such access to great men as can enable me to send you any political information. Of the agitations of an unsettled government, and the struggles of a feeble ministry, care is doubtless taken to give you more exact accounts than I can obtain. If you are inclined to interest yourself much in public transactions, it is no misfortune to you to be distant from them.

"That literature is not totally forsaking us, and that your favourite language is not neglected, will appear from the book,[1] which I should have pleased myself more with sending, if I could have presented it bound: but time was wanting. I beg, however, Sir, that you will accept it from a man very desirous of your regard; and that if you think me able to gratify you by anything more important, you will employ me.

"I am now going to take leave, perhaps a very long leave, of my dear Mr. Chambers. That he is going to live where you govern, may justly alleviate the regard of parting; and the hope of seeing both him and you again, which I am not willing to mingle with doubt, must, at present, comfort as it can, Sir,

"Your most humble servant,

"SAM. JOHNSON.

"*March 30, 1774.*"

"TO THE SAME.

"SIR,—

"Being informed that, by the departure of a ship, there is now an opportunity of writing to Bengal, I am unwilling to slip out of your memory by my own negligence, and therefore take the liberty of reminding you of my existence, by sending you a book which is not yet made public.

"I have lately visited a region less remote, and less illustrious than India, which afforded some occasions for speculation; what has occurred to me I have put into the volume,[2] of which I beg your acceptance.

"Men in your station seldom have presents totally disinterested; my book is received, let me now make my request.

"There is, Sir, somewhere within your government, a young adventurer, one Chauncey Lawrence, whose father is one of my oldest friends. Be pleased to show the young man what countenance is fit, whether he wants to be restrained by your authority, or encouraged by your favour. His father is now President of the College of Physicians, a man venerable for his knowledge, and more venerable for his virtue.

[1][Sir William] Jones's "Persian Grammar."
[2]"Journey to the Western Islands of Scotland."

"I wish you a prosperous government, a safe return, and a long enjoyment of plenty and tranquillity.

"I am, Sir,

"Your most obedient

"And most humble servant,

"SAM. JOHNSON.

"London, Dec. 20, 1774."

"TO THE SAME.

"Jan. 9, 1781.

"SIR,—

"Amidst the importance and multiplicity of affairs in which your great office engages you, I take the liberty of recalling your attention for a moment to literature, and will not prolong the interruption by an apology which your character makes needless.

"Mr. Hoole, a gentleman long known, and long esteemed in the India-House, after having translated Tasso, has undertaken Ariosto. How well he is qualified for his undertaking, he has already shown. He is desirous, Sir, of your favour in promoting his proposals, and flatters me by supposing that my testimony may advance his interest.

"It is a new thing for a clerk of the India-House to translate poets; —it is new for a Governor of Bengal to patronise learning. That he may find his ingenuity rewarded, and that learning may flourish under your protection, is the wish of, Sir,

"Your most humble servant,

"SAM. JOHNSON."

I wrote to him in February, complaining of having been troubled by a recurrence of the perplexing question of liberty and necessity;— and mentioning that I hoped soon to meet him again in London.

On Monday, March 19, I arrived in London, and on Tuesday, the 20th, met him in Fleet-street, walking, or rather indeed moving along; for his peculiar march is thus described in a very just and picturesque manner, in a short Life of him published very soon after his death:—"When he walked the streets, what with the constant roll of his head, and the concomitant motion of his body, he appeared to make his way by that motion, independent of his feet." That he was often much stared at while he advanced in this manner, may easily be believed; but it was not safe to make sport of one so robust as he was. Mr. Langton saw him one day, in a fit of absence, by a sudden start, drive the load off a porter's back, and walk forward briskly, without being conscious of what he had done. The porter was very angry, but stood still, and eyed the huge figure with much earnestness, till he was satisfied that his wisest course was to be quiet, and take up his burden again.

Our accidental meeting in the street, after a long separation, was a pleasing surprise to us both. He stepped aside with me into Falcon-court, and made kind inquiries about my family; and, as we were in a hurry going different ways, I promised to call on him next day; he said he was engaged to go out in the morning. "Early, Sir?" said I. JOHNSON: "Why, Sir, a London morning does not go with the sun."

I waited on him next evening, and he gave me a great portion of his original manuscript of his "Lives of the Poets," which he had preserved for me.

I found, on visiting his friend, Mr. Thrale, that he was now very ill, and had removed, I suppose by the solicitation of Mrs. Thrale, to a house in Grosvenor-square. I was sorry to see him sadly changed in his appearance.

He told me I might now have the pleasure to see Dr. Johnson drink wine again, for he had lately returned to it. When I mentioned this to Johnson, he said, "I drink it now sometimes, but not socially." The first evening that I was with him at Thrale's, I observed he poured a large quantity of it into a glass, and swallowed it greedily. Everything about his character and manners was forcible and violent; there never was any moderation; many a day did he fast, many a year did he refrain from wine; but when he did eat, it was voraciously; when he did drink wine, it was copiously. He could practise abstinence, but not temperance.

Johnson's profound reverence for the Hierarchy made him expect from Bishops the highest degree of decorum; he was offended even at their going to taverns. "A bishop (said he) has nothing to do at a tippling-house. It is not indeed immoral in him to go to a tavern; neither would it be immoral in him to whip a top in Grosvenor-square: but, if he did, I hope the boys would fall upon him, and apply the whip to *him*. There are gradations in conduct; there is morality—decency—propriety. None of these should be violated by a bishop. A bishop should not go to a house where he may meet a young fellow leading out a wench." BOSWELL: "But, Sir, every tavern does not admit women." JOHNSON: "Depend upon it, Sir, any tavern will admit a well-dressed man and a well-dressed woman; they will not perhaps admit a woman whom they see every night walking by their door, in the street. But a well-dressed man may lead in a well-dressed woman to any tavern in London. Taverns sell meat and drink, and will sell them to anybody who can eat and can drink. You may as well say that a mercer will not sell silks to a woman of the town."

"Poh! (said Mrs. Thrale), the Bishop of [St. Asaph] is never minded at a rout." BOSWELL: "When a bishop places himself in a situation where he has no distinct character, and is of no consequence, he degrades the dignity of his order." JOHNSON: "Mr. Boswell, Madam, has said it as correctly as it could be."

On Friday, March 30, I dined with him at Sir Joshua Reynolds's, with the Earl of Charlemont, Sir Annesley Stewart, Mr. Eliot, of Port Eliot, Mr. Burke, Dean Marlay, Mr. Langton; a most agreeable day, of which I regret that every circumstance is not preserved; but it is unreasonable to require such a multiplication of felicity.

Mr. Eliot mentioned a curious liquor, peculiar to his country, which the Cornish fishermen drink. They call it *mahogany;* and it is made of two parts gin, and one part treacle, well beaten together. I begged to have some of it made, which was done with proper skill by Mr. Eliot. I thought it very good liquor; and said it was a counterpart of what is called *Athol porridge* in the Highlands of Scotland, which is a mixture of whisky and honey. Johnson said "that must be a better liquor than the Cornish, for both its component parts are better." He also observed, *"Mahogany* must be a modern name; for it is not long since the wood called mahogany was known in this country." I mentioned his scale of liquors:—claret for boys—port for men—brandy for heroes. "Then (said Mr. Burke), let me have claret: I love to be a boy; to have the careless gaiety of boyish days." JOHNSON: "I should drink claret too, if it would give me that: but it does not; it neither makes boys men, nor men boys. You'll be drowned by it, before it has any effect upon you."

I ventured to mention a ludicrous paragraph in the newspapers, that Dr. Johnson was learning to dance of Vestris. Lord Charlemont, wishing to excite him to talk, proposed, in a whisper, that he should be asked whether it was true. "Shall I ask him?" said his Lordship. We were, by a great majority, clear for the experiment. Upon which his Lordship very gravely, and with a courteous air, said, "Pray, Sir, is it true that you are taking lessons of Vestris?" This was risking a good deal, and required the boldness of a General of Irish Volunteers to make the attempt. Johnson was at first startled, and in some heat answered, "How can your Lordship ask so simple a question?" But immediately recovering himself, whether from unwillingness to be deceived, or to appear deceived, or whether from real good humour, he kept up the joke: "Nay, but if anybody were to answer the paragraph, and contradict it, I'd have a reply, and would say that he who contradicted it was no friend either to Vestris or me. For why should not Dr. Johnson add to his other powers a little corporeal agility? Socrates learnt to dance at an advanced age, and Cato learnt Greek at an advanced age. Then it might proceed to say that this Johnson, not content with dancing on the ground, might dance on the rope; and they might introduce the elephant dancing on the rope. A nobleman wrote a play called 'Love in a Hollow Tree.' He found out that it was a bad one, and therefore wished to buy up all the copies and burn them. The Duchess of Marlborough had kept one; and when he was against her at an election, she had a new edition of it printed, and prefixed to it, as a frontispiece, an elephant dancing on a rope; to show that his Lordship's writing comedy was as awkward as an elephant dancing on a rope."

On Sunday, April 1, I dined with him at Mr. Thrale's, with Sir Philip Jennings Clerk and Mr. Perkins, who had the superintendence of Mr. Thrale's brewery, with a salary of five hundred pounds a year. Sir Philip had the appearance of a gentleman of ancient family, well advanced in life. He wore his own white hair, in a bag of goodly size, a black velvet coat, with an embroidered waistcoat, and very rich laced ruffles; which Mrs. Thrale said were old-fashioned, but which, for that reason, I thought the more respectable, more like a Tory; yet Sir Philip was then in Opposition in Parliament. "Ah, Sir (said Johnson), ancient ruffles and modern principles do not agree."

Mrs. Thrale mentioned a gentleman who had acquired a fortune of £4,000 a year in trade, but was absolutely miserable, because he could not talk in company; so miserable that he was impelled to lament his situation in the street to *****, whom he hates, and who he knows despises him. "I am a most unhappy man (said he). I am invited to conversations. I go to conversations; but, alas! I have no conversation." JOHNSON: "Man commonly cannot be successful in different ways. This gentleman has spent, in getting £4,000 a year, the time in which he might have learnt to talk; and now he cannot talk." Mr. Perkins made a shrewd and droll remark: "If he had got his £4,000 a year as a mountebank, he might have learnt to talk at the same time that he was getting his fortune."

Mr. Thrale appeared very lethargic to-day. I saw him again on Monday evening, at which time he was not thought to be in immediate danger; but early in the morning of Wednesday, the 4th, he expired. Johnson was in the house, and thus mentions the event: "I felt almost the last flutter of his pulse, and looked for the last time upon the face that for fifteen years had never been turned upon me but with respect and benignity." Upon that day there was a *call* of the Literary Club; but Johnson apologised for his absence by the following note:

"Mr. Johnson knows that Sir Joshua Reynolds and the other gentlemen will excuse his incompliance with the call, when they are told that Mr. Thrale died this morning.
"Wednesday."

Mr. Thrale's death was a very essential loss to Johnson, who, although he did not foresee all that afterwards happened, was sufficiently convinced that the comforts which Mr. Thrale's family afforded him would now in a great measure cease. He, however, continued to show a kind attention to his widow and children as long as it was acceptable: and he took upon him, with a very earnest concern, the office of one of his executors, the importance of which seemed greater than usual to him, from his circumstances having been always such, that he had scarcely any share in the real business of life. His friends of the Club were in hopes that Mr. Thrale might have made a liberal provision for him for his life, which, as Mr. Thrale left no son, and a very large fortune, it would have been highly to his honour to have done; and, considering Dr. Johnson's age, could not have been of long duration; but he bequeathed him only two hundred pounds, which was the legacy given to each of his executors.

On Thursday, April 12, I dined with Johnson at a bishop's, where were Sir Joshua Reynolds, Mr. Berenger, and some more company. He had dined the day before at another bishop's. I have unfortunately recorded none of his conversation at the bishop's where we dined together: but I have preserved his ingenious defence of his dining twice abroad in Passion-week; a laxity in which I am convinced he would not have indulged himself at the time when he wrote his solemn paper in the *Rambler* upon that awful season. It appeared to me that by being much more in company, and enjoying more luxurious living, he had contracted a keener relish for pleasure, and was consequently less rigorous in his religious rites. This he would not acknowledge;

but he reasoned, with admirable sophistry, as follows: "Why, Sir, a bishop's calling company together in this week, is, to use the vulgar phrase, not *the thing*. But you must consider laxity is a bad thing; but preciseness is also a bad thing; and your general character may be more hurt by preciseness than by dining with a bishop in Passion-week. There might be a handle for reflection. It might be said, 'He refuses to dine with a bishop in Passion-week, but was three Sundays absent from church.'" BOSWELL: "Very true, Sir. But suppose a man to be uniformly of good conduct, would it not be better that he should refuse to dine with a bishop in this week, and so not encourage a bad practice by his example?" JOHNSON: "Why, Sir, you are to consider whether you might not do more harm by lessening the influence of a bishop's character by your disapprobation in refusing him, than by going to him."

"TO MRS. LUCY PORTER, IN LICHFIELD.

"DEAR MADAM,—

"Life is full of troubles. I have just lost my dear friend Thrale. I hope he is happy; but I have had a great loss. I am otherwise pretty well. I require some care of myself, but that care is not ineffectual; and when I am out of order, I think it often my own fault.

"The spring is now making quick advances. As it is the season in which the whole world is enlivened and invigorated, I hope that both you and I shall partake of its benefits. My desire is to see Lichfield; but being left executor to my friend, I know not whether I can be spared; but I will try, for it is now long since we saw one another; and how little we can promise ourselves many more interviews, we are taught by hourly examples of mortality. Let us try to live so as that mortality may not be an evil. Write to me soon, my dearest; your letters will give me great pleasure.

"Be so kind as to make my compliments to my friends; I have a great value for their kindness, and hope to enjoy it before summer is past. Do write to me.

"I am, dearest love,
"Your most humble servant,
"SAM. JOHNSON.

"*London, April 12, 1781.*"

On Friday, April 13, being Good Friday, I went to St. Clement's Church with him, as usual. There I saw again his old fellow-collegian,

Edwards, to whom I said, "I think, Sir, Dr. Johnson and you meet only at church."—"Sir (said he), it is the best place we can meet in, except heaven, and I hope we shall meet there too." Dr. Johnson told me that there was very little communication between Edwards and him, after their unexpected renewal of acquaintance. "But (said he, smiling), he met me once, and said, 'I am told you have written a very pretty book called the *Rambler*.' I was unwilling that he should leave the world in total darkness, and sent him a set."

Mr. Berenger visited him to-day, and was very pleasing. We talked of an evening society for conversation at a house in town, of which we were all members, but of which Johnson said, "It will never do, Sir. There is nothing served about there, neither tea, nor coffee, nor lemonade, nor anything whatever; and depend upon it, Sir, a man does not love to go to a place from whence he comes out exactly as he went in." I endeavoured, for argument's sake, to maintain that men of learning and talents might have very good intellectual society, without the aid of any little gratifications of the senses. Berenger joined with Johnson, and said that without these any meeting would be dull and insipid. He would therefore have all the slight refreshments; nay, it would not be amiss to have some cold meat, and a bottle of wine upon a sideboard. "Sir (said Johnson to me with an air of triumph), Mr. Berenger knows the world. Everybody loves to have good things furnished to them without any trouble. I told Mrs. Thrale once that as she did not choose to have card-tables, she should have a profusion of the best sweetmeats, and she would be sure to have company enough come to her." I agreed with my illustrious friend upon this subject; for it has pleased God to make man a composite animal, and where there is nothing to refresh the body, the mind will languish.

On Sunday, April 15, being Easter-day, after solemn worship in St. Paul's Church, I found him alone; Dr. Scott, of the Commons, came in. He talked of its having been said that Addison wrote some of his best papers in the *Spectator,* when warm with wine. Dr. Johnson did not seem willing to admit this. Dr. Scott, as a confirmation of it, related that Blackstone, a sober man, composed his "Commentaries" with a bottle of port before him; and found his mind invigorated and supported in the fatigue of his great work by a temperate use of it.

Dr. Scott left us, and soon afterwards we went to dinner. Our company consisted of Mrs. Williams, Mrs. Desmoulins, Mr. Levett, Mr. Allen the printer [Mr. Macbean], and Mrs. Hall, sister of the Reverend Mr. John Wesley, and resembling him, as I thought, both in figure and manner. Johnson produced now, for the first time, some handsome silver salvers, which he told me he had bought fourteen years ago; so it was a great day. I was not a little amused by observing Allen perpetually struggling to talk in the manner of Johnson, like the little frog in the fable blowing himself up to resemble the stately ox.

CHAPTER L—1781

Mrs. Garrick's Dinner

ON FRIDAY, APRIL 20, I spent with Johnson one of the happiest days that I remember to have enjoyed in the whole course of my life. Mrs. Garrick, whose grief for the loss of her husband was, I believe, as sincere as wounded affection and admiration could produce, had this day, for the first time since his death, a select party of his friends to dine with her. The company was Miss Hannah More, who lived with her, and whom she called her Chaplain; Mrs. Boscawen, Mrs. Elizabeth Carter, Sir Joshua Reynolds, Dr. Burney, Dr. Johnson, and myself. We found ourselves very elegantly entertained at her house in the Adelphi, where I have passed many a pleasing hour with him "who gladdened life." She looked well, talked of her husband with complacency, and, while she cast her eyes on his portrait, which hung over the chimneypiece, said that "death was now the most agreeable object to her." The very semblance of David Garrick was cheering.

We were all in fine spirits; and I whispered to Mrs. Boscawen, "I believe this is as much as can be made of life." In addition to a splendid entertainment, we were regaled with Lichfield ale, which had a peculiar appropriate value. Sir Joshua and Dr. Burney and I drank cordially of it to Dr. Johnson's health; and though he would not join us, he as cordially answered, "Gentlemen, I wish you all as well as you do me."

The general effect of this day dwells upon my mind in fond remembrance; but I do not find much conversation recorded.

In the evening we had a large company in the drawing-room; several ladies, the Bishop of Killaloe, Dr. Percy, Mr. Chamberlayne,

[533]

of the Treasury, etc., etc. Talking of a very respectable author, he told us a curious circumstance in his life, which was, that he had married a printer's devil. REYNOLDS: "A printer's devil, Sir! Why, I thought a printer's devil was a creature with a black face and in rags." JOHNSON: "Yes, Sir. But I suppose he had her face washed, and put clean clothes on her. (Then looking very serious, and very earnest.) And she did not disgrace him;—the woman had a bottom of good sense." The word *bottom,* thus introduced, was so ludicrous when contrasted with his gravity, that most of us could not forbear tittering and laughing; though I recollect that the Bishop of Killaloe kept his countenance with perfect steadiness, while Miss Hannah More slyly hid her face behind a lady's back who sat on the same settee with her. His pride could not bear that any expression of his should excite ridicule, when he did not intend it; he therefore resolved to assume and exercise despotic power, glanced sternly around, and called out in a strong tone, "Where's the merriment?" Then collecting himself, and looking awful, to make us feel how he could impose restraint, and as it were searching his mind for a still more ludicrous word, he slowly pronounced, "I say the *woman* was *fundamentally* sensible"; as if he had said, hear this now, and laugh if you dare. We all sat composed as at a funeral.

For some time after this day, I did not see him very often, and of the conversation which I did enjoy, I am sorry to find I have preserved but little. I was at this time engaged in a variety of other matters, which required exertion and assiduity, and necessarily occupied almost all my time.

On Tuesday, May 8, I had the pleasure of again dining with him and Mr. Wilkes, at Mr. Dilly's. No *negotiation* was now required to bring them together; for Johnson was so well satisfied with the former interview, that he was very glad to meet Wilkes again, who was this day seated between Dr. Beattie and Dr. Johnson (between *Truth* and *Reason,* as General Paoli said when I told him of it). WILKES: "I have been thinking, Dr. Johnson, that there should be a bill brought into Parliament that the controverted elections for Scotland should be tried in that country, at their own abbey of Holyrood House, and not here; for the consequence of trying them here is that we have an inundation of Scotchmen, who come up and never go back again. Now, here is Boswell, who is come upon the election for his own county, which will not last a fortnight." JOHNSON: "Nay, Sir, I see no reason why they should be tried at all; for, you know one Scotchman is as good as another." WILKES: "Pray, Boswell, how much may be got in a year by an Advocate at the Scotch bar?" BOSWELL: "I believe, two thousand pounds." WILKES: "How can it be possible to spend that money in Scotland?" JOHNSON: "Why, Sir, the money may be spent in England; but there is a harder question. If one man in Scotland gets possession of two thousand pounds, what remains for all the rest of the nation?" WILKES: "You know, in the last war, the immense booty which Thurot carried off by the complete plunder of seven Scotch isles; he re-embarked with *three and sixpence*." Here again Johnson and Wilkes joined in extravagant sportive raillery upon the supposed poverty of Scotland, which Dr. Beattie and I did not think it worth our while to dispute.

He gave us an entertaining account of *Bet Flint,* a woman of the town, who, with some eccentric talents and much effrontery, forced herself upon his acquaintance. "Bet (said he) wrote her own Life in verse, which she brought to me, wishing that I would furnish her with a preface to it. (Laughing.) I used to say of her that she was generally slut and drunkard;—occasionally, whore and thief. She had, however, genteel lodgings, a spinnet on which she played, and a boy that walked before her chair. Poor Bet was taken up on a charge of stealing a counterpane, and tried at the Old Bailey. Chief Justice [Willes], who loved a wench, summed up favourably, and she was acquitted. After which, Bet said, with a gay and satisfied air, 'Now that the counterpane is *my own,* I shall make a petticoat of it.' "

Mr. Wilkes observed how tenacious we are of forms in this country; and gave, as an instance, the vote of the House of Commons for remitting money to pay the army in America *in Portugal pieces,* when, in reality, the remittance is made not in Portugal money, but in our specie. JOHNSON: "Is there not a law, Sir, against exporting the current coin of the realm?" WILKES: "Yes, Sir; but might not the House of Commons, in case of real evident necessity, order our own current coin to be sent into our own colonies?"—Here Johnson, with that quickness of recollection which distinguished him so eminently, gave the *Middlesex Patriot* an admirable retort upon his own ground. "Sure, Sir, *you* don't think a *resolution of the House of Commons* equal to *the law of the land.*" WILKES (at once perceiving the application): "God forbid, Sir."—To hear what had been treated with such violence in "The False Alarm," now turned into pleasant repartee, was extremely agreeable. Johnson went on:—"Locke observes well, that a prohibition to export the current coin is impolitic; for when the balance of trade happens to be against a state, the current coin *must* be exported."

Mr. Wilkes said to me, loud enough for Dr. Johnson to hear, "Dr. Johnson should make me a present of his 'Lives of the Poets,' as I am a poor patriot, who cannot afford to buy them." Johnson seemed to take no notice of this hint; but in a little while he called to Mr. Dilly, "Pray, Sir, be so good as to send a set of my 'Lives' to Mr. Wilkes, with my compliments." This was accordingly done; and Mr. Wilkes paid Dr. Johnson a visit, was courteously received, and sat with him a long time.

The company gradually dropped away, Mr. Dilly himself was called down stairs upon business; I left the room for some time; when I returned, I was struck with observing Dr. Samuel Johnson and John Wilkes, Esq., literally *tête-à-tête;* for they were reclined upon their chairs, with their heads leaning almost close to each other, and talking earnestly, in a kind of confidential whisper, of the personal quarrel between George the Second and the King of Prussia. Such a scene of perfectly easy sociality, between two such opponents in the war of political controversy, as that which I now beheld, would have been an excellent subject for a picture. It presented to my mind the happy days which are foretold in Scripture, when the lion shall lie down with the kid.

After this day there was another pretty long interval, during which Dr. Johnson and I did not meet. When I mentioned it to him with regret, he was pleased to say, "Then, Sir, let us live double."

About this time it was much the fashion for several ladies to have evening assemblies, where the fair sex might participate in conversation with literary and ingenious men, animated by a desire to please. These societies were denominated *Blue-stocking Clubs,* the origin of which title being little known it may be worth while to relate it. One of the most eminent members of those societies, when they first commenced, was Mr. Stillingfleet, whose dress was remarkably grave, and in particular it was observed that he wore blue stockings. Such was the excellence of his conversation that his absence was felt as so great a loss, that it used to be said, "We can do nothing without the *blue-stockings*"; and thus by degrees the title was established. Miss Hannah More has admirably described a *Blue-stocking Club* in her *"Bas Bleu,"* a poem in which many of the persons who were most conspicuous there are mentioned.

Johnson was prevailed with to come sometimes into these circles,

Gordon Ross del.   New York, 1945

"If I had no duties I would spend my life.
driving a post chaise with a pretty woman."

JOHNSON

and did not think himself too grave even for the lively Miss Monckton (now Countess of Cork), who used to have the finest *bit of blue* at the house of her mother, Lady Galway. Her vivacity enchanted the Sage, and they used to talk together with all imaginable ease. A singular instance happened one evening, when she insisted that some of Sterne's writings were very pathetic. Johnson bluntly denied it. "I am sure (said she) they have affected *me*."—"Why (said Johnson, smiling, and rolling himself about), that is because, dearest, you're a dunce." When she some time afterwards mentioned this to him, he said, with equal truth and politeness, "Madam, if I had thought so, I certainly should not have said it."

Another evening, Johnson's kind indulgence towards me had a pretty difficult trial. I had dined at the Duke of Montrose's with a very agreeable party, and his Grace, according to his usual custom, had circulated the bottle very freely. Lord Graham and I went together to Miss Monckton's, where I certainly was in extraordinary spirits, and above all fear or awe. In the midst of a great number of persons of the first rank, amongst whom I recollect, with confusion, a noble lady of the most stately decorum, I placed myself next to Johnson, and thinking myself now fully his match, talked to him in a loud and boisterous manner, desirous to let the company know how I could contend with *Ajax*. I particularly remember pressing him upon the value of the pleasures of the imagination, and as an illustration of my argument, asking him, "What, Sir, supposing I were to fancy that the —— (naming the most charming duchess in his Majesty's dominions) were in love with me, should I not be very happy?" My friend, with much address, evaded my interrogatories, and kept me as quiet as possible; but it may easily be conceived how he must have felt. However, when a few days afterwards I waited upon him and made an apology, he behaved with the most friendly gentleness.

While I remained in London this year, Johnson and I dined together at several places. I recollect a placid day at Dr. Butter's, who had now removed from Derby to Lower-Grosvenor-street, London; but of his conversation on that and other occasions during this period, I neglected to keep any regular record, and shall therefore insert here some miscellaneous articles which I find in my Johnsonian notes.

Goldsmith could sometimes take adventurous liberties with him, and escape unpunished. Beauclerk told me that when Goldsmith talked of a project for having a third lecture in London solely for the exhibition of new plays, in order to deliver authors from the supposed tyranny of managers, Johnson treated it slightingly, upon which Goldsmith said, "Ay, ay, this may be nothing to you, who can now shelter yourself behind the corner of a pension"; and Johnson bore this with good-humour.

I asked him if he was not dissatisfied with having so small a share of wealth, and none of those distinctions in the state which are the objects of ambition. He had only a pension of three hundred a year. Why was he not in such circumstances as to keep his coach? Why had he not some considerable office? JOHNSON: "Sir, I have never complained of the world; nor do I think that I have reason to complain. It is rather to be wondered at that I have so much. My pension is more out of the usual course of things than any instance that I have known. Here, Sir, was a man avowedly no friend to Government at the time, who got a pension without asking for it. I never courted the great; they sent for me; but I think they now give me up. They are satisfied: they have seen enough of me." Upon my observing that I could not believe this, for they must certainly be highly pleased by his conversation; conscious of his own superiority, he answered, "No, Sir; great lords and great ladies don't love to have their mouths stopped." This was very expressive of the effect which the force of his understanding and brilliancy of his fancy could not but produce; and, to be sure, they must have found themselves strangely diminished in his company. When I warmly declared how happy I was at all times to hear him:— "Yes, Sir (said he); but if you were Lord Chancellor, it would not be so: you would then consider your own dignity."

On Saturday, June 2, I set out for Scotland, and had promised to pay a visit, in my way, as I sometimes did, at Southill, in Bedfordshire, at the hospitable mansion of Squire Dilly, the elder brother of my worthy friends, the booksellers, in the Poultry. Dr. Johnson agreed to be of the party this year, with Mr. Charles Dilly and me, and to go and see Lord Bute's seat at Luton Hoe. He talked little to us in the carriage, being chiefly occupied in reading Dr. Watson's second volume of "Chemical Essays," which he liked very well, and his own "Prince of Abyssinia," on which he seemed to be intensely fixed; having told us, that he had not looked at it since it was first published. I happened to take it out of my pocket this day, and he seized upon it with avidity.

Upon the road we talked of the uncertainty of profit with which authors and booksellers engage in the publication of literary works. JOHNSON: "My judgment I have found is no certain rule as to the sale of a book." BOSWELL: "Pray, Sir, have you been much plagued with authors sending you their works to revise?" JOHNSON: "No, Sir; I have been thought a sour, surly fellow." BOSWELL: "Very lucky for you, Sir —in that respect." I must, however, observe that notwithstanding what he now said, which he no doubt imagined at the time to be the fact, there was, perhaps, no man who more frequently yielded to the solicitations even of very obscure authors, to read their manuscripts, or more liberally assisted them with advice and correction.

He found himself very happy at Squire Dilly's, where there is always abundance of excellent fare, and hearty welcome.

Although upon most occasions I never heard a more strenuous advocate for the advantages of wealth than Dr. Johnson, he this day, I know not from what caprice, took the other side. "I have not observed (said he) that men of very large fortunes enjoy anything extraordinary that makes happiness. What has the Duke of Bedford? What has the Duke of Devonshire? The only great instance that I have ever known of the enjoyment of wealth was that of Jamaica Dawkins, who going to visit Palmyra, and hearing that the way was infested by robbers, hired a troop of Turkish horse to guard him."

When I observed that a housebreaker was in general very timorous; —JOHNSON: "No wonder, Sir; he is afraid of being shot getting *into* a house, or hanged when he has got *out* of it."

He told us that he had in one day written six sheets of a translation from the French; adding, "I should be glad to see it now. I wish that I had copies of all the pamphlets written against me, as it is said Pope had. Had I known that I should make so much noise in the world, I should have been at pains to collect them. I believe there is hardly a day in which there is not something about me in the newspapers."

On Monday, June 4, we all went to Luton Hoe, to see Lord Bute's magnificent seat, for which I had obtained a ticket. As we entered the Park, I talked in a high style of my old friendship with Lord Mountstuart, and said, "I shall probably be much at this place." The Sage, aware of human vicissitudes, gently checked me: "Don't you be too sure of that." He made two or three peculiar observations; as when shown the botanical garden, "Is not *every* garden a botanical garden?" When told that there was a shrubbery to the extent of several miles; "That is making a very foolish use of the ground; a little of it is very well." When it was proposed that we should walk on the pleasure-ground; "Don't let us fatigue ourselves. Why should we walk there? Here's a fine place, let's go to the top of it." But upon the whole, he was very much pleased. He said, "This is one of the places I do not regret having come to see. It is a very stately place, indeed; in the house magnificence is not sacrificed to convenience, nor convenience to magnificence. The library is very splendid; the dignity of the rooms is very great; and the quantity of pictures is beyond expectation, beyond hope."

It happened without any previous concert, that we visited the seat of Lord Bute upon the King's birthday; we dined and drank his Majesty's health at an inn, in the village of Luton.

In the evening I put him in mind of his promise to favour me with a copy of his celebrated letter to the Earl of Chesterfield, and he was at last pleased to comply with this earnest request, by dictating it to me from his memory; for he believed that he himself had no copy. There was an animated glow in his countenance while he thus recalled his high-minded indignation.

On Tuesday, June 5, Johnson was to return to London. He was very pleasant at breakfast; I mentioned a friend of mine having resolved never to marry a pretty woman. JOHNSON: "Sir, it is a very foolish resolution to resolve not to marry a pretty woman. Beauty is of itself very estimable. No, Sir, I would prefer a pretty woman, unless there are objections to her. A pretty woman may be foolish; a pretty woman may be wicked; a pretty woman may not like me. But there is no such danger in marrying a pretty woman as is apprehended; she will not be persecuted if she does not invite persecution. A pretty woman, if she has a mind to be wicked, can find a readier way than another; and that is all."

I accompanied him in Mr. Dilly's chaise to Shefford, where, talking of Lord Bute's never going to Scotland, he said, "As an Englishman, I should wish all the Scotch gentlemen should be educated in England; Scotland would become a province; they would spend all their rents in England."

At Shefford I had another affectionate parting from my revered friend, who was taken up by the Bedford coach, and carried to the metropolis. I went with Messieurs Dilly to see some friends at Bedford; dined with the officers of the militia of the county, and next day proceeded on my journey.

CHAPTER LI—1781–1782

Death of Robert Levett

"TO BENNET LANGTON, ESQ.

"DEAR SIR,—

"How welcome your account of yourself and your invitation to your new house was to me, I need not tell you, who consider our friendship not only as formed by choice, but as matured by time. We have been now long enough acquainted to have many images in common, and therefore to have a source of conversation which neither the learning nor the wit of a new companion can supply.

"My 'Lives' are now published; and if you will tell me whither I shall send them, that they may come to you, I will take care that you shall not be without them.

"You will, perhaps, be glad to hear that Mrs. Thrale is disencumbered of her brewhouse; and that it seemed to the purchaser so far from an evil, that he was content to give for it a hundred and thirty-five thousand pounds. Is the nation ruined?

"Please to make my respectful compliments to Lady Rothes, and keep me in the memory of all the little dear family, particularly Mrs. Jane.

"I am, Sir,
"Your affectionate humble servant,
"SAM. JOHNSON.

"Bolt-court, June 16, 1781."

In autumn he went to Oxford, Birmingham, Lichfield, and Ashbourne, for which very good reasons might be given in the conjectural yet positive manner of writers, who are proud to account for every event which they relate. He himself, however, says, "The motives of my journey I hardly know; I omitted it last year, and am not willing to miss it again." But some good considerations arise, amongst which is the kindly recollection of Mr. Hector, surgeon of Birmingham. "Hector is likewise an old friend, the only companion of my childhood

[541]

that passed through the school with me. We have always loved one another; perhaps we may be made better by some serious conversation, of which, however, I have no distinct hope."

He says too, "At Lichfield, my native place, I hope to show a good example by frequent attendance on public worship."

My correspondence with him during the rest of this year was, I know not why, very scanty, and all on my side. I wrote him one letter to introduce Mr. Sinclair (now Sir John) the Member for Caithness, to his acquaintance; and informed him in another that my wife had again been affected with alarming symptoms of illness.

In 1782 his complaints increased, and the history of his life this year is little more than a mournful recital of the variations of his illness, in the midst of which, however, it will appear from his letters that the powers of his mind were in no degree impaired.

"TO JAMES BOSWELL, ESQ.

"DEAR SIR,—

"I sit down to answer your letter on the same day in which I received it, and am pleased that my first letter of the year is to you. No man ought to be at ease while he knows himself in the wrong; and I have not satisfied myself with my long silence. The letter relating to Mr. Sinclair, however, was, I believe, never brought.

"My health has been tottering this last year: and I can give no very laudable account of my time. I am always hoping to do better than I have ever hitherto done.

"My journey to Ashbourne and Staffordshire was not pleasant; for what enjoyment has a sick man visiting the sick?—Shall we ever have another frolic like our journey to the Hebrides?

"I hope that dear Mrs. Boswell will surmount her complaints; in losing her you will lose your anchor, and be tossed, without stability, by the waves of life. I wish both her and you very many years, and very happy.

"For some months past I have been so withdrawn from the world that I can send you nothing particular. All your friends, however, are well, and will be glad of your return to London.

"I am, dear Sir,

"Yours most affectionately,

"SAM. JOHNSON.

"*January 5, 1782.*"

At a time when he was less able than he had once been to sustain a shock, he was suddenly deprived of Mr. Levett, which event he thus communicated to Dr. Lawrence.

"SIR,—

"Our old friend, Mr. Levett, who was last night eminently cheerful, died this morning. The man who lay in the same room, hearing an uncommon noise, got up and tried to make him speak, but without effect. He then called Mr. Holder, the apothecary, who, though when he came he thought him dead, opened a vein, but could draw no blood. So has ended the long life of a very useful and very blameless man.

"I am, Sir,

"Your most humble servant,

"SAM. JOHNSON.

"January 17, 1782."

In one of Johnson's registers of this year, there occurs the following curious passage: "Jan. 20. The Ministry is dissolved. I prayed with Francis, and gave thanks." It has been the subject of discussion, whether there are two distinct particulars mentioned here? Or that we are to understand the giving of thanks to be in consequence of the dissolution of the Ministry? In support of the last of these conjectures may be urged his mean opinion of that Ministry, which has frequently appeared in the course of this work; and it is strongly confirmed by what he said on the subject to Mr. Seward:—"I am glad the Ministry is removed. Such a bunch of imbecility never disgraced a country. If they sent a messenger into the City to take up a printer, the messenger was taken up instead of the printer, and committed by the sitting Alderman. If they sent one army to the relief of another, the first army was defeated and taken before the second arrived. I will not say that what they did was always wrong; but it was always done at a wrong time."

"TO EDMUND MALONE, ESQ.

"SIR,—

"I have for many weeks been so much out of order, that I have gone out only in a coach to Mrs. Thrale's, where I can use all the freedom that sickness requires. Do not, therefore, take it amiss that I am not with you and Dr. Farmer. I hope hereafter to see you often.

"I am, Sir,

"Your most humble servant,

"SAM. JOHNSON.

"*Feb. 27, 1782.*"

"TO THE SAME.

"DEAR SIR,—

"I hope I grow better, and shall soon be able to enjoy the kindness of my friends. I think this wild adherence to Chatterton more unaccountable than the obstinate defence of Ossian. In Ossian there is a national pride, which may be forgiven, though it cannot be applauded. In Chatterton there is nothing but the resolution to say again what has once been said.

"I am, Sir,

"Your humble servant,

"SAM. JOHNSON.

"*March 2, 1782.*"

These short letters show the regard which Dr. Johnson entertained for Mr. Malone, who the more he is known is the more highly valued. It is much to be regretted that Johnson was prevented from sharing the elegant hospitality of that gentleman's table, at which he would in every respect have been fully gratified. Mr. Malone, who has so ably succeeded him as an Editor of Shakspeare, has, in his preface, done great and just honour to Johnson's memory.

"TO MRS. LUCY PORTER, IN LICHFIELD.

"DEAR MADAM,—

"I went away from Lichfield ill, and have had a troublesome time with my breath; for some weeks I have been disordered by a cold, of which I could not get the violence abated, till I had been let blood three times.

"I have not, however, been so bad but that I could have written, and am sorry that I neglected it.

"My dwelling is but melancholy; both Williams, and Desmoulins, and myself, are very sickly: Frank is not well; and poor Levett died in his bed the other day, by a sudden stroke; I suppose not one minute passed between health and death: so uncertain are human things.

"Such is the appearance of the world about me: I hope your scenes are more cheerful. But whatever befalls us, though it is wise to be serious, it is useless and foolish, and perhaps sinful, to be gloomy. Let us, therefore, keep ourselves as easy as we can; though the loss of friends will be felt, and poor Levett had been a faithful adherent for thirty years.

"Forgive me, my dear love, the omission of writing; I hope to mend that and my other faults. Let me have your prayers.

"Make my compliments to Mrs. Cobb, and Miss Adey, and Mr. Pearson, and the whole company of my friends.

"I am, my dear,

"Your most humble servant,

"SAM. JOHNSON.

"London, March 2, 1782."

"TO CAPTAIN LANGTON, IN ROCHESTER.

"DEAR SIR,—

"It is now long since we saw one another; and, whatever has been the reason, neither you have written to me, nor I to you. To let friendship die away by negligence and silence, is certainly not wise. It is voluntarily to throw away one of the greatest comforts of this weary pilgrimage, of which when it is, as it must be taken finally away, he that travels on alone, will wonder how his esteem could be so little. Do not forget me; you see that I do not forget you. It is pleasing in the silence of solitude to think that there is one at least, however distant, of whose benevolence there is little doubt, and whom there is yet hope of seeing again.

"Of my life, from the time we parted, the history is mournful. The spring of last year deprived me of Thrale, a man whose eye for fifteen years had scarcely been turned upon me but with respect or tenderness; for such another friend, the general course of human things will not suffer man to hope. I passed the summer at Streatham, but there was no Thrale; and having idled away the summer with a weakly body and neglected mind, I made a journey to Staffordshire on the edge of winter. The season was dreary, I was sickly, and found the friends sickly whom I went to see. After a sorrowful sojourn, I returned to a habitation possessed for the present by two sick women, where my dear old friend, Mr. Levett, to whom as he used to tell me, I owe your acquaintance, died a few weeks ago, suddenly in his bed; there passed not, I believe, a minute between health and death. At night, as at Mrs. Thrale's, I was musing in my chamber, I thought with uncommon earnestness, that however I might alter my mode of life, or whithersoever I might remove, I would endeavour to retain Levett about me; in the morning my servant brought me word that Levett was called to another state, a state for which, I think, he was not unprepared, for he was very useful to the poor. How much soever I valued him, I now wish that I had valued him more.

"I have myself been ill more than eight weeks of a disorder, from which, at the expense of about fifty ounces of blood, I hope I am now recovering.

"You, dear Sir, have, I hope, a more cheerful scene; you see George fond of his book, and the pretty misses airy and lively, with my own little Jenny equal to the best; and in whatever can contribute to your quiet or pleasure, you have Lady Rothes ready to concur. May whatever you enjoy of good be increased, and whatever you suffer of evil be diminished.

"I am, dear Sir,

"Your humble servant,

"SAM. JOHNSON.

"Bolt-court, Fleet-street,
    "March 20, 1782."

"TO MR. HECTOR, IN BIRMINGHAM.

"DEAR SIR,—

"I hope I do not very grossly flatter myself to imagine that you and dear Mrs. Careless will be glad to hear some account of me. I performed the journey to London with very little inconvenience, and came safe to my habitation, where I found nothing but ill health, and, of consequence, very little cheerfulness. I then went to visit a little way into the country, where I got a complaint by a cold which has hung eight weeks upon me, and from which I am, at the expense of fifty ounces of blood, not yet free. I am afraid I must once more owe my recovery to warm weather, which seems to make no advances towards us.

"Such is my health, which will, I hope, soon grow better. In other respects I have no reason to complain. I know not that I have written anything more generally commended than the 'Lives of the Poets'; and have found the world willing enough to caress me, if my health had invited me to be in much company; but this season I **have been** almost wholly employed in nursing myself.

"When summer comes I hope to see you again, and will not put off my visit to the end of the year. I have lived so long in London that I did not remember the difference of seasons.

"Your health, when I saw you, was much improved. You will be prudent enough not to put it in danger. I hope, when we meet again, we shall congratulate each other upon fair prospects of longer life; though what are the pleasures of the longest life, when placed in comparison with a happy death?

"I am, dear Sir,

"Yours most affectionately,

"SAM. JOHNSON.

"London, March 21, 1782."

I wrote to him at different dates; regretted that I could not come to London this spring, but hoped we should meet somewhere in the summer; mentioned the state of my affairs, and suggested hopes of some preferment; informed him, that as "The Beauties of Johnson" had been published in London, some obscure scribbler had published at Edinburgh what he called "The Deformities of Johnson."

"TO JAMES BOSWELL, ESQ.

"DEAR SIR,—

"The pleasure which we used to receive from each other on Good Friday and Easter Day we must be this year content to miss. Let us, however, pray for each other, and hope to see one another yet from time to time with mutual delight. My disorder has been a cold, which impeded the organs of respiration, and kept me many weeks in a state of great uneasiness; but by repeated phlebotomy it is now relieved: and next to the recovery of Mrs. Boswell, I flatter myself that you will rejoice at mine.

"What we shall do in the summer, it is yet too early to consider. You want to know what you shall do now; I do not think this time of bustle and confusion like to produce any advantage to you. Every man has those to reward and gratify who have contributed to his advancement. To come hither with such expectations at the expense of borrowed money, which, I find, you know not where to borrow, can hardly be considered prudent. I am sorry to find, what your solicitations seem to imply, that you have already gone the whole length of your credit. This is to set the quiet of your whole life at hazard. If you anticipate your inheritance, you can at last inherit nothing; all that you receive must pay for the past. You must get a place, or pine in penury, with the empty name of a great estate. Poverty, my dear friend, is so great an evil, and pregnant with so much temptation, and so much misery, that I cannot but earnestly enjoin you to avoid it. Live on what you have; live if you can on less; do not borrow either for vanity or pleasure; the vanity will end in shame, and the pleasure in regret: stay therefore at home, till you have saved money for your journey hither.

" 'The Beauties of Johnson' are said to have got money to the collector; if 'the Deformities' have the same success, I shall be still a more extensive benefactor.

"Make my compliments to Mrs. Boswell, who is, I hope, reconciled to me; and to the young people, whom I have never offended.

"I am, dear Sir,

"Your most affectionate,

"Sam. Johnson.

"London, March 28, 1782."

Notwithstanding his afflicted state of body and mind this year, the following correspondence affords a proof not only of his benevolence and conscientious readiness to relieve a good man from error, but by his clothing one of the sentiments in his *Rambler* in different language, not inferior to that of the original, shows his extraordinary command of clear and forcible expression.

A clergyman at Bath wrote to him that, in the *Morning Chronicle,* a passage in "The Beauties of Johnson," article Death, had been pointed out as supposed by some readers to recommend suicide, the words being, "To die is the fate of man; but to die with lingering anguish is generally his folly"; and respectfully suggesting to him that such an erroneous notion of any sentence in the writings of an acknowledged friend of religion and virtue, should not pass uncontradicted.

Johnson thus answered the clergyman's letter:

"TO THE REVEREND MR. ——, AT BATH.

"Sir,—

"Being now in the country in a state of recovery, as I hope, from a very oppressive disorder, I cannot neglect the acknowledgment of your Christian letter. The book called 'The Beauties of Johnson' is the production of I know not whom; I never saw it but by casual inspection, and considered myself as utterly disengaged from its consequences. Of the passage you mention, I remember some notice in some paper; but knowing that it must be misrepresented, I thought of it no more, nor do I know where to find it in my own books. I am accustomed to think little of newspapers; but an opinion so weighty and serious as yours has determined me to do, what I should, without your seasonable admonition, have omitted: and I will direct my thought to be shown in its true state. If I could find the passage I would direct you to it. I suppose the tenor is this:—'Acute diseases are the immediate and inevitable strokes of Heaven; but of them the pain is short, and the conclusion speedy; chronical disorders, by which we are suspended in tedious torture between life and death, are commonly the effect of our own misconduct and intemperance. To die, etc.'—This, Sir, you see is all true and all blameless. I hope some time in the next week to have all rectified. My health has been lately much shaken; if you favour me with any answer, it will be a comfort to me to know that I have your prayers.

"I am, etc.,

"Sam. Johnson.

"*May 15, 1782.*"

This letter, as might be expected, had its full effect, and the clergyman acknowledged it in grateful and pious terms.

On the 30th of August, I informed him that my honoured father had died that morning; a complaint under which he had long laboured having suddenly come to a crisis, while I was upon a visit at the seat of Sir Charles Preston, from whence I had hastened the day before, upon receiving a letter by express.

"TO JAMES BOSWELL, ESQ.

"DEAR SIR,—

"I have struggled through this year with so much infirmity of body, and such strong impressions of the frailty of life, that death, whenever it appears, fills me with melancholy; and I cannot hear without emotion of the removal of anyone, whom I have known, into another state.

"Your father's death had every circumstance that could enable you to bear it; it was at a mature age, and it was expected; and as his general life had been pious, his thoughts had doubtless for many years past been turned upon eternity. That you did not find him sensible must doubtless grieve you; his disposition towards you was undoubtedly that of a kind, though not of a fond father. Kindness, at least actual, is in our power, but fondness is not; and if by negligence or imprudence you had extinguished his fondness, he could not at will rekindle it. Nothing then remained between you but mutual forgiveness of each other's faults, and mutual desire of each other's happiness.

"I shall long to know his final disposition of his fortune.

"You, dear Sir, have now a new station, and have therefore new cares, and new employments. Life, as Cowley seems to say, ought to resemble a well-ordered poem; of which one rule generally received is, that the exordium should be simple, and should promise little. Begin your new course of life with the least show, and the least expense possible; you may at pleasure increase both, but you cannot easily diminish them. Do not think your estate your own, while any man can call upon you for money which you cannot pay: therefore, begin with timorous parsimony. Let it be your first care not to be in any man's debt.

"When the thoughts are extended to a future state, the present life seems hardly worthy of all those principles of conduct, and maxims of prudence, which one generation of men has transmitted to another; but upon a closer view, when it is perceived how much evil is produced, and how much good is impeded by embarrassment and distress, and how little room the expedients of poverty leave for the exercise of virtue, it grows manifest that the boundless importance of the next life enforces some attention to the interest of this.

"Be kind to the old servants, and secure the kindness of the agents and factors; do not disgust them by asperity, or unwelcome gaiety, or apparent suspicion. From them you must learn the real state of your affairs, the character of your tenants, and the value of your lands.

"Make my compliments to Mrs. Boswell; I think her expectations from air and exercise are the best that she can form. I hope she will live long and happily.

"I forgot whether I told you that Ramsay has been here; we dined cheerfully together. I entertained lately a young gentleman from Corrichatachin.

"I received your letters only this morning.

"I am, dear Sir,

"Yours, etc.,

"SAM. JOHNSON.

"*London, Sept. 7, 1782.*"

In answer to my next letter, I received one from him, dissuading me from hastening to him, as I had proposed; what is proper for publication is the following paragraph, equally just and tender:

"One expense, however, I would not have you to spare; let nothing be omitted that can preserve Mrs. Boswell, though it should be necessary to transplant her for a time into a softer climate. She is the prop and stay of your life. How much must your children suffer by losing her."

My wife was now so much convinced of his sincere friendship for me, and regard for her, that without any suggestion on my part, she wrote him a very polite and grateful letter.

"DR. JOHNSON TO MRS. BOSWELL.

"DEAR LADY,—

"I have not often received so much pleasure as from your invitation to Auchinleck. The journey thither and back is, indeed, too great for the latter part of the year; but if my health were fully recovered, I would suffer no little heat and cold, nor a wet or a rough road to keep me from you. I am, indeed, not without hope of seeing Auchinleck again; but to make it a pleasant place I must see its lady well, and brisk, and airy. For my sake, therefore, among many greater reasons, take care, dear Madam, of your health; spare no expense, and want no attendance that can procure ease, or preserve it. Be very careful to keep your mind quiet; and do not think it too much to give an account of your recovery to, Madam,

"Yours, etc.,

"SAM. JOHNSON.

"*London, Sept. 7, 1782.*"

"TO JAMES BOSWELL, ESQ.

"DEAR SIR,—

"Having passed almost this whole year in a succession of disorders, I went in October to Brighthelmstone, whither I came in a state of so much weakness, that I rested four times in walking between the inn and the lodging. By physic and abstinence I grew better, and am now reasonably easy, though at a great distance from health. I am afraid, however, that health begins, after seventy, and long before, to have a meaning different from that which it had at thirty. But it is culpable

[551]

to murmur at the established order of the creation, as it is vain to oppose it; he that lives, must grow old; and he that would rather grow old than die, has God to thank for the infirmities of old age.

"At your long silence I am rather angry. You do not, since now you are the head of your house, think it worth your while to try whether you or your friend can live longer without writing, nor suspect that after so many years of friendship, that when I do not write to you, I forget you. Put all such useless jealousies out of your head, and disdain to regulate your own practice by the practice of another, or by any other principle than the desire of doing right.

"Your economy, I suppose, begins now to be settled; your expenses are adjusted to your revenue, and all your people in their proper places. Resolve not to be poor: whatever you have, spend less. Poverty is a great enemy to human happiness; it certainly destroys liberty, and it makes some virtues impracticable, and others extremely difficult.

"Let me know the history of your life, since your accession to your estate. How many houses, how many cows, how much land in your own hand, and what bargains you make with your tenants.

*   *   *

"Of my 'Lives of the Poets,' they have printed a new edition in octavo, I hear, of three thousand. Did I give a set to Lord Hailes? If I did not, I will do it out of these. What did you make of all your copy?

"Mrs. Thrale and the three Misses are now for the winter in Argyll-street. Sir Joshua Reynolds has been out of order, but is well again; and I am, dear Sir,

"Your affectionate humble servant,

"SAM. JOHNSON.

"*London, Dec. 7, 1782.*"

"TO DR. SAMUEL JOHNSON.

"*Edinburgh, Dec. 20, 1782.*

"DEAR SIR,—

"I was made happy by your kind letter, which gave us the agreeable hopes of seeing you in Scotland again.

"I am much flattered by the concern you are pleased to take in my recovery. I am better, and hope to have it in my power to convince you, by my attention, of how much consequence I esteem your health to the world and to myself.

"I remain, Sir, with grateful respect,

"Your obliged and obedient servant,

"MARGARET BOSWELL."

The death of Mr. Thrale had made a very material alteration with respect to Johnson's reception in that family. The manly authority of the husband no longer curbed the lively exuberance of the lady; and as her vanity had been fully gratified, by having the Colossus of Literature attached to her for many years, she gradually became less assiduous to please him. Whether her attachment to him was already divided by another object I am unable to ascertain; but it is plain that Johnson's penetration was alive to her neglect or forced attention; for on the 6th of October this year we find him making a "parting use of the library" at Streatham, and pronouncing a prayer which he composed on leaving Mrs. Thrale's family.

CHAPTER LII—1783

Table Talk

IN 1783 he was more severely afflicted than ever, as will appear in the course of his correspondence; but still the same ardour for literature, the same constant piety, the same kindness for his friends, and the same vivacity, both in conversation and writing, distinguished him.

Having given Dr. Johnson a full account of what I was doing at Auchinleck, and particularly mentioned what I knew would please him—my having brought an old man of eighty-eight from a lonely cottage to a comfortable habitation within my enclosures, where he had good neighbours near to him,—I received an answer in February, of which I extract what follows:

"I am delighted with your account of your activity at Auchinleck, and wish the old gentleman, whom you have so kindly removed, may live long to promote your prosperity by his prayers. You have now a new character and new duties; think on them and practise them.

"Make an impartial estimate of your revenue, and whatever it is, live upon less. Resolve never to be poor. Frugality is not only the basis of quiet, but of beneficence. No man can help others that wants help himself; we must have enough before we have to spare.

"I am glad to find that Mrs. Boswell grows well; and hope that, to keep her well, no care nor caution will be omitted. May you long live happily together."

On Friday, March 21, having arrived in London the night before, I was glad to find him at Mrs. Thrale's house, in Argyll-street, appearances of friendship between them being still kept up. I was shown into his room, and, after the first salutation, he said, "I am glad you are come: I am very ill." He looked pale, and was distressed with a difficulty of breathing: but, after the common inquiries, he assumed his usual strong animated style of conversation. Seeing me now for the first time as a *Laird,* or proprietor of land, he began thus: "Sir, the superiority of a country gentleman over the people upon his estate is very agreeable: and he who says he does not feel it to be agreeable, lies; for it must be agreeable to have a casual superiority over those who are by nature equal with us." BOSWELL: "Yet, Sir, we see great proprietors of land who prefer living in London." JOHNSON: "Why, Sir, the pleasure of living in London, the intellectual superiority that is enjoyed there, may counterbalance the other. Besides, Sir, a man may prefer the state of the country gentleman upon the whole, and yet there may never be a moment when he is willing to make the change to quit London for it."

He sent a message to acquaint Mrs. Thrale that I was arrived. I had not seen her since her husband's death. She soon appeared, and favoured me with an invitation to stay to dinner, which I accepted. There was no other company but herself and three of her daughters, Dr. Johnson, and I. She too said she was very glad I was come, for she was going to Bath, and should have been sorry to leave Dr. Johnson before I came. This seemed to be attentive and kind, and I, who had not been informed of any change, imagined all to be as well as formerly. He was little inclined to talk at dinner, and went to sleep after it; but when he joined us in the drawing-room, he seemed revived, and was again himself.

Talking of conversation, he said, "There must, in the first place, be knowledge, there must be materials;—in the second place, there must be a command of words;—in the third place, there must be imagination, to place things in such views as they are not commonly seen in;—and in the fourth place, there must be presence of mind, and a resolution that it is not to be overcome by failures: this last is an essential requisite; for want of it, many people do not excel in conversation. Now *I* want it; I throw up the game upon losing a trick." I wondered to hear him talk thus of himself, and said, "I don't know, Sir, how this may be; but I am sure you beat other people's cards out of their hands." I doubt whether he heard this remark. While he went on talking triumphantly, I was fixed in admiration, and said to Mrs. Thrale, "O, for short-hand to take this down!"—"You'll carry it all in your head (said she); a long head is as good as short-hand."

After musing for some time, he said, "I wonder how I should have any enemies; for I do harm to nobody." BOSWELL: "In the first place, Sir, you will be pleased to recollect that you set out with attacking the Scotch; so you got a whole nation for your enemies." JOHNSON: "Why, I own, that by my definition of *oats,* I meant to vex them." BOSWELL: "Pray, Sir, can you trace the cause of your antipathy to the Scotch?" JOHNSON: "I cannot, Sir." BOSWELL: "Old Mr. Sheridan says it was because they sold Charles the First." JOHNSON: "Then, Sir, old Mr. Sheridan has found out a very good reason."

Next day, Saturday, March 22, I found him still at Mrs. Thrale's, but he told me that he was to go to his own house in the afternoon. He was better, but I perceived he was an unruly patient; for Sir Lucas Pepys, who visited him, while I was with him, said, "If you were *tractable,* Sir, I should prescribe for you."

I had paid a visit to General Oglethorpe in the morning, and was told by him that Dr. Johnson saw company on Saturday evenings, and he would meet me at Johnson's that night. When I mentioned this to Johnson, not doubting that it would please him, as he had a great value for Oglethorpe, the fretfulness of his disease unexpectedly showed itself; his anger suddenly kindled, and he said, with vehemence, "Did not you tell him not to come? Am I to be *hunted* in this manner?" I satisfied him that I could not divine that the visit would not be convenient, and that I certainly could not take it upon me of my own accord to forbid the General.

I found Dr. Johnson in the evening in Mrs. Williams's room, at tea and coffee with her and Mrs. Desmoulins, who were also both ill; it was a sad scene, and he was not in a very good humour. He said of a performance that had lately come out, "Sir, if you should search all the madhouses in England, you would not find ten men who would write so, and think it sense."

I was glad when General Oglethorpe's arrival was announced, and we left the ladies. Dr. Johnson attended him in the parlour, and was as courteous as ever.

On Sunday, March 23, I breakfasted with Dr. Johnson, who seemed much relieved, having taken opium the night before. He, however, protested against it, as a remedy that should be given with the utmost reluctance, and only in extreme necessity. I mentioned how commonly it was used in Turkey, and that therefore it could not be so pernicious as he apprehended. He grew warm, and said, "Turks take opium, and Christians take opium; but Russel, in his account of Aleppo, tells us that it is as disgraceful in Turkey to take too much opium, as it is with us to get drunk. Sir, it is amazing how things are exaggerated. A gentleman was lately telling in a company where I was present, that in France as soon as a man of fashion marries, he takes an opera girl into keeping; and this he mentioned as a general custom. 'Pray, Sir (said I), how many opera girls may there be?' He answered, 'About fourscore.' 'Well then, Sir (said I), you see there can be no more than fourscore men of fashion who can do this.'"

Mrs. Desmoulins made tea; and she and I talked before him upon a topic which he had once borne patiently from me when we were by ourselves,—his not complaining of the world, because he was not called to some great office, nor had attained to great wealth. He flew into a violent passion, I confess with some justice, and commanded us to have done. "Nobody (said he) has a right to talk in this manner, to bring before a man his own character, and the events of his life, when he does not choose it should be done. I never have sought the world; the world was not to seek me. It is rather wonderful that so much has been done for me. All the complaints which are made of the world are unjust. I never knew a man of merit neglected: it was generally by his own fault that he failed of success. A man may hide his head in a hole: he may go into the country, and publish a book now and then, which nobody reads, and then complain he is neglected. There is no reason why any person should exert himself for a man who has written a good book: he has not written it for any individual. I may as well make a present to a postman who brings me a letter. When patronage was limited, an author expected to find a Mæcenas, and complained if he did not find one. Why should he complain? This Mæcenas has others as good as he, or others who have got the start of him."

In the evening I came to him again. He was somewhat fretful from his illness. A gentleman asked him whether he had been abroad to-day.

"Don't talk so childishly (said he). You may as well ask if I hanged myself to-day." I mentioned politics. JOHNSON: "Sir, I'd as soon have a man to break my bones as talk to me of public affairs, internal or external. I have lived to see things all as bad as they can be."

On Sunday, March 30, I found him at home in the evening, and had the pleasure to meet with Dr. Brocklesby, whose reading, and knowledge of life, and good spirits, supply him with a never-failing source of conversation. He mentioned a respectable gentleman, who became extremely penurious near the close of his life. Johnson said there must have been a degree of madness about him. "Not at all, Sir (said Dr. Brocklesby), his judgment was entire." Unluckily, however, he mentioned that, although he had a fortune of twenty-seven thousand pounds, he denied himself many comforts, from an apprehension that he could not afford them. "Nay, Sir (cried Johnson), when the judgment is so disturbed that a man cannot count, that is pretty well."

I shall here insert a few of Johnson's sayings, without the formality of dates, as they have no reference to any particular time or place.

"The more a man extends and varies his acquaintance the better." This, however, was meant with a just restriction; for he, on another occasion, said to me, "Sir, a man may be so much of everything, that he is nothing of anything."

"Raising the wages of day-labourers is wrong; for it does not make them live better; but only makes them idler, and idleness is a very bad thing for human nature."

Talking of an acquaintance of ours, whose narratives, which abounded in curious interesting topics, were unhappily found to be very fabulous; I mentioned Lord Mansfield's having said to me, "Suppose we believe one *half* of what he tells." JOHNSON: "Ay; but we don't know *which* half to believe. By his lying we lose not only our reverence for him, but all comfort in his conversation." BOSWELL: "May we not take it as amusing fiction?" JOHNSON: "Sir, the misfortune is that you will insensibly believe as much of it as you incline to believe."

After repeating to him some of his pointed, lively sayings, I said, "It is a pity, Sir, you don't always remember your own good things, that you may have a laugh when you will." JOHNSON: "Nay, Sir, it is better that I forget them, that I may be reminded of them, and have a laugh on their being brought to my recollection."

When I recalled to him his having said as we sailed up Loch Lomond, "That if he wore anything fine, it should be *very* fine"; I observed that all his thoughts were upon a great scale. JOHNSON: "Depend upon it, Sir, every man will have as fine a thing as he can get; as large a diamond for his ring."

He said, "How few of his friends' houses would a man choose to be at, when he is sick!" He mentioned one or two. I recollect only Thrale's.

He observed, "There is a wicked inclination in most people to suppose an old man decayed in his intellects. If a young or middle-aged man, when leaving a company, does not recollect where he laid his hat, it is nothing; but if the same inattention is discovered in an old man, people will shrug up their shoulders, and say, 'His memory is going.'"

I am very sorry that I did not take a note of an eloquent argument in which he maintained that the situation of Prince of Wales was the happiest of any person's in the kingdom, even beyond that of the Sovereign. I recollect only—the enjoyment of hope—the high superiority of rank, without the anxious care of government,—and a great degree of power, both from natural influence wisely used, and from the sanguine expectations of those who look forward to the chance of future favour.

He said, "A man should pass a part of his time with *the laughers*, by which means anything ridiculous or particular about him might be presented to his view, and corrected." I observed, he must have been a bold laugher who would have ventured to tell Dr. Johnson of any of his particularities.[1]

Having observed the vain ostentatious importance of many people in quoting the authority of dukes and lords, as having been in their company, he said, he went to the other extreme, and did not mention his authority when he should have done it, had it not been that of a duke or a lord.

Dr. Goldsmith said once to Dr. Johnson that he wished for some additional members to the Literary Club, to give it an agreeable variety; for (said he), there can now be nothing new among us: we have travelled over one another's minds. Johnson seemed a little angry,

---

[1] I am happy, however, to mention a pleasing instance of his enduring with great gentleness to hear one of his most striking particularities pointed out:—Miss Hunter, a niece of his friend Christopher Smart, when a very young girl, struck by his extraordinary motions, said to him, "Pray, Dr. Johnson, why do you make such strange gestures?"—"From bad habit (he replied). Do you, my dear, take care to guard against bad habits." This I was told by the young lady's brother at Margate.

and said, "Sir, you have not travelled over *my* mind, I promise you."
Sir Joshua, however, thought Goldsmith right; observing that "when
people have lived a great deal together, they know what each of them
will say on every subject. A new understanding, therefore, is desirable;
because, though it may only furnish the same sense upon a question
which would have been furnished by those with whom we are accustomed to live, yet this sense will have a different colouring; and
colouring is of much effect in everything else as well as painting."

Johnson used to say that he made it a constant rule to talk as well
as he could both as to sentiment and expression, by which means,
what had been originally effort became familiar and easy. The consequence of this, Sir Joshua observed, was that his common conversation in all companies was such as to secure him universal attention,
as something above the usual colloquial style was expected.

Johnson's dexterity in retort, when he seemed to be driven to an
extremity by his adversary was very remarkable. Of his power in
this respect, our common friend, Mr. Windham, of Norfolk, has been
pleased to furnish me with an eminent instance. However unfavourable to Scotland, he uniformly gave liberal praise to George Buchanan,
as a writer. In a conversation concerning the literary merits of the
two countries, in which Buchanan was introduced, a Scotchman,
imagining that on this ground he should have an undoubted triumph
over him, exclaimed, "Ah, Dr. Johnson, what would you have said
of Buchanan, had he been an Englishman?"—"Why, Sir (said Johnson, after a little pause), I should *not* have said of Buchanan, had he
been an *Englishman,* what I will now say of him as a *Scotchman*—
that he was the only man of genius his country ever produced."

Though his usual phrase for conversation was *talk,* yet he made a
distinction; for when he once told me that he dined the day before
at a friend's house, with "a very pretty company"; and I asked him
if there was good conversation, he answered, "No, Sir; we had *talk*
enough, but no *conversation;* there was nothing *discussed."*

Mr. Hoole told him he was born in Moorfields, and had received
part of his early instruction in Grub-street. "Sir (said Johnson, smiling), you have been *regularly* educated." Having asked who was his
instructor, and Mr. Hoole having answered, "My uncle, Sir, who was
a tailor"; Johnson, recollecting himself, said, "Sir, I knew him; we
called him the *metaphysical tailor.* He was of a club in Old-street,
with me and George Psalmanazar, and some others: but pray, Sir,
was he a good tailor?" Mr. Hoole having answered that he believed

he was too mathematical, and used to draw squares and triangles on his shop-board, so that he did not excel in the cut of a coat;—"I am sorry for it (said Johnson), for I would have every man to be master of his own business."

Johnson's attention to precision and clearness in expression was very remarkable. He disapproved of a parenthesis; and I believe in all his voluminous writings, not half-a-dozen of them will be found. He never used the phrases *the former and the latter,* having observed that they often occasioned obscurity; he therefore contrived to construct his sentences so as not to have occasion for them, and would even rather repeat the same words, in order to avoid them. Nothing is more common than to mistake surnames, when we hear them carelessly uttered for the first time. To prevent this, he used not only to pronounce them slowly and distinctly, but to take the trouble of spelling them; a practice which I have often followed; and which I wish were general.

Such was the heat and irritability of his blood, that not only did he pare his nails to the quick; but scraped the joints of his fingers with a penknife, till they seemed quite red and raw.

The heterogeneous composition of human nature was remarkably exemplified in Johnson. His liberality in giving his money to persons in distress was extraordinary. Yet there lurked about him a propensity to paltry saving. One day I owned to him that "I was occasionally troubled with a fit of *narrowness.*" "Why, Sir (said he), so am I. *But I do not tell it.*" He has now and then borrowed a shilling of me; and when I asked him for it again, seemed to be rather out of humour. A droll little circumstance once occurred: As if he meant to reprimand my minute exactness as a creditor, he thus addressed me;— "Boswell, *lend* me sixpence—*not to be repaid.*"

This great man's attention to small things was very remarkable. As an instance of it, he one day said to me: "Sir, when you get silver in change for a guinea, look carefully at it; you may find some curious piece of coin."

Though a stern, *true-born Englishman,* and fully prejudiced against all other nations, he had discernment enough to see, and candour enough to censure, the cold reserve too common among Englishmen towards strangers. "Sir (said he), two men of any other nation who are shown into a room together, at a house where they are both visitors, will immediately find some conversation. But two Englishmen will probably go each to a different window, and remain in obstinate silence. Sir, we as yet do not enough understand the common rights of humanity."

He was pleased to say to me one morning when we were left alone in his study, "Boswell, I think I am easier with you than with almost anybody."

He would not allow Mr. David Hume any credit for his political principles, though similar to his own; saying of him, "Sir, he was a Tory by chance."

His acute observations of human life made him remark, "Sir, there is nothing by which a man exasperates most people more, than by displaying a superior ability of brilliancy in conversation. They seem pleased at the time; but their envy makes them curse him at their hearts."

My readers will probably be surprised to hear that the great Dr. Johnson could amuse himself with so slight and playful a species of composition as a *charade*. I have recovered one which he made on Dr. *Barnard*, now Lord Bishop of Killaloe; who has been pleased for many years to treat me with so much intimacy and social ease, that I may presume to call him not only my Right Reverend, but my very dear Friend. I therefore with peculiar pleasure give to the world a just and elegant compliment thus paid to his Lordship by Johnson.

CHARADE

"My *first* shuts out thieves from your house or your room,
"My *second* expresses a Syrian perfume,
"My *whole* is a man in whose converse is shar'd,
"The strength of a Bar and the sweetness of Nard."

Johnson's love of little children, which he discovered upon all occasions, calling them "pretty dears," and giving them sweetmeats, was an undoubted proof of the real humanity and gentleness of his disposition.

His uncommon kindness to his servants, and serious concern, not only for their comfort in this world, but their happiness in the next, was another unquestionable evidence of what all, who were intimately acquainted with him, knew to be true.

Nor would it be just, under this head, to omit the fondness which he showed for animals which he had taken under his protection. I never shall forget the indulgence with which he treated Hodge, his cat; for whom he himself used to go out and buy oysters, lest the servants having that trouble, should take a dislike to the poor creature.

I am, unluckily, one of those who have an antipathy to a cat, so that I am uneasy when in the room with one; and I own I frequently suffered a good deal from the presence of the same Hodge. I recollect him one day scrambling up Dr. Johnson's breast, apparently with much satisfaction, while my friend, smiling and half-whistling, rubbed down his back, and pulled him by the tail, and when I observed he was a fine cat, saying, "Why, yes, Sir, but I have had cats whom I liked better than this"; and then, as if perceiving Hodge to be out of countenance, adding, "but he is a very fine cat, a very fine cat indeed."

On Saturday, April 12, I visited him, in company with Mr. Windham, of Norfolk, whom, though a Whig, he highly valued. One of the best things he ever said was to this gentleman; who, before he set out for Ireland as Secretary to Lord Northington, when Lord Lieutenant, expressed to the sage some modest and virtuous doubts, whether he could bring himself to practise those arts which it is supposed a person in that situation has occasion to employ. "Don't be afraid, Sir (said Johnson, with a pleasant smile); you will soon make a very pretty rascal."

On April 18 (being Good Friday), I found him at breakfast, in his usual manner upon that day, drinking tea without milk, and eating a cross bun to prevent faintness; we went to St. Clement's Church, as formerly. When we came home from church, he placed himself on one of the stone-seats at his garden door, and I took the other, and thus in the open air, and in a placid frame of mind, he talked away very easily. JOHNSON: "Were I a country gentleman, I should not be very hospitable, I should not have crowds in my house." BOSWELL: "Sir Alexander Dick tells me that he remembers having a thousand people in a year to dine at his house; that is, reckoning each person as one each time that he dined there." JOHNSON: "That, Sir, is about three a day." BOSWELL: "How your statement lessens the idea." JOHNSON: "That, Sir, is the good of counting. It brings everything to a certainty, which before floated in the mind indefinitely." BOSWELL: "But *omne ignotum pro magnifico est:* one is sorry to have this diminished." JOHNSON: "Sir, you should not allow yourself to be delighted with error." BOSWELL: "Three a day seem but few." JOHNSON: "Nay, Sir, he who entertains three a day, does very liberally. And, if there is a large family, the poor entertain those three, for they eat what the poor would get: there must be superfluous meat; it must be given to the poor, or thrown out."

BOSWELL: "I wish to have a good walled garden." JOHNSON: "I

don't think it would be worth the expense to you. We compute, in England, a park-wall at a thousand pounds a mile; now a garden-wall must cost at least as much. You intend your trees should grow higher than a deer will leap. Now let us see;—for a hundred pounds, you could only have forty-four square yards, which is very little; for two hundred pounds, you may have eighty-four square yards, which is very well. But when will you get the value of two hundred pounds of walls, in fruit, in your climate? No, Sir, such contention with Nature is not worth while. I would plant an orchard, and have plenty of such fruit as ripen well in your country. My friend, Dr. Madden, of Ireland, said that 'in an orchard there should be enough to eat, enough to lay up, enough to be stolen, and enough to rot upon the ground.' Cherries are an early fruit; you may have them; and you may have the early apples and pears."

I record this minute detail, which some may think trifling, in order to show clearly how this great man, whose mind could grasp such large and extensive subjects, as he has shown in his literary labours, was yet well-informed in the common affairs of life, and loved to illustrate them.

Mrs. Burney, wife of his friend Dr. Burney, came in, and he seemed to be entertained with her conversation.

Garrick's funeral was talked of as extravagantly expensive. Johnson, from his dislike to exaggeration, would not allow that it was distinguished by any extraordinary pomp. "Were there not six horses to each coach?" said Mrs. Burney. JOHNSON: "Madam, there were no more six horses than six phœnixes."

Time passed on in conversation till it was too late for the service of the church at three o'clock. I took a walk, and left him alone for some time; then returned, and we had coffee and conversation again by ourselves.

I stated the character of a noble friend of mine, as a curious case for his opinion:—"He is the most inexplicable man to me that I ever knew. Can you explain him, Sir? He is, I really believe, noble-minded, generous, and princely. But his most intimate friends may be separated from him for years, without his ever asking a question concerning them. He will meet them with a formality, a coldness, a stately indifference; but when they come close to him, and fairly engage him in conversation they find him as easy, pleasant, and kind, as they could wish. One then supposes that what is so agreeable will soon be renewed; but stay away from him for half a year, and he will neither call on you, nor send to inquire about you." JOHNSON: "Why, Sir, I cannot ascertain his character exactly, as I do not know him; but I should not like to have such a man for my friend. He may love study, and wish not to be interrupted by his friends; *Amici fures temporis*. He may be a frivolous man, and be so much occupied with petty pursuits, that he may not want friends. Or he may have a notion that there is a dignity in appearing indifferent, while he in fact may not be more indifferent at his heart than another."

We went to evening prayers at St. Clement's, at seven, and then parted.

CHAPTER LIII—1783

Death of Mrs. Williams

ON SUNDAY, APRIL 20, being Easter-day, after attending solemn service at St. Paul's, I came to Dr. Johnson, and found Mr. Lowe, the painter, sitting with him. Mr. Lowe mentioned the great number of new buildings of late in London, yet that Dr. Johnson had observed that the number of inhabitants was not increased. JOHNSON: "Why, Sir, the bills of mortality prove that no more people die now than formerly; so it is plain no more live. The register of births proves nothing, for not one-tenth of the people of London are born there." BOSWELL: "I believe, Sir, a great many of the children born in London die early." JOHNSON: "Why, yes, Sir." BOSWELL: "But those who do live, are as stout and strong people as any: Dr. Price says they must be naturally strong to get through." JOHNSON: "That is system, Sir. A great traveller observes that it is said there are no weak or deformed people among the Indians; but he with much sagacity assigns the reason of this, which is, that the hardship of their life as hunters and fishers, does not allow weak or disused children to grow up. Now had I been an Indian I must have died early; my eyes would not have served me to get food. I indeed now could fish, give me English tackle; but had I been an Indian I must have starved, or they would have knocked me on the head, when they saw I could do nothing." BOSWELL: "Perhaps they would have taken care of you: we are told they are fond of oratory; you would have talked to them." JOHNSON: "Nay, Sir, I should not have lived long enough to be fit to talk; I should have been dead before I was ten years old. Depend upon it, Sir, a savage, when he is hungry, will not carry about with him a looby of nine years old, who cannot help himself. They have no affection, Sir." BOSWELL: "I believe natural affection, of which we hear so much, is very small." JOHNSON: "Sir, natural affection is nothing: but affection from principle and established duty is sometimes wonderfully strong." LOWE: "A hen, Sir, will feed her chickens in preference to herself." JOHNSON: "But we don't know that the hen is hungry; let the hen be fairly hungry, and I'll warrant she'll peck the corn herself. A cock, I believe, will feed hens instead of himself; but we don't know that the cock is hungry." BOSWELL: "And that, Sir, is not from affection but gallantry. But some of the Indians have affection." JOHNSON: "Sir, that they help some of their children, is plain; for some of them live, which they could not do without being helped."

I dined with him; the company were, Mrs. Williams, Mrs. Desmoulins, and Mr. Lowe. He seemed not to be well, talked little, grew drowsy soon after dinner, and retired, upon which I went away.

On Monday, April 29, I found him at home in the forenoon, and Mr. Seward with him. I mentioned a worthy friend [Langton] of ours, whom we valued much, but observed that he was too ready to introduce religious discourse upon all occasions. JOHNSON: "Why, yes, Sir, he will introduce religious discourse without seeing whether it will end in instruction and improvement, or produce some profane jest. He would introduce it in the company of Wilkes, and twenty more such."

I mentioned Dr. Johnson's excellent distinction between liberty of conscience and liberty of teaching. JOHNSON: "Consider, Sir; if you have children whom you wish to educate in the principles of the Church of England, and there comes a Quaker who tries to pervert them to his principles, you would drive away the Quaker. You would not trust to the predomination of right; which you believe is in your opinions; you will keep wrong out of their heads. Now, the vulgar are the children of the State. If anyone attempts to teach them doctrines contrary to what the State approves, the magistrates may and ought to restrain him." SEWARD: "Would you restrain private conversation, Sir?" JOHNSON: "Why, Sir, it is difficult to say where private conversation begins, and where it ends. If we three should discuss even the great question concerning the existence of a Supreme Being by ourselves, we should not be restrained; for that would be to put an end to all improvement. But if we should discuss it in the presence of ten boarding-school girls, and as many boys, I think the magistrate would do well to put us in the stocks, to finish the debate there."

On Thursday, May 1, I visited him in the evening, along with young Mr. Burke. He seemed to be in a very placid humour, and although I have no note of the particulars of young Mr. Burke's conversation, it is but justice to mention in general, that it was such that Dr. Johnson said to me afterwards, "He did very well, indeed; I have a mind to tell his father."

I have no minute of any interview with Johnson till Thursday, May 15th, when I find what follows: BOSWELL: "I wish much to be in Parliament, Sir." JOHNSON: "Why, Sir, unless you come resolved to support any administration, you would be the worse for being in Parliament, because you would be obliged to live more expensively." —BOSWELL: "Perhaps, Sir, I should be the less happy for being in Parliament. I never would sell my vote, and I should be vexed if things went wrong." JOHNSON: "That's cant, Sir. It would not vex you more in the House, than in the gallery: public affairs vex no man." BOSWELL: "Have they not vexed yourself a little, Sir? Have not you been vexed by all the turbulence of this reign, and by that absurd vote of the House of Commons, 'That the influence of the Crown has increased, is increasing, and ought to be diminished'?" JOHNSON: "Sir, I have never slept an hour less, nor ate an ounce less meat. I would have knocked the factious dogs on the head, to be sure; but I was not *vexed*." BOSWELL: "I declare, Sir, upon my honour, I did imagine I was vexed, and took a pride in it; but it *was*, perhaps, cant; for I own I neither ate less nor slept less." JOHNSON: "My dear friend, clear your *mind* of cant. You may *talk* as other people do: you may say to a man, 'Sir, I am your most humble servant.' You are *not* his most humble servant. You may say, 'These are bad times; it is a melancholy thing to be reserved to such times.' You don't mind the times. You tell a man, 'I am sorry you had such bad weather the last day of your journey, and were so much wet.' You don't care sixpence whether he is wet or dry. You may *talk* in this manner; it is a mode of talking in society: but don't *think* foolishly."

On Saturday, May 17, I saw him for a short time. Having mentioned that I had that morning been with old Mr. Sheridan, he remembered their former intimacy with a cordial warmth, and said to me, "Tell Mr. Sheridan, I shall be glad to see him, and shake hands with him." BOSWELL: "It is to me very wonderful that resentment should be kept up so long." JOHNSON: "Why, Sir, it is not altogether resentment that he does not visit me; it is partly falling out of habit,

—partly disgust, as one has at a drug that has made him sick. Besides, he knows that I laugh at his oratory."

On Friday, May 29, being to set out for Scotland next morning, I passed a part of the day with him in more than usual earnestness; as his health was in a more precarious state than at any time when I had parted from him. He, however, was quick and lively, and critical, as usual. I mentioned one who was a very learned man. JOHNSON: "Yes, Sir, he has a great deal of learning; but it never lies straight. There is never one idea by the side of another; 'tis all entangled: and then he drives it so awkwardly upon conversation!"

He said, "Get as much force of mind as you can. Live within your income. Always have something saved at the end of the year. Let your imports be more than your exports, and you'll never go far wrong."

I assured him that in the extensive and various range of his acquaintance there never had been anyone who had a more sincere respect and affection for him than I had. He said, "I believe it, Sir. Were I in distress, there is no man to whom I should sooner come than to you. I should like to come and have a cottage in your park, toddle about, live mostly on milk, and be taken care of by Mrs. Boswell. She and I are good friends now; are we not?"

He embraced me, and gave me his blessing, as usual when I was leaving him for any length of time. I walked from his door to-day, with a fearful apprehension of what might happen before I returned.

My anxious apprehensions at parting with him this year proved to be but too well founded; for not long afterwards he had a dreadful stroke of the palsy, of which there are very full and accurate accounts in letters written by himself to show with what composure of mind, and resignation to the Divine Will, his steady piety enabled him to behave.

"TO MR. EDMUND ALLEN.

"DEAR SIR,—

"It has pleased God, this morning, to deprive me of the powers of speech; and as I do not know but that it may be his farther good pleasure to deprive me soon of my senses, I request you will, on the receipt of this note, come to me, and act for me, as the exigencies of my case may require.

"I am, sincerely yours,
"SAM. JOHNSON.

"*June 17, 1783.*"

"TO THE REVEREND DR. JOHN TAYLOR.

"DEAR SIR,—

"It has pleased God, by a paralytic stroke in the night, to deprive me of speech.

"I am very desirous of Dr. Heberden's assistance, as I think my case is not past remedy. Let me see you as soon as it is possible. Bring Dr. Heberden with you, if you can; but come yourself at all events. I am glad you are so well, when I am so dreadfully attacked.

"I think that by a speedy application of stimulants much may be done. I question if a vomit, vigorous and rough, would not rouse the organs of speech to action. As it is too early to send, I will try to recollect what I can, that can be suspected to have brought on this dreadful distress.

"I have been accustomed to bleed frequently for an asthmatic complaint; but have forborne for some time by Dr. Pepys's persuasion, who perceived my legs beginning to swell. I sometimes alleviate a painful, or more properly an oppressive constriction of my chest, by opiates; and have lately taken opium frequently, but the last, or two last times, in smaller quantities. My largest dose is three grains, and last night I took but two. You will suggest these things (and they are all that I can call to mind) to Dr. Heberden.

"I am, etc.,
"SAM. JOHNSON.

"*June 17, 1783.*"

Two days after he wrote thus to Mrs. Thrale:

"On Monday, the 16th, I sat for my picture [to Miss Reynolds], and walked a considerable way with little inconvenience. In the afternoon and evening I felt myself light and easy, and began to plan schemes of life. Thus I went to bed, and in a short time waked and sat up, as has been long my custom, when I felt a confusion and indistinctness in my head, which lasted, I suppose, about half a minute. I was alarmed, and prayed God that however he might afflict my body, he would spare my understanding. This prayer, that I might try the integrity of my faculties, I made in Latin verse. The lines were not very good, but I knew them not to be very good: I made them easily, and concluded myself to be unimpaired in my faculties.

"Soon after I perceived that I had suffered a paralytic stroke, and that my speech was taken from me. I had no pain, and so little de-

Gordon Ross del. New York, 1945

Mrs Sarah Siddons

jection in this dreadful state, that I wondered at my own apathy, and considered that perhaps death itself, when it should come, would excite less horror than seems now to attend it.

"In order to rouse the vocal organs, I took two drams. Wine has been celebrated for the production of eloquence. I put myself into violent motion, and I think repeated it; but all was vain. I then went to bed, and strange as it may seem, I think slept. When I saw light, it was time to contrive what I should do. Though God stopped my speech, He left me my hand; I enjoyed a mercy which was not granted to my dear friend Lawrence, who now perhaps overlooks me as I am writing, and rejoices that I have what he wanted. My first note was necessarily to my servant, who came in talking, and could not immediately comprehend why he should read what I put into his hands.

"I then wrote a card to Mr. Allen, that I might have a discreet friend at hand, to act as occasion should require. In penning this note, I had some difficulty; my hand, I knew not how nor why, made wrong letters. I then wrote to Dr. Taylor to come to me, and bring Dr. Heberden: and I sent to Dr. Brocklesby, who is my neighbour. My physicians are very friendly, and give me great hopes; but you may imagine my situation. I have so far recovered my vocal powers, as to repeat the Lord's Prayer with no very imperfect articulation. My memory, I hope, yet remains as it was; but such an attack produces solicitude for the safety of every faculty."

"TO JAMES BOSWELL, ESQ.

"DEAR SIR,—

"Your anxiety about my health is very friendly, and very agreeable with your general kindness. I have, indeed, had a very frightful blow. On the 17th of last month, about three in the morning, as near as I can guess, I perceived myself almost totally deprived of speech. I had no pain. My organs were so obstructed that I could say *no,* but could scarcely say *yes.* I wrote the necessary directions, for it pleased God to spare my head, and sent for Dr. Heberden and Dr. Brocklesby. Between the time in which I discovered my own disorder, and that in which I sent for the doctors, I had, I believe, in spite of my surprise and solicitude, a little sleep, and Nature began to renew its operations. They came and gave the directions which the disease required, and from that time I have been continually improving in articulation. I can now speak, but the nerves are weak, and I cannot continue discourse long; but strength, I hope, will return. The physicians consider me as cured. I was last Sunday at church. On Tuesday I took an airing to Hampstead, and dined with the Club, where Lord Palmerston was proposed, and, against my opinion, was rejected. I designed to go next week with Mr. Langton to Rochester, where I purpose to stay about ten days, and then try some other air. I have many kind invitations. Your brother has very frequently inquired after me. Most of my friends have, indeed, been very attentive. Thank dear Lord Hailes for his present.

"I hope you found at your return everything gay and prosperous, and your lady in particular quite recovered and confirmed. Pay her my respects.

> "I am, dear Sir,
> > "Your most humble servant,
> > > "SAM. JOHNSON.

"London, July 3, 1783."

Such was the general vigour of his constitution, that he recovered from this alarming and severe attack with wonderful quickness; so that in July he was able to make a visit to Mr. Langton at Rochester, where he passed about a fortnight, and made little excursions as easily as at any time of his life. In August he went as far as the neighbourhood of Salisbury, to Heale, the seat of William Bowles, Esq., a gentleman whom I have heard him praise for exemplary religious order in his family. In his diary I find a short but honourable mention of this visit:—"August 28, I came to Heale without fatigue. 30. I am entertained quite to my mind."

While he was here, he had a letter from Dr. Brocklesby, acquainting him of the death of Mrs. Williams, which affected him a good deal. Though for several years her temper had not been complacent, she had valuable qualities, and her departure left a blank in his house. Upon this occasion he, according to his habitual course of piety, composed a prayer.

I shall here insert a few particulars concerning him, with which I have been favoured by one of his friends.

"His thoughts in the latter part of his life were frequently employed on his deceased friends. He often muttered these, or suchlike sentences: 'Poor man! and then he died.' "

"A friend was one day, about two years before his death, struck with some instance of Dr. Johnson's great candour. 'Well, Sir (said he), I

will always say that you are a very candid man.'—'Will you? (replied
the Doctor); I doubt then you will be very singular. But, indeed, Sir
(continued he), I look upon myself to be a man very much misunderstood. I am not an uncandid, nor am I a severe man. I sometimes say
more than I mean, in jest; and people are apt to believe me serious:
however, I am more candid than I was when I was younger. As I know
more of mankind, I expect less of them, and am ready now to call a
man *a good man,* upon easier terms than I was formerly.' "

His fortitude and patience met with severe trials during this year.
The stroke of the palsy has been related circumstantially; but he was
also afflicted with the gout, and was besides troubled with a complaint
which not only was attended with immediate inconvenience, but
threatened him with a chirurgical operation, from which most men
would shrink. The complaint was a *sarcocele,* which Johnson bore
with uncommon firmness, and was not at all frightened while he looked
forward to amputation. He was attended by Mr. Pott and Mr. Cruikshank. I have before me a letter of the 30th of July this year, to Mr.
Cruikshank, in which he says, "I am going to put myself into your
hands"; and another accompanying a set of his "Lives of the Poets," in
which he says, "I beg your acceptance of these volumes, as an acknowledgment of the great favours which you have bestowed on, Sir, your
most obliged and most humble servant." I have in my possession several
more letters from him to Mr. Cruikshank, and also to Dr. Mudge, at
Plymouth, which it would be improper to insert, as they are filled with
unpleasing technical details. I shall, however, extract from his letters to
Dr. Mudge such passages as show either a felicity of expression or the
undaunted state of his mind.

"My conviction of your skill, and my belief of your friendship, determine me to entreat your opinion and advice."—"In this state I with
great earnestness desire you to tell me what is to be done. Excision is
doubtless necessary to the cure, and I know not any means of palliation.
The operation is doubtless painful; but is it dangerous? The pain I
hope to endure with decency; but I am loth to put life into much
hazard."—"By representing the gout as an antagonist to the palsy, you
have said enough to make it welcome. This is not strictly the first fit,
but I hope it is as good as the first; for it is the second that ever
confined me; and the first was ten years ago, much less fierce and fiery
than this."—"Write, dear Sir, what you can to inform or encourage
me. The operation is not delayed by any fears or objections of mine."

Happily the complaint abated without his being put to the torture of amputation. But we must surely admire the manly resolution which he discovered, while it hung over him.

I wrote to him, begging to know the state of his health, and mentioned that "Baxter's 'Anacreon,' which is in the library at Auchinleck, was, I find, collated by my father in 1727, with the MS. belonging to the University of Leyden, and he has made a number of notes upon it. Would you advise me to publish a new edition of it?"

His answer was dated September 30.—"You should not make your letters such rarities, when you know, or might know, the uniform state of my health. It is very long since I heard from you; and that I have not answered is a very insufficient reason for the silence of a friend.—Your 'Anacreon' is a very uncommon book; neither London nor Cambridge can supply a copy of that edition. Whether it should be reprinted, you cannot do better than consult Lord Hailes.—Besides my constant and radical disease, I have been for these ten days much harassed with the gout; but that has now remitted. I hope God will yet grant me a little longer life, and make me less unfit to appear before him."

He this autumn received a visit from the celebrated Mrs. Siddons. He gives this account of it in one of his letters to Mrs. Thrale [October 27]:—"Mrs. Siddons, in her visit to me, behaved with great modesty and propriety, and left nothing behind her to be censured or despised. Neither praise nor money, the two powerful corrupters of mankind, seem to have depraved her. I shall be glad to see her again. Her brother Kemble calls on me, and pleases me very well. Mrs. Siddons and I talked of plays; and she told me her intention of exhibiting this winter the characters of *Constance, Catharine, and Isabella,* in Shakspeare."

Mr. Kemble has favoured me with the following minute of what passed at this visit.

"When Mrs. Siddons came into the room, there happened to be no chair ready for her, which he observing, said with a smile, 'Madam, you who so often occasion a want of seats to other people, will the more easily excuse the want of one yourself.'

"Having placed himself by her, he with great good humour entered upon a consideration of the English drama; and, among other inquiries, particularly asked her which of Shakspeare's characters she was most pleased with. Upon her answering that she thought the character of *Queen Catharine* in 'Henry the Eighth' the most natural:—'I think so too, Madam (said he), and whenever you perform it, I will once more hobble out to the theatre myself.' Mrs. Siddons promised she would do herself the honour of acting his favourite part for him; but many circumstances happened to prevent the representation of 'King Henry the Eighth' during the Doctor's life."

Johnson, indeed, had thought more upon the subject of acting than might be generally supposed. Talking of it one day to Mr. Kemble, he said, "Are you, Sir, one of those enthusiasts who believe yourself transformed into the very character you represent?" Upon Mr. Kemble's answering—that he had never felt so strong a persuasion himself; "To be sure not, Sir (said Johnson); the thing is impossible. And if Garrick really believed himself to be that monster, Richard the Third, he deserved to be hanged every time he performed it."

A pleasing instance of the generous attention of one of his friends has been discovered by the publication of Mrs. Thrale's Collection of Letters. In a letter to one of the Miss Thrales, he writes, "A friend, whose name I will tell when your mamma has tried to guess it, sent to my physician to inquire whether this long train of illness had brought me into difficulties for want of money, with an invitation to send to him for what occasion required. I shall write this night to thank him, having no need to borrow." And afterwards, in a letter to Mrs. Thrale, "Since you cannot guess, I will tell you that the generous man was Gerard Hamilton. I returned him a very thankful and respectful letter."

I applied to Mr. Hamilton, by a common friend, and he has been so obliging as to let me have Johnson's letter to him upon this occasion, to adorn my collection.

"TO THE RIGHT HONOURABLE WILLIAM GERARD HAMILTON.

"Dear Sir,—

"Your kind inquiries after my affairs, and your generous offers, have been communicated to me by Dr. Brocklesby. I return thanks with great sincerity, having lived long enough to know what gratitude is due to your friendship; and entreat that my refusal may not be imputed to sullenness or pride. I am, indeed, in no want. Sickness is, by the generosity of my physicians, of little expense to me. But if any unexpected exigence should press me, you shall see, dear Sir, how cheerfully I can be obliged to so much liberality.

   "I am, Sir,
    "Your most obedient
     "And most humble servant,
      "Sam. Johnson.

"*November 19, 1783.*"

[573]

I consulted him on two questions of a very different nature: one, whether the unconstitutional influence exercised by the peers of Scotland in the election of the representatives of the Commons, by means of fictitious qualifications, ought not to be resisted?—the other, what in propriety and humanity, should be done with old horses unable to labour? I gave him some account of my life at Auchinleck; and expressed my satisfaction that the gentlemen of the county had, at two public meetings, elected me their *Præses,* or Chairman.

"TO JAMES BOSWELL, ESQ.

"DEAR SIR,—·

"Like all other men who have great friends, you begin to feel the pangs of neglected merit; and all the comfort that I can give you is, by telling you that you have probably more pangs to feel, and more neglect to suffer. You have, indeed, begun to complain too soon; and I hope I am the only confidant of your discontent. Your friends have not yet had leisure to gratify personal kindness; they have hitherto been busy in strengthening their ministerial interest. If a vacancy happens in Scotland, give them early intelligence: and as you can serve Government as powerfully as any of your probable competitors, you may make in some sort a warrantable claim.

"Of the exaltations and depressions of your mind you delight to talk, and I hate to hear. Drive all such fancies from you.

"On the day when I received your letter, I think, the foregoing page was written; to which one disease or another has hindered me from making any additions. I am now a little better. But sickness and solitude press me very heavily. I could bear sickness better, if I were relieved from solitude.

"The present dreadful confusion of the public ought to make you wrap yourself up in your hereditary possessions, which, though less than you may wish, are more than you can want; and in an hour of religious retirement return thanks to God, who has exempted you from any strong temptation to faction, treachery, plunder, and disloyalty.

"As your neighbours distinguish you by such honours as they can bestow, content yourself with your station, without neglecting your profession. Your estate and the Courts will find you full employment, and your mind well occupied will be quiet.

"The usurpation of the nobility, for they apparently usurp all the influence they gain by fraud and misrepresentation, I think it certainly lawful, perhaps your duty, to resist. What is not their own, they have only by robbery.

[574]

"Your question about the horses gives me more perplexity. I know not well what advice to give you. I can only recommend a rule which you do not want;—give as little pain as you can. I suppose that we have a right to their service while their strength lasts; what we can do with them afterwards, I cannot so easily determine. But let us consider. Nobody denies that man has a right first to milk the cow, and to shear the sheep, and then to kill them for his table. May he not, by parity of reason, first work a horse, and then kill him the easiest way, that he may have the means of another horse, or food for cows and sheep? Man is influenced in both cases by different motives of self-interest. He that rejects the one must reject the other.

"I am, etc.,

"SAM. JOHNSON.

"*London, Dec. 24, 1783.*

"A happy and pious Christmas; and many happy years to you, your lady, and children."

I shall here mention what, in strict chronological arrangement, should have appeared in my account of last year: but may more properly be introduced here, the controversy having not been closed till this. The Reverend Mr. Shaw, a native of one of the Hebrides, having entertained doubts of the authenticity of the poems ascribed to Ossian, divested himself of national bigotry; and having travelled in the Highlands and Islands of Scotland, and also in Ireland, in order to furnish himself with materials for a Gaelic Dictionary, which he afterwards compiled, was so fully satisfied that Dr. Johnson was in the right upon the question, that he candidly published a pamphlet, stating his conviction, and the proofs and reasons on which it was founded. A person at Edinburgh, of the name of Clark, answered this pamphlet with much zeal, and much abuse of its author. Johnson took Mr. Shaw under his protection, and gave him his assistance in writing a reply, which has been admired by the best judges, and by many been considered as conclusive. A few paragraphs, which sufficiently mark their great author, shall be selected.

"My assertions are for the most part, purely negative: I deny the existence of Fingal, because in a long and curious peregrination through the Gaelic regions I have never been able to find it What I could not see myself I suspect to be equally invisible to others; and I suspect with the more reason, as among all those who have seen it no man can show it.

"Mr. Clark compares the obstinacy of those who disbelieve the genuineness of Ossian to a blind man, who should dispute the reality of colours, and deny that the British troops are clothed in red. The blind man's doubt would be rational, if he did not know by experience that others have a power which he himself wants: but what perspicacity has Mr. Clark which Nature has withheld from me or the rest of mankind?

"The true state of the parallel must be this. Suppose a man, with eyes like his neighbours, was told by a boasting corporal that the troops, indeed, wore red clothes for their ordinary dress, but that every soldier had likewise a suit of black velvet, which he puts on when the King reviews them. This he thinks strange, and desires to see the fine clothes, but finds nobody in forty thousand men that can produce either coat or waistcoat. One, indeed, has left them in his chest at Port Mahon; another has always heard that he ought to have velvet clothes somewhere; and a third has heard somebody say that soldiers ought to wear velvet. Can the inquirer be blamed if he goes away believing that a soldier's red coat is all that he has?

"But the most obdurate incredulity may be shamed or silenced by facts. To overpower contradictions, let the soldier show his velvet coat, and the Fingalist the original of Ossian.

"The difference between us and the blind man is this: the blind man is unconvinced, because he cannot see; and we, because, though we can see, we find that nothing can be shown."

Notwithstanding the complication of disorders under which Johnson now laboured, he did not resign himself to despondency and discontent, but with wisdom and spirit endeavoured to console and amuse his mind with as many innocent enjoyments as he could procure. Sir John Hawkins has mentioned the cordiality with which he insisted that such of the members of the old club in Ivy-lane as survived, should meet again and dine together, which they did, twice at a tavern, and once at his house; and in order to insure himself society in the evening for three days in the week, he instituted a club at the Essex Head, in Essex-street, then kept by Samuel Greaves, an old servant of Mr. Thrale's.

"TO SIR JOSHUA REYNOLDS.

"DEAR SIR,—

"It is inconvenient to me to come out; I should else have waited on you with an account of a little evening club which we are establishing in Essex-street, in the Strand, and of which you are desired to be one.

It will be held at the Essex Head, now kept by an old servant of Thrale's. The company is numerous, and, as you will see by the list, miscellaneous. The terms are lax, and the expenses light. Mr. Barry was adopted by Dr. Brocklesby, who joined with me in forming the plan. We meet thrice a week, and he who misses forfeits twopence.

"If you are willing to become a member, draw a line under your name. Return the list. We meet for the first time on Monday at eight.

"I am, etc.,

"SAM. JOHNSON.

"Dec. 4, 1783."

In the end of this year he was seized with a spasmodic asthma of such violence, that he was confined to the house in great pain, being sometimes obliged to sit all night in his chair, a recumbent posture being so hurtful to his respiration, that he could not endure lying in bed; and there came upon him at the same time that oppressive and fatal disease, a dropsy. It was a very severe winter, which probably aggravated his complaints; and the solitude in which Mr. Levett and Mrs. Williams had left him, rendered his life very gloomy. Mrs. Desmoulins, who still lived, was herself so very ill, that she could contribute very little to his relief. He, however, had none of that unsocial shyness which we commonly see in people afflicted with sickness. He did not hide his head from the world, in solitary abstraction; he did not deny himself to the visits of his friends and acquaintances; but at all times, when he was not overcome by sleep, was ready for conversation as in his best days.

CHAPTER LIV—1784

Johnson's Illness

AND NOW I am arrived at the last year of the life of Samuel Johnson; a year in which, although passed in severe indisposition, he nevertheless gave many evidences of the continuance of those wondrous powers of mind, which raised him so high in the intellectual world. His conversation and his letters of this year were in no respect inferior to those of former years.

[577]

On the 8th of January I wrote to him, anxiously inquiring as to his health, and enclosing my "Letter to the People of Scotland, on the present State of the Nation."—"I trust (said I) that you will be liberal enough to make allowance for my differing from you on two points [the Middlesex Election, and the American War], when my general principles of government are according to your own heart, and when, at a crisis of doubtful event, I stand forth with honest zeal as an ancient and faithful Briton. My reason for introducing those two points was, that as my opinions with regard to them had been declared at the periods when they were least favourable, I might have the credit of a man who is not a worshipper of ministerial power."

"TO JAMES BOSWELL, ESQ.

"DEAR SIR,—

"I hear of many inquiries which your kindness has disposed you to make after me. I have long intended you a long letter, which perhaps the imagination of its length hindered me from beginning. I will, therefore, content myself with a shorter.

"Having promoted the institution of a new club in the neighbourhood, at the house of an old servant of Thrale's, I went thither to meet the company, and was seized with a spasmodic asthma, so violent, that with difficulty I got to my own house, in which I have been confined eight or nine weeks, and from which I know not when I shall be able to go even to church. The asthma, however, is not the worst. A dropsy gains ground upon me; my legs and thighs are very much swollen with water, which I should be content if I could keep there, but I am afraid that it will soon be higher. My nights are very sleepless and very tedious. And yet I am extremely afraid of dying.

"My physicians try to make me hope that much of my malady is the effect of cold, and that some degree at least of recovery is to be expected from vernal breezes and summer suns. If my life is prolonged to autumn, I should be glad to try a warmer climate; though how to travel with a diseased body, without a companion to conduct me, and with very little money, I do not well see. Ramsay has recovered his limbs in Italy; and Fielding was sent to Lisbon, where, indeed, he died; but he was, I believe, past hope when he went. Think for me what I can do.

"I received your pamphlet, and when I write again may perhaps tell you some opinion about it; but you will forgive a man struggling with disease his neglect of disputes, politics, and pamphlets. Let me have your prayers. My compliments to your lady, and young ones. Ask your physicians about my case: and desire Sir Alexander Dick to write me his opinion.

"I am, dear Sir, etc.,

"SAM. JOHNSON.

"Feb. 11, 1784."

"TO JAMES BOSWELL, ESQ.

"DEAR SIR,—

"I have just advanced so far towards recovery as to read a pamphlet; and you may reasonably suppose that the first pamphlet which I read was yours. I am very much of your opinion, and, like you, feel great indignation at the indecency with which the King is every day treated. Your paper contains very considerable knowledge of history and of the constitution, very properly produced and applied. It will certainly raise your character, though perhaps it may not make you a Minister of State.

*   *   *

"I desire you to see Mrs. Stewart once again, and tell her that in the letter-case was a letter relating to me, for which I will give her, if she is willing to give it me, another guinea. The letter is of consequence only to me.

"I am, dear Sir, etc.,

"SAM. JOHNSON.

"London, Feb. 27, 1784."

In consequence of Johnson's request that I should ask our physicians about his case, and desire Sir Alexander Dick to send his opinion, I transmitted him a letter from that very amiable baronet, then in his eighty-first year, with his faculties as entire as ever; and mentioned his expressions to me in the note accompanying it,—"With my most affectionate wishes for Dr. Johnson's recovery, in which his friends, his country, and all mankind have so deep a stake"; and at the same time a full opinion upon his case by Dr. Gillespie, who, like Dr. Cullen, had the advantage of having passed through the gradations of surgery and pharmacy, and by study and practice had attained to such skill, that my father settled on him two hundred pounds a year for five years, and fifty pounds a year during his life, as an *honorarium* to secure his particular attendance. The opinion was conveyed in a letter to me, beginning, "I am sincerely sorry for the bad state of health your very learned and illustrious friend, Dr. Johnson, labours under at present."

"TO JAMES BOSWELL, ESQ.

"DEAR SIR,—

"Presently after I had sent away my last letter, I received your kind medical packet. I am very much obliged both to you and to your physicians for your kind attention to my disease. Dr. Gillespie has sent me an excellent *consilium medicum*, all solid practical experimental knowledge. I am at present in the opinion of my physicians (Dr. Heberden and Dr. Brocklesby) as well as my own, going on very hopefully. I have just begun to take vinegar of squills. The powder hurt my stomach so much, that it could not be continued.

"Return Sir Alexander Dick my sincere thanks for his kind letter; and bring with you the rhubarb which he so tenderly offers me.

"I hope dear Mrs. Boswell is now quite well, and that no evil, either real or imaginary, now disturbs you.

"I am, etc.,
"SAM. JOHNSON.

"*London, March 2, 1784.*"

"TO JAMES BOSWELL, ESQ.

"DEAR SIR,—

"I am too much pleased with the attention which you and your dear lady show to my welfare, not to be diligent in letting you know the progress which I make towards health. The dropsy, by God's blessing, has now run almost totally away by natural evacuation: and the asthma, if not irritated by cold, gives me little trouble. While I am writing this, I have not any sensation of debility or disease. But I do not yet venture out, having been confined to the house from the 13th of December, now a quarter of a year.

"When it will be fit for me to travel as far as Auchinleck, I am not able to guess; but such a letter as Mrs. Boswell's might draw any man, not wholly motionless, a great way. Pray tell the dear lady how much her civility and kindness have touched and gratified me.

"Our parliamentary tumults have now begun to subside, and the King's authority is in some measure re-established. Mr. Pitt will have great power; but you must remember that what he has to give, must, at least for some time, be given to those who gave, and those who preserve, his power. A new minister can sacrifice little to esteem or friendship; he must, till he is settled, think only of extending his interest.

"I wish you an easy and happy journey; and hope I need not tell you that you will be welcome to, dear Sir, your most affectionate humble servant,

"SAM. JOHNSON.

"*London, March 18, 1784.*"

I wrote to him, March 28, from York, informing him that I had a high gratification in the triumph of monarchical principles over aristocratical influence, in that great county, in an address to the King; that I was thus far on my way to him, but that news of the dissolution of Parliament having arrived, I was to hasten back to my own county, where I had carried an Address to his Majesty by a great majority, and had some intention of being a candidate to represent the county in Parliament.

"TO JAMES BOSWELL, ESQ.

"DEAR SIR,—

"You could do nothing so proper as to hasten back when you found the Parliament dissolved. With the influence which your address must have gained you, it may reasonably be expected that your presence will be of importance, and your activity of effect.

"Your solicitude for me gives me that pleasure which every man feels from the kindness of such a friend; and it is with delight I relieve it by telling that Dr. Brocklesby's account is true, and that I am, by the blessing of God, wonderfully relieved.

"You are entering upon a transaction which requires much prudence. You must endeavour to oppose without exasperating; to practise temporary hostility, without producing enemies for life. This is, perhaps, hard to be done; yet it has been done by many, and seems most likely to be effected by opposing merely upon general principles, without descending to personal or particular censures or objections. One thing I must enjoin you, which is seldom observed in the conduct of elections;—I must entreat you to be scrupulous in the use of strong liquors. One night's drunkenness may defeat the labours of forty days well employed. Be firm, but not clamorous; be active, but not malicious; and you may form such an interest as may not only exalt yourself, but dignify your family.

"We are, as you may suppose, all busy here. Mr. Fox resolutely stands for Westminster, and his friends say will carry the election. However that be, he will certainly have a seat. Mr. Hoole has just told me that the City leans towards the King.

"Let me hear, from time to time, how you are employed, and what progress you make.

"Make dear Mrs. Boswell, and all the young Boswells, the sincere compliments of, Sir, your affectionate humble servant,

"SAM. JOHNSON.

"*London, March 30, 1784.*"

"TO THE REVEREND DR. TAYLOR, ASHBOURNE, DERBYSHIRE.

"DEAR SIR,—

"What can be the reason that I hear nothing from you? I hope nothing disables you from writing. What I have seen, and what I have felt, gives me reason to fear everything. Do not omit giving me the comfort of knowing that after all my losses I have yet a friend left.

"I want every comfort. My life is very solitary and very cheerless. Though it has pleased God wonderfully to deliver me from the dropsy, I am yet very weak, and have not passed the door since the 13th of December. I hope for some help from warm weather, which will surely come in time.

"I could not have the consent of the physicians to go to church yesterday; I therefore received the holy sacrament at home, in the room where I communicated with dear Mrs. Williams, a little before her death. Oh! my friend, the approach of death is very dreadful. I am afraid to think on that which I know I cannot avoid. It is vain to look round and round for that help which cannot be had. Yet we hope and hope, and fancy that he who has lived to-day may live to-morrow. But let us learn to derive our hope only from God.

"In the mean time, let us be kind to one another. I have no friend now living but you and Mr. Hector, that was the friend of my youth. Do not neglect,

"Dear Sir,
"Yours affectionately,
"SAM. JOHNSON.

"*London, Easter-Monday,*
"*April 12, 1784.*"

What follows is a beautiful specimen of his gentleness and complacency to a young lady, his godchild, one of the daughters of his friend Mr. Langton, then I think in her seventh year. He took the trouble to write it in a large round hand, nearly resembling printed characters, that she might have the satisfaction of reading it herself. The original lies before me, but shall be faithfully restored to her; and I dare say will be preserved by her as a jewel, as long as she lives.

"TO MISS JANE LANGTON, IN ROCHESTER, KENT.

"My dearest Miss Jenny,—

"I am sorry that your pretty letter has been so long without being answered; but, when I am not pretty well, I do not always write plain enough for young ladies. I am glad, my dear, to see that you write so well, and hope that you mind your pen, your book, and your needle, for they are all necessary. Your books will give you knowledge, and make you respected; and your needle will find you useful employment when you do not care to read. When you are a little older, I hope you will be very diligent in learning arithmetic; and above all, that through your whole life you will carefully say your prayers, and read your Bible.

"I am, my dear,
"Your most humble servant,
"SAM. JOHNSON.

"*May 10, 1784.*"

On Wednesday, May 5, I arrived in London, and next morning had the pleasure to find Dr. Johnson greatly recovered. I but just saw him; for a coach was waiting to carry him to Islington, to the house of his friend the Reverend Mr. Strahan, where he went sometimes for the benefit of good air, which, notwithstanding his having formerly laughed at the general opinion upon the subject, he now acknowledged was conducive to health.

On Saturday, May 15, I dined with him at Dr. Brocklesby's, where were Colonel Vallancy, Mr. Murphy, and that ever-cheerful companion Mr. Devaynes, Apothecary to his Majesty. Of these days, and others on which I saw him, I have no memorials, except the general recollection of his being able and animated in conversation, and appearing to relish society as much as the youngest man. I find only these three small particulars:—When a person was mentioned, who said, "I have lived fifty-one years in this world, without having had ten minutes of uneasiness"; he exclaimed, "The man who say so, lies: he attempts to impose on human credulity." The Bishop of Exeter in vain observed that men were very different. His Lordship's manner was not impressive: and I learnt afterwards that Johnson did not find out that the person who talked to him was a prelate; if he had, I doubt not that he would have treated him with more respect: for once talking of George Psalmanazar, whom he reverenced for his piety, he said, "I should as soon think of contradicting a Bishop." One of the company provoked him greatly by doing what he could least of all bear, which was quoting something of his own writing, against what he then maintained. "What, Sir (cried the gentleman), do you say to—

'The busy day, the peaceful night,
Unfelt, uncounted, glided by'?"

Johnson finding himself thus presented as giving an instance of a man who had lived without uneasiness, was much offended, for he looked upon such a quotation as unfair. His anger burst out in an unjustifiable retort, insinuating that the gentleman's remark was a sally of ebriety; "Sir, there is one passion I would advise you to command: when you have drunk out that glass, don't drink another." Here was exemplified what Goldsmith said of him, with the aid of a very witty image from one of Cibber's Comedies: "There is no arguing with Johnson: for if his pistol misses fire, he knocks you down with the butt end of it."

On the evening of Saturday, May 15, he was in fine spirits, at our Essex Head Club. BOSWELL: "Mr. Burke has a constant stream of conversation." JOHNSON: "Yes, Sir; if a man were to go by chance at the same time with Burke under a shed, to shun a shower, he would say—'this is an extraordinary man.' If Burke should go into a stable to see his horse dressed, the ostler would say—'we have had an extraordinary man here.' " BOSWELL: "Foote was a man who never failed in conversation. If he had gone into a stable——" JOHNSON: "Sir, if he had gone into the stable, the ostler would have said, 'here has been a comical fellow'; but he would not have respected him." BOSWELL: "And, Sir, the ostler would have answered him, would have given him as good as he brought, as the common saying is." JOHNSON: "Yes, Sir; and Foote would have answered the ostler.—When Burke does not descend to be merry, his conversation is very superior indeed. There is no proportion between the powers which he shows in serious talk and in jocularity. When he lets himself down to that, he is in the kennel." I have in another place opposed, and I hope with success, Dr. Johnson's very singular and erroneous notion as to Mr. Burke's pleasantry. Mr. Windham now said low to me that he differed from our great friend in this observation; for that Mr. Burke was often very happy in his merriment. It would not have been right for either of us to have contradicted Johnson at this time, in a society all of whom did not know and value Mr. Burke as much as we did. It might have occasioned something more rough, and at any rate would probably have checked the flow of Johnson's good-humour. He called to us with a sudden air of exultation, as the thought started into his mind, "O! gentlemen, I must tell you a very great thing. The Empress of Russia has ordered the *Rambler* to be translated into the Russian language: so I shall be read on the banks of the Wolga. Horace boasts that his fame would extend as far as the banks of the Rhone; now the Wolga is farther from me than the Rhone was from Horace." BOSWELL: "You must certainly be pleased with this, Sir." JOHNSON: "I am pleased, Sir, to be sure. A man is pleased to find he has succeeded in that which he has endeavoured to do."

One of the company mentioned his having seen a noble person driving in his carriage, and looking exceedingly well, notwithstanding his great age. JOHNSON: "Ah, Sir; that is nothing. Bacon observes that a stout healthy old man is like a tower undermined."

On Wednesday, May 19, I sat a part of the evening with him, by ourselves. I observed that the death of our friends might be a consolation against the fear of our own dissolution, because we might have more friends in the other world than in this. He perhaps felt this as a reflection upon his apprehension as to death; and said, with heat, "How can a man know *where* his departed friends are, or whether they will be his friends in the other world. How many friendships have you known formed upon principles of virtue? Most friendships are formed by caprice or by chance, mere confederacies in vice, or leagues in folly."

We talked of our worthy friend Mr. Langton. He said, "I know not who will go to Heaven, if Langton does not. Sir, I could almost say, *Sit anima mea cum Langtono.*" I mentioned a very eminent friend as a virtuous man. JOHNSON: "Yes, Sir; but ——— has not the evangelical virtue of Langton. ———, I am afraid, would not scruple to pick up a wench."

He, however, charged Mr. Langton with what he thought want of judgment upon an interesting occasion. "When I was ill (said he), I desired he would tell me sincerely in what he thought my life was faulty. Sir, he brought me a sheet of paper, on which he had written down several texts of Scripture, recommending Christian charity. And when I questioned him what occasion I had given for such an animad-version, all that he could say amounted to this,—that I sometimes contradicted people in conversation. Now what harm does it do to any man to be contradicted?" BOSWELL: "I suppose he meant the *manner* of doing it; roughly and harshly." JOHNSON: "And who is the worse for that?" BOSWELL: "It hurts people of weaker nerves." JOHNSON: "I know no such weak-nerved people." Mr. Burke, to whom I related this conference, said, "It is well, if when a man comes to die, he has nothing heavier upon his conscience than having been a little rough in conversation."

Johnson, at the time when the paper was presented to him, though at first pleased with the attention of his friend, whom he thanked in an earnest manner, soon exclaimed in a loud and angry tone, "What is your drift, Sir?" Sir Joshua Reynolds pleasantly observed that it was a scene for a comedy, to see a penitent get into a violent passion and belabour his confessor.

I have preserved no more of his conversation at the times when I saw him during the rest of this month, till Sunday, the 30th of May, when I met him in the evening at Mr. Hoole's, where there was a large company both of ladies and gentlemen. Sir James Johnston happened to say that he paid no regard to the arguments of counsel at the bar of the House of Commons, because they were paid for speaking. JOHNSON: "Nay, Sir, argument is argument. You cannot help paying regard to their arguments, if they are good. If it were testimony, you might disregard it, if you knew that it were purchased. There is a beautiful image in Bacon upon this subject: testimony is like an arrow shot from a long bow; the force of it depends on the strength of the hand that draws it. Argument is like an arrow from a crossbow, which has equal force though shot by a child."

He had dined that day at Mr. Hoole's, and Miss Helen Maria Williams being expected in the evening, Mr. Hoole put into his hands her beautiful "Ode on the Peace": Johnson read it over, and when this elegant and accomplished young lady was presented to him, he took her by the hand in the most courteous manner, and repeated the finest stanza of her poem; this was the most delicate and pleasing compliment he could pay. Her respectable friend, Dr. Kippis, from whom I had this anecdote, was standing by, and was not a little gratified.

Miss Williams told me that the only other time she was fortunate enough to be in Dr. Johnson's company, he asked her to sit down by him, which she did; and upon her inquiring how he was, he answered, "I am very ill indeed, Madam. I am very ill even when you are near me; what should I be were you at a distance?"

He had now a great desire to go to Oxford, as his first jaunt after his illness; we talked of it for some days, and I had promised to accompany him. He was impatient and fretful to-night, because I did not at once agree to go with him on Thursday. When I considered how ill he had been, and what allowance should be made for the influence of sickness upon his temper, I resolved to indulge him, though with some inconvenience to myself, as I wished to attend the musical meeting in honour of Handel, in Westminster Abbey, on the following Saturday.

CHAPTER LV—1784

Dr. William Adams

ON THURSDAY, JUNE 3, the Oxford post-coach took us up in the morning at Bolt-court. The other two passengers were Mrs. Beresford and her daughter, two very agreeable ladies from America; they were going to Worcestershire, where they then resided. Frank had been sent by his master the day before to take places for us; and I found from the way-bill that Dr. Johnson had made our names be put down. Mrs. Beresford, who had read it, whispered me, "Is this the great Dr. Johnson?" I told her it was; so she was then prepared to listen. As she soon happened to mention in a voice so low that Johnson did not hear it that her husband had been a member of the American Congress, I cautioned her to beware of introducing that subject, as she must know how very violent Johnson was against the people of that country. He talked a great deal. But I am sorry I have preserved little of the conversation. Miss Beresford was so much charmed that she said to me aside, "How he does talk! Every sentence is an essay." She amused herself in the coach with knotting; he would scarcely allow this species of employment any merit. "Next to mere idleness (said he) I think knotting is to be reckoned in the scale of insignificance; though I once attempted to learn knotting. Dempster's sister (looking at me) endeavoured to teach me it; but I made no progress."

I was surprised at his talking without reserve in the public post-coach of the state of his affairs: "I have (said he) about the world, I think, above a thousand pounds, which I intend shall afford Frank an annuity of seventy pounds a year." Indeed his openness with people at a first interview was remarkable. He said once to Mr. Langton, "I think I am like Squire Richard in 'The Journey to London,' *I'm never strange in a strange place.*" He was truly *social.* He strongly censured what is much too common in England among persons of condition,—maintaining an absolute silence, when unknown to each other; as for instance, when occasionally brought together in a room before the master or mistress of the house has appeared. "Sir, that is being so uncivilized as not to understand the common rights of humanity."

At the inn where we stopped he was exceedingly dissatisfied with some roast mutton which we had for dinner. The ladies, I saw, wondered to see the great philosopher, whose wisdom and wit they had been admiring all the way, get into ill-humour from such a cause. He scolded the waiter, saying, "It is as bad as bad can be: it is ill-fed, ill-killed, ill-kept, and ill-dressed."

He bore the journey very well, and seemed to feel himself elevated as he approached Oxford, that magnificent and venerable seat of Learning, Orthodoxy, and Toryism. Frank came in the heavy coach, in readiness to attend him; and we were received with the most polite hospitality at the house of his old friend Dr. Adams, Master of Pembroke College, who had given us a kind invitation. Before we were set down, I communicated to Johnson my having engaged to return to London directly, for the reason I have mentioned, but that I would hasten back to him again. He was pleased that I had made this journey merely to keep him company. He was easy and placid, with Dr. Adams, Mrs. and Miss Adams, and Mrs. Kennicot, widow of the learned Hebræan, who was here on a visit. He soon dispatched the inquiries which were made about his illness and recovery, by a short and distinct narrative; and then assuming a gay air, repeated from Swift,

> "Nor think on our approaching ills,
> And talk of spectacles and pills."

I fulfilled my intention by going to London, and returned to Oxford on Wednesday, the 9th of June, when I was happy to find myself again in the same agreeable circle at Pembroke College, with the comfortable prospect of making some stay. Johnson welcomed my return with more than ordinary glee.

Next morning at breakfast, he pointed out a passage in Savage's

"Wanderer," saying, "These are fine verses."—"If (said he) I had written with hostility of Warburton in my 'Shakspeare,' I should have quoted this couplet:

> 'Here Learning blinded first and then beguil'd,
> Looks dark as Ignorance, as Frenzy wild.'

You see they'd have fitted him to a *T*" (smiling). DR. ADAMS: "But you did not write against Warburton." JOHNSON: "No, Sir, I treated him with great respect both in my Preface and in my Notes."

Mrs. Kennicot spoke of her brother, the Reverend Mr. Chamberlayne, who had given up great prospects in the Church of England on his conversion to the Roman Catholic faith. Johnson, who warmly admired every man who acted from a conscientious regard to principle, erroneous or not, exclaimed fervently, "God bless him."

On the Roman Catholic religion he said, "If you join the Papists externally, they will not interrogate you strictly as to your belief in their tenets. No reasoning Papist believes every article of their faith. There is one side on which a good man might be persuaded to embrace it. A good man of a timorous disposition, in great doubt of his acceptance with God, and pretty credulous, may be glad to be of a church where there are so many helps to get to Heaven. I would be a Papist if I could. I have fear enough; but an obstinate rationality prevents me. I shall never be a Papist, unless on the near approach of death, of which I have a very great terror. I wonder that women are not all Papists." BOSWELL: "They are not more afraid of death than men are." JOHNSON: "Because they are less wicked." DR. ADAMS: "They are more pious." JOHNSON: "No, hang 'em, they are not more pious. A wicked fellow is the most pious when he takes to it. He'll beat you all at piety."

After dinner, when one of us talked of there being a great enmity between Whig and Tory;—JOHNSON: "Why, not so much, I think, unless when they come into competition with each other. There is none when they are only common acquaintance, none when they are of different sexes. A Tory will marry into a Whig family, and a Whig into a Tory family, without any reluctance. But, indeed, in a matter of much more concern than political tenets, and that is religion, men and women do not concern themselves much about difference of opinion; and ladies set no value on the moral character of men who pay their addresses to them; the greatest profligate will be as well received as the man of the greatest virtue, and this by a very good woman, by a woman who says her prayers three times a day." Our ladies endeavoured to defend their sex from this charge; but he roared them down; "No, no, a lady will take Jonathan Wild as readily as St. Austin, if he has threepence more; and, what is worse, her parents will give her to him. Women have a perpetual envy of our vices; they are less vicious than we, not from choice, but because we restrict them; they are the slaves of order and fashion; their virtue is of more consequence to us than our own, so far as concerns this world."

Miss Adams mentioned a gentleman of licentious character, and said, "Suppose I had a mind to marry that gentleman, would my parents consent?" JOHNSON: "Yes, they'd consent, and you'd go. You'd go, though they did not consent." MISS ADAMS: "Perhaps their opposing might make me go." JOHNSON: "O, very well; you'd take one whom you think a bad man, to have the pleasure of vexing your parents. You put me in mind of Dr. Barrowby, the physician, who was very fond of swine's flesh. One day, when he was eating it, he said, 'I wish I was a Jew.'—'Why so? (said somebody); the Jews are not allowed to eat your favourite meat.'—'Because (said he), I should then have the gust of eating it, with the pleasure of sinning.'"

Miss Adams soon afterwards made an observation that I do not recollect, which pleased him much; he said with a good-humoured smile, "That there should be so much excellence united with so much *depravity*, is strange."

Indeed, this lady's good qualities, merit, and accomplishments, and her constant attention to Dr. Johnson, were not lost upon him. She happened to tell him that a little coffee-pot, in which she had made him coffee was the only thing she could call her own. He turned to her with a complacent gallantry, "Don't say so, my dear; I hope you don't reckon my heart as nothing."

I asked him if it was true as reported that he had said lately, "I am for the King against Fox; but I am for Fox against Pitt." JOHNSON: "Yes, Sir; the King is my master; but I do not know Pitt; and Fox is my friend."

Dr. Wall, physician at Oxford, drank tea with us. Johnson had in general a peculiar pleasure in the company of physicians, which was certainly not abated by the conversation of this learned, ingenious, and pleasing gentleman. Johnson said, "It is wonderful how little good Radcliffe's travelling fellowships have done. I know nothing that has been imported by them; yet many additions to our medical knowledge might be got in foreign countries. Inoculation, for instance, has saved more lives than war destroys; and the cures performed by the Peruvian bark are innumerable. But it is in vain to send our travelling physicians to France, and Italy, and Germany, for all that is known there is known here: I'd send them out of Christendom; I'd send them among barbarous nations."

On Friday, June 11, we talked at breakfast of forms of prayer. JOHNSON: "I know of no good prayers but those in the 'Book of Common Prayer.'" DR. ADAMS (in a very earnest manner): "I wish, Sir, you would compose some family prayers." JOHNSON: "I will not compose prayers for you, Sir, because you can do it for yourself. But I have thought of getting together all the books of prayers which I could, selecting those which should appear to me the best, putting out some, inserting others, adding some prayers of my own, and prefixing a discourse on prayer." We all now gathered about him, and two or three of us at a time joined in pressing him to execute this plan. He seemed to be a little displeased at the manner of our importunity, and in great agitation called out, "Do not talk thus of what is so awful. I know not what time God will allow me in this world. There are many things which I wish to do." Some of us persisted, and Dr. Adams said, "I never was more serious about anything in my life." JOHNSON: "Let me alone, let me alone; I am overpowered." And then he put his hands before his face, and reclined for some time upon the table.

Dr. Johnson and I went in Dr. Adams's coach to dine with Mr. Nowell, Principal of St. Mary Hall, at his beautiful villa at Iffley, on the banks of the Isis, about two miles from Oxford. While we were upon the road, I had the resolution to ask Johnson whether he thought that the roughness of his manner had been an advantage or not, and if he would not have done more good if he had been more gentle. I proceeded to answer myself thus: "Perhaps it has been of advantage, as it has given weight to what you said: you could not, perhaps, have talked with such authority without it." JOHNSON: "No, Sir; I have done more good as I am. Obscenity and impiety have always been repressed in my company." BOSWELL: "True, Sir; and that is more than can be said of every bishop. Greater liberties have been taken in the presence of a bishop, though a very good man, from his being milder, and therefore not commanding such awe. Yet Sir, many people who might have been benefited by your conversation, have been frightened away. A worthy friend of ours has told me that he has often been afraid to talk to you." JOHNSON: "Sir, he need not have been afraid, if he had anything rational to say. If he had not, it was better he did not talk."

I censured the coarse invectives which were become fashionable in the House of Commons, and said that if members of Parliament must attack each other personally in the heat of debate, it should be done more genteelly. JOHNSON: "No, Sir; that would be much worse. Abuse is not so dangerous when there is no vehicle of wit or delicacy, no subtle conveyance. The difference between coarse and refined abuse is as the difference between being bruised by a club, and wounded by a poisoned arrow."

On Sunday, June 13, our philosopher was calm at breakfast. There was something exceedingly pleasing in our leading a college life, without restraint, and with superior elegance, in consequence of our living in the Master's House, and having the company of ladies. Mrs. Kennicot related, in his presence, a lively saying of Dr. Johnson to Miss Hannah More, who had expressed a wonder that the poet who had written "Paradise Lost," should write such poor sonnets:—"Milton, Madam, was a genius that could cut a Colossus from a rock, but could not carve heads upon cherry-stones."

On Monday, June 14, and Tuesday, 15, Dr. Johnson and I dined, on one of them, I forget which, with Mr. Mickle, translator of the "Lusiad," at Wheatley, a very pretty country place a few miles from Oxford; and on the other with Dr. Wetherell, Master of University College. From Dr. Wetherell's he went to visit Mr. Sackville Parker, the bookseller; and when he returned to us, gave the following account of his visit, saying, "I have been to see my old friend, Sack. Parker; I find he has married his maid; he has done right. She had lived with him many years in great confidence, and they had mingled minds; I do not think he could have found any wife that would have made him so happy. The woman was very attentive and civil to me. She pressed me to fix a day for dining with them, and to say what I liked, and she would be sure to get it for me. Poor Sack.! He is very ill, indeed. We parted as never to meet again. It has quite broken me down." This pathetic narrative was strangely diversified with the grave and earnest defence of a man's having married his maid. I could not but feel it as in some degree ludicrous.

In the morning of Tuesday, June 15, while we sat at Dr. Adams's, we talked of a printed letter from the Reverend Herbert Croft, to a young gentleman who had been his pupil, in which he advised him to read to the end of whatever books he should begin to read. JOHNSON: "This is surely a strange advice; you may as well resolve that whatever men you happen to get acquainted with, you are to keep to them for life. A book may be good for nothing; or there may be only one thing in it worth knowing: are we to read it all through? These voyages (pointing to the three large volumes of 'Voyages to the South Sea,' which were just come out) *who* will read them through? A man had better work his way before the mast than read them through; they will be eaten by rats and mice, before they are read through. There can be little entertainment in such books; one set of savages is like another." BOSWELL: "I do not think the people of Otaheité can be reckoned savages." JOHNSON: "Don't cant in defence of savages." BOSWELL: "They have the art of navigation." —JOHNSON: "A dog or a cat can swim." BOSWELL: "They carve very ingeniously." JOHNSON: "A cat can scratch, and a child with a nail can scratch." I perceived this was none of the *mollia tempora fandi,* so desisted.

Upon his mentioning that when he came to college he wrote his first exercises twice over, but never did so afterwards. MISS ADAMS: "I suppose, Sir, you could not make them better?" JOHNSON: "Yes, Madam, to be sure, I could make them better. Thought is better than no thought." MISS ADAMS: "Do you think, Sir, you could make your *Ramblers* better?" JOHNSON: "Certainly I could." BOSWELL: "I'll lay a bet, Sir, you cannot." JOHNSON: "But I will, Sir, if I choose. I shall make the best of them you shall pick out, better." BOSWELL: "But you may add to them. I will not allow of that." JOHNSON: "Nay, Sir, there are three ways of making them better;—putting out, adding, or correcting."

CHAPTER LVI—1784

Boswell's Farewell to Johnson

ON WEDNESDAY, JUNE 19, Dr. Johnson and I returned to London; he was not well to-day, and said very little, employing himself chiefly in reading Euripides. He expressed some displeasure at me, for not observing sufficiently the various objects upon the road. "If I had your eyes, Sir (said he), I should count the passengers." It was wonderful how accurate his observation of visual objects was, notwithstanding his imperfect eyesight, owing to a habit of attention.—That he was much satisfied with the respect paid to him at Dr. Adams's is thus attested by himself: "I returned last night from Oxford, after a fortnight's abode with Dr. Adams, who treated me as well as I could expect or wish; and he that contents a sick man, a man whom it is impossible to please, has surely done his part well."

After his return to London from this excursion, I saw him frequently, but have few memorandums; I shall therefore here insert some particulars which I collected at various times.

It having been mentioned to Dr. Johnson that a gentleman who had a son whom he imagined to have an extreme degree of timidity, resolved to send him to a public school, that he might acquire confidence;—"Sir (said Johnson), this is a preposterous expedient for removing his infirmity; such a disposition should be cultivated in the shade. Placing him at a public school is forcing an owl upon day."

Speaking of a gentleman whose house was much frequented by low company; "Rags, Sir (said he), will always make their appearance, where they have a right to do it."

A dull country magistrate gave Johnson a long tedious account of his exercising his criminal jurisdiction, the result of which was having sentenced four convicts to transportation. Johnson, in an agony of impatience to get rid of such a companion, exclaimed, "I heartily wish, Sir, that I were a fifth."

Johnson having argued for some time with a pertinacious gentleman: his opponent, who had talked in a very puzzling manner, happened to say, "I don't understand you, Sir"; upon which Johnson observed, "Sir, I have found you an argument; but I am not obliged to find you an understanding."

I have mentioned Johnson's general aversion to pun. He once, however, endured one of mine. When we were talking of a numerous company in which he had distinguished himself highly, I said, "Sir, you were a Cod surrounded by smelts. Is not this enough for you? at a time too when you were not *fishing* for a compliment?" He laughed at this with a complacent approbation. Old Mr. Sheridan observed, upon my mentioning it to him, "He liked your compliment so well, he was willing to take it with *pun sauce.*" For my part, I think no innocent species of wit or pleasantry should be suppressed: and that a good pun may be admitted among the smaller excellences of lively conversation.

When I pointed out to him in the newspaper one of Mr. Grattan's animated and glowing speeches in favour of the freedom of Ireland,

in which this expression occurred (I know not if accurately taken):
"We will persevere, till there is not one link of the English chain left
to clank upon the rags of the meanest beggar in Ireland";—"Nay,
Sir (said Johnson), don't you perceive that *one* link cannot clank?"

It may be worth remarking, among the *minutiæ* of my collection,
that Johnson was once drawn to serve in the militia, the Trained
Bands of the City of London, and that Mr. Rackstraw, of the Museum
in Fleet-street, was his Colonel. It may be believed he did not serve in
person; but the idea, with all its circumstances, is certainly laughable.
He upon that occasion provided himself with a musket, and with a
sword and belt, which I have seen hanging in his closet.

The difference, he observed, between a well-bred and an ill-bred
man is this: "One immediately attracts your liking, the other your
aversion. You love the one till you find reason to hate him; you hate
the other till you find reason to love him."

The wife of one of his acquaintance had fraudulently made a purse
for herself out of her husband's fortune. Feeling a proper compunction in her last moments, she confessed how much she had secreted;
but before she could tell where it was placed, she was seized with a
convulsive fit and expired. Her husband said he was more hurt by
her want of confidence in him, than by the loss of his money. "I told
him (said Johnson) that he should console himself: for *perhaps* the
money might be *found,* and he was *sure* that his wife was *gone.*"

He seemed to take a pleasure in speaking in his own style; for when
he had carelessly missed it, he would repeat the thought translated
into it. Talking of the Comedy of "The Rehearsal," he said, "It has
not wit enough to keep it sweet." This was easy;—he therefore caught
himself, and pronounced a more round sentence, "It has not vitality
enough to preserve it from putrefaction."

No man was more ready to make an apology when he had censured unjustly, than Johnson. When a proof-sheet of one of his works
was brought to him, he found fault with the mode in which a part
of it was arranged, refused to read it, and in a passion desired that the
compositor might be sent to him. The compositor was Mr. Manning,
a decent, sensible man, who had composed about one-half of his
Dictionary, when in Mr. Strahan's printing-house; and a great part of
his "Lives of the Poets," when in that of Mr. Nichols; and who (in
his seventy-seventh year) when in Mr. Baldwin's printing-house, composed a part of the first edition of this work concerning him. By producing the manuscript, he at once satisfied Dr. Johnson that he was

not to blame. Upon which Johnson candidly and earnestly said to him, "Mr. Compositor, I ask your pardon; Mr. Compositor, I ask your pardon, again and again."

His generous humanity to the miserable was almost beyond example. The following instance is well attested: Coming home late one night, he found a poor woman lying in the street, so much exhausted that she could not walk; he took her upon his back, and carried her to his house, where he discovered that she was one of those wretched females who had fallen into the lowest state of vice, poverty, and disease. Instead of harshly upbraiding her, he had her taken care of with all tenderness for a long time, at a considerable expense, till she was restored to health, and endeavoured to put her into a virtuous way of living.

He had a great aversion to gesticulating in company. He called once to a gentleman who offended him in that point, "Don't *attitudinise.*" And when another gentleman thought he was giving additional force to what he uttered, by expressive movements of his hands, Johnson fairly seized them, and held them down.

Mr. Steevens, who passed many a social hour with him during their long acquaintance, which commenced when they both lived in the Temple, has preserved a good number of particulars concerning him, most of which are to be found in the department of Apophthegms, etc., in the Collection of "Johnson's Works." But he has been pleased to favour me with the following, which are original:

"One evening, previous to the trial of Baretti, a consultation of his friends was held at the house of Mr. Cox, the solicitor, in Southampton-buildings, Chancery-lane. Among others present were Mr. Burke and Dr. Johnson, who differed in sentiments concerning the tendency of some part of the defence the prisoner was to make. When the meeting was over, Mr. Steevens observed that the question between him and his friend had been agitated with rather too much warmth. 'It may be so, Sir (replied the Doctor), for Burke and I should have been of one opinion, if we had had no audience.'"

"It has been supposed that Dr. Johnson, so far as fashion was concerned, was careless of his appearance in public. But this is not altogether true, as the following slight instance may show:—Goldsmith's last comedy was to be represented during some court-mourning; and Mr. Steevens appointed to call on Dr. Johnson, and carry him to the tavern where he was to dine with others of the poet's friends. The Doctor was ready dressed, but in coloured clothes; yet being told that he would find every one else in black, received the intelligence with a profusion of thanks, hastened to change his attire, all the while repeating his gratitude for the information that had saved him from an appearance so improper in the front row of a front box. 'I would not (added he) for ten pounds have seemed so retrograde to any general observance.' "

On Tuesday, June 22, I dined with him at the Literary Club, the last time of his being in that respectable society. The other members present were the Bishop of St. Asaph, Lord Eliot, Lord Palmerston, Dr. Fordyce, and Mr. Malone. He looked ill; but had such a manly fortitude, that he did not trouble the company with melancholy complaints. They all showed evident marks of kind concern about him, with which he was much pleased, and he exerted himself to be as entertaining as his indisposition allowed him.

The anxiety of his friends to preserve so estimable a life, as long as human means might be supposed to have influence, made them plan for him a retreat from the severity of a British winter, to the mild climate of Italy. This scheme was at last brought to a serious resolution at General Paoli's, where I had often talked of it. One essential matter, however, I understood was necessary to be previously settled, which was obtaining such an addition to his income as would be sufficient to enable him to defray the expense in a manner becoming the first literary character of a great nation, and, independent of all his other merits, the Author of The Dictionary of the English Language. The person to whom I above all others thought I should apply to negotiate this business was the Lord Chancellor, because I knew that he highly valued Johnson, and that Johnson highly valued his Lordship; so that it was no degradation of my illustrious friend to solicit for him the favour of such a man. I have mentioned what Johnson said of him to me when he was at the Bar; and after his Lordship was advanced to the seals, he said of him, "I would prepare myself for no man in England but Lord Thurlow. When I am to meet with him, I should wish to know a day before." How he would have prepared himself, I cannot conjecture. Would he have selected certain topics, and considered them in every view, so as to be in readiness to argue them at all points? and what may we suppose those topics to have been? I once started the curious inquiry to the great man who was the subject of this compliment: he smiled, but did not pursue it.

I first consulted with Sir Joshua Reynolds, who perfectly coincided in opinion with me; and I therefore, though personally very little known to his Lordship, wrote to him, stating the case, and requesting his good offices for Dr. Johnson. I mentioned that I was obliged to set out for Scotland early in the following week, so that if his Lordship should have any commands for me as to this pious negotiation, he would be pleased to send them before that time; otherwise Sir Joshua Reynolds would give all attention to it.

This application was made not only without any suggestion on the part of Johnson himself, but was utterly unknown to him, nor had he the smallest suspicion of it. Any insinuations, therefore, which since his death have been thrown out, as if he had stooped to ask what was superfluous, are without any foundation. But, had he asked it, it would not have been superfluous; for though the money he had saved proved to be more than his friends imagined, or than I believe he himself, in his carelessness concerning worldly matters knew it to be, had he travelled upon the Continent, an augmentation of his income would by no means have been unnecessary.

On Thursday, June 24, I dined with him at Mr. Dilly's, where were the Rev. Mr. (now Dr.) Knox, master of Tunbridge-school, Mr. Smith, Vicar of Southill, Dr. Beattie, Mr. Pinkerton, author of various literary performances, and the Rev. Dr. Mayo. At my desire old Mr. Sheridan was invited, as I was earnest to have Johnson and him brought together again by chance, that a reconciliation might be effected. Mr. Sheridan happened to come early, and having learnt that Dr. Johnson was to be there, went away; so I found, with sincere regret, that my friendly intentions were hopeless.

On Friday, June 25, I dined with him at General Paoli's, where he says, in one of his letters to Mrs. Thrale, "I love to dine." There was a variety of dishes much to his taste, of all which he seemed to me to eat so much, that I was afraid he might be hurt by it, and I whispered to the General my fear, and begged he might not press him. "Alas! (said the General) see how very ill he looks; he can live but a very short time. Would you refuse any slight gratifications to a man under sentence of death? There is a humane custom in Italy, by which persons in that melancholy situation are indulged with having whatever they like best to eat and drink, even with expensive delicacies."

On Sunday, June 27, I found him rather better: I mentioned to him a young man who was going to Jamaica with his wife and children, in expectation of being provided for by two of her brothers settled in that island, one a clergyman, and the other a physician.

JOHNSON: "It is a wild scheme, Sir, unless he has a positive and deliberate invitation. There was a poor girl, who used to come about me, who had a cousin in Barbadoes, that, in a letter to her, expressed a wish she should come out to that island, and expatiated on the comforts and happiness of her situation. The poor girl went out: her cousin was much surprised, and asked her how she could think of coming. 'Because (said she), you invited me.'—'Not I,' answered the cousin. The letter was then produced. 'I see it is true (said he) that I did invite you: but I did not think you would come.' They lodged her in an out-house, where she passed her time miserably; and as soon as she had an opportunity she returned to England. Always tell this, when you hear of people going abroad to relations, upon a notion of being well received. In the case which you mention, it is probable the clergyman spends all he gets, and the physician does not know how much he is to get."

We this day dined at Sir Joshua Reynolds's, with General Paoli, Lord Eliot (formerly Mr. Eliot, of Port Eliot), Dr. Beattie, and some other company. He put Lord Eliot in mind of Dr. Walter Harte. "I know (said he) Harte was your Lordship's tutor, and he was also tutor to the Peterborough family. Pray, my Lord, do you recollect any particulars that he told you of Lord Peterborough? He is a favourite of mine, and is not enough known; his character has been only ventilated in party pamphlets." Lord Eliot said, if Dr. Johnson would be so good as to ask him any questions, he would tell what he could recollect. Accordingly some things were mentioned. "But (said his Lordship) the best account of Lord Peterborough that I have happended to meet with is in 'Captain Carleton's Memoirs.' Carleton was descended of an ancestor who had distinguished himself at the siege of Derry. He was an officer; and, what was rare at that time, had some knowledge of engineering." Johnson said he had never heard of the book. Lord Eliot had it at Port Eliot; but, after a good deal of inquiry, procured a copy in London, and sent it to Johnson, who told Sir Joshua Reynolds that he was going to bed when it came, but was so much pleased with it, that he sat up till he had read it through, and found in it such an air of truth, that he could not doubt of its authenticity; adding with a smile (in allusion to Lord Eliot's having recently been raised to the peerage), "I did not think a *young Lord* could have mentioned to me a book in the English history that was not known to me."

He now said, "He wished much to go to Italy, and that he dreaded passing the winter in England." I said nothing; but enjoyed a secret satisfaction in thinking that I had taken the most effectual measures to make such a scheme practicable.

On Monday, June 28, I had the honour to receive from the Lord Chancellor the following letter:

"TO JAMES BOSWELL, ESQ.

"SIR,—

"I should have answered your letter immediately; if (being much engaged when I received it) I had not put it in my pocket, and forgot to open it till this morning.

"I am much obliged to you for the suggestion, and I will adopt and press it as far as I can. The best argument, I am sure, and I hope it is not likely to fail, is Dr. Johnson's merit.—But it will be necessary, if I should be so unfortunate as to miss seeing you, to converse with Sir Joshua on the sum it will be proper to ask,—in short, upon the means of setting him out. It would be a reflection on us all, if such a man should perish for want of the means to take care of his health.

"Yours, etc.,
"THURLOW."

This letter gave me a very high satisfaction; I next day went and showed it to Sir Joshua Reynolds, who was exceedingly pleased with it. He thought that I should now communicate the negotiation to Dr. Johnson, who might afterwards complain if the attention with which he had been honoured should be too long concealed from him. I intended to set out for Scotland next morning; but Sir Joshua cordially insisted that I should stay another day, that Johnson and I might dine with him, that we three might talk of his Italian tour, and, as Sir Joshua expressed himself, "have it all out." I hastened to Johnson, and was told by him that he was rather better to-day. BOSWELL: "I am very anxious about you, Sir, and particularly that you should go to Italy for the winter, which I believe is your own wish." JOHNSON: "It is, Sir." BOSWELL: "You have no objection, I presume, but the money it would require." JOHNSON: "Why no, Sir."—Upon which I gave him a particular account of what had been done, and read to him the Lord Chancellor's letter. He listened with much attention; then warmly said, "This is taking prodigious pains about a man."—"O, Sir (said I with most sincere affection), your friends would do everything for you." He paused,—grew more and more agitated,—till tears started into his eyes, and he exclaimed with fervent emotion, "God bless you all." I was so affected that I also shed tears.—After a short silence, he renewed and extended his grateful benediction, "God bless you all, for Jesus Christ's sake." We both remained for some time unable to speak.—He rose suddenly and quitted the room, quite melted in tenderness. He stayed but a short time, till he had recovered his firmness; soon after he returned I left him, having first engaged him to dine at Sir Joshua Reynolds's next day.—I never was again under that roof, which I had so long reverenced.

On Wednesday, June 30, the friendly confidential dinner with Sir Joshua Reynolds took place, no other company being present. Had I known that this was the last time that I should enjoy in this world, the conversation of a friend whom I so much respected, and from whom I derived so much instruction and entertainment, I should have been deeply affected. When I now look back to it, I am vexed that a single word should have been forgotten.

Both Sir Joshua and I were so sanguine in our expectations, that we expatiated with confidence on the liberal provision which we were sure would be made for him, conjecturing whether munificence would be displayed in one large donation, or in an ample increase of his pension. He himself catched so much of our enthusiasm, as to allow himself to suppose it not impossible that our hopes might in one way or other be realised. He said that he would rather have his pension doubled than a grant of a thousand pounds; "For (said he), though probably I may not live to receive as much as a thousand pounds, a man would have the consciousness that he should pass the remainder of his life in splendour, how long soever it might be." Considering what a moderate proportion an income of six hundred pounds a year bears to innumerable fortunes in this country, it is worthy of remark that a man so truly great should think it splendour.

As an instance of extraordinary liberality of friendship, he told us that Dr. Brocklesby had upon this occasion offered him a hundred a year for his life. A grateful tear started into his eye, as he spoke this in a faltering tone.

Sir Joshua and I endeavoured to flatter his imagination with agreeable prospects of happiness in Italy. "Nay (said he), I must not expect much of that; when a man goes to Italy merely to feel how he breathes the air, he can enjoy very little."

I accompanied him in Sir Joshua Reynolds's coach to the entry of Bolt-court. He asked me whether I would not go with him to his house; I declined it, from an apprehension that my spirits would sink. We bade adieu to each other affectionately in the carriage. When he had got down upon the foot-pavement, he called out, "Fare you well"; and without looking back, sprung away with a kind of pathetic briskness, if I may use that expression, which seemed to indicate a struggle to conceal uneasiness, and impressed me with a foreboding of our long, long separation.

I remained one day more in town, to have the chance of talking over my negotiations with the Lord Chancellor; but the multiplicity of his Lordship's important engagements did not allow of it; so I left the management of the business in the hands of Sir Joshua Reynolds.

Soon after this time, Dr. Johnson had the mortification of being informed by Mrs. Thrale, that "what she supposed he never believed," was true; namely, that she was actually going to marry Signor Piozzi, an Italian music-master. He endeavoured to prevent it; but in vain. If she would publish the whole of the correspondence that passed between Dr. Johnson and her on the subject, we should have a full view of his real sentiments. As it is, our judgment must be biassed by that characteristic specimen which Sir John Hawkins has given us: "Poor Thrale, I thought that either her virtue or her vice would have restrained her from such a marriage. She is now become a subject for her enemies to exult over; and for her friends, if she has any left, to forget, or pity."

It must be admitted that Johnson derived a considerable portion of happiness from the comforts and elegances which he enjoyed in Mr. Thrale's family; but Mrs. Thrale assures us he was indebted for these to her husband alone, who certainly respected him sincerely. Her words are, *"Veneration for his virtue, reverence for his talents,* delight *in his conversation, and* habitual endurance of a yoke my husband first put upon me, *and of which he contentedly bore his share for sixteen or seventeen years, made me go on so long with* Mr. Johnson; *but the perpetual confinement I will own to have been* terrifying *in the first years of our friendship, and* irksome *in the last; nor could I pretend to support it without help, when my coadjutor was no more."* Alas! how different is this from the declarations which I have heard Mrs. Thrale make in his lifetime, without a single murmur against any peculiarities, or against any one circumstance which attended their intimacy.

As a sincere friend of the great man whose Life I am writing, I think it necessary to guard my readers against the mistaken notion of Dr. Johnson's character which this lady's "Anecdotes" of him suggest; for from the very nature and form of her book, "it lends deception lighter wings to fly."

I have had occasion several times, in the course of this work, to point out the incorrectness of Mrs. Thrale, as to particulars which consisted with my own knowledge. But indeed she has, in flippant terms enough, expressed her disapprobation of that anxious desire of authenticity which prompts a person who is to record conversations, to write them down *at the moment*. Unquestionably, if they are to be recorded at all, the sooner it is done the better. This lady herself says, *"To recollect, however, and to repeat the sayings of* Dr. Johnson, *is almost all that can be done by the writers of his Life; as his life, at least since my acquaintance with him, consisted in little else than talking, when he was not employed in some serious piece of work."* She boasts of her having kept a commonplace book; and we find she noted, at one time or other, in a very lively manner, specimens of the conversation of Dr. Johnson, and of those who talked with him; but had she done it recently, they probably would have been less erroneous; and we should have been relieved from those disagreeable doubts of their authenticity, with which we must now peruse them.

She says of him, *"He was the most charitable of mortals, without being what we call an* active *friend. Admirable at giving counsel; no man saw his way so clearly: but he would not stir a finger for the assistance of those to whom he was willing enough to give advice."* And again on the same page, *"If you wanted a* slight *favour, you must apply to people of other dispositions; for* not a step would Johnson move *to obtain a man a vote in a society, to repay a compliment which might be useful or pleasing, to write a letter of request, etc., or to obtain a hundred pounds a year more for a friend who perhaps had already two or three. No force could urge him to diligence, no importunity could conquer his resolution to stand still."*

It is amazing that one who had such opportunities of knowing Dr. Johnson should appear so little acquainted with his real character. I am sorry this lady does not advert that she herself contradicts the assertion of his being obstinately defective in the *petites morales*, in the little endearing charities of social life, in conferring smaller favours; for she says, "Dr. Johnson *was liberal enough in granting literary assistance to others, I think; and innumerable are the prefaces, sermons, lectures, and dedications which he used to make for people who begged of him."* I am certain that *a more active friend* has rarely been found in any age. This work, which I fondly hope will rescue his memory from obloquy, contains a thousand instances of his benevolent exertions in almost every way that can be conceived; and particularly in employing his pen with a generous readiness for those to whom its aid could be useful.

I certainly, then, do not claim too much in behalf of my illustrious friend in saying, that however smart and entertaining Mrs. Thrale's "Anecdotes" are, they must not be held as good evidence against him; for, wherever an instance of harshness and severity is told, I beg leave to doubt its perfect authenticity; for though there may have been *some* foundation for it, yet, like that of his reproof to the "very celebrated lady," it may be so exhibited in the narration as to be very unlike the real fact.

It is with concern that I find myself obliged to animadvert on the inaccuracies of Mrs. Piozzi's "Anecdotes," and perhaps I may be thought to have dwelt too long upon her little collection. But as from Johnson's long residence under Mr. Thrale's roof, and his intimacy with her, the account which she has given of him may have made an unfavourable and unjust impression, my duty, as a faithful biographer, has obliged me reluctantly to perform this unpleasing task.

Having left the *pious negotiation,* as I called it, in the best hands, I shall here insert what relates to it. Johnson wrote to Sir Joshua Reynolds on July 6, as follows: "I am going, I hope, in a few days, to try the air of Derbyshire, but hope to see you before I go. Let me, however, mention to you what I have much at heart.—If the Chancellor should continue his attention to Mr. Boswell's request, and confer with you on the means of relieving my languid state, I am very desirous to avoid the appearance of asking money upon false pretences. I desire you to represent to his Lordship what, as soon as it is suggested, he will perceive to be reasonable,—That, if I grow much worse, I shall be afraid to leave my physicians, to suffer the inconveniences of travel, and pine in the solitude of a foreign country; —That, if I grow much better, of which indeed there is now little appearance, I shall not wish to leave my friends and my domestic comforts; for I do not travel for pleasure or curiosity; yet if I should recover, curiosity would revive.—In my present state, I am desirous to make a struggle for a little longer life, and hope to obtain some help from a softer climate. Do for me what you can." He wrote to me July 26: "I wish your affairs could have permitted a longer and continued exertion of your zeal and kindness. They that have your kindness may want your ardour. In the meantime I am very feeble, and very dejected."

By a letter from Sir Joshua Reynolds, I was informed that the Lord Chancellor had called on him, and had acquainted him that the application had not been successful; but that his Lordship, after speaking highly in praise of Johnson, as a man who was an honour to his country, desired Sir Joshua to let him know that on granting a mortgage of his pension, he should draw on his Lordship to the amount of five or six hundred pounds; and that his Lordship explained the meaning of the mortgage to be, that he wished the business to be conducted in such a manner that Dr. Johnson should appear to be under the least possible obligation. Sir Joshua mentioned that he had by the same post communicated all this to Dr. Johnson.

How Johnson was affected upon the occasion will appear from what he wrote to Sir Joshua Reynolds:

Ashbourne, Sept. 9. "Many words I hope are not necessary between you and me, to convince you what gratitude is excited in my heart by the Chancellor's liberality, and your kind offices. * * * * * *

"I have enclosed a letter to the Chancellor, which, when you have read it, you will be pleased to seal with a head, or any other general seal, and convey it to him: had I sent it directly to him, I should have seemed to overlook the favour of your intervention."

"TO THE LORD HIGH CHANCELLOR.

"MY LORD,—

"After a long and not inattentive observation of mankind, the generosity of your Lordship's offer raises in me not less wonder than gratitude. Bounty, so liberally bestowed, I should gladly receive, if my condition made it necessary; for to such a mind, who would not be proud to own his obligations? But it has pleased God to restore me to so great a measure of health, that if I should now appropriate so much of a fortune destined to do good, I could not escape from myself the charge of advancing a false claim. My journey to the continent, though I once thought it necessary, was never much encouraged by my physicians; and I was very desirous that your Lordship should be told of it by Sir Joshua Reynolds, as an event very uncertain; for if I grew much better, I should not be willing, if much worse, not able, to migrate. Your Lordship was first solicited without my knowledge; but, when I was told that you were pleased to honour me with your patronage, I did not expect to hear of a refusal; yet, as I have had no long time to brood hope, and have not rioted in imaginary opulence, this cold reception has been scarce a disappointment; and, from your Lordship's kindness, I have received a benefit, which only men like you are able to bestow. I shall now live *mihi carior,* with a higher opinion of my own merit. I am, my Lord,

"Your Lordship's most obliged,

"Most grateful, and

"Most humble servant,

"SAM. JOHNSON.

"September, 1784."

Upon this unexpected failure I abstain from presuming to make any remarks, or to offer any conjectures.

CHAPTER LVII—1784

Johnson's Last Visit to Lichfield

HAVING, after repeated reasonings, brought Dr. Johnson to agree to my removing to London, and even to furnish me with arguments in favour of what he had opposed; I wrote to him requesting he would write them for me; he was so good as to comply, and I shall extract that part of his letter to me of June 11, as a proof how well he could exhibit a cautious yet encouraging view of it:

"I remember, and entreat you to remember, that *virtus est vitium fugere;* the first approach to riches is security from poverty. The condition upon which you have my consent to settle in London is, that your expense never exceeds your annual income. Fixing this basis of security, you cannot be hurt, and you may be very much advanced. The loss of your Scottish business, which is all that you can lose, is not to be reckoned as any equivalent to the hopes and possibilities that open here upon you. If you succeed, the question of prudence is at an end; everybody will think that done right which ends happily; and though your expectations, of which I would not advise you to talk too much, should not be totally answered, you can hardly fail to get friends who will do for you all that your present situation allows you to hope; and if, after a few years, you should return to Scotland, you will return with a mind supplied by various conversation, and many opportunities of inquiry, with much knowledge, and materials for reflection and instruction."

Next day he set out on a jaunt to Staffordshire and Derbyshire, flattering himself that he might be in some degree relieved.

During his absence from London he kept up a correspondence with several of his friends, from which I shall select what appears to me proper for publication, without attending nicely to chronological order.

To Dr. Brocklesby, he writes, Ashbourne, July 20. "The kind attention which you have so long shown to my health and happiness makes it as much a debt of gratitude as a call of interest to give you an account of what befalls me, when accident recovers me from your immediate care. The journey of the first day was performed with very little sense of fatigue; the second day brought me to Lichfield, without much lassitude; but I am afraid that I could not have borne such violent agitation for many days together. * * * "

August 12. "Pray be so kind as to have me in your thoughts, and mention my case to others as you have opportunity. I seem to myself neither to gain nor lose strength. I have lately tried milk, but have yet found no advantage, and I am afraid of it merely as a liquid. My appetite is still good, which I know is dear Dr. Heberden's criterion of the *vis vitæ.*—As we cannot now see each other, do not omit to write, for you cannot think with what warmth of expectation I reckon the hours of a post-day."

August 14. "I have hitherto sent you only melancholy letters; you will be glad to hear some better account. Yesterday the asthma remitted, perceptibly remitted, and I moved with more ease than I have enjoyed for many weeks. May God continue his mercy. This account I would not delay, because I am not a lover of complaints, or complainers, and yet I have, since we parted, uttered nothing till now but terror and sorrow. Write to me, dear Sir."

August 19. "The relaxation of the asthma still continues, yet I do not trust it wholly to itself, but soothe it now and then with an opiate. I not only perform the perpetual act of respiration with less labour, but I can walk with fewer intervals of rest, and with greater freedom of motion. I never thought well of Dr. James's compounded medicines; his ingredients appear to me sometimes inefficacious and trifling, and sometimes heterogeneous and destructive of each other. This prescription exhibits a composition of about three hundred and thirty grains, in which there are four grains of emetic tartar, and six drops [of] thebaic tincture. He that writes thus surely writes for show. The basis of his medicine is the gum ammoniacum, which dear Dr. Lawrence used to give, but of which I never saw any effect. We will, if you please, let this medicine alone. The squills have every suffrage, and in the squills we will rest for the present."

August 21. "The kindness which you show by having me in your thoughts upon all occasions, will, I hope, always fill my heart with gratitude. Be pleased to return my thanks to Sir George Baker for the consideration which he has bestowed upon me. Is this the balloon that has been so long expected, this balloon to which I subscribed, but without payment? It is pity that philosophers have been disappointed, and shame that they have been cheated; but I know not well how to prevent either. Of this experiment I have read nothing; where was it exhibited? and who was the man that ran away with so much money?—Continue, dear Sir, to write often and more at a time, for none of your prescriptions operate to their proper uses more certainly than your letters operate as cordials."

Sept. 9. "Do you know the Duke and Duchess of Devonshire? And have you ever seen Chatsworth? I was at Chatsworth on Monday: I had seen it before, but never when its owners were at home: I was very kindly received, and honestly pressed to stay; but I told them that a sick man is not a fit inmate of a great house. But I hope to go again some time."

Lichfield, Sept. 29. "On one day I had three letters about the air balloon: yours was far the best, and has enabled me to impart to my friends in the country an idea of this species of amusement. In amusement, mere amusement, I am afraid it must end, for I do not find that its course can be directed so as that it should serve any purposes of communication; and it can give no new intelligence of the state of the air at different heights, till they have ascended above the height of mountains, which they seem never likely to do.—I came hither on the 27th. How long I shall stay, I have not determined. My dropsy is gone, and my asthma much remitted, but I have felt myself a little declining these two days, or at least to-day; but such vicissitudes must be expected. One day may be worse than another; but this last month is far better than the former: if the next should be as much better than this, I shall run about the town on my own legs."

October 6. "The fate of the balloon I do not much lament: to make new balloons, is to repeat the jest again. We now know a method of mounting into the air, and, I think, are not likely to know more. The vehicles can serve no use till we can guide them; and they can gratify no curiosity till we mount with them to greater heights than we can reach without; till we rise above the tops of the highest mountains, which we have not yet done. We know the state of the air in all its regions, to the top of Teneriffe, and therefore learn nothing from those who navigate a balloon below the clouds. The first experiment, however, was bold, and deserved applause and reward. But since it has been performed, and its event is known, I had rather now find a medicine that can ease an asthma."

October 25. "You write to me with a zeal that animates, and a tenderness that melts me. I am not afraid either of a journey to London, or a residence in it. I came down with little fatigue, and am now not weaker. In the smoky atmosphere I was delivered from the dropsy, which I considered as the original and radical disease. The town is my element; there are my friends, there are my books, to which I have not yet bid farewell, and there are my amusements. Sir Joshua told me long ago, that my vocation was to public life, and I hope still to keep my station, till God shall bid me *Go in peace.*"

To Dr. Burney, August 2. "The weather, you know, has not been balmy; I am now reduced to think, and am at last content to talk of the weather. Pride must have a fall.—I have lost dear Mr. Allen; and wherever I turn, the dead or the dying meet my notice, and force my attention upon misery and mortality. Mrs. Burney's escape from so much danger, and her ease after so much pain, throws, however, some radiance of hope upon the gloomy prospect. May her recovery be perfect, and her continuance long. I struggle hard for life. I take physic, and take air; my friend's chariot is always ready. We have run this morning twenty-four miles, and could run forty-eight more. *But who can run the race with death?*"

Nov. 1. "Our correspondence paused for want of topics. I had said what I had to say on the matter proposed to my consideration; and nothing remained but to tell you that I waked or slept; that I was more or less sick. I drew my thoughts in upon myself, and supposed yours employed upon your book.—That your book has been delayed I am glad, since you have gained an opportunity of being more exact.— Of the caution necessary in adjusting narratives there is no end. Some tell what they do not know that they may not seem ignorant, and others from mere indifference about truth. All truth is not, indeed, of equal importance; but if little violations are allowed, every violation will in time be thought little: and a writer should keep himself vigilantly on his guard against the first temptations to negligence or supineness.—I had ceased to write, because respecting you I had no more to say, and respecting myself could say little good. I cannot boast of advancement, and in case of convalescence it may be said, with few exceptions, *non progredi, est regredi*. I hope I may be excepted.—My great difficulty was with my sweet Fanny, who, by her artifice of inserting her letter in yours, had given me a precept of frugality which I was not at liberty to neglect; and I know not who were in town under whose cover I could send my letter. I rejoice to hear that you are so well, and have a delight particularly sympathetic in the recovery of Mrs. Burney."

"TO THE RIGHT HON. WILLIAM GERARD HAMILTON.

"DEAR SIR,—

"Considering what reason you gave me in the spring to conclude that you took part in whatever good or evil might befall me, I ought not to have omitted so long the account which I am now about to give you.

"My diseases are an asthma and a dropsy, and, what is less curable, seventy-five. Of the dropsy, in the beginning of the summer, or in the spring, I recovered to a degree which struck with wonder both me and my physicians; the asthma now is likewise, for a time, very much relieved. I went to Oxford, where the asthma was very tyrannical, and the dropsy began again to threaten me; but seasonable physic stopped the inundation: I then returned to London, and in July took a resolution to visit Staffordshire and Derbyshire, where I am yet struggling with my disease. The dropsy made another attack, and was not easily ejected, but at last gave way. The asthma suddenly remitted in bed, on the 13th of August, and, though now very oppressive, is, I think, still something gentler than it was before the remission. My limbs are miserably debilitated, and my nights are sleepless and tedious.—When you read this, dear Sir, you are not sorry that I wrote no sooner. I will not prolong my complaints. I hope still to see you *in a happier hour,* to talk over what we have often talked, and perhaps to find new topics of merriment, or new incitements to curiosity.

"I am, dear Sir, etc.,

"SAM. JOHNSON.

"*Lichfield, Oct. 20, 1784.*"

Johnson's Last Visit to Lichfield

"TO JOHN PARADISE, ESQ.

"DEAR SIR,—

"Though in all my summer's excursions I have given you no account of myself, I hope you think better of me than to imagine it possible for me to forget you, whose kindness to me has been too great and too constant not to have made its impression on a harder breast than mine. —Silence is not very culpable, when nothing pleasing is suppressed. It would have alleviated none of your complaints to have read my vicissitudes of evil. I have struggled hard with very formidable and obstinate maladies; and though I cannot talk of health, think all praise due to my Creator and Preserver for the continuance of my life. The dropsy has made two attacks, and has given way to medicine; the asthma is very oppressive; but that has likewise once remitted. I am very weak, and very sleepless; but it is time to conclude the tale of misery.—I hope, dear Sir, that you grow better, for you have likewise your share of human evil, and that your lady and the young charmers are well.

"I am, dear Sir, etc.,

"SAM. JOHNSON.

"*Lichfield, Oct. 27, 1784.*"

To Sir Joshua Reynolds. Ashbourne, July 21. "The tenderness with which I am treated by my friends makes it reasonable to suppose that they are desirous to know the state of my health, and a desire so benevolent ought to be gratified.—I came to Lichfield in two days without any painful fatigue, and on Monday came hither, where I purpose to stay and try what air and regularity will effect. I cannot yet persuade myself that I have made much progress in recovery. My sleep is little, my breath is very much encumbered, and my legs are very weak. The water has increased a little, but has again run off. The most distressing symptom is want of sleep."

Sept. 2. "I am glad that a little favour from the Court has intercepted your furious purposes. I could not in any case have approved such public violence of resentment, and should have considered any who encouraged it as rather seeking sport for themselves, than honour for you. Resentment gratifies him who intended an injury, and pains him unjustly who did not intend it. But all this is now superfluous.—I still continue by God's mercy to mend. My breath is easier, my nights are quieter, and my legs are less in bulk, and stronger in use. I have, however, yet a great deal to overcome, before I can yet attain even an old man's health.—Write, do write to me now and then; we are now old acquaintances, and perhaps few people have lived so much and so long together, with less cause of complaint on either side. The retrospection of this is very pleasant, and I hope we shall never think on each other with less kindness."

Sept. 9. "I could not answer your letter before this day, because I went on the sixth to Chatsworth, and did not come back till the post was gone.—Many words, I hope, are not necessary between you and me, to convince you what gratitude is excited in my heart by the Chancellor's liberality and your kind offices. I did not indeed expect that what was asked by the Chancellor would have been refused, but since it has, we will not tell that anything has been asked.—I have enclosed a letter to the Chancellor, which, when you have read it, you will be pleased to seal with a head, or other general seal, and convey it to him; had I sent it directly to him, I should have seemed to overlook the favour of your intervention. My last letter told you of my advance in health, which, I think, in the whole still continues. Of the hydropic tumour, there is now very little appearance; the asthma is much less troublesome, and seems to remit something day after day. I do not despair of supporting an English winter.—At Chatsworth, I met young Mr. Burke, who led me very commodiously into conversation with the Duke and Duchess. We had a very good morning. The dinner was public."

October 2. "I am always proud of your approbation, and therefore was much pleased that you liked my letter. When you copied it, you invaded the Chancellor's right rather than mine. The refusal I did not expect, but I had never thought much about it, for I doubted whether the Chancellor had so much tenderness for me as to ask. He, being keeper of the King's conscience, ought not to be supposed capable of an improper petition.—All is not gold that glitters, as we have often been told; and the adage is verified in your place and my favour; but if what happens does not make us richer, we must bid it welcome, if it makes us wiser.—I do not at present grow better, nor much worse; my hopes, however, are somewhat abated, and a very great loss is the loss of hope, but I struggle on as I can."

This various mass of correspondence, which I have thus brought together, is valuable, both as an addition to the store which the public already has of Johnson's writings, and as exhibiting a genuine and noble specimen of vigour and vivacity of mind, which neither age nor sickness could impair or diminish.

It may be observed that his writings in every way, whether for the public, or privately to his friends, was by fits and starts; for we see frequently that many letters are written on the same day. When he had once overcome his aversion to begin, he was, I suppose, desirous to go on, in order to relieve his mind from the uneasy reflection of delaying what he ought to do.

While in the country, notwithstanding the accumulation of illness which he endured, his mind did not lose its powers. He translated an ode of Horace, which is printed in his works, and composed several prayers.

And here I am enabled fully to refute a very unjust reflection, by Sir John Hawkins, both against Dr. Johnson, and his faithful servant, Mr. Francis Barber; as if both of them had been guilty of culpable neglect towards a person of the name of Heely, whom Sir John chooses to call a *relation* of Dr. Johnson's. The fact is, that Mr. Heely was not his relation; he had indeed been married to one of his cousins, but she had died without having children, and he had married another woman; so that even the slight connexion which there once had been by *alliance* was dissolved. Dr. Johnson, who had shown very great liberality to this man, while his first wife was alive, as has appeared in a former part of this work, was humane and charitable enough to continue his bounty to him occasionally; but surely there was no strong call of duty upon him or upon his legatee to do more. The following letter, obligingly communicated to me by Mr. Andrew Strahan, will confirm what I have stated:

"TO MR. HEELY, NO. 5, IN PYE STREET, WESTMINSTER.

"SIR,—

"As necessity obliges you to call so soon again upon me, you should at least have told the smallest sum that will supply your present want; you cannot suppose that I have much to spare. Two guineas is as much as you ought to be behind with your creditor.—If you wait on Mr. Strahan, in New Street, Fetter Lane, or in his absence, on Mr. Andrew Strahan, show this, by which they are entreated to advance you two guineas, and to keep this as a voucher. I am, Sir,

"Your humble servant,
"SAM. JOHNSON.

"*Ashbourne, Aug. 12, 1784.*"

Indeed it is very necessary to keep in mind that Sir John Hawkins has unaccountably viewed Johnson's character and conduct in almost every particular, with an unhappy prejudice.

We now behold Johnson for the last time in his native city, for which he ever retained a warm affection, and which, by a sudden apostrophe, under the word *Lich,* he introduces with reverence, into his immortal Work, The English Dictionary:—*"Salve, magna parens!"*

To Mr. Henry White, a young clergyman, with whom he now formed an intimacy so as to talk to him with great freedom, he mentioned that he could not in general accuse himself of having been an undutiful son. "Once, indeed (said he), I was disobedient; I refused to attend my father to Uttoxeter-market. Pride was the source of the refusal, and that remembrance of it was painful. A few years ago I desired to atone for this fault; I went to Uttoxeter in very bad weather, and stood for a considerable time bareheaded in the rain, on the spot where my father's stall used to stand. In contrition I stood, and I hope the penance was expiatory."

"I told him (says Miss Seward) in one of my latest visits to him of a wonderful learned pig, which I had seen at Nottingham; and which did all that we have observed exhibited by dogs and horses. The subject amused him. 'Then (said he) the pigs are a race unjustly calumniated. *Pig* has, it seems, not been wanting to *man,* but *man* to *pig.* We do not allow *time* for his education; we kill him at a year old.' Mr. Henry White, who was present, observed that if this instance had happened in or before Pope's time, he would not have been justified in instancing the swine as the lowest degree of grovelling instinct. Dr. Johnson seemed pleased with the observation, while the person who made it proceeded to remark that great torture must have been employed ere the indocility of the animal could have been subdued.—'Certainly (said the Doctor), but (turning to me) how old is your pig?' I told him, three years old. 'Then (said he) the pig has no cause to complain; he would have been killed the first year if he had not been *educated,* and protracted existence is a good recompense for very considerable degrees of torture.' "

As Johnson had now very faint hopes of recovery, and as Mrs. Thrale was no longer devoted to him, it might have been supposed that he would naturally have chosen to remain in the comfortable house of his beloved wife's daughter, and end his life where he began it. But there was in him an animated and lofty spirit, and however complicated diseases might depress ordinary mortals, all who saw him beheld and acknowledged the *invictum animum Catonis*. Such was his intellectual ardour even at this time, that he said to one friend, "Sir, I look upon every day to be lost, in which I do not make a new acquaintance"; and to another, when talking of his illness, "I will be conquered; I will not capitulate." And such was his love of London, so high a relish had he of its magnificent extent, and variety of intellectual entertainment, that he languished when absent from it, his mind having become quite luxurious from the long habit of enjoying the metropolis; and, therefore, although at Lichfield, surrounded with friends who loved and revered him, and for whom he had a very sincere affection, he still found that such conversation as London affords could be found nowhere else. These feelings, joined, probably, to some flattering hopes of aid from the eminent physicians and surgeons in London, who kindly and generously attended him without accepting fees, made him resolve to return to the capital.

Johnson then proceeded to Oxford, where he was again kindly received by Dr. Adams, who was pleased to give me the following account in one of his letters (Feb. 17th, 1785): "His last visit was, I believe, to my house, which he left, after a stay of four or five days. We had much serious talk together, for which I ought to be the better as long as I live. You will remember some discourse which we had in the summer upon the subject of prayer, and the difficulty of this sort of composition. He reminded me of this, and of my having wished him to try his hand, and to give us a specimen of the style and manner that he approved. He added that he was now in a right frame of mind, and as he could not possibly employ his time better, he would in earnest set about it. But I find upon inquiry that no papers of this sort were left behind him, except a few short ejaculatory forms suitable to his present situation."

CHAPTER LVIII—1784

Last Days

HE ARRIVED IN LONDON on the 16th of November, and next day sent to Dr. Burney the following note, which I insert as the last token of his remembrance of that ingenious and amiable man, and as another of the many proofs of the tenderness and benignity of his heart:

"Mr. Johnson, who came home last night, sends his respects to dear Dr. Burney, and all the dear Burneys, little and great."

"TO MR. HECTOR, IN BIRMINGHAM.

"DEAR SIR,—

"I did not reach Oxford until Friday morning, and then I sent Francis to see the balloon fly, but could not go myself. I stayed at Oxford till Tuesday, and then came in the common vehicle easily to London. I am as I was, and having seen Dr. Brocklesby, am to ply the squills; but whatever be their efficacy, this world must soon pass away. Let us think seriously on our duty.—I send my kindest respects to dear Mrs. Careless: let me have the prayers of both. We have all lived long, and must soon part. God have mercy on us, for the sake of our Lord Jesus Christ. Amen.

"I am, etc.,

"SAM. JOHNSON.

"*London, Nov. 17, 1784.*"

His correspondence with me, after his letter on the subject of my settling in London, shall now, as far as is proper, be produced in one series.

July 26, he wrote to me from Ashbourne: "On the 14th I came to Lichfield, and found everybody glad enough to see me. On the 20th I came hither, and found a house half-built, of very uncomfortable appearance; but my own room has not been altered. That a man worn with diseases, in his seventy-second or -third year, should condemn part of his remaining life to pass among ruins and rubbish, and that no inconsiderable part, appears to me very strange.—I know that your kindness makes you impatient to know the state of my health, in which I cannot boast of much improvement. I came through the journey without much inconvenience, but when I attempt self-motion I find my legs weak, and my breath very short; this day I have been much disordered. I have no company; the Doctor is busy in his fields, and goes to bed at nine, and his whole system is so different from mine, that we seem formed for different elements; I have, therefore, all my amusement to seek within myself."

I unfortunately was so much indisposed during a considerable part of the year, that it was not, or at least I thought it was not, in my power to write to my illustrious friend as formerly, or without expressing such complaints as offended him. Having conjured him not to do me the injustice of charging me with affectation, I was with much regret long silent. His last letter to me then came, and affected me very tenderly.

"TO JAMES BOSWELL, ESQ.

"DEAR SIR,—

"I have this summer sometimes amended, and sometimes relapsed, but, upon the whole, have lost ground very much. My legs are extremely weak, and my breath very short, and the water is now increasing upon me. In this uncomfortable state your letters used to relieve; what is the reason that I have them no longer? Are you sick, or are you sullen? Whatever be the reason, if it be less than necessity, drive it away; and of the short life that we have, make the best use for yourself and for your friends. . . . I am sometimes afraid that your omission to write has some real cause, and shall be glad to know that you are not sick, and that nothing ill has befallen dear Mrs. Boswell, or any of your family.

"I am, Sir, yours, etc.,

"SAM. JOHNSON.

"*Lichfield, Nov. 5, 1784.*"

Yet it was not a little painful to me to find that in a paragraph of this letter, which I have omitted, he still persevered in arraigning me as before, which was strange in him who had so much experience of what I suffered. I, however, wrote to him two as kind letters as I could; the last of which came too late to be read by him, for his illness increased more rapidly upon him than I had apprehended; but I had the consolation of being informed that he spoke of me on his death-bed with affection, and I look forward with humble hope of renewing our friendship in a better world.

I now relieve the readers of this work from any farther personal notice of its author; who, if he should be thought to have obtruded himself too much upon their attention, requests them to consider the peculiar plan of his biographical undertaking.

Soon after Johnson's return to the metropolis, both the asthma and dropsy became more violent and distressful. He had for some time kept a journal in Latin of the state of his illness, and the remedies which he used, under the title of *Ægri Ephemeris,* which he began on the 6th of July, but continued it no longer than the 8th of November; finding, I suppose, that it was a mournful and unavailing register. It is in my possession, and is written with great care and accuracy.

During his sleepless nights he amused himself by translating into Latin verse, from the Greek, many of the epigrams in the *"Anthologia."* These translations, with some other poems by him in Latin, he gave to his friend Mr. Langton, who, having added a few notes, sold them to the booksellers for a small sum to be given to some of Johnson's relations, which was accordingly done; and they are printed in the collection of his works.

A very erroneous notion has circulated as to Johnson's deficiency in the knowledge of the Greek language, partly owing to the modesty with which, from knowing how much there was to be learnt, he used to mention his own comparative acquisitions. When Mr. Cumberland talked to him of the Greek fragments which are so well illustrated in the *Observer,* and of the Greek dramatists in general, he candidly acknowledged his insufficiency in that particular branch of Greek literature. Yet it may be said that, though not a great, he was a good Greek scholar. Dr. Charles Burney, the younger, who is universally acknowledged, by the best judges, to be one of the few men of this age who are very eminent for their skill in that noble language, has assured me that Johnson could give a Greek word for almost every English one; and that although not sufficiently conversant in the niceties of the language, he, upon some occasions discovered, even in these, a considerable degree of critical acumen. Mr. Dalzel, Professor of Greek at Edinburgh, whose skill in it is unquestionable, mentioned to me, in very liberal terms, the impression which was made upon him by Johnson, in a conversation which they had in London concerning that language. As Johnson, therefore, was undoubtedly one of the first Latin scholars in modern times, let us not deny to his fame some additional splendour from Greek.

The ludicrous imitators of Johnson's style are innumerable. Their general method is to accumulate hard words, without considering that although he was fond of introducing them occasionally, there is not a single sentence in all his writings where they are crowded together, as in the first verse of the following imaginary ode by him to Mrs. Thrale, which appeared in the newspapers:

> "*Cervisial coctor's viduate* dame,
> *Opins't* thou his gigantic fame,
>   *Procumbing* at that shrine;
> Shall, *catenated* by thy charms,
> A captive in thy *ambient* arms,
>   *Perennially* be thine?"

This, and a thousand other such attempts, are totally unlike the original, which the writers imagined they were turning into ridicule. There is not similarity enough for burlesque or even for caricature.

Mr. Colman, in his "Prose on several occasions," has "A Letter from Lexiphanes; containing proposals for a *Glossary* or *Vocabulary* of the *Vulgar Tongue:* intended as a supplement to a larger *Dictionary.*" It is evidently meant as a sportive sally of ridicule on Johnson, whose style is thus imitated, without being grossly overcharged. "It is easy to foresee that the idle and illiterate will complain that I have increased their labours by endeavouring to diminish them; and that I have explained what is more easy by what is more difficult—*ignotum per ignotius.* I expect, on the other hand, the liberal acknowledgments of the learned. He who is buried in scholastic retirement, secluded from the assemblies of the gay, and remote from the circles of the polite, will at once comprehend the definitions, and be grateful for such a seasonable and necessary elucidation of his mother-tongue." Annexed to this letter is a short specimen of the work, thrown together in a vague and desultory manner, not even adhering to alphabetical concatenation.[1]

The serious imitators of Johnson's style, whether intentionally, or by the imperceptible effect of its strength and animation, are, as I have had already occasion to observe, so many, that I might introduce quotations from a numerous body of writers in our language, since he appeared in the literary world.

---

[1] "*Higgledy-piggledy,*—Conglomeration and confusion.

"*Hodge-podge,*—A culinary mixture of heterogeneous ingredients: applied metaphorically to all discordant combinations.

"*Tit for Tat,*—Adequate retaliation.

"*Shilly Shally,*—Hesitation and irresolution.

"*Fee! Fa! Fum!*—Gigantic intonations.

"*Rigmarole,*—Discourse, incoherent and rhapsodical.

"*Crinkum-crancum,*—Lines of irregularity and involution.

"*Ding dong,*—Tintinnabulary chimes, used metaphorically to signify dispatch and vehemence."

A distinguished author in the *Mirror,* a periodical paper, published at Edinburgh, has imitated Johnson very closely. Thus, in No. 16: "The effects of the return of spring have been frequently remarked, as well in relation to the human mind as to the animal and vegetable world. The reviving power of this season has been traced from the fields to the herds that inhabit them, and from the lower classes of beings up to man. Gladness and joy are described as prevailing through universal Nature, animating the low of the cattle, the carol of the birds, and the pipe of the shepherd."

But I think the most perfect imitation of Johnson is a professed one, entitled "A Criticism on Gray's 'Elegy in a Country Churchyard,'" said to be written by Mr. Young, Professor of Greek, at Glasgow, and of which let him have the credit, unless a better title can be shown. It has not only the particularities of Johnson's style, but that very species of literary discussion and illustration for which he was eminent.— Having already quoted so much from others, I shall refer the curious to this performance, with an assurance of much entertainment.

Yet whatever merit there may be in any imitations of Johnson's style, every good judge must see that they are obviously different from the original; for all of them are either deficient in its force, or overloaded with its peculiarities; and the powerful sentiment to which it is suited is not to be found.

Johnson's affection for his departed relations seemed to grow warmer as he approached nearer to the time when he might hope to see them again. It probably appeared to him that he should upbraid himself with unkind inattention, were he to leave the world without having paid a tribute of respect to their memory.

"TO MR. GREEN, APOTHECARY, AT LICHFIELD.

"DEAR SIR,—

"I have enclosed the epitaph for my father, mother, and brother, to be all engraved on the large size, and laid in the middle aisle in St. Michael's church, which I request the clergyman and churchwardens to permit.

"The first care must be to find the exact place of interment, that the stone may protect the bodies. Then let the stone be deep, massy, and hard; and do not let the difference of ten pounds, or more, defeat our purpose.

"I have enclosed ten pounds, and Mrs. Porter will pay you ten more, which I gave her for the same purpose. What more is wanted shall be sent; and I beg that all possible haste may be made, for I wish to have it done while I am yet alive. Let me know, dear Sir, that you receive this.

"I am, Sir,
"Your most humble servant,
"Sam. Johnson.

"*Dec. 2, 1784.*"

My readers are now, at last, to behold Samuel Johnson preparing himself for that doom, from which the most exalted powers afford no exemption to man. Death had always been to him an object of terror; so that, though by no means happy, he still clung to life with an eagerness at which many have wondered. At any time when he was ill, he was very much pleased to be told that he looked better. An ingenious member of the *Eumelian Club* informs me that upon one occasion, when he said to him that he saw health returning to his cheek, Johnson seized him by the hand and exclaimed, "Sir, you are one of the kindest friends I ever had."

His own state of his views of futurity will appear truly rational; and may, perhaps, impress the unthinking with seriousness.

"You know (says he), I never thought confidence, with respect to futurity, any part of the character of a brave, a wise, or a good man. Bravery has no place where it can avail nothing; wisdom impresses strongly the consciousness of those faults, of which it is, perhaps, itself an aggravation; and goodness, always wishing to be better, and imputing every deficiency to criminal negligence, and every fault to voluntary corruption, never dares to suppose the condition of forgiveness fulfilled, nor what is wanting in the crime supplied by penitence.

"This is the state of the best; but what must be the condition of him whose heart will not suffer him to rank himself among the best, or among the good?—Such must be his dread of the approaching trial, as will leave him little attention to the opinion of those whom he is leaving for ever; and the serenity that is not felt, it can be no virtue to feign."

His great fear of death, and the strange dark manner in which Sir John Hawkins imparts the uneasiness which he expressed on account of offences with which he charged himself, may give occasion to injurious suspicions, as if there had been something of more than ordinary criminality weighing upon his conscience. On that account, therefore, as well as from the regard to truth which he inculcated, I am to mention (with all possible respect and delicacy, however) that his conduct, after he came to London, and had associated with Savage and others, was not so strictly virtuous, in one respect, as when he was a younger man. It was well known that his amorous inclinations were uncommonly strong and impetuous. He owned to many of his friends that he used to take women of the town to taverns, and hear them relate their history. In short, it must not be concealed that, like many other good and pious men, among whom we may place the apostle Paul upon his own authority, Johnson was not free from propensities which were ever "warring against the law of his mind,"—and that in his combats with them, he was sometimes overcome.

Here let the profane and licentious pause; let them not thoughtlessly say that Johnson was an *hypocrite,* or that his *principles* were not firm, because his *practice* was not uniformly conformable to what he professed.

Let the question be considered independent of moral and religious associations; and no man will deny that thousands, in many instances, act against conviction. Is a prodigal, for example, an *hypocrite,* when he owns he is satisfied that his extravagance will bring him to ruin and misery? We are *sure* he *believes* it; but immediate inclination, strengthened by indulgence, prevails over that belief in influencing his conduct. Why then shall credit be refused to the *sincerity* of those who acknowledge their persuasion of moral and religious duty, yet sometimes fail of living as it requires? I heard Dr. Johnson once observe, "There is something noble in publishing truth, though it condemns one's self." And one who said in his presence, "he had no notion of people being in earnest in their good professions, whose practice was not suitable to them," was thus reprimanded by him: "Sir, are you so grossly ignorant of human nature as not to know that a man may be very sincere in good principles, without having good practice?"

But let no man encourage or soothe himself in "presumptuous sin," from knowing that Johnson was sometimes hurried into indulgences which he thought criminal. I have exhibited this circumstance as a shade in so great a character, both from my sacred love of truth, and to show that he was not so weakly scrupulous as he had been represented by those who imagine that the sins, of which a deep sense was upon his mind, were merely such little venial trifles as pouring milk into his tea on Good Friday. His understanding will be defended by my statement, if his consistency of conduct be in some degree impaired.

But what wise man would, for momentary gratifications, deliberately subject himself to suffer such uneasiness as we find was experienced by Johnson in reviewing his conduct as compared with his notion of the ethics of the gospel?

I am conscious that this is the most difficult and dangerous part of my biographical work, and I cannot but be very anxious concerning it. I trust that I have got through it, preserving at once my regard to truth,—to my friend,—and to the interests of virtue and religion. Nor can I apprehend that more harm can ensue from the knowledge of the irregularities of Johnson, guarded as I have stated it, than from knowing that Addison and Parnell were intemperate in the use of wine; which he himself, in his Lives of those celebrated writers and pious men, has not forborne to record.

CHAPTER LIX—1784

Johnson's Last Illness and Death

IT IS NOT MY INTENTION to give a very minute detail of the particulars of Johnson's remaining days, of whom it was now evident that the crisis was fast approaching, when he must *"die like men, and fall like one of the princes."* Yet it will be instructive, as well as gratifying to the curiosity of my readers, to record a few circumstances, on the authenticity of which they may perfectly rely, as I have been at the utmost pains to obtain an accurate account of his last illness, from the best authority.

Dr. Heberden, Dr. Brocklesby, Dr. Warren, and Dr. Butter, physicians, generously attended him, without accepting any fees, as did Mr. Cruikshank, surgeon; and all that could be done from professional skill and ability was tried, to prolong a life so truly valuable. He himself, indeed, having, on account of his very bad constitution, been perpetually applying himself to medical inquiries, united his own efforts with those of the gentlemen who attended him; and imagining that the dropsical collection of water which oppressed him might be drawn off by making incisions in his body, he, with his usual resolute defiance of pain, cut deep, when he thought that his surgeon had done it too tenderly.

About eight or ten days before his death, when Dr. Brocklesby paid him his morning visit, he seemed very low and desponding, and said, "I have been as a dying man all night." He then emphatically broke out in the words of Shakspeare:

> "Canst thou not minister to a mind diseas'd;
> Pluck from the memory a rooted sorrow;
> Raze out the written troubles of the brain;
> And, with some sweet oblivious antidote,
> Cleanse the stuff'd bosom of that perilous stuff,
> Which weighs upon the heart?"

To which Dr. Brocklesby readily answered, from the same great poet:

> ". . . therein the patient
> Must minister to himself."

Johnson expressed himself much satisfied with the application.

Having no other relations, it had been for some time Johnson's intention to make a liberal provision for his faithful servant, Mr. Francis Barber, whom he looked upon as particularly under his protection, and whom he had all along treated truly as an humble friend. It is strange, however, to think that Johnson was not free from that general weakness of being averse to execute a will, so that he delayed it from time to time; and had it not been for Sir John Hawkins's repeatedly urging it, I think it probable that his kind resolution would not have been fulfilled.

The consideration of numerous papers of which he was possessed, seems to have struck Johnson's mind with a sudden anxiety, and as they were in great confusion, it is much to be lamented that he had not intrusted some faithful and discreet person with the care and selection of them; instead of which, he, in a precipitate manner, burnt large masses of them, with little regard, as I apprehend, to discrimination. Not that I suppose we have thus been deprived of any compositions which he had ever intended for the public eye; but from what escaped the flames, I judge that many curious circumstances relating to both himself and other literary characters, have perished.

Two very valuable articles, I am sure, we have lost, which were two quarto volumes, containing a full, fair, and most particular account of his own life, from his earliest recollection. I owned to him that, having accidentally seen them, I had read a great deal in them; and apologizing for the liberty I had taken, asked him if I could help it. He placidly answered, "Why, Sir, I do not think you could have helped it." I said that I had, for once in my life, felt half an inclination to commit theft. It had come into my mind to carry off these two volumes, and never see him more. Upon my inquiring how this would have affected him, "Sir (said he), I believe I should have gone mad."

During his last illness, Johnson experienced the steady and kind attachment of his numerous friends. Mr. Hoole has drawn up a narrative of what passed in the visits which he paid him during that time, from the 10th of November to the 13th of December, the day of his death, inclusive, and has favoured me with a perusal of it, with permission to make extracts, which I have done. Nobody was more attentive to him than Mr. Langton, to whom he tenderly said, *Te teneam moriens deficiente manu*. And I think it highly to the honour of Mr. Windham that his important occupations as an active statesman did not prevent him from paying assiduous respect to the dying Sage whom he revered. Mr. Langton informs me that "one day he found Mr. Burke and four or five more friends sitting with Johnson. Mr. Burke said to him, 'I am afraid, Sir, such a number of us may be oppressive to you.'—'No, Sir (said Johnson), it is not so; and I must be in a wretched state, indeed, when your company would not be a delight to me.' Mr. Burke, in a tremulous voice, expressive of being very tenderly affected, replied, 'My dear Sir, you have always been too good to me.' Immediately afterwards he went away. This was the last circumstance in the acquaintance of these two eminent men."

The following particulars of his conversation within a few days of his death, I give on the authority of Mr. John Nichols:

"He said that the Parliamentary Debates were the only part of his writings which then gave him any compunction: but that, at the time he wrote them, he had no conception he was imposing upon the world, though they were frequently written from very slender materials, and often from none at all,—the mere coinage of his own imagination. He never wrote any part of his works with equal velocity. Three columns of the Magazine in an hour was no uncommon effort, which was faster than most persons could have transcribed that quantity.

"He said at another time, three or four days only before his death, speaking of the little fear he had of undergoing a chirurgical operation, 'I would give one of these legs for a year more of life, I mean of comfortable life, not such as that which I now suffer';—and lamented much his inability to read during his hours of restlessness. 'I used formerly (he added), when sleepless in bed, *to read like a Turk.*'

"Whilst confined by his last illness, it was his regular practice to have the church service read to him, by some attentive and friendly divine. The Rev. Mr. Hoole performed this kind office in my presence for the last time, when by his own desire, no more than the litany was read; in which his responses were in the deep and sonorous voice which Mr. Boswell has occasionally noticed, and with the most profound devotion that can be imagined. His hearing not being quite perfect, he more than once interrupted Mr. Hoole with 'Louder, my dear Sir, louder, I entreat you, or you pray in vain!'—and, when the service was ended, he, with great earnestness, turned round to an excellent lady who was present, saying, 'I thank you, madam, very heartily for your kindness in joining me in this solemn exercise. Live well, I conjure you; and you will not feel the compunction at the last which I now feel.' So truly humble were the thoughts which this great and good man entertained of his own approaches to religious perfection.

"He was earnestly invited to publish a volume of 'Devotional Exercises,' but this (though he listened to the proposal with much complacency, and a large sum of money was offered for it) he declined, from motives of the sincerest modesty."

Amidst the melancholy clouds which hung over the dying Johnson, his characteristical manner showed itself on different occasions.

When Dr. Warren, in the usual style, hoped that he was better, his answer was "No, Sir; you cannot conceive with what acceleration I advance towards death."

A man whom he had never seen before was employed one night to sit up with him. Being asked next morning how he liked his attendant, his answer was, "Not at all, Sir: the fellow's an idiot; he is as awkward as a turnspit when first put into the wheel, and as sleepy as a dormouse."

Mr. Windham having placed a pillow conveniently to support him, he thanked him for his kindness, and said, "That will do,—all that a pillow can do."

As he opened a note which his servant brought to him, he said, "An odd thought strikes me—we shall receive no letters in the grave."

He requested three things of Sir Joshua Reynolds: To forgive him thirty pounds which he had borrowed of him; to read the Bible; and never to use his pencil on a Sunday. Sir Joshua readily acquiesced.

Johnson, with that native fortitude, which, amidst all his bodily distress and mental sufferings, never forsook him, asked Dr. Brocklesby, as a man in whom he had confidence, to tell him plainly whether he could recover. "Give me (said he) a direct answer." The Doctor having first asked him if he could bear the whole truth, which way soever it might lead, and being answered that he could, declared that, in his opinion, he could not recover without a miracle. "Then (said Johnson) I will take no more physic, not even my opiates; for I have prayed that I may render up my soul to God unclouded." In this resolution he persevered, and, at the same time, used only the weakest kinds of sustenance. Being pressed by Mr. Windham to take somewhat more generous nourishment, lest too low a diet should have the very effect which he dreaded, by debilitating his mind, he said, "I will take anything but inebriating sustenance."

Having, as has been already mentioned, made his will on the 8th and 9th of December, and settled all his worldly affairs, he languished till Monday, the 13th of that month, when he expired, about seven o'clock in the evening, with so little apparent pain, that his attendants hardly perceived when his dissolution took place.

Of his last moments, my brother, Thomas David, has furnished me with the following particulars:

"The Doctor, from the time that he was certain his death was near, appeared to be perfectly resigned, was seldom or never fretful or out of temper, and often said to his faithful servant, who gave me this account, 'Attend, Francis, to the salvation of your soul, which is the object of greatest importance'; he also explained to him passages in the scripture, and seemed to have pleasure in talking upon religious subjects.

"On Monday, the 13th of December, the day on which he died, a Miss Morris, daughter to a particular friend of his, called, and said to Francis that she begged to be permitted to see the Doctor, that she might earnestly request him to give her his blessing. Francis went into his room, followed by the young lady, and delivered the message. The Doctor turned himself in the bed, and said, 'God bless you, my dear!' These were the last words he spoke.—His difficulty of breathing increased till about seven o'clock in the evening, when Mr. Barber and Mrs. Desmoulins, who were sitting in the room, observing that the noise he made in breathing had ceased, went to the bed, and found he was dead."

About two days after his death, the following very agreeable account was communicated to Mr. Malone, in a letter by the Honourable

John Byng, to whom I am much obliged for granting me permission to introduce it in my work.

"DEAR SIR,—

"Since I saw you, I have had a long conversation with Cawston, who sat up with Dr. Johnson from nine o'clock on Sunday evening till ten o'clock on Monday morning. And, from what I can gather from him, it should seem that Dr. Johnson was perfectly composed, steady in hope, and resigned to death. At the interval of each hour, they assisted him to sit up in his bed, and move his legs, which were in much pain, when he regularly addressed himself to fervent prayer; and, though sometimes his voice failed him, his sense never did, during that time. The only sustenance he received was cider and water. He said his mind was prepared, and the time to his dissolution seemed long. At six in the morning, he inquired the hour, and, on being informed, said that all went on regularly, and he felt he had but a few hours to live.

"At ten o'clock in the morning, he parted from Cawston, saying, 'You should not detain Mr. Windham's servant; I thank you; bear my remembrance to your master.' Cawston says that no man could appear more collected, more devout, or less terrified at the thoughts of the approaching minute.

"This account, which is so much more agreeable than, and somewhat different from, yours, has given us the satisfaction of thinking that that great man died as he lived, full of resignation, strengthened in faith, and joyful in hope."

A few days before his death, he had asked Sir John Hawkins, as one of his executors, where he should be buried, and on being answered, "Doubtless in Westminster Abbey," seemed to feel a satisfaction very natural to a poet; and indeed in my opinion very natural to every man of any imagination, who has no family sepulchre in which he can be laid with his fathers. Accordingly, upon Monday, December 20, his remains were deposited in that noble and renowned edifice; and over his grave was placed a large blue flag-stone, with this inscription:

"SAMUEL JOHNSON, LL.D.
Obiit XIII *die Decembris*
Anno Domini
M. DCC. LXXXIV.
Ætatis suæ LXXV."

His funeral was attended by a respectable number of his friends, particularly such of the members of the Literary Club as were then in town; and was also honoured with the presence of several of the Reverend Chapter of Westminster. Mr. Burke, Sir Joseph Banks, Mr. Windham, Mr. Langton, Sir Charles Bunbury, and Mr. Colman, bore his pall. His schoolfellow, Dr. Taylor, performed the mournful office of reading the burial service.

I trust I shall not be accused of affectation, when I declare that I find myself unable to express all that I felt upon the loss of such a "Guide, Philosopher, and Friend." I shall, therefore, not say one word of my own, but adopt those of an eminent friend, which he uttered with an abrupt felicity, superior to all studied compositions: "He has made a chasm, which not only nothing can fill up, but which nothing has a tendency to fill up. Johnson is dead. Let us go to the next best; there is nobody; no man can be said to put you in mind of Johnson."

The character of Samuel Johnson has, I trust, been so developed in the course of this work, that they who have honoured it with a perusal may be considered as well acquainted with him. As, however, it may be expected that I should collect into one view the capital and distinguishing features of this extraordinary man, I shall endeavour to acquit myself of that part of my biographical undertaking, however difficult it may be to do that which many of my readers will do better for themselves.

His figure was large and well formed, and his countenance of the cast of an ancient statue; yet his appearance was rendered strange and somewhat uncouth by convulsive cramps, by the scars of that distemper which it was once imagined the royal touch could cure, and by a slovenly mode of dress. He had the use only of one eye; yet so much does mind govern and even supply the deficiency of organs, that his visual perceptions, as far as they extended, were uncommonly quick and accurate. So morbid was his temperament that he never knew the natural joy of a free and vigorous use of his limbs: when he walked, it was like the struggling gait of one in fetters; when he rode he had no command or direction of his horse, but was carried as if in a balloon. That with his constitution and habits of life he should have lived seventy-five years, is a proof that an inherent *vivida vis* is a powerful preservative of the human frame.

Johnson exhibited an eminent example of this remark which I have made upon human nature. At different times he seemed a different man, in some respects; not, however, in any great or essential article, upon which he had fully employed his mind, and settled certain principles of duty, but only in his manners, and in the display of argument and fancy in his talk. He was prone to superstition, but not to credulity. Though his imagination might incline him to a belief of the marvellous and the mysterious, his vigorous reason examined the evidence with jealousy. He was a sincere and zealous Christian, of high Church-of-England and monarchical principles, which he would not tamely suffer to be questioned; and had, perhaps, at an early period, narrowed his mind somewhat too much, both as to religion and politics. His being impressed with the danger of extreme latitude in either, though he was of a very independent spirit, occasioned his appearing somewhat unfavourable to the prevalence of that noble freedom of sentiment which is the best possession of man. Nor can it be denied that he had many prejudices; which, however, frequently suggested many of his pointed sayings, that rather show a playfulness of fancy than any settled malignity. He was steady and inflexible in maintaining the obligations of religion and morality; both from a regard for the order of society, and from a veneration for the Great Source of all order; correct, nay stern in his taste; hard to please, and easily offended; impetuous and irritable in his temper, but of a most humane and benevolent heart, which showed itself not only in a most liberal charity, as far as his circumstances would allow, but in a thousand instances of active benevolence. He was afflicted with a bodily disease which made him often restless and fretful; and with a constitutional melancholy, the clouds of which darkened the brightness of his fancy, and gave a gloomy cast to his whole course of thinking: we, therefore, ought not to wonder at his sallies of impatience and passion at any time; especially when provoked by obtrusive ignorance, or presuming petulance; and allowance must be made for his uttering hasty and satirical sallies even against his best friends. He loved praise when it was brought to him, but was too proud to seek for it. He was somewhat susceptible of flattery. As he was general and unconfined in his studies, he cannot be considered as master of any one particular science; but he had accumulated a vast and various collection of learning and knowledge, which was so arranged in his mind, as to be ever in readiness to be brought forth. But his superiority over other learned men consisted chiefly in what may be called the art of thinking, the art of using his mind; a certain continual power of seizing the useful substance of all that he knew, and exhibiting it in a clear and forcible manner; so that knowledge, which we often see to be no better than lumber in men of dull understanding, was, in him, true, evident, and actual wisdom. His moral precepts are practical; for they are drawn from an intimate acquaintance with human nature. His maxims carry conviction; for they are founded on the basis of common sense, and a very attentive and minute survey of real life. His mind was so full of imagery that he might have been perpetually a poet; yet it is remarkable that, however rich his prose is in this respect, his poetical pieces, in general, have not much of that splendour but are rather distinguished by strong sentiment and acute observation, conveyed in harmonious and energetic verse, particularly in heroic couplets. Though usually grave, and even awful in his deportment, he possessed uncommon and peculiar powers of wit and humour; he frequently indulged himself in colloquial pleasantry; and the heartiest merriment was often enjoyed in his company; with this great advantage, that it was entirely free from any poisonous tincture of vice or impiety, it was salutary to those who shared in it. He had accustomed himself to such accuracy in his common conversation, that he at all times expressed his thoughts with great force, and an elegant choice of language, the effect of which was aided by his having a loud voice, and a slow deliberate utterance. In him were united a most logical head with a most fertile imagination, which gave him an extraordinary advantage in arguing; for he could reason close or wide, as he saw best for the moment. Exulting in his intellectual strength and dexterity, he could, when he pleased, be the greatest sophist that ever contended in the lists of declamation; and, from a spirit of contradiction and a delight in showing his powers, he would often maintain the wrong side with equal warmth and ingenuity; so that, when there was an audience his real opinions could seldom be gathered from his talk; though when he was in company with a single friend, he would discuss a subject with genuine fairness; but he was too conscientious to make error permanent and pernicious, by deliberately writing it; and, in all his numerous works, he earnestly inculcated what appeared to him to be the truth; his piety being constant, and the ruling principle of all his conduct.

Such was Samuel Johnson, a man whose talents, acquirements, and virtues, were so extraordinary, that the more his character is considered, the more he will be regarded by the present age, and by posterity, with admiration and reverence.